THE VISUAL GUIDE TO
PARADOX®
FOR WINDOWS

The Pictorial
Companion to
Windows Database
Management
& Programming

Patrick J. Burns,
Jan Weingarten
& Ted Clifford

VENTANA
PRESS

The Ventana Press Visual Guide™ Series

The Visual Guide to Paradox for Windows: The Pictorial Companion to Windows Database Management & Programming
Copyright © 1994 by Patrick J. Burns, Jan Weingarten & Ted Clifford

Library of Congress Cataloging-in-Publication Data

Burns, Patrick (Patrick J.)
        The visual guide to Paradox for Windows : the pictorial companion to Windows database management & programming / Pat Burns. -- 1st ed.
            p.   cm.
        Includes index.
        ISBN 1-56604-150-3
        1. Database management. 2. Paradox for Windows   (Computer file) I. Title.
QA76.9.D3B89 1994
005.75'65--dc20   94-28999
                                                          CIP

Book design: Marcia Webb
Cover design: One-of-a-Kind Design; Adaptation: Robert Harris
Index service: Stephen Bach
Technical review: Greg de Vries
Editorial staff: Angela Anderson, Walt Bruce, Diana Merelman, Marion Laird, Pam Richardson
Production staff: John Cotterman, Dan Koeller, Dawne Sherman, Marcia Webb, Mike Webster
Proofreader: Lynn Jaluvka

First Edition 9 8 7 6 5 4 3 2 1
Printed in the United States of America

Ventana Press, Inc.
P.O. Box 2468
Chapel Hill, NC 27515
919/942-0220
FAX 919/942-1140

Limits of Liability and Disclaimer of Warranty

Trademarks

Trademarked names appear throughout this book. Rather than list the names and entities that own the trademarks or insert a trademark symbol with each mention of the trademarked name, the publisher states that it is using the names only for editorial purposes and to the benefit of the trademark owner with no intention of infringing upon that trademark.

About the Authors

Patrick J. Burns is a firmly established computer book author and university lecturer. His work in the computer field also includes Beta site testing, confidential review and program development of software packages for major publishers.

Author of the bestselling books *Windows, Word & Excel Office Companion* (Ventana Press), *CD Morph™!* (Addison-Wesley) and *Using Quattro Pro 5.0, Special Edition* (Que), he has written and contributed to 30 other books on Windows, Word, Excel, 1-2-3 and Quattro Pro.

Pat holds a Bachelor of Science degree in finance with a minor in economics. A native of Pennsylvania, he is a worldwide traveler who has lived in Europe and Asia. He is a founder and principal of Burns & Associates, a professional writers group based in Incline Village, Nevada.

Jan Weingarten is a software trainer, consultant and writer in Seattle, Washington. Her most recent book is *Teach Yourself WordPerfect 6.0 for Windows*. In addition, she has authored or coauthored books on Windows, Microsoft Word for Windows, Lotus 1-2-3 for Windows, Excel for Windows and CorelDRAW.

Ted Clifford is a WordPerfect and Paradox consultant and writer based in Seattle, Washington. He has been a contributing writer on several Paradox for DOS and Paradox for Windows books. In his consulting practice, Mr. Clifford focuses on office automation. One of his notable recent projects was the creation of a Paradox for Windows contact management application to automatically generate letters and reports based on information created by sales reps using Paradox for DOS on laptops.

Acknowledgments

A humongous THANK YOU to everyone at Ventana Press, especially Pam Richardson, Walt Bruce and (last but most definitely not least!) our wonderful editor, Marion Laird, who managed to stay reasonably sane through all the last-minute craziness. Without the invaluable guidance and steadfast patience of all the staff at Ventana Press, we never could have made it to the end of this book.

Thanks to Rick Schultz, the talented and slightly wacky cartoonist who did the drawings at the beginning of Chapter 2.

Thanks to Ted Clifford for kindly donating the two slick Paradox applications that appear at the end of the book.

Finally, warmest thanks to Matt Wagner, our literary agent-in-common, and all the gang at Waterside Productions. You got us this gig and brought the three of us together in the first place.

CONTENTS

INTRODUCTION

Paradox is without a doubt the brawniest, gut-busting database program around. (That's a good thing.) No sense in purchasing a puny, kick-sand-in-your-face flat file database program when what you really want is raw, bicep-flexing relational database power that's as simple to plug into as an electrical outlet. From the moment you double-click the Paradox icon in Program Manager to the instant a report rolls off your printer, Paradox will work parts of your mind you never knew you had. (That's a good thing, too.)

Paradox really is a gentle giant, though. You don't have to be a programmer and you don't need to be brilliant to wield this tool. In fact, you can go only as far as you need to with the program and then stop without fear of reprisal. Suppose all you want to do is reorganize your address book. Or maybe you need a full blown, self-running program that resembles one of those mega-buck programs sold at the software stores. Perhaps what you really need falls somewhere in between those two extremes.

Whatever your data organizing needs, this book has something for you. The first third of the book is structured to benefit the beginning user who needs up front counseling about the *database* concept. More seasoned database users will benefit from the hands-on exercises presented in the latter two-thirds of the book. Users of all levels will benefit from our philosophy that although Paradox may offer three ways of accomplishing the same task, most of us just want to know the one easiest way to get the job done.

TAKING THE VISUAL APPROACH

Attempting to learn everything about Paradox in a single sitting is like trying to wrap your arms around a redwood tree. There's just too much girth to grip onto. When you need help—and you will need it eventually—it can get confusing knowing where to turn. There's on-line help, the Experts, those Coaches, $5.00 per minute assistance lines, friends, family, dial-a-prayer, and so on. (Here comes the loaded question.) Maybe you've wondered out loud once or twice, "Isn't there a more visual way of learning Paradox?"

Paradox for Windows is a very visual program by nature. That's why we've taken a primarily visual approach in this book; our goal has always been to find that perfect balance between anecdotal messages, reference material, and practical hands-on exercises. As a result you'll find more illustrations and screen captures in our book than in most other computer books. Our figures show critical points along the path of developing the sample Paradox elements contained in the hands-on exercises. Use the screen captures as your personal Paradox road map—you'll know you're headed in the right direction when your screen resembles what's shown in our screens.

WHAT'S INSIDE

The Visual Guide to Paradox for Windows, is divided into 21 chapters and a single appendix:

○ Chapters 1 and 2 take you on a whirlwind tour of Paradox. You'll get a bird's-eye view of what working with a database program is all about. Important concepts such as learning to recognize what's what in Paradox and how to think intelligently when designing a database receive prominent coverage.

○ Chapters 3 through 8 take you on a Paradox table-hunting safari. Being that tables are the basic unit of a Paradox database, you'll quickly discover how to do things like creating and saving tables, borrowing table structures, examining the nitty gritty details of fields, and creating a system of checks and balances to keep *bad* data out of an otherwise decent database. Then you'll see exactly how to shuffle your data to produce more useful ways of reporting and analyzing records. Finally, you'll get a first-hand look at creating queries to ask questions about your database.

○ Chapters 9 through 14 show you what to do with a big game database once you've bagged one. Forms, reports, graphs and objects are the buzzwords of the day in this section of the book. Each of these items makes it easier for you and for anyone else using your database to manage and report on the data in your tables.

○ Chapters 15 through 21 contain information you'll need to know when you're ready to play with the big boys. This group of chapters tackles the ObjectPal programming language, perhaps the most powerful aspect of the Paradox program. Program code snippets will help you understand what's really going on in the background of a professionally designed Paradox application. The book concludes with two Paradox applications, designed by a real-world Paradox developer.

○ Appendix A is a guide to hiring a professional database developer. If you have the money, why not hire the best?

HOW TO USE THIS BOOK

Our book is primarily a hands-on tutorial. To get the most out of this Paradox learning experience you should work through all the exercises included in the book. Don't fudge. To minimize the amount of rekeying you need to do, this book comes with a disk that contains all the files you need to successfully complete each exercise. We've also thrown in (at no extra cost) two full-blown, stand-alone, knock-your-socks-off Paradox applications. Feel free to explore the inner workings of these applications to see what makes them tick. You're welcome!

Before moving on to Chapter 1, install the contents of the disk onto your computer. The setup utility is a breeze to use, just follow the simple instructions on the disk's label.

WHERE TO REACH US

Interested in contacting the authors? If you have any questions, comments or criticisms regarding anything that appears in this book please feel free to contact us via any of the following on-line services:

America Online: YodaDude

Compuserve: 70733,406

We'll get back to you as soon as is humanly possible.

Burns, Weingarten & Clifford

1

INTRODUCING . . . PARADOX

What is paradox? Ah yes, the question of the ages. It has puzzled scholars and philosophers ever since there were scholars and philosophers who puzzled. The American Heritage Dictionary defines a paradox as "A seemingly contradictory statement that may nonetheless be true. . . . A statement contrary to received opinion." Paradoxes are indeed a puzzlement. How can something be true and not true?

But wait a minute. I just remembered–this is about *Paradox, the program*, not *paradox, the word*. Well, since I already wrote that stuff about lowercase paradox, might as well leave it in. Anyway, for the most part it does apply to Paradox, the program (except for the "since the beginning of time" bit). You see, Paradox actually *is* a paradox.

Here's why: databases are complex, but Paradox is easy. How can this be? How can something be incredibly complex while at the same time simple to learn and work with? I'll leave that for future puzzled scholars, but that's why Paradox is called Paradox. It's a paradox.

What it means to you is that Paradox harnesses almost unimaginable power and puts that power within the reach of anyone with a computer. You don't have to be a techno-nerd to create tables, forms and reports to handle your database needs. But if you are a techno-nerd (or are inspired to move in that direction by the time you finish this book), you can use Paradox's full-featured programming language, ObjectPAL, to create entire applications complete with their own menus and interactive buttons. The sky's the limit–check out the applications in the last eight chapters of this book.

A database is just a collection of information. You might keep a bunch of names, addresses and phone numbers on scraps of paper and matchbook covers stuffed into a desk drawer. That's a database. Problem is, it's not a very manageable database. There's no easy way to find a particular phone number, or to determine how many of your friends live in Seattle, or to update an address when someone moves. That's where Paradox comes in. As a *relational database management system* (which just means that you work with information that's in a whole bunch of related tables), Paradox can make short work of any database management task.

Without further ado, let's open Paradox and start exploring.

STARTING PARADOX

You start Paradox for Windows from the Windows Program Manager. (You can also start Paradox from the Windows File Manager by switching to your Paradox directory and double-clicking on PDOXWIN.EXE.) Here's what you do to start Program Manager:

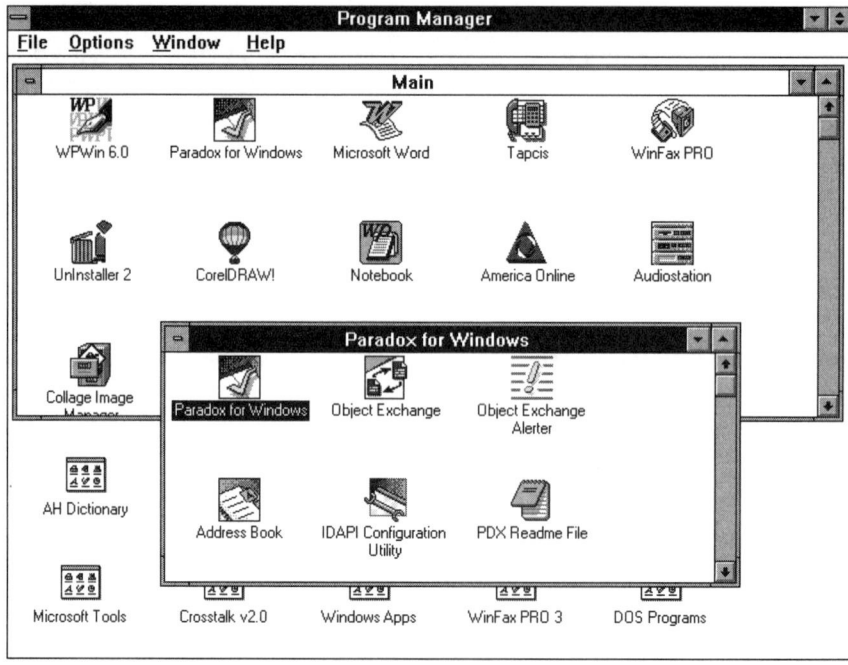

Figure 1-1: Start from the Program Manager.

1. Double-click on the Paradox for Windows group icon to open the Paradox for Windows group window.
2. Double-click on the Paradox for Windows program icon inside the Paradox for Windows group window.

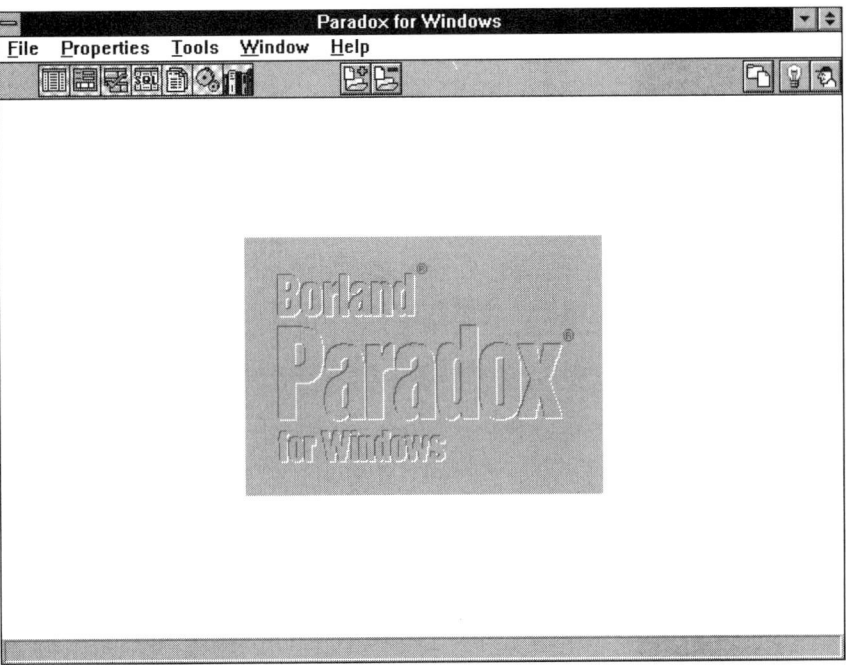

Figure 1-2: Your screen should look something like this.

Inside Scoop

You might think that starting Paradox is the first step in creating a database. Well, you might think wrong. There's a reason that the chapter on database design (Chapter 2) comes before the chapters that show you how to create and work with Paradox tables, forms and reports. And the reason is: Planning and design are important. You can learn to sling around all the fancy techno-babble words in the world (and even learn to understand them), but your database ain't a happenin' thing if you don't take the time to plan it out before you sit down at the computer.

LEAVING PARADOX

You can use any standard Windows technique to exit Paradox:

○ Choose File, Exit.

○ Double-click on the application window's Control-menu box.

○ Choose Close from the application window's Control menu.

○ Press Alt+F4.

OBJECTIVELY SPEAKING

Here's a word you're going to hear a lot (at least while you're working with Paradox)—*object*. If you treat a woman as an object, you'll probably get a well-deserved slap in the face (or worse). But Paradox items love to be treated as objects—in fact, they proudly bear the name. So what is an object? In Paradox, just about everything you work with.

What's an Object?

Tables, forms, reports, queries and scripts are all objects. And when you get into forms and reports, you'll encounter lots of *design objects*: buttons, graphics, fields and much more. So an object is anything that contains information. Or any item that you put in a form or report to display information or pictures.

What's the Object Inspector?

The Object Inspector is something that inspects an object. Simple enough. And when the Object Inspector inspects the object, it tells you what *properties* can be changed for that object. And what are properties? An object's properties are the qualities that make it look or act as it does.

And just how do you inspect an object? You right-click on it (or select the object and press F6) to open an Object Inspector menu that gives you easy access to all of the stuff that can be done to that object.

The following are two typical examples:

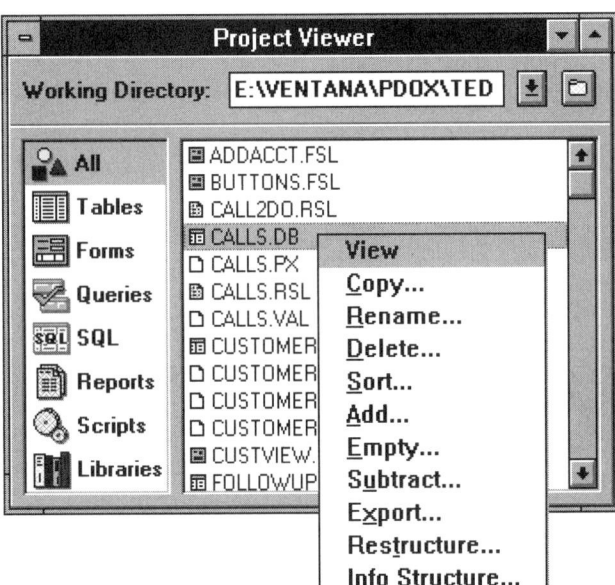

Figure 1-3: Right-click on a table name in the Project Viewer to get this Object Inspector menu.

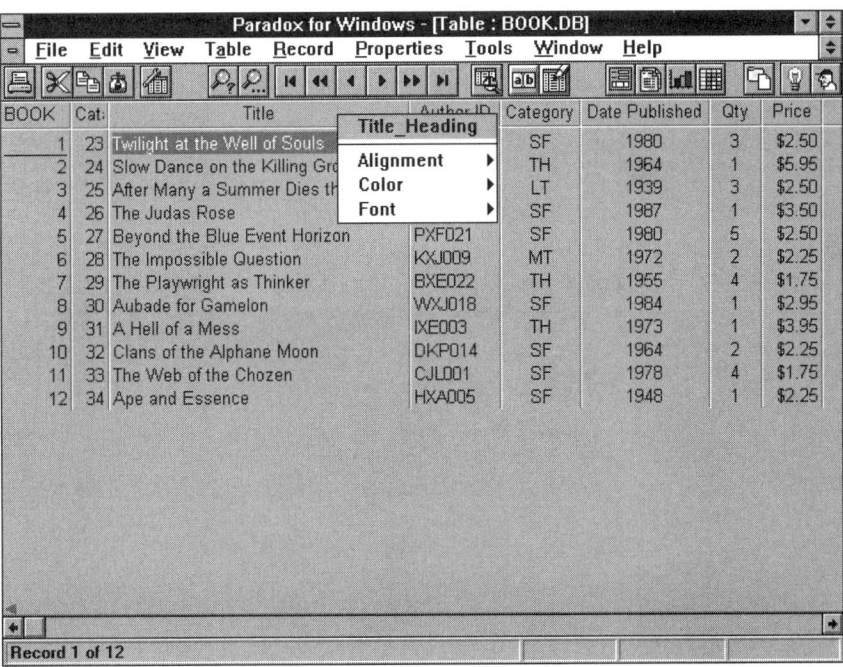

Figure 1-4: Right-click on a table's field heading to get this Object Inspector menu.

The Object Inspector is really handy—when in doubt, right-click on whatever you want to work with. You'll discover all sorts of cool Object Inspector menus that keep you from having to wade your way through a bunch of regular menus. And if the item doesn't have an Object Inspector, all you've wasted is one right-click.

LOOKING AT THE DESKTOP

Check out Figure 1-5. What you see is the Paradox desktop with the Project Viewer dialog box open. By default, the Project Viewer appears whenever you open Paradox (I'll talk about the Project Viewer in the next section). The Desktop is the foundation for everything that happens in Paradox—much like the way the Program Manager is the foundation for all of your Windows goings-on. If you close Program Manager, Windows is out of business; likewise, if you close the Desktop, Paradox is out of business. In Paradox lingo, the Desktop is the *parent* to any other windows (*children*) that you open inside Paradox.

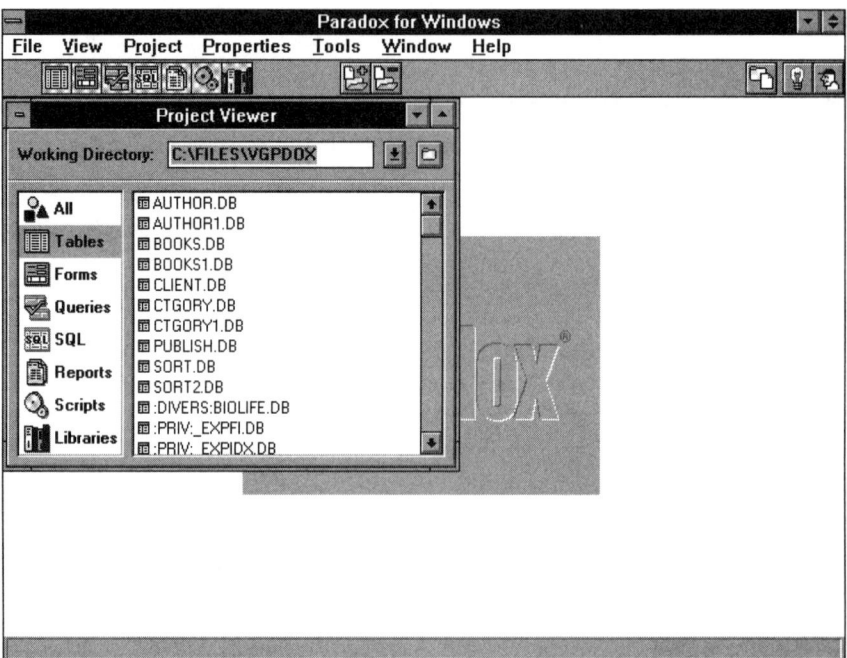

Figure 1-5: This is what you see when you open Paradox for the first time.

Let's take a look at the ingredients that make up the Desktop "pie." In the process, you'll get a quick review of some standard Windows stuff—a lot of the Desktop's (and Paradox's) elements will be very familiar to you if you've used Windows for any time at all. And a peek at the Desktop is also a good intro to Paradox itself. Most of the items (and the techniques you use on them) are repeated throughout Paradox. All of the stuff you can do from the Desktop is available to you from anywhere in Paradox.

The Title Bar

We're in basic Windows territory here. The Title bar tells you what program you're working in. The Control-menu box at the left edge of the Title bar lets you move, size, restore, minimize or maximize the Paradox window. You can also choose Switch To from the Control menu, which opens Windows's Task List. From the Task List you can open and close other programs and arrange program windows on your screen.

Inside Scoop

You can press Ctrl+Esc from anyplace in Windows to open the Task List.

On the right edge of the Title bar you've got your basic Minimize and Maximize or Restore buttons. All of this works just like it does in any Windows program—click on the Minimize button to reduce Paradox to an icon; click on the Maximize button to expand Paradox so it takes up your whole screen; click on the Restore button (which replaces the Maximize button when a program's maximized) to return the Paradox window to the size it was before you maximized it. And of course you can move or size the Paradox window (except when it's maximized) just like you can any other program or document window.

I know this sounds like run-of-the-mill stuff, but the Title bar is capable of one special feat of magic. In Figure 1-5, notice that the Project Viewer window has its own Title bar, Control-menu box and Minimize and Maximize buttons. Well, take a look at what happens when you maximize the Project Viewer.

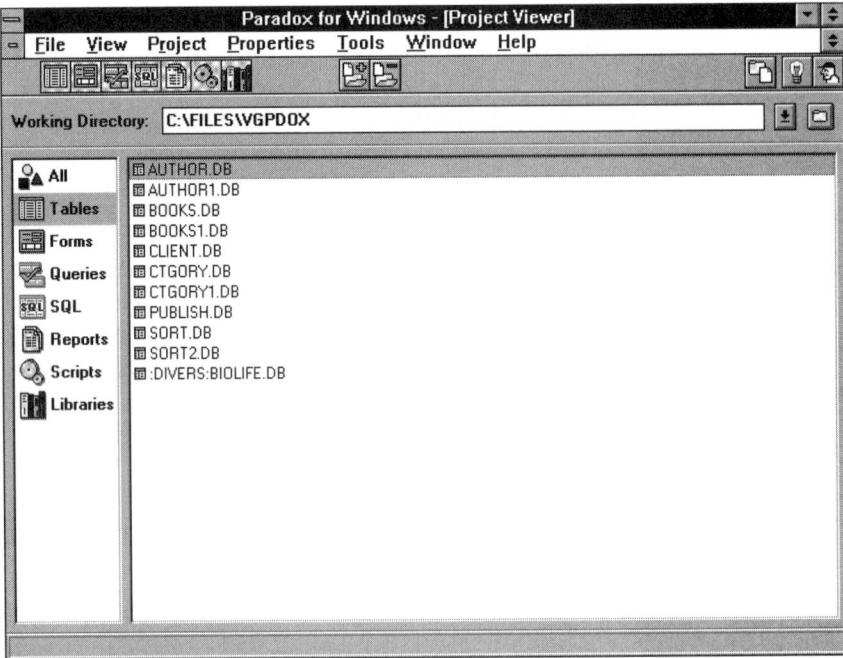

Figure 1-6: Project Viewer maximized.

Now there's only one title bar—Project Viewer's title bar has been magically absorbed by Paradox's title bar, and the combined title bar now says *Paradox for Windows - (Project Viewer)*. Project Viewer still has its own Control-menu box and Minimize/Restore buttons—they've been moved to the left and right edges of the Menu bar.

The Menu Bar

Again, basic Windows stuff. Menus in Paradox work just like menus in any Windows program. You click on a main menu item (or press Alt+[the underlined letter]) to open the pull-down menu for that item. Then click on the item you want from the pull-down menu (or press the underlined letter). If there are three dots after the item's name, that means you'll get a dialog box when you choose the item. If there's a right-pointing triangle after the name, choosing the item gives you a cascading menu (a submenu with additional choices). If there's a function key (or key combination) displayed next to the item, that means that pressing the keys will have the same effect as choosing the item on the menu.

The important thing to know about Paradox menus is that you get a different one for each object type. For example, when you open a table, you get a menu that has options specific to tables (like Edit Data and Restructure Table); when you're working with queries, you get a menu with query-specific options (like Run Query and Answer Sort).

You'll learn about the specific menu options as we get to the different features. But there are some common items on the Desktop menu that carry over to most of the other menus. The File, Properties, Window and Help menus are always there. Depending on where you are, you may have some additional choices on the Properties menu, but the Desktop option, which lets you make changes to your Desktop configuration (like changing the wallpaper or choosing a different screen font), is always available.

The File menu contains options that allow you to open, close, save and print files. You can also change your printer setup from the File menu. The Working Directory, Private Directory and Aliases options, which we'll talk about in just a bit, are also on the File menu. The three items just above Exit—Publish, Send and Subscribe—have to do with Paradox's new OBEX technology, a workgroup management feature that lets many users share Paradox project files. These options are beyond the scope of this book. Finally, you can exit Paradox from the File menu.

The View menu is available only when the Project Viewer is open. When you select an object type from the View menu, only objects of that type are listed in the Project Viewer.

If the Project Viewer is closed, the Desktop's Tools menu displays a Project Viewer item. Just click on it to open the Project Viewer. You also use the Tools menu to get to the Data Model Designer, which will be covered when we talk about forms in Chapters 9 and 10. When you choose Utilities, you get a submenu that lets you do all sorts of things: add records to a table, rename a file, sort, view a table's structure and other stuff. (All of the options on the Utilities submenu can also be found on the Project Viewer's Object Inspector menus.) The other options on the Tools menu have to do with more advanced programming-type stuff and working in a network environment, all of which are covered later in this book. The items you see on the Tools menu are available throughout Paradox; additional items are added to the Tools menu depending on what kind of object you're dealing with.

The Window menu is pretty much like the Window menu in most Windows programs. You can arrange your open windows in a cascaded or tiled format. You can close all open windows. When the Project Viewer is open, there's an option that lets you refresh (update) the Project Viewer. And the Window menu lists all of your open windows. You can move among windows by choosing Window and selecting the window you want to move to. (Of course, you can also move to a different window just by clicking in that window or pressing Ctrl+Tab to cycle through your open windows.)

The Help menu is all about getting the help you need when you need it. I'll expand on this help stuff a little later in the chapter.

The Toolbar

You might have encountered similar animals with different names in other programs–for example, "Button Bars," "Ribbons" and "SmartIcons." They all have their own unique features, but they all work essentially the same: their sole purpose in life is to give you one-click access to commonly used features.

Inside Scoop

If you want to know what a Toolbar button does, just point to it with your mouse and look at the status bar. No clicking necessary.

Just like menus, the Toolbar layout changes depending on what kind of object you're working with. And just like menus, we'll talk about the different Toolbars in the applicable chapters. Since this is the applicable chapter for talking about the Desktop Toolbar, here goes.

Figure 1-7: The Desktop Toolbar.

The following list explains what you get when you left-click on the pictured button. The seven buttons on the left are for opening and creating new files. Each of them has an Object Inspector that gives you a choice of opening an existing file or creating a new one.

 The Open Table dialog box.

 The Open Document dialog box defaulted to display files with FSL and FDL extensions (forms).

 The Select Query dialog box, defaulted to display files with QBE extensions (queries).

 The Select File dialog box defaulted to display files with SQL extensions (SQL scripts).

The Open Document dialog box defaulted to display files with RSL and RDL extensions (reports).

 The Open Document dialog box defaulted to display files with SSL and SDL extensions (scripts).

 The Open Document dialog box defaulted to display files with LSL and LDL extensions (libraries).

The two icons in the middle are for adding items to or removing items from the Project Viewer list.

 Opens the Select File dialog box, from which you can choose a *reference* (an object) to add to your current Project Viewer list.

 With a reference selected, opens the Remove Item from Project Viewer dialog box, which lets you delete a reference from the Project Viewer.

The three icons on the far right have to do with project management and help.

 Opens the Project Viewer if it's closed.

 Opens the Expert Control Panel dialog box, from which you can choose to run the Form, Mailing Labels or Report Expert.

 Opens the Coaches window. You can choose from several topics that lead you step by step through the process of completing various tasks.

Putting the Toolbar in Its Place

By default, the Toolbar sits at the top of your screen, just below the menu bar. But you can change it from its fixed position to a floating Toolbar that goes wherever you want it to.

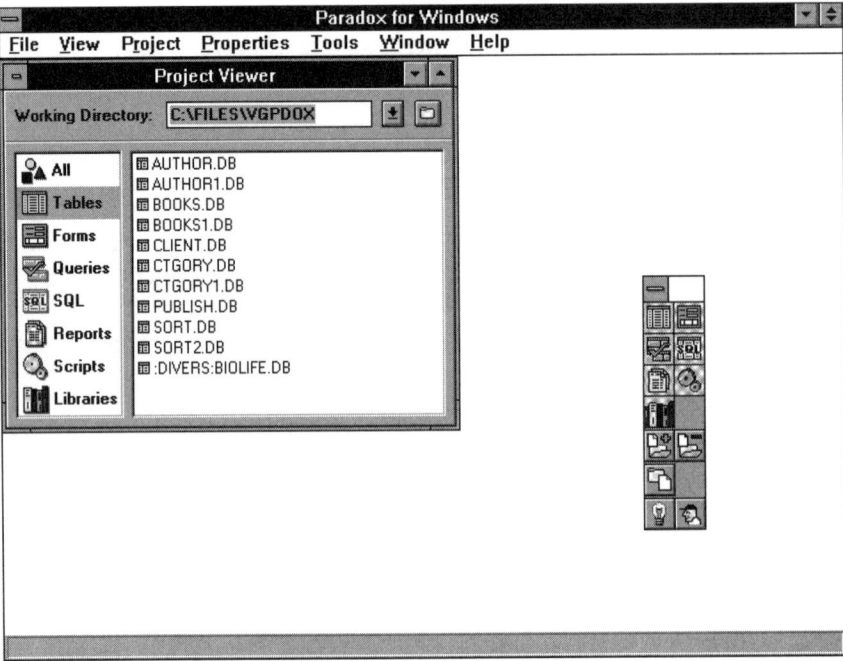

Figure 1-8: A floating Toolbar with two columns.

How did I make the Toolbar float?

1. I chose Properties, Desktop to open the Desktop Properties dialog box shown in Figure 1-9.

2. I selected Floating, and specified two columns. (You can choose from one column, two columns, one row or two rows—the default nonfloating Toolbar is displayed in one row.)

3. Drag the Toolbar to a new location by pointing to the solid area to the right of the Toolbar's Control-menu box. You can also use your keyboard to move the Toolbar. Choose Move from the Toolbar's Control menu, use the keyboard arrow keys to position the Toolbar where you want it, then press Enter.

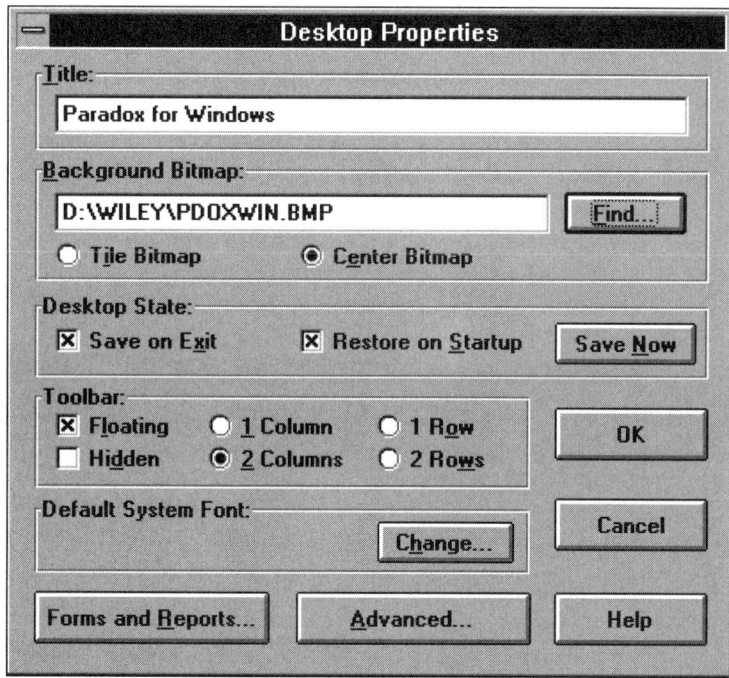

Figure 1-9: The Desktop Properties dialog box lets you change the position of the Toolbar.

4. To move the Toolbar back to its home base below the menu bar, choose Fix from the Toolbar's Control menu. (Or deselect Floating in the Desktop Properties dialog box.)

The Status Bar

The *status bar* is that innocent-looking strip at the bottom of the Paradox window. Although it may appear innocuous, please give it the respect it deserves and keep an eye on it while you work in Paradox. It boasts an ever-changing array of invaluable information. When you move your mouse pointer over a Toolbar button, the status bar tells you what the tool does. When you're in a table, the status bar tells you when you've made an error, what record you're on and whether you're in Edit mode (to name but a few of the too-numerous-to-enumerate messages you'll see on the status bar)—but only if you look at it.

Let's hear it for the status bar.

CHECKING OUT THE PROJECT VIEWER

Paradox gives you a whole bunch of ways to perform just about every task. As you've just seen, you've got Toolbars, pull-down menus and the Object Inspector (not to mention the keyboard). If all of the different options seem a little overwhelming, get to know the Project Viewer. It's a cool way of accessing all of your tables, forms, reports, queries and other Paradox objects. Not only can you use the Project Viewer to open different objects; you can also use the Project Viewer's Object Inspector menu to do different things to the objects.

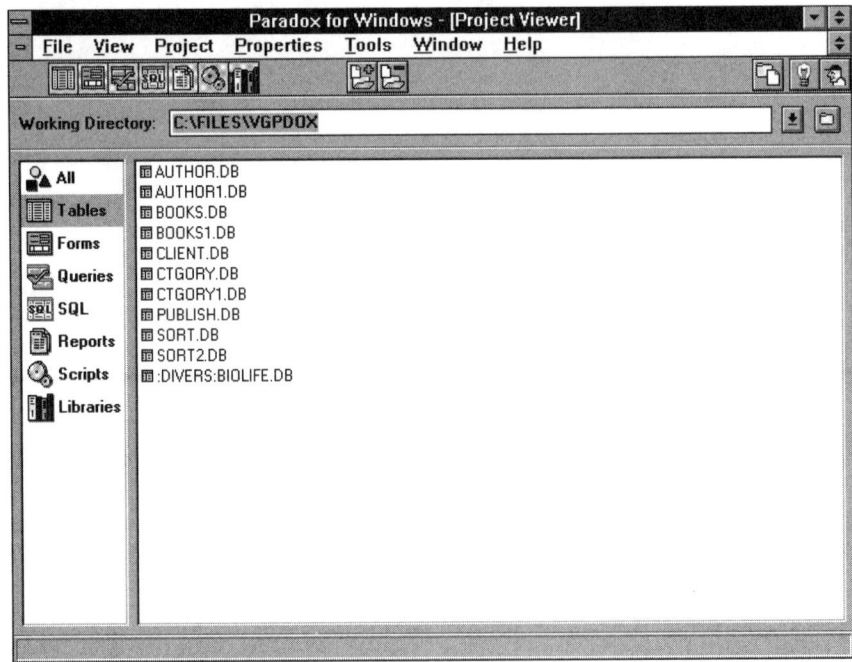

Figure 1-10: The Project Viewer (maximized).

O Each icon on the left side of the Project Viewer represents a different Paradox object type, except for the one with the cute little colored shapes (which represents all of the objects). These icons should already be familiar to you–they're the same as the group on the left side of the Toolbar. And if you have trouble figuring out what the icons stand for, try reading what it says to the right of the icon. Yup, you get pictures *and* words. What more could a person want?

O Click on an icon to see a list of all files in the current directory for that type of object.

○ Right-click on an icon to open the Object Inspector menu for that icon. These Object Inspector menus are the same as the ones for the first seven items on the Desktop Toolbar—you can choose to open existing files or create new files.

○ Right-click on any object's name (in the right column of the Project Viewer) to get an Object Inspector menu that lets you choose options specific to that type of object. For example, if you right-click on a table's name, you get the menu shown in Figure 1-11.

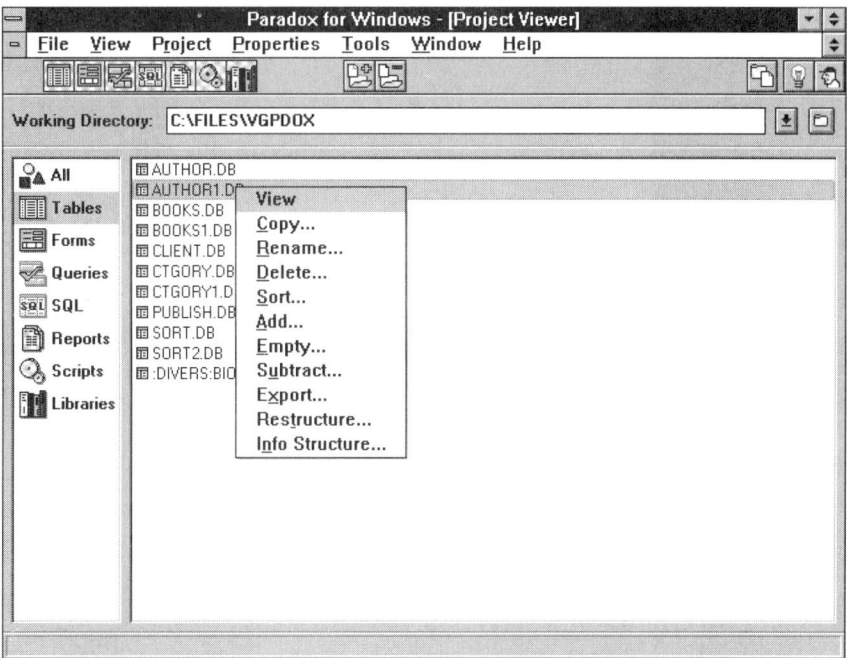

Figure 1-11: I right-clicked on AUTHOR.DB to get this menu.

○ Double-click on an object's name to do whatever's first on the Object Inspector menu. For example, if you double-click on AUTHOR.DB, Paradox will open the AUTHOR.DB table, since View is the first item on the menu.

○ Double-click on the Project Viewer's Control-menu box to close the Project Viewer.

○ Click on the Open Project Viewer Toolbar button to open the Project Viewer.

TRAVELING INCOGNITO (WITH ALIASES)

Aliases cut right to the chase when you change directories or refer to a directory when you're working with tables, reports and other Paradox objects. An alias is a nickname you give a directory so that you don't have to type a path name longer than the muddy Mississippi is wide. Who wants to type this over and over:

C:\PDOXWIN\BOOKS\VGPDOX\INVENTRY

Sure, you could use the Directory Browser to select the directory, but that could take an awful lot of hunting and clicking.

So here's what you do:

You give C:\PDOXWIN\BOOKS\VGPDOX\INVENTRY an *alias*. A nice short one that describes the project. Like INVENTORY. Then, whenever you're anyplace in Paradox where you need to choose a directory, you'll be able to choose the alias instead.

To create an alias:

1. Choose File, Aliases to open the Alias Manager dialog box shown in Figure 1-12.

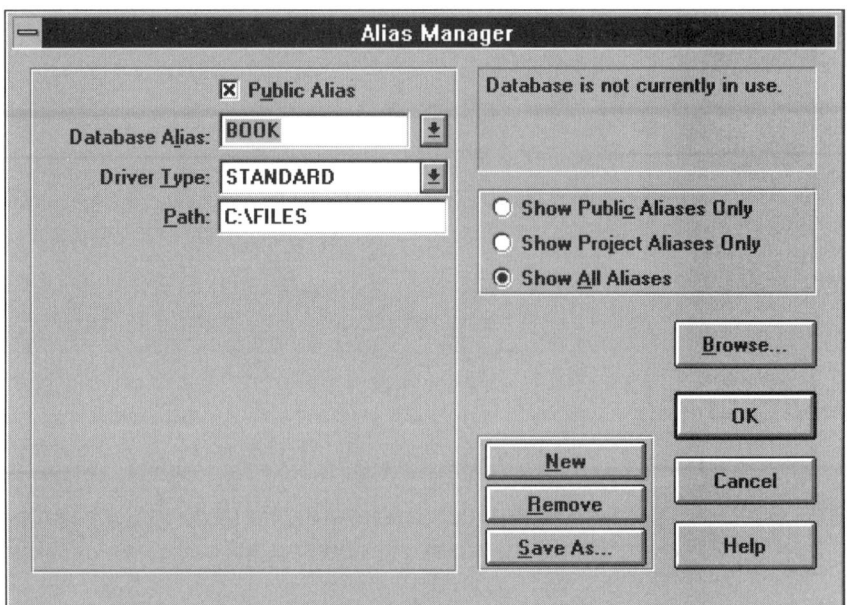

Figure 1-12: The Alias Manager dialog box.

2. Choose New. The New button is replaced by a Keep New button, and the Database Alias text box is cleared and ready for you to type in.

3. Make sure the Public Alias check box is selected if you want the alias to be available from any working directory. If you want to create a Project Alias, which means that the alias is available only from whichever working directory is current when you create the alias, deselect Public Alias.

4. Type the full path name in the Path text box (or click on the Browse button, choose the directory you want from the Directory Browser dialog box and choose OK).

5. Type the alias name in the Database Alias text box. The name can include spaces and combinations of upper- and lowercase letters (such as My Project).

   You can use an existing alias as a starting point. Just choose one of your aliases from the Database Alias drop-down list.

6. If you want to create more aliases while you're in the Alias Manager dialog box, choose Keep New. The Keep New button changes back into a New button—just follow steps 1 through 6 to create as many aliases as you want.

7. To save your aliases, choose OK, then choose Yes to confirm that you want to overwrite the IDAPI.CFG or the PDOXWORK.CFG file.

   Note: The IDAPI.CFG file contains all sorts of information about the way Paradox is set up on your system. In this case, overwriting the file just adds your new public alias to your setup. When you create a project alias, it gets saved to the PDOXWORK.CFG file in your current working directory. This file contains information specific to that directory.

You can change the path for an alias at any time. Just open the Alias Manager, choose the alias from the Database Alias drop-down list, enter a new path in the Path text box, and choose OK. When you change the directory that an alias stands for, Paradox takes care of rerouting any references to that alias. For example, you might have created a form that references files in a particular directory to which you've assigned an alias. If you change the path for the alias, the form will automatically be updated to reflect your change.

To delete an alias:

1. Open the Alias Manager dialog box (choose File, Aliases).

2. Choose the alias you want to delete from the Database Alias drop-down list.

3. Choose Remove.

4. Choose OK, and choose OK again to confirm that you want to update the IDAPI.CFG file.

DO NOT DISTURB—DIRECTORY AT WORK

Working directories? Well, it's about time. Finally, a directory that does some work. Uh, wait, that's not quite what this is all about (even though your working directory does end up taking the brunt of the workload).

Working Directory is Paradox's way of saying *default directory* or *current directory*. It's the directory that all the files you create get dumped into, unless you specifically tell Paradox to put them somewhere else. And when you access any dialog box that gives you a list of files (like Open Table or Select File), the list of files that gets presented to you by default is from your working directory.

Why Do You Need One?

What's so important about having a working directory? Well, for one thing, Paradox doesn't give you a choice. When you install Paradox, a directory called WORKING is created just below your main Paradox directory. Unless you assign a different working directory, Paradox automatically uses WORKING as your working directory.

Since Paradox has already created a working directory, should you just use it for all of your work? No. Unless, of course, you're only going to create one application and you know you'll never use Paradox for anything else. Directories in Paradox are just like directories anywhere else—they're there to organize your stuff. And where your files are located can even affect different links and connections in Paradox. So create a new directory (you can do that from Windows File Manager) whenever you start a new project. And make that directory your working directory whenever you're working on the project.

Inside Scoop

It's a good idea to assign a working directory at the beginning of every Paradox session. That way you can be sure that all of your work on a particular project will be saved in the same place.

Changing Working Directories

No problem. The only thing to keep in mind is that the directory must already exist before you can use it as a working directory.

1. Choose File, Working Directory to open the Set Working Directory dialog box shown in Figure 1-13.

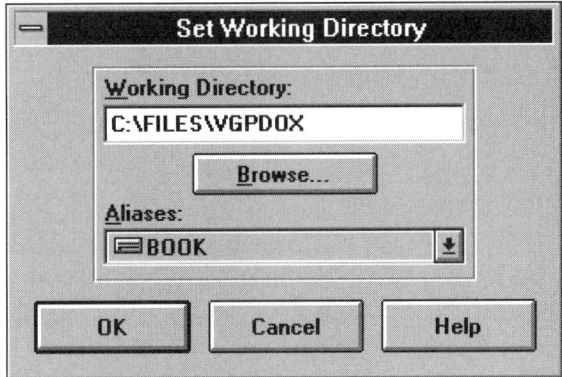

Figure 1-13: The Set Working Directory dialog box.

2. Do one of the following:
   ○ Type the directory's name (including its full path) in the Working Directory text box.
   ○ Click on the Browse button to open the Directory Browser dialog box. Use the Directories and Drive (or Alias) list to find the directory you want. Then select the directory and choose OK.
   ○ Choose an alias from the Aliases drop-down list.
3. Choose OK.

Pitfall Ahead

This isn't much of a pitfall—just something you should be aware of. Whenever you change working directories, Paradox closes any tables, forms or reports that are open. The reason this isn't a big problem is that Paradox doesn't close any objects that you've changed without asking you if you want to save them first.

Inside Scoop

The Project Viewer keeps track of the last ten directories you've used (whether or not they have aliases). So if the working directory you want to switch to has been used recently, just choose the directory or alias name from the Working Directory drop-down list in the Project Viewer.

PRIVATE—KEEP OUT

During installation, Paradox creates a directory called PRIVATE directly under your main Paradox directory and at the same time creates an alias for it: PRIV. Paradox uses this directory to store all sorts of temporary files that get created while you're working. You'll learn more about temporary files throughout the book. For now, you don't have to worry too much about all this "private" stuff except to know that anything you see in your private directory will get deleted as soon as you exit Paradox. If you've got a keeper in there, you have to save it with a different name before you leave Paradox.

Note: In a network installation, Paradox doesn't automatically create the PRIVATE directory. When you install Paradox on a network, you can specify a private directory for each user, or you can allow Paradox to use the Windows temporary directory.

You can tell Paradox to use a different directory for your private directory (there's really no reason to if you're on a stand-alone system, but I'll tell you how to do it just in case).

1. Choose File, Private Directory.

Figure 1-14: The Private Directory dialog box.

2. Enter the directory name (including the full path) in the Private Directory text box. Or use the Browser to select the directory you want.

3. Choose OK.

LOOKING AT TABLES

Tables are the basic building blocks of Paradox applications. As you'll see in the next few chapters, you can put just about any kind of information in a table. Tables can even include pictures and sounds. At the most basic level, tables are just rows and columns filled with stuff. But add a little Paradox magic to those rows and columns, and there are few limits to what you can do with that stuff. Read all about it in Chapters 3, 4 and 5.

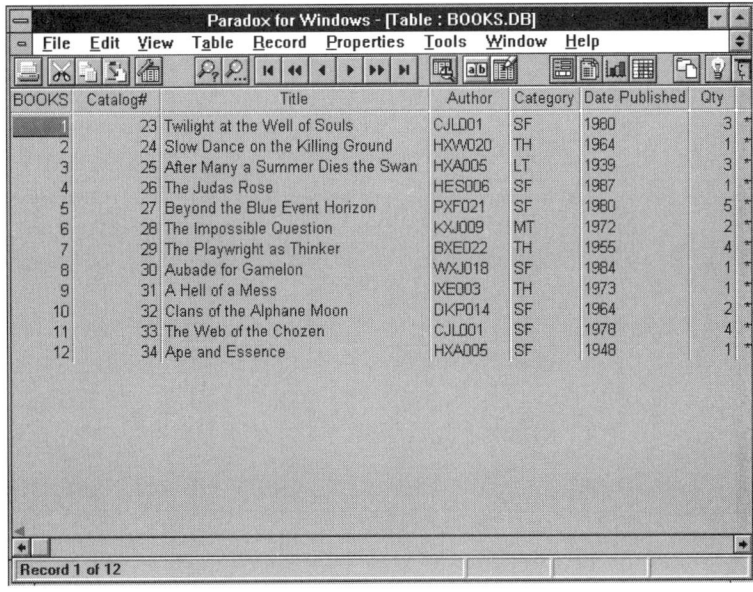

Figure 1-15: A sample table.

LOOKING AT QUERIES

If tables are the basic building blocks of Paradox, you might say that queries are the glue that holds the blocks together. (Or you might not.) A query's just a question—like "How many science fiction books with a list price over $5.50 did we sell last month?" Or, "Do we have any customers named Smith who live in Seattle?" Or, "How much wood could a woodchuck chuck if a woodchuck could chuck wood?"

Some of the other tasks that queries can accomplish include performing calculations on your data; adding specified information to or deleting specified information from a table; and comparing groups of records. You'll learn all about queries in Chapters 7 and 8.

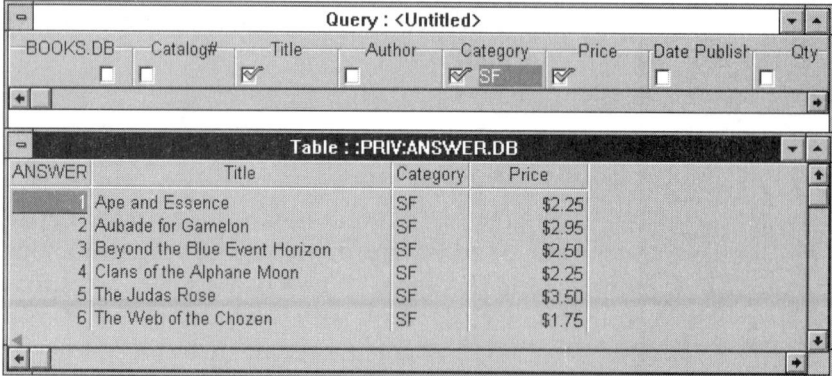

Figure 1-16: This figure shows a query followed by the answer table that resulted when I ran the query.

LOOKING AT FORMS

Forms are another way of looking at your data, and they can make it much easier to enter and work with information by enabling you to zero in on one record at a time. Whenever you create a table, you can access a ready-made QuickForm, which is just a default form without any bells and whistles.

And forms can get as fancy as you want them to be. You can create customized forms with Paradox's form designer. Add colors, lines and boxes, graphic objects and lots of other stuff. And with a little ObjectPAL programming, you can create forms that carry out all sorts of complicated instructions, depending on which button gets clicked.

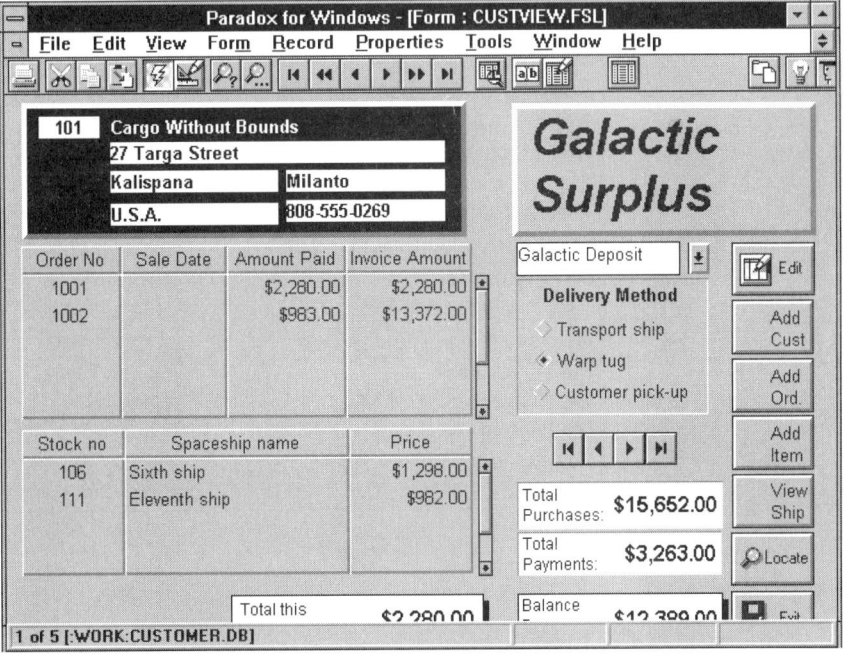

Figure 1-17: A sample form.

You'll learn all about forms in Chapters 9 and 10.

LOOKING AT REPORTS

What good is all of your hard work without the ability to print out a fancy report to wow your bosses and make your points crystal clear? Paradox's Report Designer is similar to the Forms Designer. You can design custom reports and include information from multiple tables. If you've created a form you want to use as a report, you can borrow the form's layout by opening the form as a report. No need to re-invent the wheel. You'll learn all about reports in Chapters 11 and 12.

Book List

Title	Last Name	First Name
A Hell of a Mess	Ionesco	Eugene
After Many a Summer Dies the Swan	Huxley	Aldous
Ape and Essence	Huxley	Aldous
Aubade for Gamelon	Willett	John
Beyond the Blue Event Horizon	Pohl	Frederik
Clans of the Alphane Moon	Dick	Phillip K.
Slow Dance on the Killing Ground	Hanley	William
The Impossible Question	Krishnamurti	J.
The Judas Rose	Haden Elgin	Suzette
The Playwright as Thinker	Bentley	Eric
The Web of the Chozen	Chalker	Jack L.
Twilight at the Well of Souls	Chalker	Jack L.

Figure 1-18: A sample report.

GETTING HELP

We all need a little help from our friends, and Paradox wants to be *your* friend. So it's right there lending you a helping hand. If you're already familiar with Windows's help screens, a lot of this'll be old hat (but some of it won't, so keep reading).

This is arguably the most important thing you'll learn in this book. Sure, we'll clue you in on all sorts of earth-shattering stuff and fill you with words of wisdom, but what happens when we're not around? What if (horror of horrors) you leave this book on the bus, but you need to complete an important project and your boss doesn't buy your excuse that you absolutely must have this incredibly wonderful book by your side in order to accomplish anything at all?

Here's what. You use Paradox's comprehensive help system, complete the project ahead of schedule, and get a raise. (Truth in advertising–I can't promise you the raise.) There are five main ways of getting help:

○ The Help menu

○ Context-sensitive Help

○ Coaches

○ Experts

○ Bug the person at the next desk (just checking to see if you're paying attention).

The Help Menu

You choose items from Paradox's Help menu just like you do from any other menu. And wherever you are in Paradox, the Help menu is there (it's not one of those menus that changes depending on what you're doing).

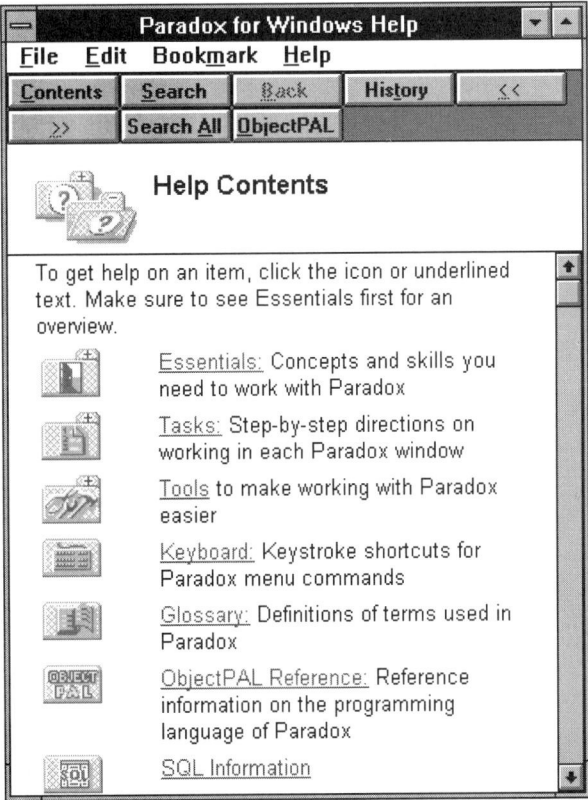

Figure 1-19: When you choose Help, Contents, you get a Help window that lists all of the different Paradox Help options.

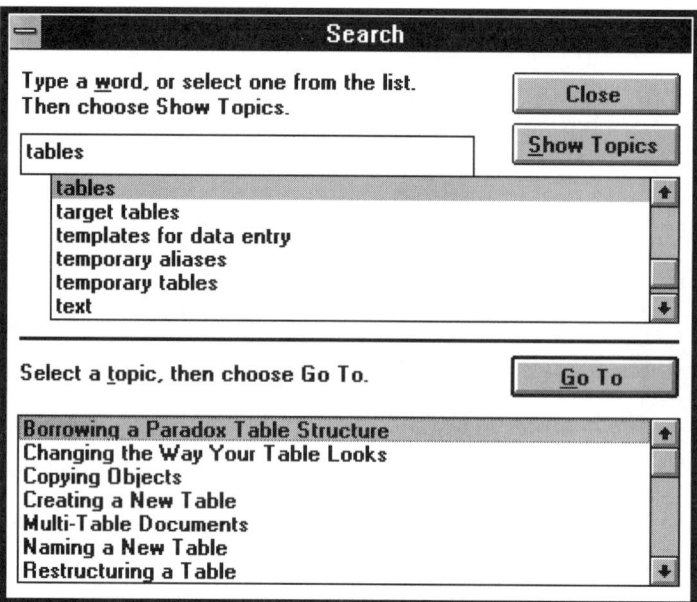

Figure 1-20: When you choose Help, Search For Help On, you get this Search dialog box, which lets you search for topics in Paradox Help's index.

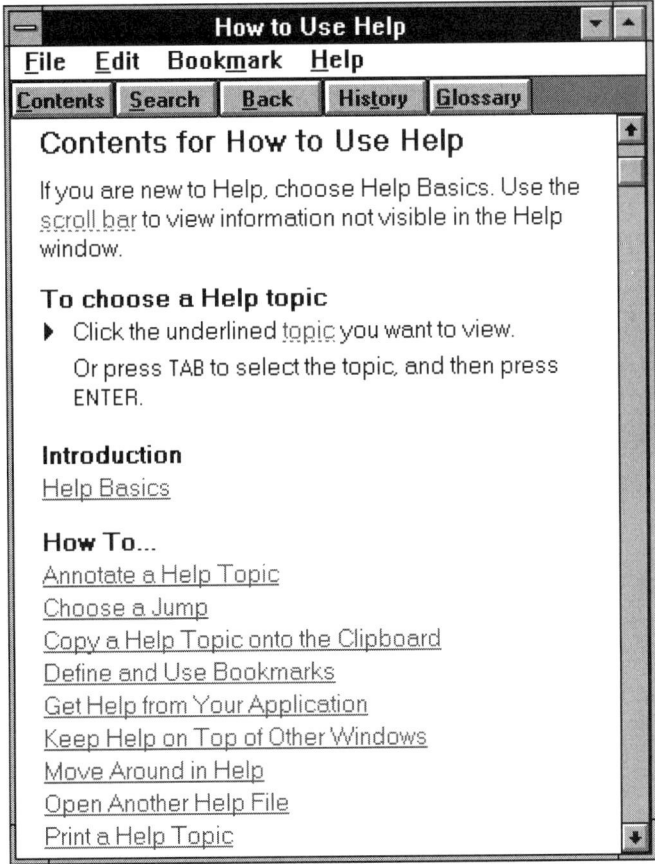

Figure 1-21: If you're not familiar with Windows Help systems, from any Help window choose Help, How to Use Help, follow the instructions and just play around a bit.

Context-Sensitive Help

Context-sensitive just means that the help you get depends on what you're working on at the time. And there are two ways to get it:

○ Press F1. When a menu item is selected, or when you're using a particular Paradox object, you'll usually get help that's specific to that item or object.

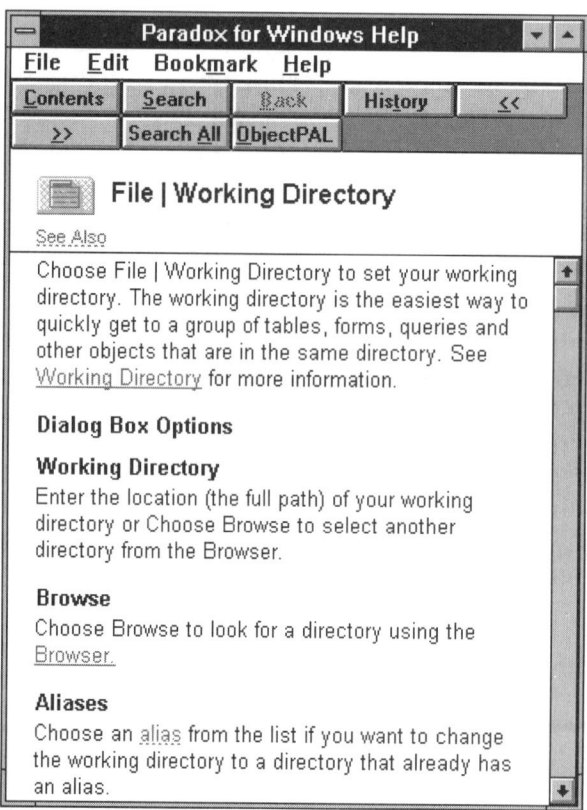

Figure 1-22: When I highlight Working Directory on the File menu and press F1, I get the Help window that tells me all about working directories.

Note: To highlight Working Directory on the File menu, I have to use the arrow keys to get there. If I click on Working Directory instead, I'll just open the Set Working Directory dialog box.

○ The other way to get context-sensitive help is to choose the Help button that's included in most dialog boxes. If there's a Help button in the dialog box you're using, just click on it to get information about that dialog box.

Inside Scoop

When in doubt, press F1. If context-sensitive help is available for the dialog box or selected menu item, you'll get it; if there's no context-sensitive help, you'll get Help Contents, which'll take you wherever you want to go in Help.

Coaches

Want a little hand-holding (but no hanky-panky!)? Paradox's new Coaches will take you by the hand and lead you step by step through an assortment of tasks. Just choose Coaches from the main Help menu to open the window you see in Figure 1-23.

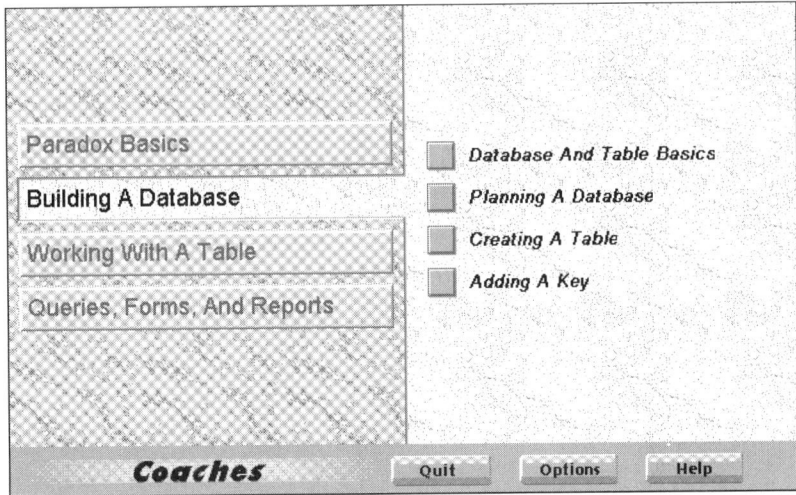

Figure 1-23: This is what you get when you choose Help, Coaches or click on the Coaches Toolbar icon (the little no-neck guy at the right end of the Toolbar).

Click on any of the four main topics on the left (Paradox Basics, Building A Database, Working With A Table or Queries, Forms, And Reports) to display a list of the available Coaches for that topic. In Figure 1-23, I clicked on Building a Database, so I get to choose from a list of Coaches designed to help with the basics of designing and creating a database. I want to create a table, but I'm not sure of all the steps, so I'll click on Creating A Table. Figure 1-24 shows a sample Coach window.

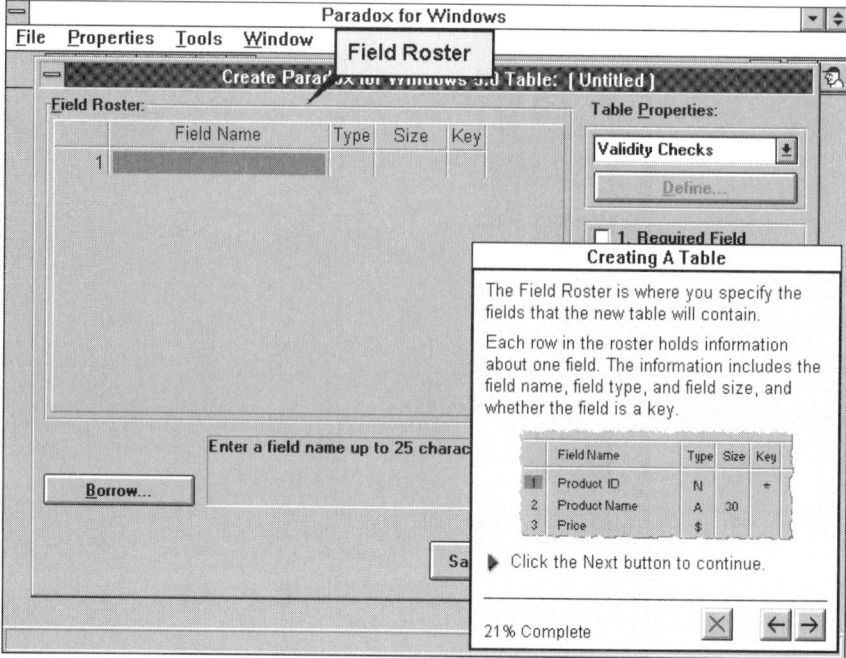

Figure 1-24: This Coach is all set to guide you through the process of creating a table.

What's really cool about Coaches is that you're actually entering and changing your own data as you move through the tutorial. A lot of tutorials use examples that don't have anything to do with what you're trying to accomplish.

○ You can exit a Coach at any time by clicking on the button with the red X. When you quit the Coach, any work you created during the tutorial remains on your screen.

○ Move forward or backward one step at a time by clicking on the Next (right arrow) or Previous (left arrow) button.

○ When you do something the Coach doesn't like, you'll see a little "Try Again" window that tells you what you're supposed to do.

Experts

And if Coaches aren't cool enough for you, give Experts a try. Coaches actually make you do some of the work—Experts do all the work for you. Paradox includes Experts for forms, mailing labels and reports. We'll talk more about Experts in the appropriate chapters, but here's a little taste of what they can do.

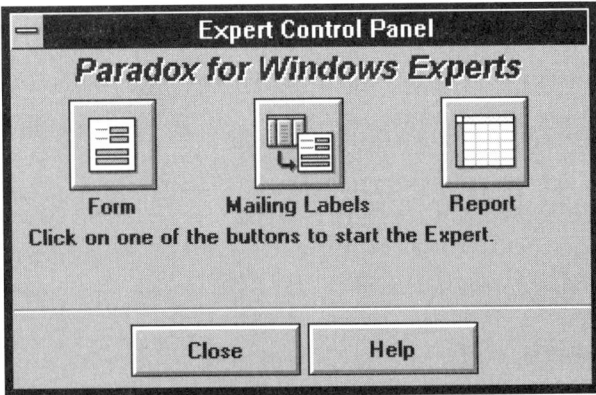

Figure 1-25: Choose Experts from the Help menu or click on the Expert button (the light bulb icon next to the Coaches button) to open the Expert Control Panel dialog box.

Note: You can also access the Form Expert from the New Form dialog box and the Report and Label Experts from the New Report dialog box.

From the Expert Control Panel dialog box, choose the Expert you want to run.

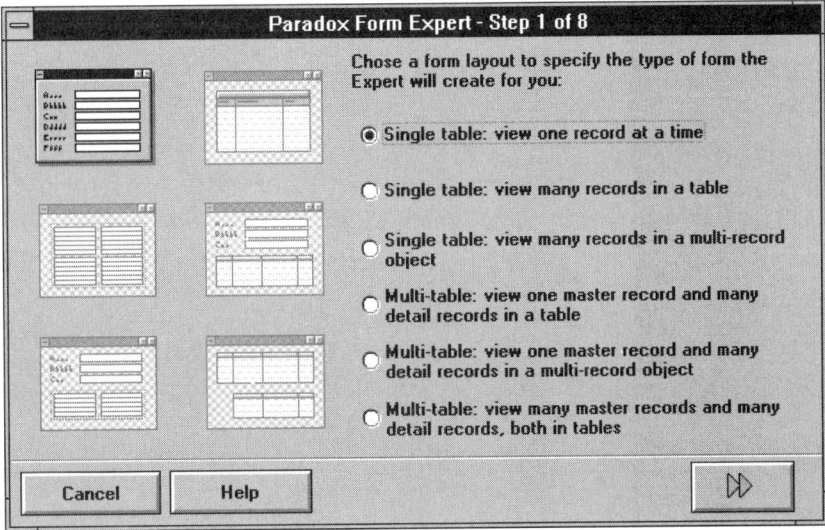

Figure 1-26: The first screen of the Form Expert.

As you can see in Figure 1-26, the Form Expert leads you through the process of designing a form. Just choose from the available options and click on the Next button (the double right arrows) to move to the next screen. When you've answered all of the Expert's questions, the Next button turns into a lightning bolt, which is Paradox's standard Design icon. Click on the Design button to instruct Paradox to go ahead and create the form.

Once you've used an Expert to create a form or report, you can make any changes you want. The end result is a plain vanilla Paradox form or report—no special tricks. The only trick is in the process Paradox takes to get to that point. So Experts can be a great shortcut for the initial form and report design processes—just use an Expert to build the basic design and modify to your heart's content.

MOVING ON

At this point, consider yourself properly outfitted for the Paradox trek. As we traverse the next several chapters and work through the gory details, you'll discover a world of possibilities. For now, though, you know your way around the desktop and you can recognize a whole bunch of Paradox objects (and you even know what objects are).

Now that you're chomping at the bit, just bursting to get your hands dirty with Paradox—slow down. In the next chapter we step backward to take a look at the essential task of planning your database. I know it's tempting to skip over this chapter and get right to what seems to be the meat of Paradox—creating tables, designing forms and reports, working with queries and all sorts of other fun stuff. But take the time to read through Chapter 2 (it's really not that long) to get a sense of how important design and planning are to the whole process.

2 THE DESIGN'S THE THING

Once upon a time, a very long time ago, in that all-but-forgotten age before 486's were considered entry-level computers—yes, before there were even any computers at all (can you conceive of such a time?)—there were databases. Yes, even in that primitive era of carbon paper and "white-out," people had to keep track of information. Some of the methods they used may have been clumsy and inflexible, but folks did what they could with the available technology.

Fortunately, you have Paradox, which gives you high-powered tools to create databases that meet your needs and grow as your needs change. But even with all of Paradox's power at your disposal, it's still possible to create clumsy and inflexible databases. In order to get the most out of Paradox, you have to spend time planning and designing your database. That's what this chapter is all about; by the end of it, you'll know the secrets of designing databases that do everything you want them to.

ALL THE WORLD'S A DATABASE

What's a database? It's a phone book, a recipe collection, a list of your videos or cassettes—just about anything. And if your handwritten lists allow you to find what you want and you're happy, they're serving their purpose. So at what point would you need to move beyond your handwritten database? When you're not happy with your current system, when you want to be able to search for information that's not readily accessible in its current fragmented form.

Figure 2-1: All of these are databases.

Example—you collect names and addresses on paper napkins, matchbook covers and corners torn off of magazine pages. And your storage system consists of dropping the data wherever you happen to be when you jot it down or empty your pockets. This system may work great for you—until you spend 20 minutes looking for that phone number you put *somewhere*.

The first step in simplifying your database might be simply to gather up all of the miscellaneous scraps and put them in a box. That way, you're no longer searching through the whole house—you have only one place to look. This might work for a while, but finding a particular piece of info is still no easy task.

Figure 2-2: Some data-storage techniques.

So your next step might be to organize all of the data into alphabetical order. That's cool, and you might think it will solve all your problems. But what about company names versus people's names? If you file by company name, how do you quickly find the name of a person at that company? And what if you want to find all of the people who live in Seattle? Or all of the people and companies that do computer consulting? Or all those who are in your area code?

This is where you start thinking (or should start thinking) about automating—dumping your data into a computer program that can reorganize and retrieve the stuff for you. And since this book's about Paradox, why don't we assume that Paradox is the computer program you decided to use. (If it's not, you bought the wrong book.)

Inside Scoop

Your database needs might be simple enough that you can get away without doing any programming, but don't rule it out without reading and trying out the last few chapters of this book. Paradox's programming language, ObjectPAL, is easy when you get the hang of it, and a little programming can really expand your database horizons. For example, you can have a menu like the one in Figure 2-3 that's the first thing you see when you load the database. Use ObjectPAL to customize your application and make it much easier on yourself and others who will use it.

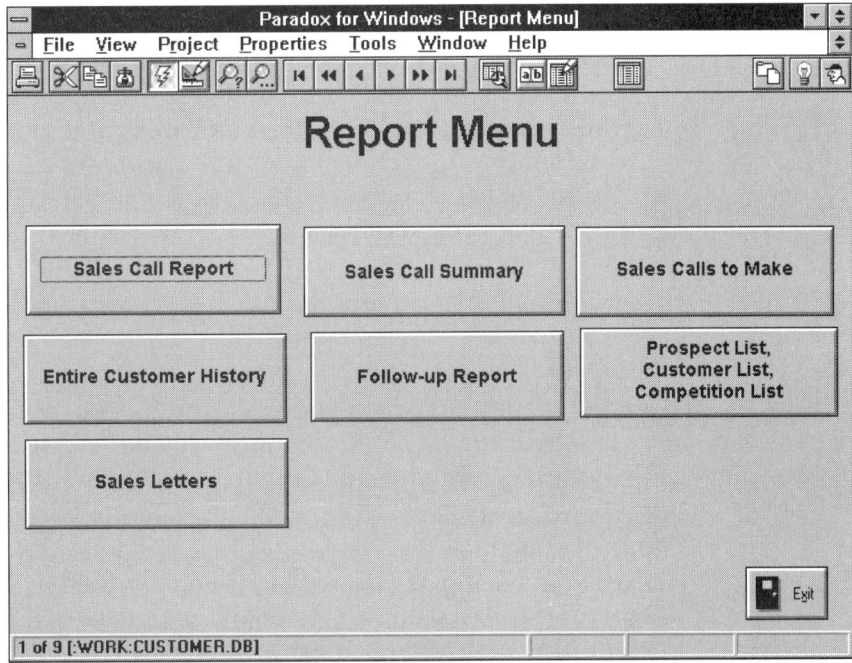

Figure 2-3: A menu like this means that users can easily get where they want to go, even if they don't know much about Paradox.

Now you see the advantages of a database program. And after careful consideration, you buy Paradox for Windows. (Smart move!) So what's the first thing you do? Install Paradox? Learn just enough to create simple tables, and immediately start entering all your data? No. Stop and THINK.

Figure 2-4: Don't touch that computer yet—put on your thinking cap.

Yup, that's the first step—thinking.

THINK ABOUT IT: MAKE A PLAN

The most important part of creating a database happens long before you even turn on the computer. It's natural to be impatient and want to just *get it done*, but rein in those impulses. The time you spend planning and designing your database will pay off in the long run. Don't get freaked out about the idea of *database design*. It sounds like a huge and complicated concept, but it's just a matter of thinking about what you want to do before you do it, instead of doing it first and making awkward adjustments afterward. Designing a database correctly means never having to say you're sorry (at least not as often).

○ Start by thinking about the end result: what problem are you trying to solve? Don't even think about the data itself until you're clear about what you want it to do.

○ Allow more time than you think you'll need—if your entire project is scheduled to take four months, it's not unreasonable to allow a month for planning and design.

There are a couple of ways to approach the design process. The one that might at first seem most logical is to start with data entry: figure out what data you need to input, proceed to design tables and input forms based on that data and then create reports as you need them. This is an approach many people take. Do you see anything wrong with it? Okay, here's a hint. What happens if you find you need a certain report, but your tables aren't structured in a way that allows you to create the report? Or maybe the data you need for the report isn't even included in your tables. Yeah, that's the problem. When you start with the details, you're ignoring (at your potential peril) the larger purpose—what your database is supposed to accomplish in the first place.

Another approach is to design from the top down—work backward from the reports and other output that you want to end up with, and use those reports to determine how the database should be structured. The advantage here is that by looking at the big picture first, you're less likely to bump up against surprises down the road. By working from output needs, you'll design a database that's capable of producing the right results.

TALK ABOUT IT

Gather information. Unless you're the only one who'll be using the data, it's important to bring other people into the process. Have meetings that include people who will be using the database from both ends of the spectrum—and the middle, too. In too many cases, databases are planned by committees of executives without taking the needs of the lower echelons (the ones who do most of the work) into account. (And even if no one but you will ever look at the data, read this section anyway. Whether or not groups of people are involved in the process, everything in this section should be part of your planning process.)

Brainstorm

The first step is to get everyone together and brainstorm about the project. Make sure the group includes at least one representative from each of the following types of users: those who gather the data, those who input the data, those who need to work with the data (write queries, reports, etc.) and those who receive the final results.

Figure 2-5: These people are serious—they came prepared with all their notes and reports.

Inside Scoop

Obviously, your group meetings can't include *everyone* who will end up working with the database (unless the entire group consists of no more than five or six members). If your database will be used by a large group, consider distributing a questionnaire to help you get information from a wider user base. The questionnaire should be developed *after* your initial group meeting.

Ask people to come to the meeting with anything they can think of that might relate to the project. Any data entry forms, reports, *anything* that could contribute to the discussion. And tell them not to worry at this point about whether the information makes sense or is really relevant. You could start the meeting by spreading all of the current printed output on a table and letting everyone take a look at how things are handled now.

Start by asking some of these questions (the more open-ended at first, the better):

○ What do you want to be able to do that you can't do with your current system?

○ Do you have access to this information right now?

○ If so, how do you get it? On a computer or manually?

○ Who collects the information?

○ How do you store the information?

○ Who will use the system, and should data-entry people or others be prevented from viewing certain confidential data that needs special protection?

You should come out of this first meeting with a basic game plan and a consensus about general goals.

Make Lists

At your next meeting, make a whole bunch of lists. Write down everything that needs to be included (don't worry yet about breaking the information down into any kind of structure). Use all the pieces you've gathered so far to put the lists together. Go over every report and form that's currently being used.

Preliminary List

Books
Authors
Invoices
Orders
Publishers
Customers
Purchase Orders
Customer Address
Titles
Book Categories
Price
Date Published
Book Summaries
Quantity in Stock

Figure 2-6: A preliminary list for Bookfinders.

Once you have the list, go through it with a fine-tooth comb and decide which items might not be necessary. And, in the process, you'll probably come up with items you need to add.

Now you just need a bit more information before you can go into hibernation and put it all together. Using your lists as guides, talk about the connections between items. Don't confuse anyone with database lingo—just talk in plain English about how the information has to work together.

SKETCH IT OUT

Work out a preliminary design. Here's where the fun begins. You get to take all these lists and accumulated data and turn them into a workable application. But no sweat—you've read this book, you're happenin', you're cool—you're a budding database designer!

But before you get going (hold on, we're almost there), there are a few rules and concepts we need to talk about.

How Many Tables?

You might need only one table if you know (absolutely positively for sure) that the database will be used for one purpose and one purpose only. For example, you might have a Christmas card list of names and addresses that's used *only* for Christmas mailings. The problem here is that what you're absolutely positively sure of today can change tomorrow (or even later this afternoon). Better to prepare for other eventualities. Get out that crystal ball. Get feedback from people who will use the system (at all levels). What if you decide to keep track of who sent you a Christmas card back? Or you want to track the names and ages of the children?

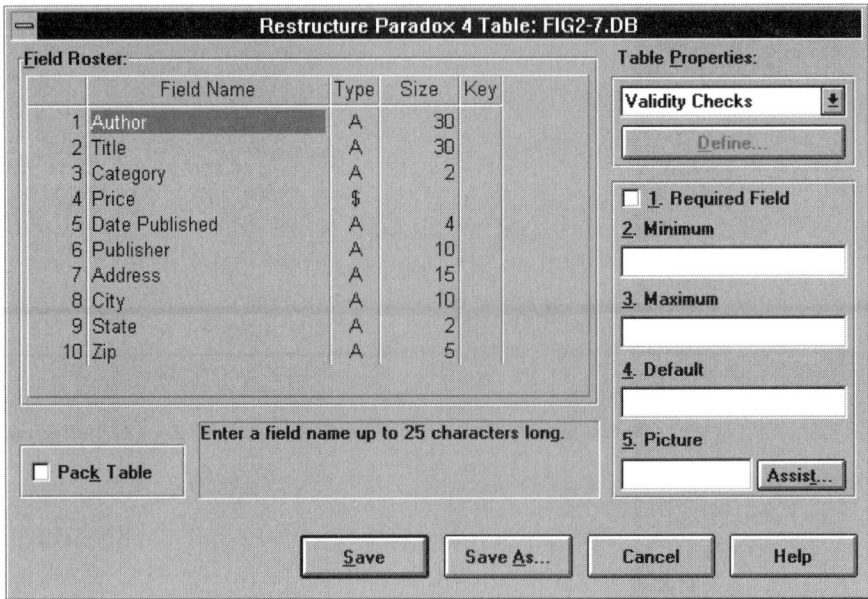

Figure 2-7: One table that contains all of Bookfinders's data.

In Figure 2-7, all of the fields for the Bookfinders application are in one table. It might seem like that's the easiest way to do it—everything in one place. But Paradox doesn't care whether your data is in 1 table or 50. By linking tables, you can easily cross-reference data in different locations.

Are They Normal?

Most stuff, even if it's simple, needs at least two tables. And the reason is...normalization. (You do want to be normal, don't you? Well, even if you don't, your databases do, so keep reading.)

Normalization is a fancy database term that stands for something simple and logical. Normalization helps to ensure accuracy, prevent duplicate entries that cause errors and simplify retrieval. If you're entering a name and address in several different places, what are the chances that you won't *ever* make a mistake? You don't have to answer that one. Addresses are prime examples: if they're spread out all over the place, you can't be sure you're using the most current one. If the address is on a particular order form, it's the address that was correct at the time that order was placed. That address might have been updated in the main customer table but not changed in all of the other places where you've entered the address.

Author	Title	Price	Date	Publisher	Address	City	State	Zip
Eugene Ionesco	A Hell of a Mess	$3.95	1973	Grove	53 E. 11th	New York	NY	10003
Sheri S. Tepper	Grass	$4.95	1989	Bantam	666 5th Ave.	New York	NY	10022
Ursula K. LeGuin	The Beginning Place	$2.25	1980	Bantam	666 5th Ave.	New York	NY	10022
Robert Silverberg	Tower of Glass	$1.25	1970	Bantam	666 5th Ave.	New York	NY	10022
Ben Bova	To Save the Sun	$4.99	1992	Tor	175 5th Ave.	New York	NY	10010

Table : FIG2-8.DB

Figure 2-8: Unnormalized.

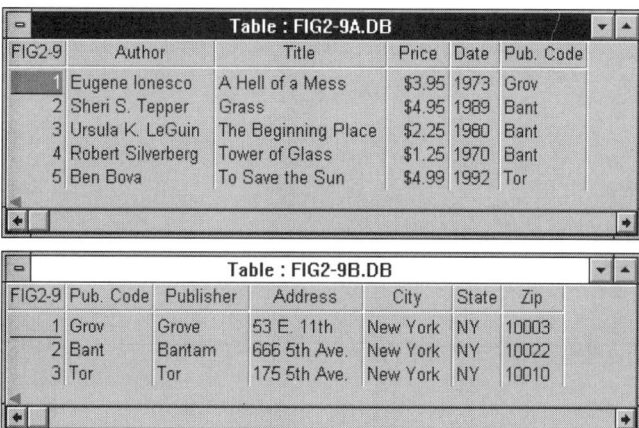

Table : FIG2-9A.DB

FIG2-9	Author	Title	Price	Date	Pub. Code
1	Eugene Ionesco	A Hell of a Mess	$3.95	1973	Grov
2	Sheri S. Tepper	Grass	$4.95	1989	Bant
3	Ursula K. LeGuin	The Beginning Place	$2.25	1980	Bant
4	Robert Silverberg	Tower of Glass	$1.25	1970	Bant
5	Ben Bova	To Save the Sun	$4.99	1992	Tor

Table : FIG2-9B.DB

FIG2-9	Pub. Code	Publisher	Address	City	State	Zip
1	Grov	Grove	53 E. 11th	New York	NY	10003
2	Bant	Bantam	666 5th Ave.	New York	NY	10022
3	Tor	Tor	175 5th Ave.	New York	NY	10010

Figure 2-9: Normalized.

A couple of rules of thumb will help you figure out when you should use more tables:

○ This is the most important rule: If you find yourself repeating information in several records, you probably need a new table. In Figure 2-8 (the unnormalized table), notice that the publisher name and address fields are repeated for each book. You can simplify data entry and reduce errors by putting the publisher information in a separate table and including a field in the books table that refers to the publisher table.

○ Any time a table has so many fields that it's difficult to view your data, consider breaking it down into more than one table.

○ Does your table have more than one "theme"? Does it try to accomplish more than one goal? One way to find out is by jotting down all the different elements (types of people, things, events, orders, etc.). Then take a look at your records. Do they have any data that overlaps into another category? If so, then you have too much stuff in the table. (When I say "overlaps," I'm not referring to a field that refers to another table, like a customer ID number inside an order table. I'm talking about duplicating all of the customer data inside the order table—including the customer's name, address and phone number—with each order.)

○ If you're entering the same data into two or more records, think about splitting off a new table. For example, you wouldn't want to include detailed order information in a customer table—the same customer could place lots of orders (you hope), so the customer and order information should be in separate, linked tables.

Figure 2-10: This table is repetitive fields personified.

○ Are fields repeated within the table? Take a look at Figure 2-10. In this table, there's a field for each of the author's books. Notice that there are four separate book fields. To search this table for a particular book, you'd have to search through each of the four book fields. And what if an author has the audacity to write more than five books? Where does it end? I'll tell ya—with a separate book table that's linked to the author table.

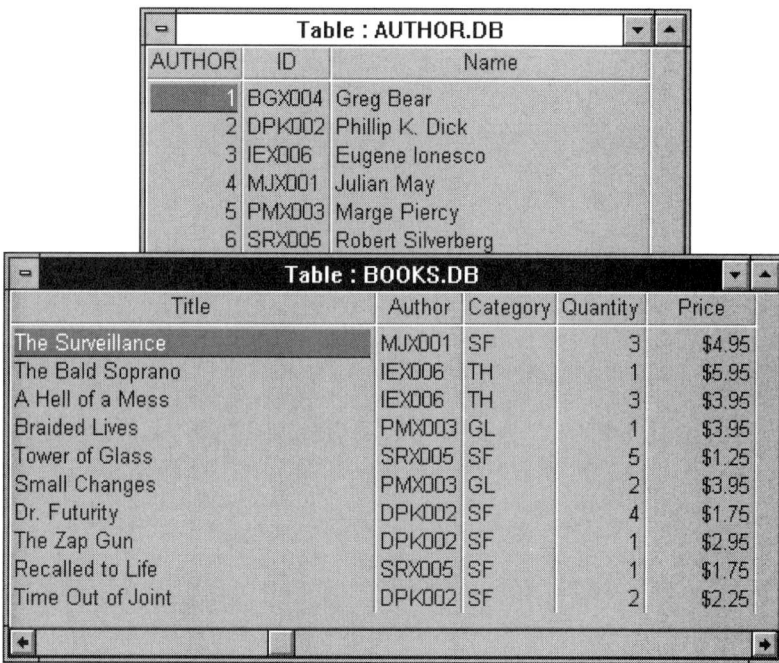

Figure 2-11: Books and authors broken down into logical groups of tables.

Let's examine Figure 2-11 further. It still has a lot of problems.

Chunkify & Sift

In AUTHOR.DB, notice that the first and last names are in the same field. Not a good idea. If you want to sort on last names or print a report that includes all of the last names that begin with A through D, you're out of luck. As a general rule, break each piece of data into its smallest meaningful chunk. What's meaningful? Any chunk that you might want to do something with. You definitely want to have the street address, city, state and ZIP Code items in separate fields, but splitting the street address into two fields (one for the street number, one for the street name) wouldn't accomplish anything.

AUTHOR	Author ID	Last Name	First Name
1	AXI007	Asimov	Isaac
2	BXE022	Bentley	Eric
3	CJL001	Chalker	Jack L.
4	DKP014	Dick	Phillip K.
5	HES006	Haden Elgin	Suzette
6	HXA005	Huxley	Aldous
7	HXW015	Hanley	William
8	IXE003	Ionesco	Eugene
9	KXJ009	Krishnamurti	J.
10	LCS010	Lewis	C.S.
11	LUK013	LeGuin	Ursula K.
12	LXD002	Lessing	Doris
13	PXF021	Pohl	Frederik
14	RXJ006	Russ	Joanna
15	SJP004	Sartre	Jean Paul
16	SXI012	Salajan	Ionna
17	WXJ018	Willett	John
18	ZXE008	Zamiatin	Eugene

Table : AUTHOR.DB

Figure 2-12: This table's chunkified.

Inside Scoop

Ask yourself if you'll *ever* want to sort on part of a field. If the answer's yes, the portion that you want to sort on needs to be in its own field.

The next big question here is: Do you have any fields that can be calculated based on other fields? If so, you might be able to do away with some of those fields.

Pick a Primary Key

We're still picking on poor old Figure 2-11. Do you see any field that contains unique information (information that can't be duplicated in any other record)? Okay, I won't make you puzzle this out for yourself. The answer is—you don't. The name fields aren't unique—two or more people could certainly have the same name. And what if your list includes several people who are employed (or live) at the same place? The way it stands, there's no way to uniquely identify each record.

Almost every table (with few exceptions) should have a field (or fields) containing a value that doesn't exist in any other record. This field is called the *primary key*, and it's used to sort your table and keep you from duplicating records. You'll learn more about primary keys in Chapter 3, but the main thing for now is just to be aware that they're a good thing.

So what field should be the primary key? If none of the current fields will work, what should you do? That's easy—make one up. In fact, the best kind of primary key is one that doesn't contain any meaningful (or changeable) information. Paradox's new Autoincrement field is ideal for this purpose. Figure 2-13 shows a new field called Catalog# that uses an Autoincrement field (the numbers are assigned sequentially as you input the data for each record).

Catalog#	Title	Author ID	Category	Price	Date Pub	Qty
1	Twilight at the Well of Souls	CJL001	SF	$2.50	1980	3
2	Slow Dance on the Killing Ground	HXW020	TH	$5.95	1964	1
3	After Many a Summer Dies the Swan	HXA005	LT	$2.50	1939	3
4	The Judas Rose	HES006	SF	$3.50	1987	1
5	Beyond the Blue Event Horizon	PXF021	SF	$2.50	1980	5
6	The Impossible Question	KXJ009	MT	$2.25	1972	2
7	The Playwright as Thinker	BXE022	TH	$1.75	1955	4
8	Aubade for Gamelon	WXJ018	SF	$2.95	1984	1
9	A Hell of a Mess	IXE003	TH	$3.95	1973	1
10	Clans of the Alphane Moon	DKP014	SF	$2.25	1964	2
11	The Web of the Chozen	CJL001	SF	$1.75	1978	4

Figure 2-13: Catalog# is the key field in this table.

It's All Relative

Your tables get to know each other intimately through all sorts of links and references. Here's some info that will help you guide your charges through the maze of relationship types:

First thing. *Foreign keys*: A key that's a primary field in one table but it's being used as a reference in another table, so it's *foreign*. For example, the Author ID field is a primary key when it's in the AUTHOR table, but it becomes a foreign key when you use it in the BOOKS table. The foreign key is what links the BOOKS table to the AUTHOR table. And speaking of links, they come in the three following relationship flavors:

○ **One-to-one:** That's where each record in a table corresponds to one record in another table. In most cases, one-to-one relationships aren't necessary and may even be a warning that you have some design problems. One reason to use one-to-one relationships would be to split a table that has too many fields into two or more tables, to make it more workable.

○ **One-to-many:** Each record in the table can refer to multiple records in another table. In the case of AUTHOR and BOOKS, there's only one record for each author, but the same author could have written many books, so the same Author ID could appear in many records in the BOOKS table. In a one-to-many relationship, there has to be a common field that links the tables. Notice that both AUTHOR and BOOKS use the Author ID field. One-to-many is probably the most common type of link.

Inside Scoop

In some types of links, the table that only has one record is called the *parent* table, and the table that has many linked entries is called the *child* table. Referential integrity links (which you'll learn about in Chapter 4) use this terminology. In the example we're using here, AUTHOR is the parent and BOOKS is the child.

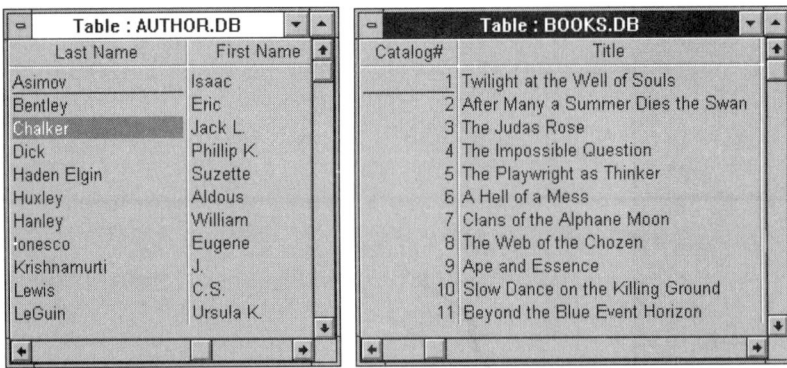

Figure 2-14: There's a one-to-many relationship between these two tables.

○ **Many to many:** Any number of records in a table can relate to any number of records in another table. With a many-to-many relationship, you don't actually link the two tables directly. You have to have a third table that acts as an intermediary. As you can see in

Figure 2-14, one publisher can represent many books, and one customer can buy from many publishers.

Linking Tips

○ When you're creating links, make sure the fields you're linking on are the same type and length.

○ It's a good idea to give linked fields the same name. Paradox doesn't require it, but using the same name makes it much easier to keep track of your links, especially in a complex structure.

○ In one-to-many relationships, the linked field in the parent table (the table that's on the *one* side of the relationship) should be the primary key.

In Figure 2-15, note that both Author ID fields are alphanumeric with a length of six characters (and they have the same name). The Author ID field in the AUTHOR table is the primary key.

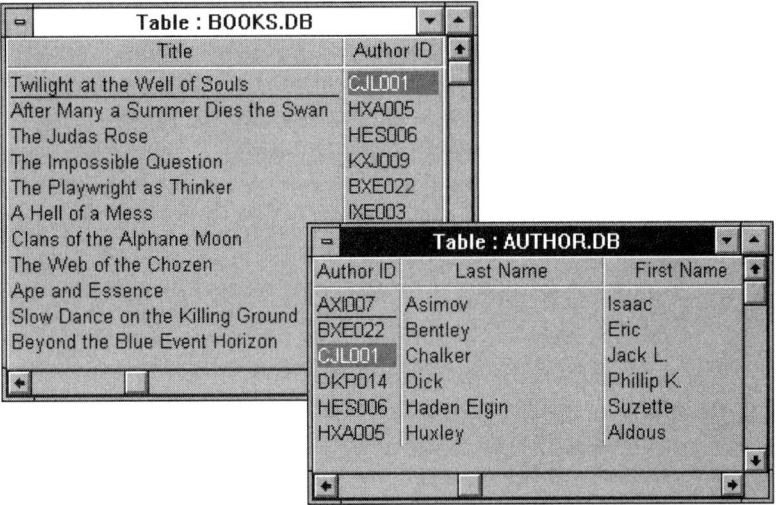

Figure 2-15: This example illustrates the points under "Linking Tips."

GET DOWN TO WORK

Figure out which fields you need, their types and how long each field needs to be. This is where *all* the information you've gathered comes into play. By this point, you should be able to zero in on your needs for a particular field. For example, if you have a ZIP Code field, will all of your ZIP Codes be five digits, or will they include extended (seven- or nine-digit) codes? And do you need to allow for Canadian codes or foreign addresses? The answers to these questions will determine how you set up the field.

○ Name your fields. Think about the links between tables. Whenever possible, linked fields should use the same names.

○ Sketch out your tables, forms and reports by hand, or use your favorite word processor or desktop publishing program. The idea is to work in a medium that's comfortable for you. You want to concentrate on the actual design process without worrying about how to implement that design in an unfamiliar program.

○ To secure your data, think about locking primary key fields. Also, use meaningless values for key fields. If you use names or some other potentially changeable data, you can mess up any links you have whenever you change the data.

IMPLEMENT & TEST IT

This is where you get to start playing with Paradox—creating tables, forms and reports. All of these elements are sketched out. Now all you have to do is create them. I won't get into the technical details of building Paradox tables and other objects—the next nine chapters lead you through the actual process.

Input your test data. Once you've built the application, you'll probably get a lot of pressure to immediately put it into use (especially if you're dealing with tight deadlines or if people have been waiting a long time for easy access to this data). Withstand that pressure. A database that doesn't get tested is a database that can end up with major problems. And who bears the brunt of any dissatisfaction (even if you were strong-armed into releasing the database before you were ready)? Yeah, you. And who has to untangle the mess after 30,000 records have already been entered? You again.

Inside Scoop

If you make it clear during your initial meetings that testing is an important process and explain your reasons, you'll meet with less resistance when it comes to crunch time.

So how do you test, and what are you looking for? You test by entering a small (but representative) amount of sample data. Your goal is to put the database through its paces with a little bit of data and discover any problems before you spend a ton of time dumping all of your company's data into it. You're looking for anything that could interfere with the smooth running of the database.

Be sloppy. Yes, I really meant that. The thing is, you're trying to uncover problems, and the way to do that is by making every data-entry mistake you can think of. Enter words in number fields, enter invalid data in fields that use referential integrity or lookup tables (both of these are covered in Chapter 4), etc.

Inside Scoop

As part of the testing process, go back to your initial planning group for input. Ask them to come up with off-the-wall, pie-in-the-sky requests—anything they think they might want out of the database even if it wasn't covered in your planning sessions. Then try to create the forms, reports or queries they request. This'll be the supreme test, because it's exactly what happens in real life. Everything is planned, all nice and neat, all contingencies covered, and then some department head decides she *must* have a certain report structured in a certain way (even though she was the one who categorically stated that she would *never* need a report like that).

○ If you have a name field, try the longest name you can think of to see if it fits in the field you designed.

○ Enter duplicate records to see what happens.

○ Create a bunch of queries (*querying* just means asking questions about your data, and it's covered in Chapters 7 and 8). Make sure your tables are set up so that you can ask the questions you need to ask.

○ Check out all links and validity checks.

○ Run all of the reports you've designed to make sure they work properly and that nothing was overlooked in the initial design process. Double-check any calculations in the reports.

Who should do all this testing? You? Believe it or not, you're not the best person to test the database you created. You're too close to it, you know what everything's *supposed* to do, and by now, your database knowledge goes way beyond that of most of the people who'll be using the system.

Get some volunteers from the groups that will actually be using the data—if possible, the least experienced users. You want to find problems the people doing the work may encounter. Take their feedback seriously, not only about actual errors, but about how easy or difficult the system is to use.

REFINE IT

Use the feedback you've received to work out problems, and modify your design as necessary. At this point, you're still working with sample data. Once you make all of your corrections, test it again just to make sure you haven't introduced any new glitches.

Now you can wave the green flag and tell the users they can start inputting all 59,000 records. But don't feel that's the end of it. Work with it. Use the database, but continue the feedback process. A database is always a work in progress.

Even if you've tested for every possible eventuality and everything works perfectly, new eventualities have a way of developing (eventualities are sneaky that way). Continue to solicit feedback, and modify your design to keep up with changing needs. This may sound ominous, but if you've gone through all the design steps and included everything you need, while at the same time retaining as much flexibility as possible, making changes will be easy. It's only when you've slapped together a haphazard design that making changes can pose problems.

MOVING ON

This chapter introduced you to database design and brought in a bunch of concepts to think about. It may seem like I've put the tail before the head. You might think the design information should come *after* you learn how to create tables, forms, reports and queries. But I put this chapter where it is to emphasize the importance of the design process. Don't worry if everything in the chapter isn't crystal clear right now. Just move on to the next chapter, where you'll start learning how to create tables. And when you've worked through the book and are ready to start creating your own application, come back to this chapter for a review.

3 TABLES 101

In the previous chapter, you learned how important it is to put in the effort to plan your database. Now it's time to get your feet wet and start creating tables.

Tables are the building blocks for your databases—all of the information you want to organize and use has to first be entered into a table (or, as is usually the case, several tables that contain different sets of related data). As with wooden or metal tables, Paradox tables are the foundation upon which you build—in this case, your database application. Hmmm, let's see how far I can stretch that analogy. Well, after you build (or buy) a table for your home, you put stuff on it, right? And you can move it around, pile books on it, dance on it—you get the idea. Once you've built a Paradox table, you can pile stuff *into* it—lots of useful stuff.

In this chapter you'll create the structure for a table that will contain information for Bookfinders, a small company that specializes in science-fiction, theatre and metaphysical books. In the next chapter, you'll add more tables to the database.

Begin by opening Paradox if you haven't already, and, so we'll all be starting from the same place, make sure you're at a blank Desktop (or that the only thing on your Desktop is the Project Viewer). That's right, clear the deck. See, you can always have a clean desktop somewhere (even if your furniture is buried under a mountain of rubble and your boyfriend calls you "Tornado"). Your screen should look like Figure 3-1 or Figure 3-2 on the next page. If it doesn't, choose Window, Close All to clear any open files from the Desktop.

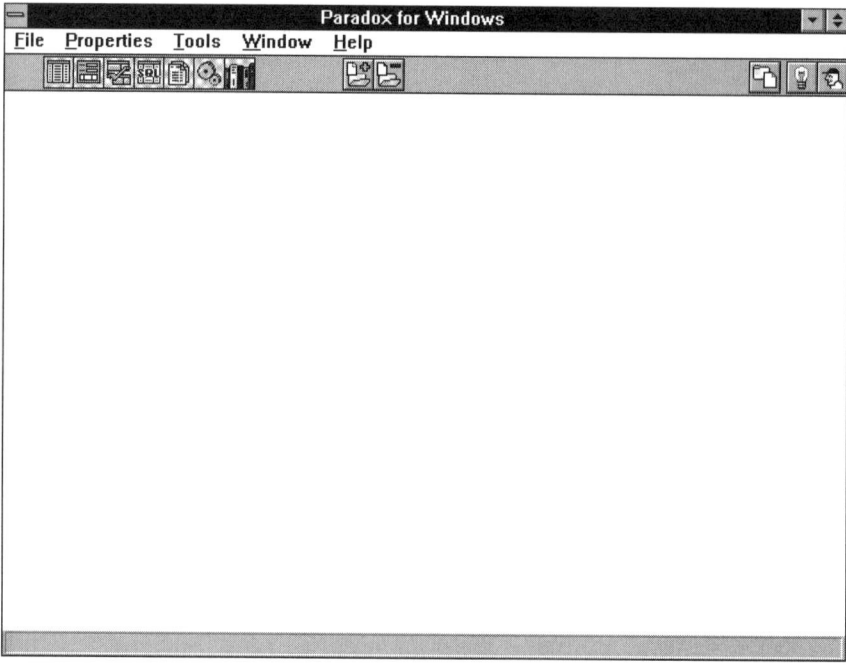

Figure 3-1: Your screen should look like this.

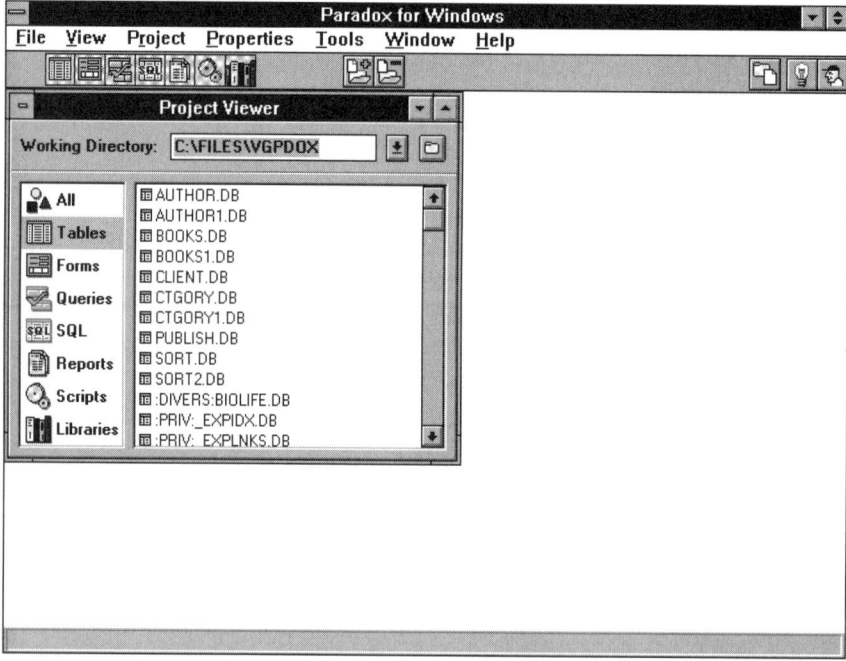

Figure 3-2: Or like this.

CREATING A NEW TABLE

In this chapter, I want you to dip your toe into the basics of creating a table structure before you jump into the deep end. Don't worry—by the time you're done with this chapter, you'll be comfortable enough with the basics that you'll be ready and eager to move on and find out what else you can do. The first step in creating a new table is setting up the table's structure. (Of course, before you even think about actually creating a table, I trust you've done all the preliminary design work!)

Next, it's a good idea to make sure your working directory is set the way you want it before you start creating your table. Yes, you can save your table to a different directory after you create it, but it's much easier and more efficient to set your working directory ahead of time so you're certain that all of the files you create for a particular database will end up in the same place.

To set your working directory, follow these steps:

1. Choose File, Working Directory to open the Set Working Directory dialog box shown in Figure 3-3.

Figure 3-3: The Working Directory dialog box.

2. In the Working Directory text box, enter the full path name of the directory you want to use.

    Or choose an alias from the Aliases drop-down list. Figure 3-4 shows the Set Working Directory dialog box with the Aliases drop-down list open.

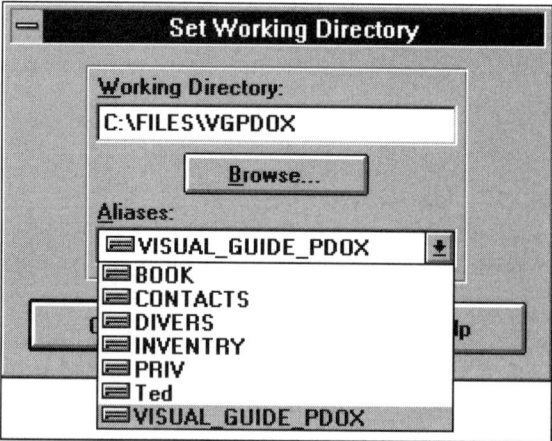

Figure 3-4: The Set Working Directory dialog box with the Aliases drop-down list open. Choose the alias you want from the drop-down list.

3. Choose OK once if you typed the directory name in the Working Directory text box.

Inside Scoop

The instructions above are meant to serve as a quick cheat sheet on working directories. For more detailed information about working directories and aliases, see Chapter 1, "Introducing . . . Paradox."

If the Project Viewer is open, you can save steps by using Project Viewer's Working Directory area. The drop-down list lets you choose one of the last ten working directories you've used, and the file icon takes you to the Directory Browser, where you can pick any drive or directory on your hard drive.

Choosing the Table Type

By default, Paradox tables are created in Paradox for Windows 5.0 format, but Paradox also allows you to create tables in Paradox 4, Paradox 3.5, dBase for Windows, dBase IV and dBase III+ formats. You choose the table type when you first create a new table.

Note: All of the examples in this chapter use the Paradox for Windows 5.0 format.

Inside Scoop

So why would you want a table that's not a Paradox for Windows table? I'll tell you. See, you might be working on a project with someone who uses Paradox for DOS or a version of dBase. Creating your table from scratch in the appropriate format means you don't have to mess around with a bunch of conversions or worry about which features will translate to a different program. And love means never having to say you're sorry (NOT!).

To open a new table:

1. Right-click on the Open Table Toolbar icon and choose New from the Object Inspector (or choose File, New, Table) to open the Table Type dialog box shown in Figure 3-5.

   Note: If the Project Viewer's open, you can right-click on its Table icon and choose New from the Object Inspector menu.

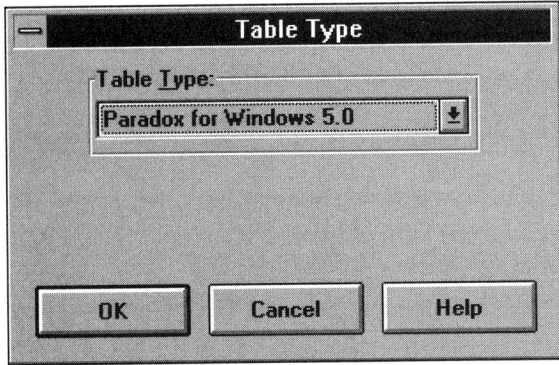

Figure 3-5: The Table Type dialog box.

2. Choose OK to accept Paradox for Windows 5.0 (the default) as the table type.
     If you want to select another table type, open the Table Type drop-down list and choose the type you want before you choose OK.
3. When you choose OK, the Create Paradox for Windows 5.0 Table dialog box appears, as shown in Figure 3-6.

The Field Roster section   The Table Properties section

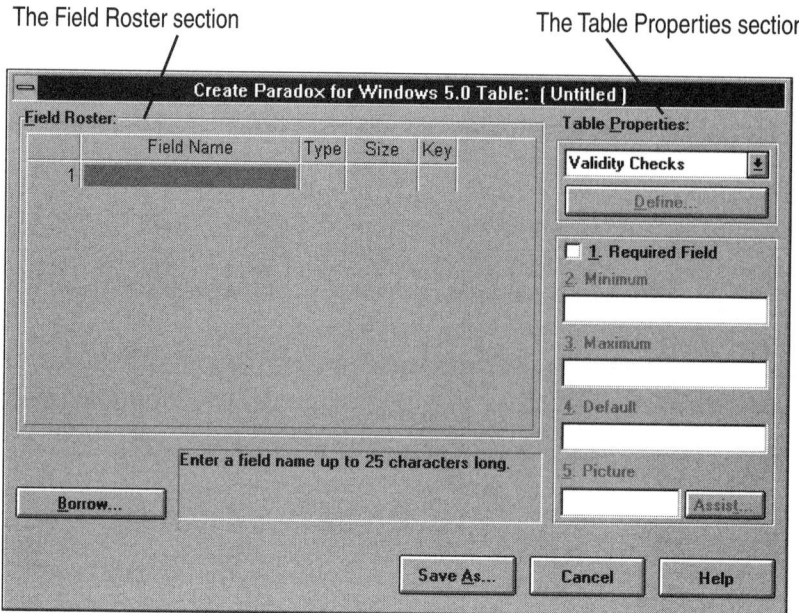

Figure 3-6: The Create Table dialog box.

In Figure 3-6 above, notice that the title bar says "Create Paradox for Windows 5.0 Table: (Untitled)." The title bar reflects the table type you chose and lets you know that the table hasn't been given a name yet.

Defining Fields

Take another look at Figure 3-6. The Field Roster section is where you enter the information for the fields you want to use. The Table Properties section contains options for adding validity checks, table lookups, secondary indexes, referential integrity, password security and changing the table language. This chapter focuses only on the Field Roster section—you'll find details about the various Table Properties options (and more information on field types) in Chapter 4.

Building the table structure is simply a matter of entering the information for each field on a separate line in the Field Roster.

To move around in the Field Roster with the keyboard:

○ Press Enter, Tab or the Right arrow key to move to the next column.

○ Press Shift+Tab or the Left arrow key to move to the previous column.

○ Press the Up arrow to move up one row.

○ Press the Down arrow to move down one row.

To move around in the Field Roster with your mouse, just click in the column you want. Whether you use the keyboard or the mouse, you'll notice that Paradox won't let you move into an area until you've entered all of the data that leads up to that area. For example, if you click on the Type column for Record 1 before you enter your field name, your computer will beep rudely at you, and the selection bar won't move. But once you've created Record 1 and moved on to Record 2, you can move back into any column in Record 1 to make changes. Also, you'll see that you don't have to do anything special to create a new row—as soon as you finish entering information for one field, Paradox automatically adds a new row when you press Enter, Tab, or the Down arrow.

Assigning Field Names

Paradox gives you a lot of latitude in naming your fields—field names can even include spaces, which makes it much easier to come up with names that don't look like hieroglyphics. But there are a few rules. Here goes:

○ You can have up to 25 characters in a field name.

○ A field name can include spaces, but it can't start with a space.

○ You can't have duplicate field names in a table, and you can't get around this by entering one name in uppercase and one in lower-case. Paradox doesn't differentiate between uppercase and lower-case in field names.

○ Field names can include any printable character, including letters, numbers and keyboard symbols. However, a few characters shouldn't be used in field names: " [ ] { } ( ) and ->. The number sign (#) can be used as part of a field name (ITEM#, for example), but it can't be used by itself.

○ Paradox automatically capitalizes the first letter of each field name.

Choosing the Field Type

You can choose among 17 types of fields (all of which are discussed in detail in Chapter 4). But don't sweat it—you don't have to remember the field type choices. When your insertion point's in the Type column, you can press the Spacebar or click the right mouse button to display an Object Inspector menu that lists all of the available field types. Just choose the type you want from the Type Inspector. Of course, if you already know which type you want and what it's called, you can just type the letter in the Type column.

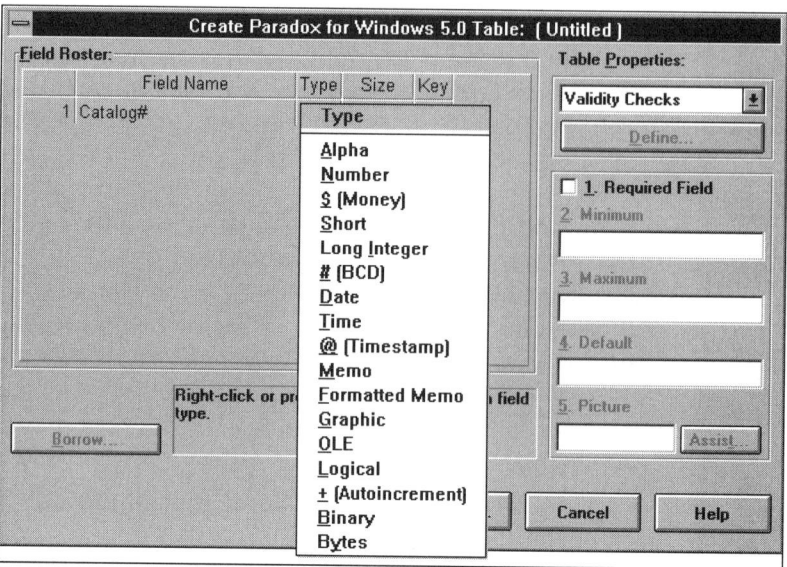

Figure 3-7: The Type Inspector menu in the Create Table dialog box. Just click on the field type you want or type the underlined letter or character.

Specifying the Field Size

You probably think (and logically so) that you can tell how big a field is by how wide the column for that field is. Well, whatcha see ain't always whatcha get. The size you specify determines how much data you can put in the field (and, as you'll soon see, for some field types it doesn't even do that), but the amount of data that shows up onscreen is decided in a totally separate operation. You'll learn how to change the way your table looks onscreen in Chapter 5, but for now I just don't want you to get hung up the notion that field size has anything to do with a table's appearance. You might designate 30 characters for a particular field but only have 10 characters visible at one time in the table. When you enter data for that field, Paradox allows you to enter all 30 characters—you just won't be able to see all of them without scrolling through the field (or changing the column width for the table so that more of the field is visible).

We'll get into field specifics in the next chapter (probably more of them than you ever thought you wanted to know). Right now I'll just tell you how Paradox handles the size issue for different field types.

○ The only types that force you to enter a size are Alpha, Memo and Bytes. With alpha fields, the size you specify actually determines the amount of data you're allowed to enter in the field (up to 255 characters). With memo fields, the size is just the amount of the memo that gets stored in the file with your table (up to 240 characters). A memo field can contain as much information as you want—until you run out of disk space. (You might, however, want to control yourself a bit and leave some room on your hard disk just in case you ever decide to write another memo or do anything else with your computer.)

○ So what happens to your colossal memo if only 240 characters are stored with your table? Paradox stores your whole memo in a separate file with an MB extension and retrieves the file when you view the memo field. This is a really cool way of handling it—the memo's there when you need it, but it's not taking up a bunch of space in your table and slowing things down.

○ None of the number-type fields let you specify a size. These fields are Number, Money, Date, Short Number, BCD, Timestamp and Long Integer. Most of the number-type fields allow you to enter up to 15 significant digits. You can control the length of entries in a particular field by defining a validity check, as you'll see in the next chapter.

○ Formatted Memo, Graphic, OLE and Binary fields work just the same as Memo fields in that up to 240 characters can be stored in the table's file, and the entire field is stored in a separate file with an MB extension. The only difference is that you're not required to specify a size for these four field types.

Defining Key Fields

Pop quiz. Anyone remember the song "Brand-New Key" (careful, you might be giving away your age) that Melanie sang (a lot) in the early 70's? There's a line, "I got a brand-new pair of roller skates, you got a brand-new key. . ." So, who thinks she's really talking about roller skates?? Nudge, nudge, wink, wink. But the point is that there's only one key that could possibly unlock her "roller skates." In other words, it's unique. There's no other key like it in the world (or at least in her neighborhood).

And so it goes with Paradox key fields. When you make a field a key field, you're saying that every entry in that field must be unique. If you try to make a duplicate entry in a key field, you get a key violation error message and you must make a different entry before you can move on to another record. Paradox uses the key field to create a primary index. All of the records in your table get sorted according to the primary index, and it's also used to ensure that every record in your table is unique.

So what kind of field should you turn into a key field? Name? Nope. The problem there is that more than one person can have the same name. Address? Nope again—you might have several people from the same company on your list. A part number or some similar identifier is a perfect candidate for a key field. And if your table doesn't include a part number, catalog number, employee number or some other unique identifier, you can always create an arbitrary field in which you enter a number or code to identify each record.

Inside Scoop

Paradox's new Autoincrement field type is perfect for key fields. Read all about it in the next chapter.

But you're not limited to one key field. By specifying more than one field, you can create a composite key. This allows you to have duplicate entries in any of the specified fields, but the sum of the composite keys has to be unique.

To specify your key fields, all you do is place an asterisk in the Key column for each field that you want to be part of your primary key. You do that by double-clicking the left mouse button or pressing any character on the keyboard. You remove a key the same way—if you set a key field by mistake, just double-click or press any character.

And again, some rules:

○ All of the fields that are keyed have to be the first ones in the table structure. As you can see in Figure 3-8, Catalog#, which is keyed, is at the top of the list. If I wanted to make Author ID the key, I'd have to move it above Catalog#. (Rearranging the Field Roster is covered in the next chapter.)

○ If you want to define more than one field as a key, the first key field needs to be at the top and the others must follow it.

○ If you're planning to use referential integrity links, each table in the link has to be keyed. (I know, you're not planning any right now. How could you? You don't even know what they are yet. But you'll learn all about them in the next chapter, and this information will become extremely valuable.)

Building the Sample Table

We've covered the basic info—all that's left to it is to do it. We're going to create a table called BOOKS for Bookfinders. BOOKS will be used to keep track of inventory. (Figure 3-8 shows the finished table structure. Use this figure as you work through the steps.)

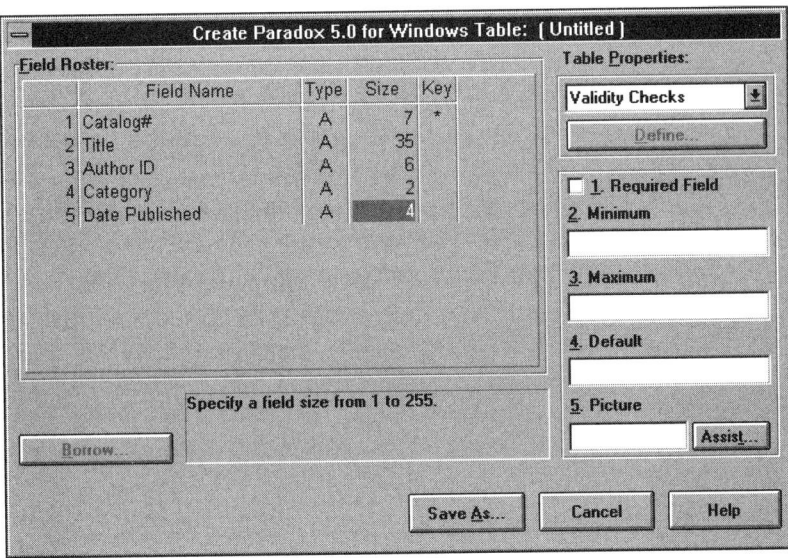

Figure 3-8: The table structure for the sample table. The selection bar tells you where you are. Check out the area to the right of the Borrow button for important messages.

1. With the selection bar in the first row of the Field Name column, type **Catalog#**.

   Before you move to the next column, take a look just below the Field Roster area. You'll see a message that says "Enter a field name up to 25 characters long." For each column in the Field Roster, Paradox helps you out by displaying a message that tells you what to do. See, you don't really have to remember anything—Paradox takes all the work out of it. I'm sorry if that's not enough of a challenge for you. But don't worry, you'll find plenty of things in Paradox that will more than challenge you.

2. Move to the Type column by clicking in it or by pressing Tab, Enter or the Right arrow. (And don't forget to check out the help message.)

3. Click the right mouse button (or press the Spacebar) to display the Type Inspector menu.

4. Click on Alpha (or press A).

   If you know the letter for the field type, you don't have to choose it from the Type Inspector—you can enter it directly. The Type Inspector menu is there just to assist you.

5. Move to the Size column and type 7.

6. Double-click in the Key column to set Catalog# as a key field. You can also set a key field by pressing the Spacebar or any letter or number key.

7. Follow the instructions in steps 1 through 6 to add the rest of the fields to your table.

Here are a few tips to help you out in case you need to make some changes while you're creating the table structure.

○ Delete a field by highlighting any column in the field and pressing Ctrl+Del. That deletes the entire field, not just the column you're in.

○ Delete the data in any column of a field by highlighting the entry and pressing Del.

○ Insert a field by positioning the selection bar anywhere in the row below where you want the new field. Then press Ins. The field is inserted above the field where your cursor was located.

SAVING YOUR TABLE STRUCTURE

A penny saved is a penny earned. I know, that's a really tired cliché (and it may not be long before pennies are phased out of existence), but the idea here is that saving is a good thing. In the case of tables (and other computer stuff), saving is a very, very good thing. Actually, Paradox does a reasonable (but not perfect, as you'll see in the following Pitfall Ahead) job of warning you when you're about to do something stupid. If you use the Control-menu box to close the Create Table dialog box without saving, you'll get a message that says something like "What do you mean, you don't wanna save? Hey buddy, it's your dime. Just say no and I'm outta here." And you can't enter any data into your table without first saving the structure.

Pitfall Ahead

Sounds pretty good, right? If you try to exit without saving, Paradox warns you. Cool, no problem—as long as you use the Control-menu box to exit. But if you use the Cancel button—problem! Click on Cancel, and that structure you spent hours getting just right is a memory. No warning, no nothing. Try to keep that trigger finger (the one that's just itching to click the mouse button) off the Cancel button unless you really want to trash the table structure.

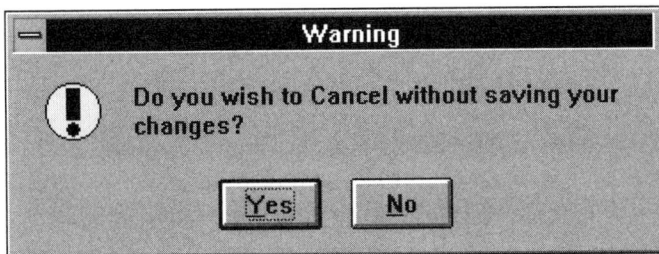

Figure 3-9: The warning message isn't quite as rude as my paraphrase in the preceding paragraph. It actually looks like this.

If you choose Yes, all of your painstaking work will be lost and you'll have to start over. I don't want you to go through that hassle, so here's what to do:

1. When you're all done with your entries in the Create Paradox for Windows dialog box, click on the Save As button.

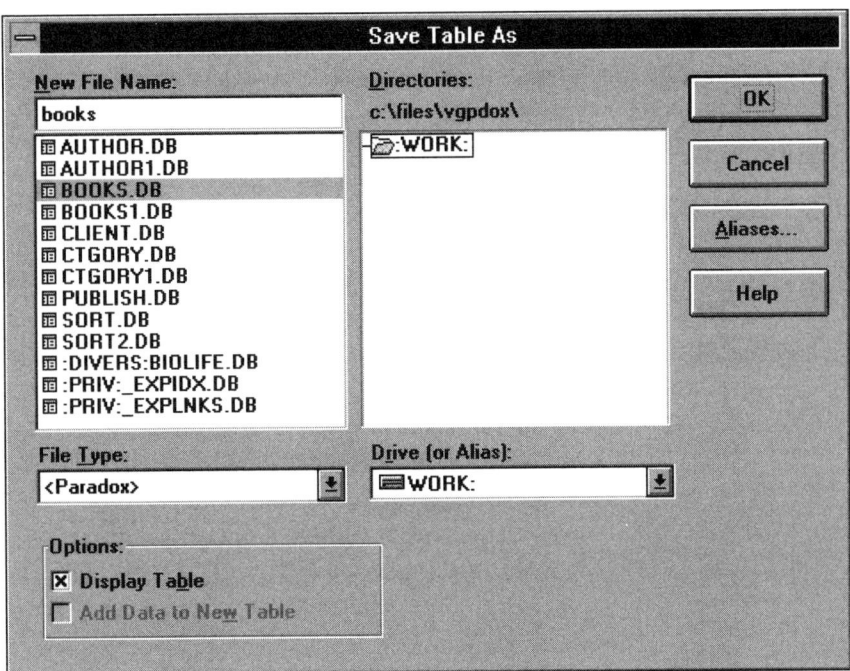

Figure 3-10: When you click on Save As, this dialog box appears.

The New File Name text box is where you type the table's name. The Options box lets you control what happens after you save the table structure. Use the Directories and Drive (or Alias) boxes if you want to save to a location other than your working directory.

2. Type **BOOKS** in the New File Name text box. Don't type an extension—Paradox will automatically add a DB extension to the table's name.

    Just a reminder: You don't have to type the name in upper-case letters—Paradox automatically converts whatever you type to uppercase. All of the filenames in this book are in uppercase just so they'll stand out from the rest of the text.

3. Check the Display Table check box.

    If you don't check this box, when you save the table structure you're returned to the Desktop window. If you want to work on the table right away, you have to open it, which would waste at least 20 seconds of your valuable time.

    If you check Display Table, as soon as you choose OK to close the Save Table As dialog box, your table is displayed in a Table View window so you can get right to work.

    The Add Data To New Table option applies only if you've already entered data in your table and you want to save it under a different name. The Save As option can also be used when you're restructuring a table; you can give it a new name at that point, and if you choose Add Data To New Table, all of the data in the original table (assuming the fields are compatible) gets copied to the new table.

4. By default, Paradox saves the table to your working directory. If you want to save the table to a different directory, use the Directories and Drive (or Alias) sections to choose the directory you want.

Inside Scoop

As you get deeper into the database world, there may be times when you want to save files to directories other than your working directory. But until you really know your way around the Paradox block, the safest course is to set your working directory at the beginning of each session. That way, all of your files for a particular database will end up in the same place.

5. When you're done, choose OK.

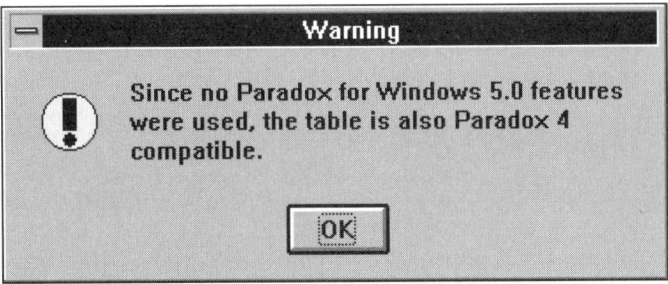

Figure 3-11: You'll probably see this warning message when you choose OK. Don't worry—it just means that the table is compatible with a previous version of Paradox. Just choose OK to accept the message.

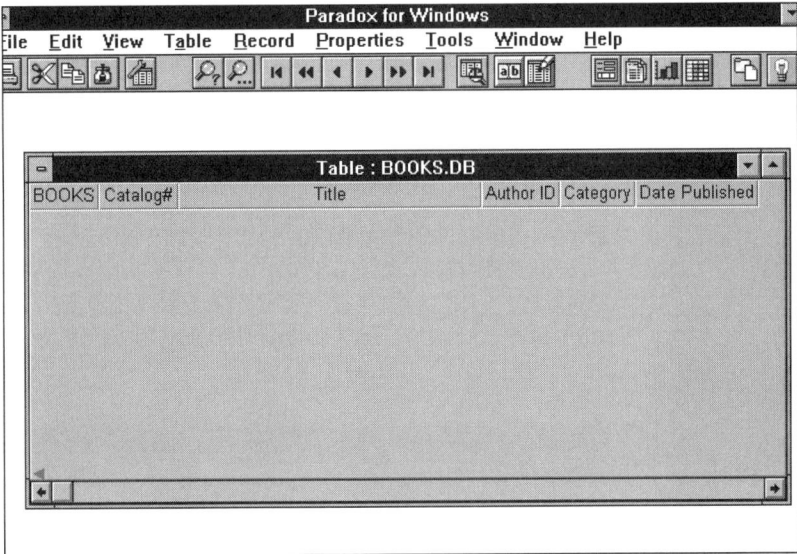

Figure 3-12: This is what your screen should look like, assuming you checked Display Table before you chose OK. (Well I told you to, didn't I?)

6. Double-click on the table's Control-menu box to return to the Desktop for now.

Before we move on, take a deep breath and pat yourself on the back (but don't do both at the same time if that would stress you out). You just created an actual table. And pretty soon you'll even know what to do with it.

The rest of this chapter covers some table miscellany. You don't need to know most of it right now, but it'll come in handy not too far down the road.

Temporary Tables

Lots of things cause Paradox to create temporary tables. Each of those situations will be covered as we get to the appropriate section, but here are a couple of examples (queries are covered in Chapters 6 and 7):

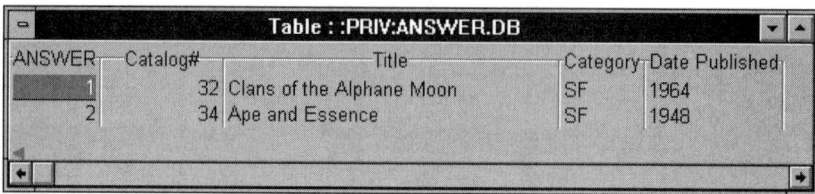

Figure 3-13: When you run a query (that is, ask your table a question), Paradox usually puts the results of the query into a table called ANSWER.DB.

If you change the structure of a table in a way that could result in key violations (this might happen if you add a key field to a table that didn't have a key when the table already contains data), Paradox deletes any records that violate the key-field rules and puts them in a table called KEYVIOL.DB.

Catalog#	Category	Title	Author	Price	Date Published
1	SF	Twilight at the Well of Souls	CJL001	$2.50	1980
2	TH	Slow Dance on the Killing Ground	HXW020	$5.95	1964
3	LT	After Many a Summer Dies the Swan	HXA005	$2.50	1939
4	SF	The Judas Rose	HES006	$3.50	1987
5	SF	Beyond the Blue Event Horizon	PXF021	$2.50	1980
6	MT	The Impossible Question	KXJ009	$2.25	1972
7	TH	The Playwright as Thinker	BXE022	$1.75	1955
8	SF	Aubade for Gamelon	WXJ018	$2.95	1984
9	TH	A Hell of a Mess	IXE003	$3.95	1973
10	SF	Clans of the Alphane Moon	DKP014	$2.25	1964
11	SF	The Web of the Chozen	CJL001	$1.75	1978
12	SF	Ape and Essence	HXA005	$2.25	1948

Figure 3-14: An example of a KEYVIOL.DB table.

Even though temporary tables are created in a bunch of different circumstances, they all share the following characteristics:

◯ They're all stored in your private directory. In the Project Viewer and the Open Table dialog box, Paradox lists the names of all of the tables in your working directory, like this: BOOKS.DB, TYPE.DB, etc. At the end of the list, any temporary tables are listed with :PRIV: in front of them—:PRIV:ANSWER.DB, :PRIV:KEYVIOL.DB, etc.

○ The data in a temporary table exists only until you exit Paradox or change your private directory. Hence the name "temporary."

○ Paradox will create more than one temporary table of the same type if you do something that generates the same temporary table more than once during a Paradox session. When this happens, Paradox adds a number to the end of the table's name. (Like KEYVIOL1.DB, KEYVIOL2.DB, KEYVIOL3.DB.)

○ Temporary tables are real-live Paradox tables. You can restructure them, query them, edit the data, and do all sorts of other table stuff. However, the only way to make all of this table stuff stick to a temporary table is to rename the table so the data doesn't get overwritten or lost. You can do whatever you want to a temporary table, but if you don't give it a different name, your efforts will be wasted.

○ You shouldn't use any of Paradox's temporary table names when you name your tables (or any other Paradox object). Otherwise you run the risk of having your table overwritten if you do something that makes Paradox create a temporary table with the same name. And when you exit Paradox or change your private directory, that table's history. Until you're familiar with the different temporary table names, it wouldn't hurt to check the following list of temporary table names before you name a new table.

Name	What's In It
ANSWER	Query results
CHANGED	Original copy of changed records
CROSSTAB	Crosstab results
DELETED	Records deleted as a result of a DELETE query
ERRCHNG	Records that Paradox was unable to change from a CHANGETO query
ERRDEL	Records that Paradox was unable to delete from a DELETE query
ERRINS	Records that Paradox was unable to insert from an INSERT query
EXPORT	Specifications for exported fixed-length text
IMPORT	Specifications for imported fixed-length text
INSERTED	Records inserted during an INSERT query
KEYVIOL	Records that violate key field rules
LOCKS	Any active locks that have been placed on a table
PAL$SRC	Source code, objects and methods in forms (I know, you really wanted to name your next table PAL$SRC, but control yourself).
PROBLEMS	Problems that Paradox couldn't keep in the table after you do a restructure or import

Changing a Table's Name

Now that I've told you what'll happen if you don't rename a temporary table, did you think I'd leave you hanging? Nah, not a chance. Here's how you keep from losing the information in a temporary table.

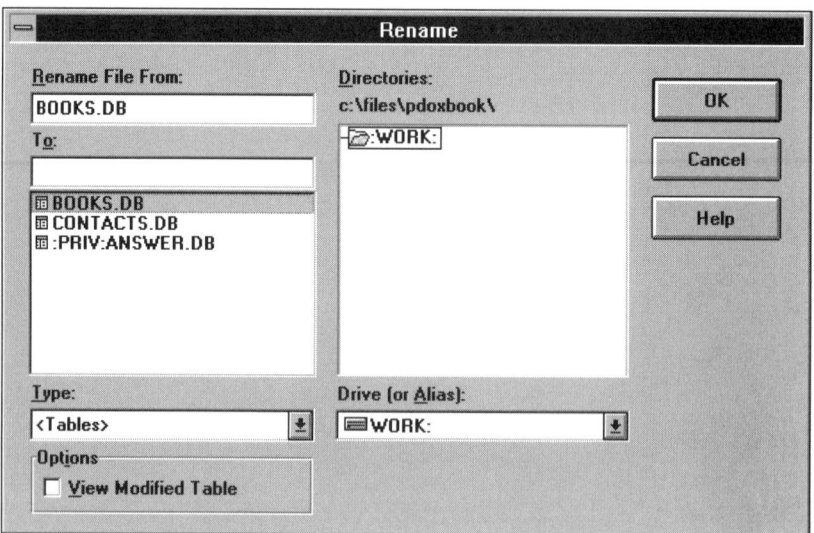

Figure 3-15: Use this dialog box to rename any Paradox file.

1. Choose Tools, Utilities, Rename to display the Rename dialog box.
    All of the files in your working and private directories of the type shown in the Type box are listed under the To text box.
2. If you want to rename another kind of file, click on the arrow next to the Type box and make a choice from the drop-down list.
3. If you want to rename a file that's not in your working directory, change to the directory you want by using the Directories and Drive (or Alias) areas.
4. When the file you want to rename is displayed in the file list, double-click on it. This copies the file name to the From text box.
    You can also type the file name directly into the Rename File From text box. This can save you some steps if the file you want to rename is in a different directory; just be sure you type the full path name if this is the case.
5. Type the new name in the To text box.
6. The View Modified Table check box is exactly like the Display Table check box in the Save Table As dialog box. If this box is checked, Paradox displays the renamed table onscreen as soon as you close the Rename dialog box.
7. When you've made all your choices, choose OK.

You can rename other Paradox objects. The example in this section is specifically about tables, since that's what we're talking about. But you use exactly the same techniques to rename forms, queries, reports or scripts.

Inside Scoop

You can also use the Project Viewer to rename a table. Just right-click on the table you want to rename and choose Rename from the Object Inspector. The Rename dialog box you get is pretty much like the one you get when you choose Tools, Utilities, Rename. The main difference is that it doesn't have Rename File From and To text boxes. It doesn't have to because Paradox already knows which file you want to rename. Also, there's no View Modified Table check box.

If you want to rename the table you're currently working on, you can skip the Utilities menu and just choose Rename from the Table menu. When you do it this way, you get an abridged version of the Rename dialog box that looks like this:

Figure 3-16: This dialog box streamlines the process. All you have to do is type the new name in the To text box.

Pitfall Ahead

Don't use the Windows File Manager, DOS, or any other method to rename Paradox tables. A table can have all sorts of related files attached to it. For example, whenever you add a validity check, a key field or a secondary index, Paradox creates a separate file that's part of the table's family. The only way to make sure all related files get renamed and all connections are retained is to use Tools, Utilities, Rename or Table, Rename from Paradox. Paradox knows what to do with its files and how everything works together. Those other guys don't.

Inside Scoop

If you try to rename a table and Paradox won't let you, it's probably because the table is a parent in a referential integrity link. (Read all about referential integrity in the next chapter.) To rename the table, you have to delete the link or delete the child table.

BORROWING ANOTHER TABLE'S STRUCTURE

If you already have a table that's similar to a new one you want to create, you can save yourself time and effort by "borrowing" the structure of the existing table. It doesn't matter if the existing table structure doesn't have everything you want to put in the new one. You can use the borrowed table as a template and make whatever changes you require. Paradox makes it easy to borrow—there's a Borrow button right in the Create Table dialog box.

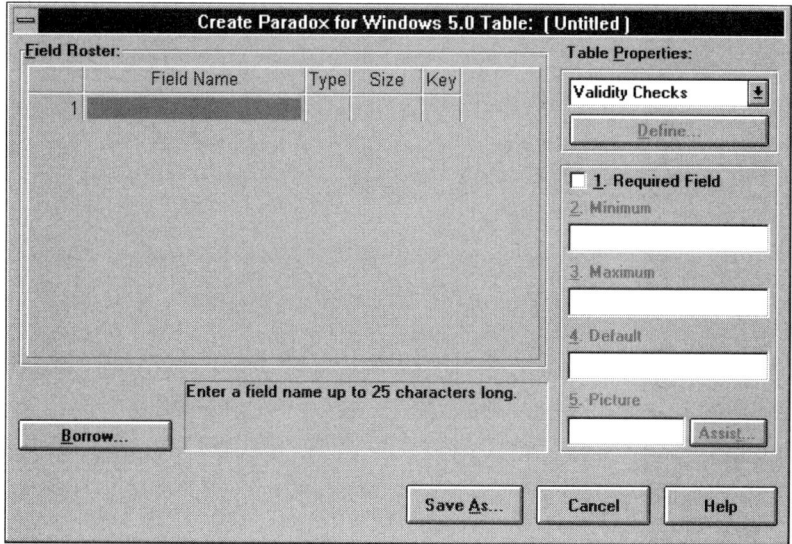

Figure 3-17: Clicking on the Borrow button in the Create Table dialog box lets you borrow the structure of a table you've already created.

Clicking on the Borrow button opens the Borrow Table Structure dialog box shown in Figure 3-18. Choose the table whose structure you want to borrow from the Source Table list box. If the table you want to borrow from is in a different directory that doesn't have an alias, click on the Browse button, select the path you want from the Browser and choose OK. Check the boxes for any options you want to transfer from the existing table.

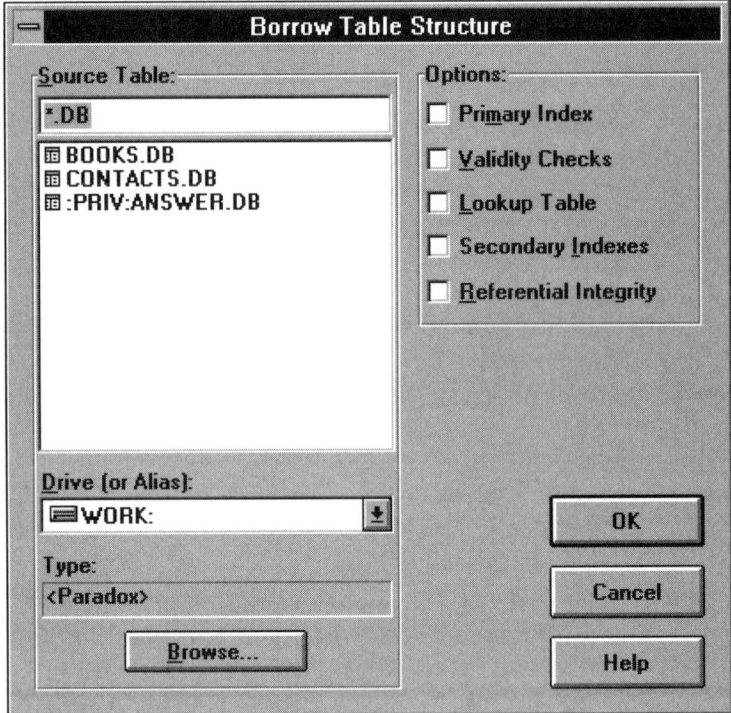

Figure 3-18: The Borrow Table Structure dialog box.

Choose OK when you've completed your selections in the Borrow Table Structure dialog box. You'll be returned to the Create Table dialog box, where the field structure, along with any Table Properties options you chose to borrow, is now displayed. At this point, you can edit the structure to meet your new needs. (I know, you don't know how to do that yet. Just hang in there, you'll learn all about restructuring tables in Chapter 4.)

CREATING TABLES FROM EXISTING DATA

But what if I've already created a database or spreadsheet in another program? Do I have to start from scratch in Paradox? Glad you asked. And the definitive answer is, probably not. Paradox can import data from several different spreadsheet file formats, including Quattro Pro, Lotus 1-2-3 and Excel. It can also import data from delimited and fixed-length text files. The basic steps follow:

1. Choose Tools, Utilities, Import.
2. To choose another file format, open the File Type drop-down list and make a choice from the list shown below:

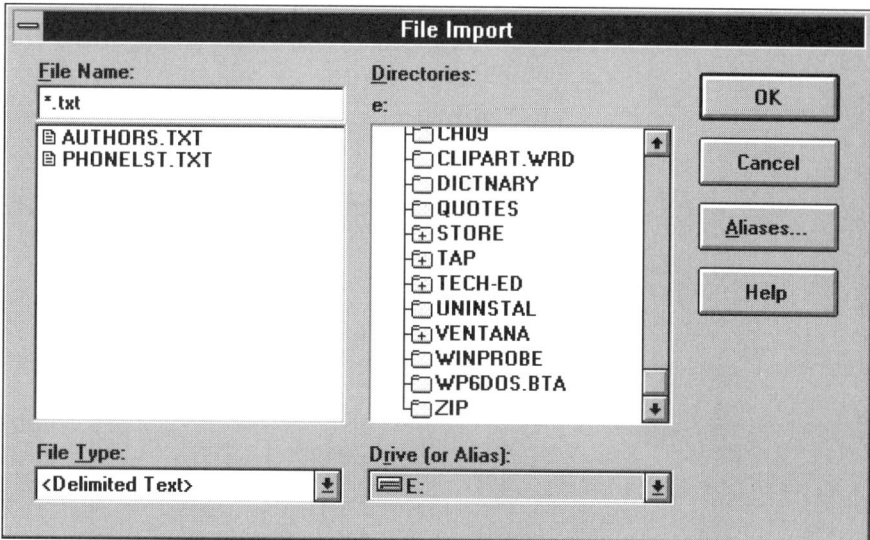

Figure 3-19A: The File Import dialog box displays any file in your working directory that has a TXT extension (the default type is <Delimited Text>).

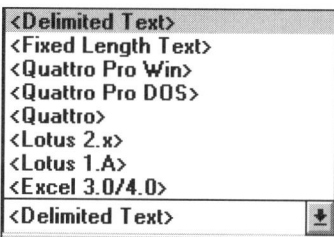

Figure 3-19B: The Type drop-down list.

3. Select the file you want to import and choose OK. Depending on where the file's located, you might have to use the Directories or Drive (or Alias) list.

What happens next depends on the kind of file you're importing.

IMPORTING SPREADSHEET DATA

If you import a spreadsheet file, you'll see the dialog box shown in Figure 3-20. In the New Table Name text box, type a name for the new table, and check either the Paradox or dBase radio button, depending on which type of table you want to create. Enter the range of cells you want to import in the From cell and To cell text boxes, or choose a named range from the Named Ranges drop-down list. If you want to use the headings in the top row of the spreadsheet as column headings in your table, select "Get field names from first row." When you choose OK, Paradox will create a table from the spreadsheet data, using the field names from the first row of imported data and automatically assigning field types according to the formula shown in the table below.

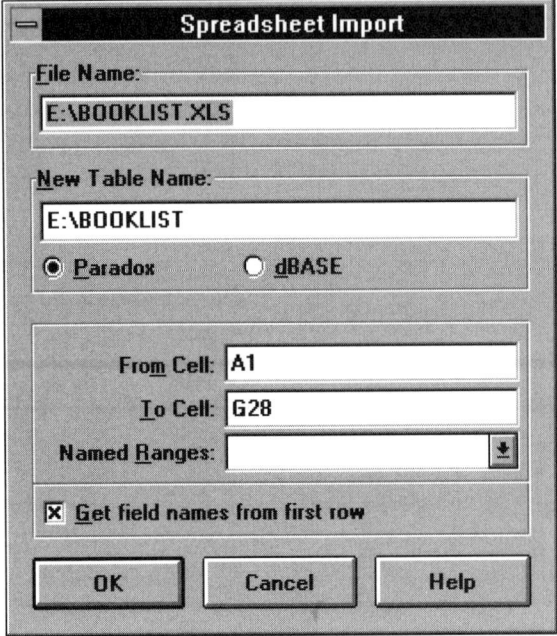

Figure 3-20: If the file you want to import is in one of the spreadsheet formats, the Spreadsheet Import dialog box opens.

How Paradox Converts Spreadsheet Values

What It Was	What Paradox Turns It Into
Label	Alpha
Whole number	Short Number
Number that uses decimal place	Number
Number formatted as currency	Money
Number formatted as date	Date

Note: If a column in the spreadsheet has both dates and whole numbers, it's converted to an alpha field. If it has both currency and numbers, it's converted to a number field.

IMPORTING DELIMITED TEXT

When you import a delimited ASCII (text) file, you see the dialog box shown in Figure 3-21. In the New Table Name text box, type a name for the new table, and check either the Paradox or dBase radio button, depending on which type of table you want to create. If the fields in the ASCII file are separated by commas, with quotes around the text fields, all you have to do is choose OK. Otherwise, choose Options.

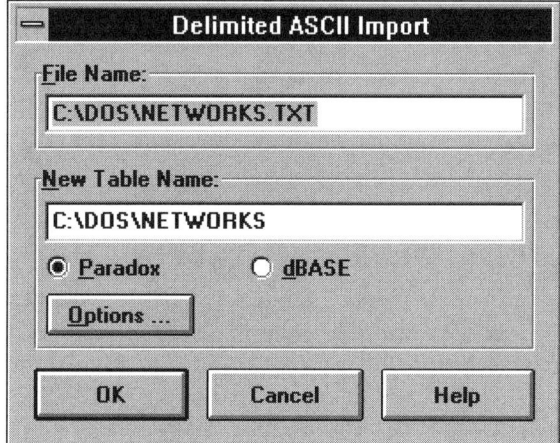

Figure 3-21: If you're importing a delimited ASCII (text) file, you get this dialog box.

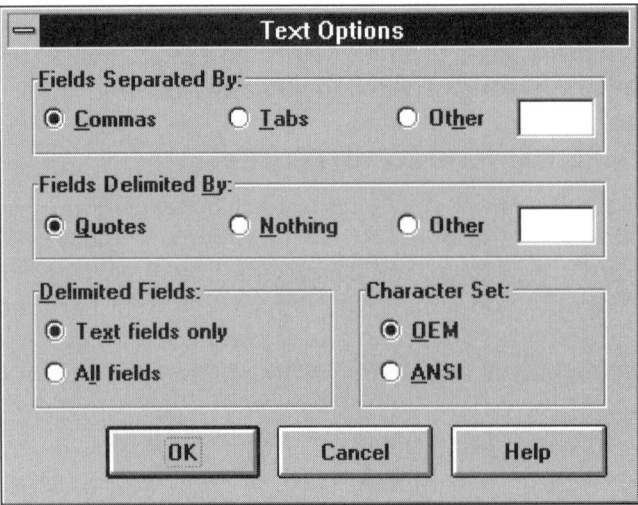

Figure 3-22: Use this dialog box to tell Paradox what field separators and delimiters are used in the ASCII file and which character set to use.

IMPORTING FIXED-LENGTH TEXT

If you're importing a fixed-length ASCII file, you get the dialog box shown in Figure 3-23. The main difference between a delimited file and a fixed-length file is that in a delimited file, the fields run together; the only way you can tell where one field begins and the next one ends is by looking at the field separators (usually commas). A fixed-length text file looks like a table—the fields are lined up nice and neat.

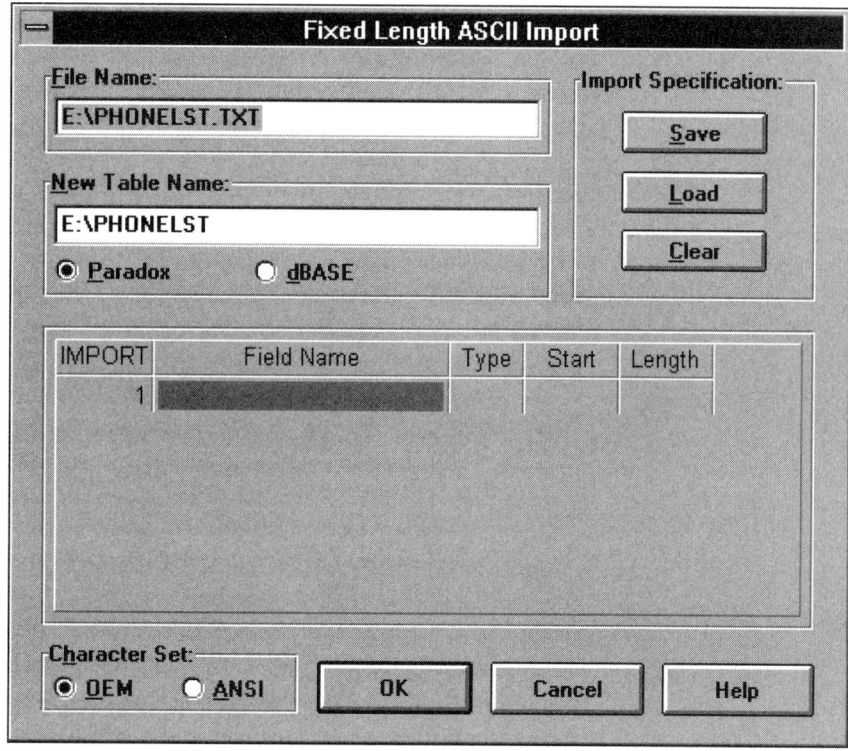

Figure 3-23: The Fixed Length ASCII Import dialog box.

EXPORTING TO OTHER FORMATS

You can export data from Paradox or dBase tables into all of the same formats that you can import from, and the procedure is very similar.

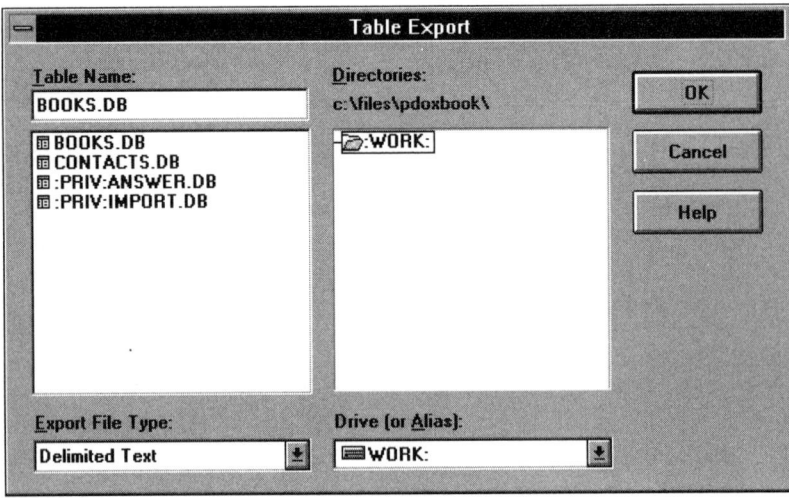

Figure 3-24: The Table Export dialog box.

1. Choose Tools, Utilities, Export.
2. Select the table you want to export from the Table Name list. If the table isn't listed, use the Directories or Drive (or Alias) list to move to the right directory.
3. Choose a file format from the Export File Type list and choose OK.

As with importing, the next step depends on the file type you're exporting to. Just follow the instructions in the dialog boxes, entering a name for the exported table and filling in other necessary options. If you're exporting to a delimited text file, there's an Options button in the Delimited ASCII Export dialog box that takes you to the same Text Options dialog box used for importing. You can change the delimiter, separator or character set.

MOVING ON

As I've been promising (or threatening) throughout this chapter, the next chapter is devoted entirely to table structure. So hold on to those questions you're just dying to ask—chances are, they're about to be answered.

4 MORE ABOUT TABLE STRUCTURE

OK, we've been through the basics—you know how to create a simple table (and in the next chapter you'll even learn how to put data into it!). Now it's time to explore the deeper meaning of all this table structure stuff.

I wish I could tell you that unraveling the secrets of table structure will make you a better person and that you'll acquire riches beyond your wildest imaginings. The truth is that unraveling the secrets of table structure will just make you someone who knows all about tables. Who's to say, though, that database knowledge won't be the determining factor in your ultimate success? Certainly not I. So read on and reap the benefits.

THE SETUP

We're going to make some changes to the table you created in the last chapter. In order to do that, we have to open up the table in a window that allows us to restructure the table. Strangely enough, the command you use to do this is called Restructure. To make sure we're all starting out with the same thing onscreen, follow along with me:

1. Switch to the Project Viewer.
2. Right-click on BOOKS.DB and choose Restructure from the Object Inspector menu.

   Note: If the table you want to restructure is already open, you have to choose Table, Restructure Table instead. And if the Project Viewer isn't open, you can choose Tools, Utilities, Restructure, and double-click on BOOKS.DB.

Everybody got that? Your screen should now look sort of like Figure 4-1. If you didn't complete the table in Chapter 3, you can use BOOKS.DB from the disk that came with your copy of this book. See, we want to make life easy for you—we'll even do some of the work so you don't have to. But the more of it you work through yourself, the more you'll get out of it. (Sorry, I couldn't help myself there—I slip into lecture mode every now and then. OK, I think I'm back in control now.)

Notice the title of the dialog box in Figure 4-1. To change a table you've already created, you restructure the table. You might wonder why it says "Paradox 4 Table" instead of "Paradox 5 Table." It's because the table structure doesn't include any field types that exist only in Version 5. Until we add field types that aren't included in Version 4, Paradox treats the table as if it were created in Version 4, but it's compatible with both versions.

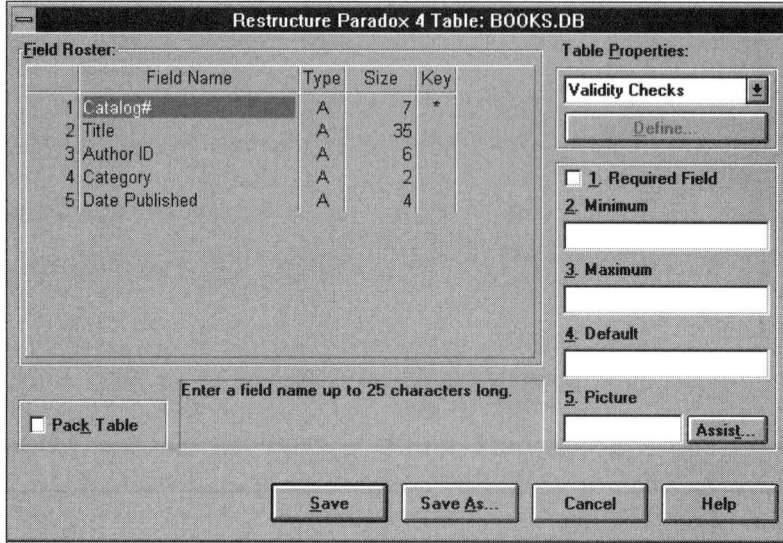

Figure 4-1: The BOOKS table you created in the last chapter.

This table's a pretty good start, but there's a whole lot of stuff we can do to it. Since I want to tell you about the types of fields, we'll add a field for some of the different types to help you get the hang of what they're all about. We'll go through all of the field types, but in some cases I'll just talk about them or show you examples instead of actually adding a field to BOOKS.DB.

Alpha Fields

All of the fields you've created so far are alpha, which means that they're made up of combinations of words and numbers. Naturally, you'll use alpha fields for names and titles and things like that. But you'll also use alpha fields for numbers you don't need to use in calculations. Notice that the Date Published field is alpha. Even though the date is a number, we don't have to do any calculations on it, so an alpha field works fine. I'll explain why Date Published isn't a date field when we talk about date fields in a little bit.

Inside Scoop

It's a good idea to use alpha fields whenever you have numbers that you know you'll never want to add, subtract, or do any other kind of calculations on. There are two reasons for this. First, alpha fields give you a whole lot more formatting options and allow you to add characters like hyphens or parentheses. Second, if you use an alpha field, there's no chance that the number could be used by mistake in a calculation or query. On the other hand, don't decide too quickly that you'll never want to calculate the information in a particular field. If the field contains a dollar amount, the safest course is to make it a money field. That way, you leave all of your options open in case you decide to do some calculations on the field.

Field Facts

❍ Alpha fields can include any combination of numbers, letters or symbols. (Any printable ASCII character can be used in an alpha field.)

❍ Alpha fields can contain up to 255 characters. You must specify a size when you create the field.

❍ You can use spaces in an alpha field, but a space can't be the first character.

❍ Alpha fields can be used to store data in files created by applications capable of being DDE servers.

Example

Title, Author, Category and Date Published are all examples of alpha fields.

Number Fields

Use number fields when you want to perform calculations on your data.

Field Facts

❍ You can put only numbers in number fields. If you try to enter a letter or symbol, your computer will beep at you and the message

"Illegal Character" will appear on the status bar at the bottom of your screen.

○ The numbers can be positive or negative.

○ Numbers can range from -10^{307} to 10^{308} and can contain up to 15 significant digits.

○ The size of number fields is fixed—you don't specify a size when you create the field.

○ You can change the way the numbers are displayed. Paradox provides six predefined number formats, and you can also define your own custom formats. Number formats are covered in the next chapter.

○ When you perform calculations on a number field, Paradox recognizes up to six decimal places. This is true even if you don't have any decimal places displayed.

○ Don't put stuff like ZIP Codes, product numbers or phone numbers in number fields. Alpha fields give you much more flexibility (unless you're planning to do a calculation to find out what all of your phone numbers add up to. Yeah, that'd be useful!).

Example

We'll add a field called Quantity in Stock to BOOKS.DB. Since this data will be used in calculations to keep track of inventory, we'll make it a number field. (Make sure you're still in the Restructure Table dialog box for BOOKS.DB.)

1. Move your cursor to the last row of the Size column. Press the Tab, Right arrow or Down arrow key to add a row at the bottom of the structure.

2. Type **Qty** in the Field Name column.

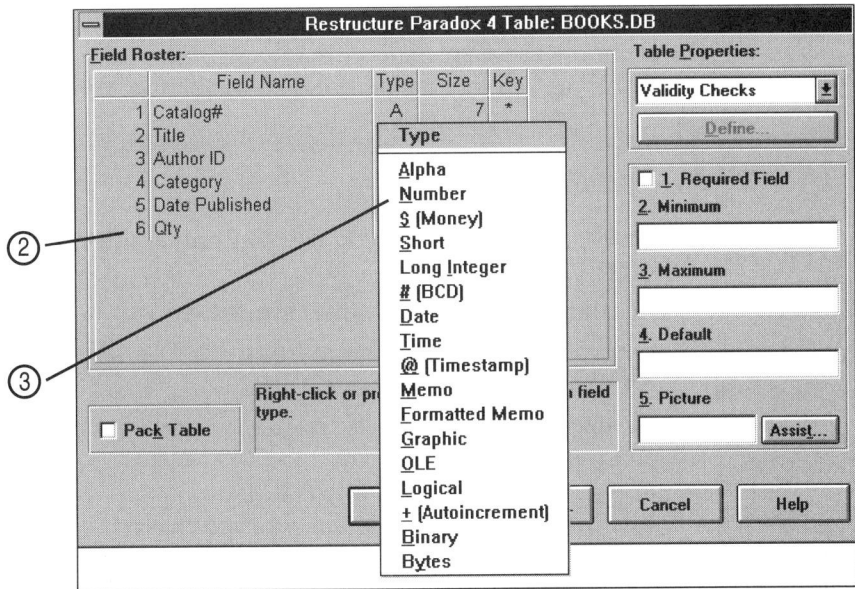

Figure 4-2: We're adding a number field called "Quantity in Stock."

3. Right-click in the Type column to display the Type Inspector menu and choose Number.

4. Press the Tab key to move to the next column. Notice that the Size and Key columns are both bypassed–number fields don't allow you to enter a size, and key fields must be at the top of the Field Roster.

Figure 4-3: BOOKS.DB with data entered in the newly created number column.

Because the Qty column is set up as a number field, we'll be able to use calculations in reports and queries to get different breakdowns of stock on hand.

Money Fields

What do you think a money field would be used for? Right–money stuff. Actually, the only real difference between money fields and number fields is the way the numbers are formatted. In money fields, the numbers are displayed with a dollar sign and two decimal places. (You can, of course, change the display format; you'll learn how to do that in the next chapter.)

Field Facts

○ Just like number fields, you can put only numbers and decimal points in money fields.

○ The numbers can be positive or negative.

○ Money field values can range from -10^{307} to 10^{308} and can contain up to 15 significant digits.

○ The size of money fields is fixed—you don't specify a size when you create the field.

○ By default, money fields display two decimal places, but Paradox stores up to six decimal places for use in calculations.

○ Negative money values are displayed in parentheses.

Example

Using the instructions for adding a number field, add a money field called "Price." The only change is that instead of choosing Number from the Type Inspector menu, you'll choose Money.

Figure 4-4: BOOKS.DB with data entered in the Price field.

We can use this Price field to get breakdowns on pricing information.

Date Fields

This might not be quite as obvious as money fields, but I have faith in you. C'mon, you can do it. A date field is for . . . dates!! But there are a couple of caveats here. By *date*, Paradox means any date that includes the month, day and year. If you want to include a field that shows only the year (like the Date Published field), you have to use another field type. That's why we made Date Published an alpha field.

Field Facts

❍ You can put any valid date (including all of those BC dates) through December 31, 9999 a.d., into a date field. *Valid* means that it has to be a real date. For example, if you try to enter February 30, 1994, the message "Bad Date Specification" appears in the status bar, and you can't leave the field until you fix it.

❍ Paradox knows all about leap years (and even leap centuries) within the allowable date range. That's why it won't let you enter February 30.

❍ There are several different date formats, and you'll learn all about them in the next chapter.

Time Fields

Use time fields to store (you guessed it again!) time information.

Field Facts

❍ The time information is stored in milliseconds.

❍ The time clock begins at midnight and is limited to a 24-hour cycle.

❍ As with date fields, you can display times in several different formats. Formatting is covered in the next chapter.

Timestamp Fields

Use timestamp fields to "stamp" your document with the date and time.

Field Facts

❍ Timestamp fields contain both date and time information.

❍ You can format timestamp fields in various ways. Field formatting is covered in the next chapter.

Short Number Fields

Short number fields are great for humongous tables where saving every bit of space you can is crucial. Since the use of these fields is limited by the range of allowable numbers and the lack of formatting options, make sure you know what you're doing before you start messing around with short number fields.

Field Facts

○ The good news—short number fields don't take up as much disk space as regular number fields. The bad news—you can't change the display format of short number fields. The moral—wait till you really know your way around Paradox before you use short number fields.

○ You can only use whole numbers from –32,767 to +32,768 in short number fields.

Long Integer Fields

Use long integer fields for whole numbers that won't fit in short number fields (larger than 32,768 or less than –32,768).

Field Facts

○ The range for long integer fields is –2,147,483,647 to +2,147,483,647.

○ Long integer fields don't store any decimal place information.

○ Long integer fields take up more space than short number fields. So if all of your numbers fall into the range supported by short number fields, that field type is a better choice than long integer.

BCD Fields

BCD fields are like number fields, except that you can store up to 32 decimal places in a BCD field. So you can use BCD fields when your calculations need to be highly precise.

Field Facts

○ Techno trivia—BCD stands for Binary Coded Decimal.

○ When you specify the size for a BCD field, you are telling Paradox how many decimal places you want to include. You must enter a number from 0 to 32.

○ You probably won't need to use BCD fields much. The main reason Paradox included them is for compatibility with other applications. Unless you want to take advantage of the BCD field's precision calculations or you need compatibility with a specific application that uses BCD data, a number field should do the trick.

Memo Fields

Hum along with me now, "If they asked me, I could write a book . . . ." When you want to include a whole bunch of text in a field, you'll quickly run out of space with plain vanilla alpha fields, which are limited to 255 characters (that's only about three lines of text). A memo field is for any text that won't fit into an alpha field. Memo fields can be as long as you want them to be (until you run out of disk space), so you could indeed "write a book."

Field Facts

○ A memo field can contain any printable character.

○ When you create a memo field, you specify a field size up to 240 characters. The size you specify is the amount of the memo field that will be stored with your table.

○ The entire memo is stored in a separate file with an MB extension.

Inside Scoop

Unfortunately, Paradox doesn't have a spelling checker, thesaurus or grammar checker. Since a memo field can contain a lot of words (and unless you *never* make mistakes), you might want to type memos in your word processing program to take advantage of its proofreading capabilities, and then paste them into your table.

Example

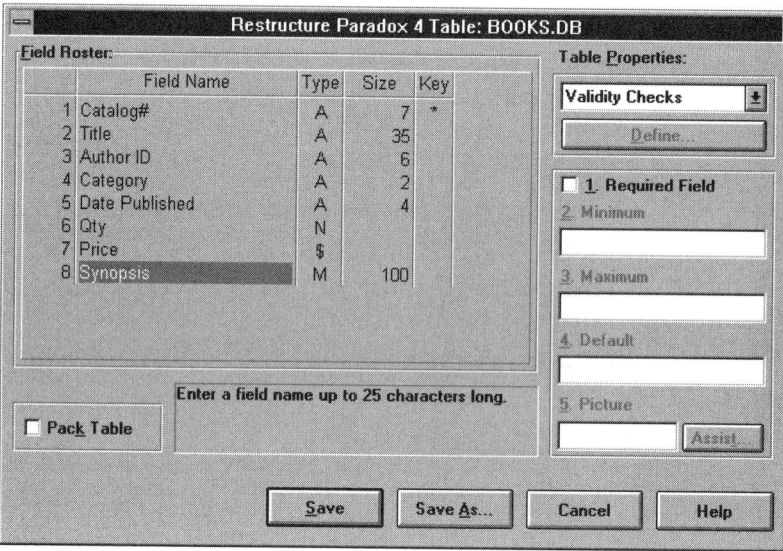

Figure 4-5: The new Synopsis field will allow Bookfinders to store and easily access a description of each book.

Add a new field to BOOKS.DB using the structure information shown in Figure 4-5 above.

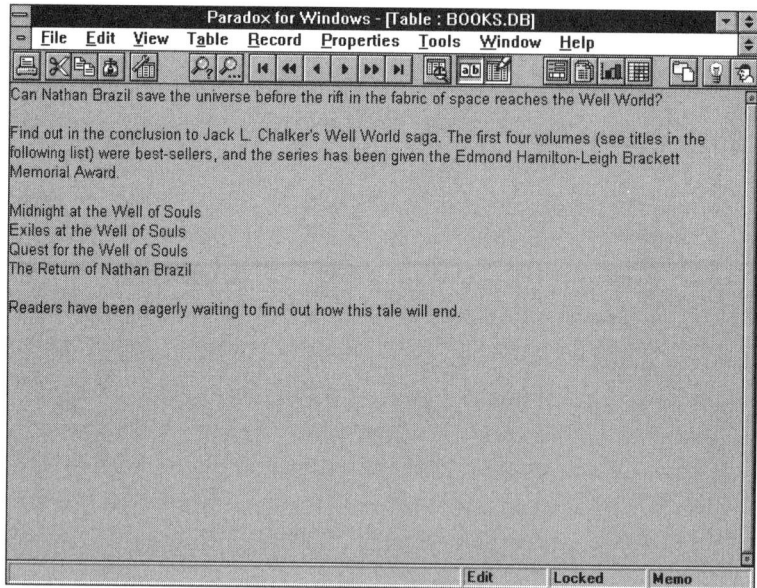

Figure 4-6: Data entered in a Memo View window.

Formatted Memo Fields

What're they for? Any text that won't fit into an alpha field *and* that you want to look pretty. The only difference between memo fields and formatted memo fields is that—surprise, surprise—you can apply formatting attributes to selected text in formatted memo fields. For example, you can change the type size, type style or text alignment for a particular word or paragraph. In a memo field, any formatting changes you make affect all text in the field.

Field Facts

○ When you create a formatted memo field, you have the option of specifying a field length up to 240 characters. The length you specify determines how much of the memo is stored with your table.

○ As with memo fields, the amount of the memo that you specify in the Size column is stored along with the table, and the entire memo is stored in a separate file with an MB extension.

○ If you don't specify a length, the field just displays <BLOB Formatted Memo> when the field isn't selected. When you select the field, Paradox shows you as much of the memo as will fit in the current column.

The BLOB That Ate the World

You won't find this one playing at a theater near you. BLOB is a cool-sounding acronym for something that's actually quite prosaic. BLOB stands for *binary large object file.* Memo, formatted memo, graphic, OLE, and binary fields are all BLOBs. Some things that BLOBs have in common: you can't sort on BLOB fields; Paradox can't identify duplicate BLOBs; you can't concatenate (combine) BLOB fields. And another thing: until you enter a value in a BLOB field (or if you don't specify a size for a BLOB field), all you see in the table is BLOB, followed by the field type.

Example

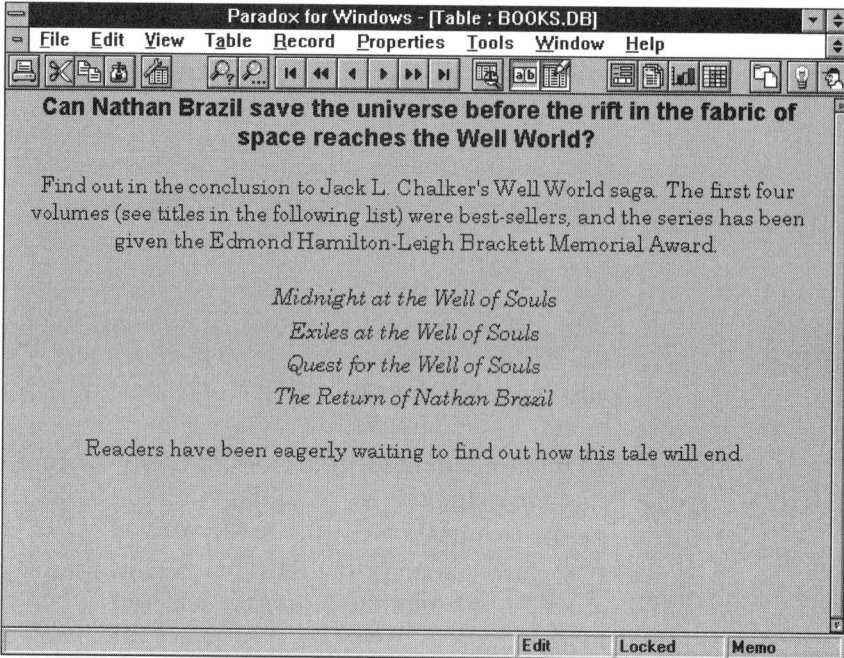

Figure 4-7: A formatted memo field.

In Figure 4-7 you see the same text that's in the memo field in Figure 4-6, but because it's a formatted memo field I was able to pretty it up.

Graphic Fields

If it's graphical, it can go into a graphic field, including scanned pictures (for example, a photo of the author), charts, clip art—you name it. Graphic fields, as the name implies, are used to store graphic images (pictures). Paradox graphic fields can use clip art or graphics created in several different formats. You can't actually create the graphics in Paradox; you just view them.

Field Facts

○ Any object or image that can be pasted from the Windows Clipboard can be placed in a graphic field. You can bring the following graphic formats directly into Paradox graphic fields: BMP, EPS, GIF, PCX and TIF. You'll learn the specifics of working with graphic fields in the next chapter.

❍ Whatever the original format, the picture gets converted to a BMP file when you bring it into a graphic field.

❍ You can specify a size up to 240 characters to store in the table's DB file.

❍ The entire graphic file is stored in a separate file with an MB extension.

Example

Figure 4-8: Here's an example of a possible use for a graphic field.

OLE Fields

No, we're not segueing into a tutorial on Flamenco dance (although I might incorporate that into my next book). OLE stands for Object Linking and Embedding, and it's just another one of those technobabble acronyms. What it is is a really cool technique that makes it possible to link objects between different Windows programs.

You can use an OLE field when you want to make changes to an object created in another program without leaving Paradox. For example, suppose you create a drawing in CorelDRAW that you want to use in a Paradox field. If you bring it in as a graphic field, you end up with a copy of the picture. If you then decide to make some changes to the picture, you have to go back to CorelDRAW, make your changes, and then edit the Paradox graphic field to bring in the modified drawing. If you had used an OLE field, you could just double-click on the field in Paradox, make changes to the drawing, return immediately to your Paradox table and the changes would be reflected in the field. No fuss, no muss.

Field Facts

❍ The only size limit is the amount of available disk space. Paradox can store up to 240 characters along with the table.

❍ The entire file is stored in a separate file with an MB extension.

Example

Figure 4-9: This field uses the same image as Figure 4-8, but take a look at the next figure (Figure 4-10) to see what's different about it.

Figure 4-10: With an OLE field, you can double-click on the field to open the program where the graphic was created.

When you're done editing the graphic, just save and close the application window to return to your Paradox table. The changes you make are immediately reflected in Paradox.

Logical Fields

Use logical fields to ask true/false or yes/no type questions in fields.

Field Facts

○ The default format for logical fields is true/false. Type **t** or **true** for True, **f** or **false** for False.

○ Logical fields are not case-sensitive. That means you can enter text in either uppercase or lowercase.

○ In addition to true/false, logical fields can be formatted to accept male/female or yes/no responses.

Autoincrement Fields

Autoincrement fields are great for key fields, where you want a unique number for each record. With an Autoincrement field, Paradox automatically assigns the number 1 to the first record you create and then increases the number by 1 for each additional record.

Field Facts

○ You can have only one Autoincrement field per table.

○ You can't edit Autoincrement fields. The number that Paradox assigns is permanent.

○ When you delete a record, Paradox doesn't renumber the other records in the table. And if you add another record, Paradox won't recycle the deleted record's number.

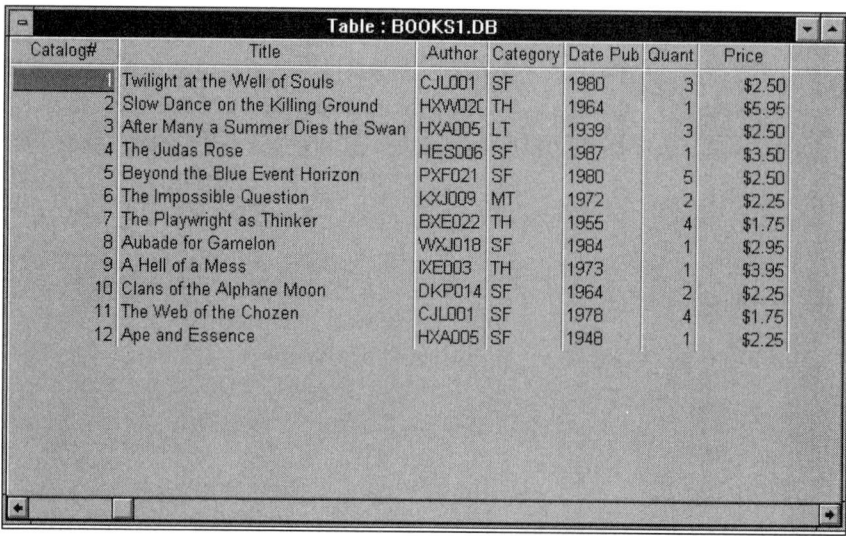

Figure 4-11: I changed the field type for Category# to Autoincrement to allow Paradox to automatically assign the numbers.

Binary Fields

A binary field is a special type of field that allows you to include information Paradox can't deal with directly.

This is heavy-duty stuff not for the faint of heart. In other words, it's for the programmer types out there. For all of you novices in the peanut gallery, don't count yourselves out—you may very well fit into the "programmer-type" category by the time you're done with this book.

Field Facts

○ Binary fields are often used to store sound files.

○ You can't access a binary field directly through Paradox; you have to use ObjectPAL programming commands.

○ You can specify a size of up to 240 characters. The size you specify determines how much of the field is stored with the table. The entire field is stored in a separate MB file.

Bytes Fields

Similar to a binary field, a bytes field contains information that Paradox can't read or interpret. And as with binary fields, bytes fields are X-rated (as in xtra-advanced).

Field Facts

❍ You must specify a size from 1 through 255 bytes.

❍ Byte field data is stored along with your table, rather than in a separate file.

❍ A typical use for a byte field would be to store bar code data.

WORKING WITH LOOKUP TABLES

As we've already discussed, one of the ways you streamline your database is by avoiding duplicate fields. What makes this workable is Paradox's ability to link data contained in multiple tables. It doesn't matter how many tables you use to contain your data, as long as there's a matching field in each of the tables involved. Throughout this book we'll make use of multiple tables for various purposes, but for now let's look at creating a table specifically for looking up information and making sure you enter the right data.

1. Create a new table using the following structure. Refer back to Chapter 3 if you need help.

Field Name	Type	Size	Key
Code	A	2	*
Description	A	30	

2. Save the table as CTGORY.DB

This table's really basic—only two fields—but it has great potential for saving you a whole bunch of time and a lot of errors. You'll begin to see what I mean as we attach CTGORY.DB to the BOOKS.DB table. And in the next chapter, you'll see the lookup table in action as you use it to enter data in the BOOKS table.

What Are They For?

Lookup tables serve three main functions: memory jogging, time saving and consistency enforcing. They can also save disk space—you don't have to repeat the same 30-character field in multiple tables. I'll use CTGORY.DB to explain what I mean:

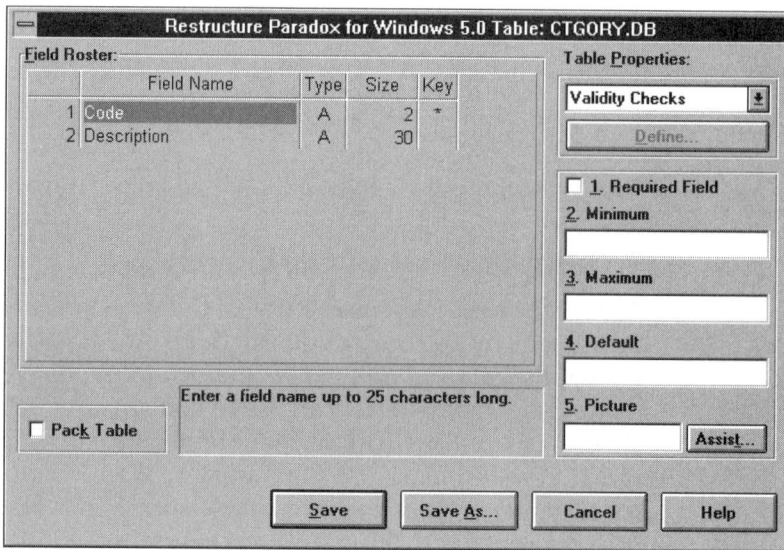

Figure 4-12: CTGORY.DB with type code and description data.

○ **Memory-jogging:** You don't have to remember the code for each different book category. When you fill in the Category field in BOOKS.DB, you can just pick the correct category from CTGORY.DB.

○ **Time-saving:** You don't even have to type the code in the Category field—you just pick it from the list in CTGORY.DB and it's automatically inserted in BOOKS.DB. In this case the codes are short, so you're not saving a whole lot of typing. But you could just as easily use a lookup table to save yourself from having to type in all of the authors' names, some of which might be long and difficult to spell correctly.

○ **Consistency-enforcing:** Once you define a lookup table for a particular field, Paradox won't let you enter a value in that field that can't be found in the lookup table. Without a lookup table, you might forget that you used LT for General Literature and enter GL instead in some of the records. Consistent entries become mega-important when you start creating reports and queries. For example, suppose you want to print a report listing all of your General Literature books. Unless all of the Category entries are consistent, you're fighting a losing battle.

Defining a Lookup Table

The first step in creating a lookup table is to create the structure for the table just like you would for any other table. As you saw with

CTGORY.DB, we followed exactly the same steps to create and save it that we did with BOOKS.DB. Once the table exists, you can link it to the table you want to use it with.

You define the link from within the main table. So start by opening BOOKS.DB:

1. If CTGORY.DB is still on your screen, close it by double-clicking on its Control-menu box. (The table you're going to use as a lookup can't be open when you define the link.)

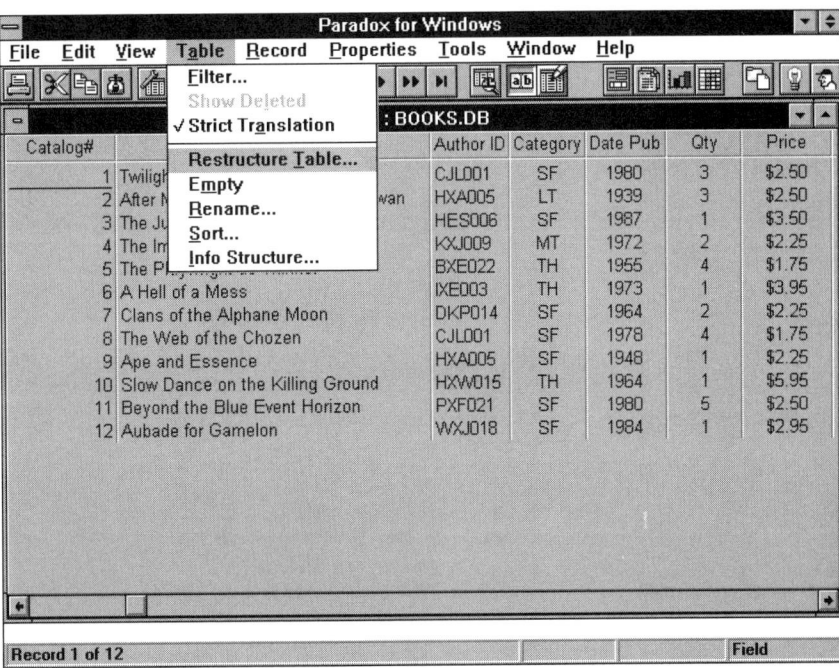

2. Click on the Open Table Toolbar button.

3. Select BOOKS.DB from the File Name list in the Open Table dialog box and choose OK.

    Note: You can also right-click on BOOKS.DB in the Project Viewer and choose Restructure from the Object Inspector menu.

Figure 4-13: BOOKS.DB with the Table menu pulled down.

4. Choose Table, Restructure Table.

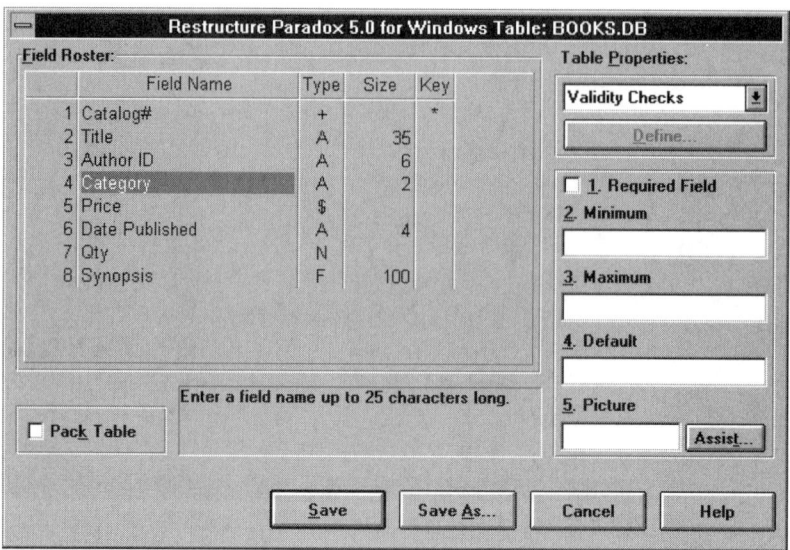

Figure 4-14: You define Table Lookups from the Restructure dialog box.

5. Select the Category field.
6. Select Table Lookup from the Table Properties drop-down list.
7. Click on the Define button. (The Define button becomes activated as soon as you choose Table Lookup.)

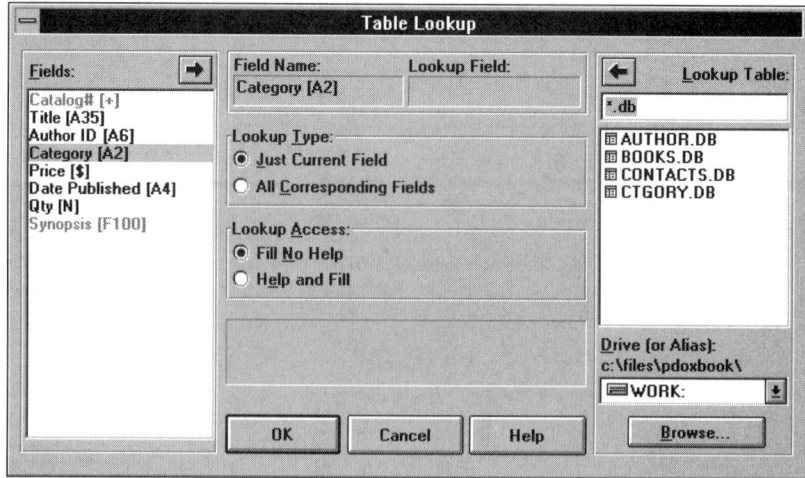

Figure 4-15: The Table Lookup dialog box. Notice that the Category field is highlighted and the name of the field appears in the Field Name box.

Inside Scoop

It doesn't matter if you forget to select the field before you open the Table Lookup dialog box. Notice that all of the fields in BOOKS.DB are listed in the Fields list. At this point you could highlight any field you want and then click on the right arrow just above the list. As with most Windows lists, you can also double-click on the field name. Whichever method you use, the field you select appears in the Field Name box and becomes the field that is used for the lookup table.

8. Select CTGORY.DB from the Lookup Table list, then click on the left arrow just above the list (or double-click on CTGORY.DB).

    Notice that the names of the fields in the Field Name and Lookup Field boxes don't match but their structures do (both are alpha with 2 characters). It's okay to have a different name for the field that you're matching in the lookup table, but if the structure of the two fields isn't exactly the same (right down to the number of characters), your computer beeps at you and the message "Field types do not match" displays near the bottom of the dialog box.

Inside Scoop

I'm using different field names in the two tables to make the point that you can do it. But whenever possible, it's a good idea to keep the linked field names the same. As you develop more complex applications, consistent naming conventions will make it easier to work with all of your links.

9. Choose Just Current Field in the Lookup Type section.

    Just Current Field means that when you select a record from the lookup table, only the value from the first field in the table is inserted in your main table. In this case, we're choosing Just Current Field because we only want the category code to appear in BOOKS.DB. If we had a field for the category description in BOOKS.DB, we could choose All Corresponding Fields to have Paradox insert data from any field in the lookup table that has a matching field in the main table.

Note: When you choose All Corresponding Fields, the matching fields must have the same names; otherwise, Paradox won't be able to find them for you.

10. Choose Help and Fill from the Lookup Access section.

Help and Fill means that you can look at the lookup table and use it to keep from having to type entries when you're entering data in the Category field in BOOKS.DB. Choose Fill No Help if you don't want people to be able to view the lookup table during data entry.

Pitfall Ahead

Think about it before you use Fill No Help, especially if you've made the field a required field (required fields are covered a little later in this chapter). If you use Fill No Help with a required field, users can't leave the field until they make a valid entry. And if they can't look up the acceptable entries, they can get awfully stuck. In fact, the only way to get out of that situation is for the person doing the entry to stop work until they can find someone who has access to the list of acceptable entries. Unless there's highly classified information in the lookup table that you don't want casual users to have access to, try to avoid Fill No Help. The time to deal with this issue is during the design process. Just make sure you don't put confidential data in any tables you plan to use as lookups.

11. Choose OK to accept your entries and close the Table Lookup dialog box. Leave the Restructure dialog box onscreen so we can do more stuff to it.

Modifying a Lookup Table

You can make changes to a lookup table by restructuring the table just as you would any other table. For example, to change CTGORY.DB, open it and choose Table, Restructure Table (or choose Restructure from the Project Viewer's Object Inspector menu for CTGORY.DB). Change the items you want and choose Save. The next section, "Using Referential Integrity," describes orphaned records and how referential integrity keeps them from being orphaned. Think about those poor orphans as you make your changes. If you change information in a linked field, any records in the main table that use the old information will lose their connection.

If you want to modify the link itself, open the main table (in our example that would be BOOKS.DB) and choose Table, Restructure Table. From the Field Roster list, select the field that's linked to the lookup table. Choose Table Lookup from the Table Properties drop-down list, then click on the Modify button. This takes you to the Table Lookup dialog box, where you can change the Lookup Type, the Lookup Access, the field to which the lookup table is linked or the table used for the lookup. Just remember that the first field in the lookup table has to be the same type and length as the field it's linked to.

Removing the Link

If you decide that you want to get rid of a link to a lookup table, no problem. Just open the Restructure dialog box for the main table (BOOKS.DB in our example), choose Table Lookup from the Table Properties drop-down list, select the field that's linked to the lookup table from the Field Roster list and click on Erase. Then choose Save to save the structure changes and close the Restructure dialog box.

Erasing the link doesn't delete the lookup table itself—it just isn't a lookup table anymore. If you want to delete the table from your disk, use the Project Viewer (right-click on the table you want to delete and choose Delete) or choose Tools, Utilities, Delete to access the Delete dialog box.

Keep in mind that you now have orphaned records in the field that used to be connected to the lookup table. Those poor orphans don't have any way of knowing where they belong.

REFERENTIAL INTEGRITY

Don't get hung up on the technobabble-sounding name—it's not as intimidating as it may seem. Referential integrity is a cool tool that can guarantee matching values between tables.

So what the heck is referential integrity? It's easier to do than talk about, so we're going to create a referential integrity link between the AUTHOR field in BOOKS.DB and the ID field in AUTHOR.DB.

Referential integrity is kinda like table lookups on steroids. Table lookups ensure that you can only enter valid data in a field, but referential integrity takes it a step further by keeping you from breaking the link between the two tables. Remember the CTGORY.DB table we used as a lookup for the Category field in BOOKS.DB? (Yeah I know, that was sooooo long ago, but you can do it.) With the link to the lookup table, you can't enter any values in the Category field in BOOKS.DB that don't exist in the Code field in CTGORY.DB. But what happens if you change the code for General Literature from LT to GL? Well, with a lookup table, nothing happens. Paradox lets you go ahead and change the code in CTGORY.DB. But it doesn't change any of the entries you've already made in BOOKS.DB where you used LT for General Literature. So you end up with a bunch of "orphaned" records that are no longer linked to anything.

Referential integrity doesn't let you abandon those poor orphans. If you try to change LT to GL when a referential link exists, one of two things happens, depending on how you set up the link (as you'll soon see): Paradox may not allow you to make the change at all; or if it does allow you to make the change, it will then update the Category field in BOOKS.DB to reflect the change. So the link survives. No orphans.

Playing by the Rules

You didn't think you'd get this cool tool without having to follow a few rules, did you? There aren't a lot, but make sure everything on the following list is in place before you define a referential integrity link:

○ The tables have to be in the same directory.

○ Both tables have to be Paradox for Windows tables (as opposed to DBIV, DBIII+ or any other type).

○ The field you're linking to in the parent table has to be a primary key field. Quick reminder: The parent table's the one that has only one record for each entry in the linked field, and the child table's the one that can have several records for each entry. We're going to create a table called AUTHOR.DB that contains information about each author. AUTHOR.DB will be the parent because there's only one record for each author, and BOOKS.DB is the child because there could be several entries for each author. Check out Chapter 2 if you want to review this parent-child stuff. (And review Chapter 3 if you need a nudge on key fields.)

○ The child table must have a primary key, but it doesn't have to be (in fact it won't work if it is) the same field you're using for the link.

○ As with lookup tables, the fields you link together must have the exact same structure (the AUTHOR/ID fields in both tables are alpha, with room for three characters), but the field names don't have to be the same.

○ No BLOBs allowed. You can't define referential integrity links to any type of BLOB field. That includes memo, formatted memo, binary, graphic and OLE.

Defining Referential Integrity

We'll start by creating the AUTHOR.DB table and then link it to BOOKS.DB using referential integrity.

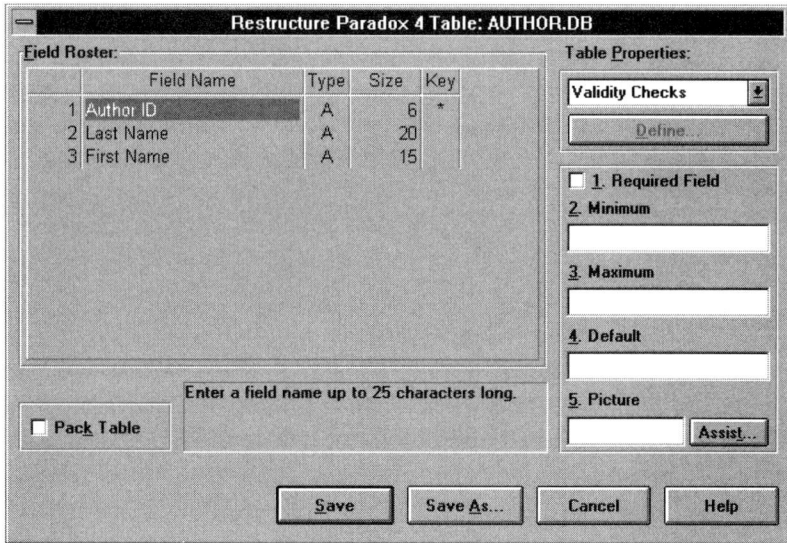

Figure 4-16: Your completed table structure should look like this.

1. Create a new table using the field names and structure shown in Figure 4-16.
2. Save the table as AUTHOR and make sure it's cleared from your screen. (As with lookup tables, you can't create a referential integrity link when the table you're linking to is open.)
3. Make sure the Restructure Paradox for Windows Table dialog box for BOOKS.DB is onscreen.
4. Choose Referential Integrity from the Table Properties dropdown list. Then click on the Define button.

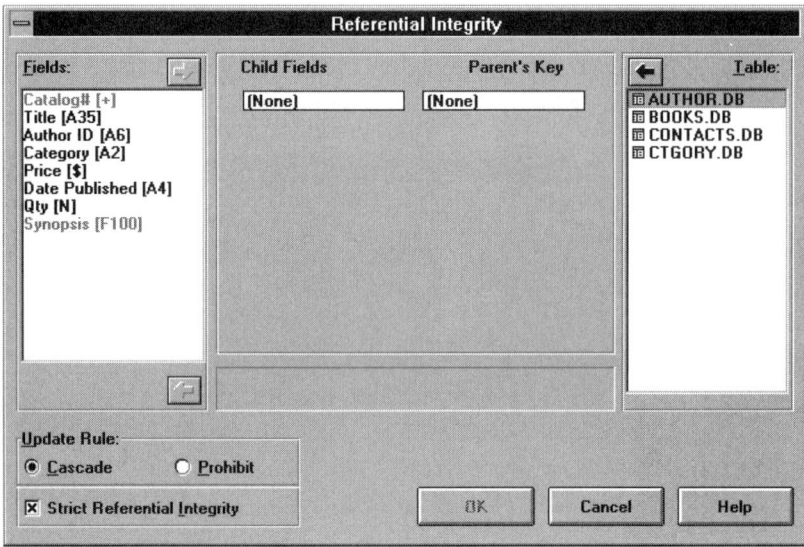

Figure 4-17: The Referential Integrity dialog box.

5. Select Author ID from the Fields list.
6. Click on the right arrow just above the Fields list to place the field name in the Child Fields box.

Fast Forward

Double-click on Author ID to combine steps 5 and 6. You can do the same thing to combine steps 7 and 8 by double-clicking on AUTHOR.DB.

If you choose the wrong field, you can just click on the left arrow below the Fields list to remove the field from the Child Fields list. Then try again.

7. Select AUTHOR.DB from the Table list.
8. Click on the left arrow just above the Table list to place the key field name from AUTHOR.DB in the Parent's Key box.

If the parent table has a composite key, all of the keyed fields will be listed in the Parent's Key list.

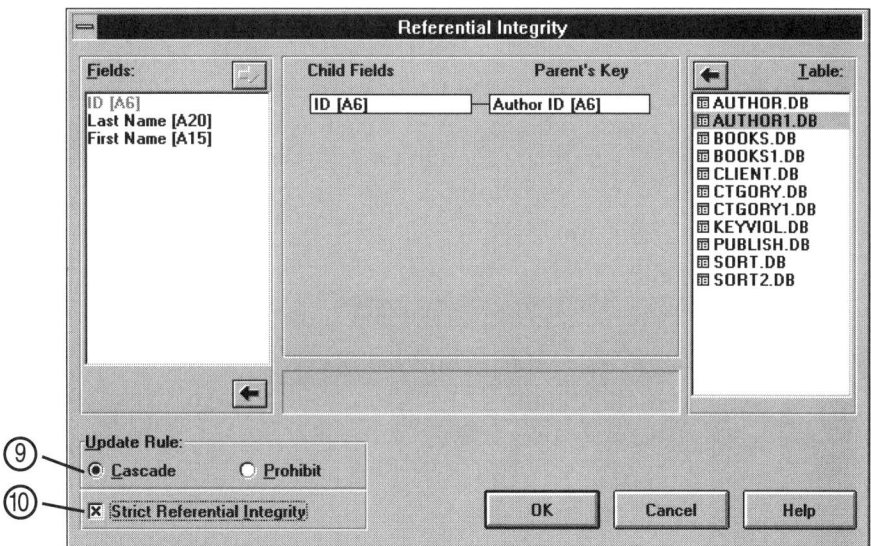

Figure 4-18: This is what your Referential Integrity dialog box should look like now. (Except for the circled numbers—we'll get to those in a minute.)

Notice a couple of things. First, Paradox doesn't let you choose a field from the AUTHOR.DB table—it automatically uses the key field from that table. Second, when the information appears in the Parent's Key box, Paradox draws a line between the Child Fields and the Parent's Key boxes to indicate that there's a valid link. If you try to use a table in which the key field doesn't match the child table's field, Paradox won't create the link. If you don't see a line between the two boxes, look for a message at the bottom of the dialog box. It'll say something like "Field types do not match" or "The parent table must be keyed" to let you know what the problem is.

9. Choose Cascade from the Update Rule area.

    The Update Rule choices determine what happens when you make changes to the primary key in the parent table. If you choose Cascade, any changes you make are also made in the child table's foreign key. If you choose Prohibit, Paradox won't let you make any changes to the primary key in the parent table if you've already entered records in the linked field in the child table.

10. Check the Strict Referential Integrity box to make absolutely sure that your data can't be messed with by someone who has a version of Paradox that doesn't support referential integrity.

    Checking Strict Referential Integrity means that no one can edit the table in an earlier version of Paradox. If you don't choose Strict Referential Integrity, the table can be opened and edited in DOS versions of Paradox. Since referential integrity doesn't exist in the DOS versions, editing a Paradox for Windows table in Paradox for DOS can breach the table's referential integrity. With Strict Referential Integrity selected, the file can be opened in DOS versions, but it's read-only (that means you can look but don't touch).

11. Choose OK.

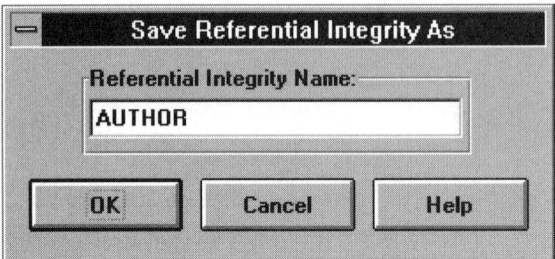

Figure 4-19: This is where you name the link.

Here you're not actually naming a table—you're just assigning a name to this particular link between two tables.

12. Type **AUTHOR** in the Referential Integrity Name text box and choose OK. The link's name appears in the Table Properties list when Referential Integrity is selected.

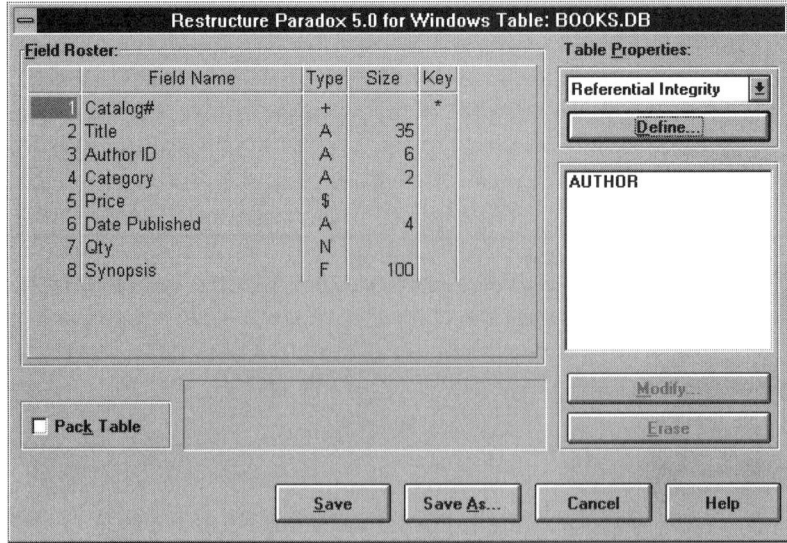

Figure 4-20: The Restructure Paradox for Windows Table dialog box with the completed link.

Modifying Referential Integrity

You can make changes to a parent table by restructuring the table just as you would any other table. For example, to change AUTHOR.DB, open it and choose Table, Restructure Table. Change the items you want and choose Save. What you can't do is make changes to any of the primary key fields without consequences in the child table. If you chose the Cascade rule when you defined the link, any changes you make to the key fields will be passed along to the child table. If you chose the Prohibit rule, you can't make any changes to the key fields without first deleting any matching records in the child table.

If you want to modify the link itself, open the child table (in our example that would be BOOKS.DB) and choose Table, Restructure Table. Choose Referential Integrity from the Table Properties drop-down list and select the link you want to modify (AUTHOR). Click on the Modify button. This takes you to the Referential Integrity dialog box, where you can change the rules, the child table's fields or the parent table.

Removing a Referential Integrity Link

If you decide you want to get rid of a referential integrity link, just open the Restructure dialog box for the child table, choose Referential Integrity from the Table Properties drop-down list, select the link that you want to delete (in this case, AUTHOR), and click on Erase. Then choose Save to save the structure changes and close the Restructure dialog box.

Self-Referential Integrity

Paradox lets you define referential integrity links between two fields in the same table. Of course, all of the standard referential integrity rules still apply—the fields have to have the same structure, no BLOBS allowed, etc. And because the linked field in the parent table always has to be a primary keyed field, the parent field in a self-referential integrity link has to be the primary key field or fields.

So why would you want to do this? What if you want to create an employee database for your company? Your employee table has one field for Employee ID and another for Supervisor ID. Since all of the supervisors are employees (or there's something wrong with this picture), you could define a self-referential integrity link from the Supervisor ID field to the Employee ID field. That would keep you from entering any IDs in the Supervisor ID field that aren't valid employee numbers.

Inside Scoop

You have to use the Prohibit Update rule for self-referential integrity links. Using the previous example, this means you can't edit data in the Employee ID field if the record you're trying to change has a link to the Supervisor ID field.

Restructuring Issues

To protect referential integrity links, Paradox won't let you make certain restructuring changes in a parent table. You can easily check to see if the table you want to restructure has any children; do this by choosing Dependent Tables from the Table Properties drop-down list in the Restructure dialog box. As you can see in Figure 4-21, that'll list any tables that are children (dependents) of the current table.

List of dependent tables —

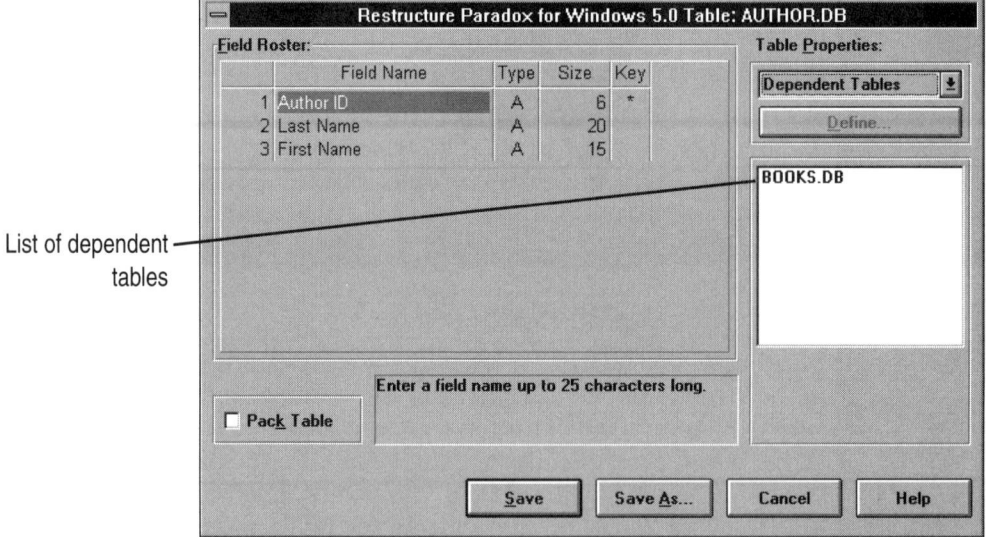

Figure 4-21: AUTHOR.DB is the parent table for BOOKS.DB because BOOKS.DB depends on AUTHOR.DB for its entry information.

It's a good idea to check for dependent tables before you make restructuring changes, especially as you start developing multitable databases with complex links.

Lookup relationships aren't listed. As discussed in the lookup tables section, Paradox will let you go ahead and make changes to a lookup table, regardless of any consequences that might result in the main table.

Once you've created a referential integrity link between two tables, you have to follow a few rules when you restructure the parent table (yeah, more rules):

○ If you make a field smaller, you have to trim data that won't fit in the new field. As you'll see when we talk about the Restructure Warning dialog box, Paradox gives you a choice about how to handle data that doesn't fit when you change the size of a field. One of the options is to put any affected records into a separate Problems table so that you can make decisions about what to do later. But you don't have that option if there's a referential integrity link.

○ If you chose Prohibit Update when you created the link in the child table, you can't change the key field for the parent table if you've entered any data in a linked field in the child table. If you want to change the key field in this situation, you have to modify the referential integrity link in the child table and change the Update Rule to Cascade.

○ You can have multiple relationships among various tables—the parent in one relationship could be the child to another parent (kinda like life). But if a table's already a parent in one relationship, you can't make it a child to another parent unless both tables are empty. In our examples, AUTHOR is the parent of BOOKS. If you want AUTHOR to be the child of CTGORY, AUTHOR and BOOKS would both have to be empty before you create the new link.

○ If you already have data in your tables, create the links in this order: first, make CTGORY the parent of AUTHOR, then make AUTHOR the parent of BOOKS. In other words, the first link is to the table that makes AUTHOR a child, which allows you to continue and make AUTHOR the parent in another relationship. This rule applies to children and parents equally (not like life).

○ If you add a validity check to either table after you've created a link, you have to choose not to apply it to existing fields when you save the structure. (This option is found in the Restructure Warning dialog box, which is discussed at the end of this chapter.)

SETTING UP VALIDITY CHECKS

Until the ubiquitous "they" manage to find a way to change human nature, I'm afraid we have to accept the fact that humans make mistakes. It's easy to forget to fill in a field or to type an invalid entry. You've just seen how lookup tables and referential integrity alleviate part of the problem, but there's more ammo in Paradox's arsenal. Paradox gives you several ways to validate your data and mitigate human error.

Required Fields

Lookup tables and referential integrity links ensure that you won't enter the *wrong* value, but they don't guarantee that you'll enter any value at all. If you want to make sure that a value is always entered in a particular field, make it a *required* field.

Let's make Author and Category required fields so that users won't be able to leave a record until they enter values in those fields.

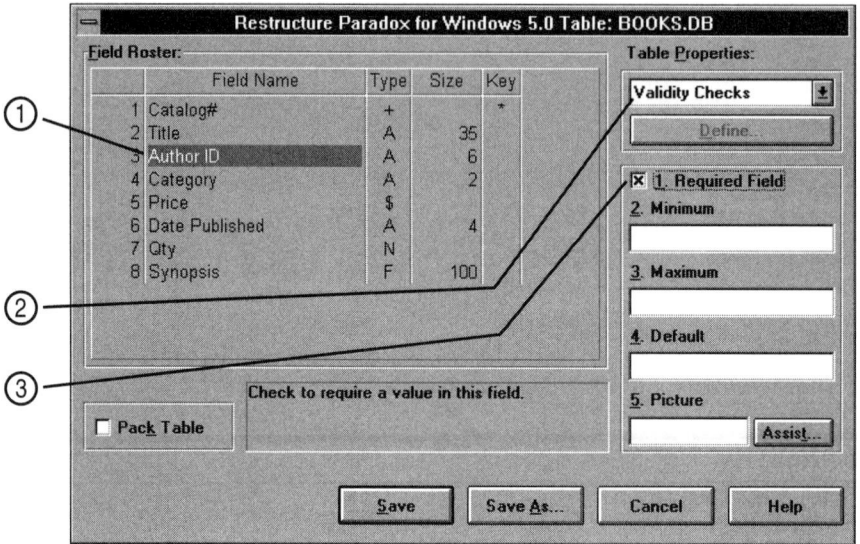

Figure 4-22: Start by opening the Restructure dialog box for BOOKS.DB.

1. Click anywhere in the Author ID field to select it.
2. Select Validity Checks from the Table Properties drop-down list.
3. Check the Required Field check box.
4. Repeat the process for the Category field.

Minimum & Maximum Values

Use Minimum and Maximum to specify a range of acceptable values for a field.

Pitfall Ahead

Setting a minimum value can get you into trouble if you're not paying attention. Whatever minimum value you specify, Paradox won't let you enter anything in the field that falls below that value. The catch here is the way Paradox treats blank fields. Any field that doesn't contain data is considered to have a lower value than *any* entered value. So setting a minimum value (even zero or a negative number) has the same effect as setting a required field. That might be okay—just be sure you're aware of what's happening.

Every customer has a credit limit of at least $100. No customer has a credit limit over $500.

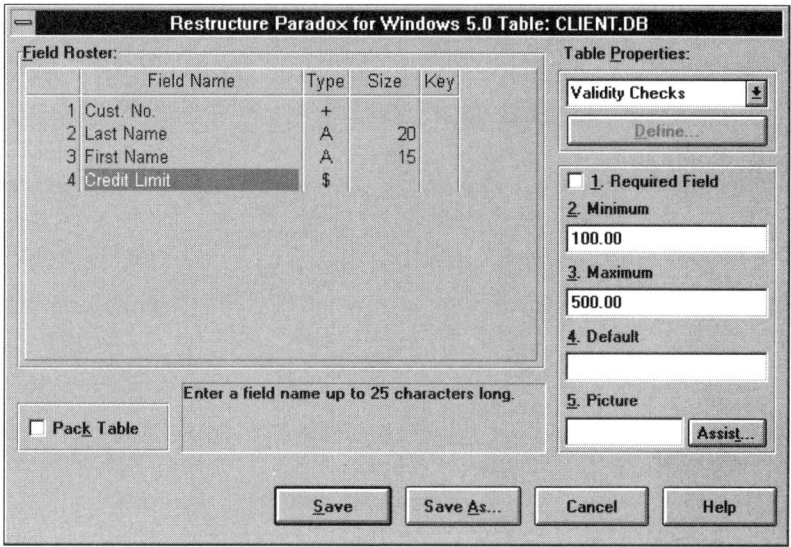

Figure 4-23: CLIENT.DB (which you haven't created yet) is part of the Bookfinders database.

This is a good example of where you would want a validity check for minimum and maximum values. Because Bookfinders doesn't allow credit for anyone who can't be trusted with a $100 limit, the minimum value is set at 100 to make sure a smaller figure can't be entered in the Credit Limit field. And since Bookfinders is a small (but growing) business, it can't deal with credit limits over $500 right now, so the maximum value is set at 500.

You can use minimum and maximum values in alpha fields too. For example, if you set a minimum value of D and a maximum of P, all of the entries in the field would have to start with letters from D to P.

Default Values

Specify a default value if most of the entries in a particular field will be the same. Since the majority of Bookfinders's books are science fiction, we'll make SF the default value for the Category field. You'll see how that can save time when we enter data in BOOKS.DB in the next chapter.

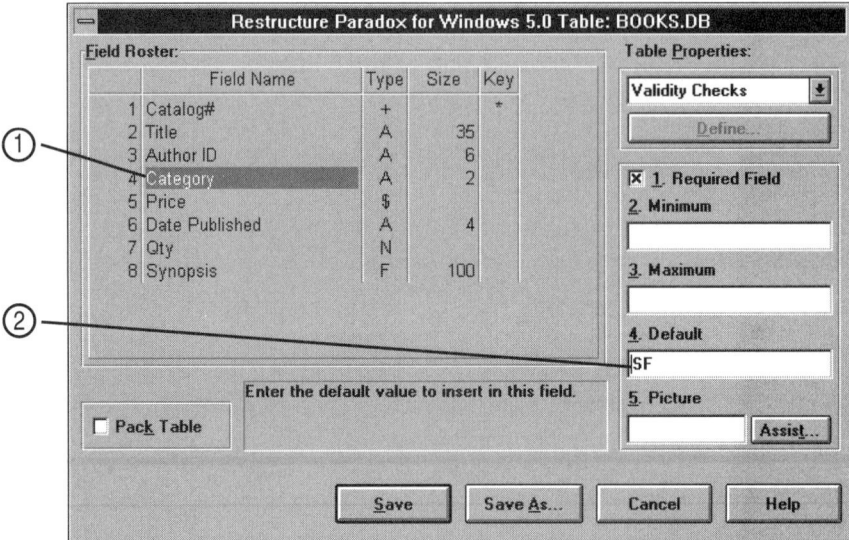

Figure 4-24: The Restructure dialog box with a default value for the Category field.

1. Click anywhere in the Category field to select it.
2. Type **SF** in the Default text box.

Inside Scoop

Notice that we're adding a default value to a field that's already a required field. You can mix and match validity check items. In the next section, we'll add a picture to the Category field to allow more flexibility in data entry while at the same time ensuring consistency. We'll do this by making it so that Paradox will accept a valid type whether you type it in uppercase or lowercase, and it will convert your entry to uppercase so all of the records match.

Pictures

The Picture option lets you get really specific about what can be put in a field. You can tell Paradox exactly how the field entry should look by "drawing a picture."

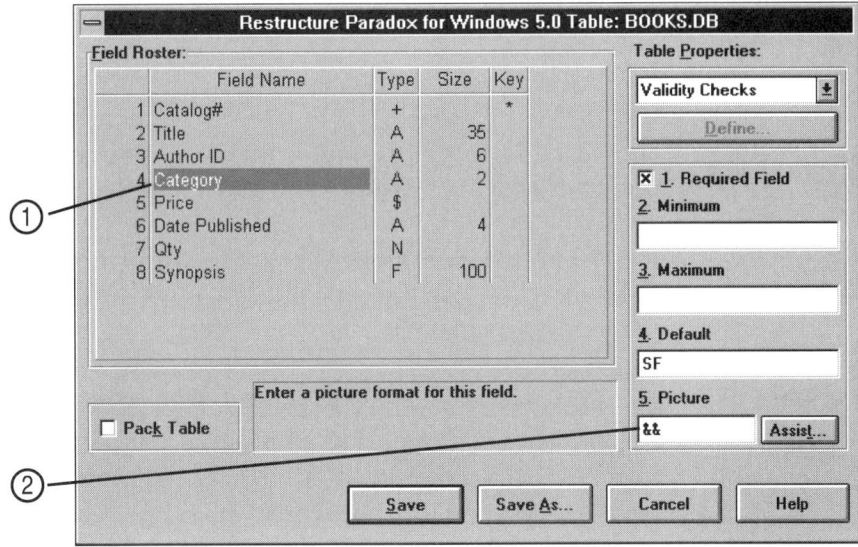

Figure 4-25: The Category field now has a picture as well as a default entry.

1. Click anywhere in the Category field to select it.
2. Type **&&** in the Picture text box.

Now you really have your bases covered for this field. When we enter data in the table in the next chapter, you'll see that there's no way you can go wrong here. If the category is science fiction, you don't have to do anything; if it's another category, just enter the initials in any combination of uppercase or lowercase; and if you can't remember the choices, press Ctrl+Spacebar to display the lookup table.

The following list tells you what each of the characters that can be used in pictures stands for.

#	One number	(Example: **####** = any four numbers.)
?	One letter	(Example: **?????** = any five letters.)
&	One letter (However it's entered, it gets converted to uppercase).	(Example; **&&** might be used for state abbreviations; you could enter ca for California, and it would be converted to CA.)

@ One character   (Example: @@@@@@ might be used for a part
  (number or letter)   number that consists of different
                                   combinations of numbers and letters.)

! One character   (Example: same as the example for @, but
  (But if you enter   any lowercase letters would end up upper-
  a letter, it gets   case.)
  converted to
  uppercase.)

; The next   (Example: ;# will result in the number
  character gets   symbol being inserted in the field.)
  inserted literally.

* The next character can be repeated as many times as you want.

*& Allows you to enter any number of letters and converts the entire
entry to uppercase.

[ ] Anything between (Example: [###-]###-#### allows you to
  the brackets   enter an area code in front of the phone
  is optional.   number, but doesn't require it.)

{ } Anything between the curly brackets is grouped together–you
have to choose one of the values in the group. (See the next
example for the comma character; the curly bracket is usually
combined with commas to separate the different choices.)

, Separates   (Example: {**Purple,Lavender**} means that
  alternative values.   you must enter either Purple or Lavender in
                        the field.)

Getting Help With Pictures

Paradox is so helpful–you don't even have to make up your own
pictures. And when you do make them up, Paradox can tell you ahead
of time whether or not they will work.

  1. Click on the Assist button next to the Picture text box.

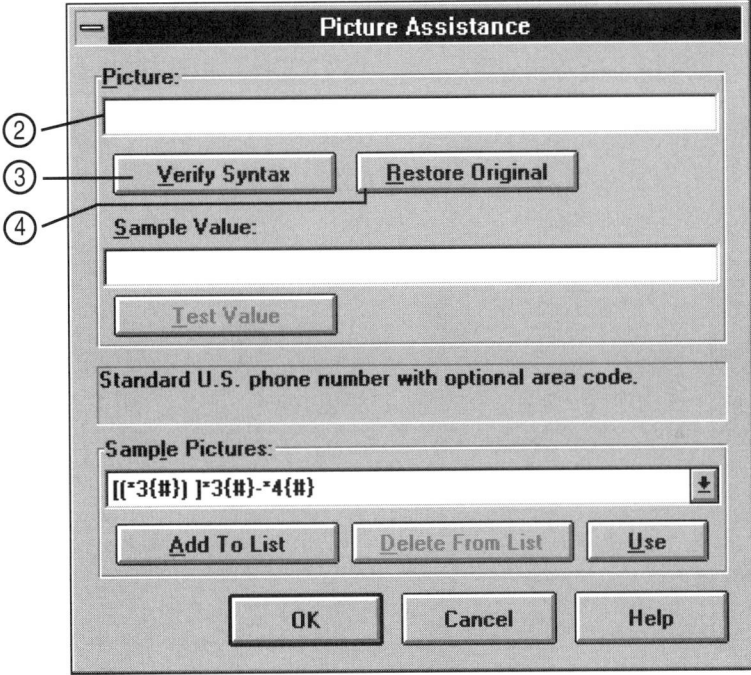

Figure 4-26: Use the Picture Assistance dialog box to create and test complex pictures or to use one of Paradox's predefined pictures.

2. Type a picture string in the Picture text box.

3. Click on the Verify Syntax button.

    If the picture is valid, the message "Value is valid." appears in the box just below the Test Value button.

4. You can click on the Restore Original button at any time to return the Picture text box to its original state. If it started out empty, clicking on Restore Original will delete anything that's been added. If you already had a picture in the Picture text box when you opened the Picture Assistance dialog box, clicking on Restore Original will return you to that original picture.

    Restore Original can be really handy if you get in too deep. Just clear the picture and start over.

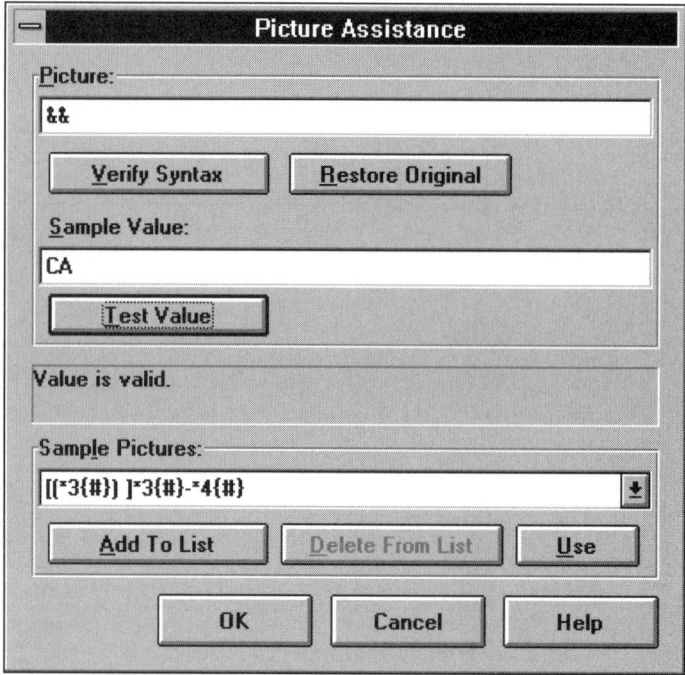

Figure 4-27: Values entered in the Picture and Sample Value text boxes.
Note the message just below the Test Value button.

5. Use Sample Value to make sure your picture will actually work
   for your situation. Verify Syntax only tells you whether the
   picture is in an acceptable format—it doesn't tell you whether
   the picture will do what you want it to. Once you have a
   picture in the Picture text box, you can enter some actual data
   in the Sample Value text box.

   Check it out. Type **&&** in the Picture text box. Then type **ca**
   (in lowercase letters) in the Sample Value text box. Notice that
   the letters are converted to uppercase as you type and that the
   message "Value is valid." is displayed in the message box just
   below the Test Value button.

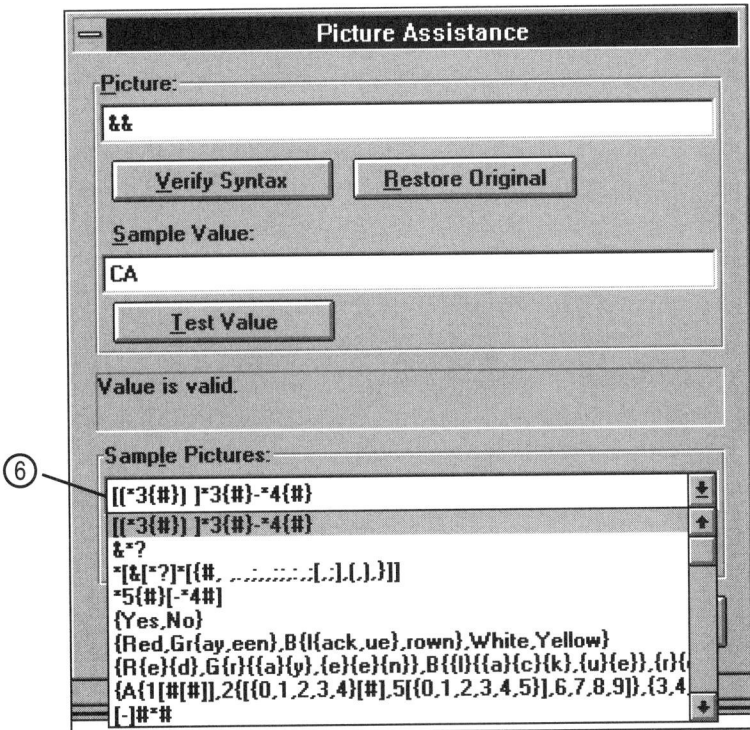

Figure 4-28: Paradox provides you with several sample pictures to choose from. These samples help you get started creating your own pictures.

6. Click on the drop-down arrow next to the Sample Pictures text box to display a list of predefined pictures.

117

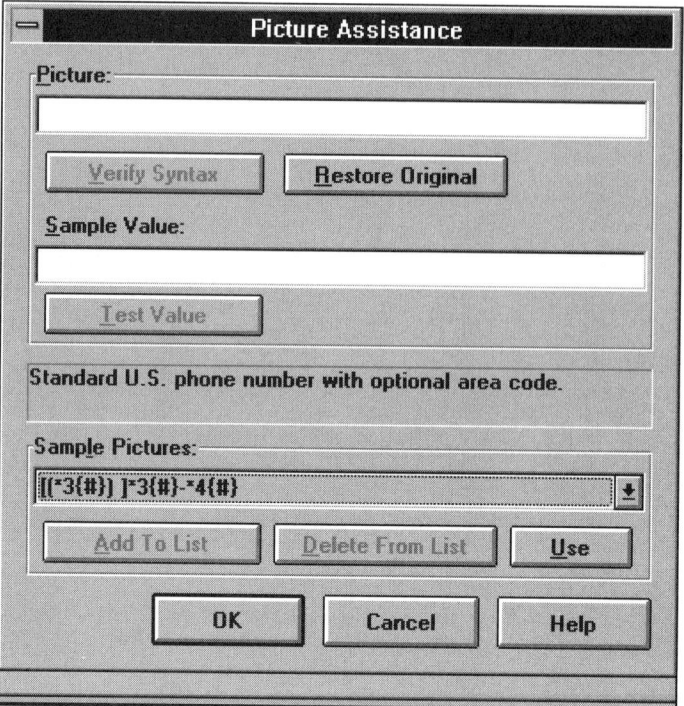

Figure 4-29: Notice the message describing the picture.

7. If you click on one of the samples, that sample is entered in the Sample Pictures text box and a description is displayed in the message area.

   You can also use your arrow keys to move through the sample list. You can view the descriptions for each sample as you move through the list. But don't press Enter—if you do, the Picture Assistance dialog box will close and whatever happens to be in the Picture text box will be inserted into the Restructure dialog box's Picture text box.

8. Click on the Use button to transfer a picture from the Sample Picture box to the Picture text box. You can then use the picture as is or edit it any way you want.

9. Click on Add To List if you create a picture that you want to be able to use in other tables. The picture in the Picture text box will be added to the Sample Pictures list and be available whenever you're in the Picture Assistance text box.

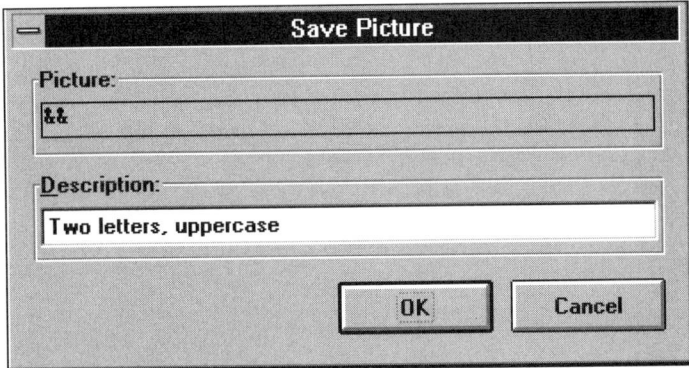

Figure 4-30: The Save Picture dialog box.

10. The Picture box displays the picture from the Picture text box. You can't change the picture in the Save Picture dialog box. If it's not what you want, choose Cancel to close the dialog box without saving the picture and make your changes in the Picture Assistance dialog box.

11. You can add a description for your picture, just like the ones Paradox uses for its predefined pictures. For this simple example, I just typed "Two letters, uppercase" so that anyone who looks at this picture will be able to tell what it does.

12. Choose OK when you're ready.

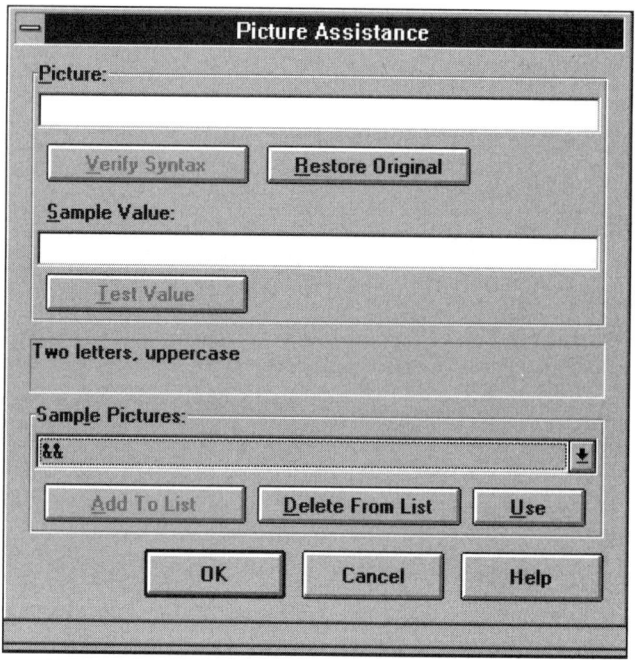

Figure 4-31: Now you can choose your picture from the Sample Pictures drop-down list, and its description appears in the message area.

Pitfall Ahead

Did you notice the Delete From List button (right between the Add To List and Use buttons)? Use it to delete pictures you've created from the Sample Pictures list. Be careful, though—as soon as you click on the Delete From List button, that picture's out of the picture without any warning messages. Paradox doesn't let you use this button to delete its own predefined pictures, so you don't have to worry about wiping them out.

RESTRUCTURING A TABLE

Everything we've done in this chapter has technically involved restructuring the table. But table lookups and validity checks are hidden behind the scenes—they don't actually affect how your table looks. In this section, we'll make changes that directly change the table: adding and deleting fields, changing the field type, and renaming fields.

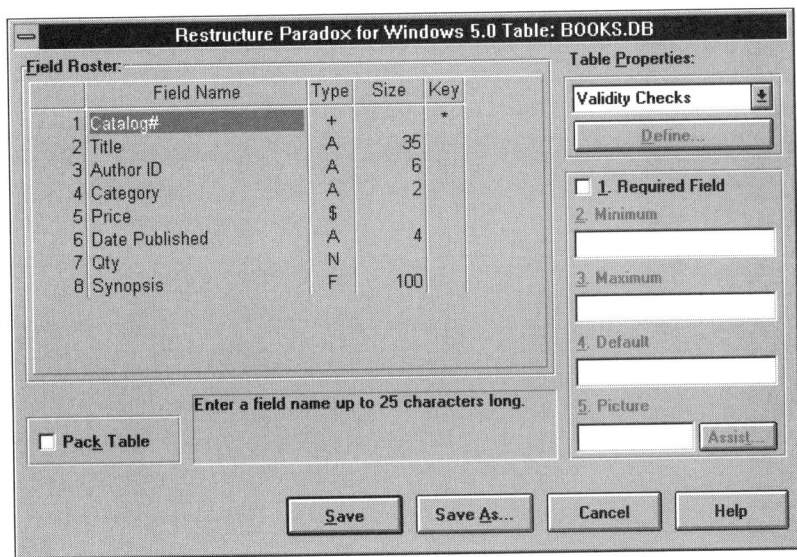

Figure 4-32: The Restructure dialog box for BOOKS.DB should be on your screen for the rest of this chapter.

You use the same technique to restructure a table that you use when you're creating the table structure in the first place. The only difference is that some of the changes have consequences after the fact. We'll get into those consequences throughout this section.

Adding, Inserting & Deleting Fields

You can always add a new field at the end of the current structure by pressing the Tab key, the Right arrow or the Down arrow when the selection bar is in the Type or Size column of the last field. Read on for more tricks:

○ To insert a field any place other than at the end, move the cursor to the row below where you want to add the new field. For example, to insert a new field between the Category and Date Published fields, move the cursor into the Date Published field. Press Insert to insert the new field just above your cursor position.

○ To delete a field, select any column in the field you want to delete and press Ctrl+Del.

If you've deleted a field from the Restructure dialog box, Paradox displays the following warning when you choose Save:

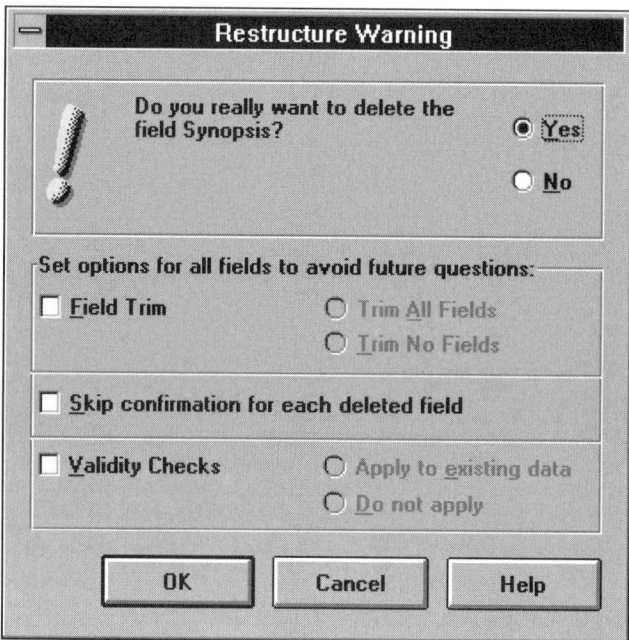

Figure 4-33: This dialog box lets you back out before you do major damage. Choose Yes and the field and its data are gone, outta here—and you can't get them back.

This dire warning isn't meant to scare you away from ever deleting a field. What I want to make perfectly clear, though, is that you should avoid at all costs sending your brain out to lunch and choosing Yes. Think first.

Changing Field Types

The mechanics of changing a field type are simple—just right-click in the Type column for the field you want to change and select a different type. The sticky part is that Paradox has a whole bunch of rules about which types can be converted to which other types. You can change the code in the Type column without a hitch, but as soon as you choose Save, you might very well see the following message:

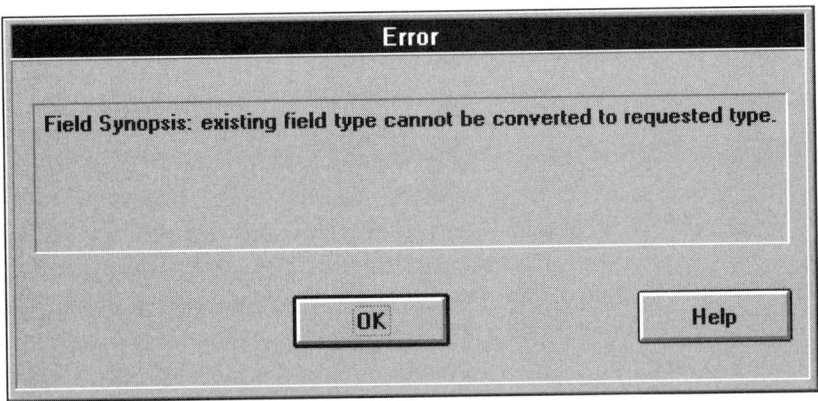

Figure 4-34: This error message box displays when you make a field type change that's a no-no. Notice that Paradox kindly lets you know which field is the problem.

This is one of those stupid Windows dialog boxes that really bugs me. The only options are OK and Help. If you choose OK, it just returns you to the Restructure dialog box so you can fix the problem. And Help doesn't give you any help—it just tells you that you're looking at an error message (like you didn't know). I want to say, "No, it's NOT OK—don't make me say everything's all right when it's not." If the button would just say something like, "You can't do that—Do not pass Go, do not collect $200—Press this button to end up right back where you started," I'd feel a lot better. OK, I'm done raving—you just got caught up in one of my pet peeves. And now back to our regularly scheduled program.

Nice person that I am, I'll try to save you the humiliation of having to encounter this warning message over and over by clueing you in on what can be changed to what:

○ Alpha fields can be changed to memo fields without any problem. Paradox will let you change alpha fields to number, money, date, short number, long integer, time or timestamp, but these conversions could cause data loss (don't worry—you get a Data Loss Warning dialog box as an out). If you convert an alpha field to one of the field types that doesn't allow you to specify a size (number, money, date, etc.), Paradox will beep at you when you try to save the structure and display this message: "You cannot specify a size for a field of this type." Just go to the Size column and delete the size information.

○ Number fields can be changed to alpha, money, logical or long integer with no hitches (except for possible data trimming if the new field type doesn't support as large a field size). Conversion to a short number type could generate the Data Warning dialog box.

○ Money fields can be changed to alpha, number, long integer or short number. Conversion to a short number type could generate the Data Warning dialog box.

○ Date fields can be changed to alpha or timestamp fields. That's it, folks. If your date field has any records that Paradox can't interpret as dates, those records are deleted from your table and moved to a temporary Problems table. You can then go through the offending records and decide what to do with them.

○ Short number fields can be changed to alpha, number, money or long integer.

○ Memo fields can be changed to alpha, formatted memo or binary.

○ Formatted memo fields can be changed to memo or binary.

○ Graphic fields can be changed to binary.

○ Binary fields can't be converted to any other type, and OLE fields can be converted only to binary.

○ Logical fields can be changed to alpha, number, short number, logical, long integer or BCD.

○ Long integer fields can be changed to alpha, number, money, short number, logical or BCD.

○ Time fields can be changed to alpha or timestamp.

○ Timestamp fields can be changed to alpha, date or time.

○ BCD fields can be changed to alpha, number, money, short number or long integer.

○ Autoincrement fields can be changed to number, money, short number, logical or long integer.

○ Bytes fields can be changed to alpha, formatted memo, binary, graphic or OLE.

○ If it ain't listed here, can't be done.

Changing the Field Size

This one's pretty straightforward. The only thing to watch out for is reducing the size of a field that already has data entered into it. If a field was set for 20 characters and you shorten the field to 10 characters, you run the risk of losing data and generating the Restructure Warning dialog box.

Changing the Field Order

To change the order of fields in the Field Roster, just point to the row number for the field you want to move and hold down the left mouse button. Thick lines appear above and below the highlighted fields.

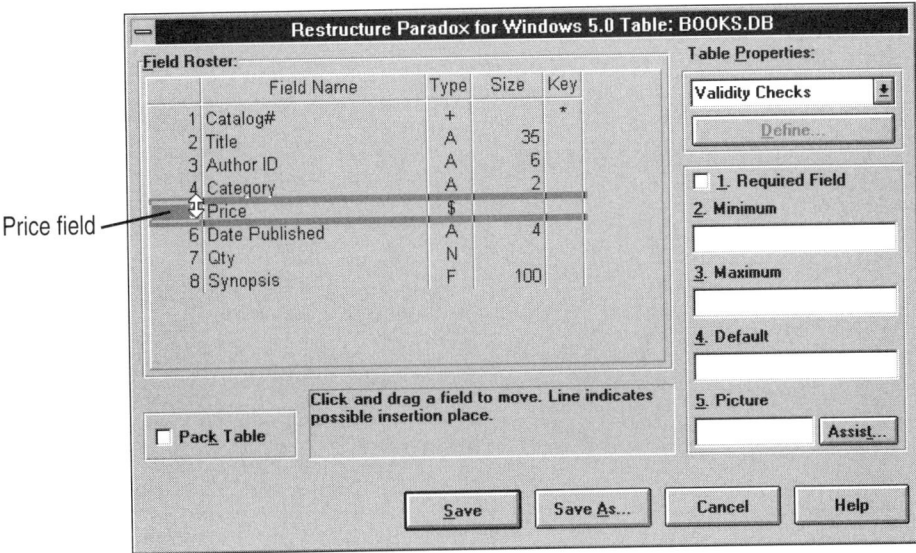

Price field ———

Figure 4-35: The Price field about to be moved.

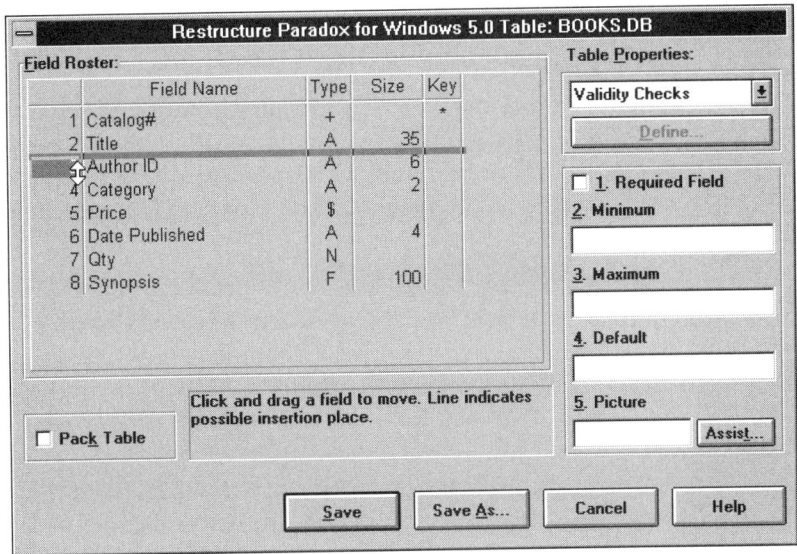

Figure 4-36: As you drag the mouse, the mouse pointer turns into a two-headed arrow and the double line turns into a single line that lets you know where the field will end up.

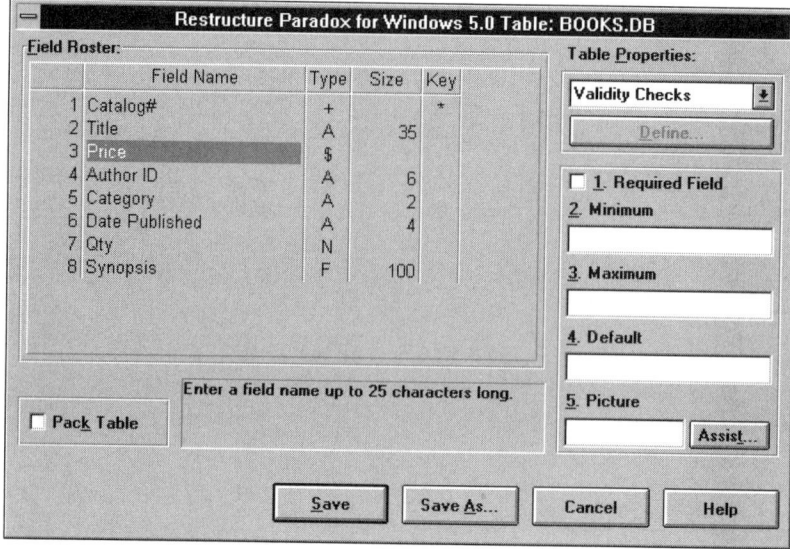

Figure 4-37: When you release the mouse button, the field is inserted at the line's position.

Saving the New Structure

Whenever you make changes to the table structure, whether it's defining a table lookup or moving some fields, you have to save the structure before the changes can be reflected in your table. To save your changes to the original table, just click on the Save button.

Oops, I Didn't Mean To!

There are a whole lot of ways to get in trouble with restructuring. You can easily end up with a convoluted mess, wishing you could just start over. Well, you can. Just choose Cancel from the Restructure dialog box. The dialog box closes without saving any changes you've made.

And there's another out. You may have noticed that I mentioned the Restructure Warning dialog box several times in this section. In any case where saving your structure changes could cause data loss, Paradox displays the Restructure Warning dialog box so that you can avert potential disasters.

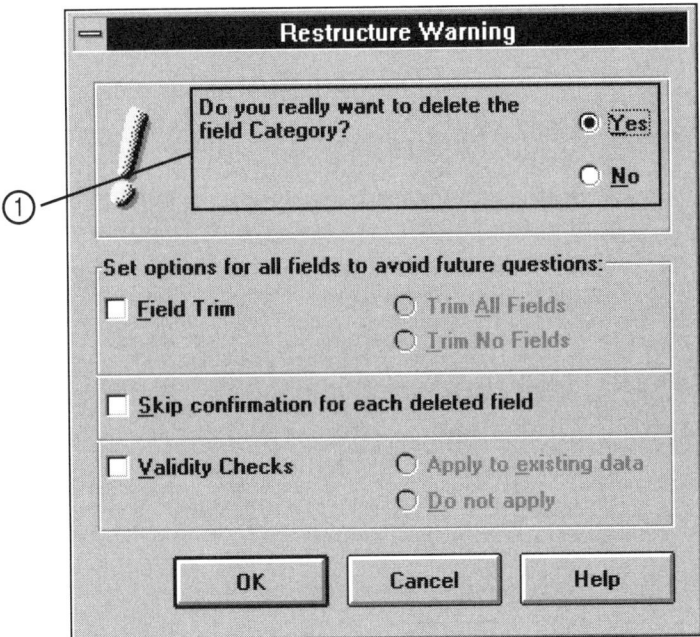

Figure 4-38: If you're trying to delete a field, the Restructure Warning dialog box looks like this.

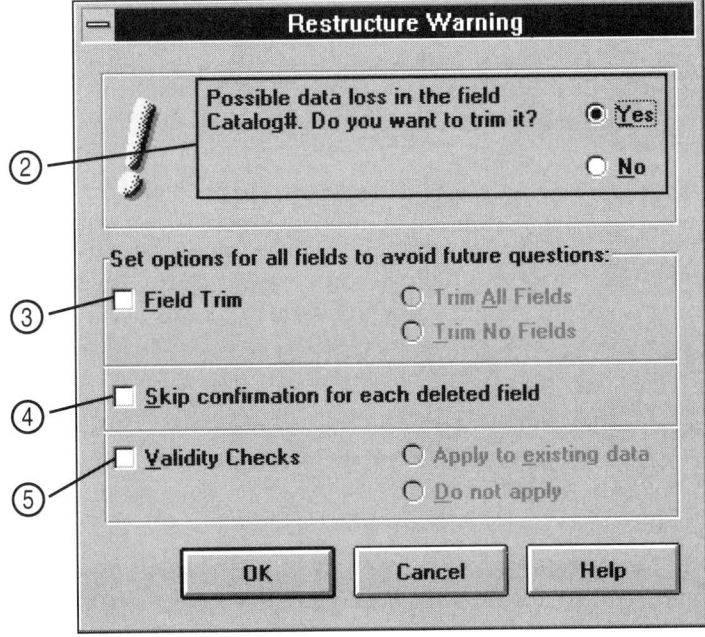

Figure 4-39: In most other cases, the dialog box looks like this.

1. Notice that the message tells you which field is about to be deleted and that your only choices are Yes and No. If you choose Yes, the field is deleted along with any data that's entered in the table. There are no more outs with this one. Make sure you answer carefully.

2. With this Restructure Warning, you get to choose whether or not to trim any records that won't fit into a reduced field length. If you choose Yes, any records that contain too many characters are deleted from your table, but they're moved into a Problems table, giving you the chance to decide what to do with each record. If you choose No, Paradox deletes any characters that won't fit into the new field length.

3. **Trim All Fields** has the same effect as choosing Yes in the message area, except that it applies to any other fields you've restructured during this session. Ditto with Trim No Fields. It's the equivalent of choosing No for all of the fields you've restructured.

4. If you select **Skip confirmation for each deleted field**, Paradox will go ahead and get rid of any other fields you've deleted during this session without asking you if it's okay.

5. Select **Apply to existing data** if you want to make sure all of the data in your table matches any new validity checks you've added during this session. Any records that don't match are moved to the KEYVIOL table.

   Select **Do not apply** if you want to leave all of the data in your table as it is. With this option, the validity checks will be applied only to new entries.

VIEWING THE TABLE STRUCTURE

Why would you want to open a dialog box that shows your table structure but doesn't allow you to do anything with it? Well, I can think of a few reasons off the top of my head:

○ Looking at the structure without being able to change it means that you can't inadvertently make changes and mess things up.

○ If you have an open table that's linked to a lookup table, Paradox won't let you restructure the lookup table. But you can get information about the lookup table's structure without leaving the main table.

○ The only way you can actually print a table's structure is by viewing the structure and then choosing Save As from the Structure Information dialog box.

To get information about a table's structure, follow these steps:

1. Choose Tools, Utilities, Info Structure.

   You can also choose Info Structure from the Project Viewer's Object Inspector menu for a selected table, or choose Table, Info Structure to view the structure of the current table. Either of these methods will save you a couple of steps.

2. Select the table whose structure you want to view from the Select File dialog box. For this exercise, choose BOOKS.DB.

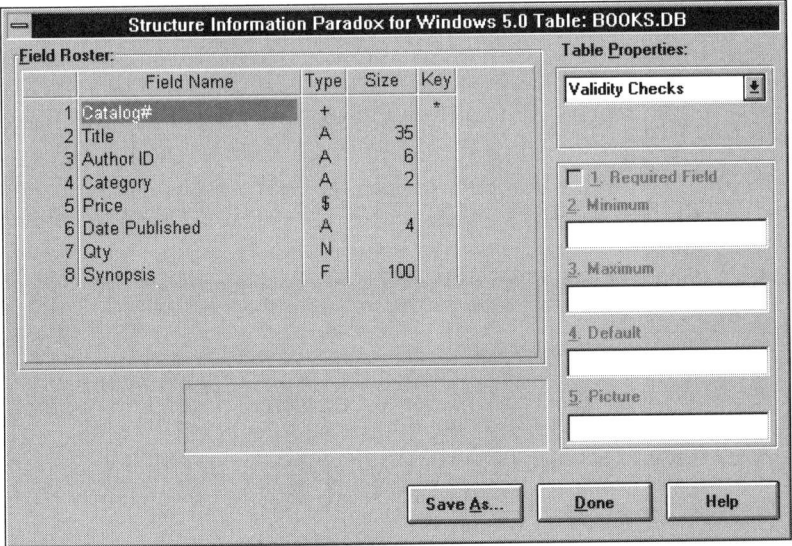

Figure 4-40: The Structure Information dialog box for BOOKS.DB.

Notice that this table looks just like the Restructure dialog box. You can select items from the Table Properties drop-down list to view different validity checks and links, and you can select different field names to find out what properties are attached to them. The only thing you can't do is change anything.

3. When you've looked to your heart's content, choose Done to close the Structure Information dialog box.

   Or, if you want to be able to print the table structure, choose Save As and give the table a name.

To view and print the table structure, follow these steps:

1. Open the table that contains the structure. This table is just like any other table. You can make changes to it, but keep in mind that any changes you make aren't actually being made to the structure of the original table.

2. Click on the Quick Report button to create a standard report. On the keyboard, press Shift+F7.

   You can also design fancier reports—you'll learn how to do that in Chapters 11 and 12.

3. Click on the Print button or choose File, Print.

4. Choose OK in the Print File dialog box to send the report to your printer.

HOW DO I GET OUT OF THIS JAM?

Jam 1

You want to define a referential integrity link, but you discover that neither table has a key field, and the field you want to link to in the parent table is the last one in the Field Roster. You end up with a message like this:

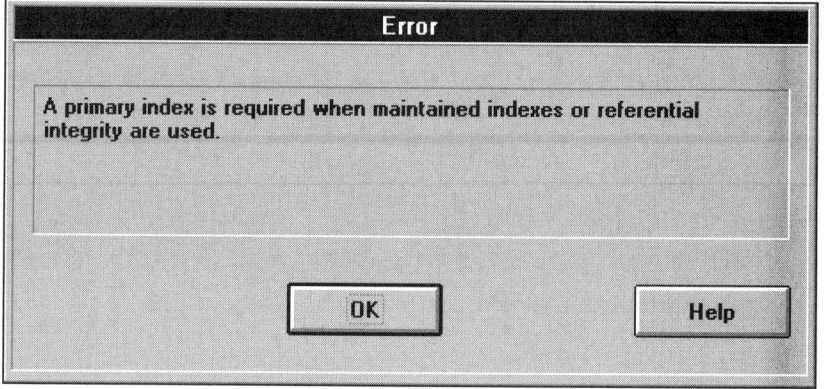

Figure 4-41 This message tells you you need to create a primary key for one (or both) of the tables before you can define the link.

Unjam

When you see this message, choose OK (even though it really isn't). Then restructure the table to include a primary key. If the table you're restructuring is the parent, you'll also have to move the field you're going to link to the top of the list.

Jam 2

You've defined a referential integrity link for a field for which you've also specified required entry, and you can't remember what you're supposed to put in it.

Unjam

You don't want to hear this, but the time to think of this was when you designed the database. At this point, all you can do is leave the table where it is until you can get the information you need. (You did write it down somewhere, didn't you?)

Jam 3

You want to make sure that the only acceptable response for a field is Yes or No.

Unjam

Use a logical field and change the format option to Yes/No.

Jam 4

You've already entered data in a table when you decide to change the name of a linked field in a lookup table.

Unjam

Here's the scoop. Paradox will let you change the field name without any problem, but the field will lose its link to the main table. The best unjammer is avoiding the problem in the first place by dealing with it in the design phase. If you do have to rename a linked field, make sure you also rename the corresponding field in the main table.

MOVING ON

You've paid your dues. You read every word of the design chapter. And you were ever so patient with all this nit-picky structure stuff. Now it's time to get down to business. (Not that everything we've covered so far isn't *incredibly* important—it's just that I know you're probably wondering if you're *ever* going to enter data into these tables we've so painstakingly prepared.)

All you have to do is turn the page. Chapter 5 will give you all the gory details about entering and editing table data, changing the way your table looks in Table View and, as a special added attraction, Chapter 6 tells you everything you ever wanted to know about sorting (but were afraid to ask because you thought it would be too gruesome—it's not). So join me in a delightful trip to the table. (Sorry, no dessert. Not even if you eat all your veggies.)

5

DOING THINGS WITH TABLES

We've spent a bunch of time designing, creating and restructuring tables. Now you'll see how all of that careful preparation pays off. We'll enter data and talk about how to work with lookup tables, referential integrity links and different field types. We'll also make changes to the data you enter and find out how to recover from mistakes—and which ones you can't recover from (always nice to know that in advance!).

ENTERING DATA

Before you can add data to a table, what do you think you might want to do first? Any guesses? Yup, you got it the first time—open the table. Remember the lookup table we created in the last chapter? And the table we connected to BOOKS.DB with a referential integrity link? Well, in order to make those links work, we have to enter data in CTGORY.DB and AUTHOR.DB, the two tables that are linked to BOOKS.DB. So we'll start by entering the categories in CTGORY.DB and then create an author list in AUTHOR.DB. This'll give us something to work with in BOOKS.DB. And there's another reason to start with CTGORY.DB and AUTHOR.DB. Their structures are much simpler than BOOKS.DB, and you'll be able to get comfortable with basic data entry before we move on to working with different field types, lookup tables and all that other good stuff.

Opening the Table

1. Just to make sure we're all starting from a clear screen, choose Close All from the Window menu (unless you're already at a clean Desktop or the Project Viewer's the only thing open).

   Just a reminder: you can open a table even if you have other tables or objects open—I'm just having you close all of your open windows to simplify the process at this point.

2. Do one of the following:

   If the Project Viewer is open, double-click on CTGORY.DB.

Or Open the Open Table dialog box by clicking on the Open Table Toolbar button or by choosing File, Open, Table. Then double-click on CTGORY.DB.

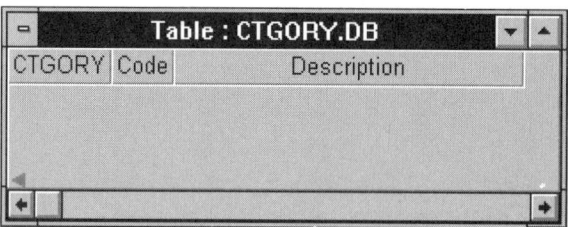

Figure 5-1: Because we haven't entered any data in CTGORY.DB, all you see is the field name heading for each field.

The Scoop on Table View

By default, Paradox opens the table in *Table View*. That's how CTGORY.DB looked right after you created the structure in Chapter 3. In this view, you can see all of your records (or at least all that will fit on your screen), just like you would in any other kind of table (except the kind you sit down at for dinner)—in other words, in a tabular format. Get it—table, tabular?? If the table doesn't have any data in it yet, you just see the field names (just like Figure 5-1).

So, you got your Table View, which is a cool way of seeing all of your records in one place (okay, there might be some scrolling in-volved—picky, picky). But what if you have about a kazillion fields in your table? It can be a giant pain to enter data when it's laid out in tabular format. Presenting . . . ta-dah . . . the Form window, which can make the process of entering and editing data virtually painless. Check out Figures 5-2 and 5-3. They show the same table in Table View and the Form window. You can arrange your fields on the form to make it easier to move from field to field. And forms are *so* much more visually appealing (we mustn't discount the emotional element here—I want you to feel *good* about your data, to feel *comfortable* with it). Enough about the Form window for now. Still to come in this chapter: stuff about entering and editing data in Paradox's default form. Still to come in Chapters 9 and 10: a form design extravaganza. By the end of Chapter 10, you—that's right, you with your nose in this book—will possess heretofore undreamed-of skills that will allow you to create your own form masterpieces.

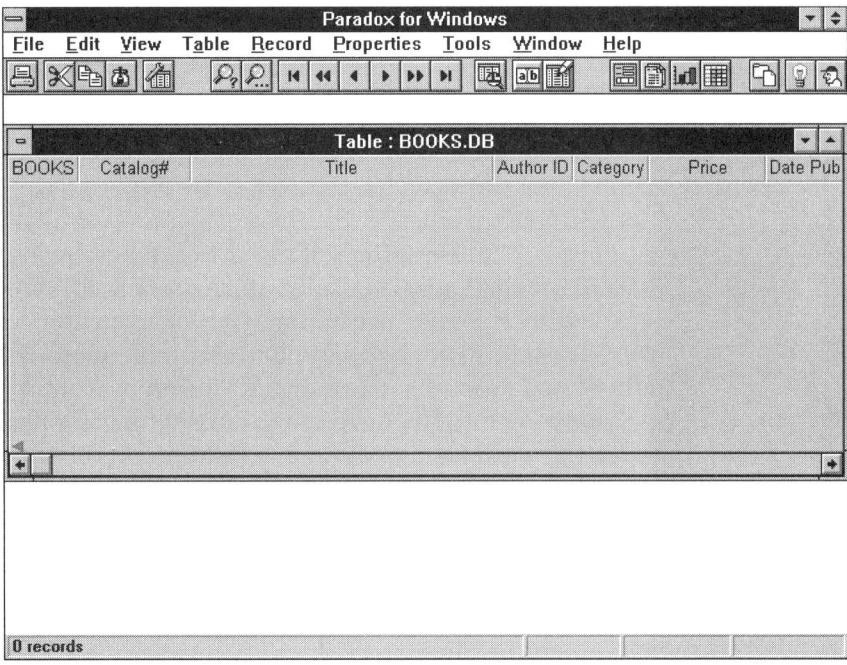

Figure 5-2: BOOKS.DB in Table View.

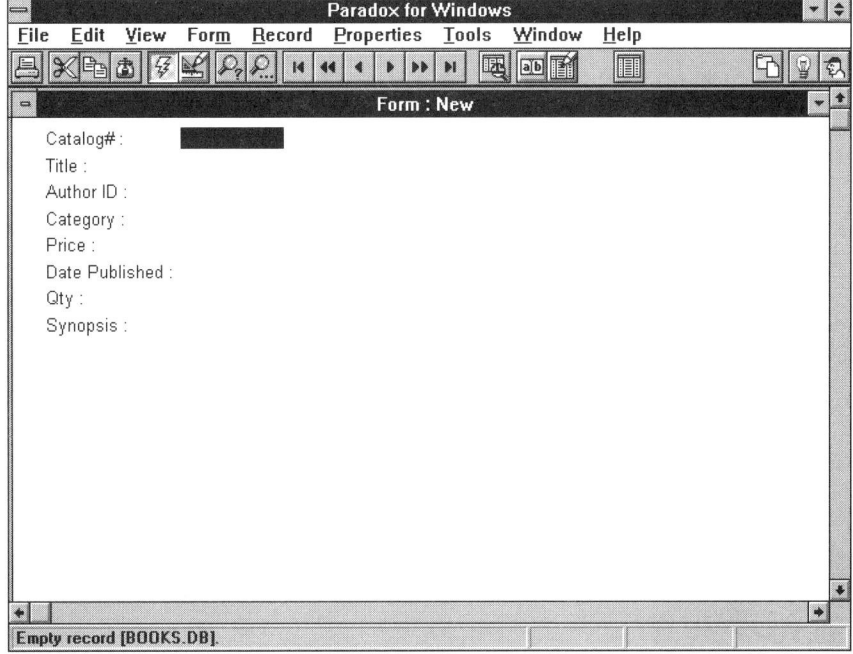

Figure 5-3: The Form window with the default form for BOOKS.DB.

A little later in this chapter, you'll learn how to alter the view in just about any way you could desire. But for now, I want you to learn all about Table View and get some practice entering information before we mess around with the view.

In case you haven't already noticed (or even if you have), take a look at the status bar in Figure 5-2. See where it says "0 records" (hint: look in the lower left corner)? When you open a table that already has stuff in it, check out the status bar to see how many records you're dealing with. And as you add information to CTGORY.DB, you'll see this number change every time you complete a record.

The other major happening in the Table window is the Toolbar. Those of you who noticed that it's different from the one on the Desktop, step to the head of the class while you pat yourself on the back (without losing your concentration on the task at hand). As we talked about in Chapter 1, Paradox displays different Toolbars depending on which window you're in, and each one will be covered in its own little section. While we're here, let's zoom in on the Table window's Toolbar and analyze it to death.

I'll tell you what each button does, how to access each option from the menu (just in case clicking on buttons makes you crazy) and which actions have keyboard shortcuts. Don't worry about the meaning of these actions for now—I'll cover all of them in the course of this chapter. This table's meant to be a handy dandy reference that you'll refer to over and over as you work with tables.

Here's the stuff you can do from the Table window's Toolbar, along with alternative keyboard methods.

Toolbar Button	What It Does	On the Menu	Keyboard Shortcut
	Opens the Print File dialog box.	File, Print	Alt+F,P
	Cuts selected data to the Clipboard.	Edit, Cut	Shift+Del
	Copies selected data to the Clipboard.	Edit, Copy	Ctrl+Ins
	Pastes data from the Clipboard.	Edit, Paste	Shift+Ins
	Opens the Restructure dialog box.	Table, Restructure Table	Alt+A,T
	Opens the Locate Value dialog box, from which you can search for specific values in fields.	Record, Locate	Ctrl+Z

Toolbar Button	What It Does	On the Menu	Keyboard Shortcut
	Repeats the last search.	Record, Locate Next	Ctrl+A
	Takes you to the first record in your table.	Record, First	Ctrl+F11
	Takes you to the previous set of records.	Record, Previous Set	Shift+F11
	Takes you to the previous record.	Record, Previous	F11
	Takes you to the next record.	Record, Next	F12
	Takes you to the next set of records.	Record, Next Set	Shift+F12
	Takes you to the last record in your table.	Record, Last	Ctrl+F12
	Opens the Filter Tables dialog box.	Table, Filter	
	Changes to Field View so you can edit within a field.	View, Field View	F2
	Changes to Edit Mode.	View, Edit Data or View, End Data (The menu option changes depending on which mode you're in.)	F9
	Switches to the Form window—displays either your custom preferred form or Paradox's default form.	Tools, Quick Form	F7
	Prepares a report using either your custom format or the default report.	Tools, Quick Report	Shift+F7
	Displays your preferred graph. If you don't have one, the Define Graph dialog box opens.	Tools, Quick Graph	Ctrl+F7

Toolbar Button	What It Does	On the Menu	Keyboard Shortcut
▦	Displays your preferred crosstab form. If you don't have one, the Define Crosstab dialog box opens.	Tools, Quick Crosstab	Alt+T,C
▤	Opens the Project Viewer.	Tools, Project Viewer	Alt+T,V
▢	Opens the Experts Control Panel dialog box.	Help, Experts	Alt+H,E
▢	Opens the Coaches window.	Help, Coaches	Alt+H,H

Inside Scoop

Don't forget about Paradox's quick reminders. Just move your mouse pointer over any Toolbar button, and the status bar tells you what that button does.

If you're really on the ball, you probably noticed that you have several additional options on the main menu. As with the Toolbars, the menu items change depending on where you are and what you're doing. As we talk about various table-related features, we'll get to most of those new menu options.

Entering Data in Table View

By now I'm sure you're rarin' to go. OK, go for it. Try to type something in the table. Anywhere. No luck, huh? That's because you're in the viewing mode, which just means look but don't touch. From this mode you can do all sorts of things to change the appearance of your table. The one thing you *can't* do is enter data. And without data, does it really matter what your table looks like? (That was a rhetorical question, in case any of you are pondering the matter.) In order to enter or edit data, you have to be in Edit mode. So, without further ado,

 Click on the Edit Data button or choose View, Edit Data.

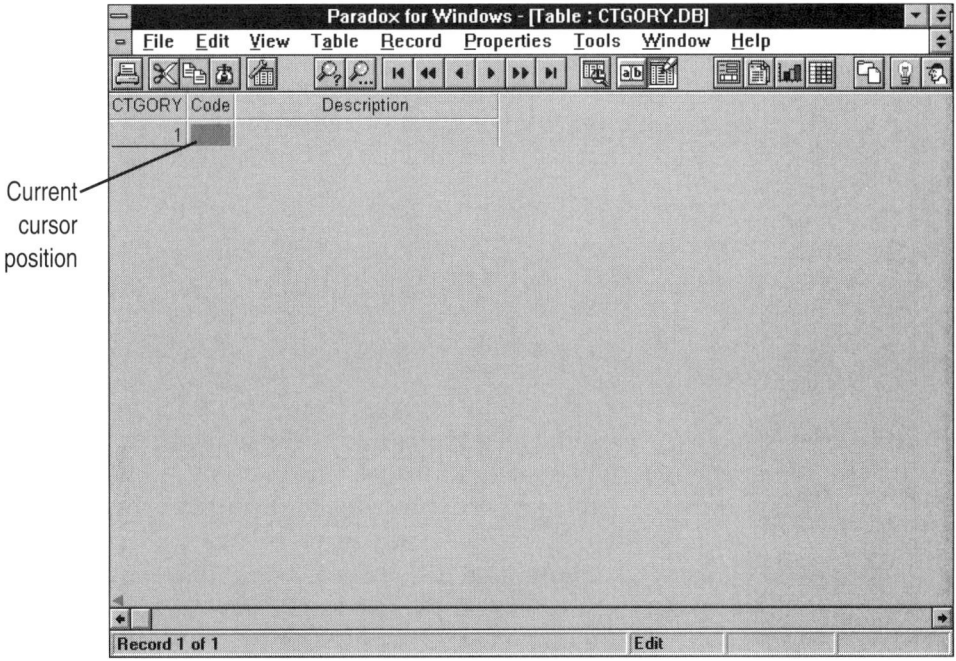

Current cursor position

Figure 5-4: Notice that there's a highlighted bar in the first field of your first record. Also notice the edit mode indicator in the status bar.

In Edit mode, that highlight lets you know where you can type. And look at the status bar. If it doesn't say Edit, you're not in Edit mode. Sounds obvious, but it's easy to forget where you are if you're bopping around between modes.

Since we're starting out nice and easy, all you have to know for now is:

❍ Type data in the field that's highlighted.

❍ To move to the next field, press the Tab, Right arrow or Enter key.

❍ When you're finished with one record, click on the Next Record button or press Tab, Right arrow or Enter to move to a new blank record. (You can also press F12.)

❍ To insert the value from the previous record, press Ctrl+D. Paradox calls this the "Ditto key." For example, if two consecutive records use the same Author ID, just enter the ID in the first record. Then move your selection bar to the Author ID field in the second record and press Ctrl+D.

There's a lot more to it—for example, if a field uses a lookup table or a validity check, there are special considerations. And you use some different techniques to enter and edit data in OLE-type fields (remember BLOBs?). We'll get to all of that in good time.

Enter the data in this table in CTGORY.DB

CODE	DESCRIPTION
TH	Theatre
LT	General Literature
SF	Science Fiction
MT	Metaphysics

Use the entries in the preceding table to fill in your CTGORY.DB table (make sure you add records in the same order they're given in the table). If you make a misteak (just kidding—I know how to spell mistache) while you're typing, make corrections before you move to the next field. You can use the arrow keys as well as Backspace and Delete. If you don't notice a mistake (see, I do know how to spell it) until after you've moved on, just leave it for now. A little later we'll talk about undoing mistakes and changing field entries.

1. Type **TH** and press Enter to move to the Description field.
   (Clicking in the Description field, pressing the Tab key and pressing the Right arrow key are all alternatives to pressing Enter.)
2. Type **Theatre** in the Description field and press Enter to save the record and move to the next one.

Figure 5-5: CTGORY.DB with one complete record.

You don't have to do anything special to save records. If you closed Paradox right now without doing anything else, the record you just entered would still be there when you came back.

3. Repeat steps 1 and 2 to complete the entries. Your finished table should look like the one shown in Figure 5-6.

Figure 5-6: This is what your table should look like now.

4. Close CTGORY.DB.

You don't have to save it—Paradox automatically posts your data as it's entered.

Pitfall Ahead

The records in Table 5-1 aren't in alphabetical order. I did that on purpose so you could see what happens when you enter them. Notice how Paradox automatically sorts the records as they're entered? That's because we made the Code field a primary key. It's easy to see what's happening in a table with just a few records. But in a really big table, a record might seem to vanish as soon as you enter it. It can seem a little weird unless you know what's happening. Anytime a table has a primary key, Paradox keeps the table sorted by the primary key, so records will jump around during data entry. The same thing happens when you change an entry.

Entering Data in the Form Window

OK, we've covered the basics of entering data in Table View. We'll use the Form window to enter the data in AUTHOR.DB.

Open the table and switch to the Form window:

1. Open AUTHOR.DB.
2. Click on the Quick Form button; choose Tools, Quick Form to open the default form and switch to the Form window; or press F7.

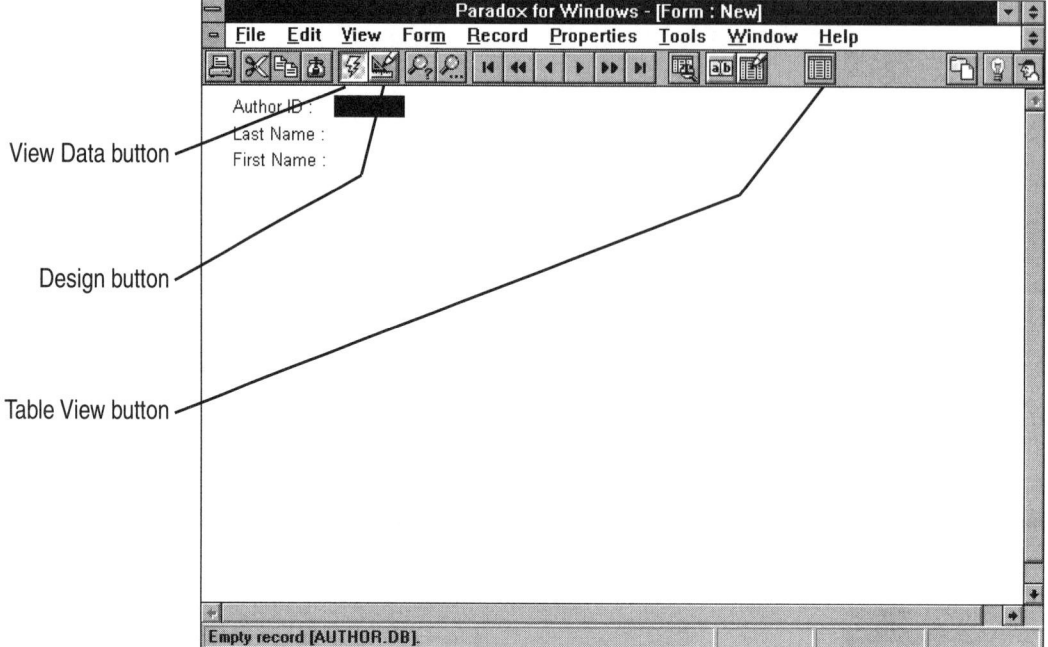

Figure 5-7: In the Form window, you can see only one record at a time, which can make it easier to enter and edit data.

And here are a few things to be aware of with the Form window:

○ When you switch to the Form window, the Table View window stays open and the Quick Form button is replaced by a Table View button. This means you can easily switch back and forth between the Form window and Table View.

○ The Form and Table View windows are both plain-vanilla Windows-type windows. You can move 'em, size 'em, juggle 'em, whatever. (Well, maybe not juggle 'em.) But so what? Who cares what kind of windows they are? You do. Because it means you can use any standard Windows technique to work with them. You could resize the windows so that both of them are visible at the same time and then just click anywhere in either window (or press Ctrl+F6) to make it the active one.

○ If you use plain old clicking or F6-ing to switch between Table View and the Form window, however, you can't take advantage of this really cool thing that Paradox does. When you use the Toolbar or press F7 to switch, Paradox automatically synchronizes the Table View window and the Form window. In plain English, this means that Paradox keeps track of which record and field you're in in one window and returns you to the exact same field in the exact same record when you switch views.

○ The Form window Toolbar's pretty much the same as the Table View Toolbar, except that the Restructure button is replaced by the View Data and Design buttons. Also, the Quick Form, Quick Graph and Quick Crosstab buttons go away. As I mentioned before, the Table View button takes the place of the Quick Form button.

Entering data in the Form window is pretty much like entering data in Table View. You get into Edit mode and type stuff in one field, then you move on to the next field and type some more. There's one little difference, which you'll see in just a moment.

OK, you're all ready to go with AUTHOR.DB on your screen, right? Let's enter some data.

ID	Last Name	First Name
CJL001	Chalker	Jack L.
LXD002	Lessing	Doris
EXI003	Ionesco	Eugene
SJP004	Sartre	Jean Paul
HXA005	Huxley	Aldous
HES006	Haden Elgin	Suzette
AXI007	Asimov	Isaac
ZXE008	Zamiatin	Eugene
KXJ009	Krishnamurti	J.
LCS010	Lewis	C.S.
RXJ011	Russ	Joanna
SXI012	Salajan	Ionna
LUK013	LeGuin	Ursula
DKP014	Dick	Phillip K.
HXW015	Hanley	William

Notice that the ID uses the author's initials followed by a three-digit code. So why don't we just use the initials? Excellent question. We need the numbers to break a tie in case two authors have the same initials. And one last thing, whenever an author doesn't have a middle initial I've used the letter X so that all the IDs will be six characters in length.

1. Type **CJL001** in the ID field.

2. Move to the Last Name field and type **Chalker**.

3. Move to the First Name field and type **Jack L.**

4. Click on the Next Record button to move to a new blank record. Or press F12 or Page Down.

    This step is the only real difference between editing in Table View and in the Form window. To get to a new blank record in the Form window, you *have* to use one of the methods in step 4. You can't use the arrow, Enter or Tab key.

5. Repeat steps 1 through 4 to enter the rest of the data shown in the table on page 141.

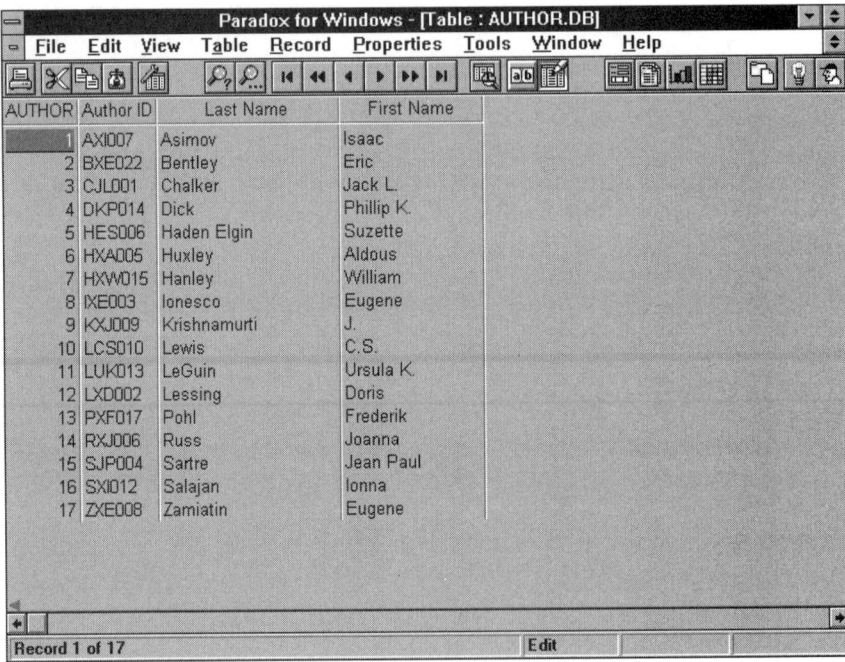

Figure 5-8: Your completed table should look like this.

6. Click on the Table View button to return to Table View and close AUTHOR.DB.

Couldn't be much simpler, could it? You just open a table, switch to the Form window if you want to, get into Edit mode and type. Well, yeah, it's really simple—as long as you never make mistakes, want to insert records in the middle of a table, need to change a name or address, work with different field types or do just about anything else. Now that you've entered data in the Table View and Form windows, let's look at some of the things you might want to do. For the rest of this chapter, you do the same thing whether you're in Table View or Form window. I'm going to use the term *table* because that's what you're always working on—you're just doing it from different views. You can assume that whatever I'm talking about applies to both views unless I tell you something else.

We'll start with the two most important things: fixing mistakes and navigating through tables and forms. (Read this section even if *you* never make mistakes, because one of your clients might have the audacity to move, in which case you would have to know how to go in and change their address.)

FIXING MISTAKES

I don't know about you, but I'm usually not fast enough on the uptake to notice mistakes until I've gone way past them. If you can catch a mistake while you're still entering data in a field, no problem. You can just use any of the standard editing techniques—Backspace or Delete to delete characters and the arrow keys to move within the field. But once you've left a field, that doesn't work anymore. The arrow keys just move you around, and if you're in Edit mode, pressing the Backspace or Delete key deletes the entire field. But you've been stringing along with me long enough that you know there's a way out of this—you *know* I wouldn't leave you hanging.

Yup, there are a couple of ways out, and here they are.

Undo

If you totally blow it in a record and want to start over, Paradox's Undo feature can do the trick. It cancels *any* changes that have been made to the record.

To use Undo, do one of the following:

○ Choose Edit, Undo.

○ Choose Record, Cancel Changes.

○ Press Alt+Backspace.

Pitfalls Ahead

○ Undo undoes *all* changes that have been made to *any field* in the current record. If you want to keep changes you've made in some fields, don't use Undo.

○ And another thing: Undo works only while you're still in the record. If you've already moved to another record, it's too late for Undo. That's because Paradox posts changes every time you move to another record. By the time you leave the record, the changes are already saved.

○ And finally: major ambush ahead if you forget that Undo can't bring back a record you've deleted.

Replacing Data in a Field

In the default Edit mode, when you move to a field, the entire field is selected. When you start typing, whatever you type replaces whatever's already there. So all you have to do to change the entire contents of a field is to move to the field and type. You could press Backspace or Del to delete the field's contents, but that's not really necessary.

If you realize that you want to start over while you're still in the field, just press Esc. Whatever was originally in the field will come back.

Using Field View

So far, we haven't come up with a way to change only part of a field. Undo operates on the whole record, and the only other way we've found to make changes to a field is to replace the original contents and start from scratch. There's got to be a better way. And Field View is it.

Getting into Field View

Here's what you do. First, move your cursor to the field you want to edit. Then use any of the following methods to get into Field View:

○ Click on the Field View button.

○ Choose View, Field View.

○ Press F2.

Click anywhere in the selected field. You can also just double-click on a field to switch to Field View. With this method, the insertion point ends up at the exact location where you click; with all of the other methods, the insertion point ends up at the end of the field. Now repeat after me: "You're not in Field View unless the status bar says "Field." In Figure 5-9, notice that the status bar gives you the Field View indicator and the instruction on how to exit Field View.

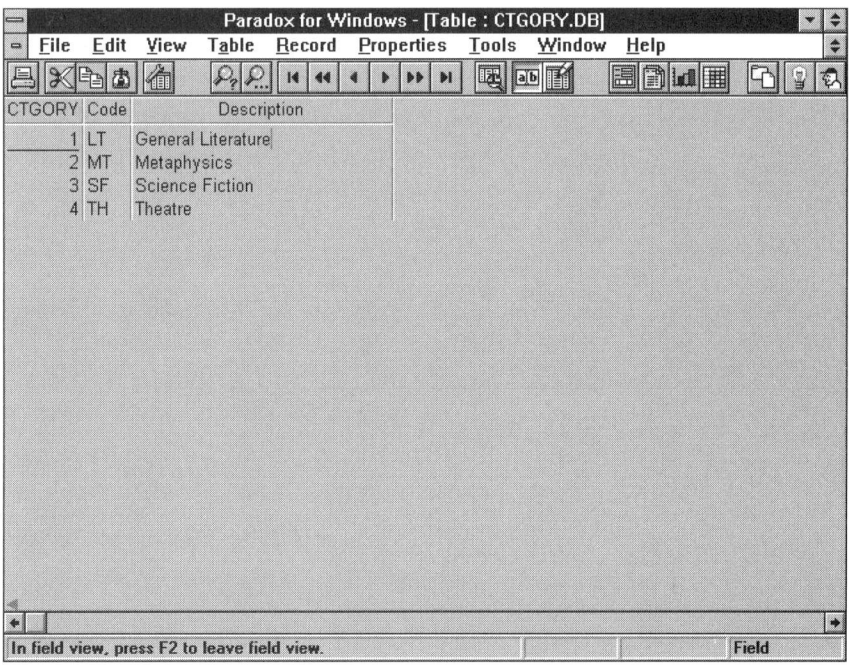

Figure 5-9: Do you think there are enough hints here to let you know which mode you're in?

Getting Out of Field View

You don't ever have to worry about how to get out of Field View—just look at the status bar in Figure 5-9.

As soon as you move to another field, you're out of Field View, so you don't have to do anything special if you're planning to move elsewhere. If you want to leave Field View but stay in the same field, just click on the Field View button or press F2.

Stick Like Glue to Field View

I just told you that moving to another field bumps you out of Field View, right? Well, what if you want to field-edit a whole bunch of fields? It's kind of a pain to keep exiting Field View and getting back into it. (Although you can easily move to Field View in another field just by double-clicking on the new field.) But if that's too much effort, press Ctrl+F2 to switch to *Persistent Field View*. When you do this, you can jump around as much as you want without leaving Field View.

And when you're ready to leave Persistent Field View, just click on the Field View button (or press Ctrl+F2 again).

Pitfall Ahead

Paradox lets you get into Field View or Persistent Field View whether or not you're in Edit mode. Even though you can see the blinking insertion point in the field, you still have to press F9 or click on the Edit Data button to do anything. Reminder: check out the status bar if you're not sure you're in Edit mode. And if you try to edit and nothing happens, look at the status bar. You'll see a message that says "Not in Edit mode. Press F9 to edit data." Are you starting to get the idea that looking at the status bar is a good thing? (You might well wonder what good it does you to be in Field View without the ability to edit. How about this? Field View allows you to scroll though a field. If you have a large field, you might not be able to see all of it at once. Just get into Field View and you can easily move around within the field.)

ADDING & DELETING RECORDS

 When you want to add records to a table that already has data in it, the easiest thing to do is click on the Last Record button (or press Ctrl+F12). This'll zip you right to the last record in your table. Then you can use any of the techniques you just learned to add a new blank record at the end of your table. If you've created a primary key in your table structure, you don't have to worry about entering your records in any particular order—as you've seen, Paradox keeps them sorted for you. (That's a good argument for using primary keys!) And even if your table doesn't have a primary key, you can still sort the table however you want whenever you want. So there's almost never a reason to insert a record at a specific place in a table.

But, if you *really* want to insert a record somewhere in the middle of a table, here's what you do:

1. Place the cursor anywhere in the record below where you want the new record inserted.

2. Choose Record, Insert. (Or press the Insert key.)

A new blank record is inserted above the row where your cursor was positioned.

Paradox makes it easy for you to delete records from a table —in fact, a little *too* easy (be sure and read the Pitfall Ahead in this section). Here's all you have to do:

1. Position your cursor anywhere in the record you want to delete.
2. Choose Record, Delete or press Ctrl+Del.

Pitfall Ahead

Be sure you want to delete the record before you do this. When you delete a record, Paradox doesn't display any cute little warning boxes or ask if you're sure you want to proceed—it just zaps the record. And you can't get it back (no Undo, no nuthin'). Of course, there's always retyping— yeah, that's always a lot of fun.

USING FIELD TYPES, LOOKUPS & REFERENTIAL INTEGRITY

We're just about to open BOOKS.DB and look at entering data in different field types. As you work with the table, use this handy little table to help you maneuver around the data using the Toolbar.

Where You Go	Toolbar	Menu	Keystroke
First record	⏮	Record, First	Alt+F11
Previous set of records	⏪	Record, Previous Set	Shift+F11 or PgUp
Previous record	◀	Record, Previous	F11
Next record	▶	Record, Next	F12
Next set of records	⏩	Record, Next Set	Shift+F12 or PgDn
Last record	⏭	Record, Last	Ctrl+F12

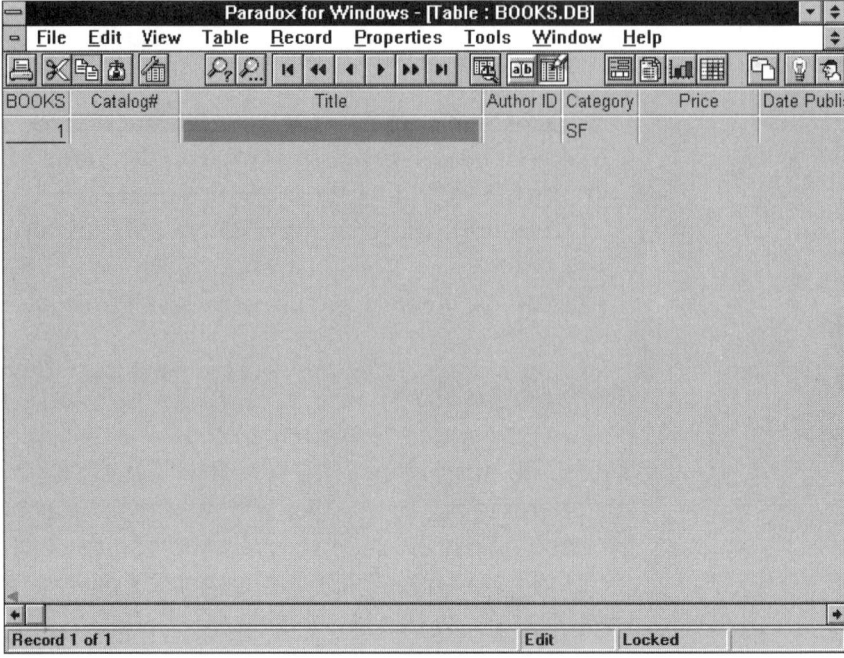

Figure 5-10: BOOKS.DB before data entry. Category is filled automatically and the status bar shows the Edit mode indicator.

Notice that as soon as you switch to Edit mode, Paradox fills in the Category field for the first record. That's because we gave it a default value. If the book is science fiction, you don't have to do anything in this field.

We'll start by entering data in the second field, which is alpha and doesn't have any validity checks, so I don't need to tell you what to do. Since the first field, Catalog#, is an Autoincrement field, Paradox doesn't let you make an entry. You'll see what happens with this field in just a minute.

1. Open BOOKS.DB (Open Table button or File, Open, Table).

2. Switch to Edit mode (Edit Data button or F9).

3. Enter the following data in the Title field:
   Twilight at the Well of Souls

4. Move your cursor to the Author ID field, but don't type anything yet.

Referential Integrity Links

Okay, just start typing the author's initials (which happen to be CJL). So far, so good. Now press the Tab key to move through the rest of the fields. When you get to the Synopsis field, try to move to the next record. Go ahead—press Tab. You just got beeped at, right? Maybe Tab's not the right key. Try pressing the Down arrow, clicking on the Next Record button or performing your favorite incantation—ain't gonna work. Now look at the status bar. You'll see "Master record missing" in the left corner. You can do whatever you want inside the record—all you can't do is get out of it. You can't even close the table or exit Paradox until you make a valid entry in the affected field. And, you may recall, the Author ID field uses a three-digit suffix after the author's initials.

But referential integrity's not the whole story here. With referential integrity, all you have to be sure of is that whatever you enter in a linked field matches an entry in the parent table. But referential integrity itself doesn't require you to enter *anything* in the field. What's happening here is that we also made Author ID a required field. So you can't leave the record without entering data in the field. And, on top of that, whatever you enter has to be correct. Sounds like a kind of "catch-22."

Inside Scoop

If you get totally stuck inside a record, Paradox does give you one out. You can delete the record (Ctrl+Del). At least that solves the problem temporarily. You can continue to work on your other data and reenter the record when you get the information you need.

"Fine, so I'll just enter the right author ID in the field and I'll be all set." You're right—but what if you can't remember the three-number suffix? One solution is to print out the information from the AUTHOR table and reference it during data entry. But there's another method that doesn't require you to keep track of a dog-eared piece of paper (and you don't even have to type the numbers). Read on.

Getting Help With Referential Integrity

The Move Help dialog box is similar to a lookup table. You can browse through the list of authors, choose the one you want, and instruct Paradox to insert it in the Author ID field in BOOKS.DB. To open and use Move Help:

1. With your cursor in the Author field, choose Record, Move Help or press Ctrl+Shift+Spacebar.

2. Select the record that contains the information for *Twilight at the Well of Souls* and choose OK. It doesn't matter which field the cursor is in—because of the referential integrity link, Paradox knows which field to insert.

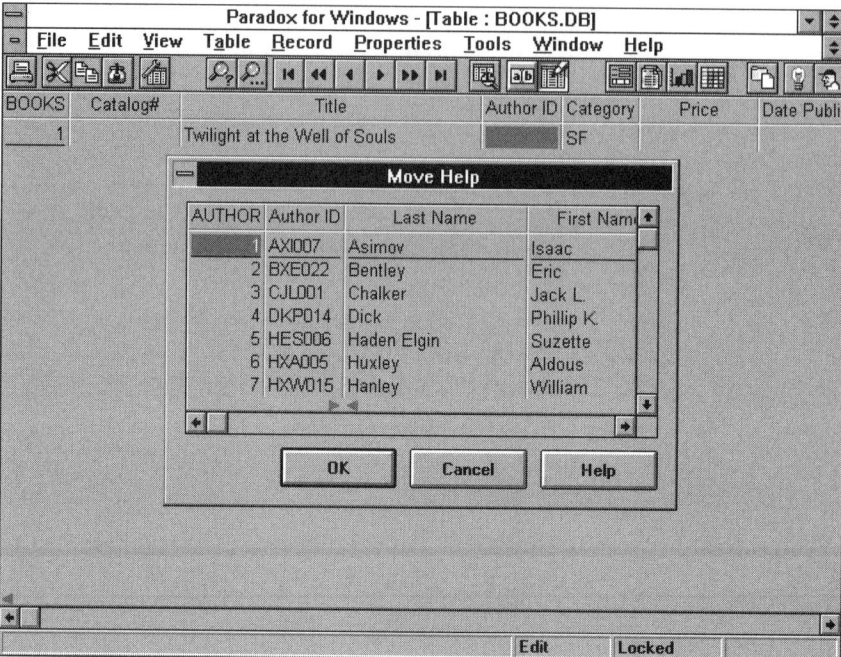

Figure 5-11: BOOKS.DB with the Move Help dialog box for the Author ID field. The Move Help dialog box contains data from the parent table for the referential integrity link.

○ You can use Locate (covered a little later in this chapter) to quickly find a record in the Move Help dialog box.

○ The data from the Author ID field in AUTHOR.DB is inserted into the Author field in BOOKS.DB.

Using Lookup Tables

Using lookup tables is just about the same as using referential integrity links. As you might remember from the last chapter, the main difference between the two is that Paradox doesn't update the main table when you edit data in lookup tables.

1. Move your cursor to the Category field.

2. Just for kicks, delete SF (leaving the field empty) and try to move to the next field. Wasn't that fun? Nothing happened, right? Look at the status bar: "Field value required. Field: Category." You're not going anywhere. I just wanted to remind you that Category is a required field.

Inside Scoop

If you don't put *something* in a required field, you're pretty much stuck there. If the field's linked by referential integrity or table lookup, about the only temporary fix is to delete the record. But if there are no links to the field, just type anything in the field so Paradox will let you keep working. You could even type some sort of code (like "FIX") to remind you to go back and fix it later.

3. Now that you know you're not leaving the field without making an entry, all you have to do is remember which categories you used. Or do you? Nah, Paradox wouldn't make you work that hard.

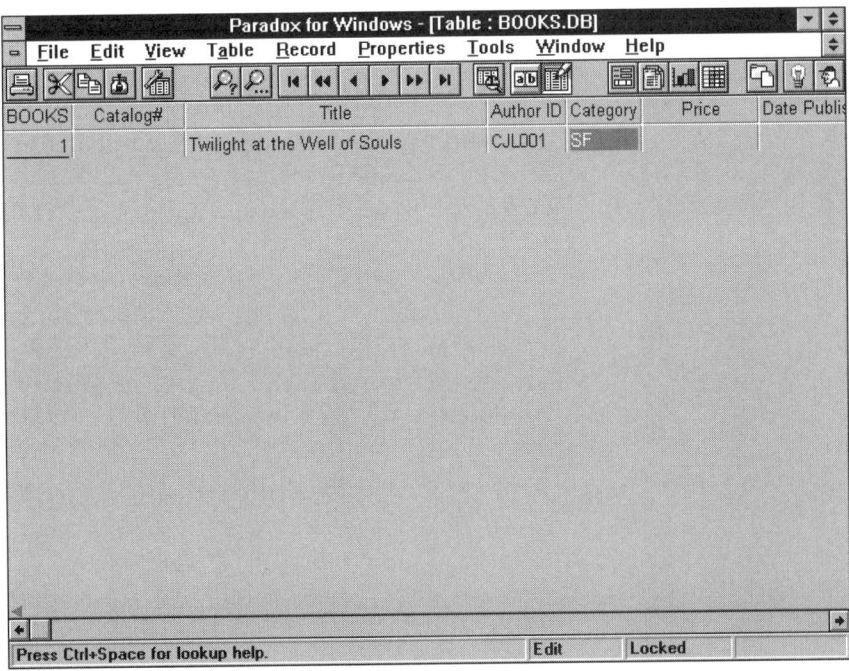

Figure 5-12: Notice the prompt ("Press Ctrl+Space for lookup table").

Paradox even tells you how to open a lookup table.

4. Just press Ctrl+Spacebar (or choose Record, Lookup Help) to open the lookup table shown in Figure 5-13.

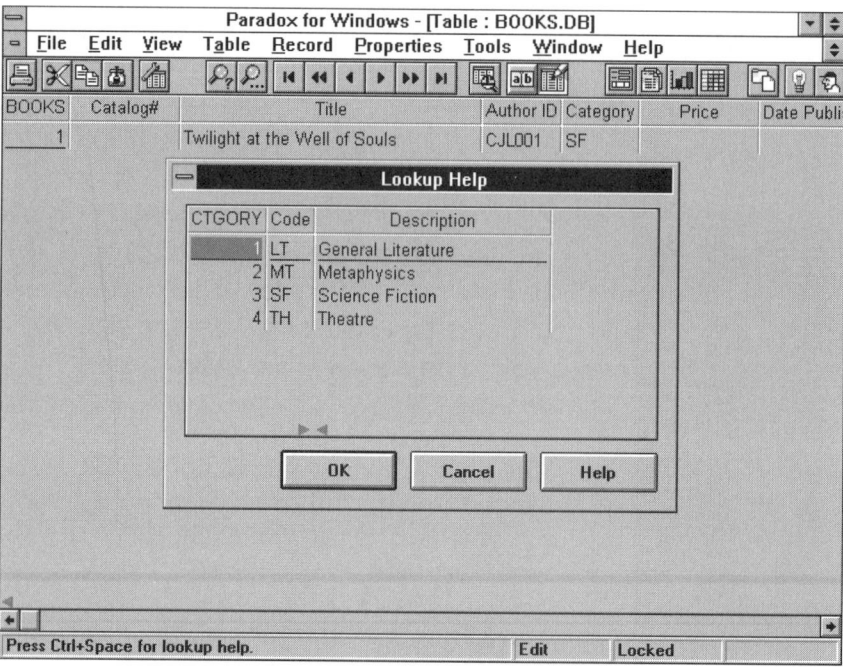

Figure 5-13: BOOKS.DB with the lookup table for the Category field.

5. This works just like the Move Help dialog box for referential integrity. Select the record you want (in this case, Science Fiction) and choose OK. Again, it doesn't matter which field you're in—Paradox takes it from there.

   As with Move Help, you can use Locate in a lookup table.

6. Of course, if you know the category code, you can just type it in. Remember the picture we created for this field? We told Paradox to turn whatever we type into uppercase letters. So if you do enter the code manually, you don't have to bother about typing it in uppercase.

7. Move to the Date Published field and type **1980**.

Entering Data in Number Fields

1. Move to the Qty in Stock field and try to type **two**. You'll hear a beep before you get to the "w." Once again, look at the status bar message: "Illegal character." Because Qty in Stock is a number field, anything other than a number is considered an illegal character (but I don't think it's a felony yet).

2. Type **3** in the Qty in Stock field and move to the Price field.
   Don't worry about how the number's displayed for now—we'll get to that when we talk about table properties later in this chapter.

Entering Data in Money Fields

1. Since the cover price is $2.50, type **2.5** and move to the Synopsis field.

2. Notice that the price is displayed as $2.50, even though you didn't type the dollar sign or the ending zero. Paradox automatically formats money fields with a dollar sign and two decimal places. So if the price is a whole number (like $15.00), all you have to type is **15**.

ENTERING & EDITING DATA IN MEMO FIELDS

1. Start typing in the Synopsis field. Uh-oh, there's that darned beep again! What is it this time? Repeat after me: "Look at the status bar." That status bar sure seems to answer a lot of questions. This time it says "Press Shift+F2 for Memo View to edit this field."
   You can't enter memo text directly in the table—you have to open a special *Memo View* window.

Inside Scoop

Even though the status bar message tells you to press Shift+F2, any of the options that take you into Field View will also work. Just double-click on the field, click on the Field View button or press F2.

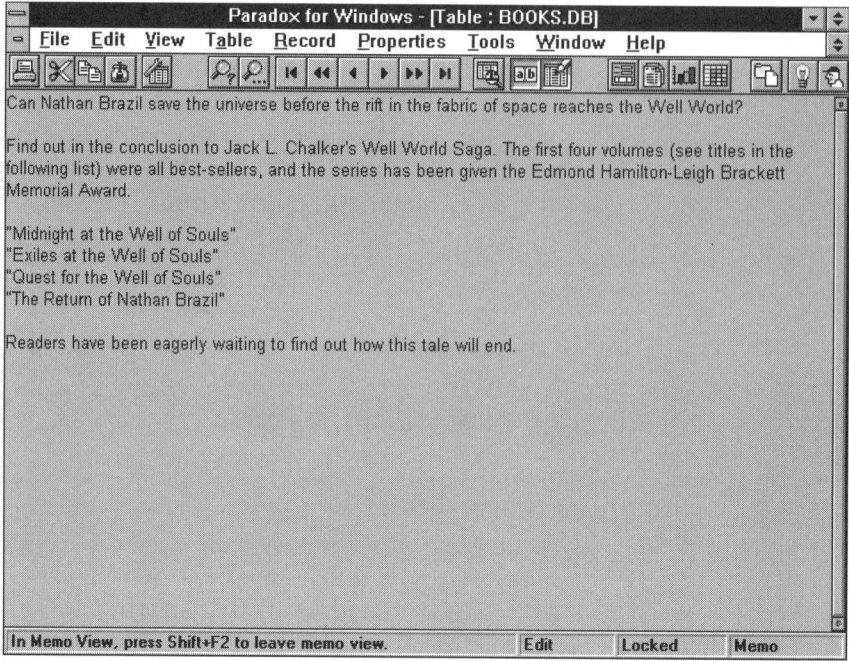

Figure 5-14: The Memo View window. The status bar message tells you you're in Memo View.

2. Enter the text shown in Figure 5-14. You can use any standard Windows techniques for moving through the text, selecting, or cutting and pasting.

3. To save the memo text, just exit Memo View and move to a new field or record. Memo text is automatically posted just like any other field.

Inside Scoop

You can create memos in your word processing program and copy them into Paradox memo fields. Because Paradox doesn't have a spell checker or thesaurus, this can help you avoid errors. The text has to be in TXT (text), RTF (rich text) or PXT (Paradox text) format, but most word processors can save files in different formats. Create the file and save it in text or rich text format. Then, when you're in Memo view, choose Edit, Paste From to open the Paste From File dialog box (Figure 5-15). Enter the full path name of the file in the File Name text box (or use the Browser) and choose OK.

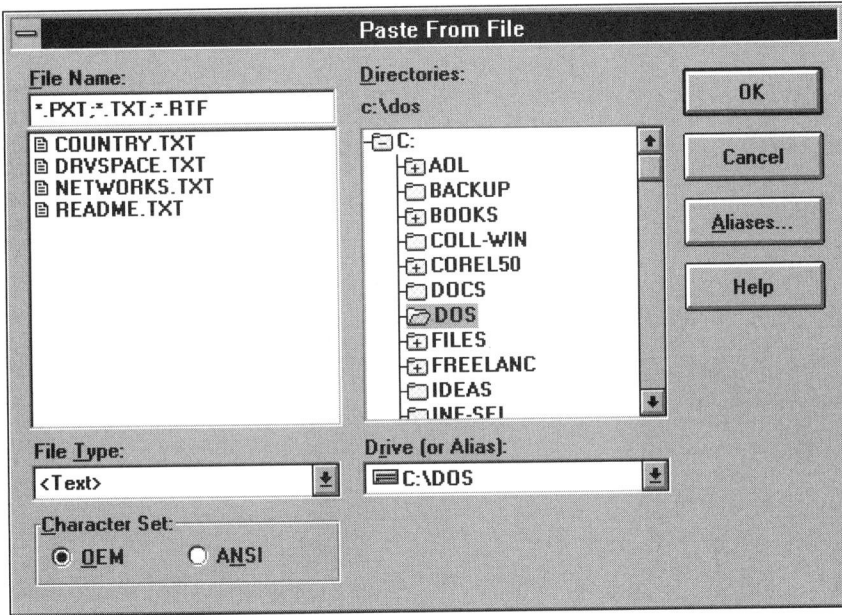

Figure 5-15: The Paste From File dialog box.

Formatted Memos

Since the Synopsis field is a regular memo field, I placed quotes around the book titles instead of using the standard italics. And it would have been nice to put the award information in boldface. Well, it's not too late. Let's just change Synopsis into a formatted memo field. Formatted memos can handle font, alignment and line spacing changes. You can also use the Tab key to indent a line of text.

1. Click on the Restructure button or choose Table, Restructure Table.

2. Type an **F** in the Type column for the Synopsis field and choose Save to close the Restructure Table dialog box.

3. Now make sure you're back in BOOKS.DB and in Edit mode. Then, with your cursor in the Synopsis field, switch to Memo View.

    There's no specific message to tell you you're in a formatted memo field.

4. Place your insertion point where you want to make a change (or select the text first if you want to change only a portion of the text) and click the right mouse button to display the text properties menu shown in Figure 5-16.

5. Make the changes you want and return to Table View.

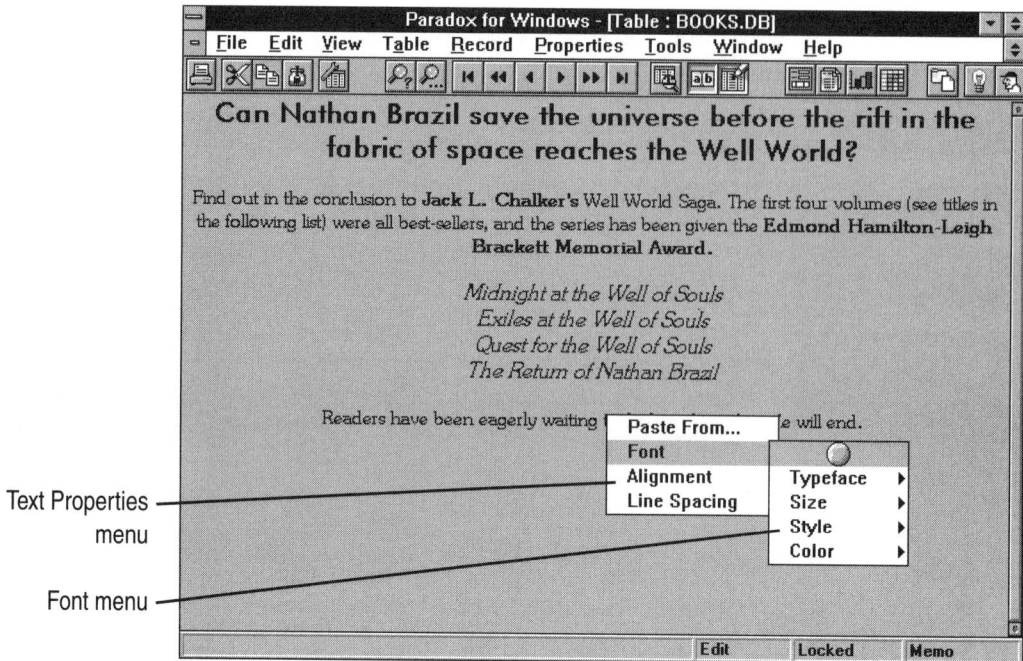

Text Properties menu

Font menu

Figure 5-16: The same memo you already typed, with formatting changes added.

Inside Scoop

See the round button on the Title bar in the Font menu? Whenever you see one of those, it means you can turn the menu into a floating palette (a dialog box with a fancy name). Just click on the button and see what happens. You should end up with a palette that looks like Figure 5-17. The palette stays open until you click the round button again. So you can make all kinds of changes without constantly having to right-click and then choose options from the text properties menu. And just like any other dialog box, you can move a floating dialog box or palette anywhere on the screen by dragging its title bar.

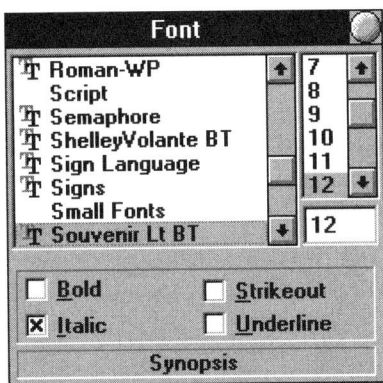

Figure 5-17: The floating Font palette.

Using Search & Replace in Memo Fields

Memo fields can be *really* long, so finding the text you want to edit can be a tedious process. That is, unless you take advantage of Paradox's Search And Replace option. This option can replace text in multiple records in a table.

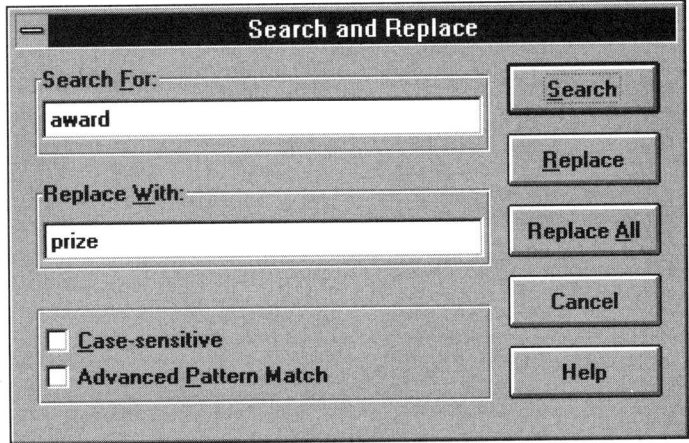

Figure 5-18: The Search And Replace dialog box.

1. With a memo or formatted memo field selected, choose Edit, Search Text to display the Search And Replace dialog box in Figure 5-18.

   You don't have to be in Memo View to do this. Paradox automatically shoots you into Memo View when it opens the Search And Replace dialog box.

Inside Scoop

If you choose Edit, Search Text from Table View, the search will begin at the top of the memo. If you want to start the search somewhere else or search through a particular section of text, first get into Memo View. Then position your insertion point where you want to start the search or select the section you want to search.

2. Type the text you want to search for in the Search For text box.

3. To replace the text with something else, enter the replacement text in the Replace With text box before you choose Search.

    To locate only text where the case is an exact match for your search string, select Case Sensitive.

    If you want to use wildcards in your search string, select Advanced Pattern Match. The search and replace feature uses the same wildcards as Locate, which is covered in the next section.

4. Now when you choose Search, Paradox finds and selects the first occurrence of what you're searching for and displays a "Match Found" message on the status bar. If you see the "Match Found" message but don't see any selected text, the Search And Replace dialog box is probably hiding the text. Just point to the Search And Replace dialog box's title bar and drag that sucker out of the way.

5. If you entered a replacement value, choose Replace to have Paradox replace the searched-for text with the new text and move to the next occurrence.

6. Choose Replace All if you want Paradox to find and replace all of the occurrences of the searched-for text without stopping at each one.

Pitfall Ahead

If you want to search and replace text within a particular section, don't choose Replace All. Replace All always searches the whole memo.

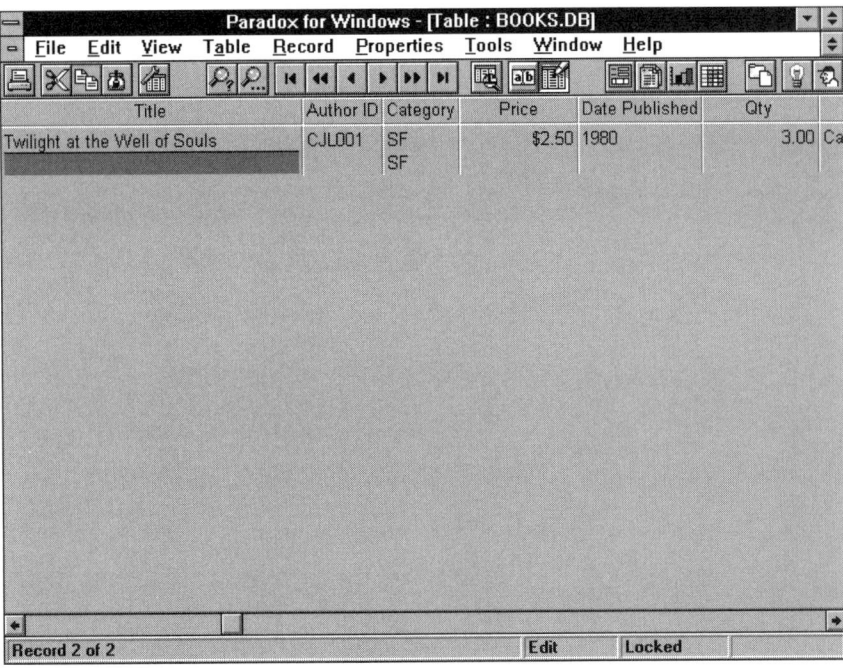

Figure 5-19: This is what your table should look like after adding data for the first record.

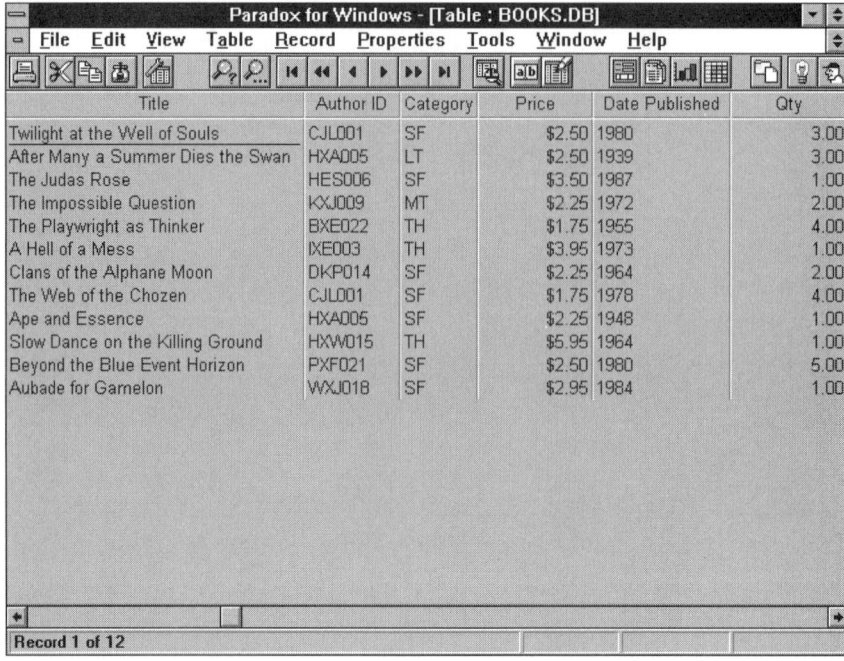

Figure 5-20: Fill in the rest of the records using this figure as an example (or open BOOKS-?.DB from the companion disk if you don't want to type).

CHANGING TABLE PROPERTIES

Table properties translates to all the stuff that makes your table look the way it does: column widths, typefaces, row heights, column order, formatting style for numbers, etc. Paradox has something it calls *direct manipulation*, which simply means you can change the size or position of certain objects just by dragging their borders. Here's what you can do with direct manipulation:

○ Drag the table name up or down to change the heading height.

○ Drag the line under the first record up or down to change the row height for all records.

○ Drag the vertical grid line in the first record in a column to the left or right to change the width of the column.

○ Drag a column heading to a new location in order to reposition the column.

○ Drag the triangle at lower left to lock specified columns in position.

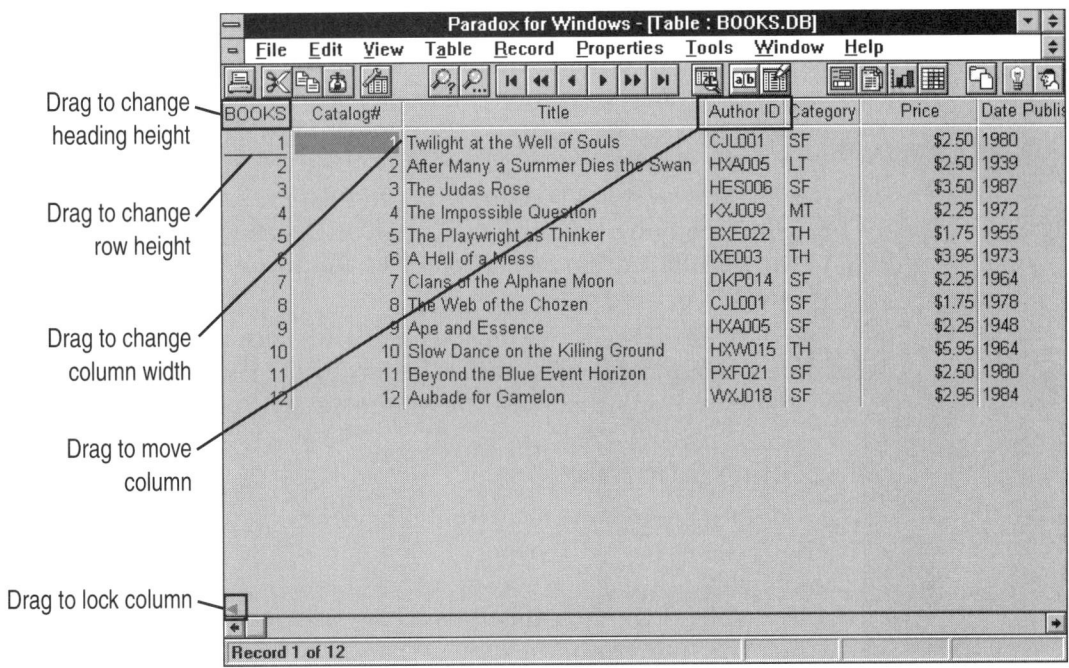

Figure 5-21: You can make changes to all of these objects through direct manipulation.

When you're making changes, you can tell when your mouse pointer is positioned in the right place because it'll turn into a two-headed arrow. Column order is the exception: for column order, the mouse pointer turns into a little box. When you hold down the mouse button and start dragging, *then* the pointer turns into a two-headed arrow.

Saving Your Changes

Before we start fooling around with Table View, I think I'd better tell you how to save the changes you like and how to back out if you make a mess.

○ To save changes to the Table View, choose Properties, View Properties, Save. It's a good idea to do this often (assuming the view is the way you want it), especially right before you try something where you're not sure what the result will be.

○ Choose Properties, View Properties, Restore if you end up with some strange and interesting results (but not the ones you want). This option takes you back to the way things were the last time you saved the properties.

○ This one's for those really big messes. Say you saved when you didn't mean to, or you decide the whole thing doesn't work and you want to start over. (Or you're just having a bad hair day and nothing looks good.) Choose Properties, View Properties, Delete. Paradox will ask if you're sure you want to delete the TV file (that's the extension Paradox gives to the file that holds the property information). If you're sure, choose OK and you'll be returned to the default properties that you had when you first installed Paradox.

I've done my duty. Now you're armed with sufficient expertise to feel free to completely mess things up, secure in the knowledge that you can clean up your messes. On your mark, get set . . . start playing!

Inspecting Properties

The Object Inspector is great, and I'll be referring to it throughout this book. Refer back to Chapter 1 for a quick introduction. As far as changing table properties goes, you can right-click on just about any part of a table to get the Object Inspector with a menu of options for that area. The title bar of the Object Inspector menu tells you what object's being inspected. For example, right-click on a column heading to get the Object Inspector menu shown in Figure 5-22.

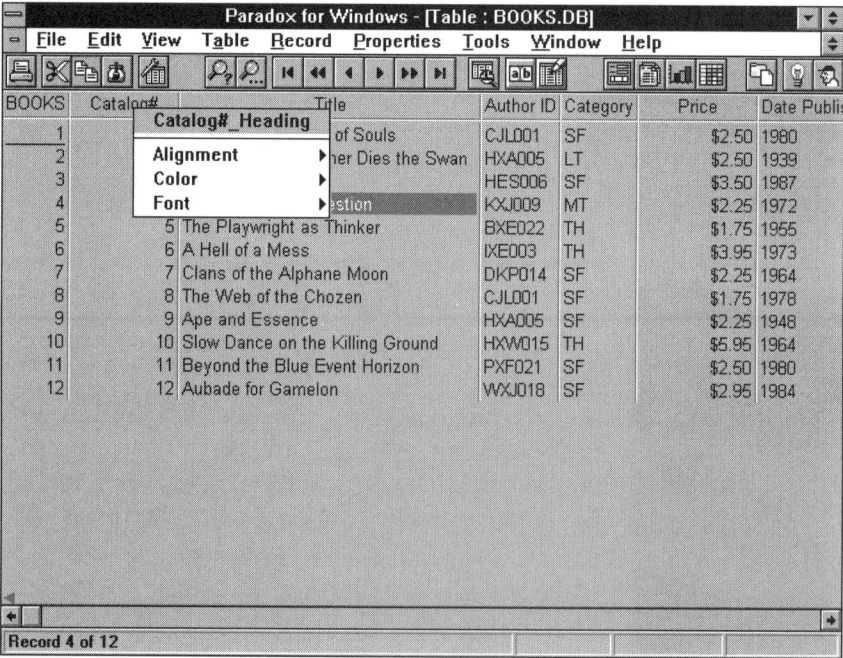

Figure 5-22: A sample Object Inspector menu.

Changing Heading Appearance

In Figure 5-21, you saw that you can change the height of the heading row. You're about to find out why you might want to do that. Suppose you want to display the headings in a larger point size? When you change the type size, the heading probably won't all fit in the heading area. So you'd have to make the heading row taller in order to display the entire heading. (This adjustment isn't made automatically as it would be in most word processing or desktop publishing programs.)

Figure 5-22 showed you the Headings Object Inspector menu. You can change the Alignment, Color or Font. And you can turn the Color and Font menus into floating palettes to make it easier to change several options in one sweep.

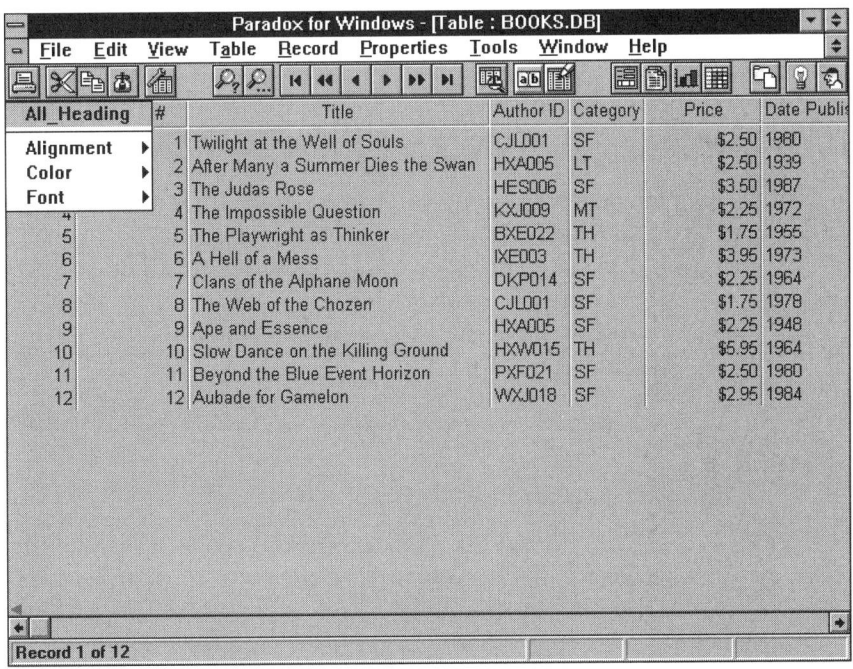

Figure 5-23: To change all headings at once, press Ctrl+Shift+H to display the All Heading Inspector menu. This works just like any other Inspector except that any changes you make will apply to all headings in the table.

Changing Column Order

This one's really handy. If you're using a composite primary key, you have to structure your table so that the fields included in the key are at the top. But that might not be how you want the fields displayed.

Just position your mouse pointer on the name of the field you want to move (the pointer turns into a little box), and drag to the left or right. As you drag, a vertical line appears, showing you where the field will end up. When you're where you want to be, release the mouse button and the field will plop into place.

The other way to move columns is by selecting the column you want to move (you can be anywhere in the column) and pressing Ctrl+R. This moves the selected column to the right end of the table. You can keep pressing Ctrl+R until your columns are in the order you want. You can definitely use this technique to arrange your columns, but it's a little like playing musical chairs. Round and round she goes, and where she'll stop, nobody knows. I mean, you know what will happen each time you press Ctrl+R, but it can take an awful lot of Ctrl+R's before everything ends up where you want it.

Locking a Field's Position

Suppose you always want to be able to see the book's title, no matter what else scrolls out of view. First move the Title column to the beginning of the table and make sure the table is scrolled all the way to the left (press Home or use the horizontal scroll bar). Then drag the triangle just below the BOOKS column. As you drag, notice that a gray box jumps to the division between each pair of fields. In this case, release the mouse button when the box is between the Title and Catalog# fields.

Now use the horizontal scroll bar to move through your fields and notice that the Title field remains in place.

Changing the Grid

The vertical lines between each column are called the *grid*. You can change the appearance of the grid lines, add a line to show which record you're on and add horizontal lines between each record. Just right-click on any grid line and make selections from the Object Inspector menu. You can also open the Object Inspector menu for grids by choosing Properties, Grid or pressing Ctrl+G.

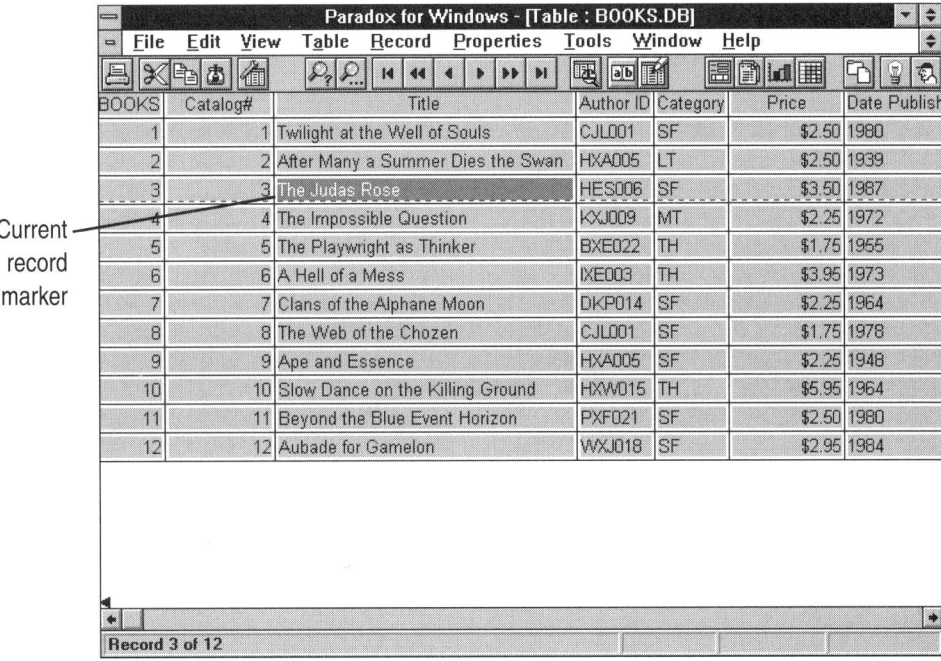

Figure 5-24: The grid has been changed to a single white line; horizontal grid lines and a current record marker have been added.

Formatting Data

The Object Inspector menus for all types of fields have these three items in common: Alignment, Color and Font.

Figure 5-25: Alignment, Color and Font are always part of the Object Inspector menu for all types of fields.

○ Choose Alignment to specify how you want your data aligned within the field. Select Left, Center or Right for horizontal alignment; Top, Center or Bottom for vertical alignment.

○ Choose Color to change the background color for the column.

○ The Color menu has a round button on its title bar (just like the Font menu). Click on the round button to display the floating color palette shown in Figure 5-26.

167

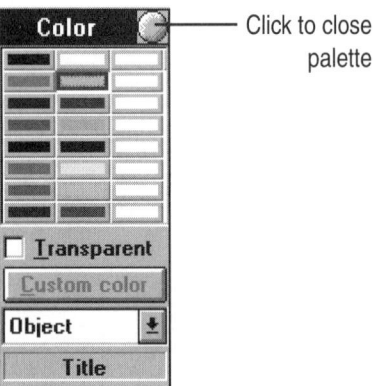

Figure 5-26: This palette remains onscreen until you click on the round button to close it.

○ Choose Font to change the typeface, size, style or color of your text.

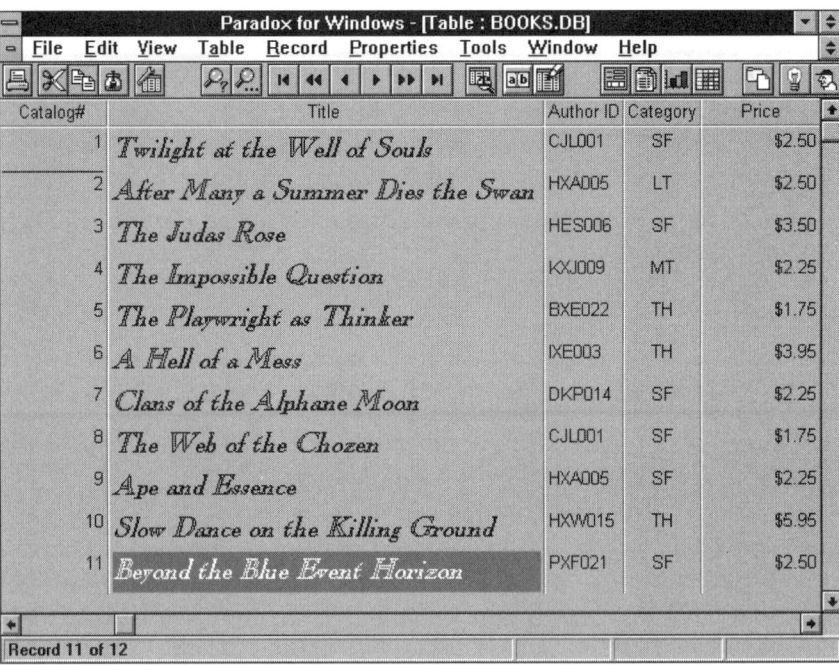

Figure 5-27: Any changes you make apply only to the current column.

If you want to make a change that affects the whole table, press Ctrl+Shift+M to open the All Inspector. Changes you make from this menu affect everything except headings.

Formatting Numbers & Dates

When you inspect a number, money or date field, there is an additional item on the Inspector menu: Number Format or Date Format (depending on which kind of field it is). When you select Number Format, you can choose from several predefined formats or click on the three dots at the top of the menu to open the Select Number Format dialog box, which allows you to fine-tune your selection or create your own custom format.

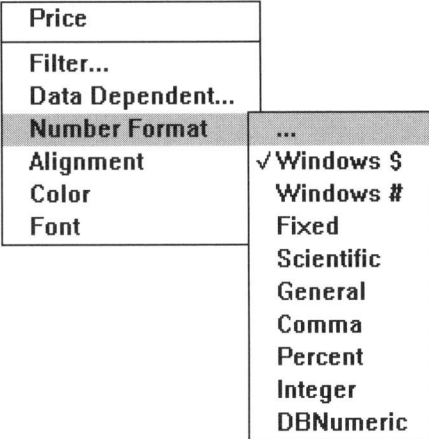

Figure 5-28: Click on the three dots at the top of the Number Format menu to open the Select Number Format dialog box.

Choose Create from the Select Number Format dialog box to open the Create Number Format dialog box shown in Figure 5-29.

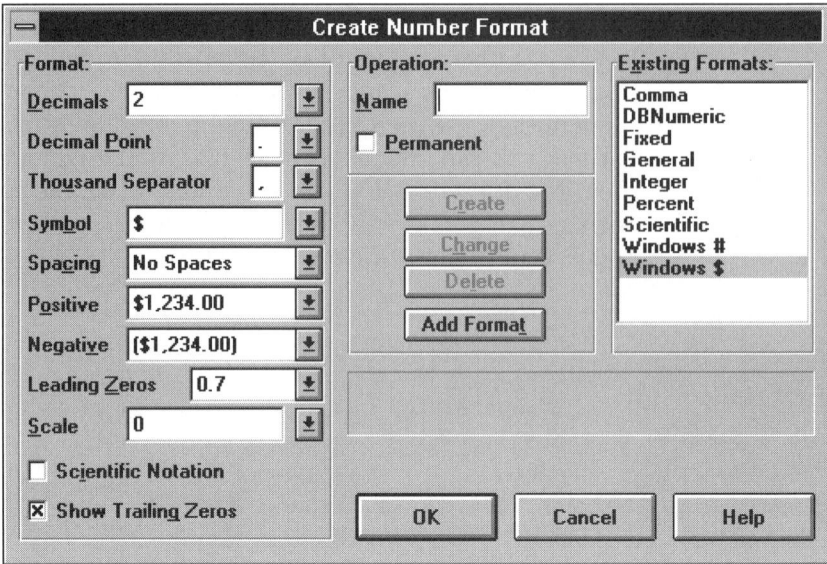

Figure 5-29: Use this dialog box to create your own custom number formats.

Choose Create from the Select Date Format dialog box to open the Create Date Format dialog box shown in Figure 5-30.

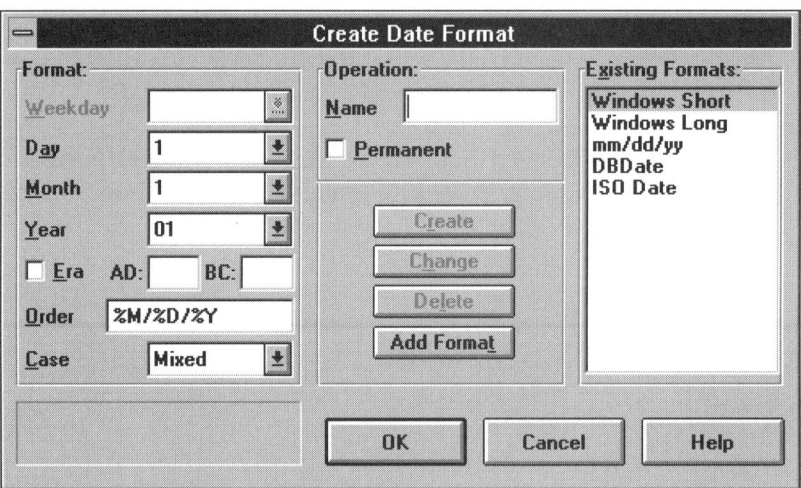

Figure 5-30: Create custom date formats here.

Inside Scoop

Two of the predefined number formats, Windows $ and Windows #, use whatever formats you've specified for currency and numbers in the Windows Control Panel (International dialog box). And the Windows Short and Windows Long date formats also rely on the settings you make in the Control Panel's International dialog box. Don't worry about it if you've never even heard of this Windows option—unless you go in and make changes, Windows uses the following standard formats:

Windows $	Dollar sign with two decimal places, negative amounts in parentheses. Example: ($50.50)
Windows #	Two decimal places, commas separating thousands. Example: 5,050,050.00
Windows Long	Day of week, followed by month, day of month and year. Example: Thursday, April 14, 1994
Windows Short	Month, day and last two digits of year, separated by slashes. Example: 4/14/94

DEFINING DEFAULT TABLE PROPERTIES

I can hear you now: "All of this property-changing is great, but do I have to do it all over for every single table?" Nope.

You might want all of your tables to use certain font, number-format or grid-line settings. To set those choices as defaults, just create a table called DEFAULT.DB in your PRIVATE directory. In the table structure, create one of each type of field. From Table View, inspect all of the objects you want to change. When the table looks just the way you want it, save the property settings (Properties, View Properties, Save). Paradox puts your settings into a file called DEFAULT.TV. Your default settings will be used for all of your tables except those that have their own TV file.

MOVING ON

I bet you think there's not much more to be said about tables. Wrong. In fact, everything in Paradox centers around tables. But more specifically, the next chapter continues the tables theme. You'll learn all about sorting, working with secondary indexes and locating records within a table.

6

FIND IT, SORT IT, FILTER IT

Now that you've learned how to enter data in your tables, we need to talk about ways of dealing with all that data without driving yourself nuts. As I've mentioned innumerable times, tables are the foundations for everything that happens in Paradox. For the rest of this book, you'll be doing stuff with basic table data. But for now, a look at four features—Locate, Sort, Secondary Index and Filter—that make it easy to find data within tables and rearrange and reorder that data.

Where did I put that darned [*fill in the blank*]? The question of the ages. If you're looking for your car keys, I can't help you out (I'm too busy trying to find mine). But if you want to find information that's buried somewhere in a table, or to rearrange the records in a table to make it easier to see the ones you want, you've come to the right place.

THE LOCATE FEATURE

One way to locate a particular record in a table or form is by scrolling around until you find it. That's okay if your table's not too big. But in a large table it's not exactly the most efficient technique. In Chapter 5, you used Paradox's Search Text feature to find text in a memo field.

The Locate feature is like the Search Text feature, in that it allows you to search for specific text in a field. But it also does a whole bunch more: you can search for a particular record number within a table or form, a specific field within a record, or a value within a field (which can include wildcards).

Locating Fields

There are lots of ways to move to the field you want within a table or form:

○ Just click anywhere in the field.

○ Use the Tab and the arrow keys to move around in the table or form.

○ Press Home to move to the first field.

○ Press End to move to the last field.

○ Press Ctrl+PgUp and Ctrl+PgDn to move through your table screen by screen.

Okay, cool. But if your table has a lot of fields, you could end up doing some mega-tabbing and clicking to get where you want. Fortunately, Paradox is right on top of this one.

1. Choose Record, Locate, Field to open the Locate Field dialog box shown in Figure 6-1.

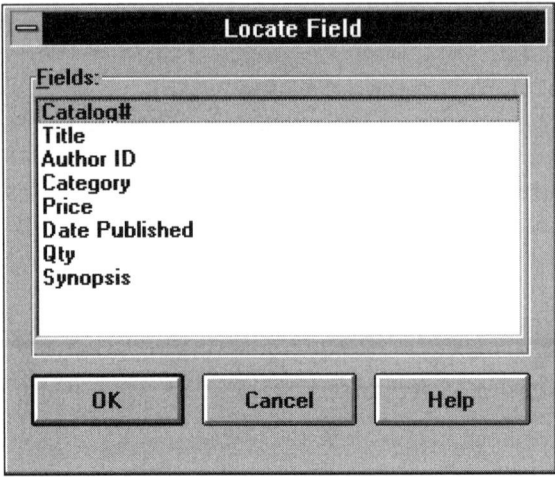

Figure 6-1: The Locate Field dialog box.

Notice that the Locate Field dialog box contains a list of all the fields in your current table (in this case, BOOKS.DB).

2. Select the field you want to move to and choose OK (for this example, choose the Price field).

As soon as you choose OK, Paradox moves your cursor directly to the selected field. How's that for quick 'n' easy?

Locating Records

As with fields, you can move to different records by clicking and scrolling. And, as with fields, this can be a pain in a really big table. So . . .

1. Choose Record, Locate, Record Number to open the Locate Record Number dialog box shown in Figure 6-2.

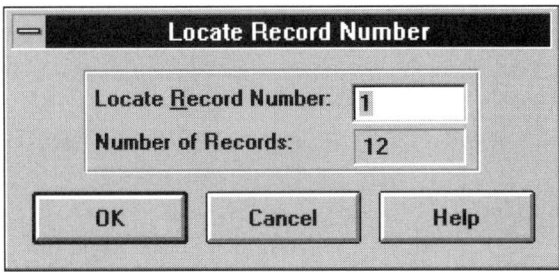

Figure 6-2: The Locate Record Number dialog box tells you which record you're currently on and how many records there are in the table.

2. Enter the record number in the Locate Record Number box and choose OK. (The record number is the number that's assigned by Paradox to specify the record's current position in the table—it doesn't have anything to do with any codes or ID numbers you've assigned.) Presto chango—there you are at the record you specified.

"Well, great," you say,"but how can I remember all of those stupid record numbers? Gimme a break!" I know, I know. This feature's useful if you happen to know the record number. But read on.

Locating Values

Here's where you can get as selective as your heart desires. You can find a specific book title or author even if you don't remember the exact spelling.

Basic steps (with more to come):

1. Choose Record, Locate, Value, or click on the Locate Field Value button on the Toolbar. Or press Ctrl+Z.

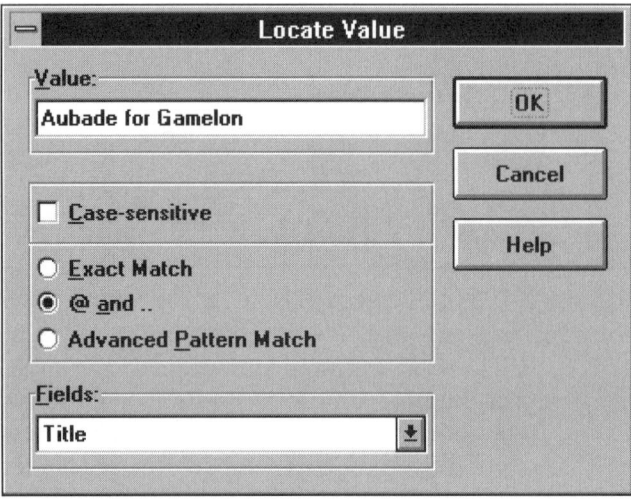

Figure 6-3: The Locate Value dialog box.

2. Enter the information you want to search for in the Value text box. Let's search for **Aubade for Gamelon**.

3. Select the field you want to search from the Fields drop-down list. In this case, select the Title field.

4. Select the Case-sensitive option if you want Paradox to find only records where the title is *exactly* the way you typed it, right down to the uppercase and lowercase letters.

5. Select Exact Match if you don't want to use any wildcards in your search. If you don't check this box, certain characters (which we'll talk about real soon) are treated as wildcards, not as actual search characters.

6. Select the "@ and .." option if you want to use the basic wildcard characters (again, coming up soon).

7. Select Advanced Pattern Match to use Paradox's extended set of wildcards (you guessed it—this is coming up soon too).

8. Choose OK.

Paradox always starts searching at the beginning of the table, *not* from your cursor location. If it finds what you're searching for, it moves your cursor to the first record that contains the value you specified.

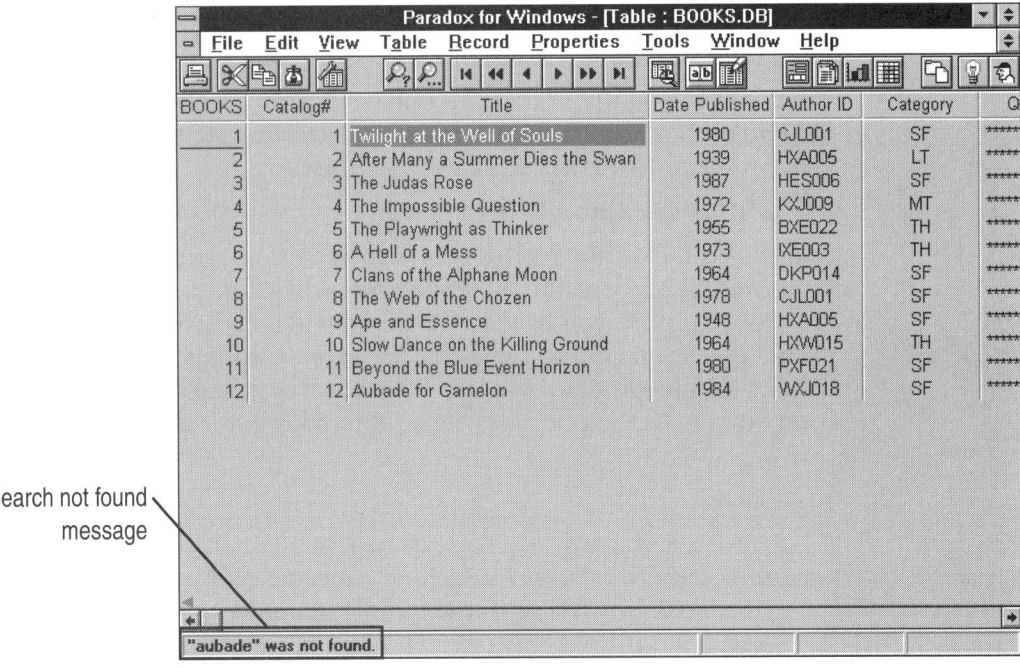

Figure 6-4: I purposely misspelled "Aubade" to show you an unsuccessful search.

Notice the message on the status bar. If your search string isn't found, this message clues you in about what's happening.

Inside Scoop

If Paradox can't find anything that matches your search string, you get dumped back into your table or form right where you started, and it looks like nothing has happened. Write this on the blackboard ten times: LOOK AT THE STATUS BAR! And when you're done writing (and cleaning the erasers), take a look at Figure 6-4.

That's all there is to it if you know exactly what you're looking for and how to spell it. Now for the fun part.

Using Wildcards

Unless you check Exact Match, you automatically have access to two wildcards (notice that the @ and .. option is selected by default in the Locate Value dialog box):

177

@ Stands in for any one character

.. Stands in for any series of characters

Suppose you know that the title you want to find is *Aubade for Gamelon* but aren't sure whether the letter following the *b* is *a* or *o*. No problem. Just enter the value like this:

Aub@de for Gamelon

This will find any record in which the title begins with *AUB*, followed by any one character and *for Gamelon*.

Now suppose you haven't the faintest idea how to spell the title—you aren't even sure of the exact name. A customer came in and said a friend told her about this really cool book, and she *thinks* it had *bade* somewhere in the title. All you need to do is enter the following string:

..bade..

This'll get you any title that has *any* number of characters (including zero) before or after *bade*. If the title starts or ends with *bade* or contains *bade* anywhere in the middle, Paradox will find it.

Now, what if the search for *bade* doesn't work?. (Remember, she said she *thought* the title had *bade* in it.) In the unlikely event that the title actually does contain something that resembles *bade*, you might get lucky by combining the @ and .. wildcards. For example, you could try this:

..b@de..

That would give you any title that begins with any number of characters, followed by *b*, followed by any single character, and so on.

Inside Scoop

When you're messing with wildcards, it's probably because you're not sure what you're looking for. So in most cases it's a good idea to make sure the Case-sensitive option isn't selected. Using the *bade* example, if it was at the beginning of a word, the first letter might be capitalized. Or it might be in the middle or at the end of a word, with all the letters in lowercase. You have no way of knowing. If Case-sensitive isn't checked, a search for *..bade..* will find *Aubade, Baden Baden*, etc.

So far, we've done all of this using only two wildcards. But Paradox lets us get much fancier with our searches. In order to use additional wildcards, first select Advanced Pattern Match in the Locate Value dialog box. Then you can include many more wildcards.

Here's a list of "advanced wildcards," their respective functions and, in some cases, an example of what they do:

@	Stands in for any single character. Check out the *Aub@de* example above.
..	Stands in for any series of characters (or no characters). Check out the *..bade..* example above.
^	Finds the search string if it's the first thing in the field. *^bade* would find the characters *bade* only if they occur at the beginning of a field.
$	Finds the search string if it's the last thing in a field. *bade^* finds the characters only if they occur at the end of a field.
*	The character or expression (an expression is any group of characters in parentheses) just before the asterisk can occur any number of times or none at all.
+	The character or expression just before the plus sign can occur one or more times.
?	The character or expression just before the question mark can occur once or not at all.
		The search will find anything that matches the characters just before or after the vertical bar.
[*abc*]	Enclose characters in brackets to match any one of the characters. With *[abc],* the search would find a, b or c.
[^*abc*]	Place a ?? in front of the characters in brackets to limit your search to any character other than the ones in brackets. With *[^abc],* the search would find anything *but* a, b or c.
(abc)	Group
\	Use the backslash to tell Paradox that you want to use one of the wildcard characters as regular text.

Do It Again

Paradox remembers the last value you searched for, so you can easily search for it again. For example, suppose you searched for Asimov in the Author field, but the first record Paradox finds isn't the one you want. Do one of the following things to find the next occurrence:

○ Press Ctrl+A (this'll get you there the fastest).

○ Click on the Locate Next button on the Toolbar.

○ Choose Record, Locate Next.

You can keep using Locate Next to find additional occurrences until you replace the search string with something else.

Locate & Replace

Did you notice the "and Replace" option under Record, Locate? And did you notice that it was grayed out? Here's why. Locate and Replace lets you search for specific values and replace them with something else. The replacement part is why this doesn't work in Table View. Anytime you do something that will change the table data, you have to be in Edit mode.

Locate and Replace is really handy if you make the same mistake on a bunch of records. For example, what if you entered *Azimof* as the author's last name in several records, and then found out that it's really spelled *Asimov*? You could go to each record and change it. Or better yet . . .

1. Get into Edit mode (F9, the Edit Data button or View, Edit Data).

2. Choose Record, Locate, and Replace. Or press Ctrl+Shift+Z.

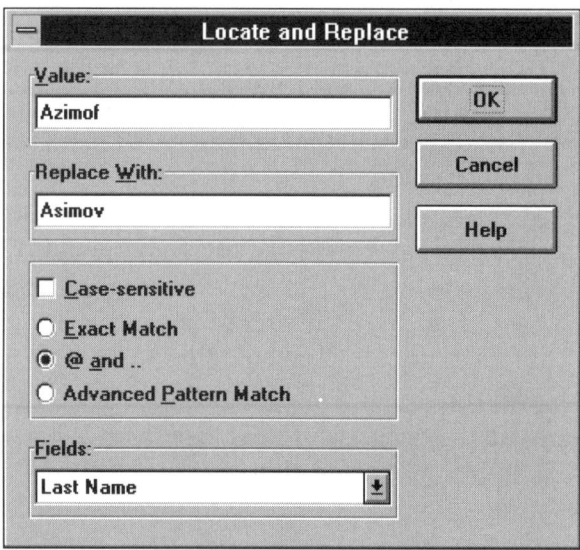

Figure 6-5: The Locate and Replace dialog box looks pretty much like the Locate Value dialog box.

3. From the Fields drop-down list, select the field you want to edit.

4. Enter your search string in the Value text box. You can use all of the options and wildcards we just talked about.

5. Enter the new text in the Replace With text box. (No wildcards here–this is the actual text that gets deposited in your record.)

6. Choose OK.

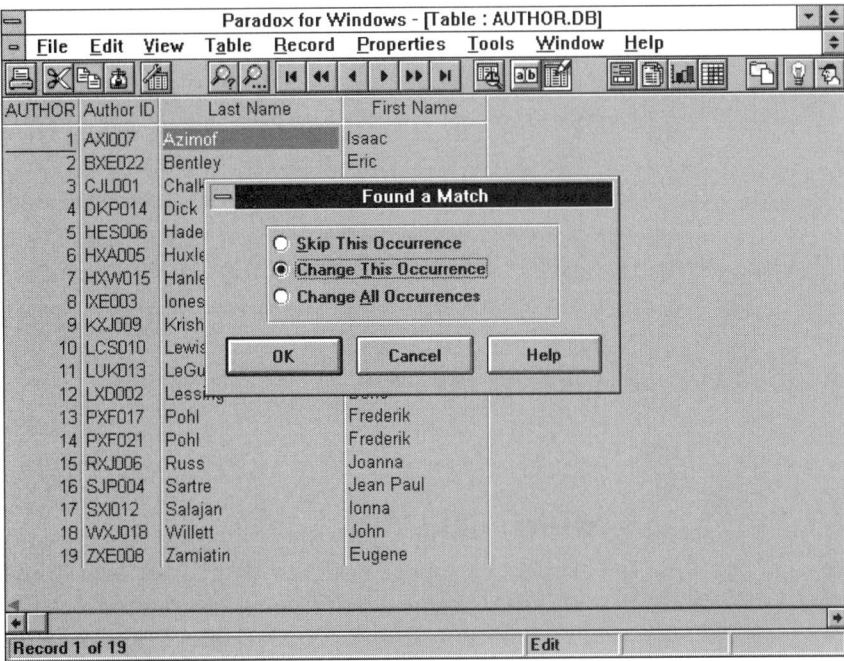

Figure 6-6: If Paradox finds a record that matches the value you entered, you'll see the Found a Match dialog box.

7. Choose Skip This Occurrence to leave the record alone but continue the search. Choose Change This Occurrence to make the replacement and move on to the next occurrence. Choose Change All Occurrences to make the replacement in the highlighted record as well as in any other records that contain the same text. Choose Cancel to leave the record alone and abandon the whole search process.

Pitfall Ahead

Be careful with wildcards when you use Locate and Replace. Depending on how you use the wildcards, you can end up locating something that never even occured to you—suppose you don't know how to spell *Sartre*, so you enter *sar..* in the Value text box. Well, you'll find Sartre, all right. But you could also find *sartorial*, *sarcophagus* and *sardonic* (those are just a few of the too-numerous-to-mention possibilities). With a plain old Locate, that's not a problem—you just move on to the next occurrence. But with Locate and Replace, you could end up changing text that you don't want to change. Before you answer Yes when Paradox asks if you want to change the occurrence, make sure you *really look* at what's in the field. Don't just space out and click that Yes button. One trick: before you begin the search, move the Locate and Replace dialog box out of the way (just drag its title bar) so that it's not covering the field you're searching in. That way, you'll be able to see the highlighted text as Paradox finds it.

SORTING RECORDS

In Chapter 3, you created a primary index by specifying a key field. In addition to making sure that each record is unique, the key is also used by Paradox to sort your records. But what if you don't always want your records sorted according to the primary key? In a lot of cases, the fields you use as the primary key (or keys) have more to do with determining which fields must have unique values than they do with how you want the table sorted. For example, in BOOKS.DB, the Catalog# is the keyed field, so every time you open the table or add records, all of your records will be sorted by catalog number. Well, you might want to be able to see your records listed according to author, or according to category. What to do? As usual, no problem.

Open BOOKS.DB so we can take a look at it.

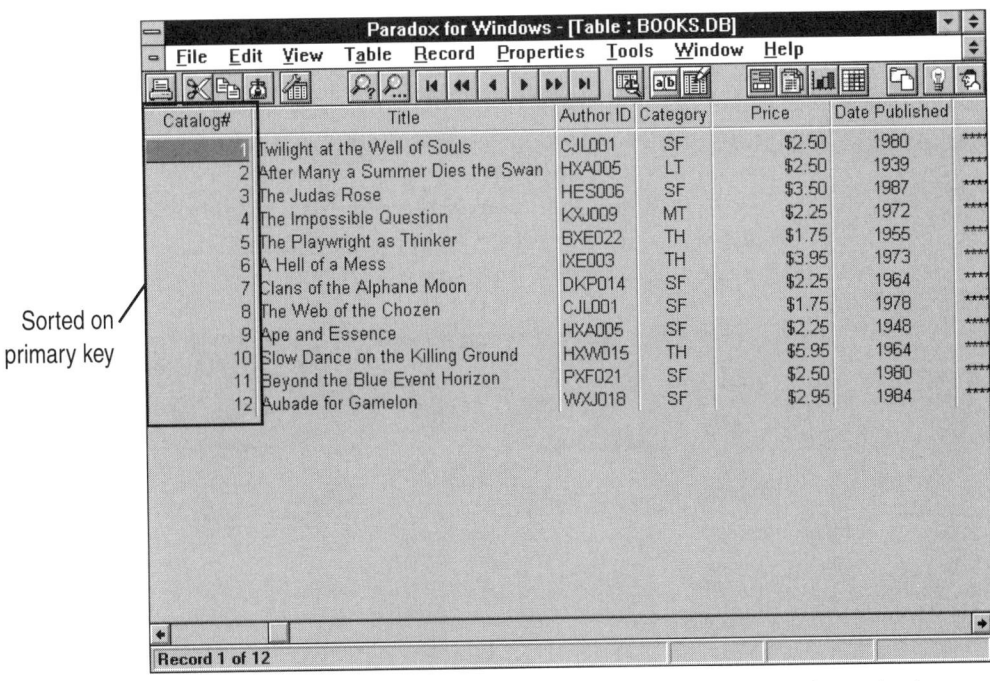

Figure 6-7: BOOKS.DB sorted on the Catalog# field (the primary key).

The table is sorted by catalog number because that's the primary key. It was chosen as the primary key to ensure that each book would have a unique ID. But that's not a very useful way of looking at the information. For reports, you might want to see the titles in alphabetical order, or group the books by category.

Inside Scoop

Sorting is quick and easy when you just want to rearrange your data for one viewing, and it's the only way you can look at one field in ascending order and another in descending order. But in most cases, secondary indexes are a better way to go. You'll learn how to create and work with secondary indexes a little later in this chapter, and we'll talk more about their advantages.

The Basics

Take a look at Figure 6-8: you'll see the key symbol if the table you're sorting has a primary key field or fields. Notice that the Same Table option under Sorted Table is dimmed. If a table has a primary key, you have to sort to a new table.

All of the fields in your table are listed. You tell Paradox which fields you want to sort on by placing them in the Sort Order list. And you use the Change Order arrows to rearrange the sort order.

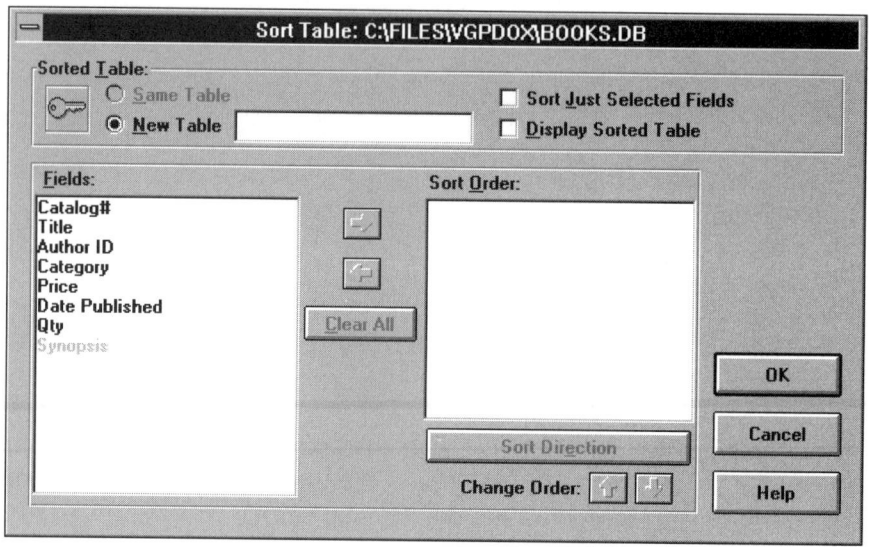

Figure 6-8: The Sort Table dialog box.

Here's the process:

1. Open the table you want to sort (in this case, BOOKS.DB).
2. Choose Table, Sort.
      Or, from the Project Viewer, right-click on the table's name and choose Sort from the Object Inspector menu. (This replaces steps 1 and 2.)
3. Choose Same Table or New Table. If you choose New Table, enter a name for the table.
4. Select the fields you want to sort on and move them into the Sort Order list.
5. Arrange the fields in the order you want them sorted.
6. Specify the sort direction (ascending or descending).
7. Choose OK to perform the sort.

And that's really all there is. You just give Paradox a name for the new table (unless the table isn't keyed, in which case you can sort the original table), specify the fields you want to sort on and arrange the sort order for the fields. Now for the details about each of these steps.

Same Table, New Table?

If your table doesn't have a primary key, you can sort to the same table or a new table. What's the difference and why does it matter?

○ When you sort to the same table, Paradox replaces the original table data with records sorted in the new order, and each record is assigned a new number. With this method, the original table is permanently changed, but you still have access to any properties you assigned to the table.

○ When you sort to a new table, the original table stays the way it was and Paradox copies all of the sorted records to a new table. With this method, the new table doesn't retain any of the validity checks or formatting that you've applied to the original table.

Pitfall Ahead

If you choose New Table to sort an unkeyed table, make sure you enter a name for the table in the New Table text box. Otherwise, Paradox will automatically use the original table for the sort. (You don't have to worry about this when you're sorting a keyed table—if you forget to specify a name, you'll get an error message telling you that "Paradox requires a new table name.")

Sorting Keyed Tables

The only thing you really need to know about sorting a keyed table is that you have to use the New Table option. For this reason, you might want to consider using a secondary index instead.

Figure 6-9: This key lets you know that the table you're sorting is keyed.

Setting Up the Sort Order

How do you figure out which fields to sort on? Well, have you ever opened up a phone book and tried to find someone whose last name is Smith? You go to the Smith section, and then you search according to the first name or initials, which are listed in alphabetical order under Smith. So, in the phone book, the last name is the *primary sort key*, which means that that's the first criterion for the sort—all of the names are sorted by last name first. The first name or initial is the *secondary sort key*. Any sort keys you define after the primary sort key are used to break ties—if more than one person has the same last name, the first name determines where the name is placed in the sorted list. The phone book is a prime example of when using more than one sort key is almost imperative. Can you imagine trying to find Sarah Smith if the first names were all listed in haphazard order under Smith?

Inside Scoop

Remember the BLOB that ate the world? Sure you do—binary, graphic, memo, formatted memo and OLE fields are all BLOBS. Well, you can't sort on any of them. Don't worry about remembering this, though—any fields you can't sort on are dimmed in the Fields list.

Sorting on One Field

First, we'll sort BOOKS.DB by category. Take a look at Figure 6-10:

1. Select New Table and assign the name SORT to the table.
2. Click on the Category field to select it.
   Notice that there's a dotted border around Category and the text is a different color.
3. Click on the right arrow to move the field into the Sort Order list. Or press Alt+A.
   The plus sign in front of Category means the records in that field will be sorted in ascending (A to Z) order. Double-click on the plus sign or click on the Sort Direction button to sort the records in descending (Z to A) order.

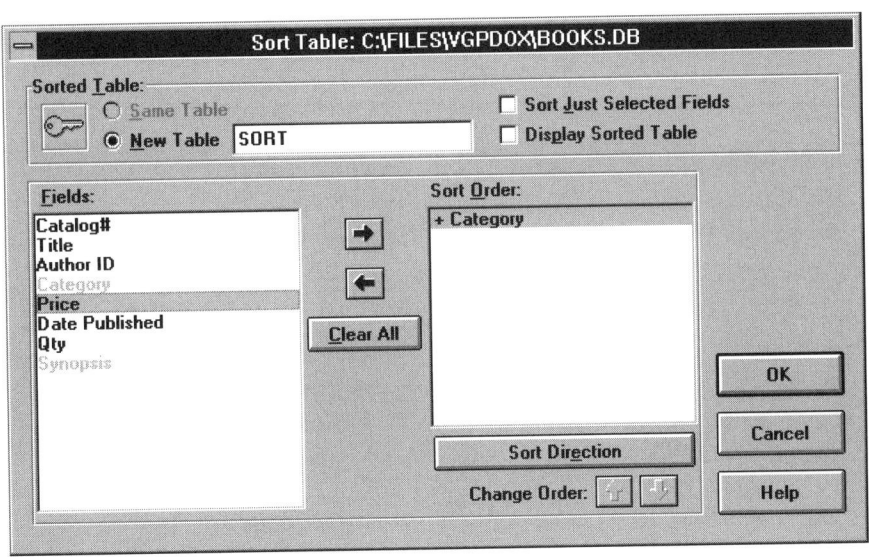

Figure 6-10: Voila! The Category field has jumped over to the Sort Order list.

4. Choose OK.

Inside Scoop

Why did you return to your original, unsorted table when you clicked on OK? I'll tell ya. See, if you don't select Display Sorted Table, Paradox does the sorting without opening the table. If you want to see the results of your handiwork without having to open the table after the sort, you need to check this box.

Since we didn't check the Display Sorted Table box, you'll have to open the table in order to look at it or work with it. Just use any technique for opening a table (the new sorted table is just like any other table).

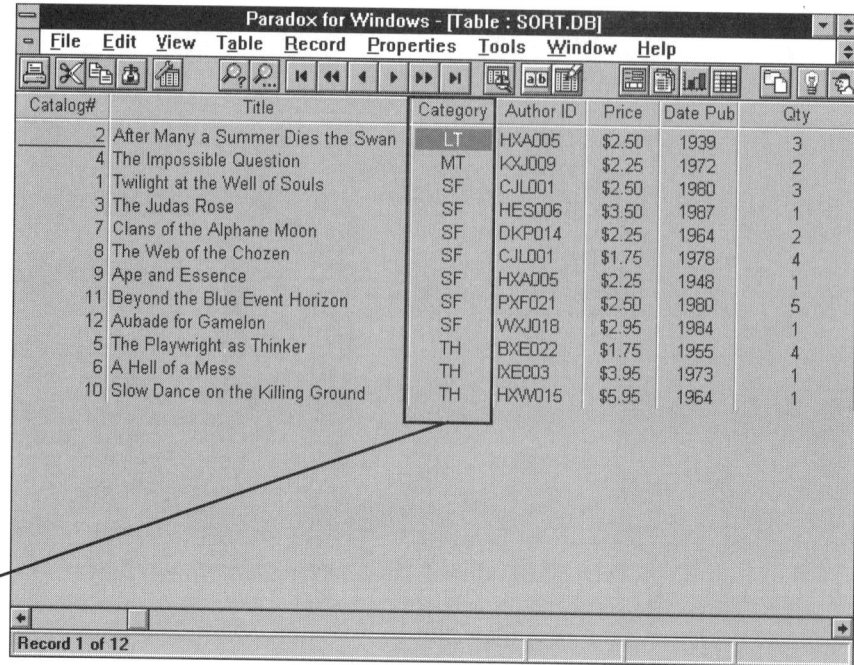

Sorted by category

Figure 6-11: Here's your new table. Remember that it's not keyed, and it doesn't have any of the properties that the original table had.

Sorting on More Than One Field

Notice anything funny about the table in Figure 6-11? Yup, it's like a nightmare phone book. You have your science fiction, theatre and other categories all arranged neatly in order, but within each category the titles were dumped unceremoniously using whatever order they were in in the original table. Maybe it's not so terrible with this particular list—after all, there aren't *that many* titles to wade through. But Bookfinders is hoping to be a growing concern, so the lack of order could very quickly become a headache.

So we'll add the Title field as a secondary sort key. And, as an added enhancement, we'll also sort on the Author field. That way, if there's more than one book with the same name in a particular category (hey, it could happen), the books will be sorted by author. I'll also show you how to add both fields at once.

1. With BOOKS.DB on your screen, choose Table, Sort.

2. Point to the Author ID field and drag down to select both Author ID and Category, but don't click on the right arrow yet.

3. Hold down the Ctrl key while you click on Title. Notice that the other fields are still selected.

4. Now, just to throw a wrench in the works, hold down the Ctrl key and click on Price.

5. *Now* you can click on the right arrow.

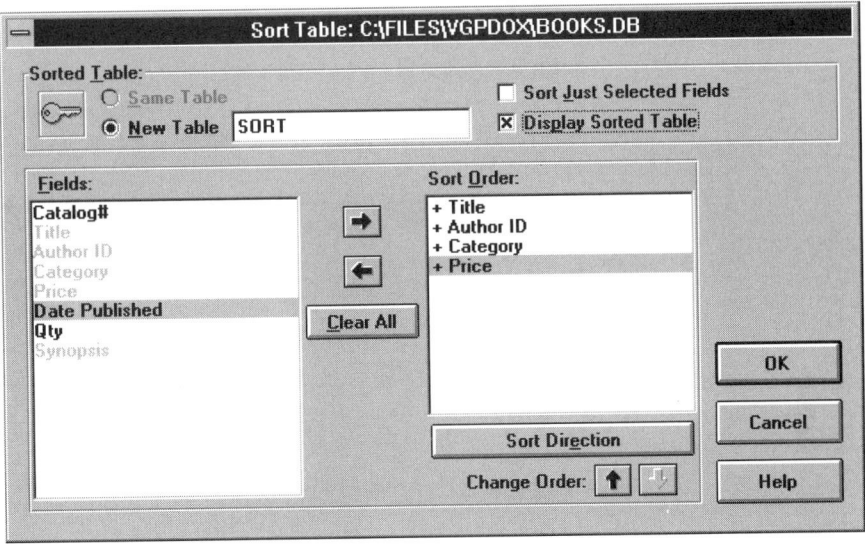

Figure 6-12: The Sort Order list should look like this.

Changing the Sort Order

Okay, everything we want is in the Sort Order list (and there's even one field we don't want—we'll deal with that in a bit). But if we performed the sort now, the list would be sorted by Title, then Author ID, then Category—not what we want. So . . .

1. Select the Category field in the Sort Order list.

2. Click on the Up arrow (next to Change Order) twice to move Category to the top.

3. Just for fun, let's sort the categories in descending order. Just select Category and click on Sort Direction (or double-click on Category).

   The Sort Direction button is a toggle—click once to switch to descending order; click again to switch back to ascending. Pay attention to the plus or minus sign in front of the field's name. That tells you which direction the sort is set for.

Removing a Field From the Sort List

I actually had a reason when I told you to add the Price field to the Sort Order List. You added it just so you could get rid of it now.

1. Select the Price field.
2. Click the left arrow or press Alt+R to move the field back to the Fields list.

And if you want to get rid of all the fields in the Sort Order list, click on the Clear All button (or press Alt+C).

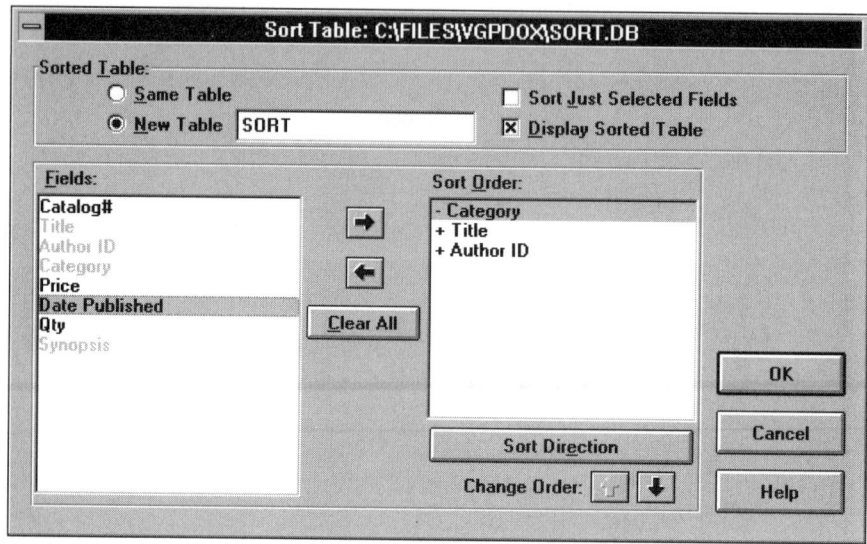

Figure 6-13: Your sort order list should now look like this.

The Final Steps

1. Select Display Sorted Table.
2. Select Sort Just Selected Fields.

   By default, Paradox uses the fields in the Sort Order list first, but it then uses all the rest of the fields in the table to break ties. If you don't want Paradox to use any fields other than the ones in the Sort Order list, select Sort Just Selected Fields.
3. Choose OK.

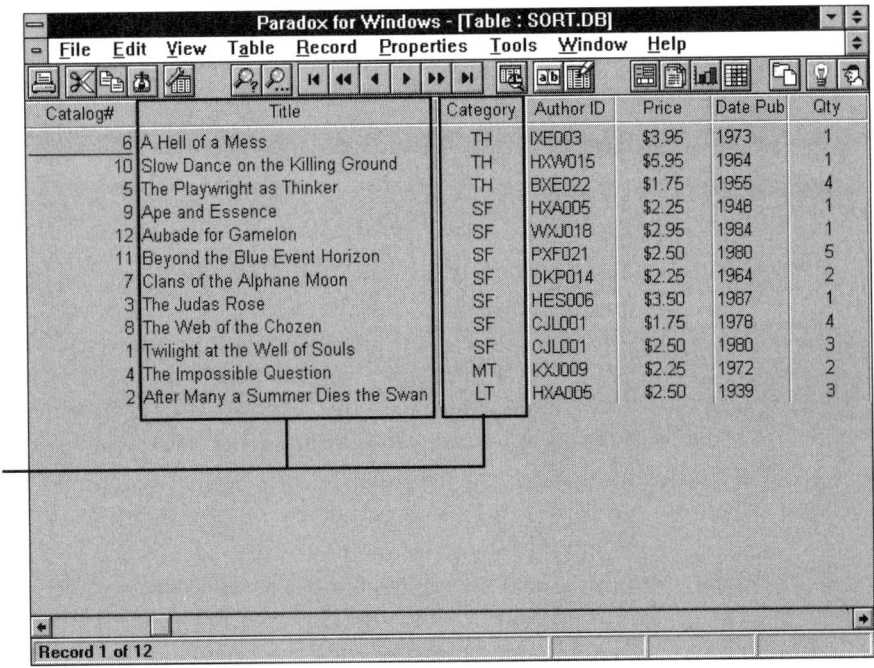

Sorted by title within
each category

Figure 6-14: Because you selected Display Sorted Table, the new table is displayed as soon as you choose OK.

Pitfall Ahead

If you sort to a new table, any changes you make to the sorted table won't be transferred to the original table. Before you make changes, make sure you know which table you're working on—just take a look at the title bar.

4. Close SORT.DB.

SECONDARY INDEXES

When you want to see your records in a different order, the most obvious solution is to perform a sort. But performing the same sort over and over can take a lot of time. Plus, a sort actually produces a separate table. So if you make editing changes while you're looking at the sorted table, you're not really changing the original data, you're just changing the sort table. And another thing—the new sorted table takes up just as much space on your hard disk as the original table. So we've still got a problem.

The solution: create a secondary index. Secondary indexes accomplish several things:

○ You can have several different secondary indexes for the same table, allowing you to view your table in various configurations.

○ You create a secondary index by restructuring the original table, and the information for the index is treated as a table property (like validity checks or referential integrity), so you don't end up with a separate table. Any changes you make while using a secondary index view are made directly on your original data.

○ You can use secondary indexes to *filter* your records. By specifying values in the Order/Range dialog box (more to come on this), you can tell Paradox that you want to see records only for the science fiction category.

○ But there's one thing you *can't* do with a secondary index that you *can* do with a sort: you can't set up a secondary index to sort some fields in descending order and others in ascending order.

Getting Started

We're going to create two secondary indexes for BOOKS.DB—one sorted by price and another sorted by title. Before you get started, though, there's one rule: You can't create a secondary index unless the table has a primary key. So, if you get into the Restructure Table dialog box and don't see any asterisks in the Key column, don't waste your time trying to create a secondary index. Refer back to Chapter 3 if you need help assigning a primary key.

1. Open BOOKS.DB.

2. Click on the Restructure button (or choose Table, Restructure Table).

    Or, with BOOKS.DB closed, double-click on BOOKS.DB in the Project Viewer.

3. Choose Secondary Indexes from the Table Properties drop-down list.

4. Click on the Define button.

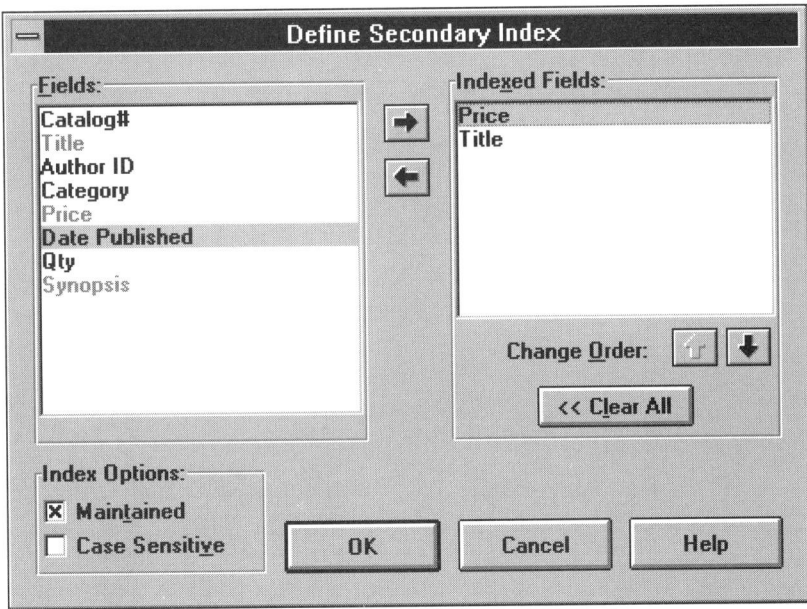

Figure 6-15: The Define Secondary Index dialog box looks a lot like the Sort Table dialog box you just worked with, so you have a head start.

5. Select the Title and Price fields and move them over to the Indexed Fields list (by clicking on the Right arrow or pressing Alt+A).

6. Move Price to the top of the list (by clicking on the Up arrow).

7. Choose OK.

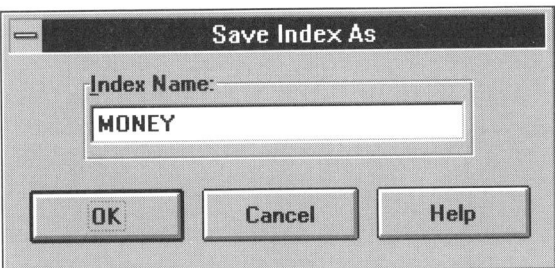

Figure 6-16: Give your index a name by typing it in the Index Name text box of the Save Index As dialog box.

8. Name this index MONEY.

Note that Paradox reserves the actual field name for indexes that use only one field, so you can't call the index PRICE.

9. Choose OK.

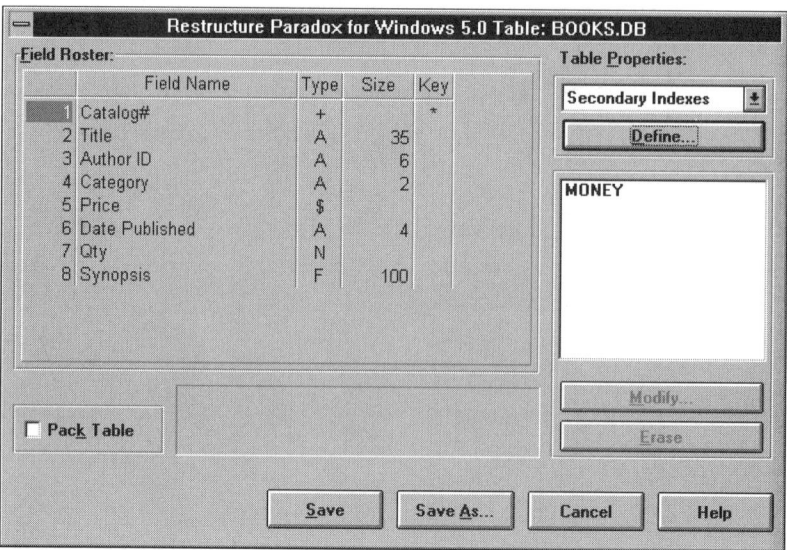

Figure 6-17: The name of the index you just created appears in the Table Properties list box when Secondary Indexes is selected.

10. Using steps 3 through 9, create another secondary index that sorts on the Title field. Call it NAME.

11. When you're back at the Restructure dialog box, choose Save to save your structure changes and close the dialog box.

Inside Scoop

A *composite secondary index* is just an index that uses more than one field. You can have up to 16 composite secondary indexes attached to a table. MONEY is a composite index—it uses the Price and Title fields. NAME uses only one field, so it's not a composite index.

Using the Indexes

Once you've defined the indexes, you need a way to tell Paradox which index you want to use, right? Of course. And here's what you do.

At this point, the Restructure Table dialog box should be closed and BOOKS.DB should be on your screen.

1. Click on the Filter button or choose Table, Filter.

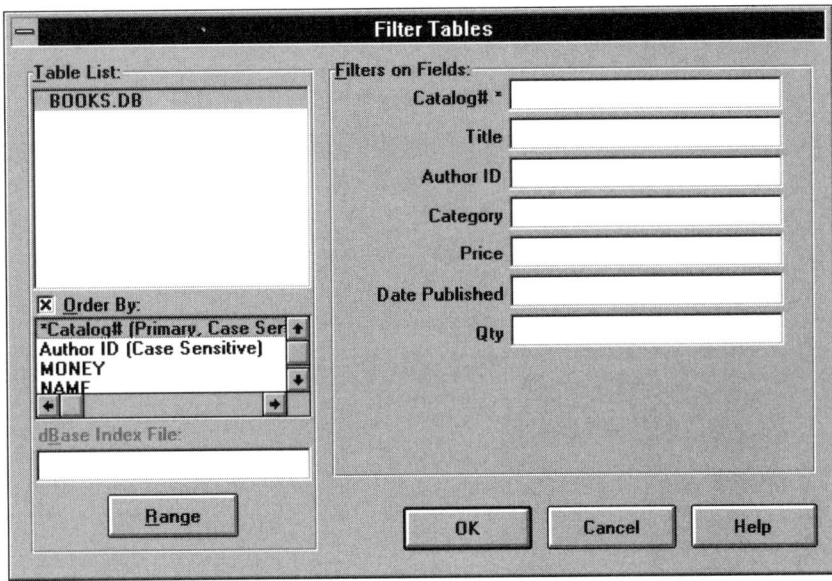

Figure 6-18: The indexes you just created are listed in the Order By list box.

In Figure 6-18, notice that the primary index is also listed there (you can tell which one it is by the asterisk in front of it). Another way to spot the primary index is that it's always at the top of the list.

    2. Select MONEY and choose OK.

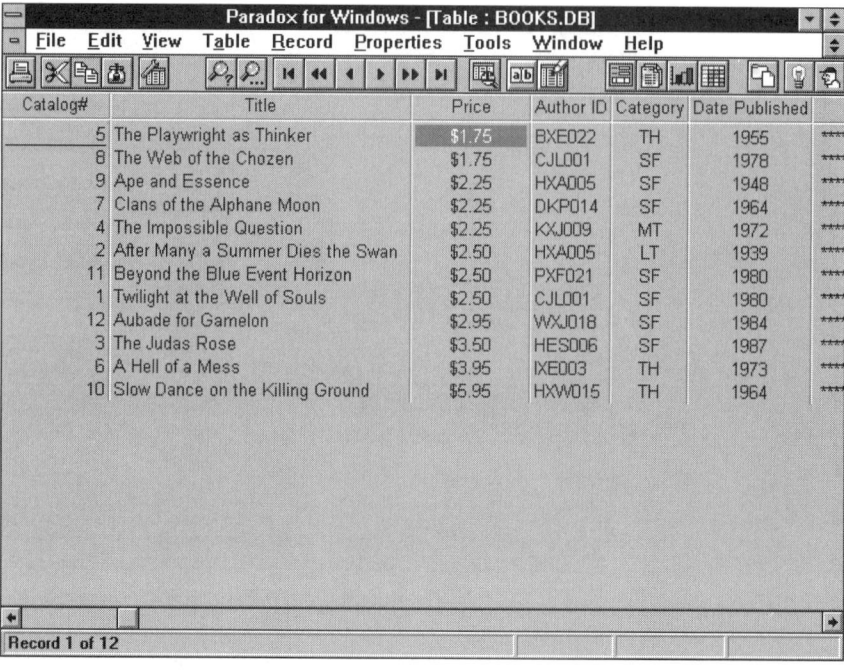

Figure 6-19: I've moved the Price field next to the Title field so you can see what's happened.

Notice in Figure 6-19 that when two or more books are priced the same, the books are sorted in alphabetical order by title within the price group.

Faster than a speeding bullet, your table's sorted according to Price and Title. As you saw with sorting, rearranging the order of records with a sort doesn't change the order of the fields. This holds true for secondary indexes too. On your screen the Title field should still be next to the Catalog field, with the Price field a few columns to the right. If you want to actually see the indexed fields together (as shown in Figure 6-19), you can move the table columns around using the techniques we covered in Chapter 5.

Remember, you haven't really done anything with your actual data. Look at the title bar—you're still in BOOKS.DB, but the records are sorted in a different order. You can make any changes you want while you're in a secondary index without worrying about updating the changes somewhere else.

Returning your table to its original order (sorted according to the primary index) is just like selecting any index. Use steps 1 and 2 above, but instead of selecting a secondary index, select the primary one (the one with the asterisk).

Inside Scoop

A common use for secondary indexes is to create reports. If that's what you're going to do, don't worry about how the fields are arranged in the table. In later chapters, you'll learn all about designing reports so that the fields appear wherever you want them.

You can define a basic secondary index and you can activate it. But there's still more. You might've noticed the Maintained and Case Sensitive options in the Define Secondary Index dialog box. And how do you modify a secondary index (or get rid of it altogether)? What's the deal? You'll find out in this section.

Modifying an Index

Nothing to it. You use most of the same steps you used to define the index in the first place. Just a couple of steps that are different:

1. When you select Secondary Indexes from the Restructure Table dialog box, you don't choose Define. That would create a whole new index.

2. Instead, select the list you want to change from the list box and choose Modify. (The Modify button is activated as soon as you select a secondary index from the list.)

3. The Define Secondary Index dialog box opens just as it did when you first defined the index. But the information you already specified is in there.

4. Just make any changes you want—add or remove fields from the Indexed Fields list (using the Right and Left arrows), rearrange the order of the fields (using the Change Order arrows) and specify any other options.

Deleting an Index

If you want to scrap the whole index, just select the index in the Restructure Table dialog box and choose Erase.

Maintain, Dude!

If you select Maintained in the Define Secondary Index dialog box, Paradox automatically updates the index whenever you make any changes to the table data. It's just like what happens with the primary index—as you add or delete records, they're automatically placed in the right order in your table. It happens so fast you usually don't even notice it's happening. If you have a whole bunch of secondary indexes, though, and your table is humongous, you might start to notice a bit of a slowdown.

With indexes you use a lot, it's a good idea to keep them maintained. But if you find your performance (no, not *yours*–the computer's!) getting sluggish, try deselecting the maintain option. If you don't have Paradox maintain the index, it gets updated whenever you activate it (through the Order/Range dialog box) or use it in a query or report.

Cases Have Feelings Too

This option's all about whether you want Paradox to pay attention to whether or not letters are capitalized. By default, indexes *are not* case-sensitive. So a list of names might look like this:

    Applebaum
    de Silva
    Douglas
    Minsky

When you select Case Sensitive, all uppercase letters are sorted first, and lowercase letters are sorted at the end. So the same list would look like this:

    Applebaum
    Douglas
    Minsky
    de Silva

THROUGH A FILTER, CLEARLY

Filtering means you tell Paradox that you want to see only certain records–all the books with prices under $15, or all of Isaac Asimov's books, or all of the science fiction and metaphysical books written before 1975, or, well you get the idea.

With this technique, we're moving into query territory, which is coming up in the next chapter. Queries let you ask your table all kinds of fancy questions and display the results in just about any way you want. But without messing with actual queries, the secondary indexes and filters let you do some simple querying.

Simple One-Field Filters

We'll start with a simple filter on one field:

1. Open BOOKS.DB.
2. Right-click anywhere in the Date Published field and choose Filter from the Object Inspector menu.

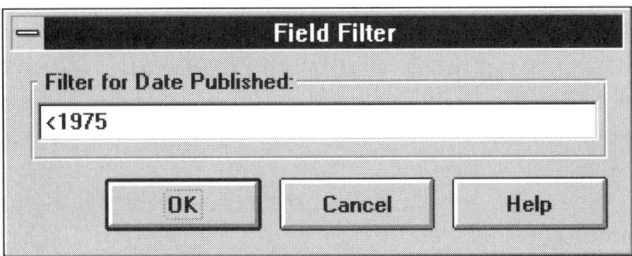

Figure 6-20: When you choose Filter from a field's Object Inspector menu, you get the Field Filter dialog box shown here.

3. Type **<1975** in the Filter for Date Published text box and choose OK.

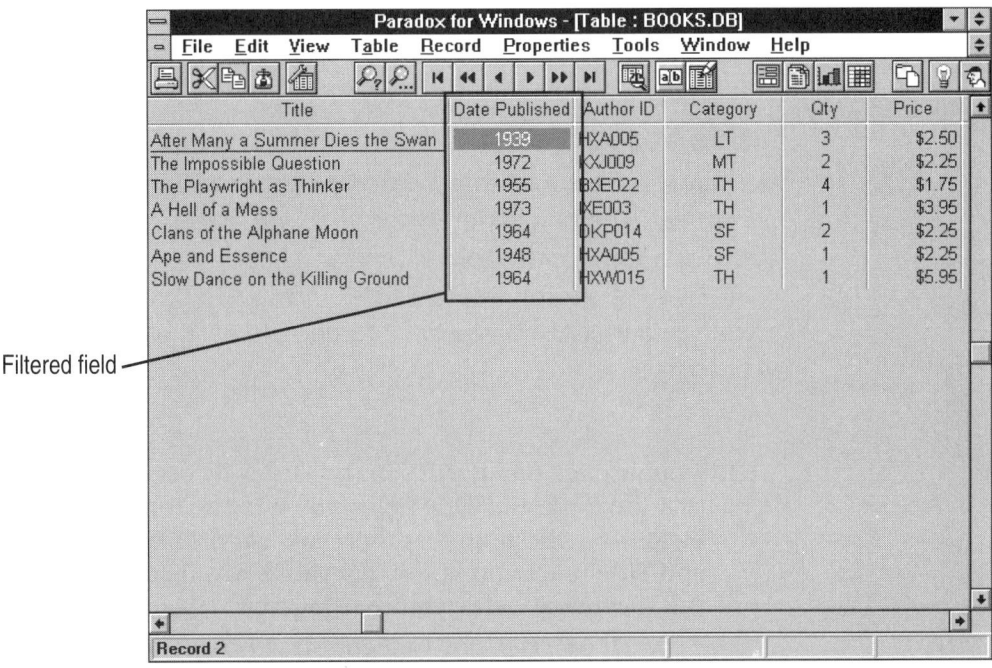

Filtered field

Figure 6-21: All you see are books published before 1975. Notice that the single-field filter didn't change the sort order; it just filtered out the records that didn't meet your criteria.

More Complex Filters

That was a quick 'n' dirty filter operation—simple and fast, but not a lot of options. If you want to set criteria for more than one field, or specify a sort order along with the filter, you have to open the Filter Tables dialog box.

First, let's get back all of the records in BOOKS.DB by removing the filter.

1. Right-click in the Date Published field and choose Filter from the Object Inspector menu.

2. Delete the information in the Filter for Date Published text box and choose OK.

Now you should be able to see all of the records. See, they didn't go away—they were just hiding.

And now for some filters that are more complex.

1. Choose Table, Filter.

Inside Scoop

You can also filter forms and reports using the instructions in this section. The only difference is that you choose Form, Filter (for a form) or Report, Filter (for a report). And if you're filtering a form, the Table List shows all of the tables in your data model, so you have to choose which table you want to filter.

2. Double-click on MONEY in the Order By list box and notice that the Price and Title fields move to the top of the Filters on Fields list. Also note that there are asterisks to the right of Price and Title to let you know that those two fields are included in the secondary index you're using.

3. Type **SF or TH** in the Category text box.

4. Type **>1950 or <1979** in the Date Published text box.
   Note: If you wanted to see all books written in 1980, you would just type **1980** in the Date Published text box to filter for an exact match.

5. Choose OK.

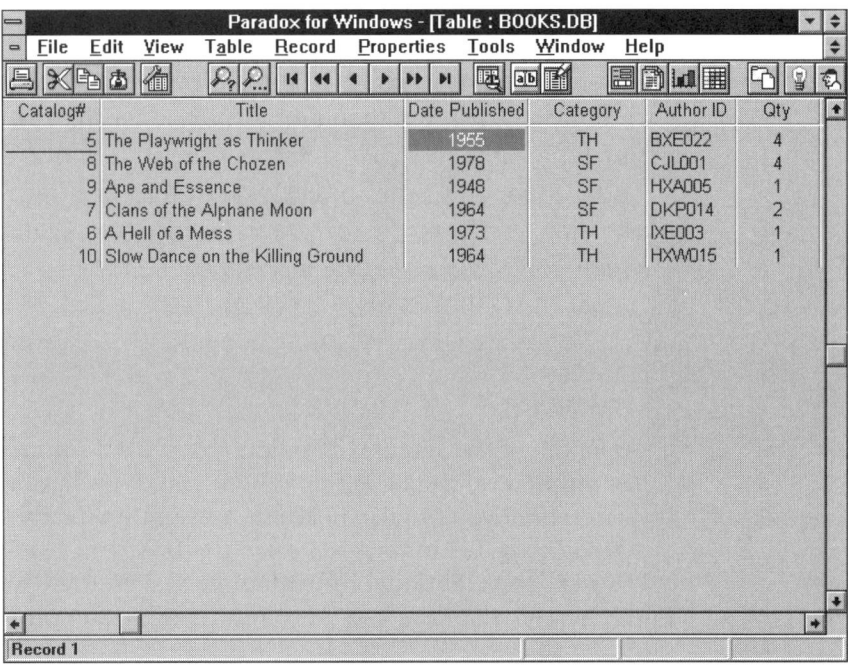

Figure 6-22: The results of the filter operation.

Take a look at Figure 6-22. It shows all of the science fiction and theatre books that were written between 1951 and 1978. Remember, though, that this is just a different view of your table. All of your records are still there, and any changes you make in the filtered view are updated with the original data.

We used the *OR* operator in the Category text box to say we wanted to see books that fit into either category. It might seem logical to use *AND* in this case—after all, we want to see both science fiction *and* theatre books. But when you use the *AND* operator, you're telling Paradox that the filtered records must meet *both* criteria rather than *either/or*. In this case, there aren't any records that are SF *and* TH, so with an SF and TH filter, you'd end up with no records at all.

Now look at the Date Published field. The dates aren't in any kind of order. Why not? Any guesses? Yeah, that's right—there's no secondary index for the date or category field. When you filter records, Paradox shows you only the records that meet your criteria, but it uses a primary or secondary index to sort the data. So if you wanted to see the filtered records arranged by date, you'd have to set up a secondary index on the Date Published field and then select that index in the Order By list before you perform the filter.

Inside Scoop

This example gave you a little taste of two comparison operators: < for less than and > for greater than. We also used the *AND* and *OR* operators. We'll talk a whole lot more about these and other operators in Chapter 8, and I'll explain the differences between queries and filters and when you should use one instead of the other.

It's Implicit

So far, all of the filters we've done have used *implicit field references*. An implicit reference is one where you don't have to tell Paradox which field you're talking about because it already knows. When you typed **SF or TH** in the Category text box, you didn't have to give Paradox any additional information. You entered your specification in the box for the field you were referring to, so nothing else was required.

But Paradox lets you perform filter operations across fields. And the way you do it is with *explicit field references.* For example, you might want to see all of the records that are *either* science fiction *or* priced under $3.75. If you type **SF** in the Category text box and **<3.75** in the Price text box, Paradox will show you all records that match *both* criteria.

Figure 6-23 shows how you put together an *OR* filter statement across fields. Notice that the field names are in brackets in front of the specification criteria. So, with explicit references, it doesn't matter which field you use to enter your criteria. Just to demonstrate that, the selection statement in Figure 6-23 isn't placed in the Category or Price text boxes—it's in the Title text box even though the Title field isn't involved in this filter.

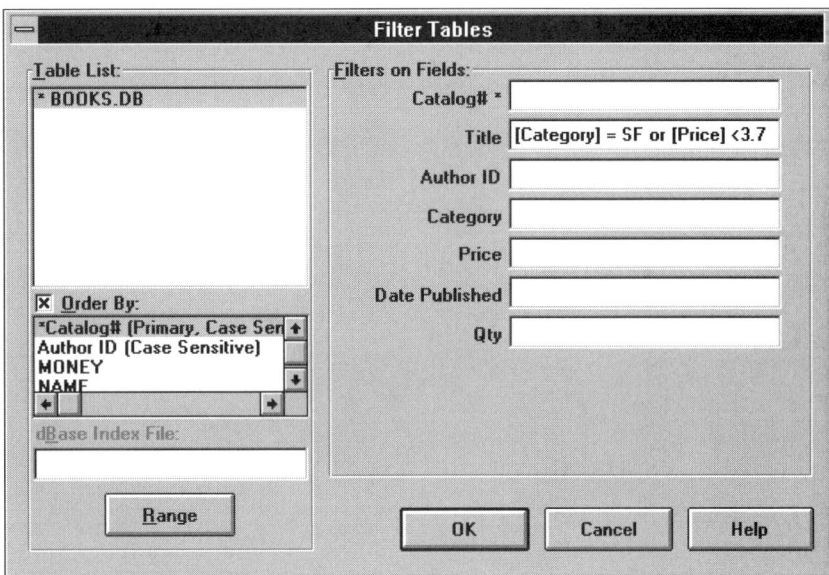

Figure 6-23: Here's what an explicit field reference looks like.

You can simplify the process by putting the selection statement in one of the fields involved in the filter. If we put the filter reference shown in Figure 6-23 in the Category field, here's what it would look like:

SF or [Price]<3.75

SF doesn't need an explicit reference because it's where Paradox expects it to be.

Riding the Range

You can specify just about anything from the Filter Tables dialog box. But the adjustments you make don't get saved with the table or form. If you want to save filter specifications with a particular secondary index for a form, select the secondary index you want and choose Range to open the Set Range for Index dialog box shown in Figure 6-24.

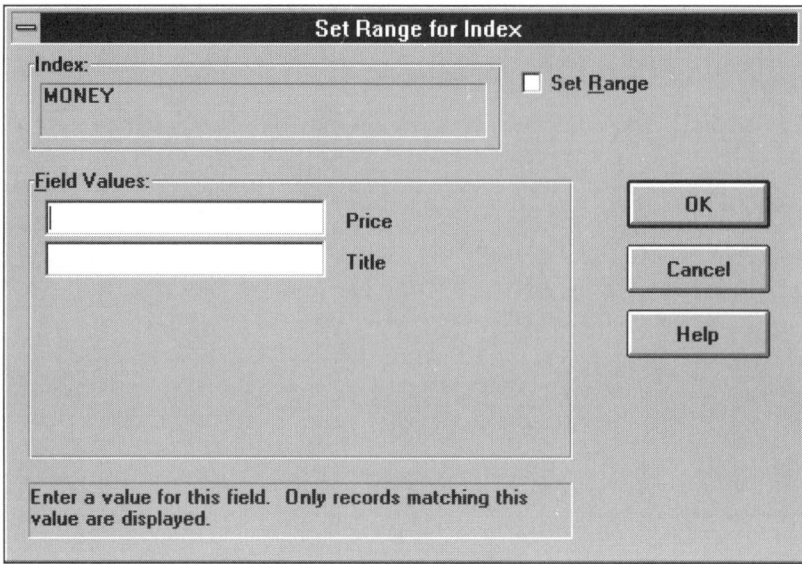

Figure 6-24: The Set Range for Index dialog box.

To get Figure 6-24, I chose MONEY from the Order By list and clicked on the Range button. Notice that only the Price and Title fields are displayed. That's because you can only set a range for fields that are included in the secondary index.

To specify an exact match for a field, just type the information in the appropriate text box. For example, to see only books priced at exactly $3.50, enter **3.50** in the Price text box.

To specify a range of values for a field, place your insertion point in the text box for that field and check the Set Range check box. Two things happen when you do this: a Match Partial Strings check box appears just below the Set Range check box, and another text box appears just below the text boxes for the field names. The additional text box allows you to enter high and low values for the field. You enter the low value in the text box with the field's name and the high value in the text box labeled "(High)." The Match Partial Strings check box tells Paradox that the values don't have to match exactly, and it appears only if the field for which you're setting a range is an alpha field.

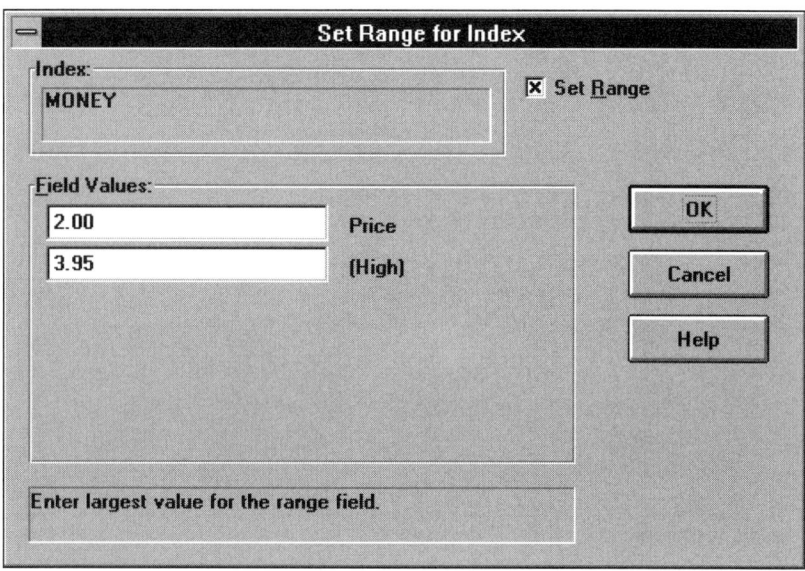

Figure 6-25: I entered **3.95** as the high value and **2.00** as the low value for the Price field.

MOVING ON

You can find stuff, and you should have everything sorted out by now (except maybe your closet). In some ways, the sort, secondary index and filter features are a build-up to querying. The techniques you learned in this chapter let you look at your data in different orders, and even look at only a specified portion of your data. Queries take all of this rearranging to new heights, and you'll learn all about them in Chapters 7 and 8.

7 QUERIES 101

What's a query? In the real world (if there is such a thing), a query is a question. In Paradox's electronic world, a query is also a question, but that's just the beginning. Suppose Bookfinders wants to track inventory by getting a list of all book titles with fewer than two copies in stock. (I'll walk you through this query in just a bit.) In a manual system, you might shout to the person in the back room, "Hey you, tell me how many books we need to reorder. If we're down to one copy of any title, give me a holler." Since you can't shout at Paradox and get a response (not this week anyway), you need to ask your question in a way that Paradox can understand.

Paradox's *QBE (query by example)* method is just the ticket. When you build a query, Paradox gives you an example of the table or tables you're querying, complete with all the fields from the original table. You just fill in the blanks—tell Paradox which fields you want included in the query and specify any conditions. Then Paradox creates an Answer table that contains all of the records that meet your conditions. That's querying in a nutshell, but that one little phrase, *specify any conditions*, is what's going to take up two whole chapters in this book.

In this chapter, we'll cover all the basics. Building and running simple queries, working with Answer tables, performing live queries, dealing with reserved words, and all the other stuff you need to build a solid foundation of query knowledge. Then, in the next chapter, we'll really take off. You'll learn how to design queries across multiple tables, how to get your queries to perform calculations, how to use queries to change data, and much more.

CREATING & RUNNING A QUERY

Let's construct a simple query—no fancy tricks—just to learn the ropes. Along the way, we'll cover a whole bunch of basic query concepts that'll stand you in good stead as we move deeper into query territory. Before we move on to the query example I used in the opening paragraph (which book titles have fewer than two copies in stock), I want you to start with something even easier.

The simplest kind of query tells Paradox to display only certain fields (much like a filter operation) without specifying any other conditions.

Suppose you want a list of book titles and categories without any of the other information in BOOKS.DB? Here's what you do:

The first step is to open the Query window:

1. Choose File, New, Query or, if the Desktop Toolbar is visible, right-click on the Open Query icon and choose New.

   Note: If the Project Viewer is open, you can also right-click on the Queries icon and choose New from the Object Inspector menu.

2. From the Select File dialog box, choose the table you want to query—either double-click on the file's name or highlight the name and choose OK. For our example, choose BOOKS.DB. (We'll talk about querying multiple tables in the next chapter.)

Inside Scoop

You'll learn about *data models* when we start talking about forms (in Chapter 9). The data model is a nifty tool that lets you establish relationships between tables in forms and reports. And why am I mentioning this here? Because you can base a query on a data model. To use an existing data model in a query, change the File Type in the Select File dialog box to "Forms" or "Reports." Then select the form or report that uses the data model.

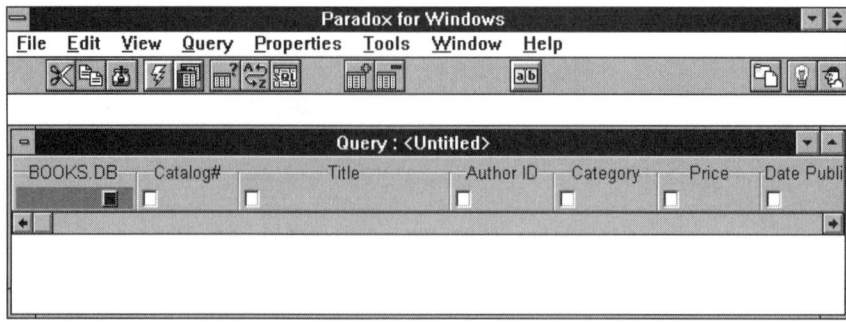

Figure 7-1: The Query window opens, along with a new menu and Toolbar.

Notice that there's now a Query item on the menu bar and a whole new Toolbar (that includes a few familiar faces).

What you're looking at is the *query image*, which is a picture of your table, with all of the fields but none of the data. Notice that there's a little check box in each field in the query image. And there's also a check box in the far-left column (the one that displays the table's name). You'll use the check boxes to tell Paradox which fields to include in the Answer table, and you'll type stuff in the area next to the check boxes to tell Paradox what conditions you want to specify.

Which Fields Do You Want?

The first thing you have to decide is which fields you want to appear in the Answer table. The easiest way to tell Paradox to display a field is to click on the check box for that field.

1. Click on the check box in the Title field.
2. Then do the same for the Category field.

As you'll soon see, we just took a shortcut for checking the fields we wanted. There are different ways of checking a field and different techniques for inserting the check marks, but a plain vanilla check can be inserted just by clicking on a check box.

Running the Query

Click on the Run Query button, choose View, Run Query, or press F8.

The Query Status dialog box appears as soon as you run the query. For a simple query like this, the Query Status dialog box will appear and disappear in a flash. But as your queries get more complex and your tables get larger, you'll find yourself staring at that status message for longer periods of time.

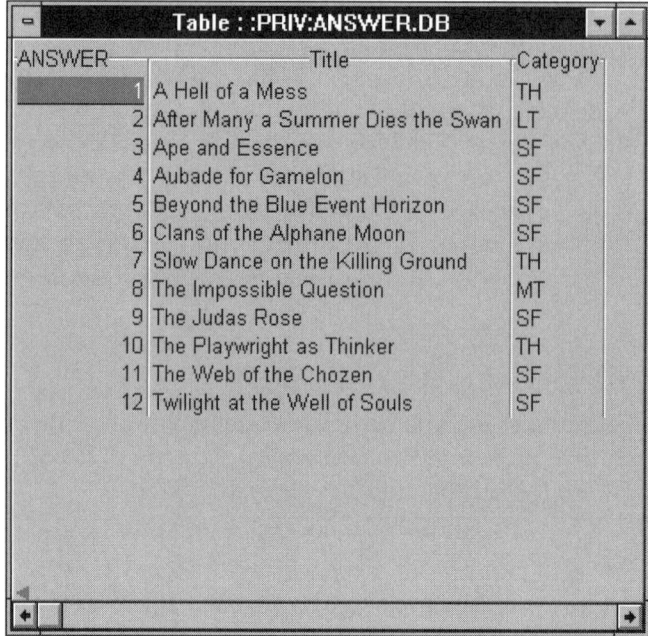

Figure 7-2: Your first Answer table. Only the fields you checked in the query image are displayed.

There. You just ran your first query. Nothing to it, right? Of course there's a whole lot more beneath the surface, but everything you'll do in this chapter and the next builds on what you just did.

THE QUERY TOOLBAR

Before we go any further, a look at the Toolbar. I'm sticking this in right now even though a lot of the options won't make a whole lot of sense at this point. You'll use some of the buttons right away, and it'll be a handy reference for you down the road. And I promise I'll cover all of the buttons in detail in the course of this chapter and the next.

Figure 7-3: The Query Toolbar.

The following list describes the action of each button on the Query Toolbar, followed by the pull-down menu alternative in parentheses.

 Removes selected data and puts it in the Clipboard (Edit, Cut).

 Puts a copy of selected data in the Clipboard (Edit, Copy).

 Puts whatever's in the Clipboard in your query (Edit, Paste).

 Runs the query (View, Run Query).

 Joins tables with example elements.

 Allows you to change the Answer table's properties (Properties, Answer Options).

 Allows you to sort the Answer table (Properties, Answer Sort).

 Translates a query into SQL (standard query language) (Query, Show SQL).

 Allows you to add tables to a query (Query, Add Table).

 Allows you to remove tables from a query (Query, Remove Table).

 Toggles between Field View and Table View (View, Field View).

The group at the far right consists of the Open Project Viewer, Expert and Run Coaches buttons that are available on every Toolbar.

CHECKING IT OUT

When you hold down the left mouse button on a check box, you get a pop-up menu like the one in Figure 7-4. Drag to select the check mark you want. Each check type sends a different message to Paradox when you run your query.

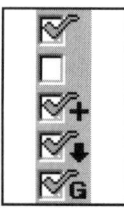

Figure 7-4: To select a check type, hold down the mouse pointer while you choose one of the options in this pop-up list.

Alternatives for Entering Check Marks:

○ Press F6 to enter a plain check mark. F6 is a toggle; if there's already a check mark of any kind, pressing F6 removes it.

○ Press Shift+F6 repeatedly to cycle through the check types. Pressing Shift+F6 in a field that's not checked will place a plain check in the box; pressing Shift+F6 again will replace the check with a Check Plus, and so on.

Check

 A plain check mark tells Paradox to display all unique records that meet your selection criteria. The records are sorted in ascending order (unless you tell Paradox something else, the sort is based on the first checked field in the table).

To get the Answer table shown in Figure 7-5, I put a plain check mark in the Category field. Because the plain check mark gets rid of duplicate entries, the Answer table displays only one listing for each category. And the categories are in alphabetical order, from A through Z.

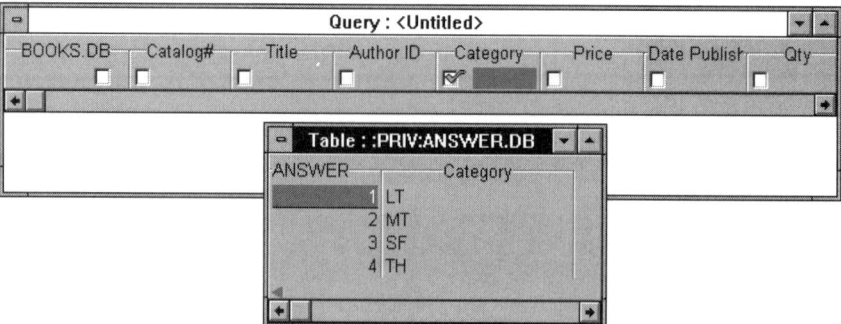

Figure 7-5: Plain check query on Category field.

Check Plus

The differences between a check and a Check Plus are that the Check Plus displays every record that meets your criteria even if there are duplicate values and that the records aren't sorted in the Answer table. If there's a Check Plus in any field, duplicate values will be displayed for all of the checked fields.

In Figure 7-6, I queried the Category field with a Check Plus.

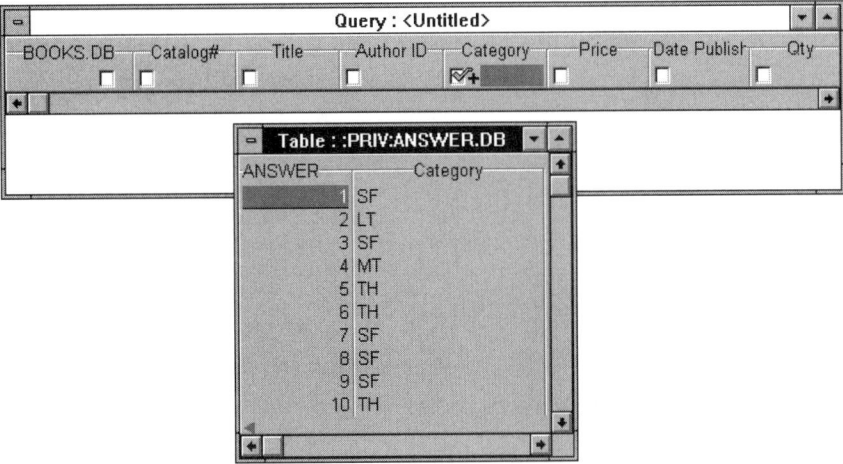

Figure 7-6: Check Plus query on Category field.

Pitfall Ahead

The Check Plus overrides any plain checks or Check Descendings in other fields. Since plain checks and Check Descendings screen out duplicates and sort the records, their functions are in conflict with the Check Plus, which doesn't sort or screen duplicates. So a Check Plus in any field takes control of the whole query.

Check Descending

Check Descending is just like the plain vanilla check, with one difference. It sorts the records in the Answer table in descending instead of ascending order. As with the plain check, Check Descending screens out duplicate entries.

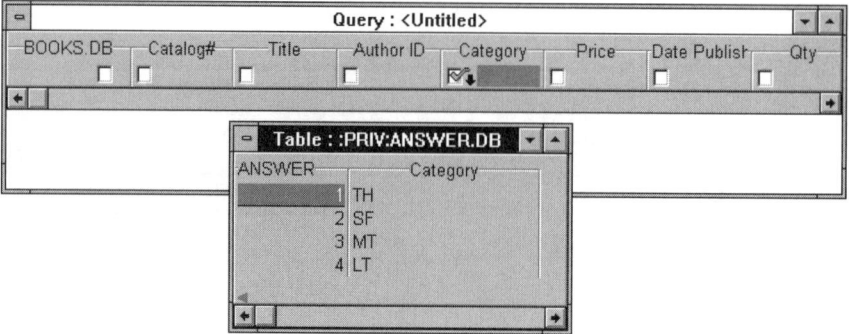

Figure 7-7: Check descending query on Category field.

Check Group

Check Group is used for SET queries, which will not be covered in this book.

Blank Check Box

Choosing the blank check box removes a check mark (of any type) from the field. You can also remove a check mark just by clicking on a box that has a check mark or by pressing Shift+F6 until all of the checks disappear.

Inside Scoop

You can check all of the fields at once by using the check box below the table's name (at the left end of the query image). Use this check box just like any other—click on the box for a plain check or make a choice from the pop-up list. This can be handy even if you don't want to check *all* of the fields. If you're planning to check eight fields in a table that contains ten fields, check all eight in one step and then individually uncheck the two you don't want to use.

Use the table name check box to clear all of the check marks if you want to start over. Just select the blank check box from the table name's pop-up check menu. This works no matter how many fields are checked.

QUERIES THAT SELECT RECORDS

The query you did at the beginning of this chapter was just the first step. Once you've checked the fields you want displayed, the fun begins. Placing a check mark in a field tells Paradox that you want the field displayed in the Answer table, but it doesn't narrow the query to find specific records within a field. To do that, you have to enter *selection conditions*. All that means is that you type something in a field to tell Paradox what you want to happen during the query.

At its most basic, a selection condition tells Paradox to find all records that are an exact match for what you type. For example, if you want to find all science fiction books, you just type "SF" in the query image's Category field. But selection conditions can get as fancy as you want—in this chapter and the next, we'll use them to do everything from finding exact matches to doing calculations across tables.

Pitfall Ahead

Queries are case-sensitive unless you use wildcards or the LIKE operator (discussed in this chapter). So a query to find SF will *only* find SF, not sf or Sf.

Finding Exact Matches

So, you know all about putting check marks in little boxes. Now, on to picking apart the table and telling Paradox exactly what you want to see. We'll start with exact matches, since they're the most straightforward.

Pitfall Ahead

You'd figure this one out soon enough on your own, but I'm just doing my job here—helping you avoid some common traps. One of the most common mistakes with queries is to enter selection conditions but forget to check any of the boxes. Another is to check only the box that contains your selection criteria. Using the example in this section, it's easy to think, "I want to see all my science fiction books, so all I have to do is type SF in the Category field and I'm all set." Not quite—a couple of problems.

If you just enter criteria in fields without checking any boxes, you'll get a dialog box that tells you there are no checked fields. The check marks tell Paradox which fields you want displayed in the Answer table. If no fields are checked, there's nothing to display, so Paradox can't run the query.

Now suppose you typed **SF** in the Category field *and* checked the box. Yeah, there's something to view, but it won't help you much. You won't see any book titles or authors or anything except a table that tells you yes, there are a whole bunch of science fiction books.

The moral: Make sure you put checks in all of the fields you want to see in the Answer table.

Okay. We want a list of science fiction books. Now you have to decide which fields you want to see. The title, of course. And it might also be nice to see the author and the price. Here's how to do it:

1. Start a new query using any of the following methods:
   - Right-click on the Desktop Toolbar's Open Query button and choose New.

   - Right-click on the Project Viewer's Query icon and choose New.
   - Choose File, New, Query.
2. From the Select File dialog box, choose BOOKS.DB.
3. Place plain check marks in the Title, Author ID, Category and Price fields.
4. Move to the Category field and type **SF**.
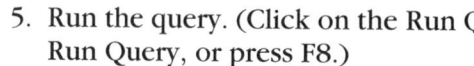
5. Run the query. (Click on the Run Query button, choose View, Run Query, or press F8.)

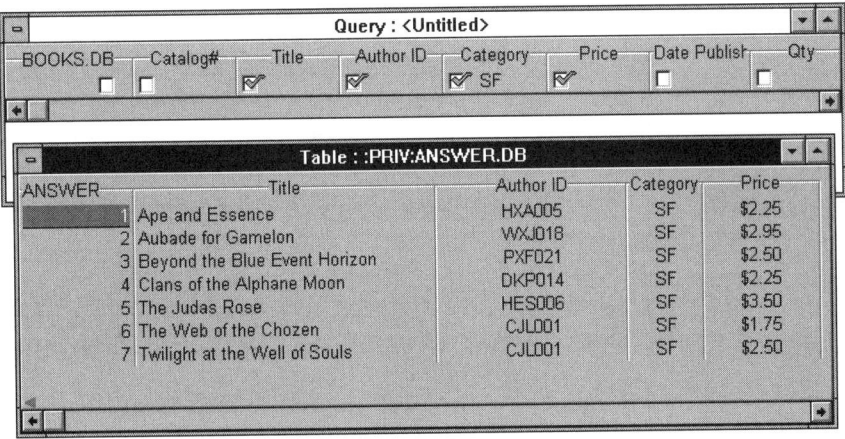

Figure 7-8: The query image and Answer table for this query.

Some Answer Table Stuff

In Figure 7-8, you have a lovely list of science fiction books. Cool. But now what do you do with it? I think a little Answer table talk is in order. Later in this chapter, we'll do some serious Answer table manipulation. You'll learn how to sort the Answer table and change its appearance before you run the query, as well as some other stuff. But there are a few things you need to know right now.

○ The Answer table is just like any other table. You can restructure it, change its properties, add data—anything you can do to a regular table. But don't do a lot of stuff to the Answer table without reading the following item.

○ The Answer table is a temporary table. As soon as you exit Paradox or run another query, the current Answer table goes bye-bye.

○ If you want to use the Answer table later on, you have to rename it, which turns it into a regular, permanent table (instructions coming up in just a bit).

○ As with any other table or window, you can move the Answer table window out of the way by dragging its title bar. When you run a query, the Answer table is displayed on top of the query image, so you have to move the Answer table window somewhere else if you want to see the query image.

 ○ You can print the Answer table in a quick report format by clicking on the Print button or choosing File, Print.

○ Any changes you make to the data in the Answer table are *not* reflected in your original table unless you perform a live query (more about that coming up).

217

Renaming the Answer Table

Use one of the following methods to rename the Answer table:

○ From the Project Viewer, right-click on :PRIV:ANSWER.DB and choose Rename from the Object Inspector menu. Enter a new name in the New File Name text box. Use the Directories and Drive (Or Alias) lists to select the directory you want the file moved to, and choose OK.

○ Choose Tools, Utilities, Rename. Type the current file name in the Rename File From text box and the new file name in the To text box. Use the Directories and Drive (Or Alias) lists to change directories. Choose OK to rename the file. If you want to display the table right away, check the View Modified Table check box before you choose OK.

Make sure you rename the table before you exit Paradox or run another query.

Inside Scoop

You can tell Paradox to assign a new name to the Answer table before you run the query. Just click on the Answer Table Properties button or choose Properties, Answer Options, to open the Answer Options dialog box. Enter the name you want in the Table text box and choose OK.

Pitfall Ahead

This pitfall is related to the preceding Inside Scoop. Using the Answer Options dialog box to assign a new name to the Answer table can save time, but it can also get you in a whole lot of trouble. Paradox hangs on to the name you assign until you close the query image. So if you plan to run more queries using the same query image, make sure you either assign a different name or select the Answer table radio button. Otherwise, your newly named table will be overwritten as soon as you run your next query.

Performing Live Queries

In most cases, running a query produces the Answer table, which has no connection with your original table. Whatever changes you make affect only the Answer table. When you go back to the original table, it'll be just the way it was. This is usually the safest course of action. If Paradox didn't work this way, it would be too easy to inadvertently make sweeping changes that could screw up an entire application. And, as you'll see in the next chapter, Paradox gives you ways to move or copy query data to your original table or to another table.

But what if you *want* your changes to be directly reflected in your original table? Answer: a *live query view*. When you perform a live query, you get a view of the actual table, rather than the Answer table. So you're working with the table itself, not a separate Answer table.

Can you perform a live query on any kind of data? Nope. You have to follow the rules:

❍ The query can involve only one table (you'll learn about multitable queries in the next chapter).

❍ You have to use a Check Plus. That's because you're dealing with the original table, so Paradox doesn't allow you to sort the query.

❍ If your query creates any fields that result from calculations, those fields can't be edited in the live query view.

❍ You can't use the @ wildcard operator.

❍ You can't use the .. wildcard operator at the beginning of a selection condition, but you can use it at the end.

So, as long as you follow the rules, you can run a query that produces a live view of your table. Here's how:

1. With your query image onscreen, click on the Answer Table Properties button or choose Properties, Answer Options.

2. From the Answer Options dialog box, select the Live Query View radio button, as shown in Figure 7-9.

    (We'll get to the rest of the stuff in this dialog box a little later in this chapter.)

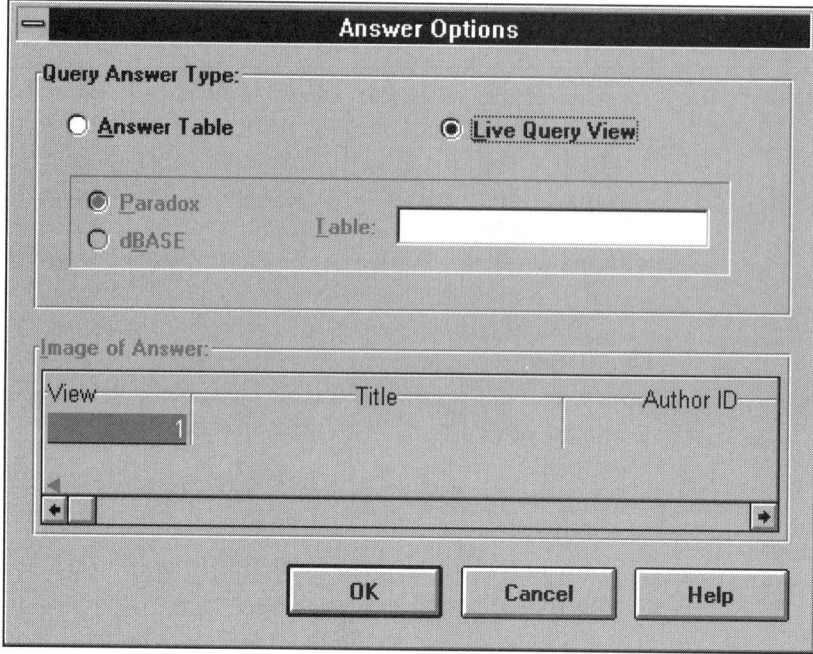

Figure 7-9: Choose Live Query View from this dialog box.

3. Run the query. (Click on the Run Query button, choose View, Run Query; or press F8.)

Instead of the Answer table, you get a Query View window like the one in Figure 7-10. The symbol to the left of each field name lets you know that you're in a live query and that the field can be edited. If there's no symbol next to the field name, the field can't be edited in live query view.

Title	Category	Price
Twilight at the Well of Souls	SF	$2.50
The Judas Rose	SF	$3.50
Clans of the Alphane Moon	SF	$2.25
The Web of the Chozen	SF	$1.75
Ape and Essence	SF	$2.25
Beyond the Blue Event Horizon	SF	$2.50
Aubade for Gamelon	SF	$2.95

Query View : <UNTITLED>

Figure 7-10: A live query window.

And Some Query Image Stuff

In the "Some Answer Table Stuff" section, you learned how to rename the Answer table so you could mess with it later. Once you've re-named it, you can use it to run reports or even as the basis for an entirely new table. But is it the Answer table itself that you want to preserve, or is it the query that got you the Answer table? Trick question.

The Answer table you have right now gives you a list of all your science fiction books. After you rename the Answer table, you can print the list as many times as you want. But suppose you want a separate list for each book category as part of your monthly report? The renamed Answer table isn't going to do you much good next month—by then, you'll probably have added some new books and gotten rid of others. The trick is to save the query so you can run it whenever you want to produce an updated list that includes all your current titles.

As you begin putting your applications to use, saved queries will become an important part of your arsenal. You'll create a required query only once, save the query and then run it when you want current data. You can even use the query to create forms and reports without having to run the query.

Saving a Query

1. With the query image onscreen, choose File, Save As.
2. Enter a name in the New File Name text box. But don't add an extension—Paradox automatically gives queries a QBE extension.

    If necessary, use the Directories and Drive (Or Alias) lists to specify a different directory.
3. Choose OK.

Using Comparison Operators

By now you should have a basic understanding of how to create and run simple queries to find exact matches, as well as how to rename the Answer table and save a query. It's time to branch out. The next step after finding exact matches is to find records that match a range of values. Which brings us back to the example I used at the beginning of the chapter—which book titles have fewer than two copies in stock?

Just as you did with filters in the last chapter, you use *comparison operators* to tell Paradox what you're looking for. The following table describes the comparison operators you can use to specify a range of values.

Operator	What It Means
=	Equal to (usually optional in queries)
<	Less than
>	Greater than
<=	Less than or equal to
>=	Greater than or equal to

Pitfall Ahead

For most of this chapter, I'm keeping the same query image onscreen and modifying it for different queries. This works great when you want to perform several queries on the same table or tables. But there's one thing to watch out for: until you close the query window, the query image keeps the criteria you used for the last search. When you construct a new query, make sure you delete checks and specifications that don't apply to your new criteria.

To create the query:

1. Make sure the query image for BOOKS.DB is onscreen, and get rid of any existing checks and selection conditions.
2. Place a plain check mark and type <2 in the Qty field.

Inside Scoop

You can move columns in your query image just like you can in any table (just drag the field heading or press Ctrl+R). In the Query Image for Figure 7-11, notice that I moved the Qty column next to the Title column so both of them are visible onscreen at the same time. Feel free to move columns so you don't have to keep scrolling back and forth through your fields—changes you make to the query image appearance don't affect the Answer table or your original table.

3. Don't forget you still have to check any other fields you want displayed; otherwise, you'll just get a list of numbers that don't relate to anything. Check the Title and Category fields.
4. Click on the Run Query button, choose View, Run Query, or press F8.

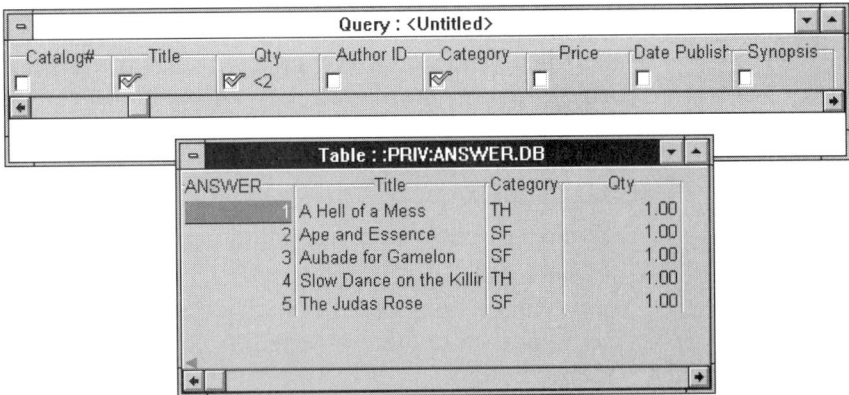

Figure 7-11: The query image and Answer table for all books with fewer than two copies in stock.

Note: In Figure 7-11, notice that the numbers aren't formatted correctly. The Answer table doesn't hold on to any property or formatting changes you made in the original table. At the end of this chapter, I'll show you how to change the Answer table properties before you run the query.

Comparison operators work with letters as well as numbers. If you want to see all book titles that begin with the letter T or higher, just enter >T in the Title field (and don't forget to check the field). That's what I did in Figure 7-12. You might wonder why you don't have to use the equal-to-or-greater-than (>=) operator in order to include titles beginning with T. The reason you don't is that Paradox considers any word that has *anything* after the T to be greater than T. The only way >T might miss a book in the T category would be if the title was T all by itself (or if any book title begins with a lowercase letter).

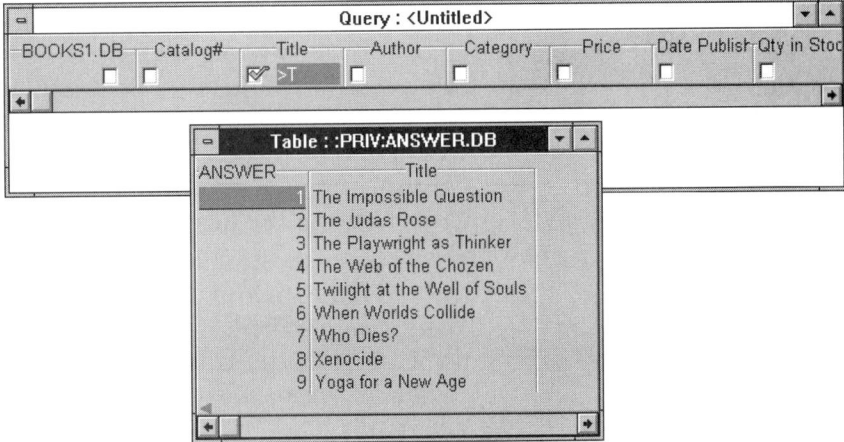

Figure 7-12: All books with titles beginning with the letter T or greater.

Using Wildcard Operators

Sometimes you don't know exactly what you want to find. Like, this morning I went into the kitchen and couldn't remember why I was there. Unfortunately, Paradox wildcards couldn't help me out in that situation. But they definitely can help when you're trying to find stuff with a Paradox query. Why use wildcards?

O You don't know the exact spelling (can't remember if it's Asimov or Azimof).

O You want to pull records with a particular number or character sequence embedded in a field (extremely useful for finding text in memo fields).

O Your search for an exact match wasn't successful. For example, you tried to search for *Marian* in a name field and came up empty. A search with a wildcard operator can broaden the search to include Marion, Marianne, etc.

The following wildcard operators work with letters and numbers, and neither one of them is case-sensitive:

..	Matches any number of characters or blank spaces (including zero)
@	Matches any one character

The following is a list of example conditions using wildcard operators and what each one finds:

..souls	Any record that ends with souls. Souls could be a complete word or the last part of a word.
..souls..	Any record with souls anywhere inside it. Souls could be a complete word or part of a word with souls at the beginning, end, or in the middle.
a@b@de	A word beginning with the letter a, followed by any one character, followed by the letter b and any one character, and ending with the letters de. If you used this condition in the Title field of BOOKS.DB, the query wouldn't find any matches. The way this is set up, it would find *only* records in which the entire field entry consists of one word. To find the title *Aubade for Gamelon*, use the next condition.
a@b@de..	This is just like the above condition, but the two dots at the end tell Paradox to include any record with *anything* after a@b@de. If you're not sure that the word (in this case, Aubade) is at the beginning of the field, use ..a@b@de.. to make sure you find Aubade no matter where it is.

Some Rules for Using Wildcards

❍ You can't use the @ wildcard by itself to find text in a memo or formatted memo field. This one makes sense when you think about it: a memo field usually contains more than one word, and the @ wildcard represents only one character. For example, enter **..well world..** if you want to find all the memos that have Well World somewhere in them. Enter **..we@@ world..** if you can't remember whether it's Well World or West World. But if you just enter **we@@**, Paradox would only find records in which the entire memo field consisted of the word *well* (or *west* or *welt* or *went*).

❍ All wildcard searches are case-insensitive.

❍ Don't type a thousands separator when you use wildcards to query number fields.

❍ When you use wildcards in date fields, the pattern you enter has to be in the same format as your current date format settings in the Windows Control panel. And the Windows date format has to match the date format in your IDAPI configuration file.

❍ You can't combine wildcards and comparison operators in the same selection statement.

SYMBOLS & RESERVED WORDS

There are a whole bunch of symbols and words that Paradox reserves for specific purposes in query statements and filters. Why do you need to know about this? Because if you use any of these symbols or reserved words in your selection condition, Paradox automatically assumes you're referring to the function that the symbol or reserved word performs and not the word itself. We'll talk about several of these symbols and words in this chapter and the next, but for now here's an example.

AND is an operator that's used to tell Paradox you want to find all values that meet both specifications in a selection condition. For example, >=1950 AND <=1980 finds records that are equal to or greater than 1950 *and* equal to or less than 1980. So whenever you use the word *and* (uppercase or lowercase) in a selection condition, Paradox thinks you're using it as an operator.

But it would be pretty silly if you could never search for *and*, *or*, *average* and a lot of other perfectly good words, just because Paradox uses them to mean something else. So of course you can use them. You just have to put the condition inside quotation marks. Like this:

"Ape and Essence"

Now Paradox knows you're talking about *and, the word*, not *and, the operator*. In the above example, the quotation marks allow you to search for the title *Ape and Essence*. Without the quotation marks, the same statement would tell Paradox to find any record that contains both *ape* and *essence*.

Inside Scoop

You don't have to enclose blank spaces between words in quotation marks. But you do have to put quotation marks around commas, periods, exclamation marks and any other characters that Paradox uses as operators.

The following table gives you a list of Paradox's symbols, query operators and reserved words.

Arithmetic Operators (Chapter 8)

+	Addition (Also joins alphanumeric values.)
-	Subtraction
*	Multiplication
/	Division
()	Use to group operators to establish precedence.

Comparison Operators (Chapter 7)

=	Equal to
>	Greater than
<	Less than
>=	Greater than or equal to
<=	Less than or equal to

Reserved Words (Chapter 8)

CALC	Display result of calculation in new calculated field.
CHANGETO	Change specified values in a field and place in temporary table.
DELETE	Delete records containing specified values and place in temporary table.
INSERT	Insert records containing specified values and place in temporary table.
SET	Define specified values as a set for use in set comparisons.

Set Comparison Operators (Chapter 8)

EVERY	Display only records that match every member of a defined set.
EXACTLY	Display only records that match every member of a defined set and no others.
NO	Display only records that don't match any values in defined set.
ONLY	Display only records that match values in defined set.

Summary Operators (Chapter 8)

ALL	Calculate summary based on all values in a group, including duplicates.
AVERAGE	Calculate average of values in a field.
COUNT	Return the number of values in a field.
MIN	Return the lowest value in a field.
MAX	Return the highest value in a field.
SUM	Calculate the total of all values in a field.
UNIQUE	Calculate summary based on all unique values in a group (no duplicates).

Special Operators (Chapters 7 and 8)

,	Display records matching both conditions (same as AND).
!	Display record even if there's no match.
AND	Display records matching both conditions (same as ,).
AS	Create a new field in the Answer table.
BLANK	Display records in which the field is blank.
LIKE	Display records that are similar to the condition (in alpha fields only).
NOT	Display records that don't match the condition.
OR	Display records that match one condition *or* another (or both conditions).
TODAY	Display records containing the current system date.

Wildcard Operators (Chapter 7)

..	Match any series of characters (including blank spaces).
@	Match any single character.

In addition to the stuff in the table, there are a couple of other things to be aware of:

❍ A single period (.) that comes just before or after the .. operator has to be enclosed in quotation marks.

○ If you want to use quotation marks as themselves rather than as instructions to Paradox, type a backslash (\) in front of the quotation marks.

○ If you want to use a backslash as itself, type another backslash in front of it.

ALTERING THE ANSWER TABLE

A little earlier, I told you how to move columns in the query image to make it easier to build a query (I moved the Qty field next to the Title field to minimize scrolling). But rearranging query image columns doesn't have any effect on the Answer table. By default, the fields in the Answer table are displayed in the order in which they appear in the original table. In Figure 7-13, notice that the Price field has been moved next to the Title field in the query image. But in the Answer table, the Price field still follows the Category field.

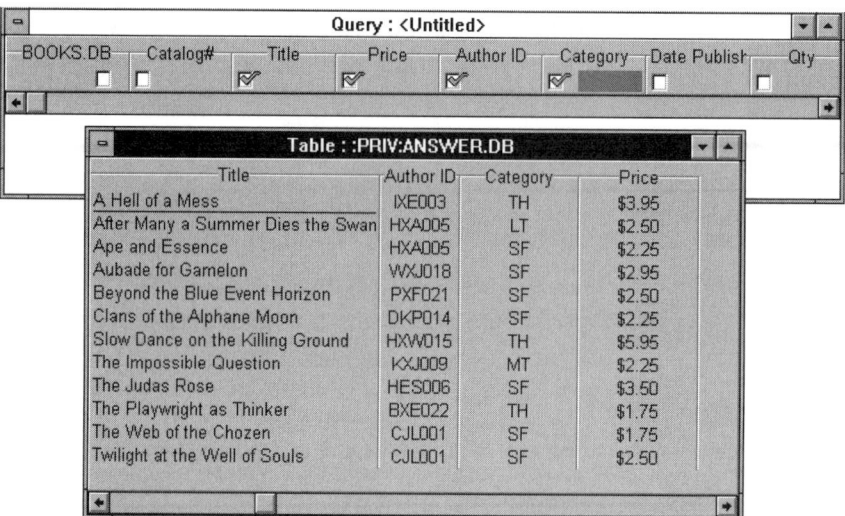

Figure 7-13: Changing column order in the query image doesn't change the Answer table.

So what to do? Easy. Just click on the Answer Table Properties button or choose Properties, Answer Options to open the Answer Options dialog box shown in Figure 7-14.

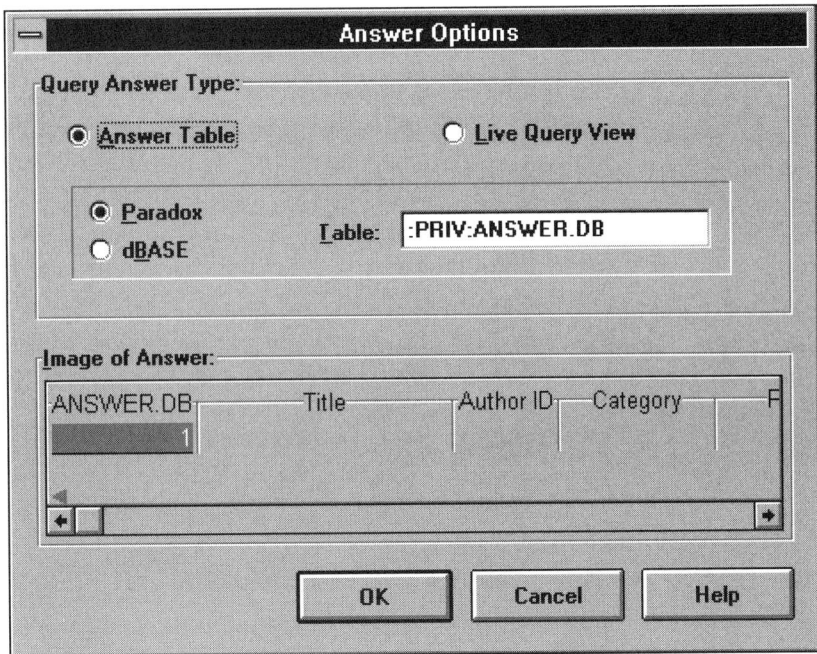

Figure 7-14: The Answer Options dialog box.

The Image of Answer section displays a copy of your table structure, showing all of the fields you checked in the query image. Treat
this image just like a table. Use direct manipulation to rearrange
column order or to change heading height, row height or column
width. Use Object Inspector menus to change specific table properties. The following list is a reminder of some of the stuff you can do.
Refer to Chapter 5 for a refresher on changing table appearance.

○ Drag the table name up or down to change the heading height.

○ Drag the line under the first record up or down to change the row
   height.

○ Drag a vertical column grid to change the column width.

○ Drag a column heading to a new location to reposition the
   column.

○ Press Shift+F6 (or Ctrl+Shift+M) to get the All Object Inspector
   menu, which lets you change properties for all columns at the
   same time.

○ Press Ctrl+Shift+H to get the All Headings Object Inspector menu,
   which lets you change properties for all column headings at the
   same time.

○ Press Ctrl+G to get the Grid Inspector menu, which lets you make changes to the appearance of the grid lines.

○ Choose Number Format from the Object Inspector menu for any number field to change the appearance of numbers in the field. Remember that any formatting you applied in the original table won't be transferred to the Answer table.

○ Choose Alignment, Color or Font from any Object Inspector menu to position data within a field or display the field data in a different color or font.

In Figure 7-15, I moved the Price field next to the Title field, widened some columns and changed the heading font.

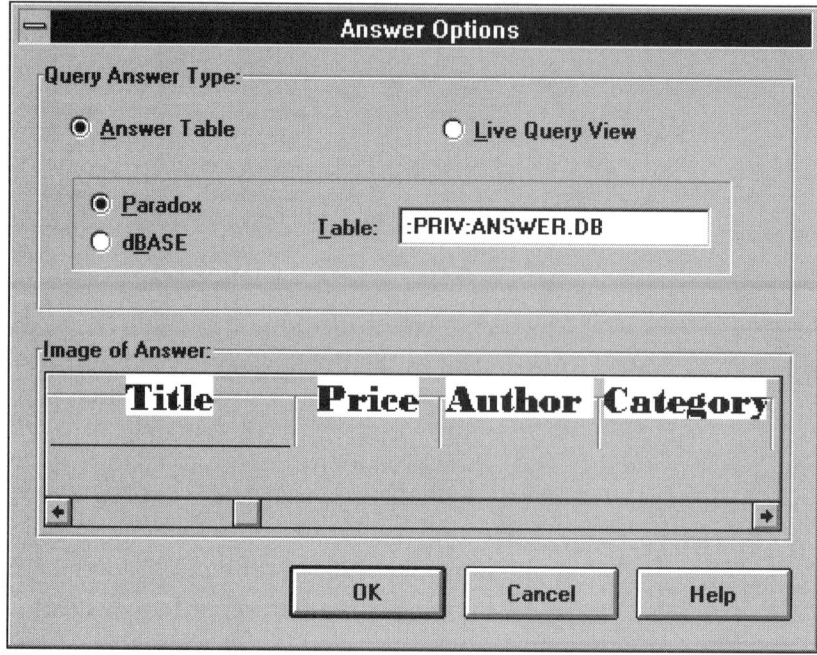

Figure 7-15: The fields in the Answer table will be displayed in this order.

The changes you make to the Answer table's properties are saved when you save the query. So when you run the same query again, the new properties are still there.

Setting the Sort Order

 You can sort the data in an Answer table using the same sorting techniques you learned in the last chapter. The only difference is that you do it from a special dialog box. With your query image onscreen, click on the Sort button or choose Properties, Answer Sort to open the Sort Answer dialog box shown in Figure 7-16.

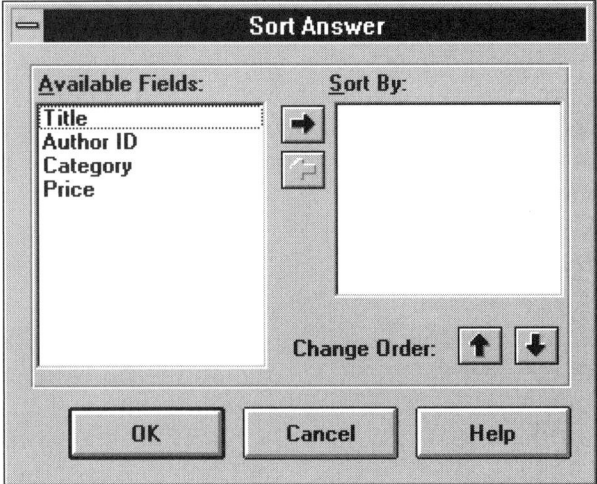

Figure 7-16: The Sort Answer dialog box.

The Available Fields list displays all of the fields you checked in the query image. Double-click on a field name (or select the field name and click on the right arrow) to move the field into the Sort By list. Use the Change Order arrows (the up and down arrows) to rearrange the fields in the Sort By list. Double-click on a field name in the Sort By list (or select the field name and click on the left arrow) to remove a field from the Sort By list. For more info about sorting, review Chapter 6.

Pitfall Ahead

You have to have at least one field checked (with any kind of check mark) before you can use the Answer Properties or Sort Answer dialog box. If you choose either one of these options before you enter anything in the query image, you get this error message: "Attempted to prepare an empty query." If you've entered selection conditions but haven't checked any fields, you get this message: "Query has no fields checked." Just choose OK to clear the Error dialog box, check the fields you want to include and try again.

INTRODUCING SOME SLICK OPERATORS

To end your introduction to queries, I want to introduce some of Paradox's special operators. We'll use lots of operators in different situations in the next chapter, but I'll start here by giving you simple examples using a few common operators.

LIKE

The LIKE operator is a lot like the @ and .. wildcards: it lets you search for values in alpha fields that are *like* your selection condition. To repeat the example I used when talking about wildcards, suppose you searched for *Abode for Gamelon* and nothing happened. You *know* the first word is *something like abode*, and you're sure about the last part of the title. To broaden the search to find words like *abode*, just type **LIKE** in front of Abode for Gamelon, as shown in Figure 7-17.

> ### Inside Scoop
>
> Just a reminder. None of Paradox's operators are case-sensitive. LIKE, Like, and like will all give you the same result. I've entered all the operators in uppercase just so they'll stand out.

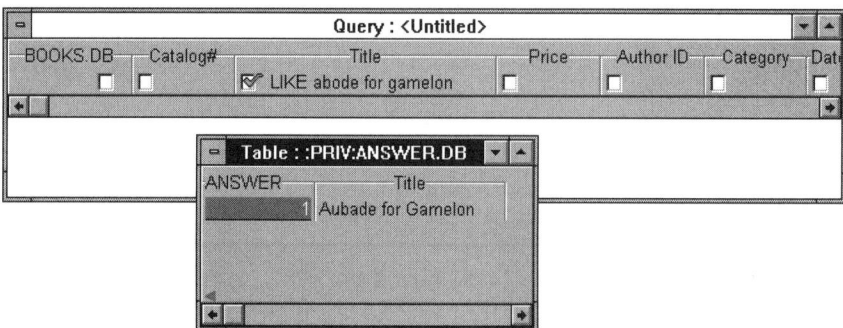

Figure 7-17: Sample query using the LIKE operator.

When you use LIKE, the first letter in your condition has to match the value you're looking for. So LIKE lsng will find Lessing, but it won't find Blessing. And for a LIKE query to be successful, the letters you type must match one-half to two-thirds of the characters in the value you want to find. And one more thing. You can't use LIKE in combination with the @ and .. wildcards.

BLANK

BLANK is a way to find records that don't have anything in specified fields. To use it, you just type BLANK in the field you want to check out. Like this:

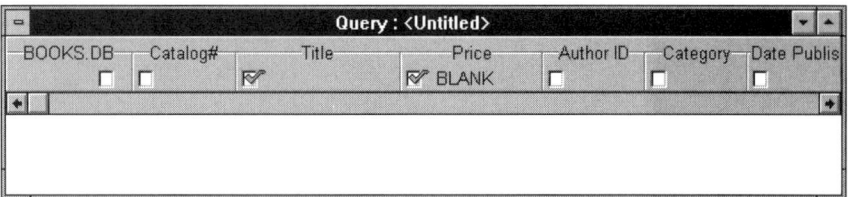

Figure 7-18: A sample query using the BLANK operator.

The query shown in Figure 7-18 gives you the following Answer table.

Figure 7-19: Now you can see which records don't have an entry in the Price field and you can take care of them.

NOT

NOT does just what you would think it does. It finds records that do *not* have the specified criteria in a field. Basically, it just reverses whatever you have in your selection condition. And you can combine NOT with the @ and .. wildcard operators. The query shown in Figure 7-20 will give you an Answer table containing all records in which "the" doesn't appear anywhere in the Title field.

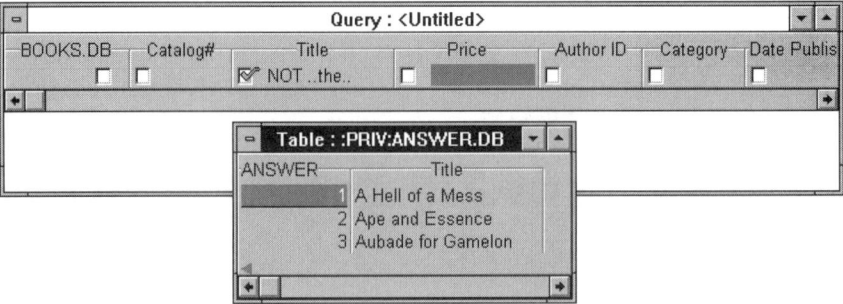

Figure 7-20: A sample query using the NOT operator.

NOT BLANK

This is actually two operators: NOT and BLANK. What do you think putting them together might accomplish? Well, BLANK finds records without any value in a specified field. And NOT reverses the action of the selection condition. So NOT BLANK screens out any blank fields. The query in Figure 7-21 will give you only records in which the Price field is filled in.

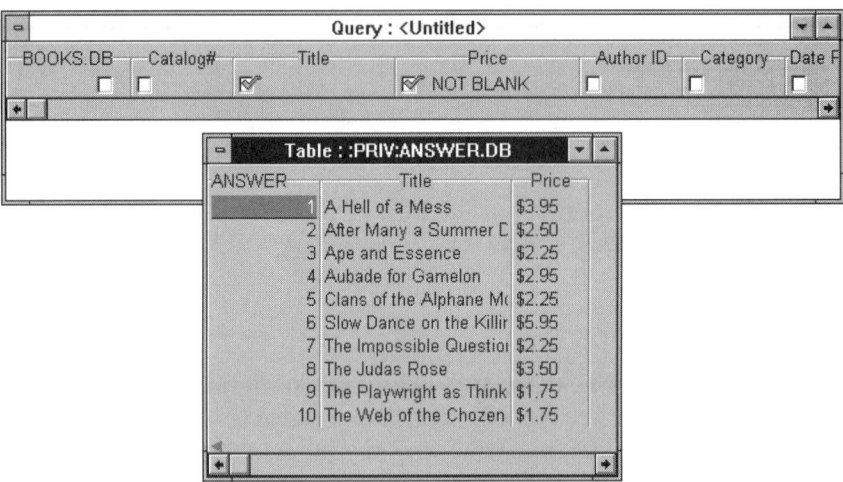

Figure 7-21: A sample query using NOT BLANK.

MOVING ON

This chapter gave you the ground rules for queries and introduced you to some simple query techniques. But we've just scratched the surface. The next chapter gets into multitable queries, queries that change data, queries that perform calculations (and lots more slick operators).

8

QUERIES, THE SEQUEL

Queries, queries, queries. Aren't we done yet? Hey, the fun's just beginning. And besides, if Rocky could go for five rounds, surely you can handle one more chapter on queries. We got all the boring basics out of the way in the last chapter. Time to find out how powerful queries can be.

We'll start slow and pick up speed. Pay attention at the beginning—I'll review the basic procedures for building a query, then we're off to the races (to thoroughly mangle my boxing metaphor).

POP QUIZ (QUERY REVIEW)

Okay, no cheating now—what do you have to do to create a query? (A little "Jeopardy" music, maestro.) Time's up. Here's the answer sheet (didn't want to make you sweat it out *too* long). It includes a few steps we haven't gotten to yet—just wanted to give you a complete picture of the process in one place.

○ Right-click on the Query button in the Project Viewer or on the Desktop Toolbar. Or choose File, New, Query.

○ From the Select File dialog box, choose the table or tables you want to query.

○ If the table's in a different directory or on a different drive, use the Directories and Drive (Or Alias) lists to get where you want to be.

○ Check the fields you want to display in the Answer table.

   Plain check screens out duplicates and sorts records in ascending order (A to Z or 1 to 10).

   Check Plus does not screen out duplicates or sort records.

   Check Descending screens out duplicates and sorts records in descending order (Z to A or 10 to 1).

   Check Group marks fields for inclusion in set queries.

○ Define your selection conditions. This is the biggest step in the process, and one that took up most of the last chapter and will consume the rest of this chapter. Selection conditions can run the gamut—from finding an exact match to performing calculations (and putting the results of the calculations into a new field) to changing values within fields.

 ○ Change Answer table options as desired. Click on the Answer Table Properties button or choose Properties, Answer Options. You can do the following stuff from the Answer Options dialog box:

   ○ Choose Live Query View to display an active view of your table instead of the Answer table.
   ○ Tell Paradox to display the Answer table in dBase format.
   ○ Rename the Answer table before you run the query.
   ○ Change the Answer table's properties (column width, row height, fonts, etc.).

 ○ Run the query. Click on the Query Toolbar's Run Query button or choose View, Run Query.

○ Rename the Answer table if you want to save it for later use. (Remember, ANSWER.DB is a temporary table; it's gone or over-written as soon as you exit Paradox or run another query.) Right-click on the table's name in the Project Viewer and choose Re-name from the Object Inspector menu. Or choose Tools, Utilities, Rename.

○ Save the query if you want to use it again. Saving the Answer table saves only a static picture of your table as it currently exists; saving the query allows you to use the same selection conditions to get current information at any time.

○ Close the query image—double-click on its Control-menu box.

QUERYING MULTIPLE FIELDS

In Chapter 7, all of the sample queries had selection conditions for only one field. Other fields were checked for display purposes, but we asked questions of only one field at a time. Time to move on. We'll start with simple AND queries (like which records meet *both* of the following conditions: fewer than two in stock *and* science fiction). Then we'll move on to multifield OR queries (like which records meet *either* condition). With multifield OR queries, you'll learn how, why and when to add rows to your query image.

AND/OR queries can be performed on one field or on multiple fields. And the way you enter the selection condition determines how Paradox interprets the query:

What You Want	How You Enter Selection Condition

AND query on single field	Separate each condition with a comma.
OR query on single field	Separate each condition with the OR operator.
AND query on multiple fields	Place all conditions on the same row (but no AND operator).
OR query on multiple fields	Place conditions on separate rows (but no OR operator).

Inside Scoop

Think about what you're trying to accomplish before you use the AND operator. Suppose you want a list of all science fiction *and* theatre books. You enter the selection condition **SF**, **TH** in the Category column, right? Wrong. Even though using the comma as an AND operator seems logical, it won't work. Because AND finds only records that match *both* conditions, SF, TH returns a list of books that are *both* science fiction and theatre. In other words, none. What you really want is to find records that meet *either* criterion: SF OR TH does the trick.

Single-Field AND Queries

As the previous Inside Scoop indicates, AND isn't always the correct operator, even when logic tells you it should be. So when *do* you use AND? Simple. When you actually *do* want the query to find records that match *both* conditions.

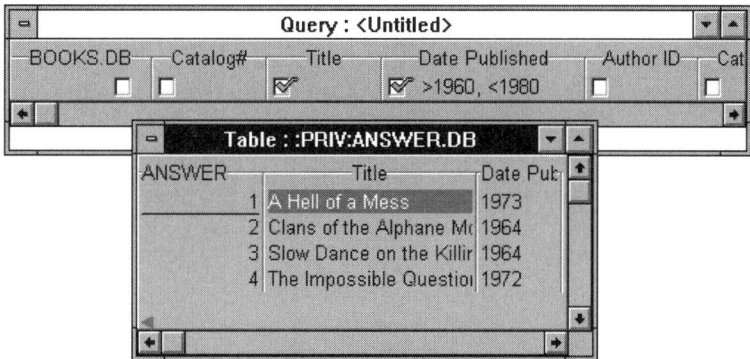

Figure 8-1: I used an AND query to find books published after 1960 *and* before 1980.

In Figure 8-1, the Answer table lists only records that meet *both*   **237** criteria: >1960 *and* <1980. In other words, any book published between those two dates.

Inside Scoop

Don't forget: if you want to enter an actual comma as part of a selection condition (in other words, you don't want the comma treated as an AND operator), make sure you enclose the comma in quotation marks.

Single-Field OR Queries

What if the selection condition for Figure 8-1 had used the OR operator instead? Think about it before you look at Figure 8-2 for the answer. The selection statement >1960 OR <1980 returns a list of books that meet *either* condition: published after 1960 *or* before 1980. Okay, now you can look.

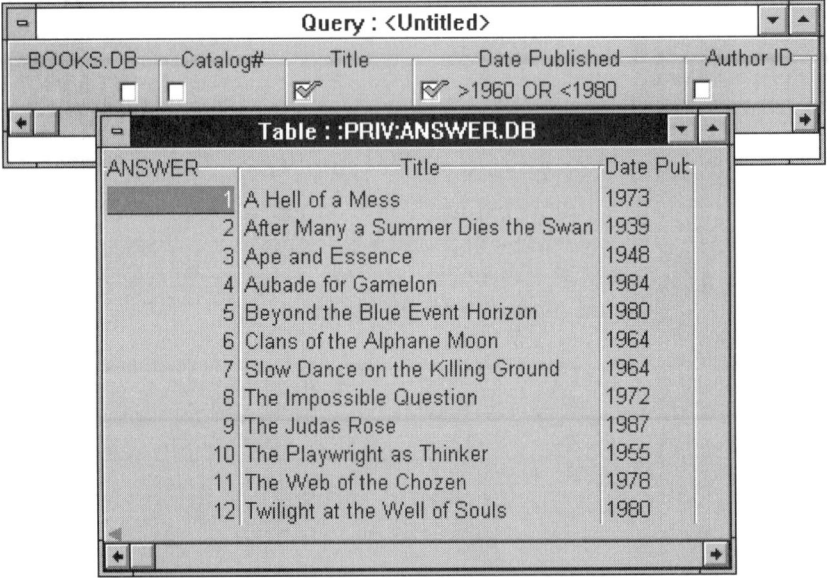

Figure 8-2: In this case, using the OR operator produced an Answer table listing every book in BOOKS.DB.

Why didn't this query screen out any books? Simple. Every single book was written either after 1960 or before 1980. So in this case, the OR operator didn't make much sense. Just another example of the importance of thinking about what you want before you construct your selection condition. Figure 8-3 shows an example of an OR query on one field that you might actually want to do. This is one of those deceptive cases where logical thought tells you to use the AND operator—after all, you want a list of all science fiction books *and* theatre books. But if you use AND, any individual record would have to be both science fiction and theatre.

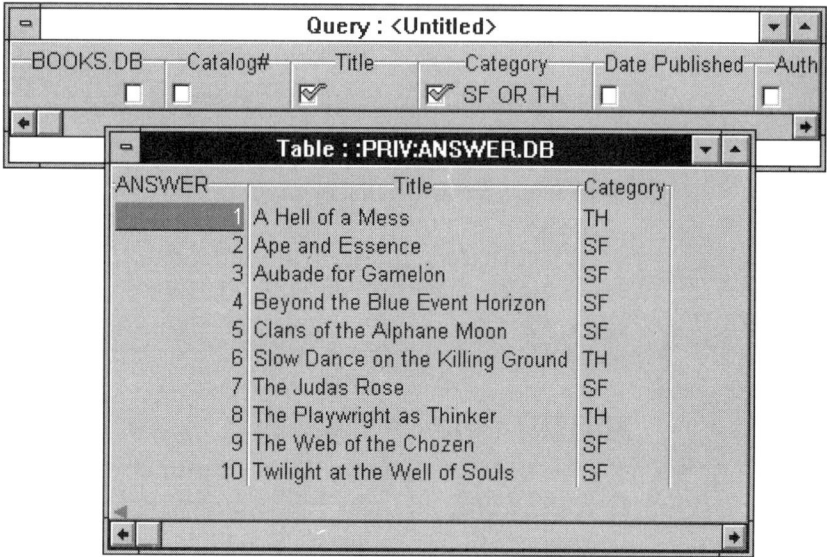

Figure 8-3: A query using the OR operator to find all science fiction and theatre books.

Multiple-Field AND Queries

An AND query across multiple fields is actually even simpler than an AND query on one field. All you have to do is enter selection conditions for the fields you want to include. As long as all of the conditions are entered on the same row in the query image, Paradox assumes you want the query to find records meeting *all* conditions. (Yeah, I know, we haven't talked about adding rows yet. That's straight ahead, when we get into multiple field OR queries.)

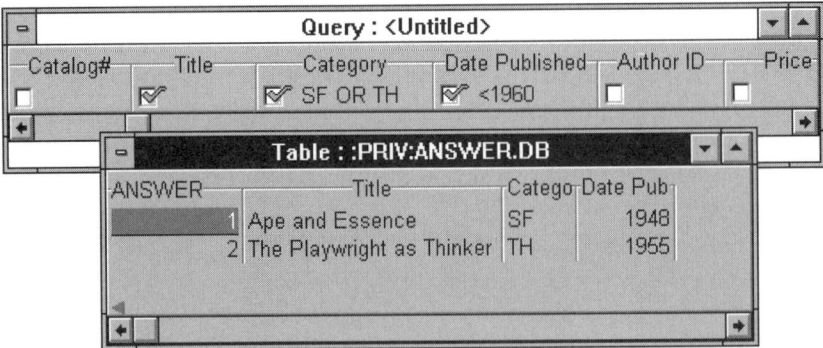

Figure 8-4: This query found books that were science fiction or theatre *and* published before 1960.

In Figure 8-4, all I did was enter SF or TH in the Category field and <1960 in the Date Published field. This process is no different than a single-field query; you're just entering single selection conditions in more than one field.

Multiple-Field OR Queries

And now for something new and different. So far, all of your queries have used only one row in the query image. But everything that's entered on the same row is assumed to be an AND condition. So, to give Paradox the OR signal, you enter selection conditions on separate rows. To use the example in Figure 8-4, suppose you wanted to find books that were science fiction *or* published before 1960?

The first thing you need to do is add a row to the query image. Just press the Down arrow to add a row below the current one, or press the Ins key to insert a new row above the current one. In Figure 8-5, I placed the SF condition on one line and the <1960 condition on another to get Paradox to treat this as an OR condition.

Pitfall Ahead

Notice that I checked the same fields in each row. I know it seems silly, but Paradox makes you check the same fields in every row of a multiple-row query. If you check different fields in each row, you'll get this error message: "Query appears to ask two unrelated questions." If you check a bunch of fields in one row and don't check any in the others, this is the message: "One or more query rows do not contribute to the ANSWER."

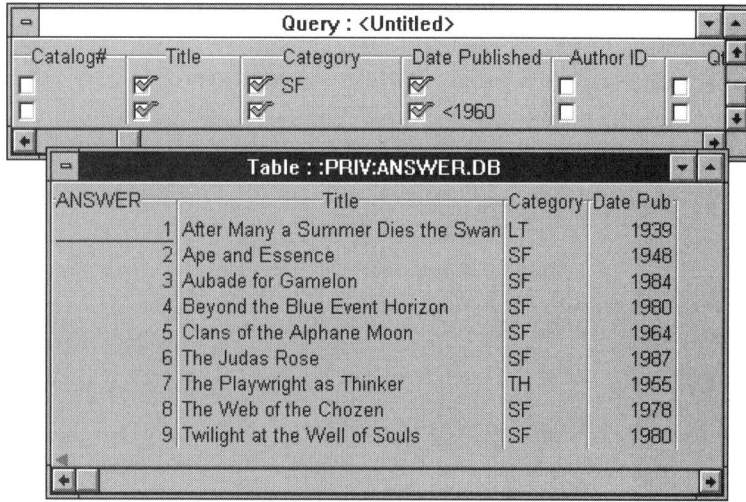

Figure 8-5: An OR query on two fields.

Combining AND & OR Conditions

You can combine AND and OR conditions on the same row or on different rows. Figure 8-6 shows a query with an AND operator in the Date Published field and an OR operator in the Category field. Because both conditions are in the same row, the entire condition is treated as an AND operation.

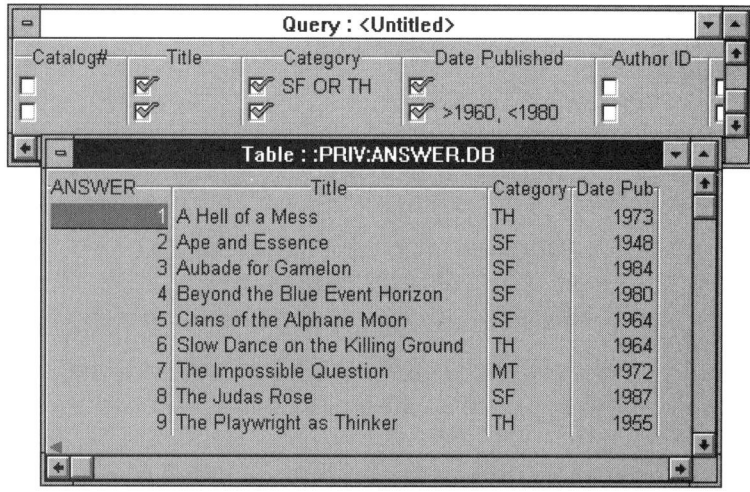

Figure 8-6: Combining AND and OR conditions in the same row.

A query can use any number of rows. Think of it like this: Each row asks a question. If a record meets *all* the criteria on one row *or* all the criteria on another row, that record will be included in the Answer table. For example, the query image in Figure 8-7 first asks the question, "Which records contain science fiction books written before 1960?" It then asks, "Which records contain theatre books written before 1960?"

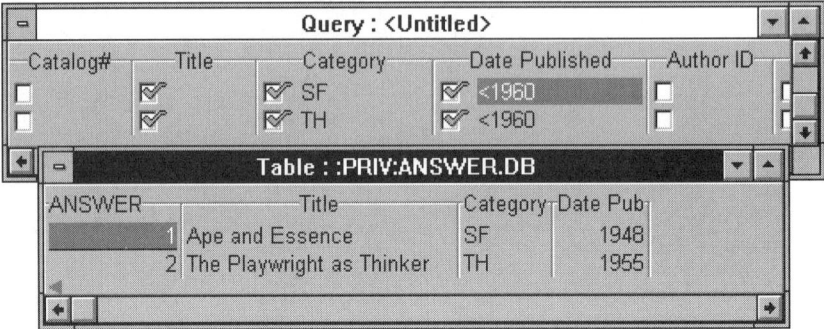

Figure 8-7: Combining AND and OR conditions on different rows.

Note: The query in Figure 8-7 could have been entered on one line. Take a look at Figure 8-8. It does exactly the same thing as the query in Figure 8-7. OR conditions for the same field can be entered on the same line or on different ones; it doesn't make any difference.

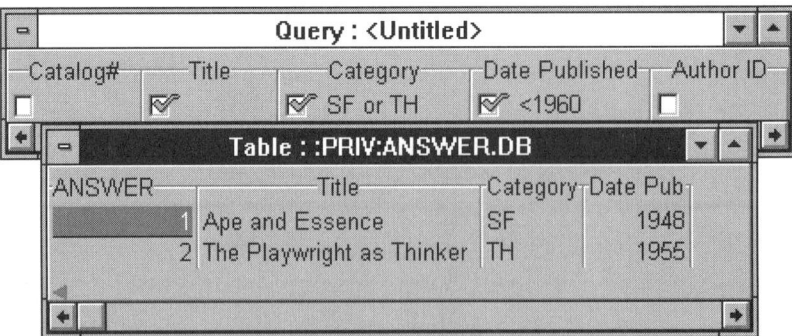

Figure 8-8: OR conditions for the same field can be entered on the same line.

QUERYING MORE THAN ONE TABLE

Ready for the big time? In the first chapter, I told you that Paradox is a relational database management system, and that *relational* just means you can link a bunch of tables together. This ability to link tables is at the heart of Paradox's power. Asking questions of multiple tables can produce powerful results, but the query process is no more difficult than what you've already done.

There are just a couple of additional steps when you query multiple tables:

❍ Add each table you want to query to the query image.

> *Note*: The tables you want to link must share a common field. The field name doesn't have to be the same, but the field types must be compatible. We talked about this in Chapter 4 when we covered referential integrity and lookup tables. The Author ID fields in BOOKS.DB and AUTHOR.DB provide a link between the two tables.

❍ Use *example elements* to tell Paradox which tables you want to link.

We'll start with these two steps. Once you understand how to add tables and use example elements, the rest of the query stuff in this chapter is just a matter of asking different kinds of questions.

Adding & Removing Tables

The easiest way to add multiple tables to a query image is to select all of the tables at once when you first create the query.

❍ Right-click on the Query button in the Project Viewer or on the Desktop Toolbar and choose New from the Object Inspector menu. Or choose File, New, Query.

❍ From the Select File dialog box, choose the table or tables you want to query. Use any standard Windows selection technique: Shift+click to select contiguous files (files that are next to each other in the list), or Ctrl+click to select noncontiguous files.

In Figure 8-9 I selected BOOKS.DB, AUTHOR.DB and PUBLISH.DB.

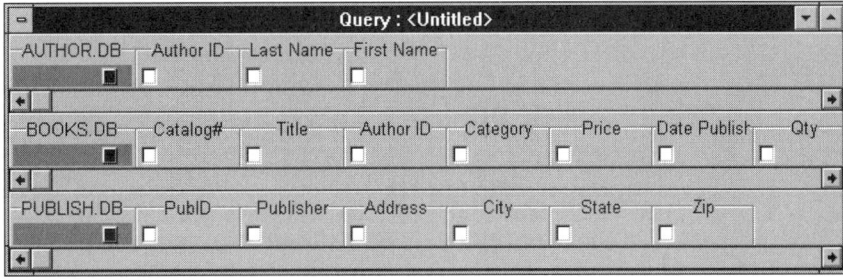

Figure 8-9: This query can ask questions of three different tables.

From the query window, you can easily add more tables or delete those you don't want.

To add a table to the query image:

○ Click on the Add Table button or choose Query, Add Table.

○ From the Select File dialog box, choose the table or tables you want to add. This is just the same as when you select tables at the beginning of a query. Shift+click or Ctrl+click to add as many tables as you want.

○ The tables you add will end up below any tables already in the query image, and they'll be displayed in alphabetical order.

To delete a table from the query image:

○ Click on the Remove Table button or choose Query, Remove Table to display the Remove Table dialog box shown in Figure 8-10.

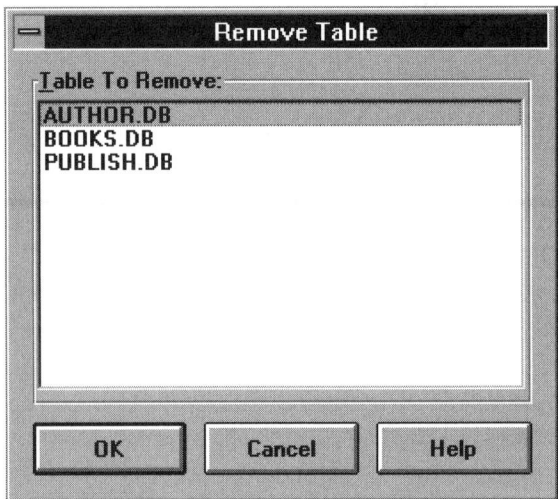

Figure 8-10: The Remove Table dialog box.

○ The Table To Remove list shows all of the tables currently in the query image. Just select the table or tables you want to remove and choose OK.

Example Elements

So far, the query image contains three separate tables. But until we do something to connect them, Paradox doesn't know what we want to do. (You'd think a fancy relational database management system would be able to figure out what you're thinking—maybe in the next version.)

We're going to link BOOKS.DB and AUTHOR.DB. Before we do that, go ahead and remove PUBLISH.DB from the query image. (Just wanted to give you a little practice in removing tables.) All set?

I know you're ready for action, but first I have to get some important explanation stuff out of the way. You wouldn't want to jump in and create example elements without understanding what they are, would you?

What's an Example Element?

Example elements are used to link tables, but they also do a whole lot more. An example element is just a name you assign to a field so that field can be referenced in a query. When we get into calculations and other advanced query stuff, example elements will play a large role.

Note: If you're already familiar with database terminology, example elements are the same as *exclusive links* or *inner joins*.

Suppose you want to add the Last Name and First Name fields together to create a field called Name? You have to give Paradox an *example* for each field. The example name doesn't have to have anything to do with the actual field name; the example element for the Last Name field could be "last" or "cartilaginous"—it doesn't make any difference. Think of it like a variable in a mathematics equation. It doesn't matter whether you use X or Y; the only thing that matters is that you use the variable consistently.

But of course there are a few rules you have to follow when assigning names for example elements:

❍ The name can include any letter or number but no punctuation marks or other symbols.

❍ No spaces allowed.

❍ Paradox will let you use reserved words as example elements, but try to avoid them. Using reserved words can get you into trouble.

❍ You can't use example elements in BLOB fields. Remember them? Graphic, memo, formatted memo, OLE and binary are all BLOB fields. (I know this doesn't have anything to do with naming example elements but I had to put it *somewhere*.)

Creating Example Elements

You can create example elements manually or you can let Paradox do it for you. So why bother doing it yourself if you can get Paradox to do the work? Here's the deal. The automatic method is good only for joining fields in two separate tables. To create example elements within tables, you have to use the manual method (which really isn't much more difficult).

The easiest way to create an example element that links two tables is by using the Join Tables button on the Query Toolbar. When you use this method, Paradox names the elements for you and takes most of the effort out of the process.

Using the Toolbar

Let's use this method to place matching example elements in the Author ID fields of BOOKS and AUTHOR.

1. Click on the Join Tables button.

2. Click in the Author ID field for BOOKS.
   Notice that an icon attaches itself to the mouse pointer and the word "Joining" is displayed on the status bar so you can tell you're in join mode.

3. Click in the Author ID field for AUTHOR.

The join tables icon disappears from your mouse pointer as soon as you place the second example element. Paradox automatically leaves join mode as soon as you click in two fields in separate tables. You can also leave join mode by clicking on the Join Tables button.

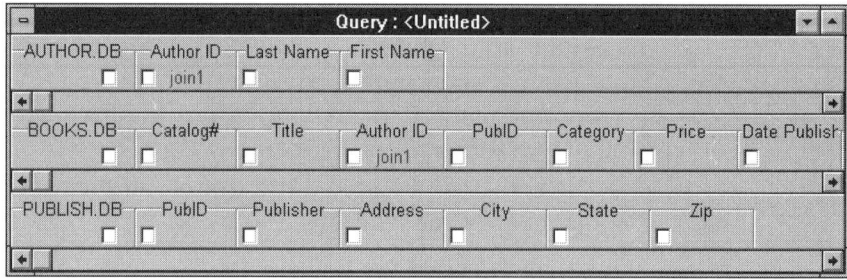

Figure 8-11: BOOKS and AUTHOR are now joined by an example element.

When you use the Join Tables button, Paradox assigns the name *join1* to the first example element. If you use the Toolbar to create more example elements for the same query image, they're named *join2, join3*, etc.

I know you can't see this in the book, but take a look at your screen. Notice that the example elements are highlighted or displayed in a different color. If your example elements aren't displayed differently, they're not example elements.

Linking More Than Two Tables

Paradox lets you link up to 24 tables in a query. Each table you use in a multitable query must contain an example element that links it with one of the other tables. You already created an example element to link BOOKS and AUTHOR. Let's add PUBLISH to the query (just click on the Add Table button and choose PUBLISH from the Select File dialog box).

Do you have to link PUBLISH to BOOKS *and* AUTHOR? Nope. Having to link every table to every other table could get cumbersome awfully fast, as well as limiting the tables that could be linked. All you have to do is link PUBLISH to *one* of the other tables. In this case, PUBLISH and BOOKS share a common field (PubID) that we can use to link the two tables.

○ Click on the Join Tables button.

○ Click in the PubID field of both the BOOKS and PUBLISH tables.

Figure 8-12: Because there's already an example element named *join1*, Paradox named the new example element *join2*.

Now you can create queries that use fields from all three tables.

Inside Scoop

You can also use data models to link tables in a query. You can use existing data models or you can create a data model when you create the query. To use an existing data model, just select the data model from the Select File dialog box that appears after you choose File, New, Query (or choose New from a query Object Inspector menu).

To create a new data model, click on the Data Model button in the Select File dialog box that's displayed as you create a new query.

Creating and using data models will be discussed when we talk about forms; I just wanted you to know that they can play a role in queries.

Doing It on Your Own

I know I've talked about the manual method versus the automatic method of creating example elements, but the manual method is actually pretty automatic. Here's all you have to do:

1. Place the selection bar in the field you want to create an example element for. For this example, move the selection bar to the Last Name field in the AUTHOR.DB table.

2. Press F5.

3. Enter a name for the example element. If you want to follow along with my examples, type **last.** If you don't care about my examples, type any nonsense word you choose.

Whew, that was tough! But seriously, that's all there is to it.

Pitfall Ahead

Just a couple of things to watch out for. Make sure the example element is highlighted or displayed in a different color. If it's not, you did something wrong. One way to mess up is to press F5 *before* you move the selection bar to the field you want. As soon as you click in a field, Paradox checks out of example element mode. So be sure your selection bar is in the right field and *then* press F5.

Here's the list of things that cause Paradox to leave example element mode: pressing the Spacebar, typing any character that can't be used in an example element (anything that's not a letter or number), or moving to another field.

Inside Scoop

What if you forget to press F5 before you type your example element? Do you have to delete it and start over? Nope—just place your insertion point in front of the word and press F5 to transform the word into an example element.

Copying Example Elements

As I mentioned earlier, the key element in example elements is consistency. If you have an example element called *name*, you can't use *names* somewhere else. If you don't have matching example elements, you'll get the Error dialog box shown in Figure 8-13.

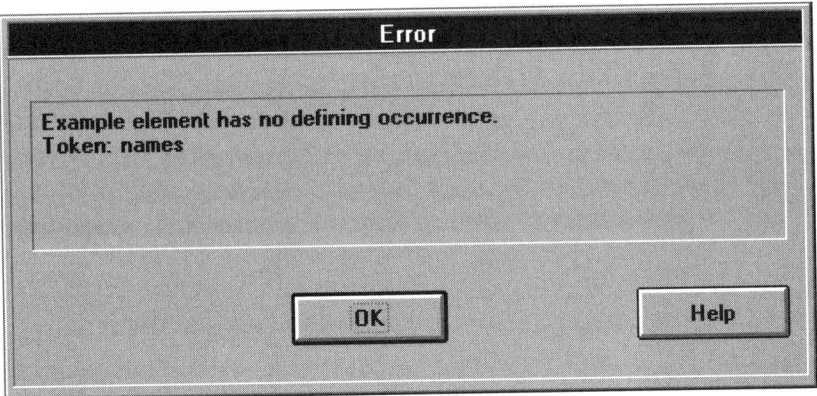

Figure 8-13: Example elements must be consistent.

Inside Scoop

Example elements do have to be consistent, but consistency doesn't include case. You can type example elements in lowercase, uppercase or mixed case—Paradox doesn't pay any attention.

The best way to ensure consistency in referencing example elements (and to save some time) is to copy the elements instead of retyping them.

○ Select the element you want to copy.

 ○ Copy the example element to the Clipboard: Click on the Copy To Clipboard button, choose Edit, Copy or press Ctrl+C (or Ctrl+Ins).

 ○ With the selection bar in the field where you want to put the copied example element, click on the Paste From Clipboard button, choose Edit, Paste or press Ctrl+V (or Shift+Ins).

Selection Conditions in Multitable Queries

In Chapter 7, we spent a lot of time talking about how to check fields and enter selection conditions. Now that we're working with multiple tables, what's different? Not much. You still have to check every field that you want to appear in the Answer table. And you can use any of the operators and wildcards in a condition.

But there's one important thing to be aware of: Don't check the same field in more than one table (unless for some reason you actually want the information displayed twice in the Answer table). For example, the Author ID fields in BOOKS and AUTHOR are linked with an example element. But if you check both fields, you'll end up with two Author ID fields in your Answer table. And don't be deceived by fields with different names. If the fields contain duplicate information, it doesn't matter what the field is called.

Selection Conditions With Example Elements

As you'll see throughout this chapter, you can combine example elements with query operators and other selection criteria. Once you've created the example element, you just refer to it as desired within a selection condition. And how do you do that?

○ With your selection bar in the field for which you want to enter the condition, press F5 and type the example element's name.

○ Or copy the example element using the techniques described earlier under "Copying Example Elements."

○ To include additional query criteria, add a comma after the example element and enter the criteria. You can add a space after the comma for display purposes, but Paradox doesn't care whether or not there's a space.

○ You can't use example elements in a single-field OR condition.

Multitable AND Queries

Now that you know how to place example elements in tables, what do you do with them? Ah, therein lies the crux of the entire query issue. (Well, not all of it. As you've seen, you can do a whole bunch without example elements. It's just that example elements take center stage in a lot of the queries we'll talk about in this chapter.)

AND queries across tables are just as easy as AND queries within one table. In a single table, all of the conditions on the same line are treated as AND conditions. In a multitable query, all of the conditions on the same line in *any* of the tables are treated as AND conditions.

Multitable OR Queries

As with OR queries in one table, OR queries across tables require a couple of extra steps. Of course, any row in the query image can contain OR conditions in a single field. And any table can contain OR conditions on separate rows. But to ask a question like "Which records in this table have titles starting with the letter T or higher?" *or* "Which records in *this* table have publishers in New York?" you have to place each question on a separate line in *each* of the tables involved, and each line must contain a different example element. It's not much different than an OR query on a single table—you just have to concentrate a little harder to make sure you match example elements and selection conditions on corresponding rows in different tables.

In Figure 8-14, the first row asks the question, "Which books have titles starting with the letter T or higher?" BOOKS and PUBLISH are linked by the example element *join1* on the PubID field. The second row asks the question, "Which books were published in New York?" The second row in both tables is linked by the example element *join2*.

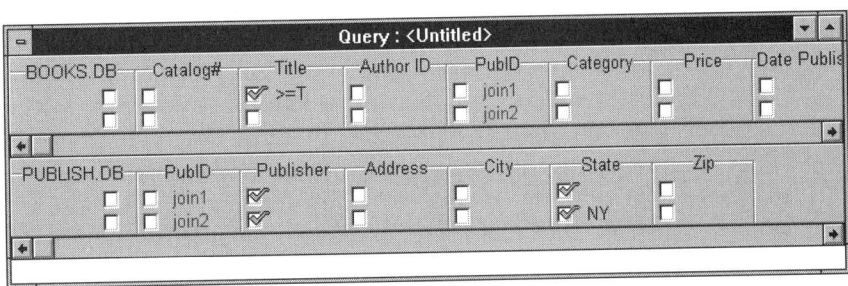

Figure 8-14: An OR query across tables.

Note: A lot of the examples in this chapter use multiple tables. But most of the techniques and operators can also be used within a single table. Some of the examples I'll use will involve single-table queries, but in those cases where I use multiple-table queries as examples, I just don't want you to think that's the only way it works.

Arithmetic Operators

Use Paradox's arithmetic operators to create *calculation expressions*. All of these operators can be used with number, short number, long integer, money and BCD fields. Addition and subtraction can be performed on date fields, and addition can be used to join values in alphanumeric fields.

Arithmetic Operators

Operator	What It's For
+	Addition (also joins alphanumeric values)
-	Subtraction
*	Multiplication
/	Division
()	Use to group operators to establish precedence

A Slick Operator

Placing a calculation expression in a field causes Paradox to include the calculation in the query. But unless you use the CALC operator, the query results won't be displayed in your Answer table. You just type **CALC** at the beginning of the expression. For example, to multiply the Qty and Price fields and display the results in a new calculated field, you would use example elements to enter the expression **CALC** *qty * price*.

Concatenation

I know I promised not to use technobabble, but *concatenation* is such a lovely word that I couldn't resist. You could live your entire life very nicely (and become a Paradox authority) without ever using the term *concatenation*. But wouldn't you rather say, "I'm using concatenation to combine these two fields" than "I'm using the addition (+) arithmetic operator to combine two alphanumeric fields into one"? Yup, that's all it means. And now at least you'll recognize the term if it pops up somewhere else in your database journey.

In addition to being a cool word, concatenation performs quite a useful function. It's easy to figure out why you'd want to perform calculations on numeric fields, but why would you want to concatenate (perform calculations on) alphanumeric fields? What's the point in combining words from one field with words from another? Take a look at Figure 8-15 and then we'll talk.

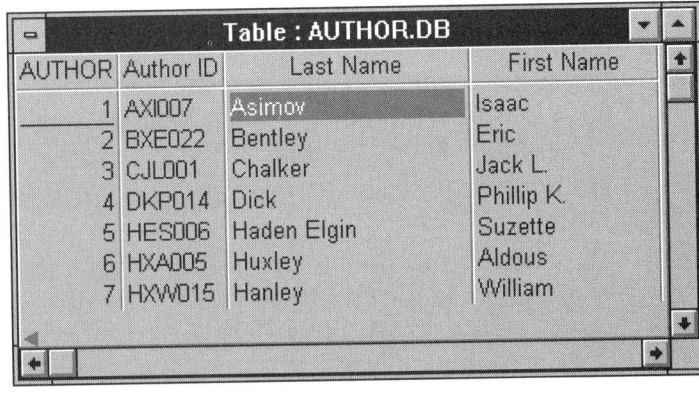

Figure 8-15: In AUTHOR.DB, each author's name is split into two fields.

In Chapter 2, I told you how important it is to chunkify–to break each piece of data into its smallest meaningful chunk. That's why we put Last Name and First Name in separate fields. And for database purposes, that's the best way to do it. It gives you a lot of flexibility in searches, forms and reports–for example, you can create a report that lists only last names.

But what if you want a list of book titles and authors? With the current configuration, you'd end up with a stilted-looking report with Last Name and First Name fields. To combine both fields so they appear together (*Isaac Asimov,* instead of *Asimov* in one field and *Isaac* in another), you use concatenation.

Here's how you do it:

1. Start a new query for AUTHOR.DB and BOOKS.DB.

2. Join AUTHOR.DB and BOOKS.DB with an example element on the Author ID field.

3. Place an example element called *last* in the Last Name field.

4. Place an example element called *first* in the First Name field.

5. Check the Title field in BOOKS.DB.

6. Don't check any fields in AUTHOR.DB.

7. Enter the following condition in any field, making sure you enter *first* and *last* as example elements. (That means you have to either press F5 before you type the example elements or copy them from the First Name and Last Name fields.)

    CALC first + " " + **last**

So what was that all about? Let's take it piece by piece:

○ CALC tells Paradox to display the results of the following calculation in a new field.

○ *first* is the example element for the First Name field. By placing this example element first, you're telling Paradox that the first name should appear in front of the last name.

○ The addition (+) operator instructs Paradox to add criteria to the expression.

○ The quotation marks enclose a space. That tells Paradox to insert a space between the first name and the last name. Without the space, the names would be bunched together. And the space has to be in quotation marks for Paradox to recognize it as an actual space. When you use a space in a selection condition, Paradox assumes you're just using it to separate criteria, unless you tell it otherwise.

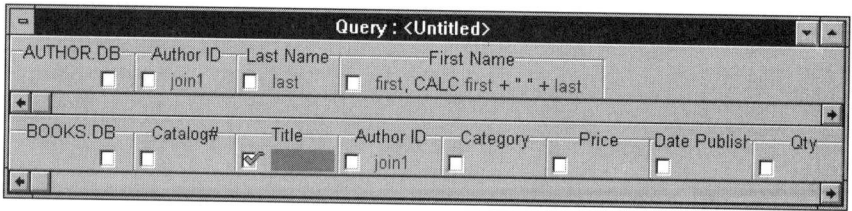

Figure 8-16: Your finished query image should look like this.

Even though you can't see it here, *first* and *last* should be highlighted or displayed in a different color.

Inside Scoop

Since a calculation expression produces a new field, it doesn't matter where you put the expression. For the calculation we're doing, you could calculate from the Last Name or First Name field, or you could use the Author ID field. The field you use is just a holding cell.

 Now run the query. (Click on the Run Query button or choose View, Run Query.) Your Answer table should look like the one in Figure 8-17.

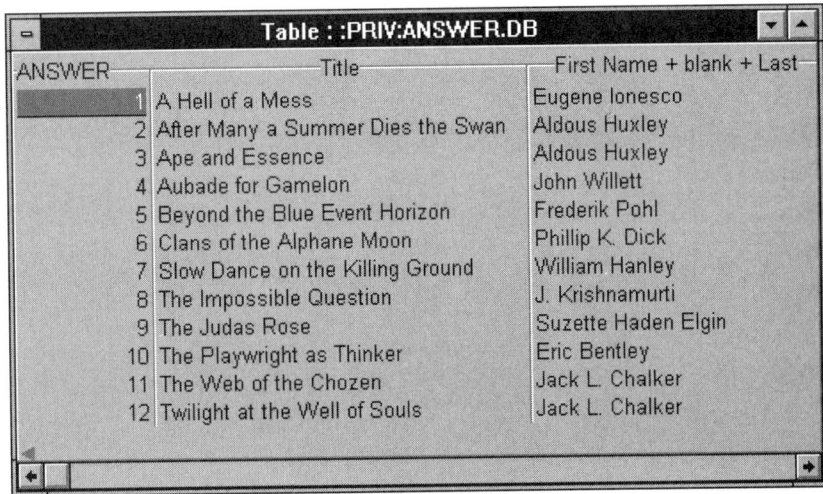

Figure 8-17: The Answer table for the concatenation query.

We're almost there. You have a respectable list of titles and authors. But take a look at the new field's name: *First Name + blank + Last*. Is that really how you want the field to appear in your report? I think not. Of course you could restructure the table and rename the field that way, but that's a lot of extra steps. Instead, how about renaming the field while you run the query?

Renaming Answer Table Fields

It's time for another slick operator. When you use CALC, Paradox automatically assigns a field name based on the fields in the calculation. Here comes AS to the rescue. The AS operator allows you to tell Paradox what you want to call the field before you run the query.

Using AS is easy—you just type **AS** followed by the field name. (Remember, AS doesn't have to be entered in uppercase characters; I'm just doing it that way so the operators stand out from the rest of the text.) Figure 8-18 shows the same calculation expression we used for Figure 8-17, with *AS Author* added to the end of the expression. This tells Paradox to perform the calculation and display the results in a new field called *Author*.

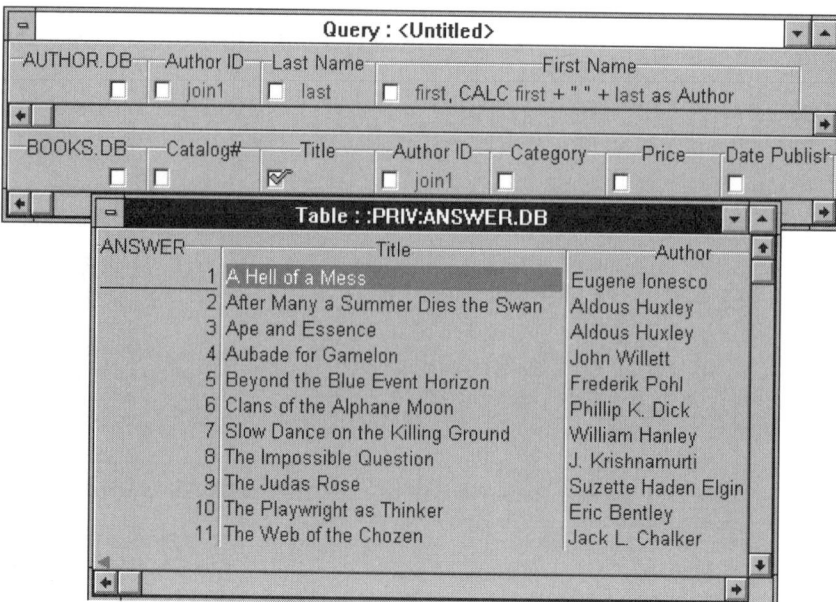

Figure 8-18: The Answer table with a new field name.

That's much better, isn't it?

You can use AS to rename *any* field in an Answer table, not just the results of calculations. If you just want to display a field with a different name, use AS without any other conditions. To get Figure 8-19, I checked the Title Field and placed the condition *AS Science Fiction* in the field. Then I placed the condition *SF* in the Category field but didn't check the field. I wanted a list of science fiction books, but I didn't want to see the category information.

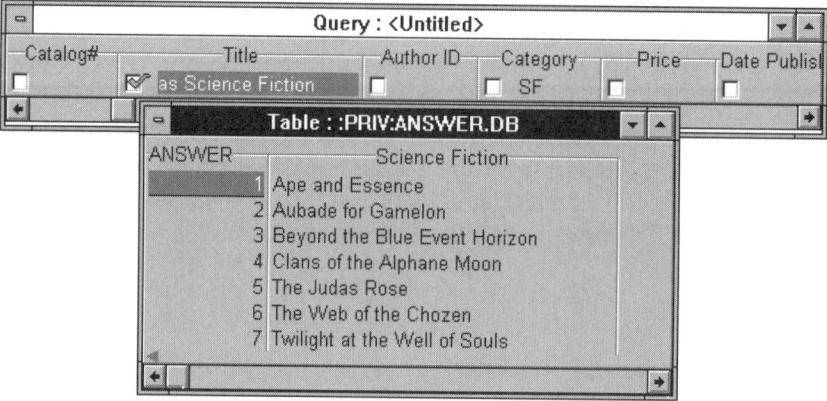

Figure 8-19: The Title field has been renamed *Science Fiction*.

This also works in multitable queries. In Figure 8-20, I renamed the Title field in BOOKS.DB and used concatenation to combine the Last Name and First Name fields in AUTHOR.DB.

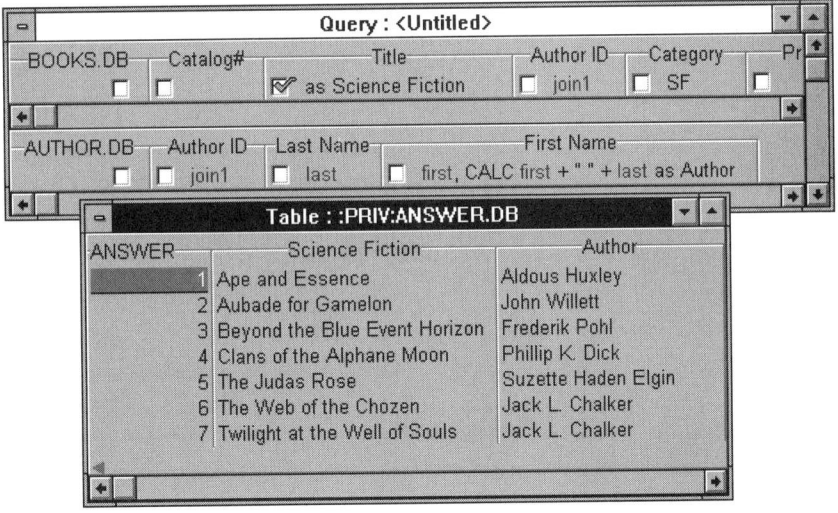

Figure 8-20: Fields have been renamed in both tables.

Calculations on Numeric Fields

Calculations with numbers aren't much different than calculations (or concatenations) with alphanumeric values. And they're also like formulas in spreadsheets. Just as you would place the formula B1 * C1 in a spreadsheet, you would use example elements and arithmetic operators to create a calculation expression in Paradox. Let's multiply the Qty field by the Price field and put the results into a new field called Total.

1. Open a new query image for BOOKS.DB.
2. Place example elements in the Qty and Price fields (I'm calling mine *qty* and *price*).
3. Don't forget to check any other fields you want displayed in the Answer table (I checked Title and Author ID).
4. In any field, enter the calculation expression shown in Figure 8-21 (I used the Author ID field).

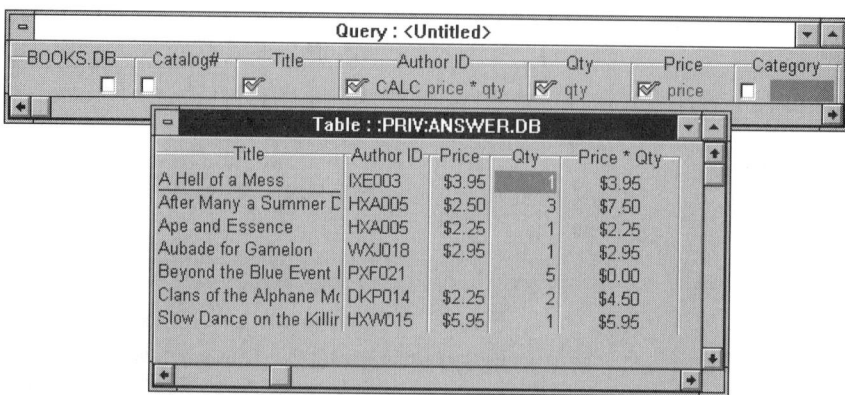

Figure 8-21: The query statement to multiply the Qty and Price fields, and the resulting Answer table.

Inside Scoop

If one of the fields in a calculated expression is blank, the calculation doesn't return a result (or it returns a blank, depending on how you look at it). For example, when you multiply Qty by Price, if the Qty *or* Price field is blank in any record, the query result for that record will be a blank field. You can tell Paradox to treat blank fields as the number zero (0) instead of as, well, blanks. Just choose Tools, System Settings, Blank As Zero.

If you use more than one arithmetic operator in a calculation expression, how does Paradox know what to do first? Simple (at least for a complex database like Paradox). First, if you use only one operator (for example, 4 + 4 + 4), Paradox has an easy time of it. It just starts from the left and works to the right. If you use more than one operator type, Paradox handles any multiplication and division first, then does any addition and subtraction. If you want Paradox to pay attention to a particular expression first, enclose the expression in parentheses.

A couple of examples:

4 + 3 * 2   The result of this expression is 9. Paradox first multiplies 3 by 2 and then adds 4 to the total.

(4 + 3) * 2   The result of this expression is 14. Because the expression 4 + 3 is grouped (by enclosing it in parentheses), Paradox first adds the numbers 4 and 3, and then multiplies the total by 2.

Calculations on Date Fields

You can use the addition (+) and subtraction (–) operators on date fields. This can be handy if you want to calculate a date that's a certain number of days earlier or later than the date in a field. For example, suppose you have a PURCHASE table that indicates the date each book was sold, and your terms are "payment within 20 days." Figure 8-22 shows a query that adds 20 days to the Date Sold field and displays the result in a field called Payment Due. (Notice that I used an example element for the Date Sold field.)

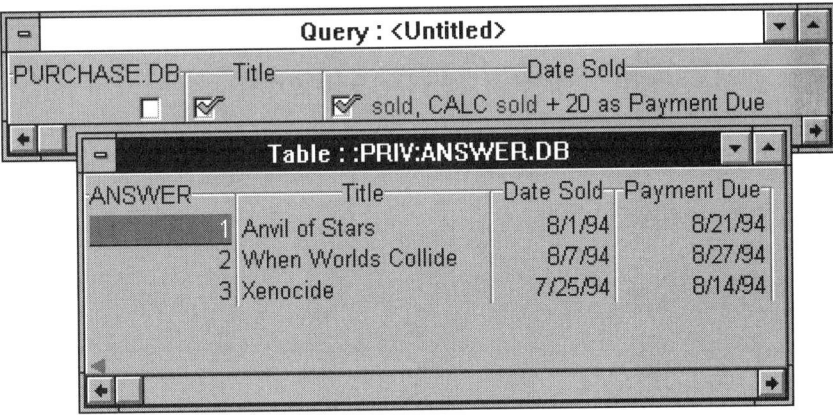

Figure 8-22: Query and Answer table for date calculation.

There's a date operator, TODAY, that allows you to search for dates relative to the current system date. Use the addition (+) or subtraction (–) operator to find dates a certain number of days earlier or later than today's date. Use comparison operators (<, >, <=, >=) to find all dates earlier or later than today's date.

Using Summary Operators

So far, all of the calculations have returned answers for particular records. But what about queries that ask questions of groups of records? You can find out stuff like the total number of science fiction books in stock. Or the average price of books. Or which book(s) are the highest priced.

The following operators can be used to return answers on groups of records:

AVERAGE	Calculates average of values in a group. Can be used with all field types except BLOBs, alpha, logical and byte.
COUNT	Returns the number of values in a field. Can be used with all field types except BLOBs.
MIN	Returns the lowest value in a field. Can be used with all field types except BLOBs.
MAX	Returns the highest value in a field. Can be used with all field types except BLOBs.
SUM	Calculates the total of all values in a field. Can be used only with number, currency, short number, long integer, BCD and Autoincrement types.

The following operators are used to modify the above summary operators (both of them can be used with all field types except BLOBs):

ALL	Calculates summary based on all values in a group, including duplicates.
UNIQUE	Calculates summary based on all unique values in a group (no duplicates).

Defining Groups

And you thought check marks were just for displaying fields in Answer tables. Nope. They do double duty. They also tell Paradox how you want to group records in summary calculations.

○ Define an entire field as a group by placing a check (of any type) in the field's check box. Figure 8-23 shows an example where a check has been placed in the Category field and the statement CALC SUM has been placed in the Qty field. Because no other conditions have been specified, the Answer table returns a total value for each category.

○ Define a group of records within a field by adding selection conditions. In Figure 8-24, to find out how many science fiction books I have in stock, I checked the Category Field and entered the condition SF; I then used the same CALC SUM statement I used in Figure 8-23.

○ To include all table records in a calculation, don't check any fields. As you can see in Figure 8-25, the statements CALC SUM in the Qty field and CALC AVERAGE in the Price field give you an Answer table with two new fields. The first field displays the total number of books in stock, and the second field displays the average price per book.

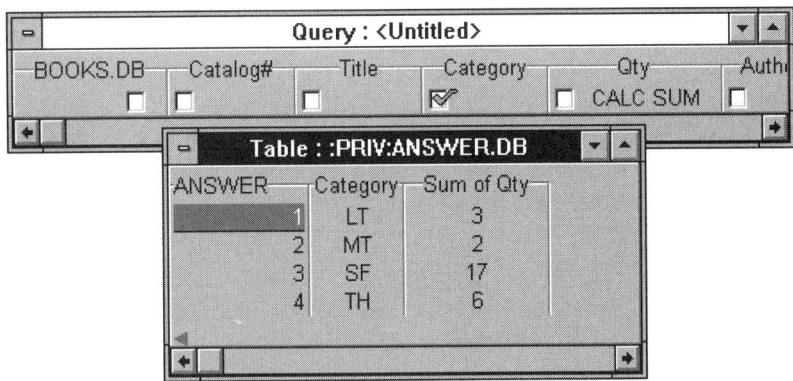

Figure 8-23: The entire Category field is defined as a group.

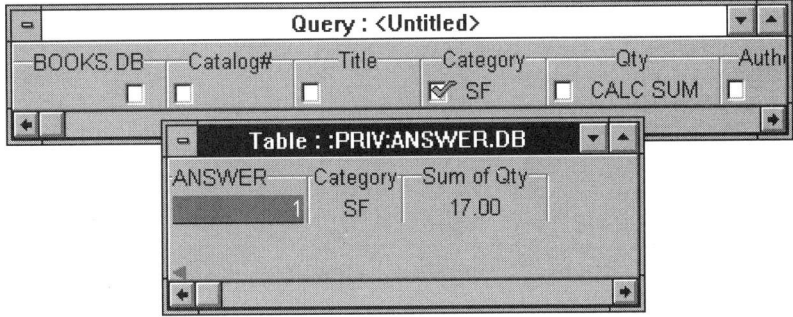

Figure 8-24: All SF records within the Category field are defined as a group.

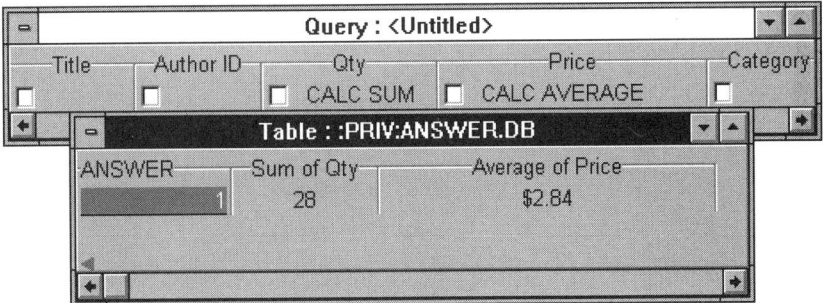

Figure 8-25: Because no fields are checked, the summary operator (SUM) works on all records in the table.

Using ALL & UNIQUE

By default, the grouping for the COUNT, MAX and MIN operators is "unique." That means that these operators will find only unique values within a group. To reverse the action of one of these unique operators, add the ALL operator. In Figure 8-26, I used CALC COUNT in the Category field to get the total number of books in each category. What happened? Well, because COUNT returns only unique values, I ended up with an answer that tells me how many different categories exist. Thus the answer *1* for each category. How helpful is that? Probably not very. To get the answer I want, I have to add ALL after the CALC COUNT statement, as shown in Figure 8-27.

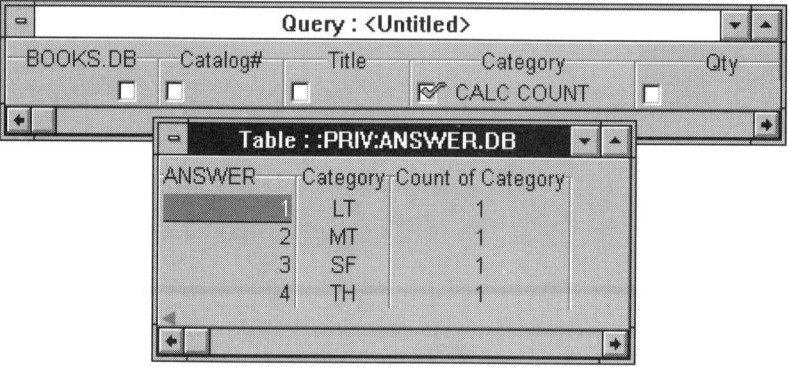

Figure 8-26: A CALC COUNT query on the Category field.

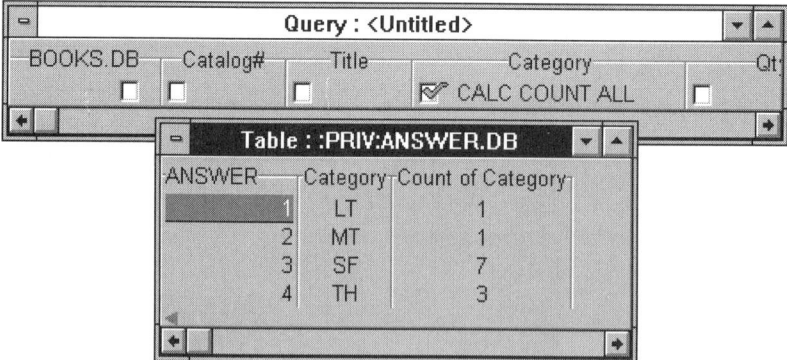

Figure 8-27: A CALC COUNT ALL query on the Category field.

The default grouping for AVERAGE and SUM is "all." The UNIQUE operator reverses the default grouping for AVERAGE and SUM the same way ALL does for COUNT, MAX and MIN.

QUERIES THAT CHANGE DATA

Paradox provides three special operators that allow you to make changes to the data in your original table: CHANGETO, DELETE and INSERT. Because it can be hard or impossible to undo these changes (except by retyping data), I'm starting this section with a Pitfall Ahead.

Pitfall Ahead

Before you perform a query that changes data, make a backup copy of your original table. Don't just copy the DB file to a floppy disk—that won't copy any files that might be associated with the table. Instead, use Paradox's Copy command. From the Project Viewer, right-click on the table's name and choose Copy from the Object Inspector menu. Or choose Tools, Utilities, Copy. Give the table a different name, something like BOOKS-BK instead of BOOKS. Then, if the query goes haywire, just rename the unchanged table—give it its original name to overwrite the changed table. Paradox does place the changed records into a temporary table called CHANGED, but because of the nature of temporary tables, I don't like to depend on the CHANGED table for my backup.

Got that? Now I can continue. You create selection conditions for queries that change data the same way you create them for any query. With one difference: You don't check any fields. CHANGETO, DELETE and INSERT queries don't create Answer tables, so checking fields to display would be meaningless (and besides, Paradox won't let you).

CHANGETO Queries

What if you assign the code SF to the science fiction category, and then your boss decides the code should be SC? Kinda stupid, but hey, the boss is always right, right? Even when she's wrong. Only problem is, you've already entered data for 952 records, 847 of which use the SF code. Do you mutter under your breath and start retyping? Do you storm out of the office? Do you put a curse on your boss? No need for any of these drastic measures; Paradox's CHANGETO operator allows you to make global changes to field data.

So what do you say to your boss? Just smile sweetly and say, "Gosh, that's a tall order, but I can handle it. And by the way, that's a *great* idea." NEVER let on that it's really a piece of cake.

Here's what you do:

1. Open a new query image for BOOKS.DB.
2. Place the condition SF in the Category field.
3. Follow SF with a comma (and a space if desired).
4. Type **CHANGETO SC**.

Figure 8-28: Your query image should look like this.

Now run the query.

Figure 8-29: The ERRORCHG table.

Hey, what happened? Why are all these records in an error table? There's a simple answer. Way back in Chapter 4, we added a validity check to the Category field—it's linked via a lookup table with CTGORY.DB. Paradox won't allow you to change data in a way that violates validity checks or referential integrity links. So instead of changing the data, Paradox put a copy of the records you were trying to change into a temporary table called ERRORCHG.

Before you can change the data in the Category field, you have to remove the link to the lookup table. Refer to Chapter 4 for more info, but here's a quick review: Restructure BOOKS.DB, choose Table Lookup from the Table Properties list, select CTGORY.DB and choose Erase. When you're done with the CHANGETO query, you can re-establish the links.

Now you can go back and run the CHANGETO query shown in Figure 8-28. Here's what happens when you run a valid CHANGETO query: all of the records containing the old data are placed in a temporary table called CHANGED, as shown in Figure 8-30. Notice that the records in the Category field still say SF. The CHANGED table is displayed as soon as you run the query. Open your original table to see what's actually been changed. As you can see in Figure 8-31, there are no entries for SF–they've all been changed to SC.

Figure 8-30: The CHANGED table.

BOOKS	Catalog#	Title	Author ID	Category
1	1	Twilight at the Well of Souls	CJL001	SC
2	2	After Many a Summer Dies the Swan	HXA005	LT
3	3	The Judas Rose	HES006	SC
4	4	The Impossible Question	KXJ009	MT
5	5	The Playwright as Thinker	BXE022	TH
6	6	A Hell of a Mess	IXE003	TH
7	7	Clans of the Alphane Moon	DKP014	SC
8	8	The Web of the Chozen	CJL001	SC
9	9	Ape and Essence	HXA005	SC
10	10	Slow Dance on the Killing Ground	HXW015	TH
11	11	Beyond the Blue Event Horizon	PXF021	SC
12	12	Aubade for Gamelon	WXJ018	SC

Figure 8-31: BOOKS.DB with changed data.

You can also use CHANGETO with calculation expressions. Suppose you want to increase the price of each book by 25 percent. Create a query like the one in Figure 8-32.

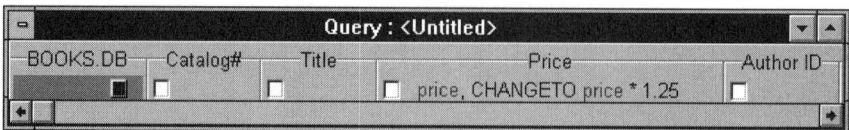

Figure 8-32: This CHANGETO query will increase the price of each book by 25 percent.

Inside Scoop

Use CHANGETO with BLANK to delete data from specified fields. To delete all data from the Category field, just enter the condition **CHANGETO BLANK**. To delete all SC codes from the Category field, enter the condition **SC, CHANGETO BLANK**.

DELETE Queries

The DELETE operator eliminates records from a table. I repeat, the DELETE operator eliminates records from a table. That means gone. Forever. If you didn't fully comprehend the Pitfall Ahead at the beginning of this section, go back immediately and don't return until you've backed up your original table.

Now that I have your attention, I can tell you that the consequences are not quite as dire as I painted them. The deleted records are placed in a temporary table called DELETED, and you can use the Add command to add records from the DELETED table back into your original table. But don't get too complacent—DELETED is a *temporary* table, and it's awfully easy to make a temporary table disappear.

As with CHANGETO, Paradox won't allow you to delete data in a way that violates validity checks or referential integrity links. Records that would cause a problem are placed in a temporary table called ERRORDEL. Before you attempt to delete records in a table that uses links or validity checks, remove the links. When you're done, you can reestablish them.

Unlike CHANGETO, the DELETE operator can be entered only in the far left column of the query image (the one that contains the table name). And you don't even have to type the whole word. When you hold down the left mouse button on the far left column, Paradox displays the pop-up menu shown in Figure 8-33.

Figure 8-33: Choose Delete from this pop-up menu.

You can also press the Spacebar to open the pop-up menu. Or, with your selection bar in the far left column, you can just type the letter *d*.

You've made your backup copy, haven't you? Because we're about to delete all of the records that contain SC in the Category field.

1. Open a new query image for BOOKS.DB.

2. Place the DELETE operator in the far left column.

3. Type **SC** in the Category field. (Remember not to check any fields.)

4. Run the query.

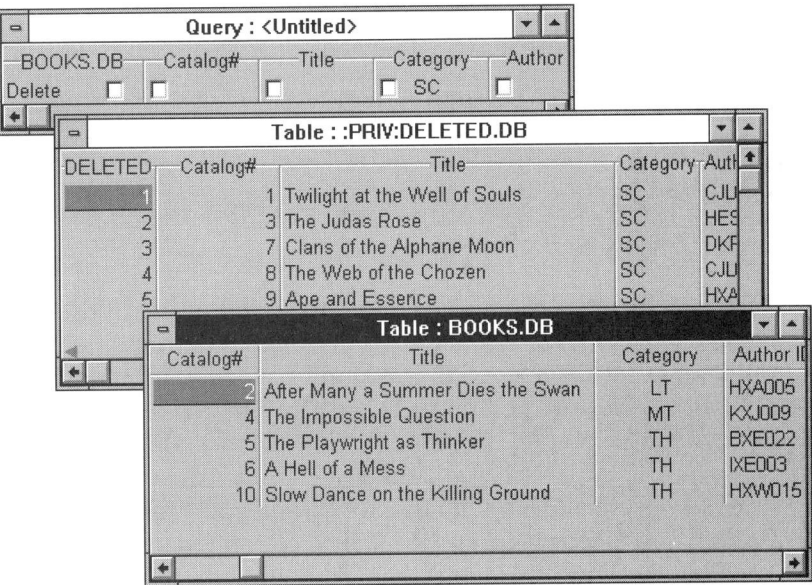

Figure 8-34: The deleted records are placed in the temporary DELETED table, and all of the science fiction books' records are gone from the BOOKS.DB.

The Inclusion Operator

When you use example elements to link tables in a query, the Answer table displays only those records that meet the conditions you specify in both tables. In other words, the records that don't match all conditions are *excluded*. That's why the use of example elements to link tables is called an exclusive link (or *inner join*). In Figure 8-35, I linked the BOOKS and PURCHASE tables by the Title field. I then checked the Title field in BOOKS and the Date Sold and Qty fields in PURCHASE. Because any books that weren't sold don't exist in the PURCHASE table, only titles that were sold are listed in the Answer table.

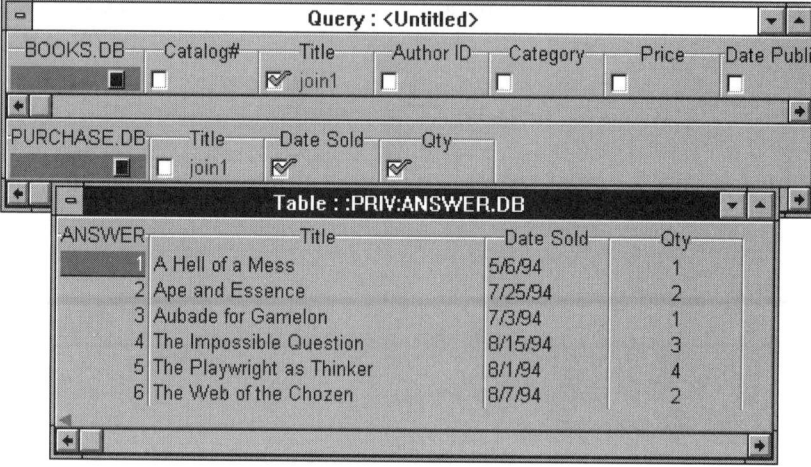

Figure 8-35: This figure shows an exclusive link between BOOKS and PURCHASE.

But what if you want to see all of the titles, even those that didn't sell? You need a way to tell Paradox to include all of the records from BOOKS, even if they don't have matching entries in PURCHASE. And how do you do that? With an *inclusive link* (or *outer join*). The *inclusion operator* (!) allows you to do just that. It's deceptively simple. All you do is place an exclamation mark after the example element in the table for which you want all records displayed. I did that in Figure 8-36. The selection conditions are exactly the same as in Figure 8-35, with one exception: the exclamation mark after the example operator in the Title field of BOOKS. But notice that the Answer table gives you a list of all books, whether or not they have matching entries in the PURCHASE table.

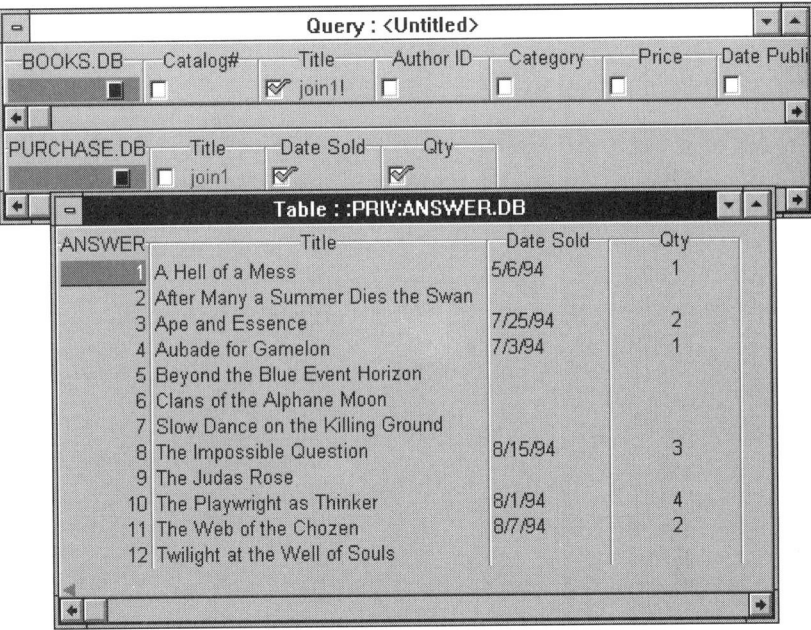

Figure 8-36: This figure shows an inclusive link between BOOKS and PURCHASE.

MOVING ON

Are we done with queries yet? Apparently you're not, if you're still asking questions. But I am. Enough, already. It's time to move on to forms. You'll like forms—we get to play around with design stuff to make the forms look pretty. And there's even a Forms Expert to do some of the grunt work for you.

9 ᖴORMS 101

ᗯe've already talked about forms a little bit. In Chapter 5, you learned how to enter data in a default form. And you learned that forms can streamline the process of entering data. But there must be more to it than that; otherwise, they wouldn't have made me write two whole chapters on forms. I'll start by giving you an expanded list of reasons to use forms:

○ A form can display more fields than you can see in Table View. Take a look at Figures 9-1 and 9-2 following this list. Figure 9-1 shows BOOKS.DB in Table View. You can't see all of the fields, so data entry would require a bunch of scrolling back and forth. Figure 9-2 shows BOOKS.DB in a Form window. Notice that all of the fields are visible.

○ You can design custom forms that match printed reports or forms that your office uses.

○ A form can include fields from more than one table.

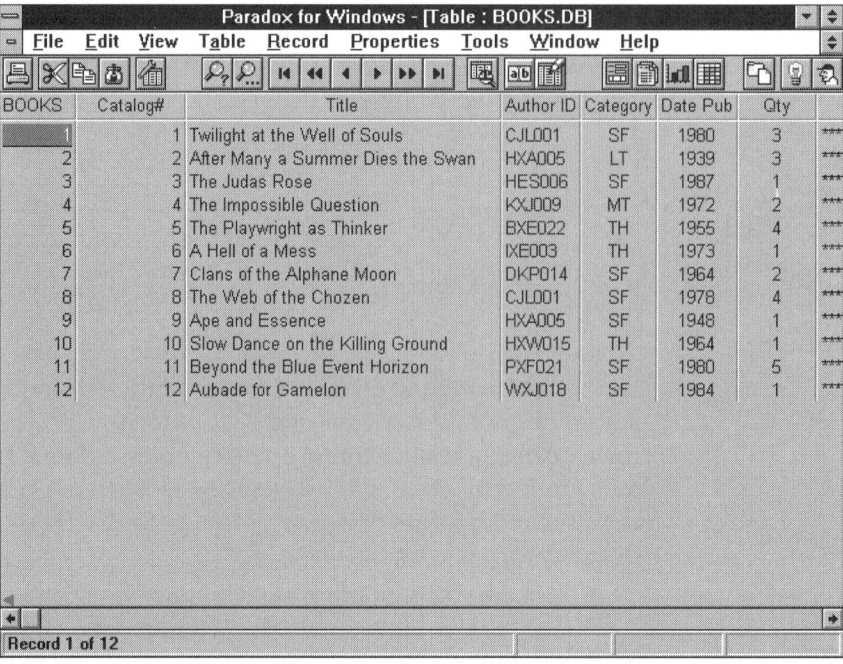

Figure 9-1: BOOKS.DB in Table View.

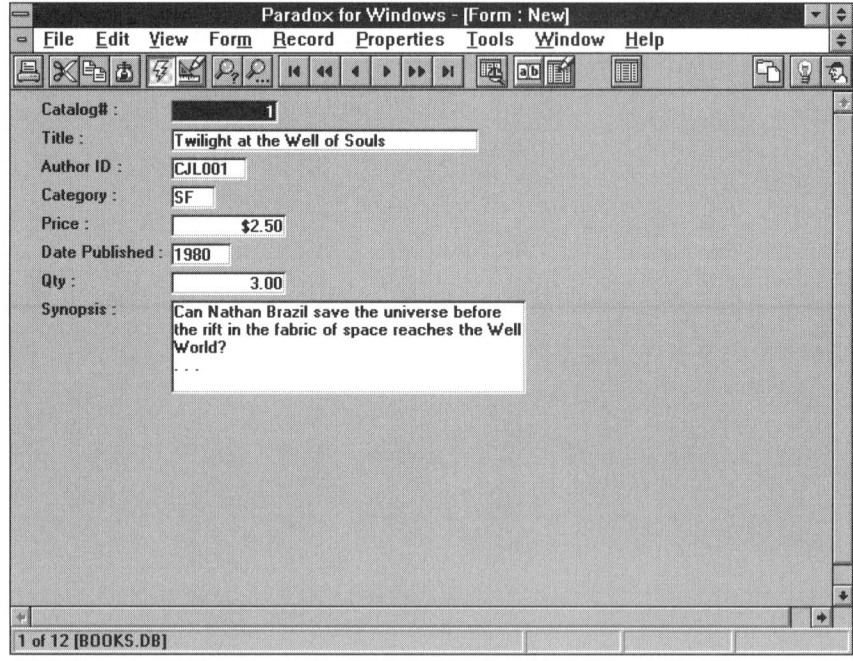

Figure 9-2: BOOKS.DB in a Form window.

In this chapter you'll learn about using Paradox's default Quick Form as a starting point for your customized form. Then we'll call on an Expert—I'll walk you though form creation using the Experts feature to guide you. And finally, we'll use the Data Model and Design Layout dialog boxes to create a basic form layout.

CREATING A FORM

There are three basic techniques for creating a new form. Here's a quick overview before we get bogged down in those messy but oh so necessary details:

1. Start with the default Quick Form and customize it as you wish.

   ○ With your table onscreen, click on the QuickForm button or press F7.

   ○ From the Form window, click on the Design button or press F8.

   ○ Customize the form.

2. Use the Forms Expert.

   ○ From any Toolbar, click on the Expert button. Or choose Help, Experts. Then click on the Form button in the Expert Control Panel.

   ○ You can also start the Form Expert by right-clicking on the Forms button from the Desktop Toolbar or the Project Viewer. Choose New from the Object Inspector menu and choose Form Expert from the New Form dialog box.

   ○ Make choices from the Form Expert windows.

   ○ When you have completed your choices for one step, click on the Next button to move to the next step.

   ○ When you've completed all the steps, click on the Create button to tell Paradox to create the form.

   ○ Customize the form as desired.

3. Do it from scratch.

   ○ Right-click on the Forms button from the Desktop Toolbar or the Project Viewer and choose New from the Object Inspector menu. Or choose File, New, Form from the pull-down menu.

   ○ Then choose Data Model/Layout Diagram from the New Form dialog box. (You can also choose Blank to create a form that's not tied to any tables.)

○ From the Data Model dialog box, choose the tables to include in the form and define links between them. Choose OK to continue.

○ In the Design Layout dialog box, choose a general layout for your form (arrange records by columns or rows; display records in tabular format, one at a time, multiple records on a page, etc.). Choose OK to continue.

○ In the Form Design window, design and customize the form.

As you can see, no matter which method you use to get going, you end up at the same place: the Form Design window. That's where all the action takes place. The technique you use to begin a new form is really a matter of choice, and by the end of this chapter you'll have enough information to make an intelligent choice.

We'll go through each method, discussing how-tos, whys and wherefores, and lots of other stuff as we take each path to its conclusion in the Form Design window. The techniques for using the Form Design window are the same no matter which path leads you to it. So once we've covered different methods for getting there, we'll zoom in on the Form Design window and stay there for the rest of this chapter and all of the next.

Inside Scoop

It doesn't matter how you get to the Form Design window. Once you're there, you can make any changes you like. You can start from a Quick Form and transform that boring default form into something entirely different. You can use the Form Expert to create a basic layout and then customize to your heart's content. Or you can use the Data Model and Design Layout dialog boxes to get you going and create your design in the Form Design window.

Starting With a Quick Form

This is the fastest way to get going with a form. That's the big plus. The minus: this method doesn't give you as much initial help as the other methods. But if you just want to make a few simple design changes to a single table form, this method can be just the ticket.

Here's what you do:

1. Open the table that you want to create the form for. For this example, open BOOKS.DB. Use one of the following methods to open the table:

    ○ From the Desktop Toolbar, click on the Open Table button and choose the table you want.

    ○ From the Project Viewer, double-click on the table's name. Or right-click on the table's name and choose View from the Object Inspector menu.

2. From Table View, click on the Quick Form button. Or press F7. This takes you to the Form window for BOOKS.DB, as shown in Figure 9-3.

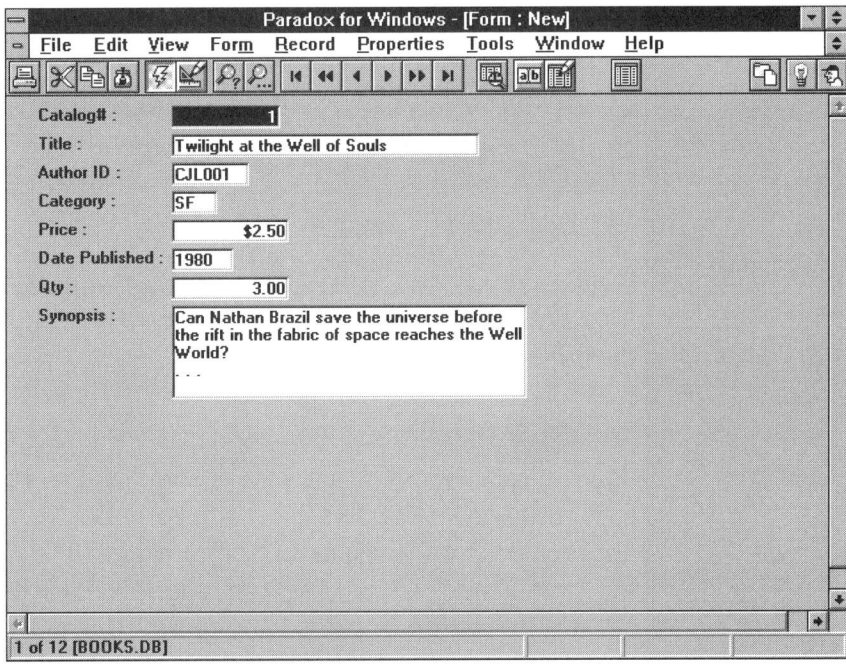

Figure 9-3: The Form window allows you to view and edit your data, but there's one more step before you can make design changes to the form.

3. Click on the Design button or press F8 to switch to the Form Design window shown in Figure 9-4.

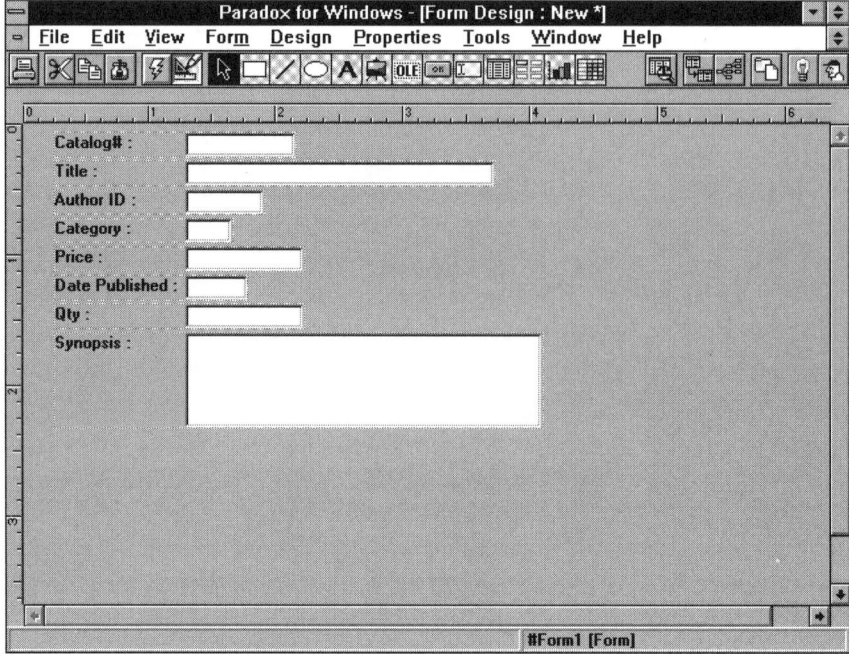

Figure 9-4: The Form Design window.

This is where you do your form design stuff—all sorts of cool things. But hold your horses for the moment—I still have to show you the other ways to get here.

Inside Scoop

You can quickly switch among the Form Design, Form View and Table View windows. From the Form Design window, just click on the View Data button or press F8 to return to the Form window. From the Form window, click on the Table View button or press F7 to return to Table View. Just reverse the process to get back to the Form Design window. Click on the Quick Form button or press F7 to switch to the Form window and click on the Design button or press F8 to switch to the Form Design window.

Using the Form Expert

The Form Expert walks you through the process of creating a form. You add tables, define links, and choose the basic style and layout. Is the Form Expert easier than the Data Model and Design Layout method? Not necessarily—it's just different, and I'll fill you in on its strengths and weaknesses as we go through it.

The main weakness as well as the major strength is that the Expert doesn't give you a whole lot of flexibility in the initial design. The style you pick contains its own design elements, some of which you might not choose on your own. This is great if one of Paradox's predefined style sheets works for you without modifications. But if that isn't the case, you don't get an opportunity to make changes until you get to the Form Designer. Depending on your needs, using the Data Model/Layout Diagram method lets you do some additional customization before you get to the Form Designer. You'll see what I mean a little later.

Opening the Form Expert

Follow these steps to open the Form Expert:

1. Click on the Expert button to open the Expert Control Panel dialog box shown in Figure 9-5.

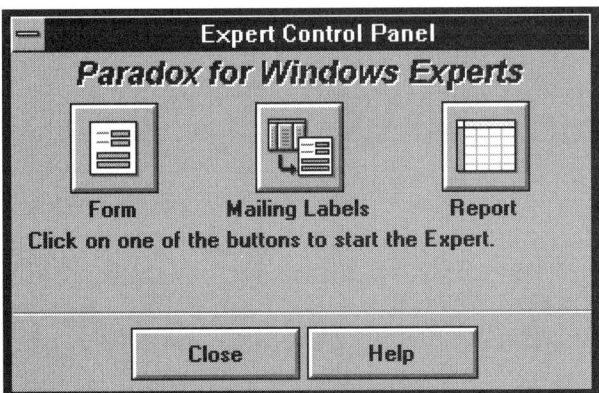

Figure 9-5: The Expert Control Panel.

2. Choose Form. This takes you to Step 1 of the Form Expert, as shown in Figure 9-6.

    You can also start the Form Expert by right-clicking on the Forms button from the Desktop Toolbar or the Project Viewer. Choose New from the Object Inspector menu and choose Form Expert from the New Form dialog box.

Now we'll go through the Form Expert. As you'll see, the Form Expert skips a few steps when you use only one table because there aren't as many decisions to make.

Choosing the Form Layout

Step 1 of the Form Expert is where you choose the basic form layout. The left side of the window displays samples of each layout choice. As you click on a radio button, the layout sample for that choice is highlighted to give you an idea of the result. You can also click directly on a design layout to activate the radio button for that option.

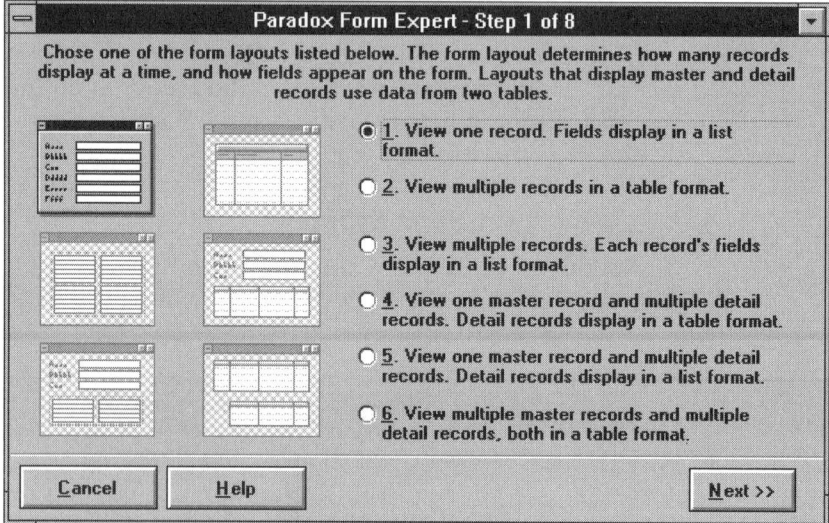

Figure 9-6: This is where you start answering questions about your form.

Notice the Cancel and Help buttons at the bottom of the window. Every Expert window contains these two buttons. You can choose Cancel from any point in the Form Expert (keep in mind that canceling abandons everything you've done in the Expert). And choosing Help takes you to an online Help window for the current step.

Also notice the Next button, which takes you to the next step. When we move to step 2, there will also be a Previous button that allows you to return to the previous step.

The following list describes your choices. Keep in mind that these layouts are just starting points—you'll be able to mess around with them later.

○ **View one record:** This format uses only one table, and only one record at a time will display on each page of your form. The fields will be arranged in a simple list format.

○ **View multiple records in a table format:** This format uses one table, but it displays multiple records on each page in a tabular format that looks sort of like what you see in Table View.

○ **View multiple records:** This format uses one table and displays multiple records with the fields in each record arranged in a list format.

○ **View one master record and multiple detail records:** The main table (we'll talk about master and detail tables in a little bit) is displayed in list format (one record at a time), and the detail (subordinate table) is displayed in tabular format (multiple records at a time).

○ **View one master record and multiple detail records:** The main table is displayed in list format (one record at a time), and the detail table is displayed with multiple records as in the above layout, but each record is displayed in list, rather than tabular, format.

○ **View multiple master records and multiple detail records, both in a table format:** The main table and detail table are both displayed in tabular format.

When you've decided which layout you want, click on the Next button. For now, choose View one record.

Choosing the Master Table

Step 2 of the Form Expert is where you choose the main table to include in the form. Notice that it asks you to select a *master table*. The master table is the main table in your form. If you use only one table in the form (if you chose any of the single-table formats in step 1), that table is considered the master.

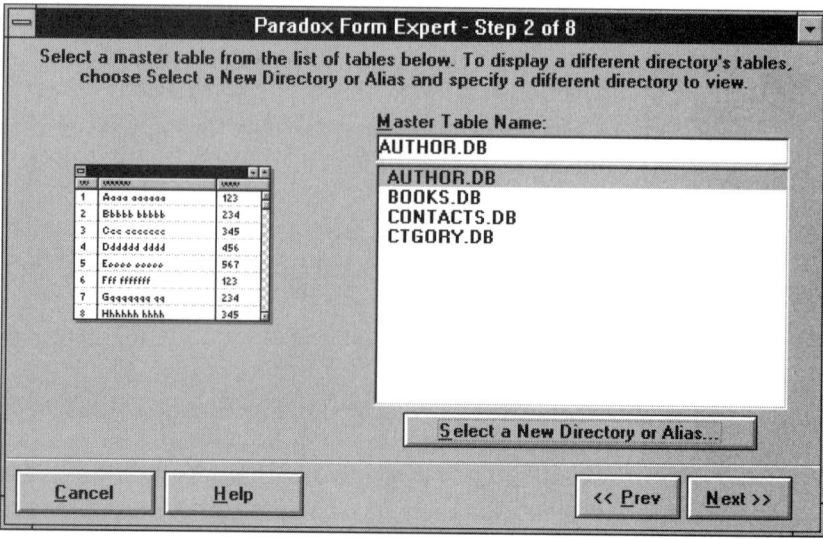

Figure 9-7: This is where you select a table for your form.

Notice that there's now a Previous button to the left of the Next button. You can click on the Previous button from any step to return to the previous step. This is great if you change your mind or think of new considerations as you work through the Expert. You can go back to any step and edit your choices.

To choose the Master table (choose BOOKS.DB):

○ Click on the table's name in the Master Table Name list.

○ Or type the name in the Master Table Name text box.

○ Or double-click on the table's name. This takes you right to the next step without clicking on the Next button.

○ If the table is in a different directory, click on the Select A New Directory Or Alias... button and choose the directory, drive and/or alias from the Directory Browser.

○ Click on the Next button when you're done.

Selecting Fields

Because we chose a single-table layout, the Form Expert skipped steps 3 and 4, which have to do with choosing detail tables and defining links between the tables. We'll return to those steps after we're done with our single-table example. One thing at a time.

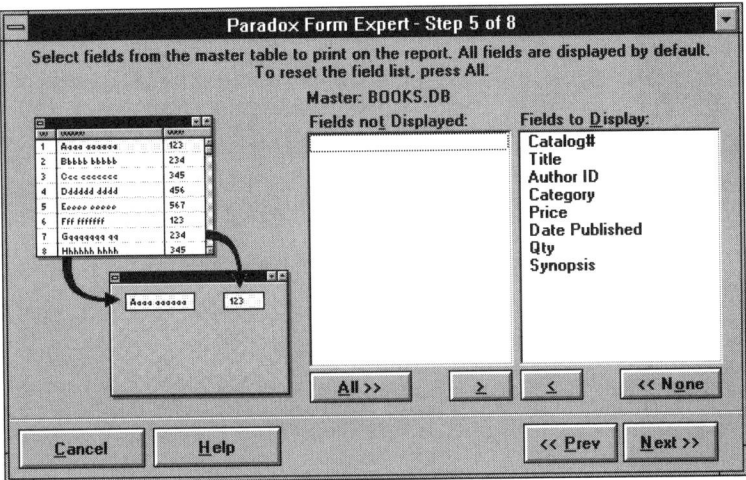

Figure 9-8: This is where you choose the fields to display on your form.

Notice that all of the fields in BOOKS.DB are listed in the Fields to Display list. By default, the form includes all of the fields from your selected table.

○ To remove a field, select the field and click on the << button just below the Fields To Display list. This moves the field into the Fields Not Displayed list. You can also double-click on a field name to move it directly to the Fields Not Displayed list.

○ Choose None to remove all fields from the Fields To Display list. This can be useful if you want the form to include only a few fields. Rather than removing a whole bunch of fields one at a time, you can start with all of your fields in the Fields Not Displayed list.

○ Move fields into the Fields To Display list by selecting the field in the Fields Not Displayed list and clicking on the >> button just below the Fields Not Displayed list. You can also double-click on a field name in the Fields Not Displayed list to move it directly to the Fields To Display list.

For our example, leave all the fields in the Fields To Display list, but before you move on, play around a bit by moving some fields back and forth. When you're ready to continue, click on the Next button.

Selecting the Display Format

Hey, we skipped another step! That's because we're working with a single table and didn't have to choose any fields for a detail table, which is what step 6 is for. So we'll have to return to step 6 later. Step 7 is where you tell Paradox how to display the form.

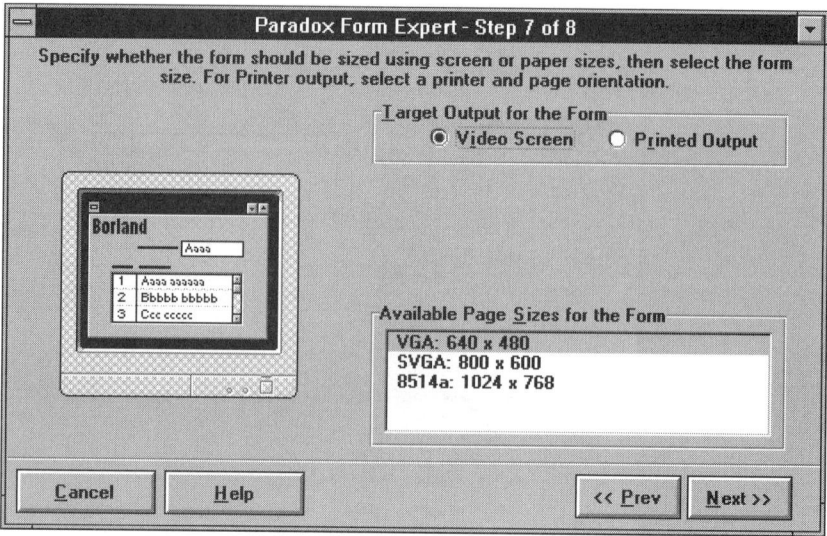

Figure 9-9: Step 7 of the Form Expert.

In this Expert window, Paradox asks you a series of questions:

○ **What is the target of the form?** Choose Video screen if you plan to use the form only for onscreen viewing and editing; choose Printed output if you plan to print the form. (If you choose Printed output, you'll still be able to view and edit the form onscreen.) For now, choose Printed output to display the questions shown in Figure 9-10.

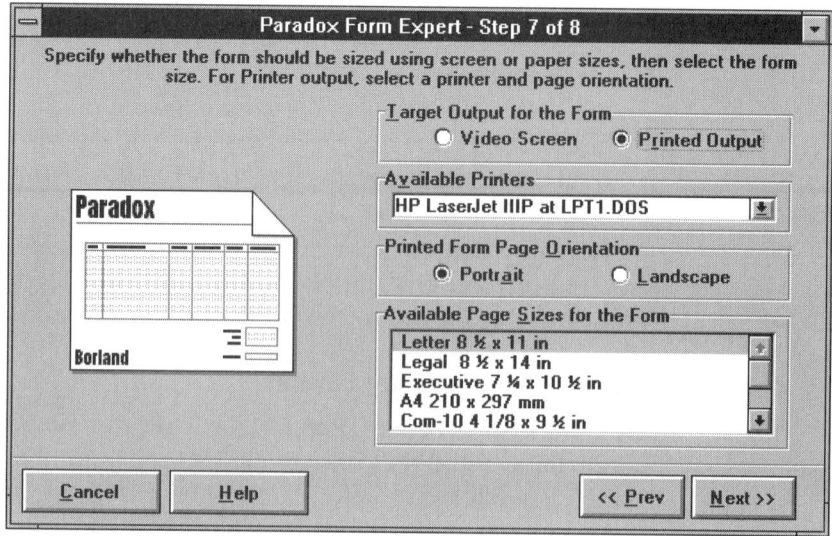

Figure 9-10: When you choose Printed output, Paradox adds a question about page orientation.

○ *How do you want to orient the page?* Choose portrait to display the form in a vertical format like the sample displayed on the left side of Figure 9-10. Choose landscape if you want the form displayed across the longer side of the page (you can see a sample by clicking on Landscape). Here's a tip for remembering which is which: Think of paintings—a portrait painting is usually taller than it is wide, and a landscape painting is usually wider than it is tall. I have these little portrait and landscape images in my head when I choose page orientation. (*Note:* You don't get to choose an orientation when Video Screen is selected.)

○ *What page size would you like?* When Printed Output is selected, you can choose from several standard paper and envelope sizes. Just pick the one you want. When Video Screen is selected, you choose among different video resolutions (the choices you get will depend on the capabilities of your monitor and video driver). Take a look back at Figure 9-9 to see a list of Video Screen page sizes.

For now, choose Video Screen, VGA: 640 x 480, and click on the Next button.

Choosing a Style

In step 8 (the final step), you choose a predefined style sheet to use for your form. When you select one of the style sheets, a sample is displayed in the left half of the window. Each style sheet contains specific appearance attributes for form objects. Once you get into the Form Design window, you can make changes, but the style sheet gives you an overall look to start with.

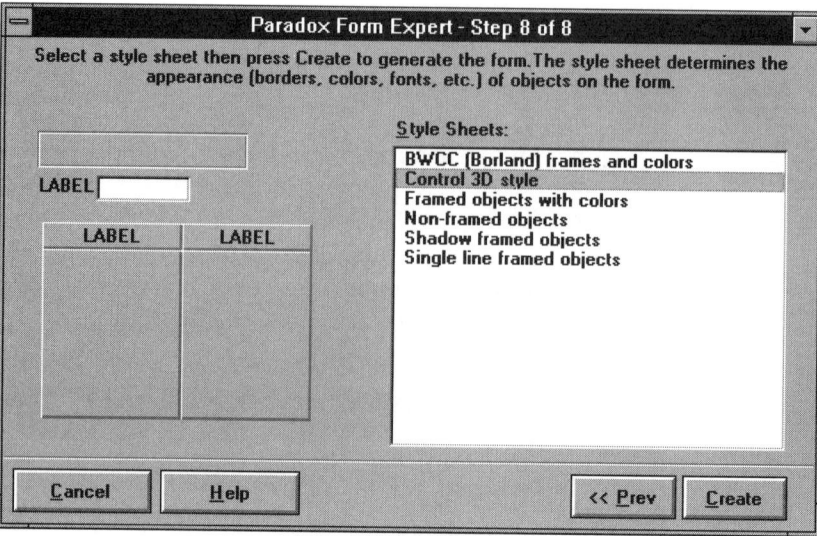

Figure 9-11: The last step of the Form Expert.

Notice that the Next button has been replaced by a Create button. When you click on the Create button, Paradox creates the form using the layout you've specified.

All you do now is select the style sheet you want to use and click on the Create button. Choose the *Shadow framed objects* option (the only reason for the choice is that I think it looks cool).

When you click on the Create button, Paradox goes through a bunch of machinations while it's creating the form. You'll see a message that tells you to "please wait" while the form is being completed. Your completed form should look like the one in Figure 9-12.

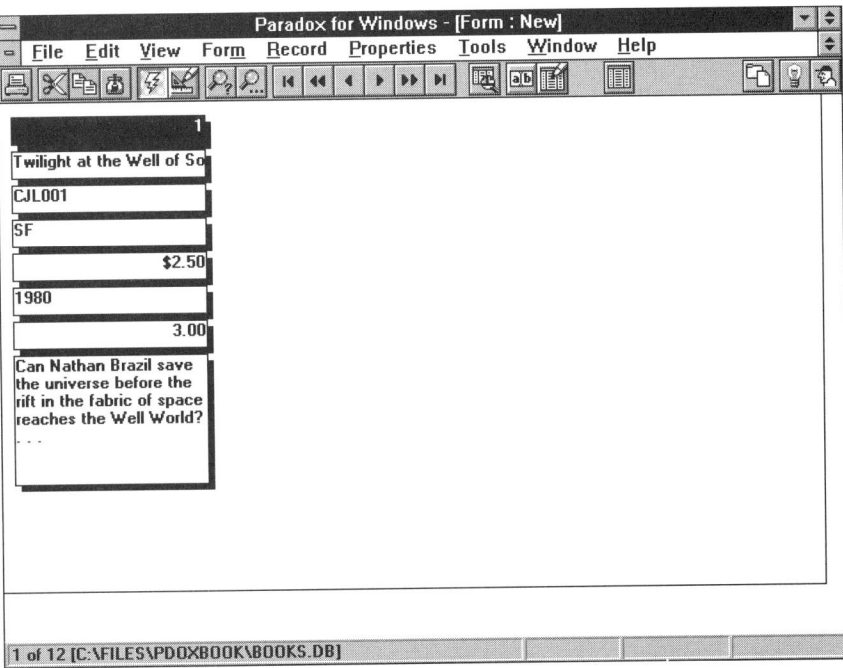

Figure 9-12: A single-table form created by the Form Expert.

You can see (at least I hope you can see) that this form has some problems. The title doesn't fit in its box, some of the text is misaligned, and you can't tell which field is which (and that's just for starters). Some adjustments are definitely in order. We'll take care of the adjustments later, but I just want you to realize that the Form Expert is only a starting point—most of the real work is done in the Form Design window.

Okay, that's it. You just used the Form Expert to create a form. We'll meet up with this form again near the end of the chapter.

Now we're going back through the parts of the Form Expert that we missed. Because we chose a single-table form, there were several things we didn't have to deal with.

Creating a Multitable Form

Since we've already gone through most of the steps in the Form Expert, I won't repeat any detailed explanations. I'll just walk you quickly through the steps, spending a little more time on the ones we haven't covered yet.

Here's the process:

1. Open the Form Expert using the techniques discussed under the "Opening the Form Expert" section.

2. In step 1, choose one of the multitable formats and move to the next step.

3. In step 2, select the table you want to use as the primary table for the form. This takes you to step 3, which we didn't run into before.

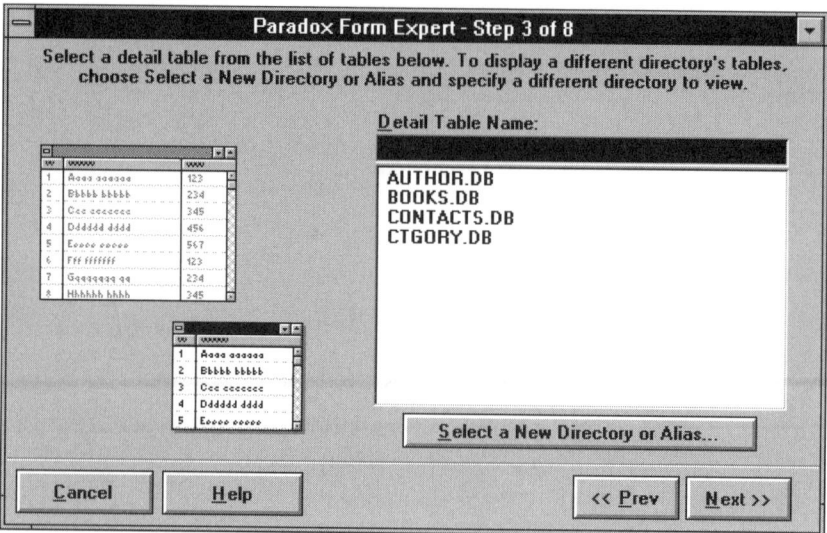

Figure 9-13: Step 3 of the Form Expert.

4. In step 3, select the detail table that will be associated with the master table.

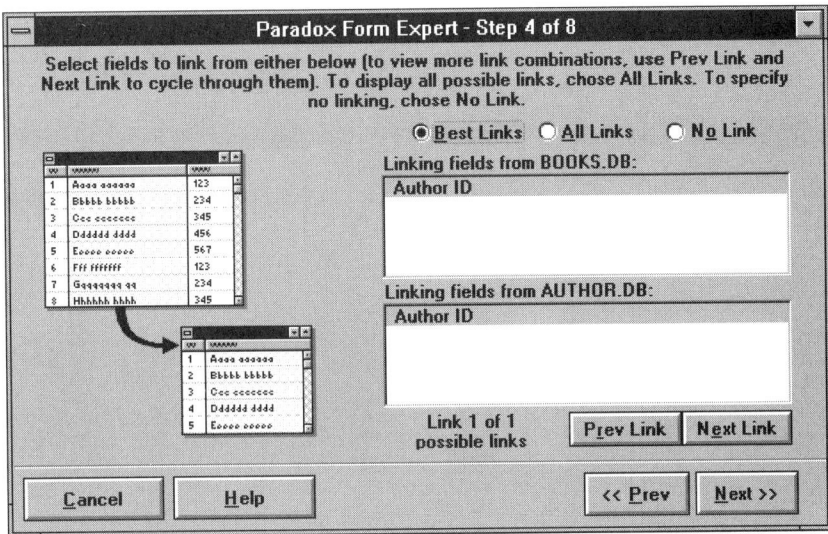

Figure 9-14: Step 4 allows you to choose how the tables will be linked.

5. Step 4 gives you the following choices for linking your master and detail tables:

○ **Select from best possible links:** Paradox determines the optimal common fields in the master table.

○ **Select from all possible links:** Paradox displays every possible common field.

○ **Don't link the tables:** Paradox doesn't display any links.

6. Step 5 is the same as it is when you use a single-table format. Choose the master table fields that you want displayed in the form.

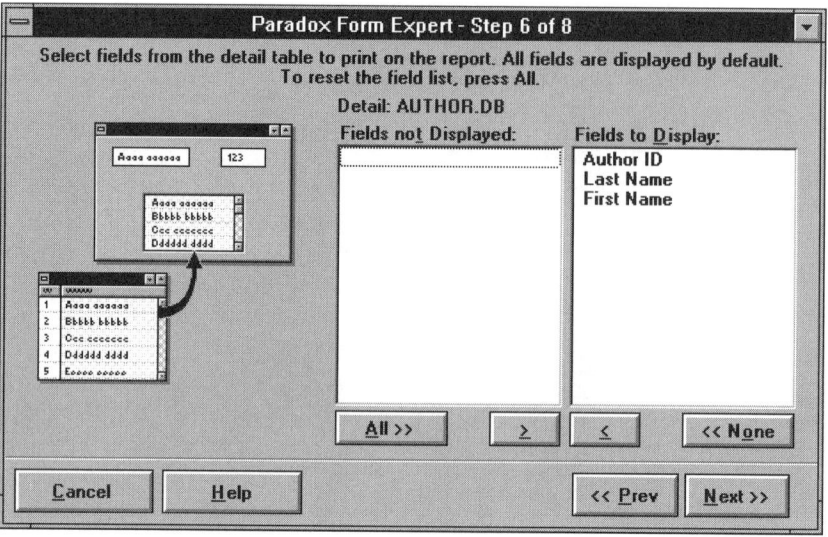

Figure 9-15: Step 6 allows you to select fields from the detail table.

7. Step 6 is just like step 5. The only difference is that you're choosing fields from the detail table instead of the master table.

8. In step 7, choose the display format, just as you did with the single-table form.

9. In step 8, choose the style sheet you want to use and click on the Create button.

That's pretty much it. You'll end up in the Form window with the form displayed according to the choices you made in the Form Expert.

Doing It on Your Own

Even though the Data Model/Layout Diagram method is considered more manual than the others, it actually provides quite a bit of assistance and in some ways can get you to the Form Design window in better shape than the Form Expert can. For one thing, you get to choose whether the fields are labeled or not. I know we haven't discussed labels yet, but you'll see what I mean shortly.

Beginning the Process

O Right-click on the Forms button from the Desktop Toolbar or the Project Viewer and choose New from the Object Inspector menu. Or choose File, New, Form from the pull-down menu. The New Form dialog box is displayed, as shown in Figure 9-16.

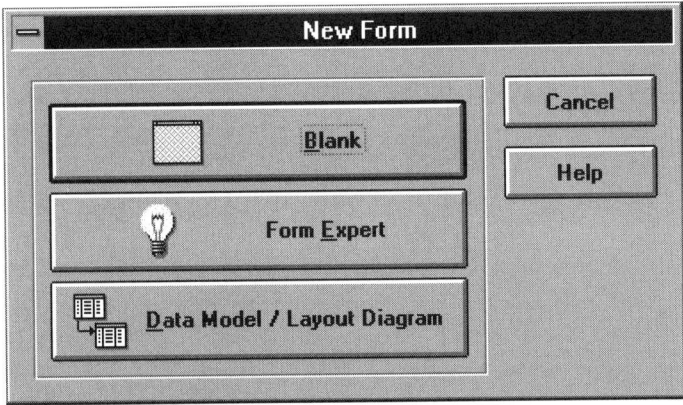

Figure 9-16: The New Form dialog box.

○ Choose Data Model/Layout Diagram from the New Form dialog box.

The Data Model Dialog Box

○ From the Data Model dialog box, you choose the tables to include in the form and define links between them. Working with data models will be covered in more detail in the next chapter when we talk about multitable forms. For now, we'll just use the Data Model dialog box as a quick way to select the table to use in a single-table form.

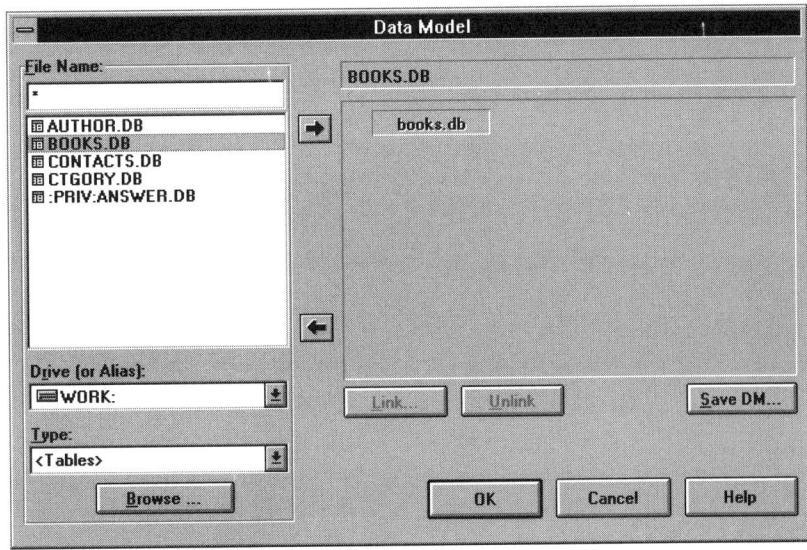

Figure 9-17: The Data Model dialog box.

1. To add a table to the data model, select the table from the File Name list or type the name in the File Name text box. For this example, choose BOOKS.DB. Then click on the right arrow button.

   ○ Click on the Browse button or use the Drive (or Alias) list if the tables you want aren't in your working directory.

   ○ If you want to use a saved query as the basis for your data model, choose <Queries> from the Type drop-down list. When the queries are displayed in the File Name list, you can move them into the data model just as you can with tables.

2. Choose OK to continue.

The Design Layout Dialog Box

The Design Layout dialog box is like having several of the Form Expert steps rolled into one. You get to decide whether you want the form displayed in single-record or multirecord format, select the fields you want included, and choose a style sheet.

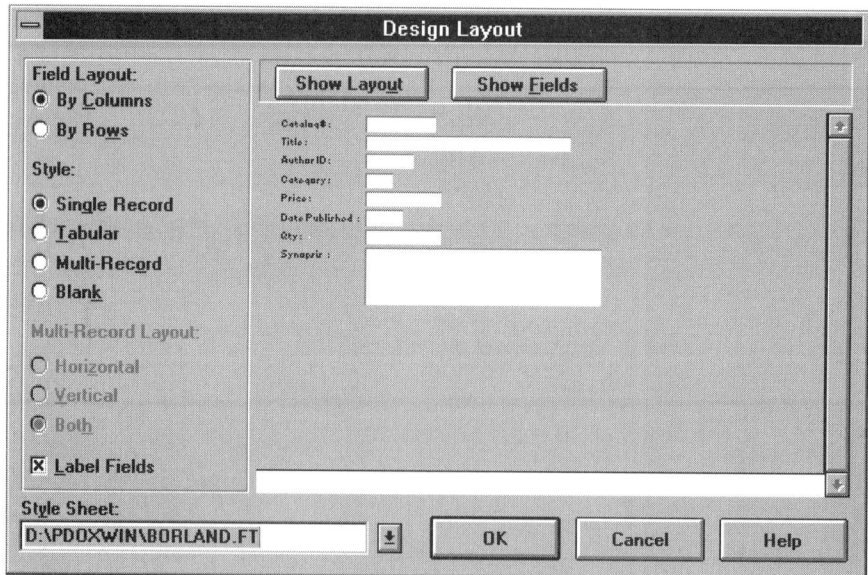

Figure 9-18: The Design Layout dialog box with Show Layout selected.

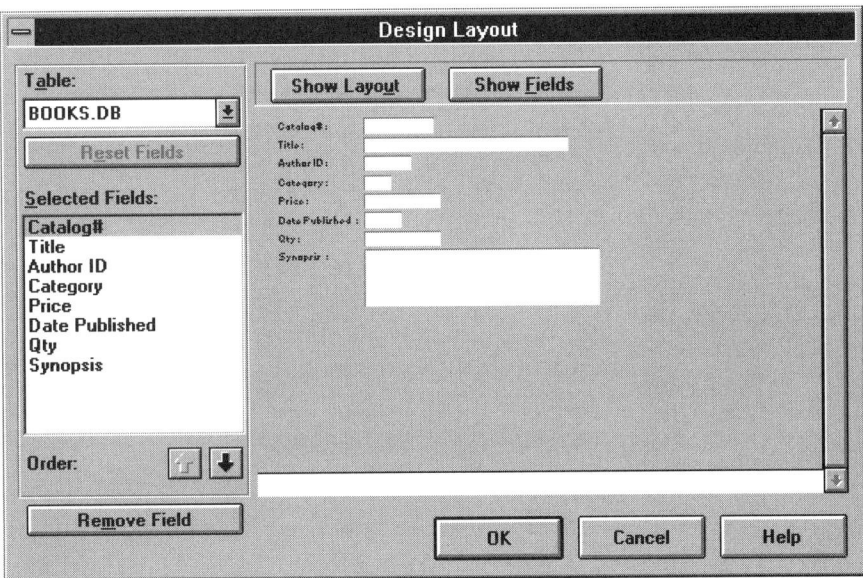

Figure 9-19: The Design Layout dialog box with Show Fields selected.

The Design Layout dialog box has two different modes. By default, it appears in Show Layout mode, as shown in Figure 9-18. From this window, you choose the Field Layout, Style and Multi-Record Layout (this option's activated only when you choose Multi-Record from the Style section). You can also choose whether you want the fields labeled or unlabeled, and you can choose a style sheet from the Style Sheet drop-down list.

When you click on the Show Fields button, the window appears as shown in Figure 9-19. Notice that all of the fields in the table are displayed. You can change the order of the fields and remove fields from the form.

I actually prefer working this way rather than using the Form Expert. I can easily change layouts, move fields around, and keep track of what's happening to the form as I go along.

Here are the options you can change when Show Layout is selected. Notice that the layout in the sample window changes to reflect any new options you select.

○ **Field Layout:** The default option is By Columns, which means that the fields are displayed in a column down the page. When no more fields will fit in the first column, the rest of the fields are displayed in a new column. Choose By Rows to display fields in horizontal rows.

○ **Style:** The default option is Single Record, which displays one record at a time in a list format. Choose Tabular to display the records in rows and columns just as they're displayed in Table

View. Choose Multi-Record to display multiple records on a page. When you select Multi-Record, you then make selections in the Multi-Record Layout section. Choosing Blank removes all fields from the form design. In essence this gives you a clean slate to start with in the Form Design window. You can then add the fields you want using the Form Design Toolbar's Field tool. When you choose Blank, the Show Fields button is dimmed.

○ **Multi-Record Layout:** The default option for a multirecord layout is Both, which means that the records are displayed both horizontally and vertically, as shown in Figure 9-20. Choose Horizontal or Vertical if you want the records displayed in only one direction.

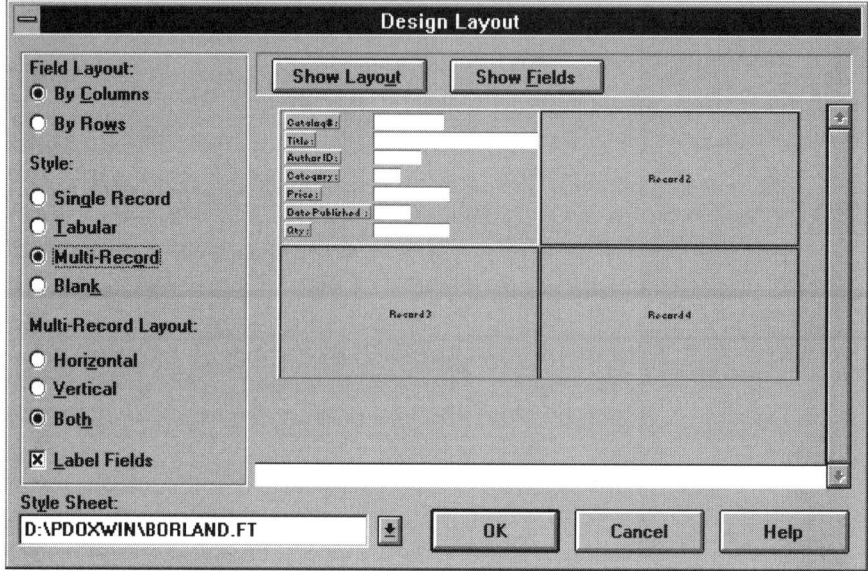

Figure 9-20: A multirecord layout, with records arranged both horizontally and vertically.

○ **Label Fields:** By default, fields are labeled, which means that the field name for each field is displayed next to the field data. Take a look at Figure 9-21. In the sample layout, there are two boxes for each field: one that contains the field's name and one that's blank. The blank box is where the field data will go.

   When you deselect the Label Fields check box, the sample layout displays only one box for each field. The box will contain the actual field data. As you can see in Figure 9-22, the text inside the boxes in the sample display is just code that tells you which field is which and how that field is structured. With no labels, field names won't appear with field data in your form.

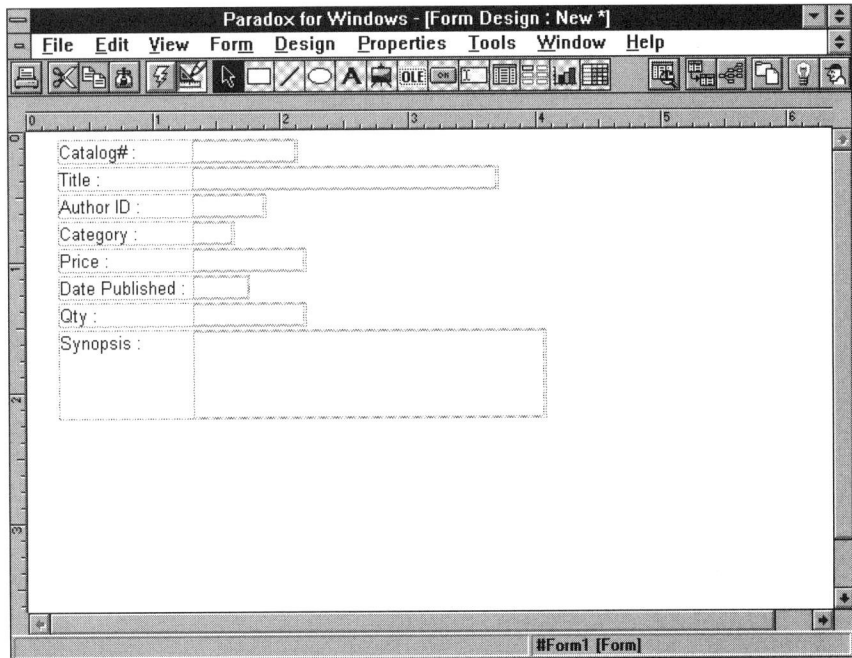

Figure 9-21: Single Record layout with labeled fields.

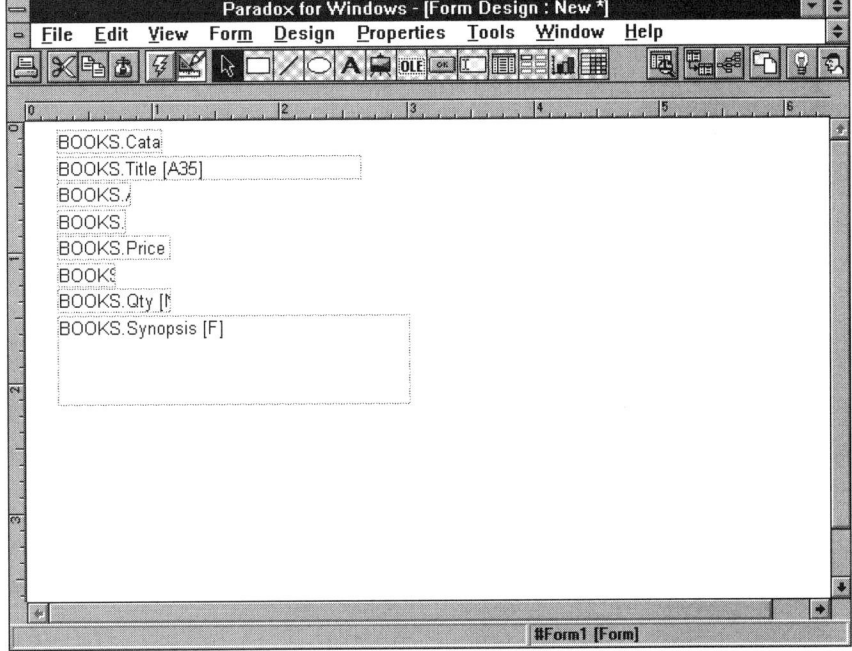

Figure 9-22: Single Record layout with unlabeled fields.

○ **Style Sheet:** From the Style Sheet drop-down list, you can choose a style sheet to attach to the form.

Here's what you can do when Show Fields is selected:

○ Remove fields from the form layout by selecting the fields from the Selected Fields list and clicking on the Remove Field button.

○ Use the up and down arrow buttons to change the order of the selected fields.

○ You can remove or change the order for more than one field at a time. Hold down the Shift key and drag to select contiguous fields, or hold down the Ctrl key while you click on noncontiguous fields.

○ If you removed a bunch of fields and want to get them back, click on the Reset fields button. This returns the Selected Fields list to its original state, with all fields in the table displayed.

For now, choose By Columns, Single Record, Label Fields, and select the Default style sheet (all of these options are in the Show Layout window). Then choose OK to go to the Form Design window, as shown in Figure 9-23.

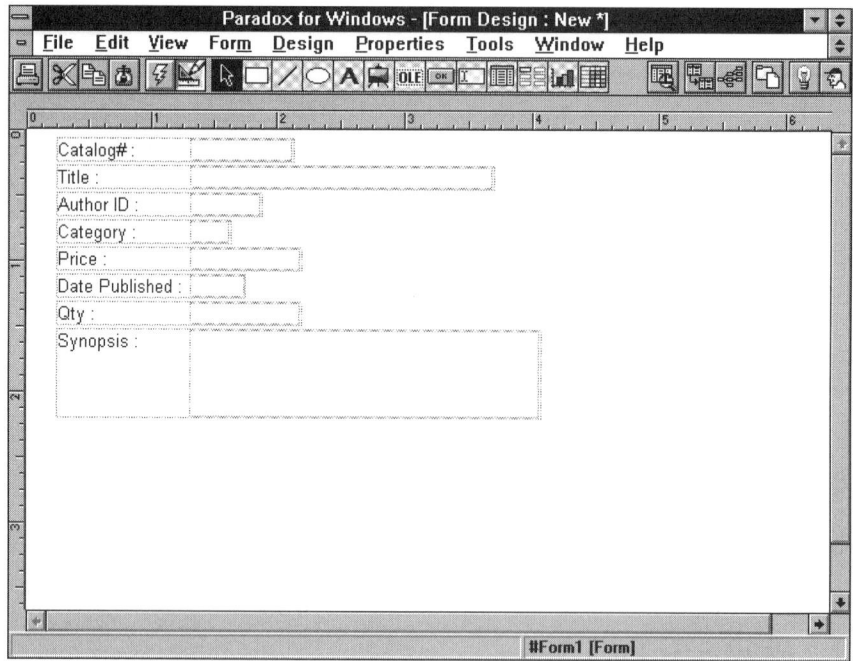

Figure 9-23: As soon as you choose OK, the form appears in the Form Design window.

Stay in the Form Design window. We'll play around with this form for the rest of the chapter.

CUSTOMIZING YOUR FORM

We've taken three different routes, but the result in each case was the same. We ended up at the Form Design window, from which we can manipulate the form design in just about any way imaginable. The rest of this chapter will get you going with some basic form-design stuff. In the process of making a few simple changes, I'll show you how to do these things:

❍ Save the form.

❍ Rearrange fields.

❍ Change field size.

❍ Switch between the Form window and the Form Design window so you can check on your work.

Saving the Form

Whichever method you took to get to the Form Design window, it's a good idea to save your form before you go any further. Even though we're going to make a lot of changes, you wouldn't want to lose the options you've already specified. To save the form,

❍ Choose File, Save As.

❍ Give the form a name (preferably something that reflects its purpose). For this example, use BOOKS1. Don't type an extension.

❍ Choose OK.

❍ Once you've given the form a name, you can choose File, Save at any time to save an updated version of the form.

❍ Notice that the name of the form is displayed on the title bar, and that it has an FSL extension.

Inside Scoop

Save frequently as you design your form. There are so many elements involved that it's easy to get way off-track. Each time you add or change something and you're sure it's the way you want it, save. Then, if you make a change that doesn't do what you want, close the form without saving and you'll be able to open the previously saved form and pick up right where you left off.

Selecting Fields

As you'll discover in the next chapter, everything in the Form Design window is an object. And objects are often contained within other objects. Why am I telling you this now? Because you can't understand how to select and work with fields without understanding that each "field" in the form design is actually a group of objects.

So what you need to know for now is that when you click on a labeled field in the Form Design window, what you're actually select-ing is the Field object that contains a Text object (the label) and an EditRegion object (for the field data). In Figure 9-24, I zoomed in on the Category field and selected the two inside objects so you can clearly see what's what.

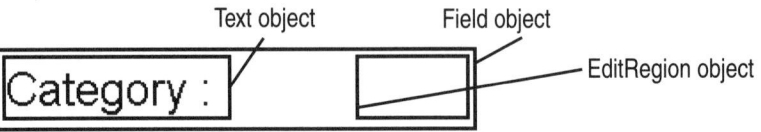

Figure 9-24: The Field object is the *container* for the Text and EditRegion objects.

I'll tell you all about containers in the next chapter. For now, just be aware that when the container object is selected, any objects within the container will be affected by whatever you do.

○ To select a field object, just click on it. Later, I'll show you how to select specific objects within a container object.

○ To select multiple objects (in this case, fields), click on the first object you want to select, then hold down the Shift key while you click on additional objects.

○ You can also select multiple objects by holding down the Shift key while you drag a "box" around the objects you want to select. For this method, the objects have to be adjacent to each other.

Rearranging Fields

In the Design Layout dialog box you were able to change the order of the displayed fields. In the Form Design window you can move fields wherever you want.

To move a field to a different position, point to the field you want to move and drag the field (which contains the Text and EditRegion objects) to a new location.

That's all there is to it. However, you'll often want to move several fields at once. Just use the techniques described earlier for selecting multiple objects, then point anywhere in the selected area and drag to move all of the selected objects.

Sizing Fields

Remember when we used the Form Expert and the title didn't fit in the field? Changing the size of a field is no problem. Just select the field object and drag one of the handles (the little boxes around the object).

In Figure 9-25, I dragged the handle on the right to make the field larger and then switched to the Form window to check my work. So why doesn't the title fit? Take a look at the same field in the Form Design window in Figure 9-26. As you can see, selecting and sizing the container (the Field object) didn't change the size of the EditRegion object inside the container.

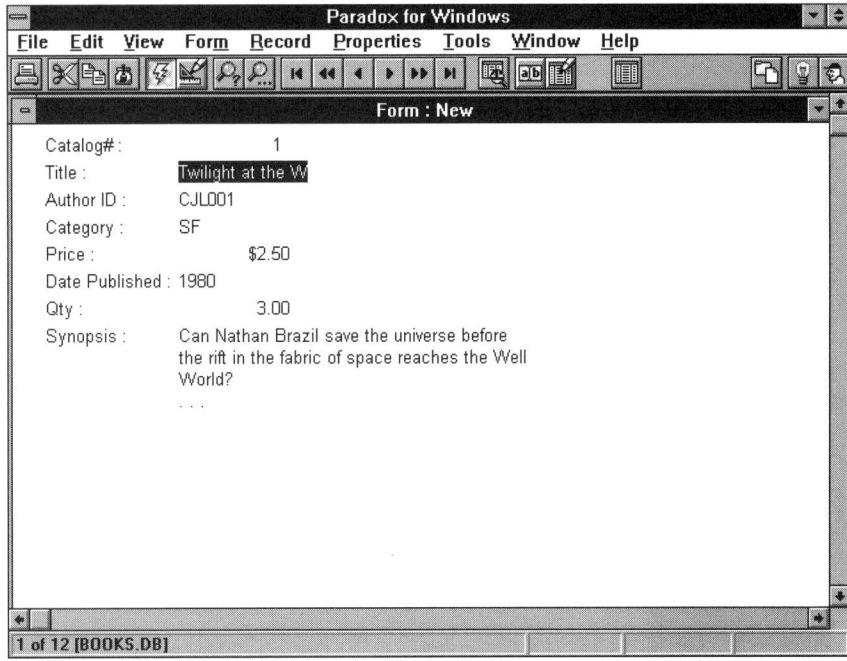

Figure 9-25: The Field object for the title has been widened.

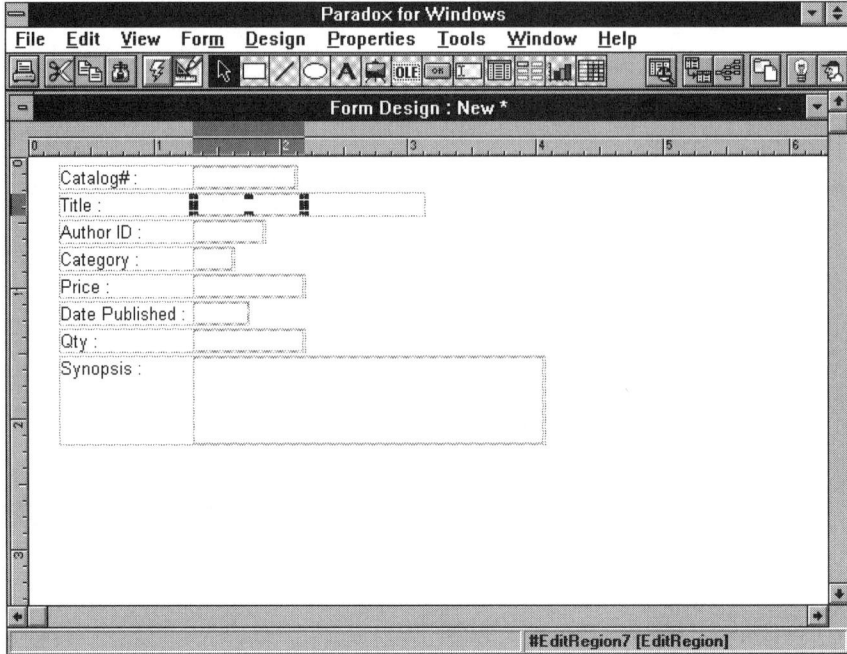

Figure 9-26: The size of the EditRegion object hasn't changed.

To select the EditRegion object, click in that area. The first time you click, the Field object will be selected. The second time you click, the EditRegion object should be selected as shown in Figure 9-26. (You can always tell which object is selected—just look at the status bar.) Now you can drag the handle and widen the EditRegion object to fill the container. In Figure 9-27, the whole title is now visible.

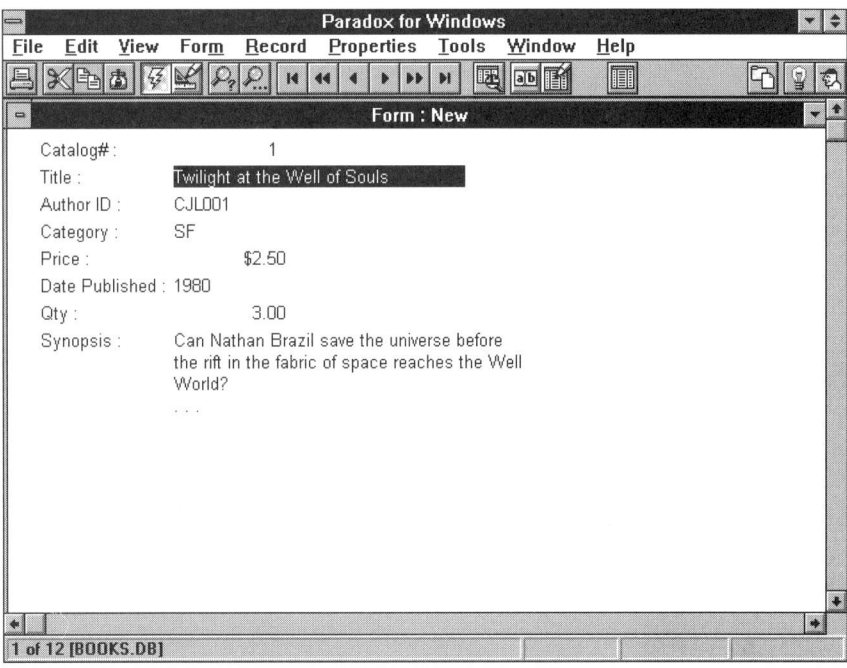

Figure 9-27: Now the title fits.

Switching Between Form & Form Design Windows

While you're designing a form, it's handy to be able to switch to the Form window to see how your changes will look on the final form.

❍ To switch to the Form window, click on the View Data button or press F8.

❍ To switch back to the Form Design window, click on the Design button or press F8.

MOVING ON

In this chapter we barely scratched the surface as far as form design goes. You know how to set up a basic layout, but there's a lot more to do. In the next chapter, you'll learn about all of the cool tools in the Form Design window's Toolbar. You'll also learn how to work with all kinds of design objects, how to zoom in on your design to make it easier to work with small objects, how to place special and calculated fields, and much, much more. See you there!

10 FORMS, THE SEQUEL

In the last chapter, you learned how to create a basic form layout and bring it into the Form Design window. Because the Form Design window consists of a huge grab bag of tricks and tools, we'll take a journey through this window's menus and Toolbar buttons. Along the way, you'll learn how to:

○ Use the Form Design window's design tools.

○ Work with objects inside other objects.

○ Group, Stack and Duplicate objects.

○ Create buttons and drop-down lists.

○ Use the Object Tree to see a diagram of your form layout.

○ And much more . . .

OPENING THE FORM

In Chapter 10, you saved your completed form layout as BOOKS1.FSL. Once you've saved a form you can open it in the Form window, which allows you to view and edit the table data, or in the Form Design window, where you can make changes to the form itself. Our main goal right now is just to open BOOKS1.FSL. But the Open Document dialog box also lets you do a few other neat tricks, so I'll cover them while we're in there.

To open a form using the Open Document dialog box, follow these steps:

1. From a blank Desktop, click on the Form button (or choose File, Open, Form).

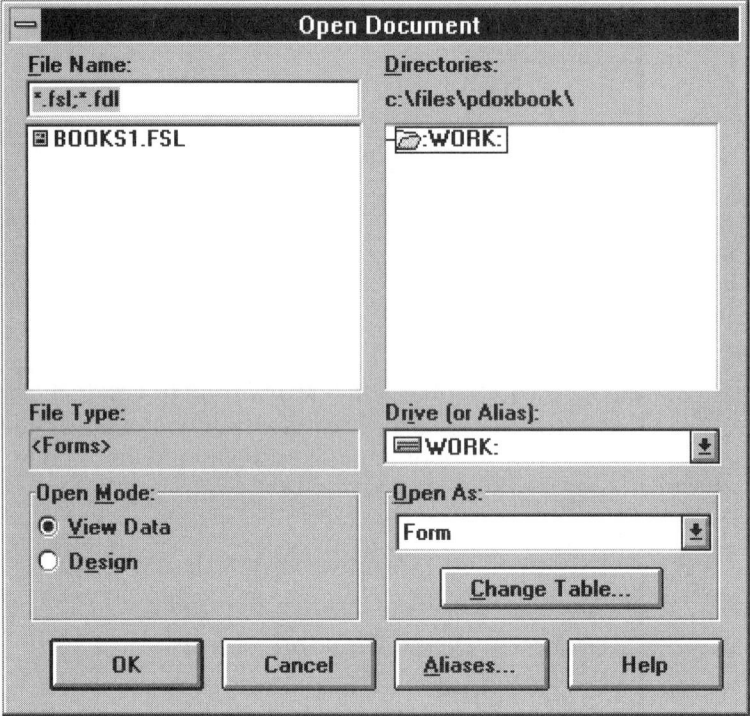

Figure 10-1: The Open Document dialog box.

2. The default Open Mode is View Data, which opens the form in a Form window for display and data entry purposes. To open the form directly in the Form Design window, select the Design radio button. (Don't worry if you forget to make this choice—as you saw in the last chapter, you can easily switch between the Form and Form Design windows by pressing F8 or clicking on the View Data or Design button.) For our example, select Design.

3. Notice the Open As drop-down list. By default, a form is opened as a form. Yeah, I hear what you're thinking, "Duh, like what else would it open as?" Well, Slick, you can also open a form as a report. To do that, just choose Report from the Open As drop-down list.

   And why do that? Because maybe you created this totally awesome form and you'd like to base a report on the form's layout. By the way, you can also do it in reverse—if you create a report that you want to turn into a form, you can open the report as a form. Pretty cool stuff, huh?

4. To base your form on a new master table, choose Change Table and make a selection from the Select File dialog box.

5. When you've selected all the options you want, click on the form you want to open (in this case, BOOKS1.FSL) and choose OK.

Note: An alternative way of opening a form is to use the Project Viewer, right-click on the form icon and then right-click on the form you want to open. From the Object Inspector menu, choose View Data to open the form in the Form window, or choose Design to open the form in the Form Design window.

Okay, all of you still with me? BOOKS1.FSL should be on your screen in the Form Design window. Let's hit the road—we have many miles to go before we sleep (unless my writing puts you to sleep before we get there).

WORKING IN THE FORM DESIGN WINDOW

Actually, this whole chapter's about working in the Form Design window, but there are a few things we need to cover now. Why now? For one thing, I don't want you wondering stuff like "What's with the rulers?" or "Those new Toolbar buttons are awfully cute, but what do they do?" You'll get your chance to play with everything, but I'll start with an overview so you feel comfortable with the Form Design window. But first, a few generic tips that will minimize your frustration factor:

○ Save your form design frequently. By its very nature, creating a form design involves a lot of playing around. And because you have so many options to play around with, it's easy to make a change that causes your form to go kaboom (it won't exactly explode, but neither will it be the form that you've slaved over). So get in the habit of choosing File, Save before you make a change that could have unexpected results. Then, if you don't like the change, just close the form (but don't save it!). When you reopen the form, you'll be able to start right where you left off.

○ Don't forget Undo! (But don't rely on it either.) If you do something that doesn't work or isn't what you intended, choose Edit, Undo (or press Alt+Backspace) *before you do anything else*. Remember, Undo undoes only your most recent action. So if you don't notice the problem until you do something else, it's too late for Undo. That's why the previous tip about saving is so important.

○ Maximize the Form Design window so it takes up your whole screen (click on the Maximize button or double-click on the form's title bar). It's much easier to work with design stuff when you can see as much as possible.

○ Take a look at your design in the Form window from time to time. Don't get so bogged down in the design that you forget what you're working toward: a form that can be displayed and edited in the Form window. So click on the View Data button (or choose View, View Data) to display your design in the Form window so you can keep track of your progress.

○ Take advantage of the Zoom feature. Zoom out for an overall look at your design, or zoom in for detailed work in a particular area. Zooming is covered later in this chapter.

○ Float the Toolbar. If you need more room onscreen, move the Toolbar from its fixed position. To turn it into a floating Toolbar that can be moved anywhere on the screen, choose Properties, Desktop and make the appropriate selections in the Desktop Properties dialog box. For more information about this, refer to Chapter 1.

The Form Design Toolbar

Let's start with the obvious: the new Toolbar buttons. Figure 10-2 shows you the Form Design window's Toolbar, and the list that follows tells you what each button does. (But don't forget about the status bar. If you forget what a particular button does, just move your mouse pointer over the button and look at the status bar.)

Figure 10-2: The Form Design Toolbar.

The first four buttons on the left are the same as those you've already seen in the Table View and Form windows: Print, Cut To Clipboard, Copy To Clipboard and Paste From Clipboard. So we'll start with the fifth button.

 The View Data button switches to the Form window, where you can edit the table data. (This button's inactive when you're in the Form window.) Menu alternative: View, View Data. Keyboard alternative: F8.

 The Design button switches from the Form window to the Form Design window. (This button's inactive when you're in the Form Design window.) Menu alternative: View, Design Form. Keyboard alternative: F8.

 The Selection arrow selects an object or multiple objects so you can do things to them (like move them around, change properties, etc.). No menu alternative as such, but you can choose Edit, Select All to select all objects onscreen or to select all objects contained within a selected object.

The next twelve buttons are all *design tools*, which just means you can use them to place different kinds of *design objects* on the form. Any design objects that you add to the form are part of the form itself but are not reflected in the table.

The Box tool draws boxes, squares and rectangles.

The Line tool draws horizontal, vertical or diagonal lines. The lines can be curved or straight, and you can turn lines into arrows.

The Ellipse tool draws circles and ellipses.

The Text tool places text objects on the form.

The Graphic tool places graphic objects on the form.

The OLE tool places OLE objects on the form.

The Button tool adds buttons to a form. You attach ObjectPAL code to a button to make it do something. In this chapter, I'll show you how to add a button, but you have to read the programming chapters later in this book before you'll be able to put the button to use.

The Field tool adds individual table fields to a form.

The Table tool adds entire table frames to a form.

The Multi-Record tool adds repeating records to a form.

The Graph tool adds graphs to a form.

The Crosstab tool adds crosstabs to a form.

The Filter button opens the Filter Tables dialog box, from which you can specify which records you want displayed when the form is run. Menu alternative: Form, Filter.

The Data Model button opens the Data Model dialog box.

The Object Tree button displays a diagram of the relationships among all of the objects on a form. Or, if a particular object is selected, you'll see a diagram that begins with that object. Menu alternative: Tools, Object Tree.

The three buttons on the far right are our old friends Project
Viewer, Expert and Coaches.

The Ruler

By default, horizontal and vertical rulers are displayed in the Form
Design window. And it's a good thing that they are. They're super-
handy when you position or size design objects. In Figure 10-3, the
Synopsis field is selected. Notice that the shaded area on each ruler
tells you the exact size and position of the object. And the little
diamonds display the current position of your mouse pointer. As you
move or size an object, the shaded area moves or changes size to
reflect your changes.

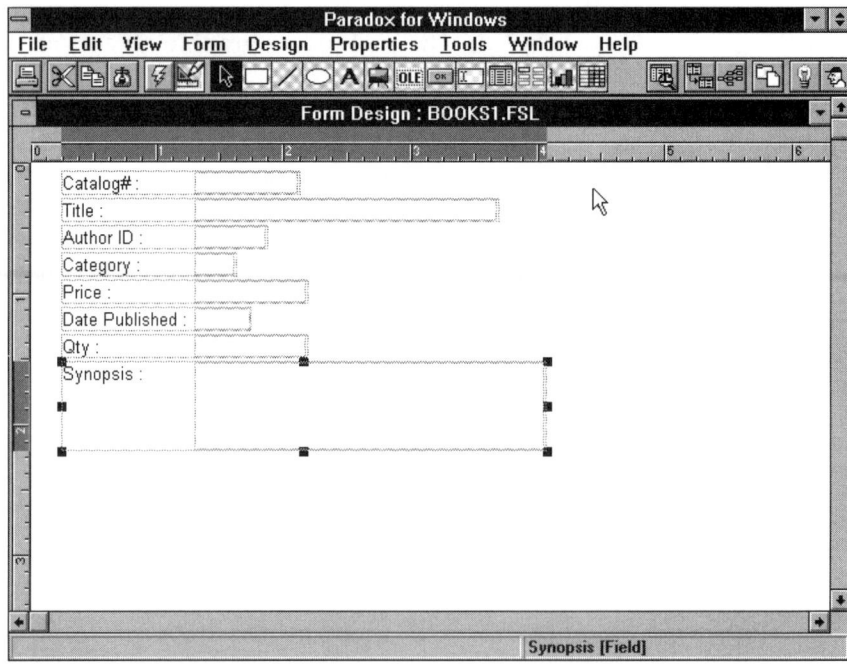

Figure 10-3: The rulers keep track of each object's size and position.

Hiding the Rulers

As handy as the rulers are, sometimes you just want more display area
on your screen. No problem. The rulers are controlled by options on
the Properties menu. These options are toggles, which means that
you use the same technique to select the option (place a check next
to it) or deselect it (get rid of the check). When the ruler options are
selected, the rulers are "turned on." To turn them off, just deselect
the options:

○ Choose Properties, Horizontal Ruler to select or deselect the horizontal ruler.

○ Choose Properties, Vertical Ruler to select or deselect the vertical ruler.

You may have noticed the Expanded Ruler option just below Vertical Ruler on the Properties menu. The Expanded ruler provides several options for working with text objects. It's really cool, and we'll discuss it at length under "Working With Text Objects."

WORKING WITH DESIGN OBJECTS

In Chapter 1, I told you that Paradox treats just about everything as objects. Tables, forms, reports and queries are all objects. And each field in each record is an object. So it stands to reason that everything you put in a form is also a design object. Understanding all this object stuff is the key to working with forms. When you use the Text tool to place text on a form, that text becomes a text object. When you use the Table tool to place an entire table on a form, the whole table becomes a design object on that form. And what does all this mean? It means that all design objects have a lot in common and that once you understand their common aspects and how objects relate to each other, you have the basic tools for working with any design object, even if it's one you've never used before.

So instead of getting into the individual design tools right away, I want to cover some important concepts and techniques that will stand you in good stead as you work with forms. By the time we get to the individual tools, you'll already have most of the knowledge you need to work with them—it will just be a matter of discussing the unique characteristics of that particular tool.

Understanding Containership

Pay attention here. Containership is one of the most important concepts in form design. Unless you understand the relationship between containers and the objects inside the containers, you'll have trouble with a lot of this form stuff. At the end of Chapter 9, you saw how important it is to have the right object selected. When you tried to get the title to fit by resizing the field object, it didn't work. Why? Because the field object is the *container*, and the EditRegion object (which contains the title data) is a *contained object* inside the container. So you had to select and resize the EditRegion object before the title would fit in the field.

Here's an illustration. In Figure 10-4, I selected the Title field and opened the Object Tree window (you'll learn about the Object Tree a little later in this chapter). Because the Object Tree shows how objects relate to each other, it's easy to see that the Title field is the main item in the relationship and that the EditRegion and Text fields "belong" to the Title field.

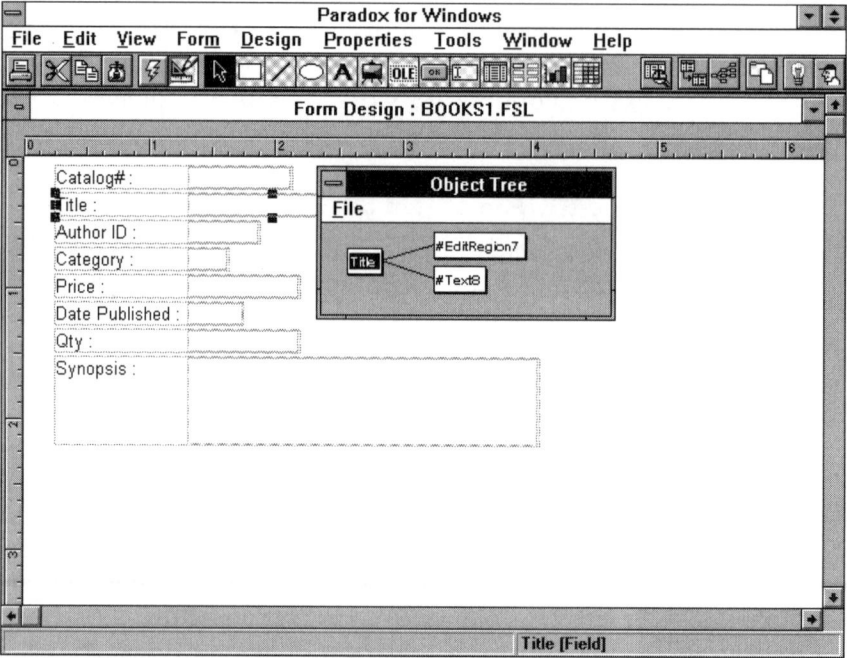

Figure 10-4: A demonstration of containership.

The containership relations in a labeled field are set up automatically: each Field object contains a Text object that displays the actual field name (the label) and an EditRegion object that displays the field data when the form is viewed. But you can also create your own contained objects.

Paradox defines a container as an object that completely surrounds other objects. Doing stuff to the container affects the contained objects. When you move or delete a container, the contained objects are automatically moved or deleted. (But you can move or delete a contained object without affecting the container.) There are several ways to place an object inside a container:

○ Create the object so it's totally inside the container object.

○ Move an object completely inside a container object.

○ Move or resize the container so that it completely surrounds the objects you want contained.

○ Paste an object inside a container.

Pitfall Ahead

It's easy to delete an object without paying attention, and before you know it the object is gone, along with any objects inside it. A couple of tips: First, if you delete an object or objects by mistake, choose Edit, Undo (or press Alt+Backspace) *before you do anything else.* But better than undoing is not doing in the first place. If you want to delete a container without deleting the objects inside it, right-click on the container object and choose Design, Contain Objects from the Object Inspector menu. Make sure that Contain Objects is not checked. Now you can work with the container without having its behavior affect the objects inside.

Another way to break the container relationship is to move contained objects so at least a portion of each object is outside the container frame.

This won't work for certain types of objects. For example, you can't break a container relationship for labeled field objects. A labeled field object *must* contain Text and EditRegion objects.

Selecting Objects

You have to select an object before you can do anything to it. To select a single object, you just click on the object. But because of containership issues, there's a little more to it. We'll start with the basics.

 Activate the Selection Arrow tool (you can tell if it's already selected—the button is highlighted) and click on an object. When you select an object, Paradox displays handles (little boxes) around the object, as shown in Figure 10-5. Use the handles to resize the object. As you move your mouse pointer over a handle, the pointer turns into a double-headed arrow, indicating the direction in which you can size the object. Just drag the handle until the object is the size you want.

Note: You can also select objects with the keyboard. Press the Tab key to select individual objects in sequence.

Figure 10-5: Notice the little black boxes around the object.

Inside or Outside?

With forms, you're often dealing with objects that are contained by other objects. By default, Paradox selects the outside object (the container) first. To make this easier to visualize, here's an example.

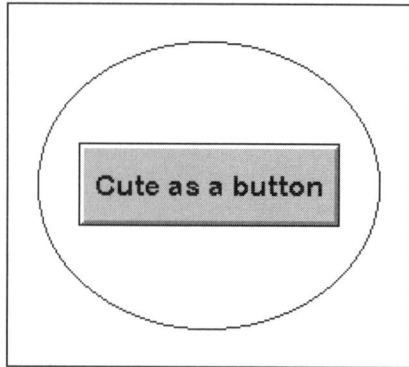

Figure 10-6: A button inside a circle inside a box.

When you click in this area (even if you click right on the button), the box is the first thing that's selected. When you click again, the circle is selected. And finally, a third click will select the button. This default selection method ensures that you will always select the container first, which is useful in many instances.

But what if you don't want to have to click two or three times before a contained object is selected? Choose Properties, Designer to open the Design Properties dialog box shown in Figure 10-7.

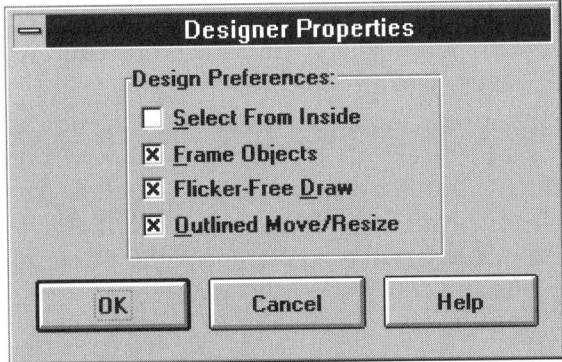

Figure 10-7: The Design Properties dialog box.

Notice that Select From Inside is not checked. To reverse the default action of selecting from the outside in, check Select From Inside and choose OK. Select From Inside gives you much greater precision in selecting objects. Now, when you click directly on the button, the button is selected. When you click on the circle, the circle is selected. And when you click on the box—well, you get the picture.

Inside Scoop

Cool selection shortcut: Press Esc to select the next outermost object. This shortcut works whether or not Select From Inside is selected. For example, when the button is selected, press Esc to select the circle, press Esc again to select the box, and press it once more to select the page. When the page is selected, pressing Esc deselects everything.

Selecting Multiple Objects

Paradox provides several techniques for selecting and deselecting more than one object. First, make sure the Selection Arrow tool is activated. Then do the following:

○ To select several individual objects, hold down the Shift key while you click on each object. To deselect one of the selected objects, hold down the Shift key while you click on the object you want to deselect. The rest of the objects will remain selected.

○ If the objects you want to select are adjacent to each other, you can *marquee select* by dragging an imaginary box around the objects. Position your mouse pointer just outside the first object.

Then hold down the Shift key while you drag a box outline around the objects. When you release the mouse button, all of the objects inside the box are selected.

○ To select all of the objects inside the currently selected object, choose Edit, Select All. Using the box, circle, button example from Figure 10-6, assume that the box is selected. Choosing Edit, Select All selects the circle and button as well. If you don't have any objects selected when you choose Edit, Select All, all of the objects in the design window are selected.

Zooming In for a Closer Look

You usually can't see your whole design onscreen (unless you have one of those super-big-screen monitors, in which case I'm jealous). Of course you can always use the scroll bars to display different portions of the design. But sometimes you need an overall view. And sometimes you need a closer look so you can more easily edit a particular area. That's where zooming comes in. Here's what you do:

Choose View, Zoom. Then make a choice from the cascading menu:

○ **25%**   Reduces display to 25% of its original size.

○ **50%**   Reduces display to 50% of its original size.

○ **100%**   Design is displayed at its normal size.

○ **200%**   Expands display to 200% of its original size.

○ **400%**   Expands display to 400% of its original size.

○ **Fit Width**   Sizes the design according to the width of the Form Design window.

○ **Fit Height**   Sizes the design according to the height of the Form Design window.

○ **Best Fit**   Sizes the design according to both the height and width of the Form Design window.

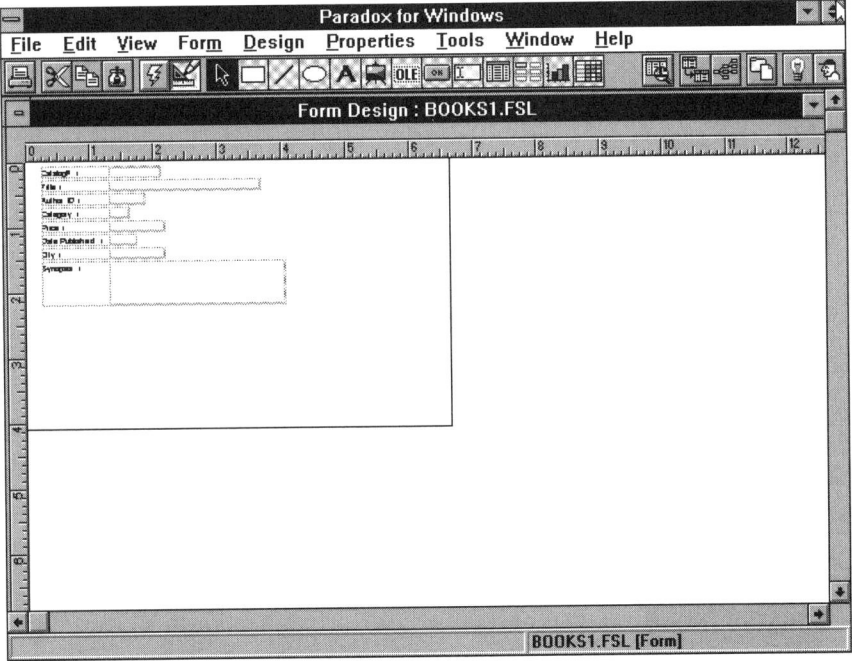

Figure 10-8: BOOKS1.FSL zoomed out to 50%.

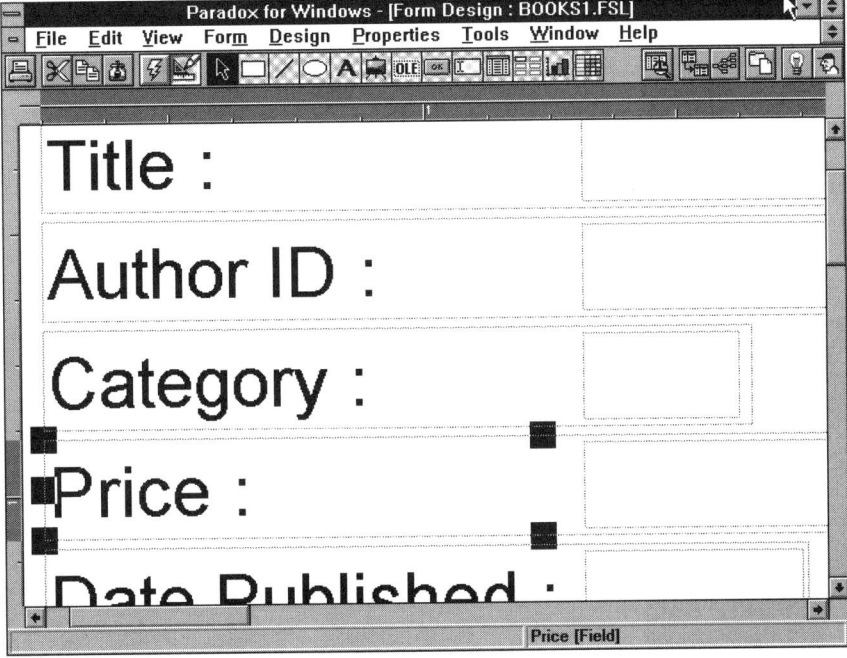

Figure 10-9: BOOKS1.FSL zoomed in to 400% with the Price field selected.

Using the Grid

Grid lines are a handy way to place objects on your form. Choose Properties, Show Grid (this is a toggle, so selecting it means making sure there's a check mark next to the option) to display the horizontal and vertical grid shown in Figure 10-10.

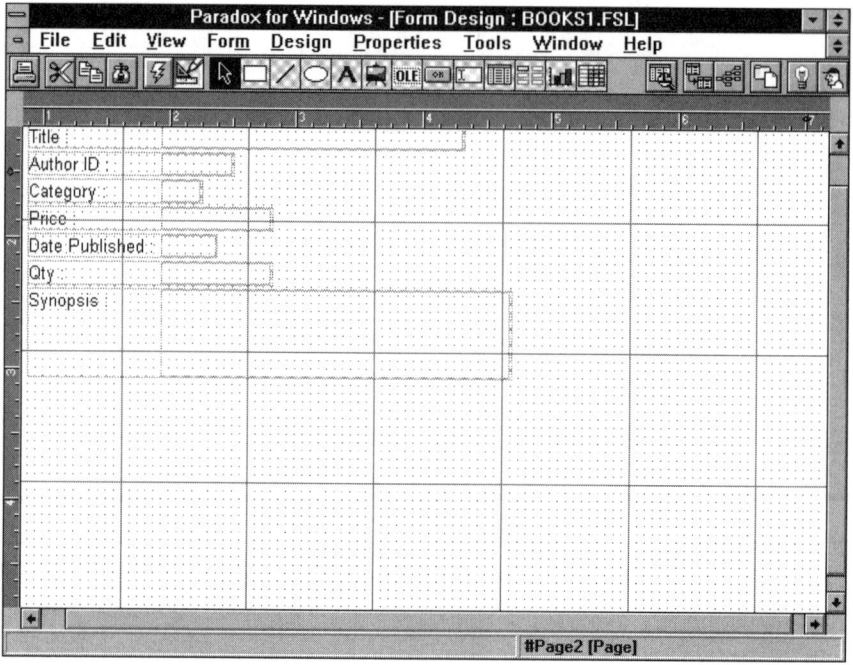

Figure 10-10: BOOKS1.FSL with visible grid lines.

Sticky Grids

The grid lines give you a visible tool for positioning and sizing objects. But they're even more helpful if you turn on the Snap To Grid option (choose Properties, Snap To Grid). With this option selected, whenever you move or resize an object, the object *snaps to* (aligns with) the nearest major or minor grid line. The solid lines are major grid lines; the dotted lines are minor grid lines.

Inside Scoop

Snap To Grid can be turned on even if the grid lines aren't visible. So even if you find the visible grid lines distracting, you can still take advantage of sticky grids. And it's kind of fun to see objects snap to invisible markers.

Changing Grid Settings

You can change the distance between grid lines by choosing Properties, Grid Settings. This displays the Grid Settings dialog box shown in Figure 10-11.

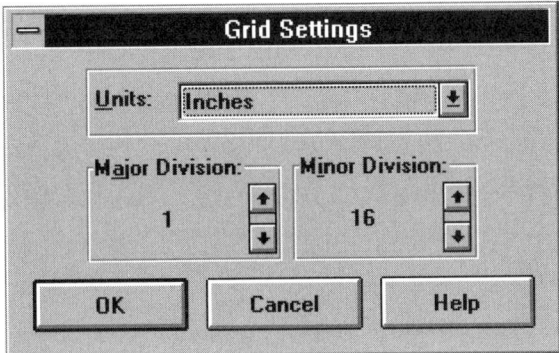

Figure 10-11: The Grid Settings dialog box.

○ **Units:** Ruler markings and grid lines are displayed in your default unit of measurement. To change the default, choose Inches or Centimeters from the Units drop-down list.

○ **Major Division:** Use the up and down arrows to change the distance between the major grid lines.

○ **Minor Division:** Use the up and down arrows to change the distance between the minor grid lines.

Aligning Objects

Paradox's ability to align objects means you don't have to get too picky when you place objects on your form. You can put objects sort of where you want them to be and then use the Align feature to fine-tune the placement. To align objects, first select the objects you want to align. Then choose Design, Align and choose one of the options on the cascading menu. Figures 10-12 through 10-17 show examples of each alignment option.

Note: If Snap To Grid is turned on, objects are aligned to the nearest grid line.

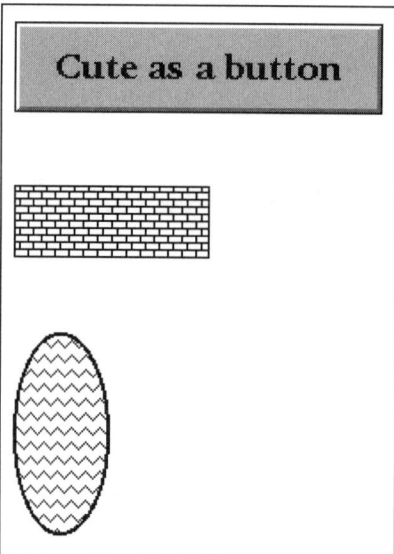

Figure 10-12: Align Left. The left sides of all selected objects are aligned with the left side of the selected object that's farthest to the left.

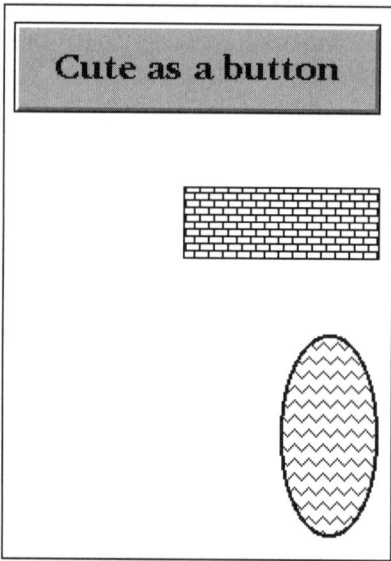

Figure 10-13: Align Right. The right sides of all selected objects are aligned with the right side of the object that's farthest to the right.

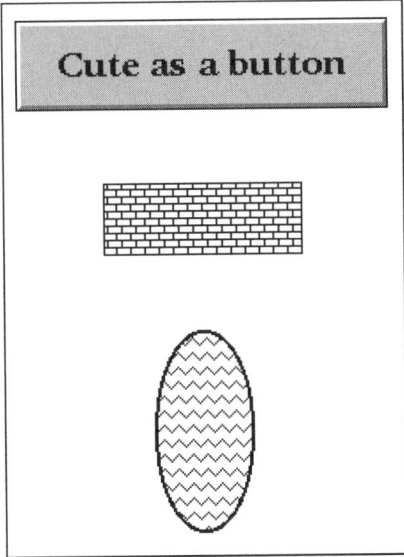

Figure 10-14: Align Center. All selected objects are centered on an imaginary vertical line that passes through the center of each object.

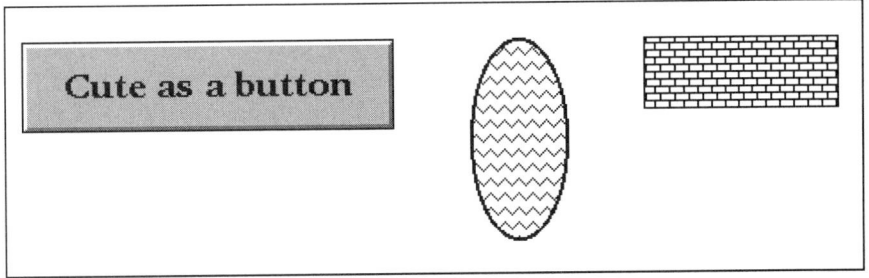

Figure 10-15: Align Top. The top of each selected object is aligned with the top of the highest selected object.

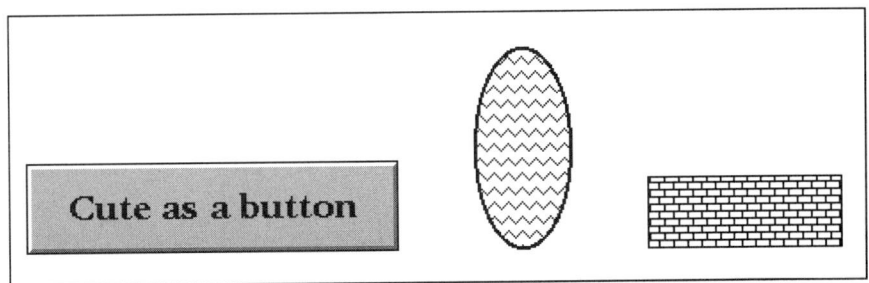

Figure 10-16: Align Bottom. The bottom of each selected object is aligned with the bottom of the lowest selected object.

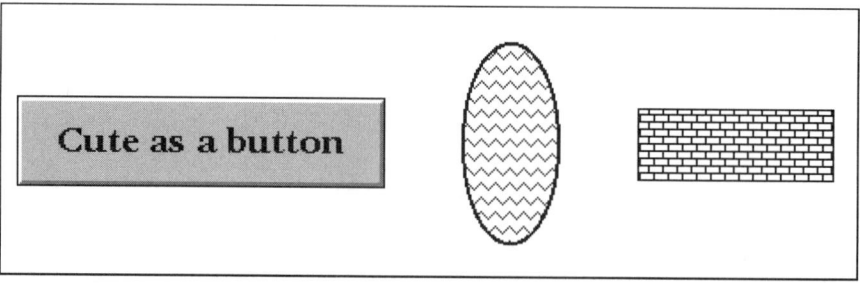

Figure 10-17: Align Middle. The middle of each object is aligned horizontally.

Adjusting Size for Multiple Objects

This option and the next, Adjust Spacing, are two of my favorites. You'll have to wait a bit to see why I think Adjust Spacing is so cool, but Adjust Size is right here, right now. Okay. What if you've created a whole bunch of buttons (or circles or boxes or whatever) and you want them to be the same size. Sure, you can drag handles to size each object. And the Ruler and grid lines can help you out, especially if Snap To Grid is turned on. But getting everything exactly the same size could be a giant pain.

But it's not a giant pain. And why not? Because of the Adjust Sizing option. In Figure 10-18 I added a bunch of buttons. They're all different sizes (and they *were* all over the place until I used the Align option to line them up by their left borders). To make them all the same size involves a couple of steps:

○ First, select all of the objects you want to change.

○ Then choose Design, Adjust Size.

○ Finally, choose one of the options from the cascading menu.
  Figures 10-19 through 10-22 illustrate the different options.

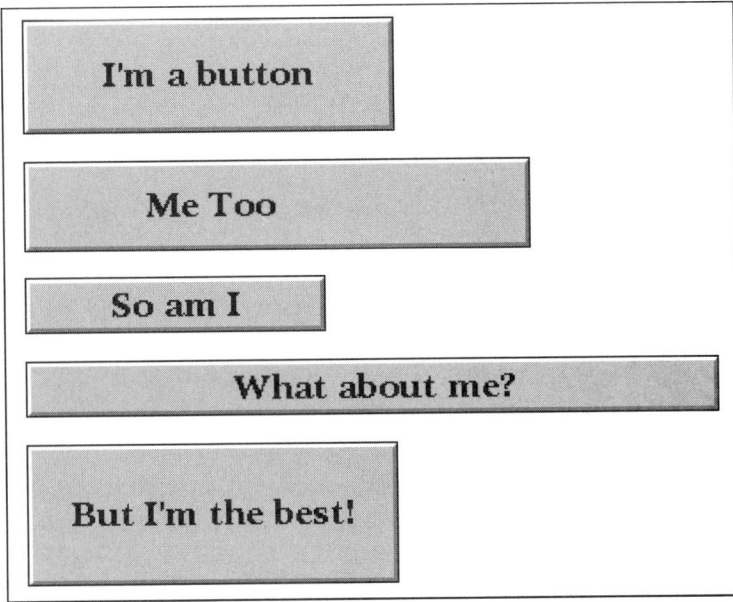

Figure 10-18: A bunch of buttons.

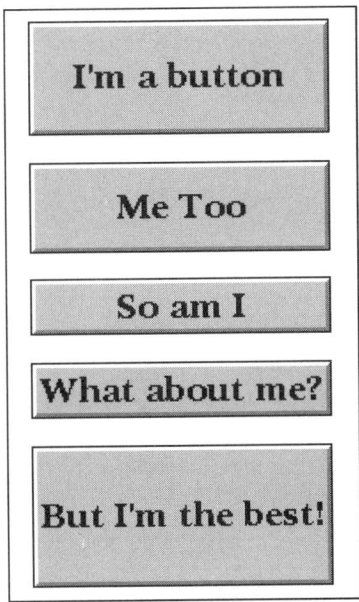

Figure 10-19: Minimum Width. All objects become as narrow as the narrowest object.

Figure 10-20: Maximum Width. All objects become as wide as the widest object.

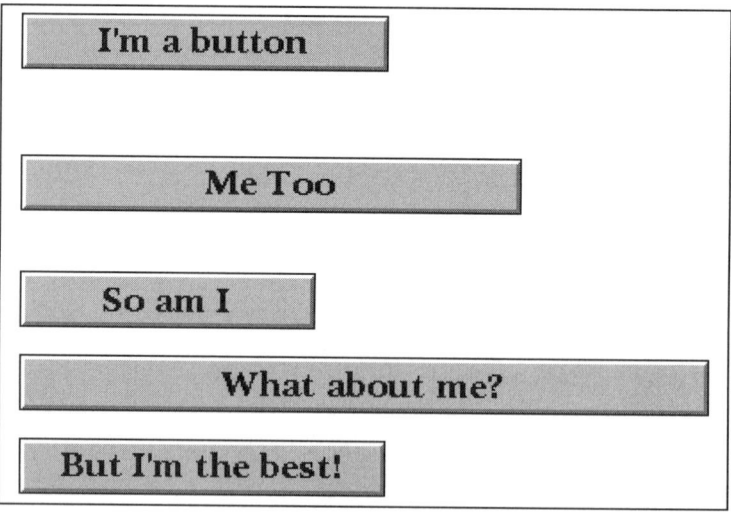

Figure 10-21: Minimum Height. All objects become as short as the shortest object.

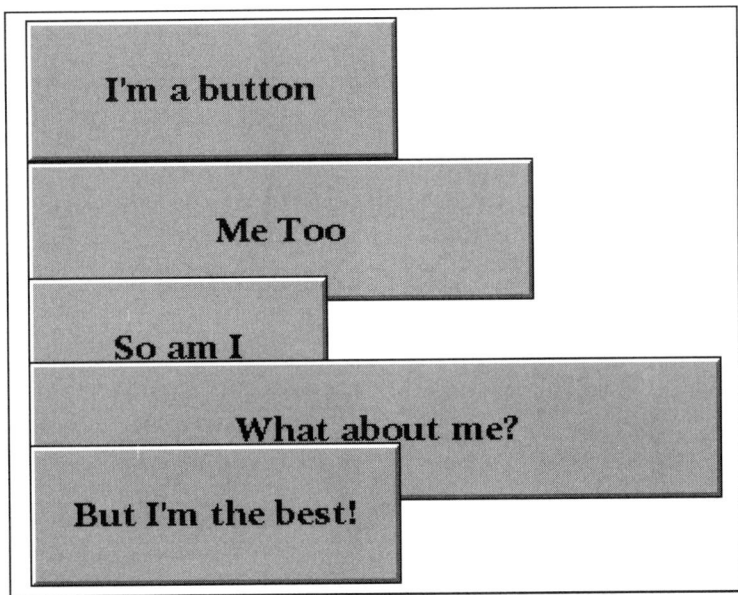

Figure 10-22: Maximum Height. All objects become as tall as the tallest object.

Combine width and height options to get the result you want. If you want all objects to be the same size as the largest object, choose Maximum Width and Maximum Height. If Paradox can't resize one of the selected objects, it just ignores that object and takes care of the rest.

Inside Scoop

With several of the design options, notice that the objects remain selected after you apply the option. This is true for the Align, Adjust Size and Adjust Spacing options we've just been talking about. The reason you should take note of this is that it means you don't have to start selecting from scratch before you can make additional changes. For example, to adjust the horizontal and vertical spacing, just select the objects and choose Design, Adjust Spacing, Horizontal. Because the objects are still selected you can then choose Design, Adjust Spacing, Vertical without having to reselect anything.

Adjusting Spacing

Now for my other favorite. This is totally cool. Suppose you want the spacing between objects to be the same. By now you know that you can laboriously move each object, using the Ruler and Snap To Grid to meticulously position each object where you want it. But there's a much easier way. Take a look at Figure 10-23. This is the *before* picture. Notice the uneven gaps between buttons.

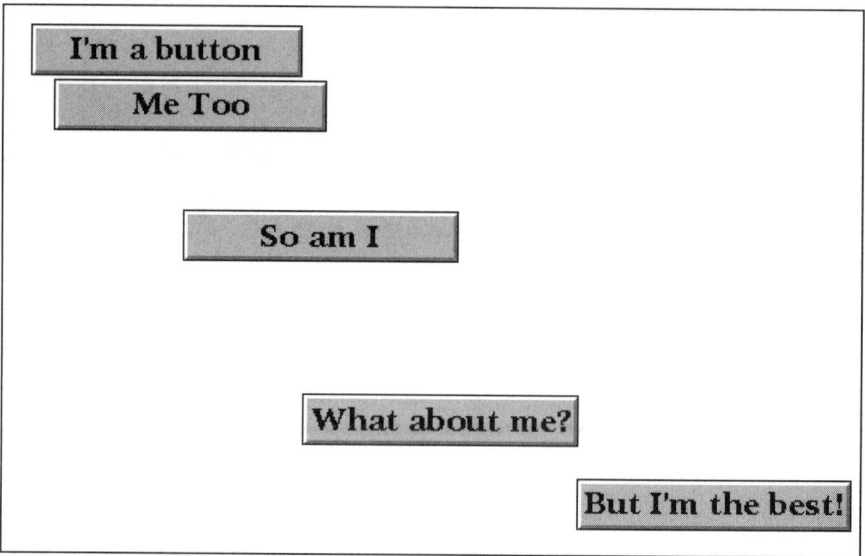

Figure 10-23: These buttons aren't evenly spaced.

To adjust the spacing:

○ Select the objects you want to change.

○ Choose Design, Adjust Spacing.

○ Choose Horizontal or Vertical.

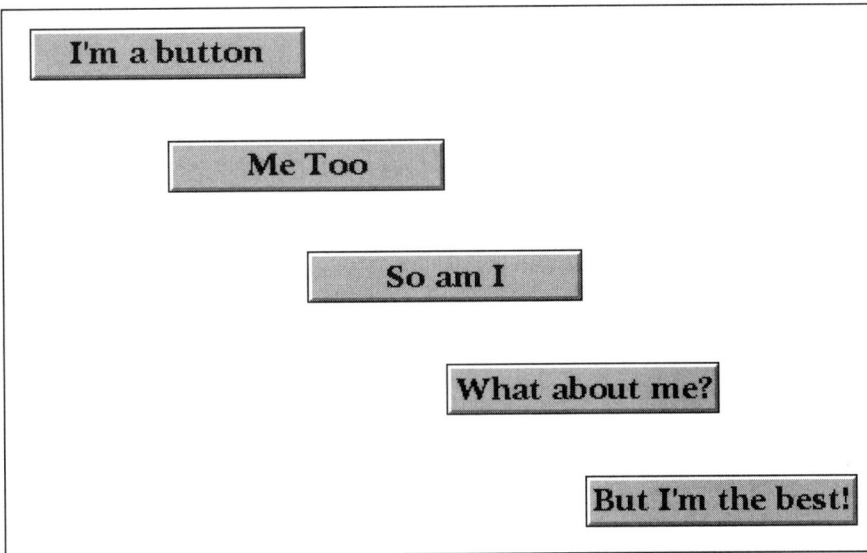

Figure 10-24: I adjusted the horizontal and vertical spacing.

Inside Scoop

Adjust Spacing works even if objects are pinned (we'll talk about pinning later—it's just a way of making sure objects stay in a particular position). For now just be aware that Adjust Spacing overrides pinning.

Grouping Objects

When we talked about containership, you saw how contained objects are treated. When you move or delete the container, the contained objects are also moved or deleted (unless you turn off the Contain Objects property). Grouped objects act very much like contained objects. You can group any number of objects and have them behave as a single object. Here's what you do:

❍ Select the objects you want to group.

❍ Choose Design, Group.

   A thin dotted line appears around the entire group, with a single set of handles. Now all of the objects will behave as if they were contained inside the group box.

❍ When you move or delete the group, all objects that are part of the group are moved or deleted.

○ You can still select individual objects within a group.

○ You can have groups within groups. Suppose you have several buttons that you've grouped. If you include the button group in another group, the button group retains its "groupness."

○ Just because an object is inside a grouped area, that object is not necessarily part of the group. A group consists *only* of the objects that were selected when you chose Design, Group. Any objects that were not selected, or that were added after the group was created, are not part of the group.

○ Grouping can be used to change the tab order (which we'll discuss in a bit). By default, Paradox moves to all of the objects inside a group or container before it moves to the next group or container.

○ To ungroup objects, select the group and choose Design, Ungroup. Or right-click on the group box and choose Ungroup from the Group Object Inspector menu.

Stacking Objects

When you start messing around with design objects, you can end up with circles on top of squares on top of lines, and other combinations too numerous to mention. In other words, more than one object can occupy the same space. Stacking gives you a way to control how objects are layered. You can move selected objects in front of or behind other objects.

Figure 10-25 shows an ellipse and a button. Notice that the ellipse is covering part of the button. To move the ellipse behind the button, choose Design, Send To Back (Figure 10-26 shows you the result). To reverse the process, just choose Design, Bring To Front.

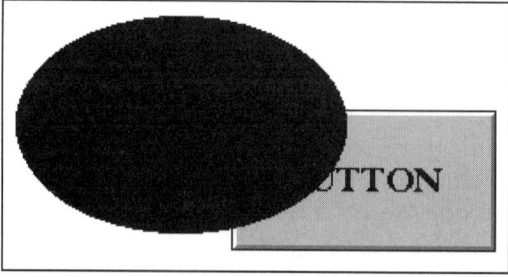

Figure 10-25: The ellipse is in front of the button.

Figure 10-26: I used Design, Send To Back to move the ellipse behind the button.

Duplicating Objects

Copying objects is an easy way to ensure consistency. For example, if you want to create several buttons that are the same size and share the same properties, just create one button that's exactly the way you want it. Then copy the button as many times as you want. There are two ways of copying design objects: you can copy selected objects to the Clipboard and then paste them back into your form, or you can choose Design, Duplicate to place a duplicate copy of selected objects on your form.

Using the Clipboard

Follow these steps to use the Clipboard method:

1. Select the object or objects you want to copy.

2. Click on the Copy To Clipboard button or choose Edit, Copy. Keyboard alternative: Ctrl+Ins.

3. Click in the Form Design window where you want the duplicate object to appear.

4. Click on the Paste From Clipboard button or choose Edit, Paste. Keyboard alternative: Shift+Ins.

5. Follow steps 3 and 4 to make additional copies. Whatever's in the Clipboard stays there until you replace it with something else; so until you cut or copy another object to the Clipboard, your original selection can be pasted in until you get sick of it.

Using the Duplicate Feature

Follow these steps to use the Duplicate feature:

1. Select the object or objects you want to duplicate.

2. Choose Design, Duplicate. The duplicate object is placed just below the original object.

As you can see, choosing Design, Duplicate saves you a few steps, especially if the object's final destination is close to the original object. The method you choose is really a matter of preference.

Changing Object Properties

Throughout this book, you've worked with Object Inspector menus. You know that when you right-click on an object (or press F6 with the object selected), you get a menu with options specific to that object. Object inspection works exactly the same way in the Form Design menu. The publishers wanted this book to weigh in under five pounds, so there won't be room to discuss every single property for every single object type. But I'll review the basics of object inspection and then talk about several of the more important properties.

Inside Scoop

You can get Help on any item in an Object Inspector menu. The only trick to getting context-sensitive Help is that you have to use the keyboard. With the menu open, use the Up or Down arrow on your keyboard to move to the item you want to find out about. If the item is followed by a right-pointing triangle, press Enter or the Right arrow key to open the submenu and use the Up or Down arrow to select the item. Then press F1 to open a Help window for the highlighted item.

Penetrating Properties

When you right-click on an object, you get an Object Inspector menu for that object. Even if you have several objects selected, the Object Inspector menu applies only to the object you right-click on. And if the object contains other objects, any changes you make apply only to the container object itself, not to the objects inside it. But what if you want to change properties for several selected objects? Or change properties for all of the objects contained within another object?

Use Paradox's *penetrating properties* option. This allows you to choose from an Object Inspector menu that contains all of the properties that can be applied to *any* of the selected objects. And when you change any property, the property is added to any selected object for which that property is valid. If the selected object is a container, property changes apply to all objects within the container.

To see a penetrating Object Inspector menu, first select the object or objects you want to inspect. Then hold down the Ctrl key while you right-click. Keyboard alternative: press Shift+F6. In Figure 10-27, I selected a box containing other objects and right-clicked. Notice that the Object Inspector menu is for the box only. In Figure 10-28, I selected the box and Ctrl+right-clicked. Notice that the Object Inspector menu header now says "Objects in Box." (When you use penetrating inspection on a group of selected objects, the header says "Objects in Selection.")

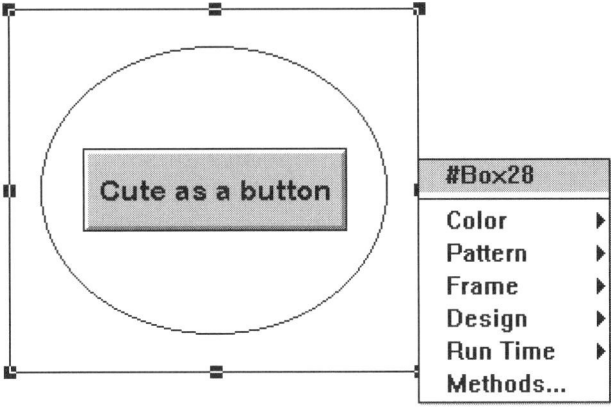

Figure 10-27: Making changes from this Object Inspector menu will affect only the box.

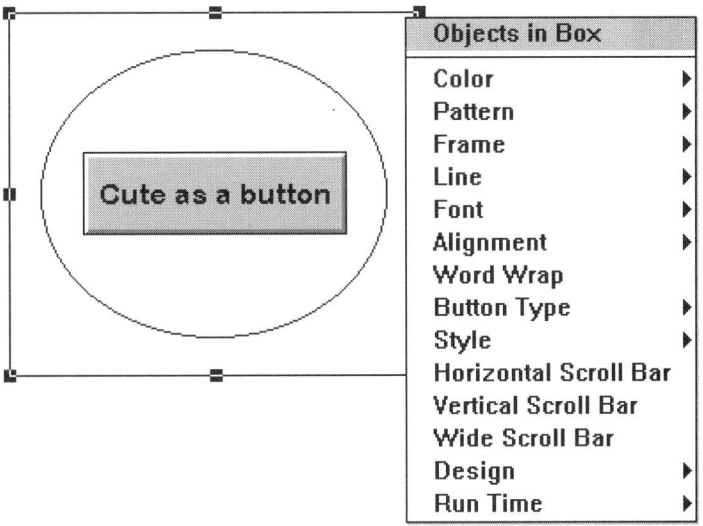

Figure 10-28: With this penetrating Object Inspector menu, you can make changes to the box *and* any objects inside the box.

327

Inside Scoop

Remember to look at the Object Inspector menu's header.
You can tell at a glance whether it's a regular or a
penetrating menu.

Using the Object Tree

Because objects can be contained within objects that are contained
within objects that are on top of or behind other objects, it can be
difficult to get to the Object Inspector menu you want. And as you get
into ObjectPAL, you'll need a way to see what all of your objects are
called so you can refer to them in your programming code. What if
you want to change the properties for several objects without having
to scroll around and select each object before you can right-click on
it? Or you want to see all of your object names at a glance, instead of
selecting each one and checking out the status bar? As you might
have guessed by now, help is on the way.

The Object Tree gives you a diagram of your form design, as shown
in Figure 10-29. To display the entire Object Tree, make sure you
don't have any objects selected and choose Tools, Object Tree. If you
want to view the Object Tree for a particular object, select the object
before you choose Tools, Object Tree.

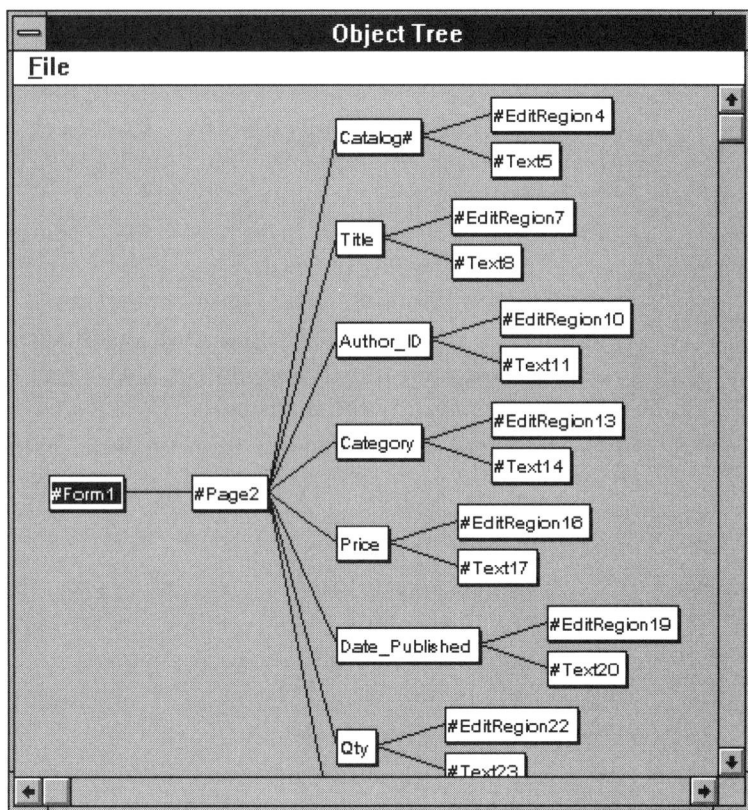

Figure 10-29: The Object Tree for BOOKS1.FSL. You can see how each object is related.

If Figure 10-29 freaks you out (too many little pieces), don't worry about it. You can do everything you need to without ever using the Object Tree. But give it a chance. The Object Tree can be an extremely useful tool. Here are a few of the things you can do with it:

○ **Select objects:** When you click on an object in the Object Tree, that object is also selected in the Form Design window. Keyboard alternative: Use the arrow keys to move to different objects.

○ **Change properties:** Right-click on any object to open the Object Inspector menu for that object. Remember that the object in the Object Tree is just a stand-in for the actual object in the Form Design window. Any changes you make are applied directly to the actual object.

○ **Apply penetrating properties:** As in the Form Design window, you can Shift-click to select multiple objects in the Object Tree and then Ctrl+right-click to access the penetrating properties menu for the selected objects.

○ **See which objects you've named:** (Naming objects is covered next.) Paradox's default name begins with a pound sign (#) followed by the object type. In Figure 10-29, notice that the field name objects are the only ones that don't have pound signs in front of them. When you created your table structure and assigned field names, you named those objects.

○ **Print the Object Tree:** Just choose File, Print from the Object Tree menu. A printout of the Object Tree can be useful for troubleshooting and documenting your form design.

○ **See which objects have ObjectPAL methods attached to them:** If a method is attached to an object, the object's name is underlined and marked with an asterisk.

Object Trees will be covered in more detail in the ObjectPAL chapters.

Renaming Design Objects

As you saw in Figure 10-29, the only objects that don't use Paradox's default naming system are the Field objects that you named when creating the table structure. Paradox assigns a sequential number to each design object. The form itself is #1, the page is #2, and additional items are numbered as they're added. The first object you place on a form is always #3. Look at the Catalog# object in Figure 10-29. It's actually the third object, so the next object is *#EditRegion4*.

The default object names are usually okay. Unless you're doing ObjectPAL programming, you don't need to refer to particular objects by name. The ins and outs of naming objects will be covered in detail in the ObjectPAL chapters; for now, I'll just show you how to do it.

1. To rename a design object, right-click on the object to open its Object Inspector menu, then click on the menu's title. The Object Name dialog box shown in Figure 10-30 will appear.

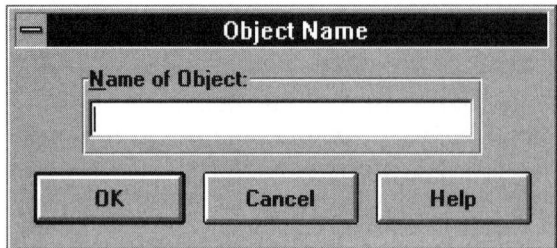

Figure 10-30: The Object Name dialog box.

2. Enter a name in the Name of Object text box and choose OK.
   The name can be up to 32 characters long. You can use only letters, numbers, the underline character and the pound sign—no spaces or other characters allowed.

Inside Scoop

How do you see an object's name? Three ways: Inspect the object and look at the Object Inspector menu's heading; select the object and look at the status bar; or display the Object Tree.

USING THE DESIGN TOOLS

At the beginning of the chapter I briefly described all of the tools on the Form Design Toolbar. But since I'm such a nice person, I won't make you go all the way back there. Figure 10-31 shows the design tools, which are the twelve buttons in the middle of the Toolbar.

Figure 10-31: The Form Design window's design tools.

You place design objects by first clicking on the design tool you want and then clicking and dragging to position and size the object in your form. You can always tell which design tool is active—its button is darker. Your mouse pointer gives you another clue. When you select a design tool, a little picture of the tool attaches itself to your mouse pointer.

Inside Scoop

By default, design tools are inactivated as soon as you use them. If you want to use the same tool to create multiple objects, just hold down the Shift key while you click on the tool. That tool remains selected until you select another tool.

Adding Boxes, Lines & Ellipses

With the Box, Line and Ellipse tools, you can draw lines and shapes (simple ones) on your form. You use each tool the same way—just click on it, then click and drag until the object is the shape and size you want. There isn't much to say about the box and ellipse except that one's square (or rectangular) and the other's round. But there are a few things you can do with lines.

Creating Curved Lines

By default, the Line tool draws a straight line. If you want a curved line, here's what you can do:

1. Right-click on the line and choose Line Type, Curved from the Object Inspector menu.
2. Drag a handle to adjust the angle of the curve.

Creating an Arrow

Lines are great for pointing to specific form objects. And what better way to point than with an arrow? It's easy to turn a line into an arrow:

1. Right-click on the line and choose Line Ends from the Object Inspector menu.
2. Choose On One End if you want an arrow on one end of the line; choose On Both Ends to place arrows on both ends of the line.

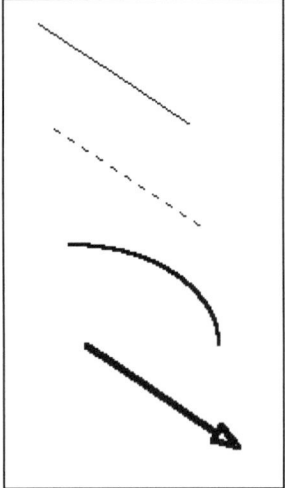

Figure 10-32: Different line styles.

The line on the top was created with the Line tool. So were the other lines. But the third line is curved and the fourth is an arrow.

Working With Text Objects

A text object is an object that contains text. Simple enough. When you select the Text tool and drag to create an outline in the design window, you're actually creating a frame into which you can put words. What do you use it for? Well, how about a title for your form?

In Chapter 5, you learned how to work with formatted memo fields, so you know how to inspect text objects and change their properties (color, font, pattern, etc.) But you can do a whole lot more with text objects in forms. A text object can expand to fit text as you enter it, or its size can be fixed. And you can set tabs and margins, change line spacing and do all sorts of other stuff.

How a text object is sized depends on how you create the object in the first place.

Creating a Fixed-Size Text Object

To create a fixed-size text object, just click on the Text tool and then click and drag to create a frame in the design window. As you type, text is displayed inside the frame. When you reach the right border of the frame, the text automatically wraps to the next line (the Word Wrap property is turned on by default). When you get to the bottom of the frame, the text onscreen scrolls up so that what you're typing continues to display.

○ Even though the size of the frame is fixed, that doesn't have any effect on the amount of text you can enter.

○ You can resize a fixed size text object by selecting the object and dragging any of its handles.

○ You can change a text object from fixed size to variable by selecting Design Sizing, Fit Text from the text object's Object Inspector menu.

Creating a Variable-Size Text Object

To create a variable-size text object, click on the Text tool, click in the design window (don't drag to create a frame) and start typing. As you type, the text object expands to the right until you press the Enter key. Pressing the Enter key defines the right border of the text object. After you type the first line, don't press Enter at the end of each line; the text will automatically wrap at your newly defined right border.

○ The height of the text object changes as you add or delete text.

○ The Word Wrap property is turned on as soon as you press Enter. With Word Wrap turned on, you can resize the text object horizontally but not vertically.

○ With Word Wrap turned off, you can't resize the text object.

○ To change a variable-size text object to a fixed-size text object so you can resize it, choose Design Sizing, Fixed Size from the text object's Object Inspector menu.

○ By default, a variable-size text object expands as you add text and shrinks when you delete text. If you want the text object to expand but not shrink, choose Design Sizing, Grow Only from the text object's Object Inspector menu.

○ If you turn Word Wrap off (by unchecking Word Wrap in the Object Inspector menu), you can enter only one line of text in the object. This goes for fixed-size objects as well.

Formatting & Editing Text

Once you've created a text object, the first thing you need to know is how to edit the text. We can get that out of the way in about two seconds—just click on the object to select it (remember, it's selected when the handles are visible), then click on the object again to place an insertion point inside the text area. When the insertion point appears, the handles disappear, and you're cleared for editing. You can also select a text object for editing by pressing the Tab key until the text object is selected, then pressing F2 to place the insertion point.

As with formatted memo fields, you can apply font attributes to all of the text or to selected portions of it. You make your selections from the text object's Object Inspector menu, but the result you get depends on what's selected when you right-click. For all text properties other than font attributes, your choices always apply to the entire object.

○ To change font properties for the entire text object, select the object and choose Font from the Object Inspector menu. Make sure you see handles around the object before you right-click, not an insertion point inside the text.

○ To change font properties for part of the text, select the text you want to change before you right-click.

○ To change font properties for new text, right-click with your insertion point inside the text object but nothing selected. The properties you change will apply to new text from your insertion point onward.

Using the Expanded Ruler

You can use the Text Object Inspector to change text alignment and line spacing, but there's an editing and layout tool that lets you change alignment and spacing at the click of a button. The expanded ruler also allows you to add tabs, create first-line and hanging indents, and change margins. To display the expanded ruler (shown in Figure 10-33, first make sure the horizontal ruler is visible (Properties, Horizontal Ruler). Then choose Tools, Expanded Ruler.

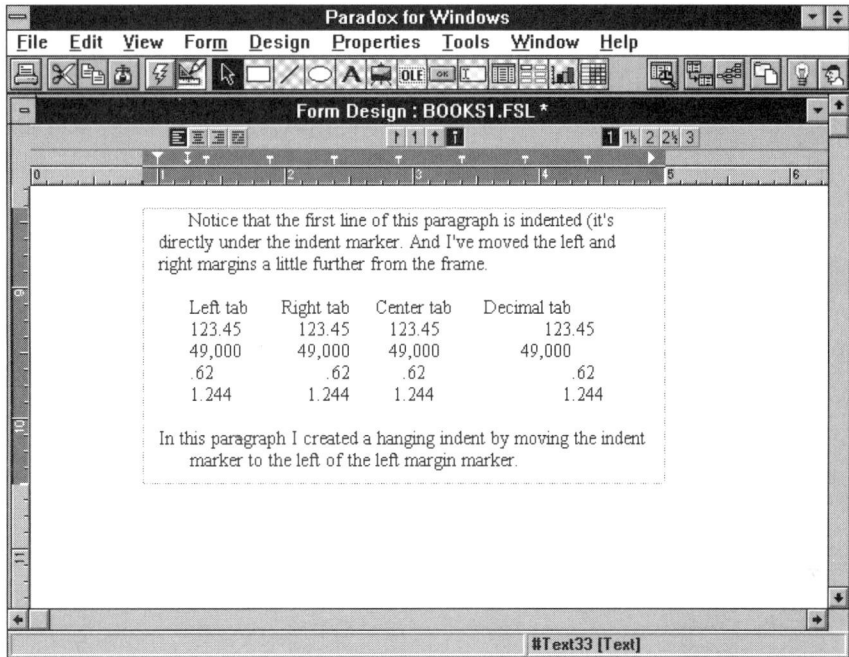

Figure 10-33: The Expanded Ruler with sample text.

Margin, indent, alignment and line spacing changes apply to the paragraph in which the insertion point is positioned. To apply one of these options to multiple paragraphs, select at least a portion of each paragraph before choosing the option.

○ To change text alignment or line spacing, just click on one of the text-alignment or line-spacing buttons.

○ To add a tab marker, click one of the tab buttons to specify a tab type, then click in the tab well (just above the horizontal ruler). Once you've placed a tab marker, you can move it by dragging it to a new location on the ruler, or delete it by dragging it off the ruler. Figure 10-33 shows examples of the different tab types.

○ You can't move or delete the default tab settings (the default tab markers are the stubby little tee-shaped ones). But as soon as you place a tab marker, Paradox deletes all of the default tabs to the left of your marker. So if you want to delete all of the default tab settings in one swipe and start from scratch, just add a tab stop to the right of the last default tab.

○ The indent marker affects the first line of each paragraph. But remember that changing the indent affects only selected paragraphs or the paragraph in which your insertion point is located. For a normal indent, drag the indent marker to the right of the left margin marker. For a hanging indent, drag the indent marker to the left of the left margin marker. See Figure 10-33 for examples.

○ To change the margins for a paragraph or selected paragraphs, drag the left or right margin marker to a new location.

Note: The indent marker and the left margin marker look like they're one piece, and it can be a bit tricky to get them to move separately. In Figure 10-33 I moved the indent marker to the right of the left margin marker so you can see what they look like. By default, both markers are in the same position. If you drag the top triangle, both objects will move. To move the indent marker by itself, drag the bottom triangle.

Inside Scoop

Add a vertical scroll bar to a text object that contains more text than is visible at one time. To add a scroll bar, just choose Vertical Scroll Bar from the text object's Object Inspector menu. A real-live scroll bar will appear in your text object, and you can use it just like any other Windows scroll bar. If you want a wider scroll bar, choose Wide Scroll Bar from the Object Inspector menu. (If Vertical Scroll Bar isn't selected, choosing Wide Scroll Bar doesn't do anything.) You can add scroll bars to most form objects—I'm just using this text object as an example of how handy they can be.

In most cases, you'll want to add a frame when you use the Vertical Scroll Bar property. Just choose Frame from the Object Inspector menu and choose the style, color and thickness you want. Figure 10-34 shows a text object to which a frame and wide scroll bar have been added.

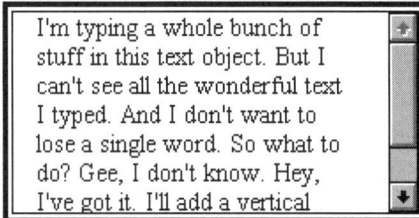

Figure 10-34: A text object with a scroll bar and frame.

Adding Graphic & OLE Objects

In Chapter 4, you learned about graphic and OLE fields. Adding graphic and OLE objects to forms is very much like adding graphic objects to a graphic or OLE field. And the same differences still hold: in a graphic field or object, the image is placed directly in your form or table and there's no connection to the program where the image was originally created; in an OLE field or object, the image is actually a copy—when you double-click on it, you can edit the image in its original format. OLE objects can also contain sound and document files. For more information about OLE, see Chapter 14.

Use the Graphic tool to create a graphic object:

1. Select the Graphic tool.

2. Drag to create a frame the size you want. When you release the mouse button, the object appears as shown in Figure 10-35.

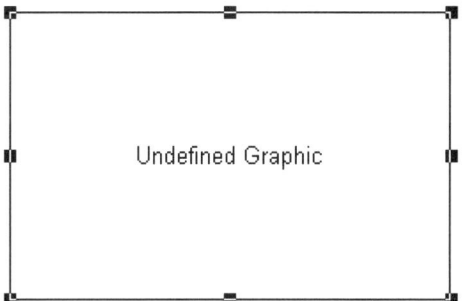

Figure 10-35: An empty graphic object.

3. By default, the Size To Fit option is turned on. That means the frame will resize to accommodate the graphic. If you don't want that to happen, choose Design from the Object Inspector menu and deselect Size To Fit.

4. To place an image in the frame, right-click on the object and choose Define Graphic from the Object Inspector menu.

5. To paste an image that has been copied to the Clipboard, choose Paste.

Or, to choose a graphic file from the Paste From Graphic File dialog box, choose Paste From, select the image you want and choose OK. You can insert BMP, PCX, TIF, GIF and EPS files.

Figure 10-36: A graphic object with an image inserted.

Use the OLE tool to create an OLE object:

1. Select the OLE tool.

2. Drag to create a frame the size you want. When you release the mouse button, the frame appears with "Undefined OLE" inside it.

3. Go to the OLE server program that contains the object you want to use and copy the object to the Clipboard. You'll find out all about OLE servers in Chapter 14.

4. Return to Paradox and choose Define OLE from the OLE object's Object Inspector menu.

5. Choose Paste. The image appears inside the frame.

Cropping a Graphic

You can crop a graphic to display only a portion of the image. Here's how:

1. Make sure Design, Size To Fit is deselected.
2. Select the container and size it so it's smaller than the graphic.
3. Move the graphic inside the container until the part of it you want to keep is displayed.

Figure 10-37: A cropped graphic image.

Changing Properties

The following properties can be applied to graphic objects (magnification also works for OLE objects). To use these properties, right click on a graphic object and make a selection from the Object Inspector menu.

○ **Magnification:** You can display the graphic at various percentages of its original size. Choose Best Fit to display the graphic at the largest possible magnification that allows the entire graphic to be displayed inside the frame.

○ **Raster Operation:** You can create special effects by making selections from the Raster menu. The options tell Paradox how the image should relate to its background. The choices will have different effects depending on the type of graphic file, so just play around with this one and see what you like.

Placing Buttons on a Form

Use the Button tool to place a Windows-style button on your form. Just select the Button tool and drag inside the Form Design window to create a button like the one shown in Figure 10-38.

Figure 10-38: A button before anything's been done to it.

In order to make the button perform an action, you have to use ObjectPAL code, which you'll learn about in the last part of this book. Here's what you can do at this point:

○ Change the button's text just as you would change text inside a text object (click to display an insertion point).

○ Choose Button Type from the Object Inspector menu and turn the button object into a radio button or a check box. By default, you get a regular push-button type.

○ If you select Radio or Check Box as the button type, you can then choose a style for the button object.

Inside Scoop

Even though the button doesn't really do anything right now, you can still have fun with it. When you switch to the Form window, you can click on a check box, push button or radio button to select and deselect it. Not very exciting, but we all need a mindless diversion now and then.

Working With Field Objects

Your form already has a bunch of field objects—the ones that came from BOOKS.DB. As we discussed, every field object consists of the field object (the container), a Text object (the label, which can be removed) and an EditRegion object (which holds the field data when the form is displayed).

You can use the Field tool to add additional fields to your form.

1. Select the Field tool.

2. Drag to place the field.

3. Choose Define Field from the Object Inspector menu.

What happens next depends on what you want to happen next. If you want to place one of the fields from the tables you're using, just select the field from the Define Field menu shown in Figure 10-39. If the field you want to place isn't listed, read on.

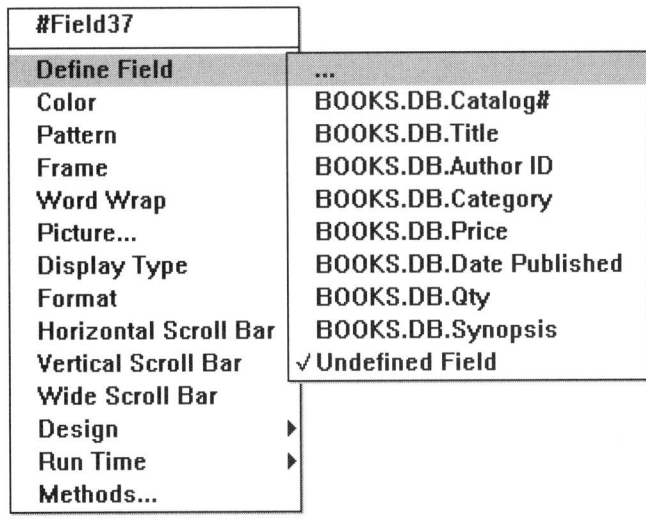

Figure 10-39: The Define Field menu.

To define special, calculated and summary fields, click on the three dots at the top of the Define Field menu to open the Define Field Object dialog box shown in Figure 10-40. For additional field choices, click on the drop-down list next to the table name.

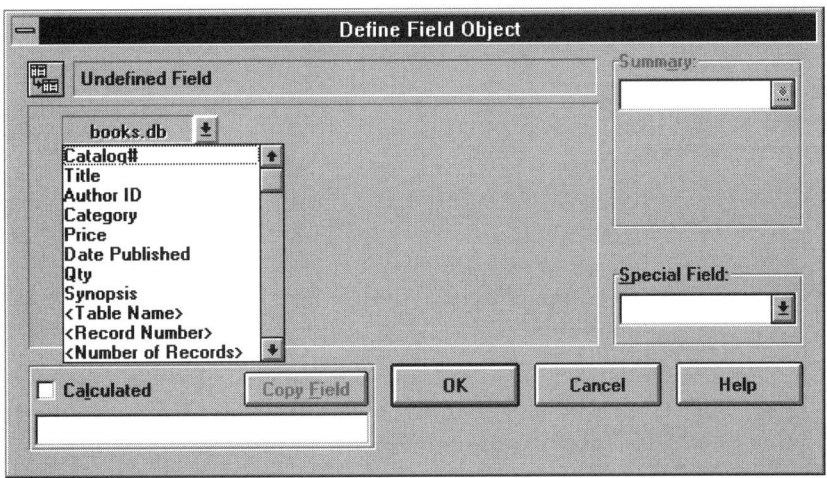

Figure 10-40: The Define Field Object dialog box with the field list displayed.

Special Fields

Notice that, in addition to the fields from the table, this list contains choices in angle brackets. These are *special* fields that allow you to place the table's name, the current record number, the total number of records or the total number of fields in a field object.

You can also choose special fields from the Special Field drop-down list shown in Figure 10-41. These special fields let you do things like place the current date, time or page number in a form.

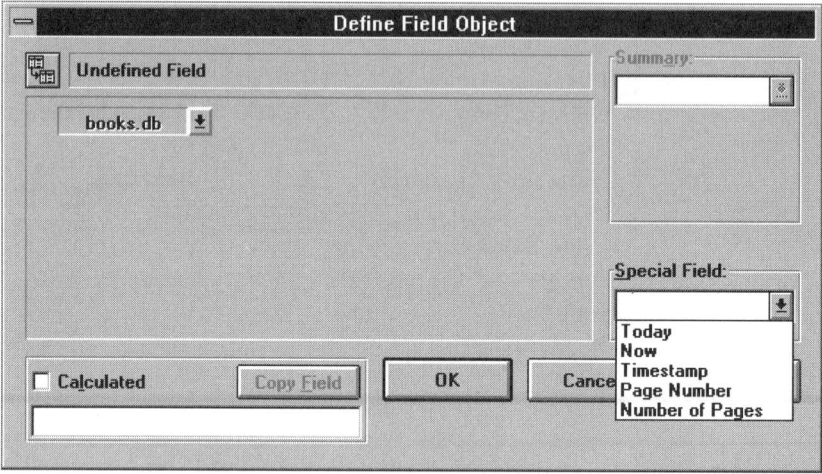

Figure 10-41: The Special Field drop-down list.

Calculated Fields

To define a calculated field, select the Calculated check box and enter a calculation formula in the text box at the bottom of the dialog box. You can perform calculations using the techniques you learned for queries in Chapter 8. To make it easier to refer to fields in your calculations, you can choose a field from the table name drop-down list and click on the Copy Field button to place the field in the calculation text box.

Summary Fields

You can also do COUNT, MIN and MAX summaries on numeric fields. If the field can handle a summary, the Summary drop-down list is activated when the field is selected. Just open the drop-down list and choose the summary type you want.

When you've defined the new field, choose OK. The field appears in the Form Design window, at which point you can do whatever you want to it.

Inside Scoop

By default, all field objects have labels. To get rid of the label, choose Field Type, Unlabeled from the field object's Object Inspector menu.

Working With Table Objects

 When you create an initial form design with a tabular layout, Paradox places a *table frame* on your form. Just as a field object consists of a container and embedded objects, a table frame consists of the frame itself (the container) and embedded objects. The field objects themselves are contained within the table frame. You can also define additional table objects using the Table tool. As with the other design tools, you just click on the Table tool, then drag to place the frame in your form.

When you release the mouse button, a table frame with undefined fields is displayed, as shown in Figure 10-42.

LABEL	LABEL	LABEL
Undefined Field	Undefined Field	Undefined Field

Figure 10-42: A table frame.

You can inspect and define individual field and record objects, but the easiest way to get information into a table object is by defining the table itself. Just right-click on the table frame object and choose Define Table. Any available tables will be listed on the Define Table menu. If the table you want to use isn't displayed, click on the three dots at the top of the menu to open the Define Table Object dialog box shown in Figure 10-43.

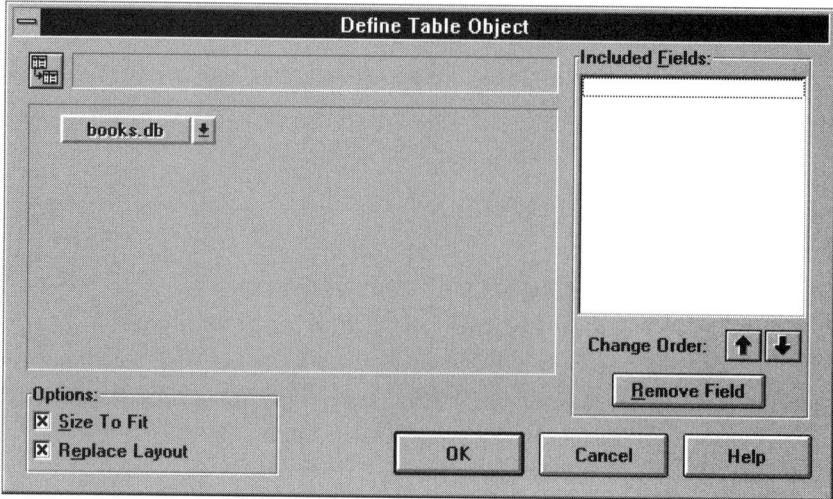

Figure 10-43: The Define Table Object dialog box.

 To add tables to your data model, click on the Data Model button, place the tables you want in the Data Model dialog box and choose OK.

Some Choice Properties

Following are descriptions of several properties that can be applied to a bunch of different object types. If the property can't be applied to a particular type of object, that option won't appear on the Object Inspector menu.

○ **Frame:** Choose from several different styles to add frames to almost any kind of object.

○ **Horizontal Scroll Bar/Vertical Scroll Bar:** Place horizontal and/ or vertical scroll bars in an object.

○ **Wide Scroll Bar:** Works in conjunction with the Horizontal Scroll Bar or Vertical Scroll Bar property to widen the displayed scroll bars.

○ **Design, Pin Vertical and Design, Pin Horizontal:** Pinning allows you to "glue" an object to a specific horizontal or vertical position. When you select Pin Vertical, the object can be moved only horizontally. When you select Pin Horizontal, the object can be moved only vertically. When both are selected the object stays exactly where it is.

○ **Design, Contain Objects:** When this option is selected, the object can act as a container for other objects. If you don't want this to happen, deselect the option.

○ **Run Time:** The Run Time menu contains options that affect what happens when you view (or *run*) the form. You'll use most of the run time properties in the ObjectPAL chapters.

DISPLAYING FIELDS

So far, all of your field objects have been plain old labeled fields. You know how to change the formatting and get rid of the label, but you can get a lot fancier. How about creating drop-down and radio button lists just like you see in most of your Windows programs? Sound hard? It's not. It's just a matter of selecting the option you want and making some entries in a dialog box. When you choose Display Type from a field object's Object Inspector menu, you get the menu shown in Figure 10-44. This section will cover the Drop-Down Edit, List, Radio Buttons and Check Box options.

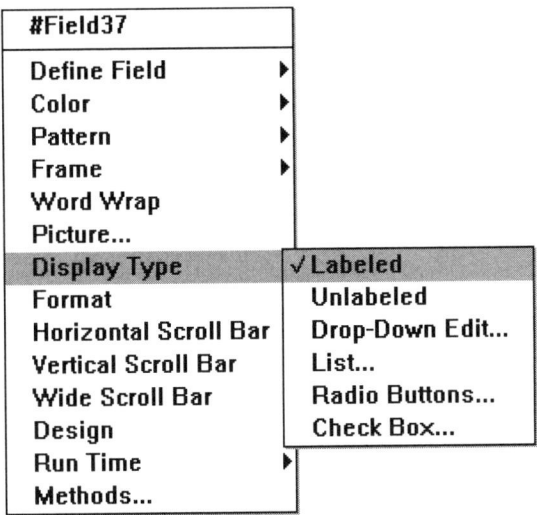

Figure 10-44: The Display Type menu.

Inside Scoop

I'm going to show you how to add data to different types of list boxes, and you'll be able to choose from the options to enter data directly in your form. But hold on before you go hog-wild with this one. In general, using ObjectPAL programming to tie a field to its referential integrity reference is preferable to simply entering the field data in a field object's list box. Suppose you create a drop-down list for the Category field that contains each category. What happens when you get a new category? Not only do you have to make the change in the CTGORY.DB file, you also have to edit the form design. This creates additional work and additional opportunities for errors. The ObjectPAL chapters discuss all of this in detail—check them out before you make final decisions on defining your field objects.

Lists, Drop-Down Lists & Radio Buttons

I'm grouping these three display types because you use the same techniques for all of them. I'll talk you through it defining a drop-down list, then show you examples of the other types.

1. From a field object's Object Inspector menu, choose Display Type, Drop-Down Edit.

Figure 10-45: The Define List dialog box. Notice that the Field Type box tells you which type is selected.

2. In the Item text box, type each item you want on the list and press Enter.

3. Click on the Sort List button to sort all of the items in the Item List in ascending order (A to Z or 1 to 10).

4. Use the up and down arrows just below the Item List to change the order of individual items.

5. Select an item and click on the Modify Item button to edit the item.

6. Select an item and click on the Remove Item button to delete the item.

7. Choose OK.

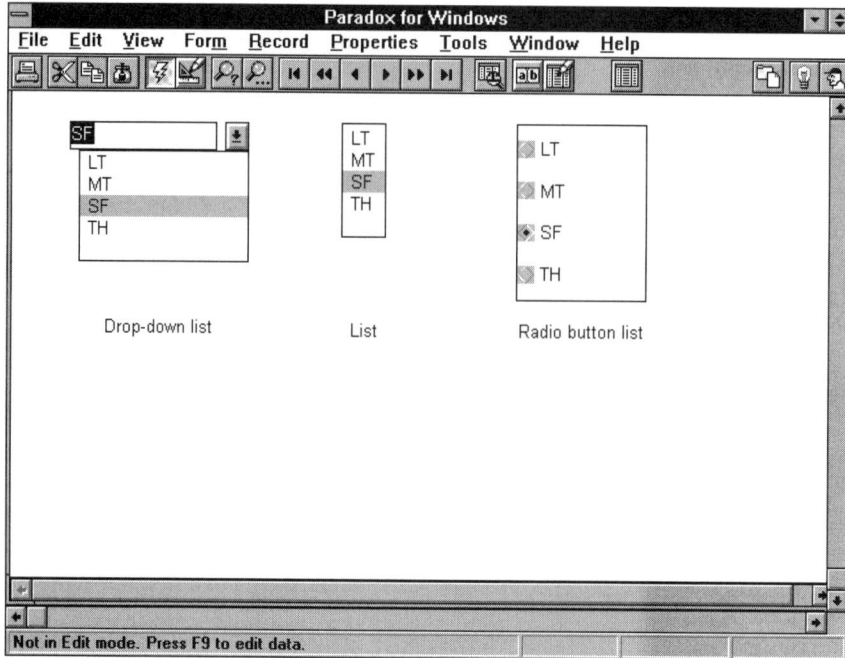

Figure 10-46: Sample drop-down, list and radio button field objects in the Form window.

Although you create each field display type the same way, there are a few differences in how they work when you run (view) the form.

○ With a drop-down field, you can make a choice from the drop-down list or type directly in the field's text box.

○ With a list field, you must make a choice from the list. You can't type your own entry.

○ With a radio button list, you just click on the button for the item you want.

Check Boxes

Check boxes are different than the other field display types. Think about how check boxes work in regular dialog boxes. For example, take a look at the Designer Properties dialog box shown in Figure 10-48 (a couple of pages down the road). Each item has a check box next to it. When the check box is selected, the item is turned on. When the check box is blank, the item is turned off. So a check box can have only two behaviors: on or off. But you get to define what the "on" and "off" values are.

To define a check box:

1. From the field object's Object Inspector menu, choose Display Type, Check Box.

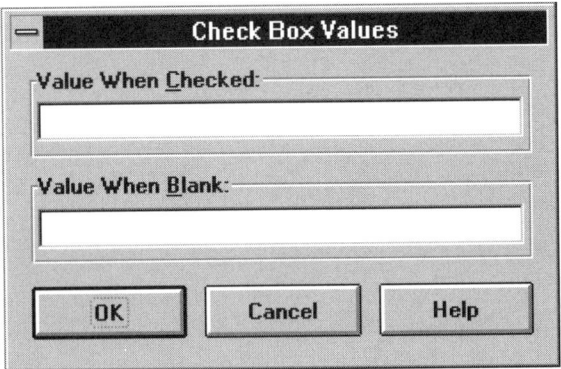

Figure 10-47: The Check Box Values dialog box.

2. Type a value in the Value When Checked text box. That will be the default value for the field.

3. Type a value in the Value When Blank text box. That's what you want displayed when the check box is empty.

MULTIPAGE FORMS

If all of your fields won't fit in one window, or if your design requires more space, you can add pages to your form. To add a page to the end of the form, just choose Form, Page. You can place new objects or copy objects from other pages. The Form, Page menu provides several options for moving among pages, including a Go To option that can take you to a specific page. To delete a page, select the entire page (make sure nothing else on the page is selected and that #Page is displayed on the status bar) and choose Edit, Delete. Be careful with this one—you're getting rid of *everything* on the page.

CHANGING FORM DESIGN WINDOW OPTIONS

Paradox has certain default ways of behaving, most of which you can change. A little earlier I told you how to deselect Select From Inside to give you greater precision in selecting objects. To change this and other *designer* properties, choose Properties, Designer.

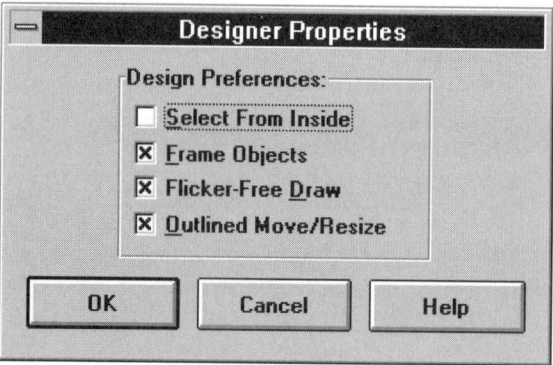

Figure 10-48: The Designer Properties dialog box.

○ **Select From Inside:** As mentioned earlier, when Select From Inside is selected, Paradox selects from the outside in.

○ **Frame Objects:** By default, design objects are displayed with a dotted-line frame so you can see the outline of the object. If you deselect Frame Objects, you won't see a frame unless you've added one by choosing Frame from the Object Inspector menu.

○ **Flicker-Free Draw:** By default, Flicker-Free draw is turned on to minimize screen flickering when you move or resize objects. This option can slow things down a bit. You can try turning it off and see if it makes a difference.

○ **Outlined Move/Resize:** By default, this option is turned on. When you move or resize an object, you see only an outline that represents the object. You can turn this option off if you want to see the actual object while it's being moved or resized. Unless the outline really bothers you, though, don't mess with this one. You pay for displaying the entire object with slower screen displays.

MOVING ON

It's time to move on to reports—a new topic with much in common with forms. You'll find yourself using the same design and layout tools, selection methods and many other options. Chapter 11 takes you through the basics of creating a report layout, using the Report and Mailing Label Experts and starting a report from a default QuickReport. After that, Chapter 12 gets into detail on advanced report stuff.

11 REPORTS 101

In the previous two chapters, you learned all about working with forms. Because forms and reports have a whole lot in common, most of what you learned will come in handy in this chapter and the next. The main thing that separates reports from forms is that reports are meant to be printed out. Of course you can print out your forms, but Paradox's Report Designer has special features that allow you to do things like adding header or footer information to each page. This is done through *report bands*, which divide your report layout into sections. You'll learn all about bands in the next chapter. For now, just be aware that by placing information in different bands, you can determine where that information will print.

CREATING A REPORT

As with forms, there are three basic techniques for creating a new report. And as I did with forms, I'll give you a quick overview before we get into the details. I'll focus on working with the three types of Experts—*Quick Report*, *Report*, and *Mailing Label*—and the Data Model and Design Layout dialog boxes.

1. Start with the default Quick Report and customize it as you wish.

   ○ With your table onscreen, click on the Quick Report button or press Shift+F7.

   ○ From the Report window, click on the Design button or press F8.

   ○ Customize the report.

2. Use the Report Expert.

   ○ From any Toolbar, click on the Expert button. Or choose Help, Experts.

   ○ Then, click on the Report (or Mailing Labels) button in the Expert Control Panel.

○ You can also start the Report Expert by right-clicking on the Reports button from the Desktop Toolbar or the Project Viewer. Choose New from the Object Inspector menu and choose Report Expert (or Label Expert) from the New Report dialog box.

○ Make choices from the Report Expert windows.

○ When you have completed your choices for one step, click on the Next button to move to the next step.

○ When you've completed all the steps, click on the Create button to tell Paradox to create the report.

○ Customize the report as desired.

 3. Do it from scratch.

○ Right-click on the Reports button from the Desktop Toolbar or the Project Viewer and choose New from the Object Inspector menu. Or choose File, New, Report from the pull-down menu.

○ Then choose Data Model/Layout Diagram from the New Report dialog box. (You can also choose Blank to create a report that's not tied to any tables.)

○ From the Data Model dialog box, choose the tables to include in the report and define links between them. Choose OK to continue.

○ In the Design Layout dialog box, choose a general layout for your report (arrange records by columns or rows; display records in tabular format, one at a time, multiple records on a page, etc.) Choose OK to continue.

○ In the Report Design window, design and customize the report.

Just as all techniques for creating forms lead to the Form Design window, all report roads lead to the Report Design window. In this chapter I'll cover the methods of getting you to the Report Design window, and in the next chapter you'll learn how to put it all together to create eye-catching reports.

Starting With a Quick Report

This is the quickest and easiest way to get started. Just open a default Quick Report and then make any changes you want. Here's how:

1. Open the table you want to create the report for. For this example, open BOOKS.DB.

2. From Table View, click on the Quick Report button. Or press Shift+F7. This takes you to the Report window for BOOKS.DB, as shown in Figure 11-1.

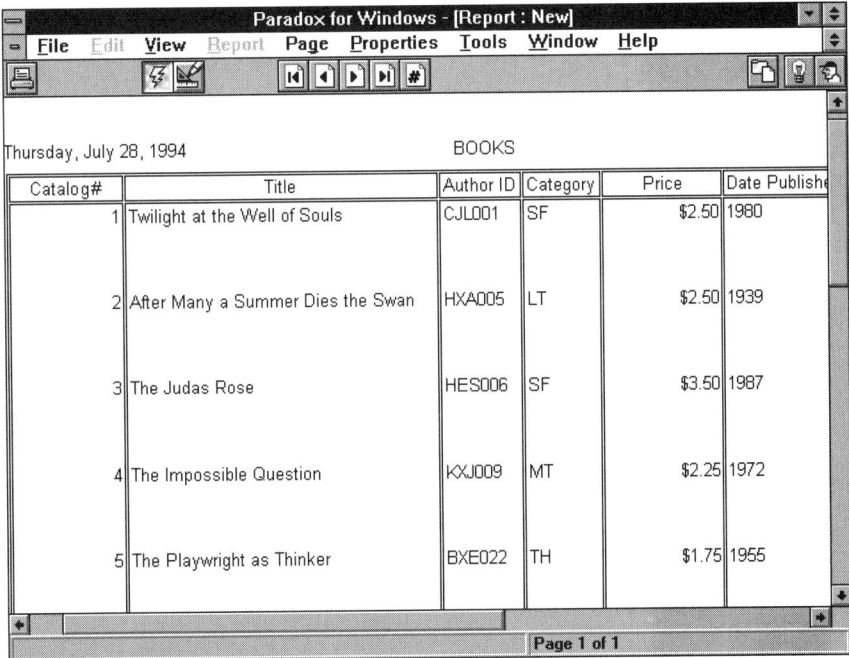

Figure 11-1: The Report window allows you to view the report data as it will look in the printed report. Notice that the default report is in a tabular format.

3. Click on the Design button or press F8 to switch to the Report Design window shown in Figure 11-2.

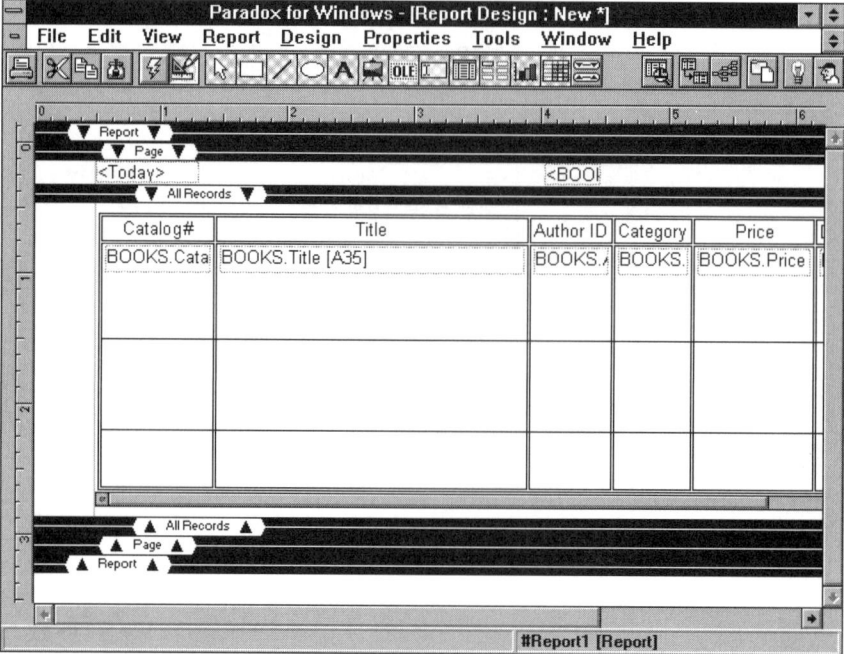

Figure 11-2: The Report Design window.

Using the Report Expert

The Report Expert walks you through the process of creating a report. You add tables, define links and choose the basic style and layout. As with the Form Expert, the Report Expert gives you a good head start, but you'll still have plenty to do in the Report Design window if you want to customize the report.

Opening the Report Expert

Follow these steps to open the Report Expert:

1. Click on the Expert button to open the Expert Control Panel dialog box.

2. Choose Report. This takes you to Step 1 of the Report Expert, as shown in Figure 11-3.

    You can also start the Report Expert by right-clicking on the Reports button from the Desktop Toolbar or the Project Viewer. Choose New from the Object Inspector menu and choose Report Expert from the New Report dialog box.

Choosing the Layout

Step 1 of the Report Expert is where you choose the basic report layout. The left side of the window displays samples of each layout choice. As you click on a radio button, the layout sample for that choice is highlighted to give you an idea of the result. You can also click directly on one of the layout samples to activate the radio button for that option.

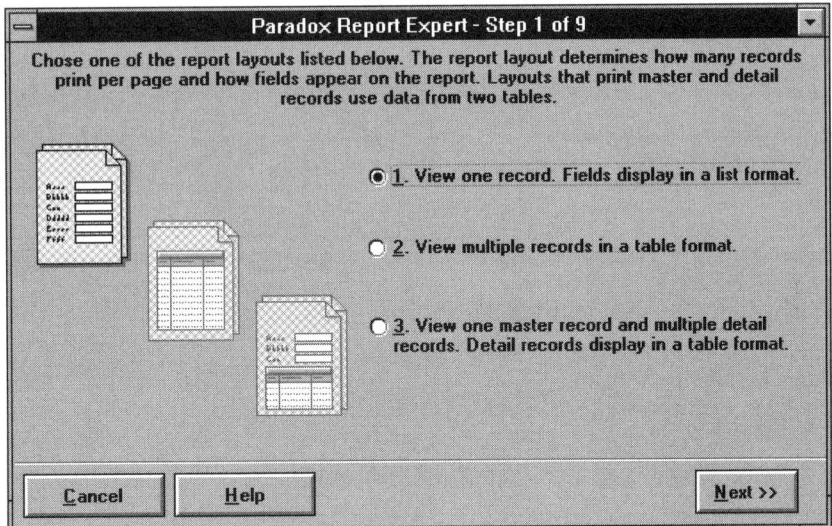

Figure 11-3: Step 1 of the Report Expert. This is where you start answering questions about your report.

Remember that you can choose Cancel from any point in the Report Expert, but be aware that in canceling you abandon everything you've done in the Expert. And choosing Help takes you to an online Help window for the current step. The Next button at the bottom right takes you to the next step.

The following list describes the layout choices. Again, these layouts are just starting points—you'll be able to change them around later.

○ Option 1 prepares a report in which you see only one record on each page, with the fields displayed top to bottom. In this layout, only one table can be used.

○ Option 2 prepares a tabular report, similar to the Quick Report in Figure 11-1. You see multiple records on one page, but only one table can be used in the report.

○ Use option 3 if you want to prepare a report using multiple tables. The main table is displayed in list format, and the detail table is displayed in tabular format.

When you've decided which layout you want, click on the Next button. For now, choose option 2, View multiple records in a table format.

Choosing the Master Table

Step 2 of the Report Expert is where you choose the main (master) table to include in the form. If you choose option 1 or 2, which are both single-table layouts, the table you choose is considered the master table.

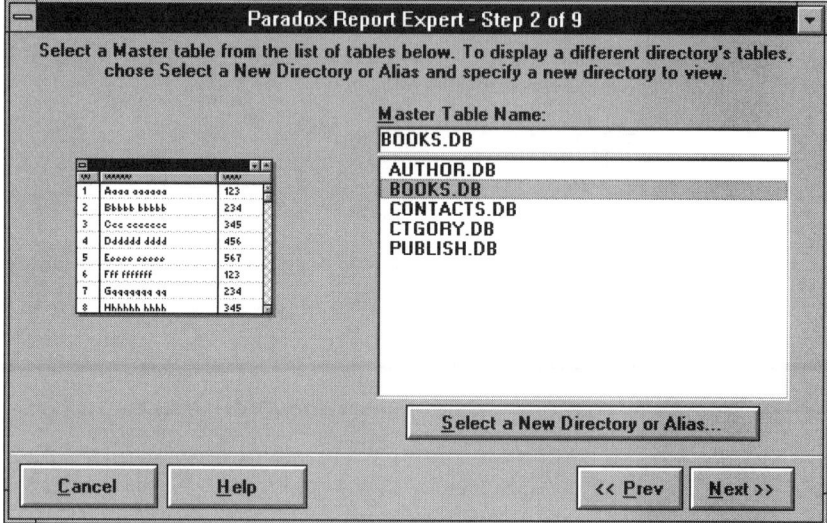

Figure 11-4: Step 2 of the Report Expert.

At this point, the Prev button appears to the left of the Next button. From any Expert window except the first, you can click on the Prev button to go back to any step you want to edit.

To choose the Master table (choose BOOKS.DB):

○ Click on the table's name in the Master Table Name list.

○ Or type the name in the Master Table Name text box.

○ Or double-click on the table's name. This takes you right to the next step without clicking on the Next button.

○ If the table is in a different directory, click on the Select A New Directory Or Alias button and choose the directory, drive and/or alias from the Directory Browser.

○ Click on the Next button when you're done.

Selecting Fields

Because we chose a single-table layout, the Report Expert skipped steps 3 and 4, which have to do with choosing detail tables and defining links between the tables. We'll return to those steps after we're done with our single-table example.

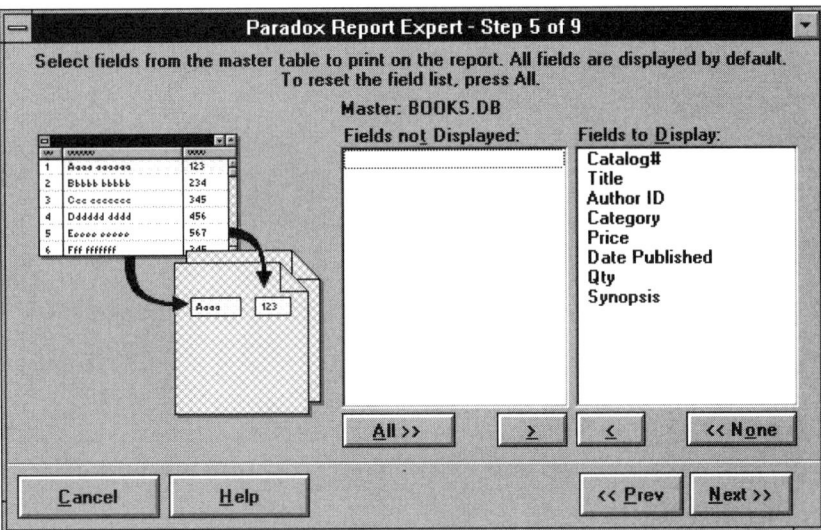

Figure 11-5: Step 5 of the Report Expert. This is where you choose the fields to display on your report.

Notice that all of the fields in BOOKS.DB are listed in the Fields To Display list. By default, the report includes all of the fields from your selected table.

○ To remove a field, select the field and click on the < button just below the Fields To Display list. This moves the field into the Fields Not Displayed list. You can also double-click on a field name to move it directly to the Fields Not Displayed list.

○ Choose None to remove all fields from the Fields To Display list. If you plan to include only a few fields, it can save you some time if you first get rid of all the fields at once and then move back only those that you need.

○ Move fields into the Fields To Display list by selecting the field in the Fields Not Displayed list and clicking on the > button just below the Fields Not Displayed list. You can also double-click on a field name in the Fields Not Displayed list to move it directly to the Fields to Display list.

○ Choose All to move all fields in the Fields Not Displayed List into the Fields To Display list.

For our example, leave all the fields in the Fields To Display list and click on the Next button.

Selecting the Print Format

Because we're working with a single table, we skipped step 6, which has to do with choosing fields for the detail table.

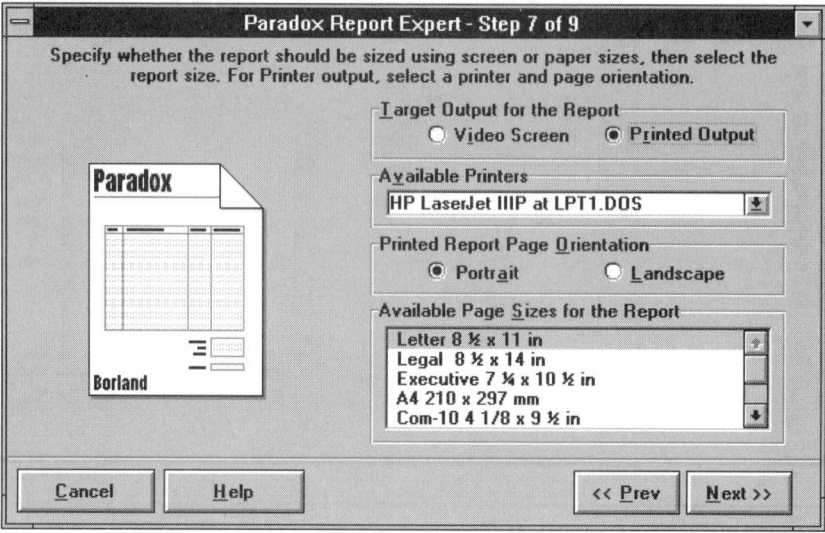

Figure 11-6: Step 7 of the Report Expert.

Step 7 is where you tell Paradox how to print the report.

○ **Target Output for the Report:** Choose Video Screen if you want a report designed for screen display; choose Printed Output (the default) to design the report for your printer.

○ **Available Printers:** If you have only one printer, its name should be displayed here. If you have more than one printer, open the Available Printers drop-down list and choose the printer you want to use for the report.

○ **Printed Report Page Orientation:** Choose Portrait to display the report in a vertical format, or choose Landscape for a report that prints across the long side of the page. When you click the Portrait or Landscape radio button, the left side of the window displays a sample report showing the selected orientation. (**Note:** You can't choose an orientation when Video Screen is selected.)

○ **Available Page Sizes for the Report:** For printed reports, you can choose from several standard paper sizes. When Video Screen is selected, you choose among different video resolutions (the choices you get will depend on the capabilities of your monitor and video driver).

For now, choose Printed Output, Landscape, Letter 8 1/2 x 11 in, and click on the Next button.

Specifying Headers & Footers

Here's where you tell Paradox whether you want header or footer information on each page of the report.

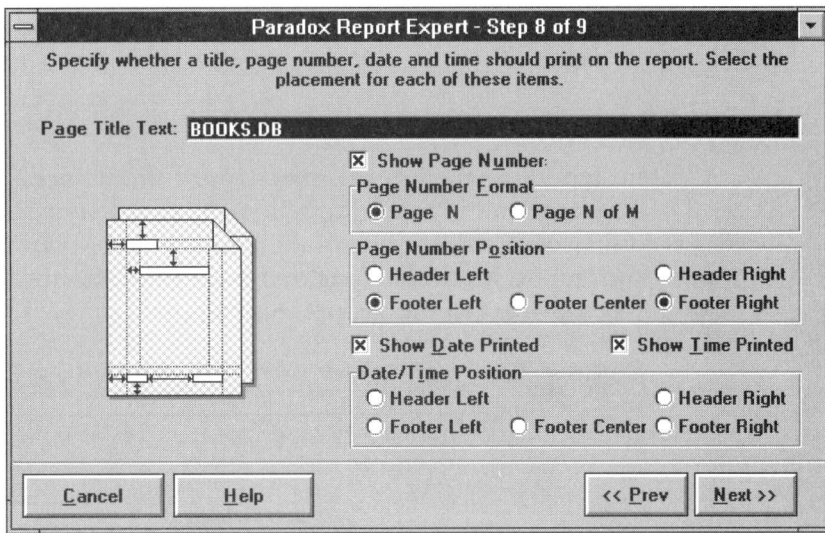

Figure 11-7: Step 8 of the Report Expert.

Use this window to include date, time and page number information in your report:

○ **Page Title Text:** The text you type in the Page Title Text box will appear on the first page of your report, and it will be centered between the left and right margins.

○ **Show Page Number:** Check this box if you want the current page number to print on each page.

○ **Page Number Format:** Tell Paradox how you want the page number to appear. The Page N option prints the word *page* followed by the page number (e.g., *Page* 2). The Page N of M option prints the word *page* followed by the page number and the total number of pages. For example, if you have a ten-page report, the second page would say *Page 2 of 10*.

○ **Page Number Position:** Tell Paradox where you want the page numbers. A header is at the top of the page; a footer is at the bottom. A page number can appear at the left or right side of the page in a header; it can appear at left, at right or centered in a footer.

○ **Show Date Printed:** Check this box if you want the date the report is printed to be displayed in the report.

○ **Show Time Printed:** Check this box if you want the time the report is printed to be displayed in the report. If both Show Date Printed and Show Time Printed are selected, the time appears immediately following the date.

○ **Date/Time Position:** Tell Paradox whether you want the date and/or time in the header or footer, and choose a position on the page.

Choosing a Style

In step 9 (the final step), you choose a predefined style sheet to use for your report. When you select one of the style sheets, a sample is displayed in the left half of the window. The style you choose gives your report an overall look, but you can make any changes you want when you get to the Report Design window.

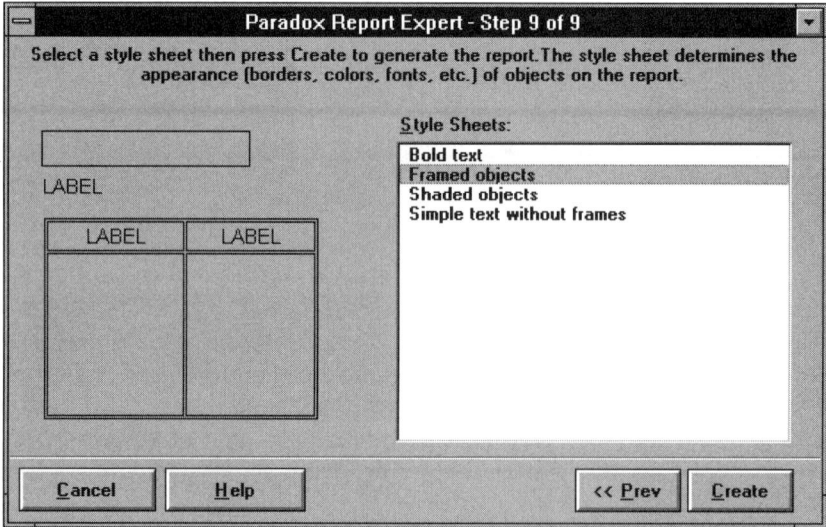

Figure 11-8: The last step of the Report Expert.

The Next button has been replaced by a Create button. When you click on it, Paradox creates the report using the layout that you've specified.

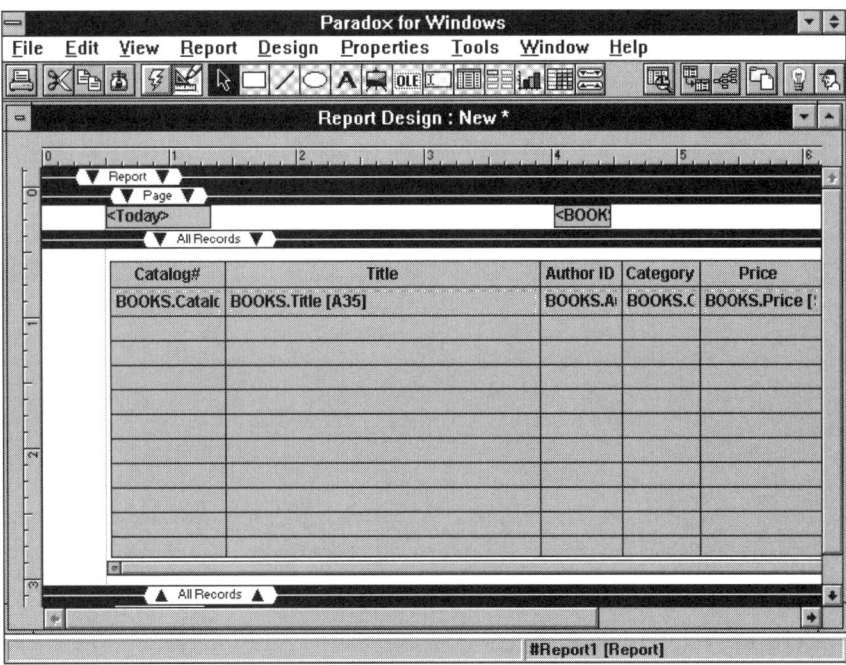

Figure 11-9: A tabular report created by the Report Expert.

Creating a Multitable Report

In this section, I'm just going to give you a quick rundown on the steps that weren't covered in the previous section. The only difference when you create a multitable report is that you have to fill in a few extra dialog boxes that ask you questions about the additional tables. To create a multitable report using the Report Expert, choose option 3 (View One Master Record and Multiple Detail Records) from step 1 and then follow through the steps as described earlier. Here's a quick look at the steps you missed:

○ Step 3 is where you select the detail table that will be associated with the master table. The techniques are the same as those for step 2.

○ Step 4 is where you choose how the tables will be linked.

○ Step 6 is just like step 5, except you're choosing fields from the detail table instead of the master table.

Doing It on Your Own

Just as you did with forms, you can create a report layout by choosing tables from the Data Model dialog box and then selecting fields to include and a report layout from the Design Layout dialog box.

Beginning the Process

 ○ Right-click on the Reports button from the Desktop Toolbar or the Project Viewer and choose New from the Object Inspector menu. Or choose File, New, Report from the pull-down menu. The New Report dialog box is displayed, as shown in Figure 11-10.

Figure 11-10: The New Report dialog box.

○ Choose Data Model/Layout Diagram from the New Report dialog box.

The Data Model Dialog Box

From the Data Model dialog box, you choose the tables to include in the report and define links between them.

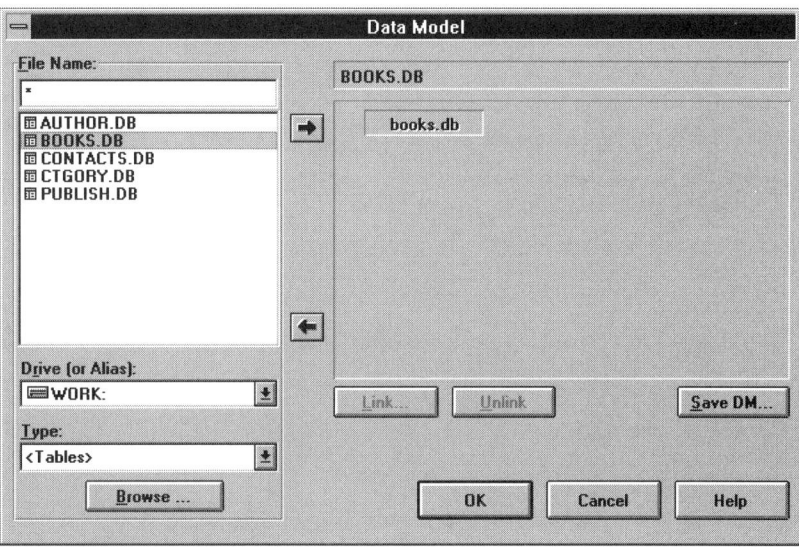

Figure 11-11: The Data Model dialog box.

To add a table to the data model, select the table from the File Name list or type the name in the File Name text box. For this example, choose BOOKS.DB. Then click on the right arrow button.

○ Click on the Browse button or use the Drive (Or Alias) list if the tables you want aren't in your working directory.

○ If you want to use a query or previously saved data model as the basis for your data model, choose <Queries> or <Data Models> from the Type drop-down list. When the queries or data models are displayed in the File Name list, you can move them into the data model just as you can with tables.

○ Choose OK to continue.

The Design Layout Dialog Box

Here's where you determine the basic layout and style and tell Paradox which fields to include in the report.

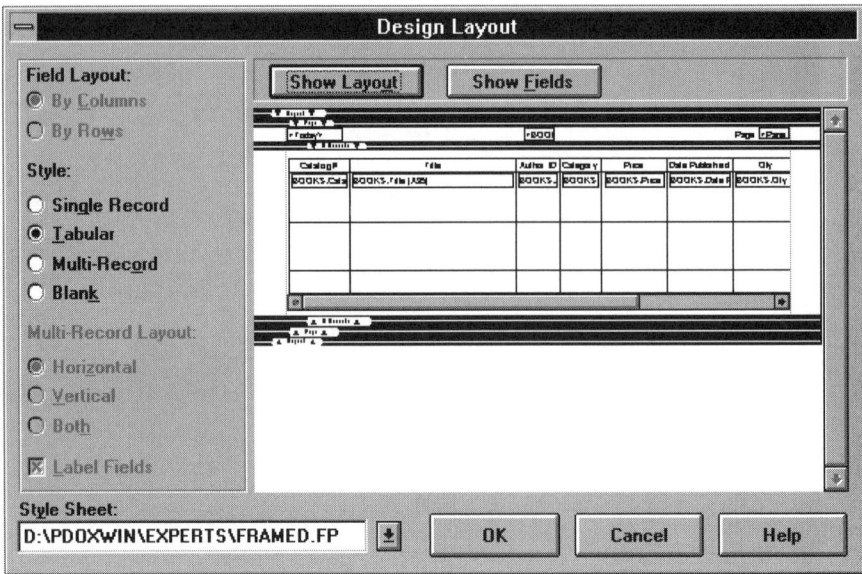

Figure 11-12: The Design Layout dialog box with Show Layout selected.

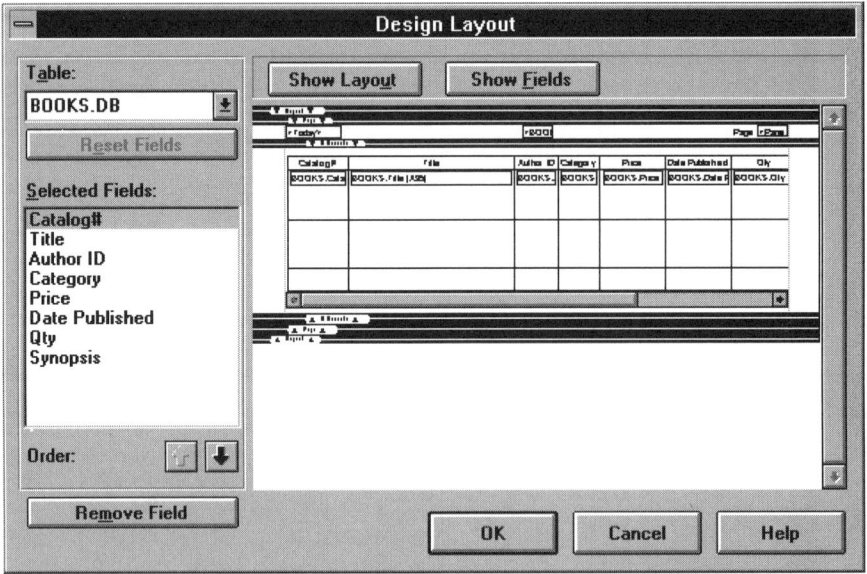

Figure 11-13: The Design Layout dialog box with Show Fields selected.

Just as when you create a form, the Design Layout box is initially displayed in Show Layout mode, as shown in Figure 11-12. This is where you choose the Field Layout, Style and Multi-Record Layout, and specify whether you want labeled fields.

Click on the Show Fields button to display the window shown in Figure 11-13. All of the fields in your table are displayed—you can choose which ones you want to include and determine their order.

For a complete description of the options in the Design Layout dialog box, see Chapter 9.

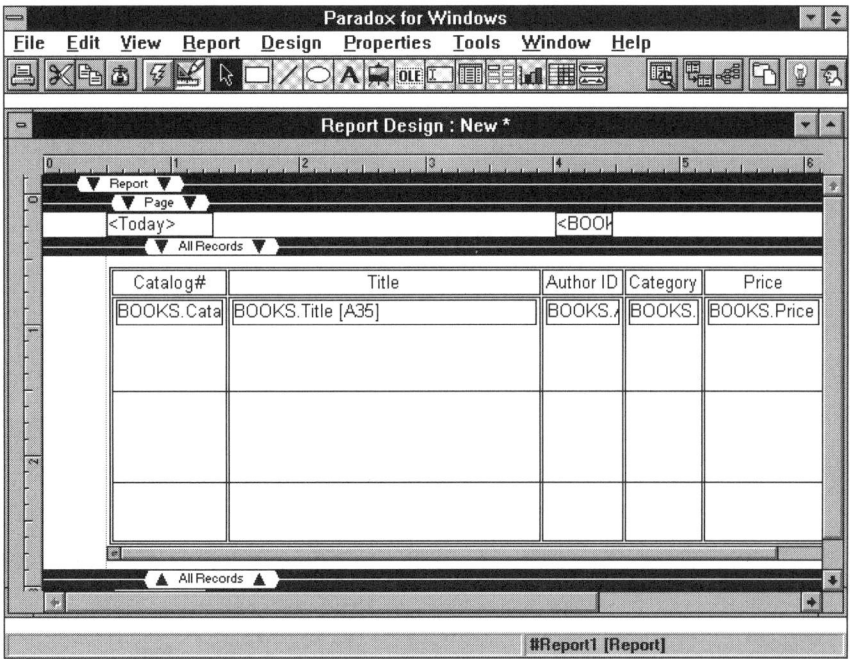

Figure 11-14: As soon as you choose OK, the report appears in the Report Design window.

Looks a little different than the Form Design window, doesn't it? The three horizontal lines at the top and bottom are those bands I referred to at the beginning of the chapter, and you'll learn all about them in the next chapter. But now we're going to take a look at a specialized kind of report: mailing labels.

CREATING MAILING LABELS

If you use Paradox to keep track of name and address information, a report that formats all that address info for mailing labels can be awfully handy. You can take any table into the Report Design window and with some customization set up such a report. But there's an easier way. Because the report-type document is so commonly used for mailing labels, Paradox has considerately included a Mailing Label Expert, and you're about to learn how to use it.

Opening the Mailing Label Expert

Follow these steps to open the Mailing Label Expert:

1. Click on the Expert button to open the Expert Control Panel dialog box.
2. Choose Mailing Labels. This takes you to step 1 of the Mailing Label Expert, as shown in Figure 11-15.

    You can also start the Mailing Label Expert by right-clicking on the Reports button from the Desktop Toolbar or the Project Viewer. Choose New from the Object Inspector menu and choose Label Expert from the New Report dialog box.

Here we go.

Choosing the Label Type

Notice that this looks a lot like the other Expert windows. There's stuff for you to specify as well as Cancel, Help and Next buttons. In this first step, you specify the type of mailing labels you want to use.

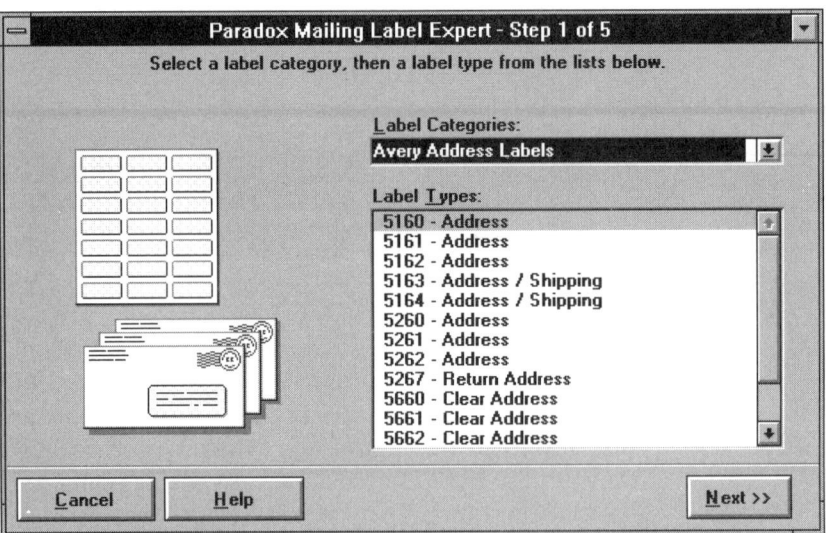

Figure 11-15: Step 1 of the Mailing Label Expert.

The Label Types list displays a whole bunch of different Avery address labels. Just select the type you're using and choose Next. (Or double-click on the label type to move directly to the next step.)

Inside Scoop

Paradox uses Avery label types because they're pretty standard. But if you use a different brand, just select the Avery type that most closely matches the measurements of yours.

Just because this Expert is called "Mailing Label," that doesn't mean you're limited to boring old address labels. Paradox provides layouts for a few zillion other label types, such as audio and video cassettes, name badges and indexes. Go ahead—label your world! To choose from a different label list, open the Label Categories drop-down list and make a selection. Here's what you get to choose from:

Avery Address Labels

Avery Address Labels - Metric

Avery Card Products

Avery Card Products - Metric

Avery Index Products

Avery Index Products - Metric

Avery Mini-Sheets

Avery Mini-Sheets - Pan European

Avery Specialty Labels

Avery Specialty Labels - Metric

For now, choose 5162-Address from the Avery Address Labels category and click on the Next button.

Selecting a Table

In step 2, you select a table to use for the report.

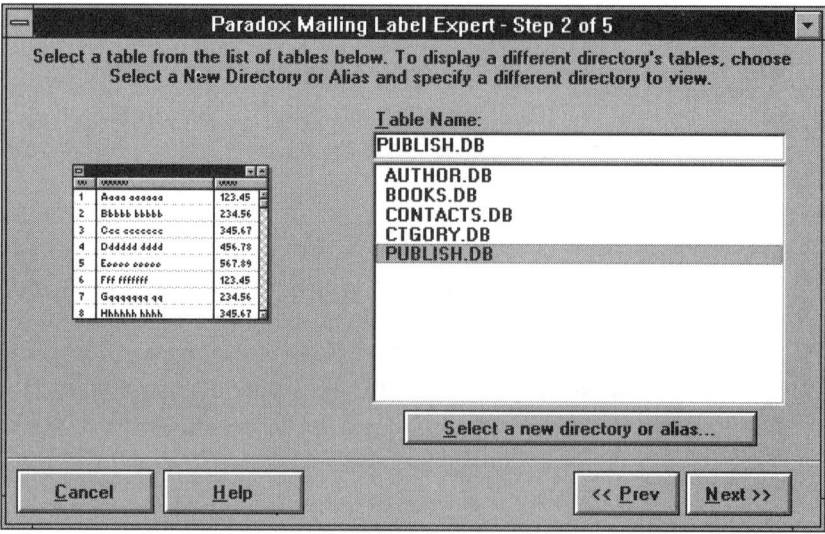

Figure 11-16: Step 2 of the Mailing Label Expert.

To choose the table you want:

○ Click on the table's name in the Table Name list (choose PUBLISH.DB).

○ Or type the name in the Table Name text box.

○ Or double-click on the table's name. This takes you right to the next step without clicking on the Next button.

○ If the table is in a different directory, click on the Select A New Directory Or Alias button and choose the directory, drive and/or alias from the Directory Browser.

○ Click on the Next button when you're ready.

Choosing the Font

This step's easy. You just select the font and size you want for the labels, and check the boxes for any attributes you want to add.

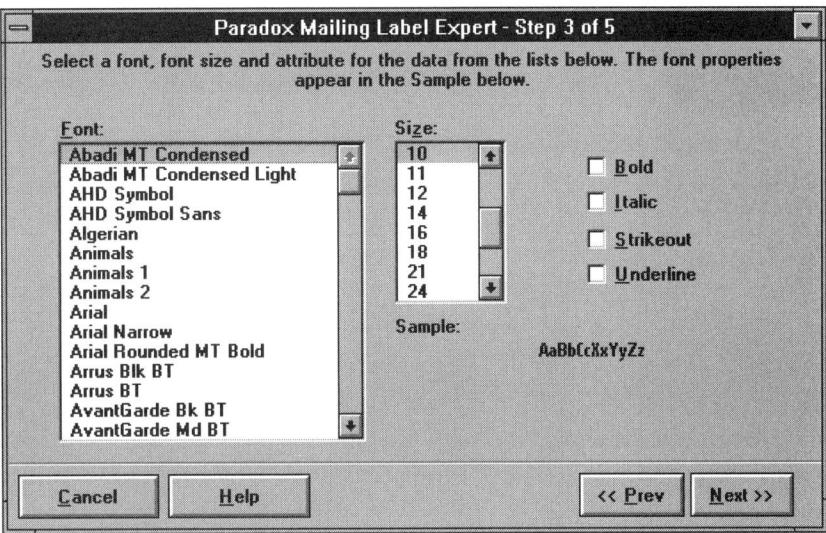

Figure 11-17: Step 3 of the Mailing Label Expert.

As you make different selections, notice that the sample area displays a preview. Go ahead and play around a bit–choose any font you like, but for our example, make it 12 points. Click on the Next button when you've chosen all your options.

Give Printing Instructions

In step 4, you give Paradox information about your labels: how the labels feed into your printer and whether the labels print left to right or top to bottom.

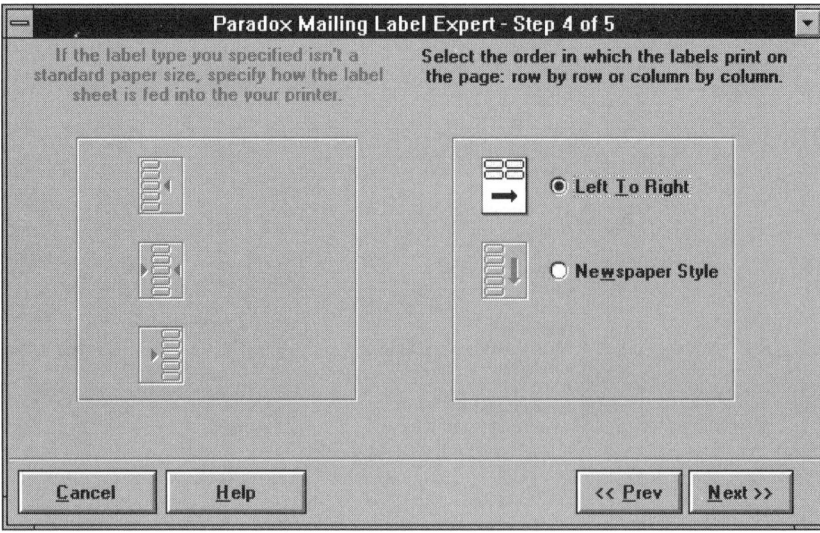

Figure 11-18: Step 4 of the Mailing Label Expert.

Putting Fields on the Label

In this last step of the Mailing Label Expert, you tell Paradox which fields to include and where to place each field on the label.

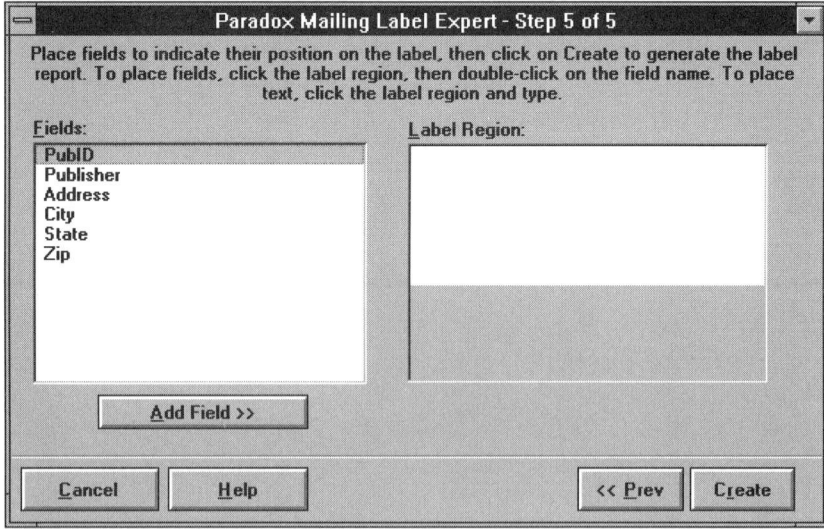

Figure 11-19: Step 5 of the Mailing Label Expert.

All of your fields are displayed in the Fields list. To include fields in the mailing label report:

1. Click in the Label Region box to tell Paradox where you want the field.

2. Double-click on the field you want to add. (Or select the field and click on the Add Field button.)

3. Repeat steps 1 and 2 for each field you want to add.

4. To add additional text to the label, click in the Label Region box and type stuff.

This may seem a bit complicated, but once you understand what's happening, there's nothing to it. See, what you want to end up with is a standard address layout, like this:

Ventana Press
P.O. Box 2468
Chapel Hill, NC 27515

The Publisher field is on the first line, the Address field is on the second line, and the City, State and ZIP fields are on the third line. Notice that the third line combines three different fields. The fields are placed by positioning the insertion point in the Label Region box and then double-clicking on the appropriate field. But what about the comma after the city and the spaces between the city and state and the state and ZIP? Easy. You just type 'em. Let's run through it with the PUBLISH fields:

1. Click in the top left corner of the Label Region box (notice that a flashing insertion point appears) and double-click on the Publisher field. Publisher is now displayed in curly brackets in the Label Region box.

2. Press the Enter key to move the insertion point to the next line.

3. Double-click on the Address field and press Enter.

4. Double-click on the City field.

5. Type a comma and then press the Spacebar to add a comma and space after the city.

6. Double-click on the State field.

7. Press the Spacebar to add a space after the state.

8. Double-click on the ZIP field.

Your Mailing Label Expert window should now look like the one in Figure 11-20.

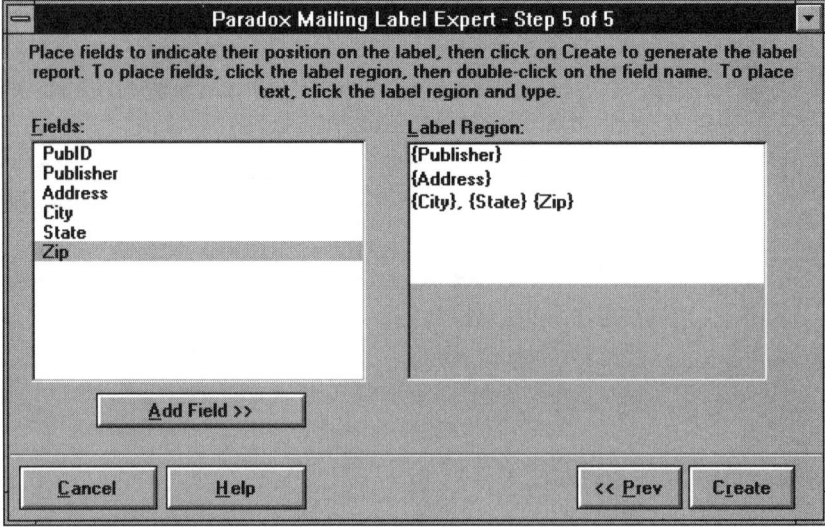

Figure 11-20: The completed Label Region box for our example.

9. Click on the Create button. Your labels will appear in the Report window. In Figure 11-21, I zoomed out to 50% so you could see more of the page layout.

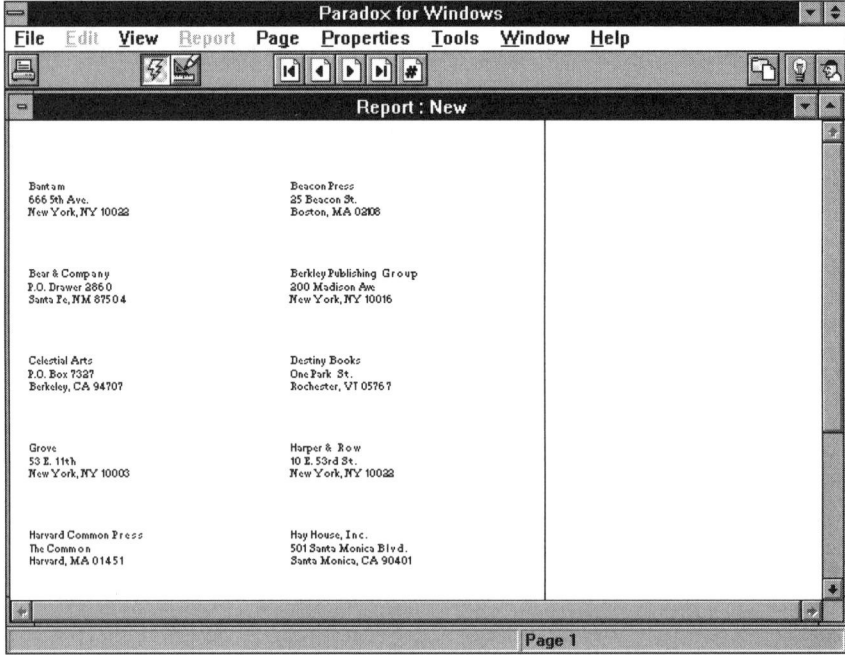

Figure 11-21: Labels in the Report window.

Click on the Design button or press F8 to switch to the Report Design window.

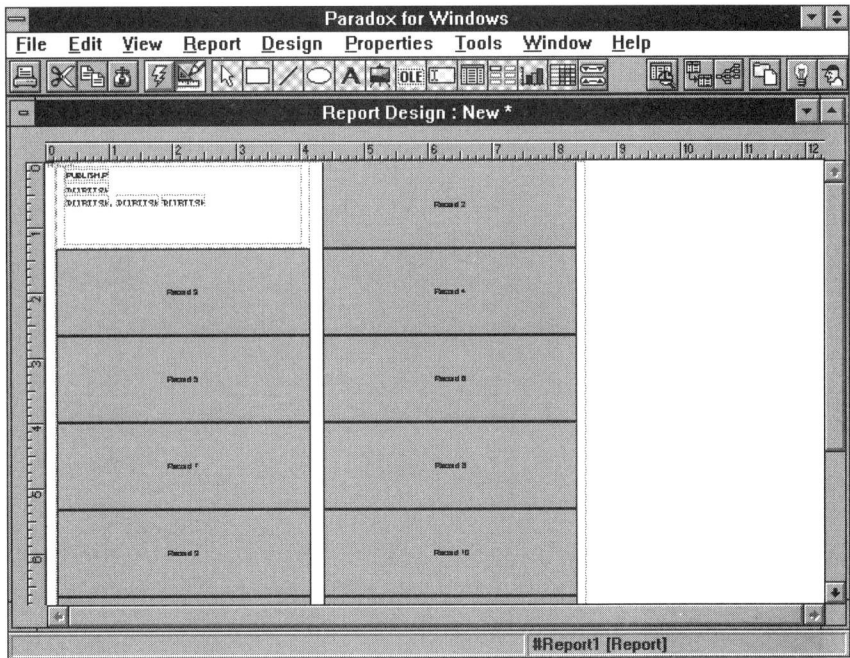

Figure 11-22: Here's what your labels look like in the Report Design window.

MOVING ON

In this chapter, you used several different methods for creating report layouts. And you learned how to use the Mailing Label Expert to create a special kind of report. Now get ready for report overdrive. In the next chapter, you'll make use of everything you learned about design tools in Chapter 10 ("Forms, the Sequel"), and learn a bunch of new stuff that relates specifically to reports.

12

REPORTS, THE SEQUEL

The report-writing technique that this chapter suggests is different than the one you learned in the last chapter. The Report Expert is a great tool when you're starting out in Paradox, but you'll soon discover that the default report layout Paradox produces for you is not right for every situation. Who wants plain Vanilla ice cream for dessert every day when there's a freezer full of Rocky Road and Double Bubble Gum Delight just around the corner?

We weren't kidding earlier in the book when we said that creating forms and reports (in their respective Design windows) is almost an identical process. Back in the forms chapters you saw how extensive an arsenal of design tools Paradox has to offer. Really, the only thing that's different between form-making and report-making is the medium where you're presenting your data. But Paradox's incredibly robust set of reporting tools can get intimidating, and we don't want to open Pandora's box if we can avoid it. Let's just peek inside.

The next pages lead you step by step through the process of creating a report from scratch. Along the way you'll learn how to do all of the following things for yourself, without any help from the so-called experts:

○ Create a data model that "links" data from two different tables.

○ Review Paradox's default report layout.

○ Customize the report layout to suit your needs.

○ Preview and then print your report.

CREATING A DATA MODEL

A *data model* is a Paradox tool for "linking" data that's stored in two or more different tables. Once you've established the data model link, you can draw specific field information from the linked tables and recombine it into a custom-designed form or report.

The sample tables you'll use in this chapter allow you to link two tables that were designed for use at a local bookstore. The ORDERS.DB table contains a record of all orders placed by the store's customers.

The STOCK.DB table contains the bookstore's accounting of the books currently in stock. Let's link them:

1. Choose the File, New, Report command. Paradox displays the New Report dialog box.

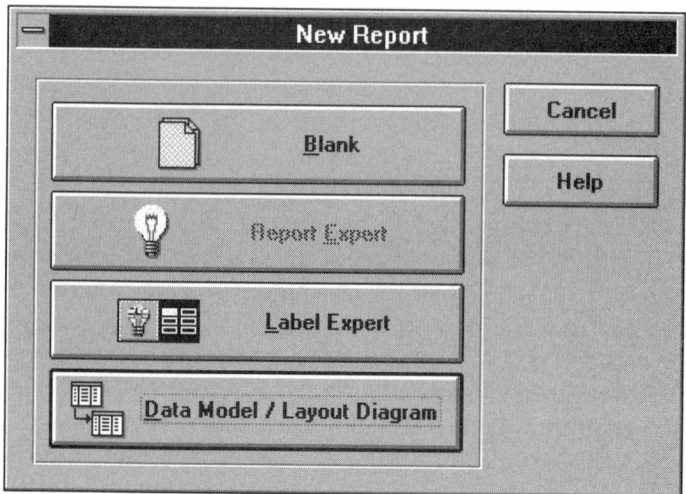

Figure 12-1: The New Report dialog box

2. Click the Data Model / Layout Diagram button. After a second, the Data Model dialog box appears. It's here that you can define the data link between your two tables.

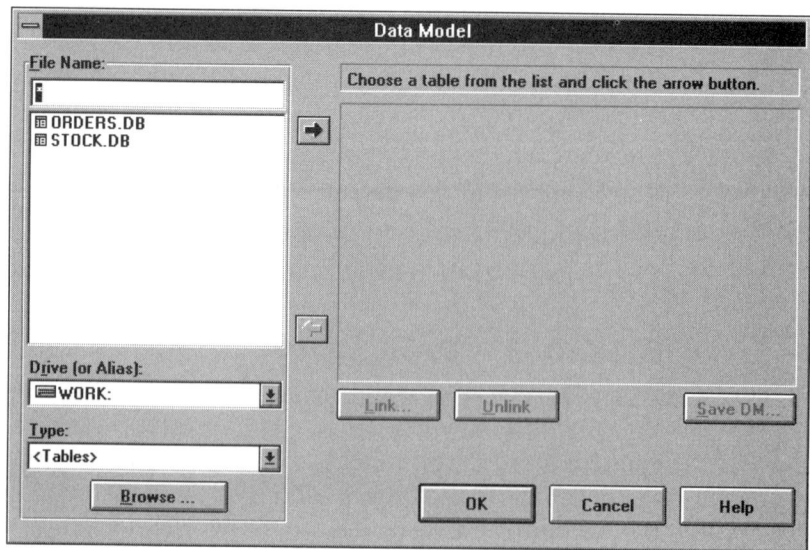

Figure 12-2: This Data Model dialog box shows the sample tables in my Paradox working directory.

3. Using the Drive drop-down list and the Browse button, locate the directory that contains ORDERS.DB and STOCK.DB, the two sample tables. Make sure the <Tables> option is active in the Type list so that Paradox displays only table names. When the tables appear in the File Name list box, you're ready to continue.

4. Double-click on the name ORDERS.DB to add this table to the data model. (Be sure to *double-click* and not *single-click*.) Paradox shows the table name in the data model panel at the right side of the Data Model dialog box.

5. Double-click on the name STOCK.DB to add this table to the data model. Paradox shows the table name in the data model panel, just below the ORDERS.DB entry.

Inside Scoop

If you accidentally add the wrong table into the data model panel, click the table's name and then click the Remove Table arrow to remove the name.

6. Drag your mouse pointer over either table name in the data model panel. Notice how the pointer changes to a linking tool (see Figure 12-3). You use this linking tool to associate the tables whose names appear in the data model panel.

7. To link the tables, click on the ORDERS.DB table name (we'll call this the *master* table) and then drag the linking tool down toward the STOCK.DB table name (which we'll call the *detail* table). Paradox draws a thin line to show that you're making a "connection" between these two tables.

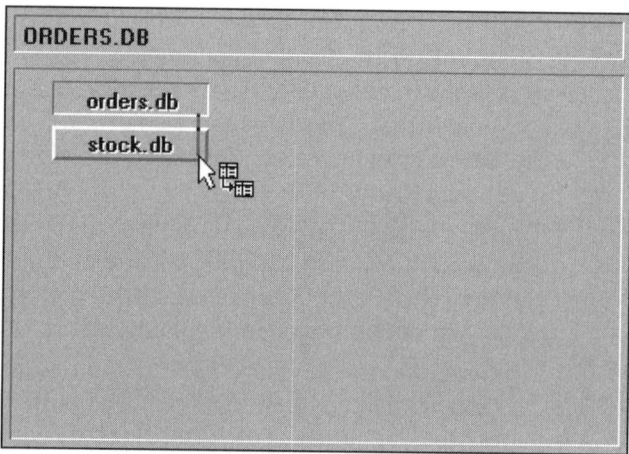

Figure 12-3: The linking tool is joining the ORDERS.DB table with the STOCK.DB table.

8. When the linking line touches both table names, release your mouse. After a moment, Paradox displays the Define Link dialog box.

Inside Scoop

Paradox displays the Define Link dialog box only if the link you're creating is a new link. If you had previously created a link between the two tables, Paradox would recognize it and display a graphic representation of that link in the data model panel.

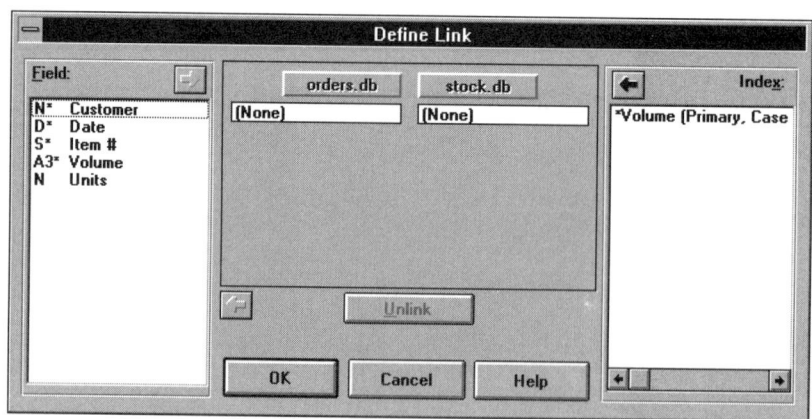

Figure 12-4: The Define Link dialog box is where you tell Paradox about the fields in the ORDERS.DB and STOCK.DB tables that you wish to link.

Notice that the fields from ORDERS.DB appear in the Field list, while only a single field from STOCK.DB appears in the Index list. That's because ORDERS.DB is a master table—this table contains all the possible fields that can be linked to. For the detail table (STOCK.DB), Paradox shows only the fields that are defined as key fields. In this case, the Volume field is the only key field in STOCK.DB.

9. To define the master table's linking field, double-click on the Volume field name shown in the Field list box. Paradox transfers the field name into the center of the Define Link dialog box underneath the table name ORDERS.DB. Because there's only one field to choose from in the Index list, and because that field is a valid one to link to, Paradox also transfers the field name underneath the table name STOCK.DB.

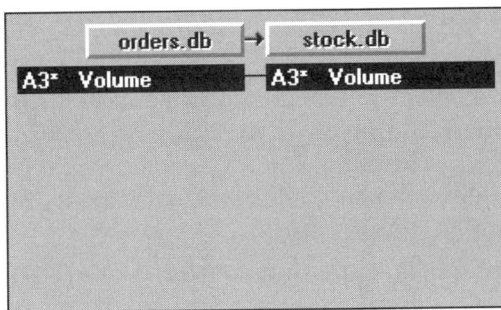

Figure 12-5: Paradox recognizes the Volume field name from the ORDERS.DB and the STOCK.DB tables as a match for linking.

10. Choose OK to accept the link described in the Define Link dialog box. Paradox returns you to the Data Model dialog box which displays, in the data model panel, a graphic representation of the link you just created.

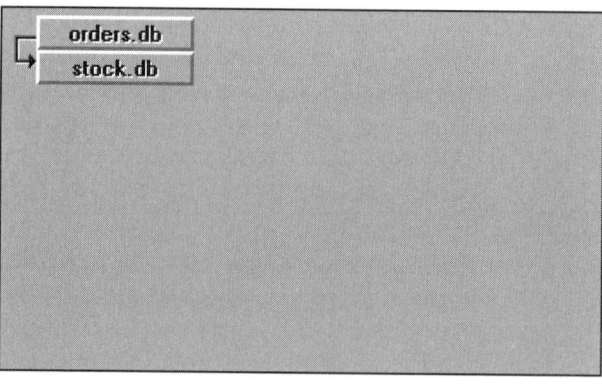

Figure 12-6: Paradox identifies the type of link by a graphic representation in the data model panel.

The particular graphic shown represents a one-to-one or many-to-one relationship. In this case, each order and stock listing identifies the books by volume.

11. To name your newly created data model, click the Save DM button. In the Save File As dialog box, type a name for your data model into the File Name text box. I named my data model *books*; you can use the same name for your data model or a different one.

12. You're finished creating your data model, so click OK. Paradox removes the Data Model dialog box from your screen, pauses for a second or two and then displays the Design Layout dialog box (see Figure 12-7).

The data model link you established between the two sample tables becomes the basis for the report you'll create in the next couple of sections of this chapter.

CHECKING OUT THE DESIGN LAYOUT

There are many different buttons and check boxes in the Design Layout dialog box. Don't let them intimidate you. Paradox is good about deciding which design layout is best for your report. Even if what you start out with is just okay, you can always customize the report to your heart's delight.. Paradox allows you to completely change the default design layout.

In this section, you'll learn how to recognize what Paradox has chosen for you in a design layout. You'll also discover that there are many different ways to proceed with your report design—what matters most is that *you* give the final approval before the report is created.

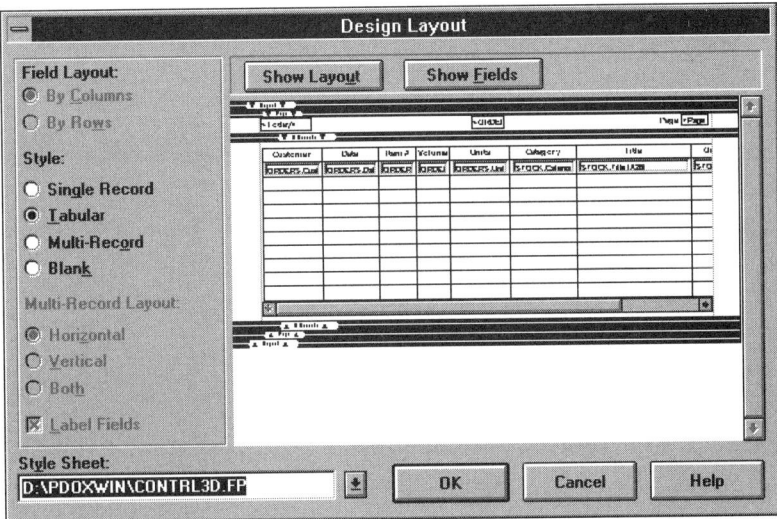

Figure 12-7: The Design Layout dialog box initially shows Paradox's best guess at the ideal report design layout for your data. Feel free to change your mind.

The thing that's most immediately striking about the report structure shown in the layout area is that it contains all of the unique fields from both your master table and your index table (the ORDERS.DB and STOCK.DB tables). You can include all the fields in your report, or you can elect to remove one or more. Right off the bat, if you know that a particular field isn't needed for the report you've been envisioning, go ahead and delete it. (When you delete a field from a report, you aren't deleting it from the table; you're only leaving it out of the report.) Or perhaps reordering the fields in the report will produce a more informative and organized layout.

To delete and rearrange fields for the sample report:

1. Click the Show Fields button. Paradox displays a list of all fields for both tables in the Selected Fields dialog box.

2. Click any field you want to remove and then click the Remove Field button.

3. Reorder your fields by clicking the Order arrows. The up arrow moves the selected field up one row in the list; and the down arrow moves the selected field down one row in the list.

4. Remove and rearrange fields in your list so that it looks just like the one shown in Figure 12-8.

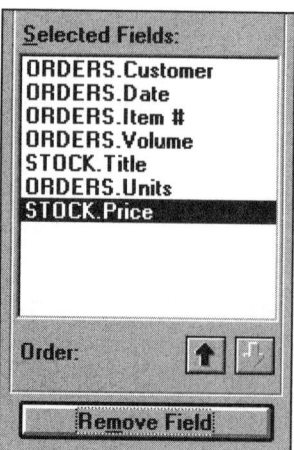

Figure 12-8: Create this organization of fields for the sample report.

5. Click OK to complete the exercise. Paradox exits the Design Layout dialog box and then displays a new Report Design window with all remaining information from your tables.

CUSTOMIZING THE REPORT LAYOUT

The deeper you delve into the design of a report, the more decisions there are to be made. It's the nature of the design game. You can spend as little or as much time as you can afford to, tweaking the layout of the default Paradox report so that it comes out looking exactly the way you want.

In this section, you'll learn how to do these things:

○ Place a new text object in the report band.

○ Remove an existing text object from the report band.

○ Widen the report band to add white space to your report.

○ Shift the positioning of the entire report object in the Report Design window.

○ Design for screen previewing or for printing.

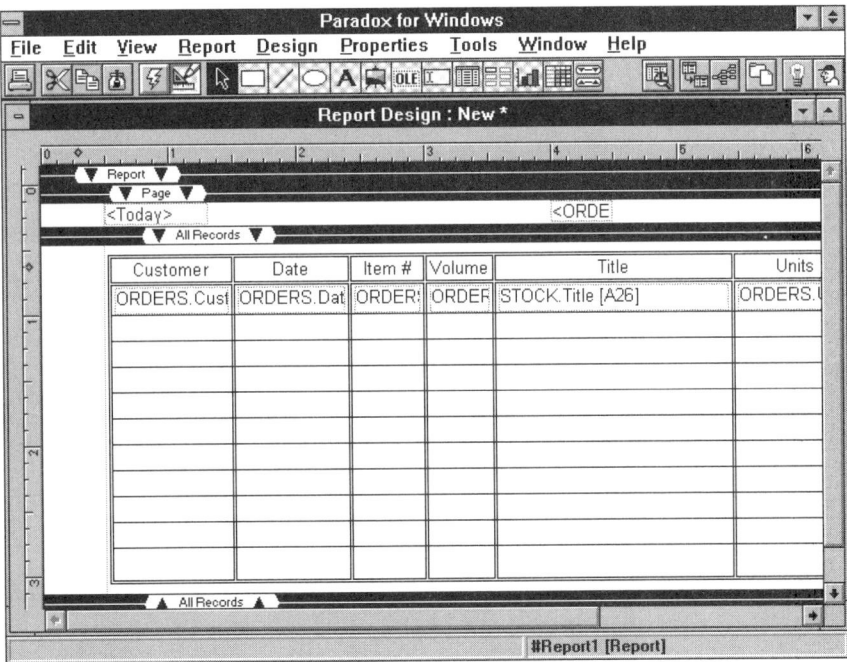

Figure 12-9: The Report Design window is where you fine-tune the design of your report layout.

As you can tell, the Report Design window is unlike anything you've seen before. Really, it's not too hard to learn what's what in this window so that you quickly can produce a final draft of the report. The prominent features in the Report Design window are the bands—those long, thick lines that run horizontally across the report page. Paradox uses bands to distinguish sections in a report.

There are four different kinds of bands in a Paradox report. The *Report band* prints information at the start and end of a report. The *Page band* prints information at the top and bottom of each page in a report. The *Group band* is an optional band that enables you to define groups (ways of ordering information) for the records in the table on which the report is based. The *Record band* encompasses the center area of a report on your screen. The information here tells Paradox how to print information for every record in the table on which the report is based.

Let's start by seeing how to enter a title into the report band. This title will appear at the start and end of your report:

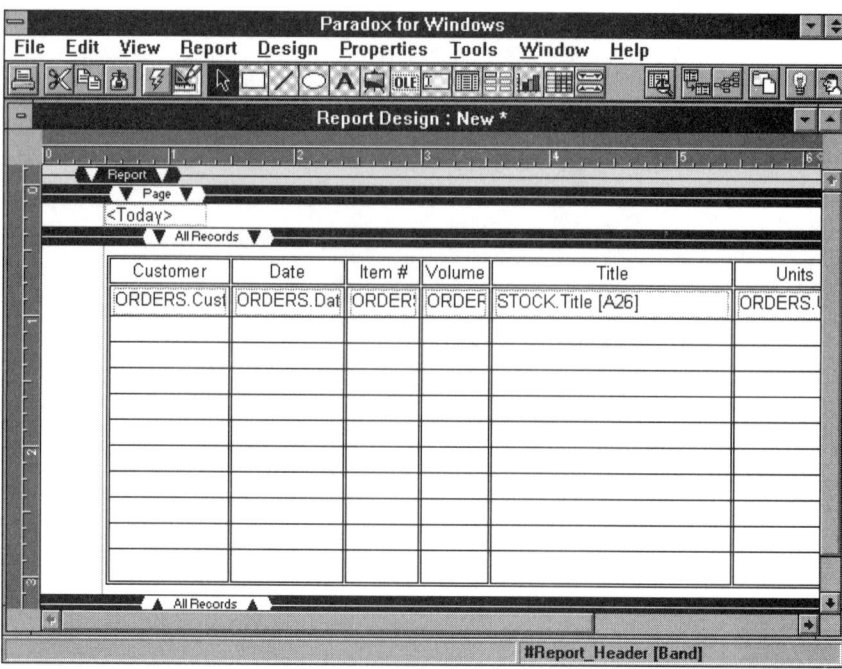

Figure 12-10: Click inside the Report band to select it. The color of a band changes when it's selected. Compare the color of the Report band to that of the Page and Record bands in this figure.

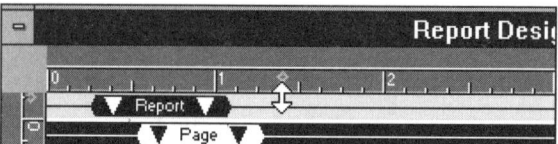

Figure 12-11: Position your mouse pointer in the upper-half of the Report band until the pointer changes to a two-headed arrow. Now drag up about an inch. Paradox adds white space in between the Report band and the Page.

Inside Scoop

If the white space in a band is not tall enough to accommodate a text object you place there, Paradox will automatically resize it for you as soon as click outside the object to affix the text.

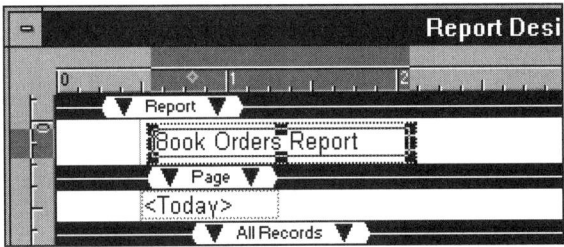

Figure 12-12: Click the Text tool in the Toolbar and place a text object at the left margin of the Report band. Type a title for the report (*Book Orders Report*) and then click outside the object to affix it.

Next, take a look at the fields inside the Page band. The *<Today>* field prints today's date, the *<ORDERS>* field prints the name of the master table and the *Page Number* field prints consecutive page numbers on each page in the report. Paradox places each of these fields into every new report

Let's see how to delete the master table field. Click the <ORDERS> field in the Page band. Paradox adds selection handles around the perimeter of the master table field object. Press Delete to remove the object from the Page band. That's it. You've just learned how to remove objects (in this case, a field object) from a Page band.

Now let's run through an exercise that illustrates how to manage your report as you prepare to preview and print. The following steps show how to format the *Customer* field data, view the full width of your report on screen and then save the report for posterity.

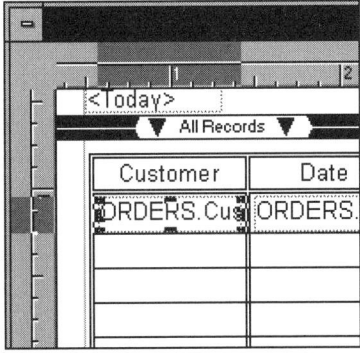

Figure 12-13: Click three times the cell containing the ORDERS.Customer field in the Records band. Paradox selects the object containing the ORDERS.Customer for the purpose of formatting.

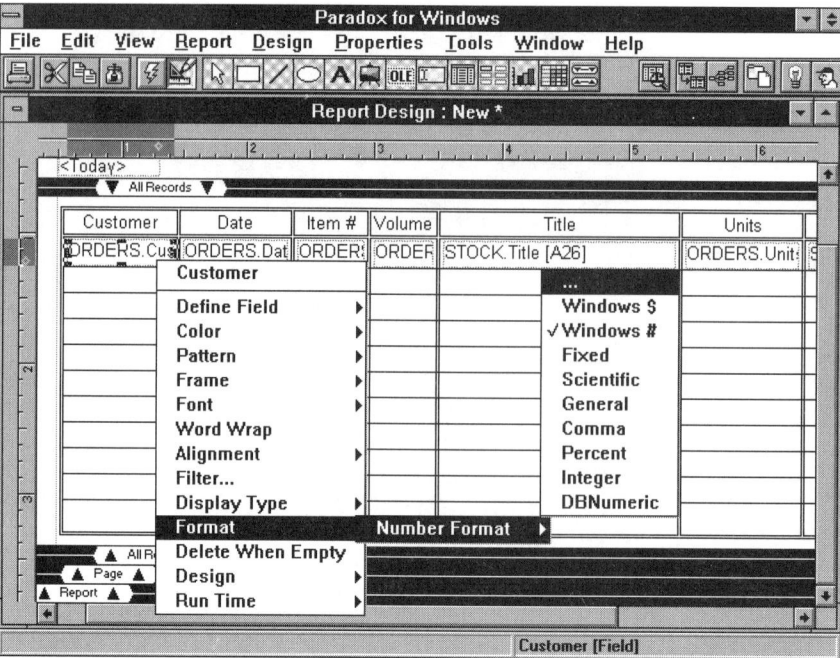

Figure 12-14: Right click the ORDERS.Customer field to inspect its properties menu and choose the Format, Number Format options. The Number Format pop-up menu shows that the current format for the *ORDERS.Customer* field is *Windows#*.

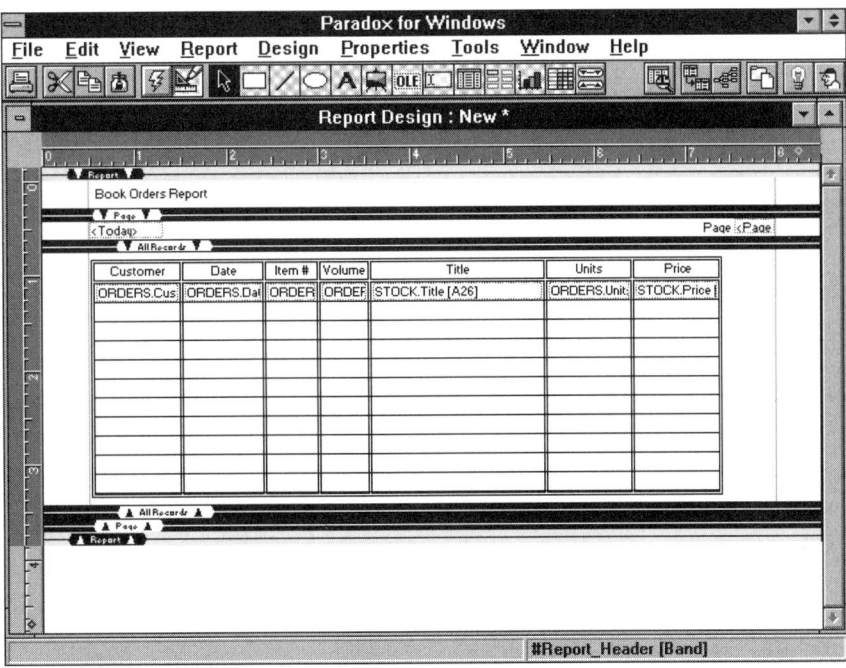

Figure 12-15: Click the Integer option (displays a customer number as 1200 instead of as 1,200.00). To view your report in full width, choose the View, Zoom, Fit Width.

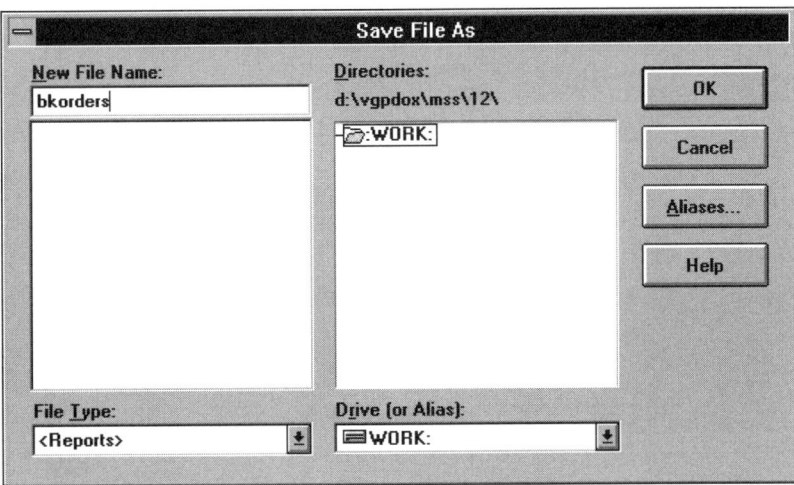

Figure 12-16: Always be sure and save a copy of your. Choose the File, Save command, type a name in the File Name text box, then click OK to save your report. (I named my report BKORDERS.)

PREVIEWING & PRINTING THE REPORT

Paradox can produce reports for two different presentation mediums: your screen display or your printer. By default, each report you design is custom-tailored for printing on a printer. It's a snap to change that so all of your reports look equally delicious on your computer's screen. (Maybe you have one of those bosses who constantly is peering over your shoulder.)

To see what printing options are available for your reports, choose the Report, Page Layout command. Paradox displays the Page Layout dialog box.

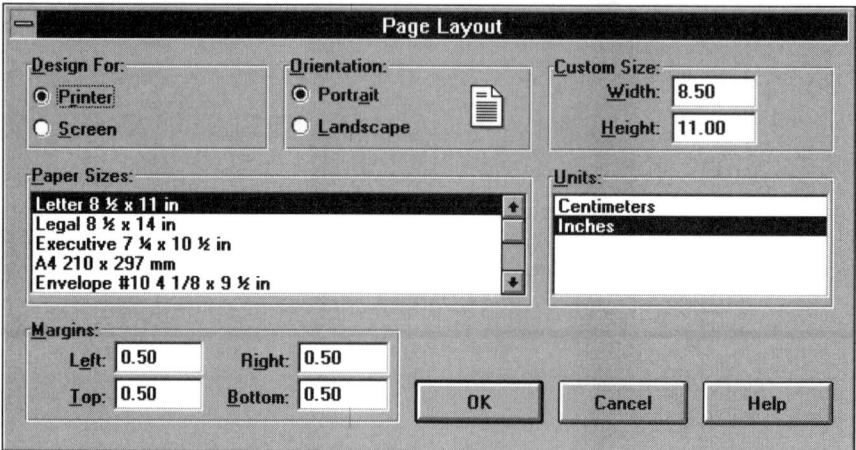

Figure 12-17: The Page Layout dialog box allows you to design your report for display on a screen or for printing on paper.

Pitfall Ahead

Not all fonts are created equal. In fact, the difference between the fonts you view on your screen and those that appear in your printed reports can be startling. The explanation for why this is so is not as important as knowing that when it happens there's nothing you can do about it. Hopefully it won't happen to you.

So, you have some decisions to make. Here are some suggestions about where to begin:

○ Do you need to show the report onscreen? Click the Screen option in the Design For area.

○ Do you need to send a printed copy of the report to headquarters? Click the Printer option in the Design For area.

○ Do you have any special page size requirements, such as legal paper size, or specific margin needs? Well, you can make all those settings in the Paper Sizes and Margins area.

○ Is your report too wide to fit on your printer paper. Try out the Landscape option in the Orientation area.

Inside Scoop

If you can't get your Landscape option to work, it's probably because you've selected Screen as your Design For setting. Unfortunately, the only Orientation setting that works when you're designing for onscreen viewing is Portrait.

○ Are you wondering where Paradox is hiding the Print Preview command? Don't wonder, it's not there. To preview a Paradox report, click the View Data button (the lightning bolt button) or choose the View, Run Report command. The end result is the same.

○ How do you get back to the Report Design window when you're done previewing? Click the Design button (the triangle-pencil-ruler button) or choose the View, Design Report command. You're back in a flash.

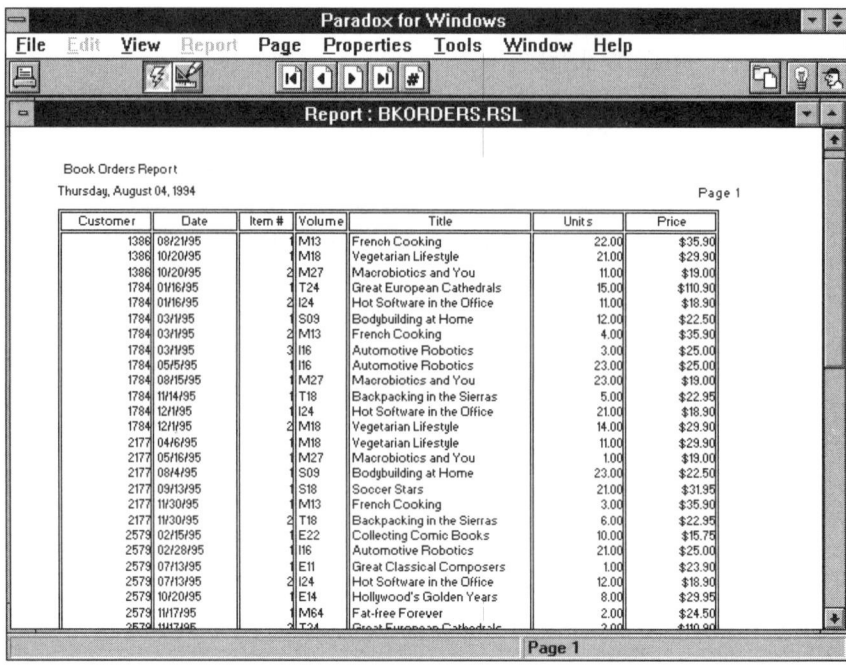

Figure 12-18: Preview the final version of your reports onscreen before you make the big commitment to send it to paper.

MOVING ON

No report is complete without some sort of eye-catching graphic or clever, probing illustration. The days of long-winded written reports are thankfully gone. With so many easily wielded design tools at our disposal, it'd be a crime to produce a report that uses a thousand words to say what can be conveyed in a single illustration. Read on, Picasso, read on.

13

WORKING WITH GRAPHS & CROSSTABS

Reports are great for showing off data, aren't they? Cool columns and rows of information so organized that even Mr. Magoo could figure out what's what. These days, though, written reports just aren't splashy enough to close the big sale or wow your board of directors. They may not even be good enough to get you that all-important raise.

It's a sign of the times. Most of us grew up watching television. Today's kids are growing up watching movies and videos with multi-million-dollar reality-bending special effects. Without the aid of visual devices—graphs, pictures and drawings—I dare say that many people would have a difficult time drawing conclusions from words and numbers in a report.

Graphs and crosstabs are visual aids that help us understand and analyze data in our Paradox reports. They help us spot trends and ferret out buried or concealed meanings in the numbers. How do graphs and crosstabs do this? Simply by offering us hundreds of different ways of categorizing, summarizing and sorting the facts and figures in a Paradox report.

Read on. This chapter's all about the simplest approach to creating graphs and crosstabs.

WHAT ARE GRAPHS & CROSSTABS?

Certainly you've seen a graph or two in your day. They're those colorful (usually) charts that show data in pies, on bars, inside columns, along a series of lines, and so on. A *crosstab* is more of a spreadsheet-style report format. For that matter, a crosstab looks a lot like a Paradox table. Whereas spreadsheet data comes from *you* (when you type it into your spreadsheet), the data for a crosstab comes from a *query* that Paradox automatically creates and runs for you.

The reason you create graphs and crosstabs is to categorize, summarize and sort your data just the way you like it. The result you expect is a better representation and understanding (hopefully) of the information you're dissecting.

```
 —              Paradox for Windows - [Table : CARSTOCK.DB]        ▼ ▲
 □  File  Edit  View  Table  Record  Properties  Tools  Window  Help      ▲
 ┌──┐┌──┐┌──┐  ┌──┐┌──┐ ┌──┐┌──┐┌──┐ ┌──┐┌──┐┌──┐  ┌──┐┌──┐┌──┐┌──┐  ┌──┐┌──┐┌──┐
```

CARSTOCK	Year	Make	Model	Mileage	Price
1	1994	Acura	Integra	9,674	$14,999
2	1994	Acura	Legend	5,000	$29,988
3	1994	Infiniti	Q45	5,000	$39,900
4	1994	Mazda	Protege	13,000	$9,695
5	1993	Honda	Accord SE	16,000	$18,500
6	1993	Honda	Del Sol Si	12,000	$13,950
7	1993	Infiniti	J30	25,000	$26,750
8	1993	Mazda	929	21,250	$22,930
9	1992	Acura	Vigor	35,410	$18,995
10	1992	Lexus	ES 300	23,000	$26,995
11	1991	Acura	NSX	16,300	$41,500
12	1991	Infiniti	G20	26,000	$12,950
13	1991	Infiniti	M30	44,000	$15,500
14	1991	Mazda	929S	44,000	$15,400
15	1991	Toyota	Celica GT	38,000	$11,500
16	1991	Toyota	Supra Turb	41,000	$16,995
17	1990	Acura	Integra	89,500	$12,000
18	1990	Acura	Legend	90,000	$13,000
19	1990	Honda	Accord EX	52,000	$11,750
20	1990	Lexus	250	55,000	$12,500

```
Record 1 of 26
```

Figure 13-1: The CARSTOCK table shows the year, make, model, mileage and price of a used car inventory.

Consider the CARSTOCK table shown in Figure 13-1. It belongs to the used car dealership where you just started working (yes, *you*). Since you are new on the job, the first matter of business is to break down the used car inventory by Make and Price so you can pick just the right car for any customer's budget. The 1D (one dimensional) crosstab shown in Figure 13-2 summarizes the CARSTOCK table data just the way you need it.

	Acura	Honda	Infiniti	Lexus	Mazda
Average Price	21,747	11,070	23,775	21,496	12,545

Figure 13-2: A simple, 1D (one-dimensional) crosstab.

You can create a graph that shows the same data. The graph in the following figure is a more visually appealing and effective medium for analyzing the same average price data.

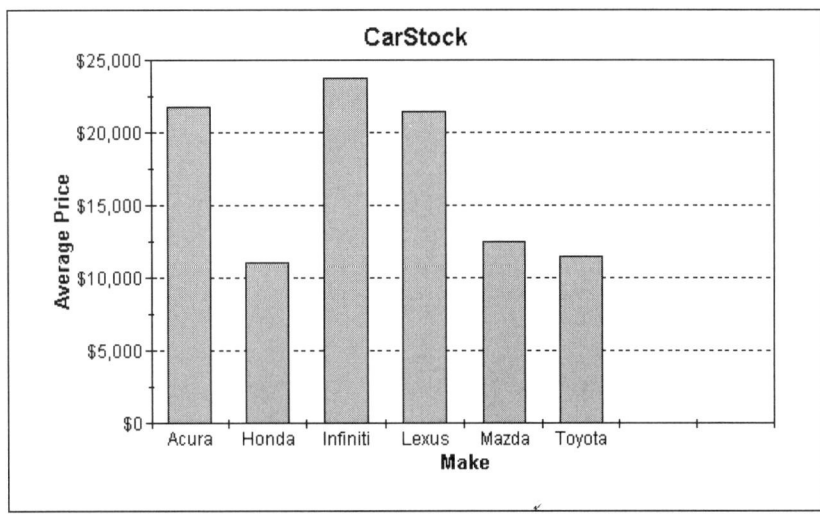

Figure 13-3: A basic, 1D graph that shows the average price of each make of car.

As you can see in Figures 13-2 and 13-3, graphs and crosstabs share a few things in common. First, they both categorize data: the column headings along the top row in the crosstab, and the labels appearing along the horizontal axis in the graph. Second, they both have a summary category: the Label "Average Price" on the vertical axis in the graph and the same label that sits all by itself at the left end of the crosstab. This mixture of categories and summary data helps you identify and understand the results of your summarizing efforts. In both the graph and crosstab, the summarizing results appear at the intersection of both category fields. The results in the crosstab are *numbers*; the results in the graph are numbers represented by *bars*.

As analytical tools, graphs are simple to understand and pleasing to the eye. They also make it easier to identify trends, spot new relationships in your data, and uncover hidden meanings that simply can't be understood by looking at numbers in a report. That's why graphs are such valuable additions to a Paradox report.

CHOOSING YOUR DATA

Choosing the data you wish to analyze in a crosstab or graph is easy. Just think of crosstabs and graphs as fraternal twins: even though they look different, they have the same parents (a Paradox table). This means that no special reorganizing of table data is required. In fact, there's another way of looking at the relationship between graph and crosstab: When you create and customize a graph, Paradox *cross-tabulates* your data and displays it in an easy-to-digest visual format.

To create a crosstab or graph, you first must identify a *summary field*—the field(s) in your table whose data you want to summarize. Paradox allows you to summarize data many different ways. You can count entries, average things, locate the minimum or maximum value in a list or even sum a list of numbers. In the CARSTOCK table example earlier, we decided to average (summarize) the Price field. There is one rigid rule concerning summarizing data: Paradox only sums and averages data in numeric fields. Makes sense, huh? You don't really want to average a list of car names, do you?

Inside Scoop

When you create a crosstab or graph, Paradox looks at the current field in your table and anticipates the type of summarizing you want to do. For instance, if the current field contains *numeric entries,* then Paradox automatically selects Sum as the summarizing option. When the current field contains alphanumeric or date entries, Paradox chooses the Count option. Remember, these are only the default settings. You can change them any time you wish.

The second step in creating a graph or a crosstab is to identify which other table field(s) you wish to associate with the summary field. These "associative" fields are called *category fields*. Going back to the CARSTOCK example, having a list of average prices is meaningless unless you can relate those prices to another piece of information, right? That's why we decided to average Price for each unique entry in the Make field. This crosstab allowed you to quickly get your finger on the pulse of your dealership's inventory.

To break it down even further, you could produce a crosstab that compared average price to each Make and Model field entry. That way, you could quickly compare the average price of a Honda Civic to the average price of an Infinity Q45. (Hey, some customers do want to know these things.) When you choose a second category by which to summarize your data, you can produce even more useful and informative graphs and crosstabs. In the following sections, we'll take a look at several different types of crosstabs and graphs. The examples build from the simple to the complex so you can decide for yourself which types will benefit you most in your Paradox reports.

Inside Scoop

The maximum number of fields (summary fields plus category fields) that Paradox allows you to add to a crosstab is 254. Who knows where that number came from. It could be a pyramid power thing. Why the heck are you trying to analyze that much data at one time anyway?

The "No Categories" Tabular Graph

The most basic type of graph you can produce in Paradox is the *tabular* graph. It's basic because it's the default graph type in Paradox, and to build one requires a minimum of effort. A tabular graph is a lot like a graph you'd create in a spreadsheet program. One category appears along a horizontal line (the x axis), one or more categories appear along a vertical line (that's the y axis), and the bars or columns in between plot out the relationship between the two sets of data. But the plot only shows how one point on the x axis relates to another point on the y axis; there is nothing in the graph that summarizes data for you.

Because "summarizing" is not part of the process of creating a tabular graph, the tabular graph has no fraternal Paradox twin (the hypothetical tabular crosstab). A tabular graph is usually large, even if the table from which it was created is small. That's because a tabular graph shows every unique relationship in your table for any two fields.

Consider the CARSTOCK table, which contains only 26 records. If you were to create a tabular graph using the Model and Price fields, you'd end up with a graph that had 26 bars, or lines or columns. (Here's where Paradox shines.) So that you can see all 26 items on the tabular graph without having to scrunch them all together, Paradox shows only the first eight bars. To get to the remaining 18 bars, you can scroll through your table by clicking the Next Record button on the Form Toolbar. Each click reveals another bar at the right side of the graph. Figure 13-4 shows a tabular graph I created for the CARSTOCK table.

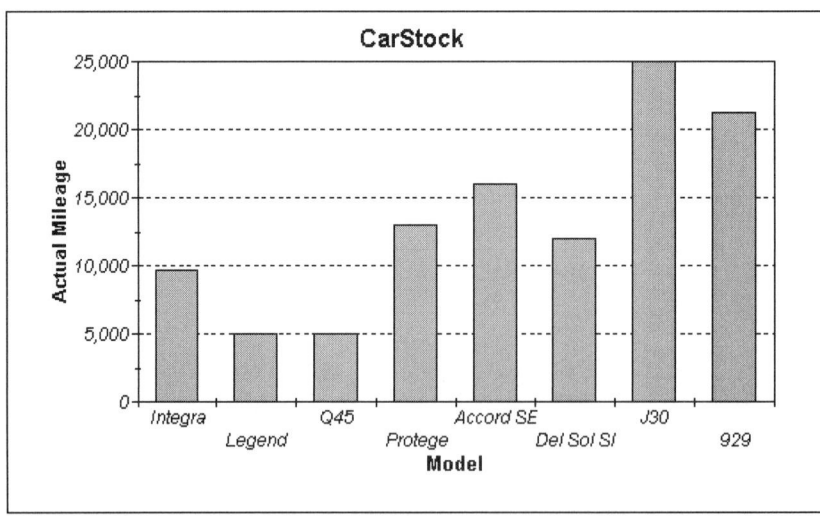

Figure 13-4: A tabular graph that charts the mileage of each car in the CARSTOCK table.

Figure 13-5 shows a different version of the tabular graph shown in Figure 13-4. In this particular graph, I added the Price field to the y axis. At first glance, you might think I'm nuts: "How can you show a value field (Mileage) on the same axis as a currency field (Price)?" you ask. All I did was change the y axis title, remove the dollar sign formatting and add a legend; Paradox handled the rest.

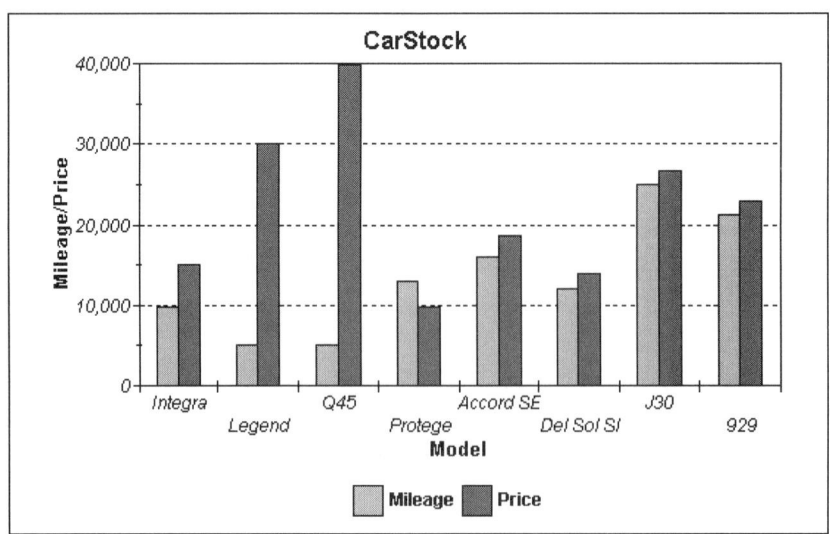

Figure 13-5: A tabular graph that charts the mileage and price for every car in the CARSTOCK table.

Please don't go away thinking that the graph in Figure 13-5 is no longer a tabular graph just because I added the Price category to the y axis. This graph is a tabular graph because it still doesn't summarize (count, sum, average, etc.) anything. Remember: tabular means never having to say you're summarizing.

The "One Category" Graph or Crosstab

Every 1D graph and 1D crosstab contains at least one category field and one summary field. For instance, the 1D crosstab in Figure 13-6 shows the total number of cars available within each Make classification of the CARSTOCK table.

This label was added in a Form Design window.

	# in Stock
Acura	6
Honda	5
Infiniti	4
Lexus	3
Mazda	5
Toyota	3

Figure 13-6: This 1D crosstab uses a vertical organization instead of the more typical horizontal arrangement of data.

Notice the description "# in Stock" at the top of the column in Figure 13-6. It doesn't correspond to any field name from the CARSTOCK table. That's because I added this label in a Form Design window. Remember, a crosstab is just a form. You'll learn in an upcoming section how easy it is to customize crosstabs using the same form design techniques you learned back in Chapters 9 and 10.

Inside Scoop

Paradox can usually create vertical 1D crosstabs (see Figure 13-6) faster than horizontal 1D crosstabs (like the one shown way back in Figure 13-2). Don't ask why, just commit this little tidbit to memory. It'll come in handy later when you perform a 56-step exercise that demonstrates how to create complex vertical crosstabs (hah, just kidding).

Checking Out a 1D Graph

Pop quiz: What's the difference between a tabular graph and a 1D graph? Yes! Tabular graphs *do not* summarize anything, while 1D graphs can summarize anything. This really is important. Imagine wanting to calculate the average price of each Acura model in stock, but accidentally creating a tabular graph in which the first occurrence of an Acura is a $41,000 NSX—the highest-priced Acura model. That would throw a monkey wrench into your analysis, huh?

Figure 13-7 shows a 1D summary graph that includes the average-price-of-each-Acura-model data. Here, the x axis values are from the Model field in the CARSTOCK table. The values graphed against the y axis are the average of the values in the Price field.

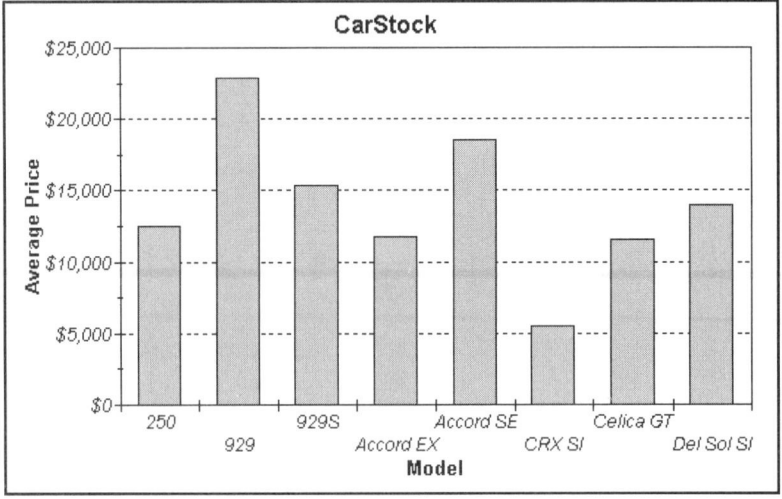

Figure 13-7: A 1D summary graph that shows the average price of each unique Model in stock.

The "Two Category" Graph or Crosstab

Mid-term exam: What's the difference between a 1D crosstab or graph and a 2D crosstab or graph? Give up? Here's a hint: You create a 1D crosstab or graph the same way you create a 2D crosstab or graph, except that you go "one D" further. That means you select *two* category fields and one summary field. The following list shows five of the many possible ways of relating CARSTOCK data in a 2D crosstab and graph:

Summary Field	Category Field #1	Category Field #2
Year (Average)	Make	Model
Mileage (Average)	Year	Price
Price (Average)	Mileage	Year
Price (Min)	Make	Model
Make (Count)	Year	Model

Checking Out a 2D Crosstab

There are several useful ways to create a 2D crosstab using the CARSTOCK table. It really depends on how you wish to relate information from each field. Figure 13-8 shows a crosstab that summarizes by average price, using the Make and Year fields as categories. This presentation makes it easy to identify which class of cars is more expensive for any particular year.

	1988	1989	1990	1991	1992
Acura			$12,500	$41,500	$18,995
Honda	$5,650	$5,500	$11,750		
Infiniti				$14,225	
Lexus			$18,747		$26,995
Mazda		$7,350		$15,400	
Toyota			$5,988	$14,248	

Figure 13-8: The summary region in this 2D crosstab tells you the average price of all cars in stock for each Make.

In Figure 13-8, the blank cells mean that there are no entries for that model year.

Or suppose you want to know the maximum price for the cars in each Make and Year class. That way, if a customer is unhappy with the price of one particular model you're showing, you can simply pick one from a Make and Year category that has less expensive cars. To produce this crosstab, you choose Year and Make as the categories, and Model as a summary. The crosstab summary region in Figure 13-9 shows the maximum price for each unique Model.

	1988	1989	1990	1991	1992
Acura			$13,000	$41,500	$18,995
Honda	$5,650	$5,500	$11,750		
Infiniti				$15,500	
Lexus			$24,993		$26,995
Mazda		$8,500		$15,400	
Toyota			$5,988	$16,995	

Figure 13-9: The summary region in this 2D crosstab tells you the maximum price of all cars in stock for each Make.

Inside Scoop

A quick comparison of the crosstabs in Figure 13-8 and 13-9 may cause you to wonder why the summary data looks the same if one is showing average price and the other maximum price. Since our sample database is quite puny, containing a whopping total of 26 records, the average price will *equal* the maximum price for any instance where there is only one car in stock for any model year. The Honda summary detail for 1988, 1989 and 1990 is the same in both crosstabs because the CARSTOCK table has only one model in stock for each of those years. You won't often encounter these analysis overlaps in your own work—that is, assuming that your databases are more of the Goliath type and less of the Davey variety.

Checking Out a 2D Graph

A 2D summary graph categorizes, or groups, the summary data being graphed by using *two* category fields. One category field appears along the x axis and the other appears along the y axis. Figures 13-10 and 13-11 show 2D summary graphs for the crosstabs that appear in the preceding two figures.

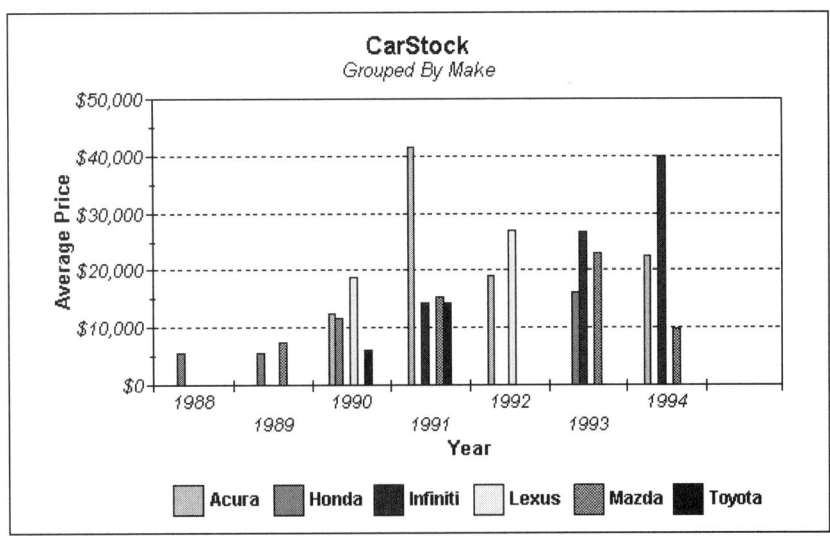

Figure 13-10: A 2D summary graph that shows the average price of all cars in stock for each Make.

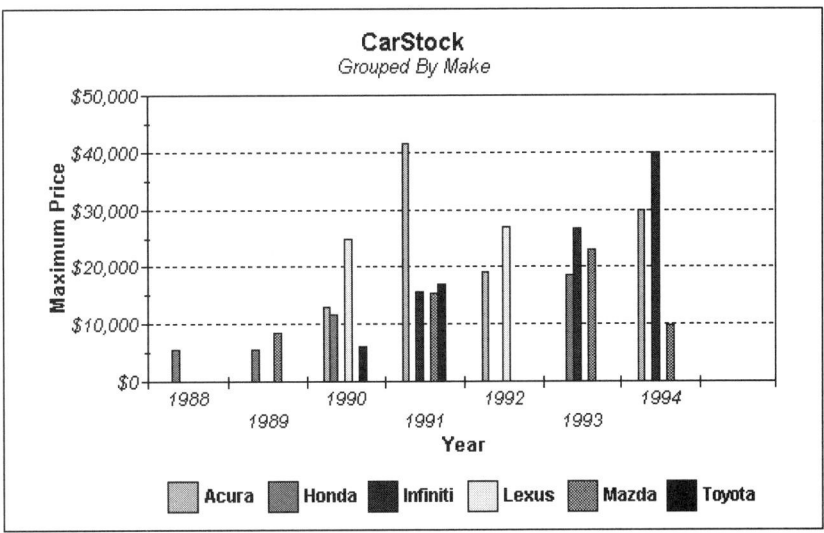

Figure 13-11: A 2D summary graph that shows the maximum price of all cars in stock for each Make and Model.

YOUR FIRST CROSSTAB

Like other important Paradox tasks, there are several ways to create a crosstab. Since our goal has always been to show you the quickest, easiest approach to doing anything in Paradox, this section focuses on creating crosstabs using the Quick Crosstab button. Does that sound fast or what?

The following exercise walks you through the steps necessary to create a simple 1D summary crosstab for the sample *CarStock* table. You can follow the same general steps to create crosstabs with other tables or other types of crosstabs (2D crosstab, multitable crosstab, etc.).

1. Choose File, Open, Table and retrieve the CARSTOCK table into your Paradox workspace.

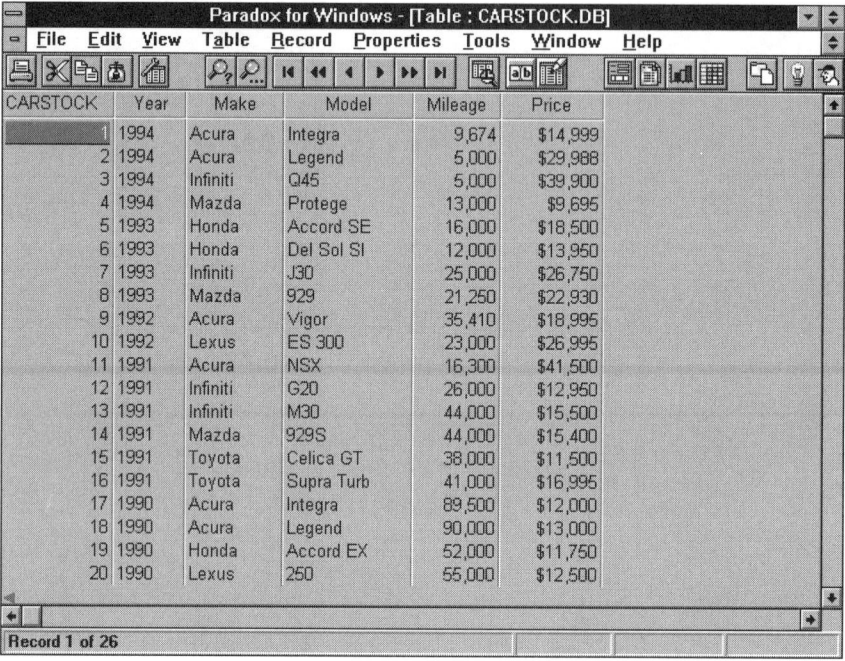

Figure 13-12: My CARSTOCK table appears in a maximized Table window.

2. Click the Quick Crosstab button on the Table window Toolbar. Paradox displays the Define Crosstab dialog box (see Figure 13-13).

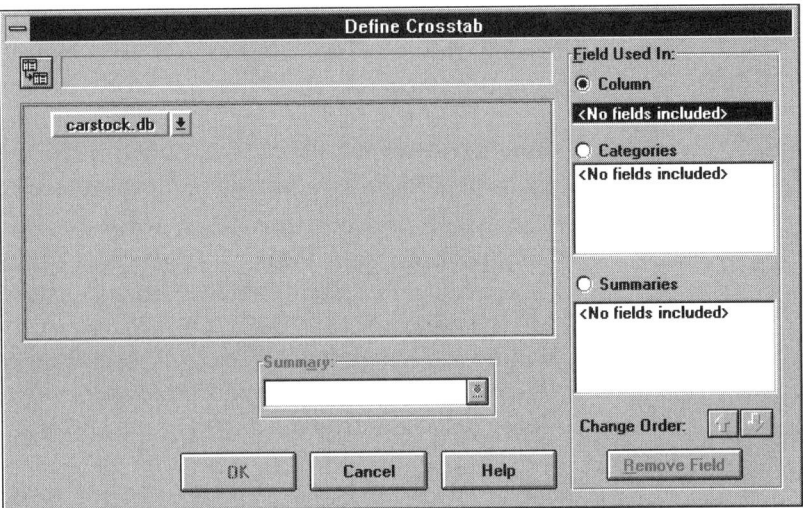

Figure 13-13: The default, blank Define Crosstab dialog box. The drop-down list (showing *carstock.db*) contains the field names for the CARSTOCK table.

Take note of several things in this dialog. First, notice the table name *carstock.db* in the upper left corner of the dialog box. This name belongs to a drop-down list that contains each field name in the CARSTOCK table. Second, the OK button at the bottom of the dialog remains dimmed until you define a valid crosstab. To do that, you must identify at least one category and one summary field. Finally, since the Column radio button in the Field Used In area is active, let's start by defining that field first.

Inside Scoop

The Column radio button really just identifies another category in your crosstab. The "category" that you define using Column, you see, is the one that you wish to show along the top row of your crosstab.

3. Click the drop-down arrow next to *carstock.db* to reveal the field name list, then click the Make field name in the list. Paradox transfers the field into the Column text box in the following form: *CARSTOCK.Make*.

4. Click the Summaries radio button in the Field Used In area. Open the field name list again and click the Price field name this time.

Paradox transfers the entry *Sum(CARSTOCK.Price)* into the Summaries text box. This code means that Paradox intends to sum the entries in the Price field for your crosstab. Remember, when Paradox first encounters a numeric field it always assumes you want to sum it. Now we'll change the Summary method so that Paradox averages the Price data.

5. Click the Summary drop-down arrow to reveal the list of summary action options. Click the Avg option.

The entry *Sum(CARSTOCK.Price)* in the Summaries text box changes to *Avg(CARSTOCK.Price)* to show that Paradox will now average the Price data. Most importantly, the OK button no longer is dimmed. That means you have correctly defined a valid crosstab (see Figure 13-14).

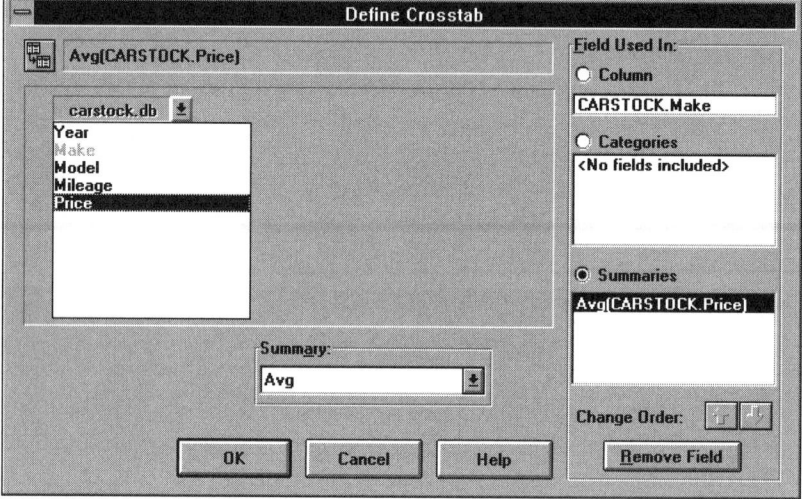

Figure 13-14: The crosstab is defined and ready to go. Use the Summary: drop-down list (showing *Avg*) to define the type of summarizing.

6. Click OK.

Pitfall Ahead

In order to create a crosstab, Paradox must first run a query that produces the summary information for your crosstab. Ninety-nine percent of the time this process completes without a hitch. There are two instances when Paradox may be unable to produce your crosstab: when the Answer table that Paradox creates during the query run contains too many fields and when your hard disk runs out of space to store the query. In both cases, the resulting crosstab will be blank.

Paradox creates a 1D crosstab based on the settings shown in the Define Crosstab dialog box of Figure 13-14.

Anatomy of a Crosstab

Paradox usually takes a few seconds to create a crosstab. When it's done summarizing and organizing the field data according to your settings, Paradox displays the crosstab on your screen in a Form window.

This is one column heading.

This is one piece of summary data.

The category description goes here.

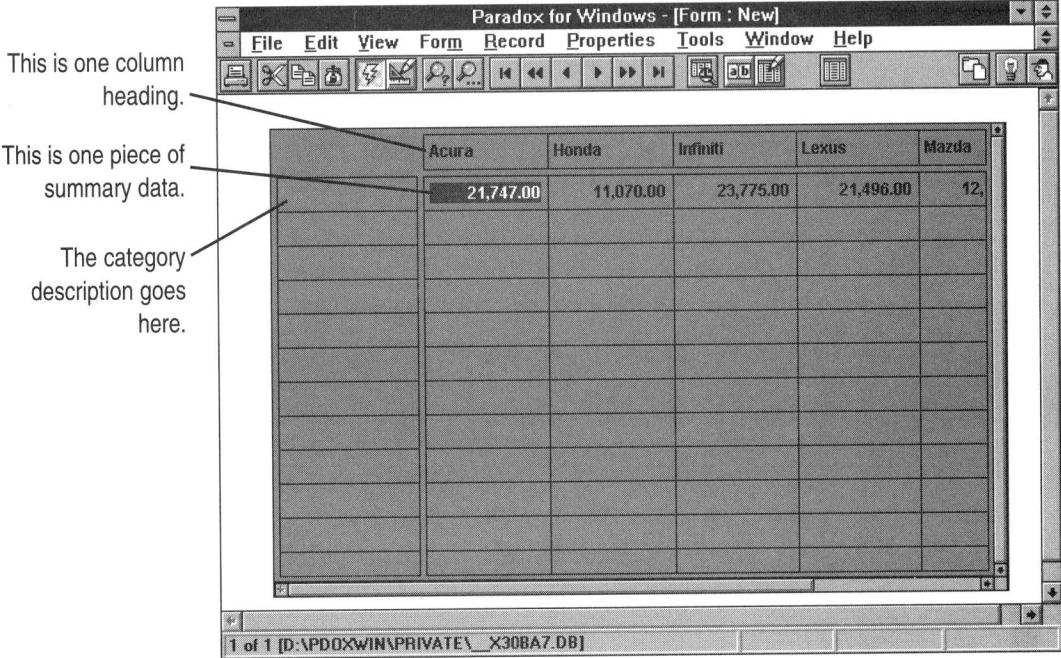

Figure 13-15: Paradox displays this 1D crosstab on your screen.

Immediately you'll be struck (but hopefully not in the forehead) by how basic the crosstab appears at first. So basic, in fact, that there's not even a descriptive label in the first column to describe what's in the crosstab. You know, something like *Average Price*. Don't fret—it's a snap to add text to your crosstab. Here's a rundown of what's in the crosstab and on your screen:

Element	What it's good for
Category description	If one were there, you'd see a description such as *Average Price.*
Column heading	In this case, the Make field is the only heading.
Summary data	These values represent the average of the Price field data.
Scroll bars	Use these tools to scroll through large crosstabs.
Form window Toolbar	Works just the same as if you had created a new form (hey, you did!).

Since your crosstab is displayed in a Form window, you can edit the structure and appearance of the crosstab as you would do for any form in the Form Design window. Once you display the crosstab in the Form Design window, simply right-click any object to inspect its Properties menu. Each menu contains commands specific to your object so that you can tweak the object in many different ways.

Inspecting a Crosstab

To edit properties in a crosstab, you must first move your crosstab into a Form Design window. To do that, choose the View, Design Form command; better yet, just press F8 to get there immediately.

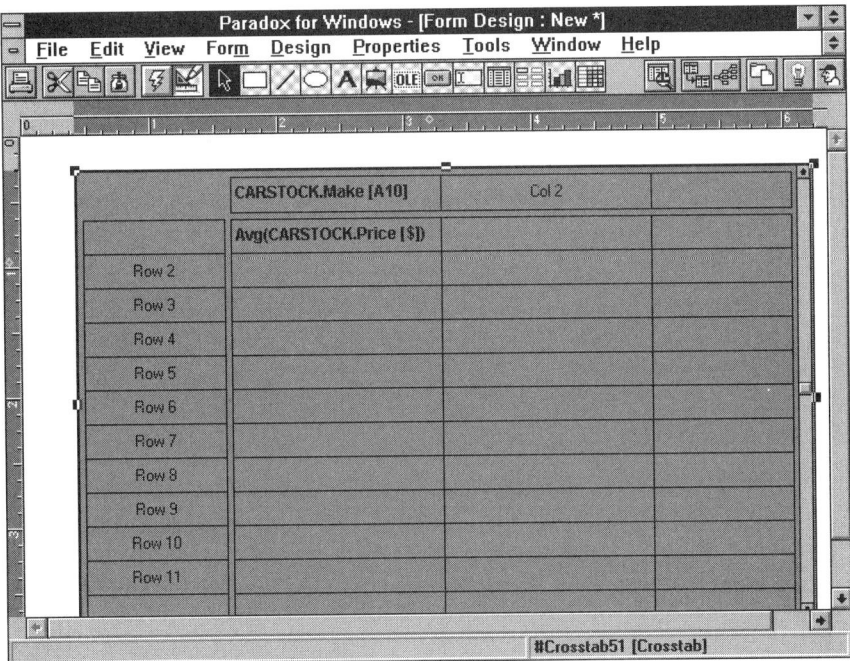

Figure 13-16: Viewing the sample crosstab in the Form Design window.

Let me mention that I've widened the first column in the crosstab shown above so that you can see exactly what's inside. Notice that each field object contains one of the codes you created back in the Crosstab Design dialog box. A field type description appears next to each of these codes so you remember what type of data they contain. That's important because you may wish to format the numeric entries in your crosstab; in order to do that, you need to know what type of number it is you're formatting.

To change the properties of any object that appears in your crosstab, select the object and right-click it. Here's a short list of common tasks you can perform. Refer back to Figure 13-16 for specific mouse positioning information:

❍ To add the label *Average Price* to the blank description area just above *Row 2*, click the Text tool, drag the outline of the text box and release your mouse, type in the text, then click anywhere outside the new text element.

❍ To widen or narrow the rows, position your mouse pointer on the top border of *Row 2* until you see a two-headed arrow, then drag down or up to simultaneously resize all rows.

❍ To widen or narrow the columns, position your mouse pointer on the left border of *Col 2* until you see a two-headed arrow, then drag right or left to simultaneously resize all rows.

○ To change the number format for the summary Price data, right-click the object that contains the *Avg(CARSTOCK.Price[$])* code, choose Format, Number Format, then click one of the formatting options.

○ To change the alignment of the column headings of the summary Price data, right-click the *CARSTOCK.Make[A10]* object or choose Alignment and then click one of the alignment options.

○ When you're finished making changes to the crosstab and you're ready to leave the Form Design window, press F8 again. Paradox displays the newly modified crosstab in a Form window.

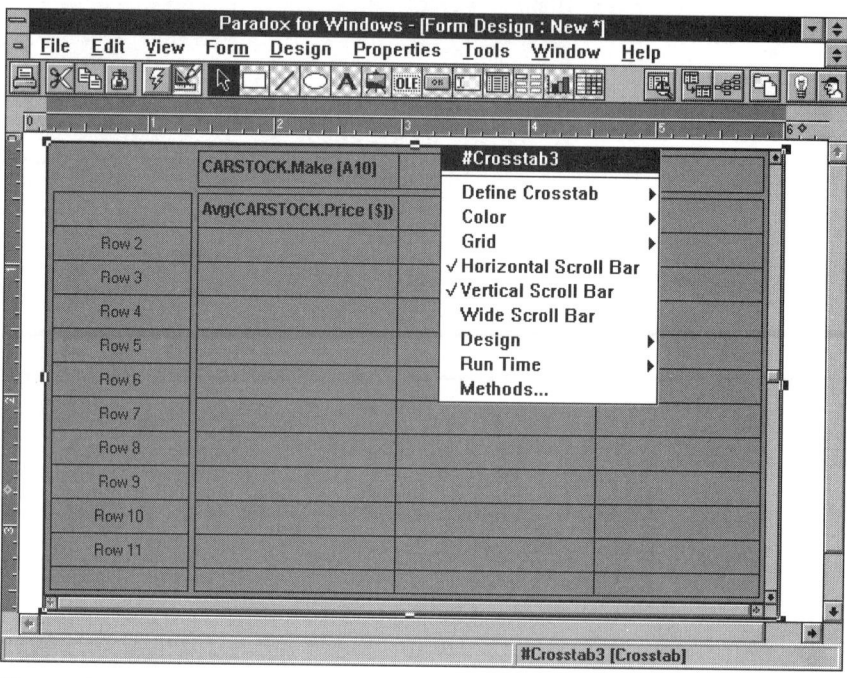

Figure 13-17: Inspecting the property menu for the crosstab as a whole.

For in-depth coverage of how to inspect and alter the properties of elements in a form, flip back to Chapter 9, "Forms 101," and Chapter 10, "Forms: the Sequel."

Now What To Do With It?

At this point there are a couple of different things you can do with your crosstab. Here are four fun things to do with a crosstab once you've got one:

❍ When Paradox creates a crosstab, it also creates a temporary table that contains the data shown in the crosstab. You can save the temporary table and use it as any other table if you wish. To do this, choose the Edit, Save Crosstab command. When Paradox displays the Save Crosstab Table As dialog box, type a name into the File Name text box, then click OK.

❍ Perhaps you'd like to save the crosstab form. To do so, choose File, Close and click Yes in the ensuing dialog box, then type a name in the File Save As dialog box.

❍ To print the crosstab, choose the File, Print command.

❍ To discard the current crosstab so that you can create a new one, start by choosing the File, Close command and clicking the No option in the Next dialog box. Now click the Quick Crosstab button again.

YOUR FIRST GRAPH

Creating a Paradox graph is just as rewarding as creating a crosstab. Even more so. Like other Paradox tasks, you can assemble the graph from the ground up using your intimate knowledge of working in the Form and Report windows, creating elements, defining fields, and so on. Or you can try your hand at the quickest, easiest approach to creating a graph: the Quick Graph button. Let me guess.

In the following exercise you will learn how to create a simple 1D summary graph for the ever-present sample CARSTOCK table. As with the crosstab exercise, you'll easily be able to adapt these steps to create graphs with other tables or with other types of graphs (tabular, 2D graph, etc.).

1. Choose File, Open, Table and retrieve the CARSTOCK table into your Paradox workspace. If you just popped in from the last section, then this table may still be on your screen. If that sounds like you, then you won't have to open it up again.

2. Click the Quick Graph button on the Table window Toolbar. Paradox displays the Define Graph dialog box (see Figure 13-18).

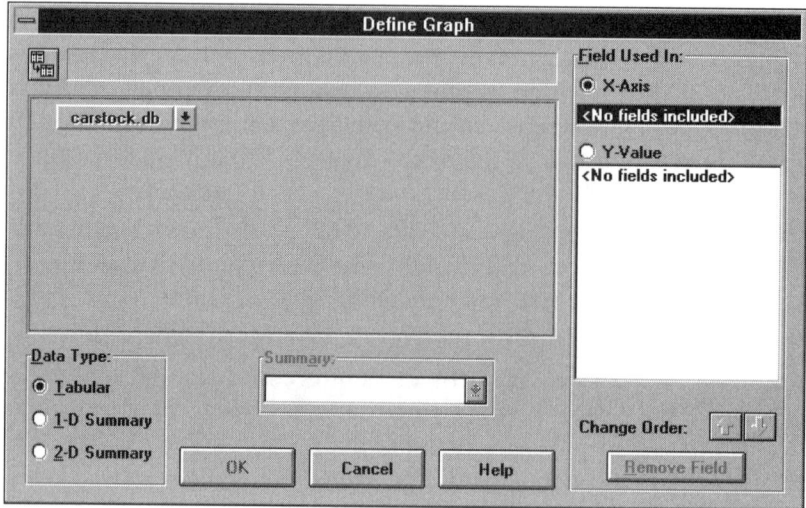

Figure 13-18: The default, blank Define Graph dialog box.

You'll immediately feel as if you've found a lost friend. That's because the Define Graph dialog box is nearly identical to the Define Crosstab dialog box from the last section. The table name *carstock.db is* still there in the upper left corner of the dialog box and the OK button at the bottom. In this dialog, though, you must identify the X-Axis field and at least one Y-Value category (that's the summary field). Finally, you must tell Paradox which type of graph to construct by making a choice inside the Data Type area. Let's start there.

Inside Scoop

When you click the 2-D Summary radio button in the Data Type area, Paradox shows an extra category list in the Field Used In area. Click the 2-D Summary now so you can see it. It's called the Grouped By list, and it's here that you identify the field you wish to group your data by (take a peek back at Figure 13-10 if you don't remember this feature).

3. Click the 2-D Summary button in the Data Type area. Paradox adds the Grouped By list box to the middle of the Field Used In area.

4. Click the X-Axis radio button, then click the drop-down arrow next to *carstock.db* to reveal the field name list. Click the Year field name in the list. Paradox transfers the Year field into the X-Axis box as the code *CARSTOCK.Year.*

5. Click the Grouped By radio button in the Field Used In area. Open the field name list again and click the Make field name this time.

6. Now click the Y-Value radio button in the Field Used In area. Open the field name list one last time and click the Mileage field name.

    Paradox transfers the entry *Sum(CARSTOCK.Mileage)* into the Y-Value text box. This code means that Paradox intends to sum the entries in the Mileage field for your crosstab. Remember, when Paradox first encounters a numeric field, it always assumes you want to sum it. Since we're more interested in identifying the minimum mileage for each make, we'll change the Summary method so that Paradox locates the minimum Mileage data.

7. Click the Summary drop-down arrow to reveal the list of summary action options. Click the Min option.

    The entry *Sum(CARSTOCK.Mileage)* in the Summaries text box changes to *Min(CARSTOCK.Mileage)* to show that Paradox will now locate the minimum Mileage data. The OK button is no longer dimmed, so you have correctly defined a 2-D summary graph (see Figure 13-14).

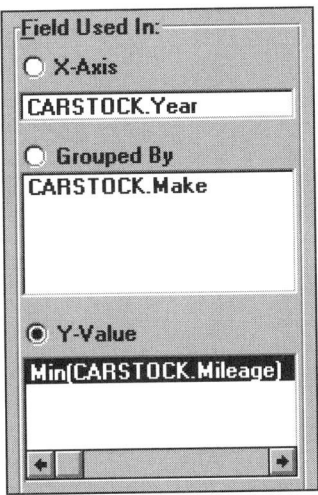

Figure 13-19: The Field Used In area contains all the information Paradox needs to calculate your 2D summary graph.

8. Click OK.

Paradox creates the 2D summary graph based on the settings shown in the Field Used In area of Figure 13-19.

Anatomy of a Graph

Paradox only requires a couple of seconds to create a graph. When Paradox finishes summarizing and organizing the field data according to your settings, it displays the graph on your screen in a Form window.

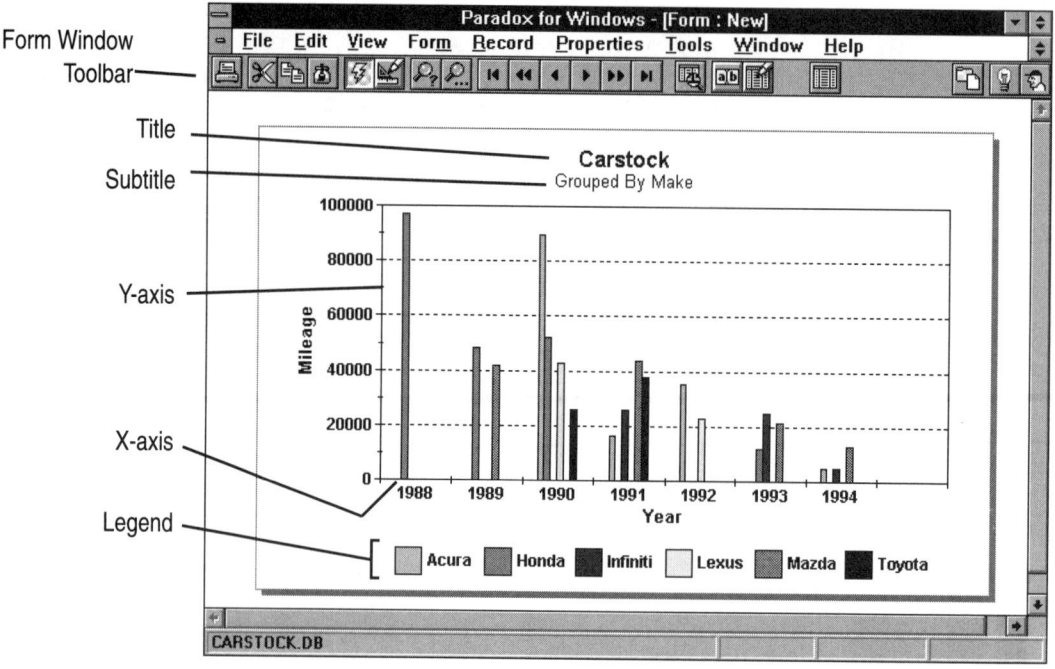

Figure 13-20: This 2D summary graph shows the minimum mileage for each model year grouped by make.

The initial reaction to a Paradox graph usually is one of glee: "Hey, I created a graph!" The real challenge comes when you want to spiff up the graph and make it truly custom. For instance, maybe you'd like to change the text labels a bit to make them more descriptive, or play around with the number scale on the y axis so it's easier to recognize. Yes, you can do these (and a whole slew of other things) to your graph. Here's a quick glance at what's in the graph on your screen:

Element	What it's good for
Title	That's the name of the table; you can make it more descriptive.
Subtitle	That's how you can make the title more descriptive.
X Axis	In this case, the Year field appears here.
Y Axis	These values represent the minimum of the Mileage field data.
Legend	The key to figuring out what's what in complex graphs.
Form window Toolbar	Works just the same as if you had created a new form (hey, you did!)

Paradox displays your graph in a Form window, just as with crosstabs. You can edit the structure and appearance of the graph just as you can edit other forms in the Form Design window. Once you display the graph in the Form Design window, simply right-click any object to inspect the properties for that object.

Inspecting a Graph

To edit a graph's properties you must first display the graph in the Form Design window. To do that, choose the View, Design Form command; better yet, just press F8 to get there immediately. To change the properties of any object that appears in your graph, select the object and right-click it.

Here's a short list of common tasks you can perform:

❍ To change the y axis label *Mileage* to *Minimum Mileage*, right-click the *Mileage* label in the graph, choose Title, Text, type *Minimum Mileage* into the Enter Title dialog box, then click OK.

❍ To change the graph type from 2D Bar to 3D Rotated Bar, right-click the graph outside of the bar display area, then choose the Graph Type, 3D Rotated bar option. Remember that when you choose any of the rotated graph types, the y axis and x axis swap locations on the graph.

❍ To move the legend from the bottom of the graph to the right side of the graph, right-click just outside the perimeter of the legend, then choose Legend Pos, Right.

❍ To format the number formatting scale for the y axis, right-click near the y axis, choose Ticks, Number Format, and then choose a number formatting option.

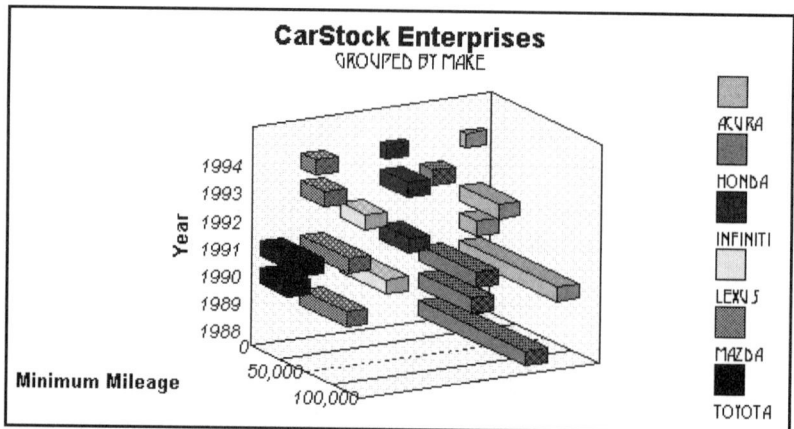

Figure 13-21: This version of the 2-D summary graph is formatted more professionally.

For in-depth coverage of how to inspect and alter the properties of elements in a form, flip back to Chapter 9, "Forms 101," and Chapter 10, "Forms: the Sequel."

Now What To Do With It?

At this point there are a couple of different things you can do with your graph. Here are three fun things to do with a graph once you've got one:

○ Perhaps you'd like to save the graph form you just created. To do so, choose File, Close and click Yes in the ensuing dialog box, then type a name in the File Save As dialog box.

○ To print the graph, choose the File, Print command.

○ To discard the current graph so that you can create a new one, start by choosing the File, Close command and clicking the No option in the Newly Created Document dialog box. Then click the Quick Graph button again.

MOVING ON

That's it for crosstabs and graphs. Hopefully we satisfied your curiosity for creating and working with these important visual aids. Keep in mind that using the Quick Crosstab and Quick Graph buttons are the fastest way to create crosstabs and graphs. Once you're more familiar with changing the properties of crosstabs and graphs in the Form Design window, try your hand at actually modifying the category and summary fields themselves. (This saves you the trouble of recreating crosstabs or graphs that go awry.) Just right-click one of the category or summary field elements and look for a "Define ..." option; for example, Define Y-Value (for a graph) or Define Column Field (for a crosstab).

For even more cool fun with graphic objects, go right on ahead to the next chapter where you'll learn how to share and link data in your Paradox applications.

14

THE ABC's OF DDE & OLE

ome like their acronyms hot! It's hard to believe, but yes, you're about to embark upon a chapter dedicated to two acronyms so powerful and friendly that you'll eventually come to know them by their pet names: DDE (dee-dee-eee) and OLE (oh-lay). These innocent-looking abbreviations describe technologies that make it incredibly— no amazingly—simple to exchange, link and share data from all your favorite Windows programs, including Paradox, of course.

DDE and OLE are essentially different flavors of the same sort of tool. The most important trait they share is their love for giving you access to all sorts of data from all sorts of places. Chronologically speaking, DDE arrived on the scene earlier than OLE, and today many Windows programs continue to use both. So how do you know when it makes sense to use one or the other of these tools?

Good question. This chapter introduces you to both DDE and OLE technology and shows you how and when you're likely to bump into these tools. Along the way, we'll check out some cool ways to take advantage of them in Paradox.

DDE VERSUS OLE

So what's the big difference? DDE, or *Dynamic Data Exchange* to those in the know, lets you grab data from programs such as Quattro Pro for Windows, 1-2-3 for Windows, Excel and other assorted num-ber-crunching beasties, and devour that data in Paradox, using all of the table-managing and querying skills you've learned so far in the book. It's only fair that this relationship should be a two-way street, so DDE also allows you to send your Paradox table data over into those programs too.

When DDE first appeared in an early version of Windows, most of us were still wowed by the ability to cut, copy and paste stuff inside a single program. With DDE on the scene, it was possible to copy data from one program's document (like a Paradox table) and paste it *as a data link* to another program's document (like the cell in a Quattro Pro for Windows spreadsheet). Sure, Paradox was okay for doing basic run-of-the-mill math gymnastics, but some of us really wanted to get our hands on the number-juggling tools available in programs like Quattro Pro for Windows. DDE made it so. When we copied a Paradox table value and pasted it into a Quattro Pro for Windows spreadsheet, Windows created a "hot link" between the two programs. These hot links were all the rage: "Hey Joe, watch me create a hot link between my computer and the IRS's computer."

OLE, or *Object Linking and Embedding*, is one of the most abused and joked-about acronyms known to man. Let me say now that it is not a reference to a Spanish bullfight cheer nor is it a clinical term for animal husbandry. OLE is simply everything that DDE is and a lot more. Instead of shuttling data back and forth between programs (like with DDE), OLE actually lets you store a file from one program inside a Paradox table, or vice versa. The method to this madness? Well, when you *embed* a Word for Windows document inside a Paradox table, you can instantly retrieve that Word for Windows document by double-clicking it. Whoosh! In a flash, your Word for Windows document appears in Paradox—no Alt+Tab-ing back out to Program Manager, launching the Word for Windows program, retrieving the file, copying and pasting it and so on.

Think of OLE as the computer software equivalent of gene-splicing. You get a bigger and better Paradox that has the analytical capabilities of spreadsheet programs like Quattro Pro for Windows and Excel; the text and document-handling genius of word processing programs like Word for Windows and WordPerfect for Windows; and the image-making power of graphics programs like Paintbrush and PowerPoint. You can even link up to other database programs like dBASE and Access (they need all the help they can get).

Inside Scoop

You may have noticed that many of the program names I've listed are followed by "for Windows" (Word-Perfect for Windows and Quattro Pro for Windows) while some do not (Excel and PowerPoint). In most cases, publishers that have released a Windows version of a program originally designed for DOS distinguish their products by adding "for Windows" after the name. In the case of Excel, PowerPoint and Paintbrush, you won't see the "for Windows" designation because there never was an original DOS version of those programs. This tidbit of history is important because *only* programs specifically designed to run under Windows support the DDE and OLE technologies.

BREAKING IT DOWN INTO LAYMAN'S TERMS

Now that you have a general idea of what DDE and OLE are about, let's talk a little bit about how these tools actually work. To orient ourselves, we should take a moment to learn a few new terms. You see, in addition to being famous acronyms, DDE and OLE each has a language all its own. It's not a hard language to learn; in fact, the terminology is built upon a metaphor that has existed since the beginning of time.

Living To Give & Aching To Take

The DDE language is based on the familiar notion of giving and taking. The premise is this: one application *gives* data while another application *takes* the data. When DDE first appeared in Windows, the euphemistic terms s*erver* and *client* were used to describe the roles played by any two applications that took part in this unique symbiotic relationship. The server, of course, *supplied* the information for the DDE link while the client *took* that information. I always liked to think of the roles as more of a master-slave relationship (Microsoft didn't agree). You can imagine the roles any way you like so long as you understand that one application gives information and another application takes it.

The OLE language, also based upon the idea of giving and taking, resembles the language of DDE—with one small exception. To clarify what actually transpires in an OLE link, Microsoft chose the term *container* to describe any application that takes a file (document) from another application. That's because the taking application really is a sort of container that houses the embedded file. In formal settings and at officious gatherings, the application giving the file is called the *OLE server* while the application that takes and embeds the file is called the *OLE container*.

Even more important, you should know that Paradox is capable of both giving and taking DDE and OLE information (the sign of a proper upbringing). This is significant because some cheesy software publishers decided that it really wasn't too important to adopt this give-and-take philosophy for their own products. Consequently, not all Windows programs are capable of sharing information as generously as Paradox does. When you're wondering if a particular program you own supports DDE or OLE technology, go straight to the index in your user's guide. If these famous acronyms are not there, you're out of luck.

In the following example, Paradox is a *container* application and Word for Windows is a *server* application.

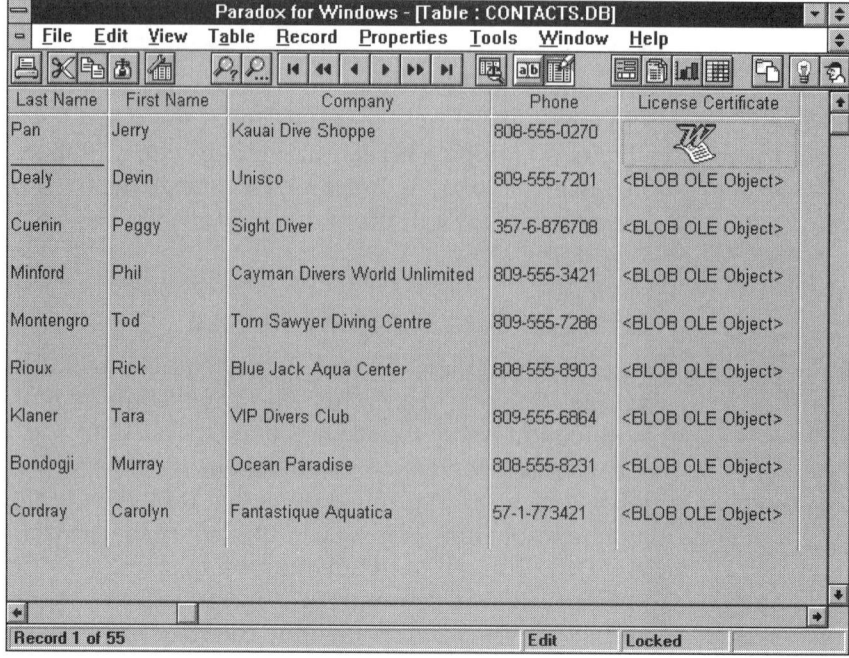

Figure 14-1: Paradox takes information that Word for Windows is giving. In this view, a Word for Windows document, represented by the familiar Word icon (upper right screen area), is embedded into a field in a Paradox table.

OLE Then & OLE Now

Today, DDE looks and acts pretty much like it did way back in the dark ages (of computers). OLE technology, on the other hand, has undergone some changes since its debut as OLE 1.0. You need to know a little bit about how OLE has changed because some programs still don't support OLE 2.0, the newest and greatest version of this object-embedding technology.

As you read through the following sections, don't worry if the procedures and tasks seem foreign. Later in the chapter we'll run through several short exercises designed to quickly demonstrate how DDE and OLE work in Paradox. It's at that time that the stuff you're about to read will gel.

How Embedded Objects Are Updated

Suppose you embedded an object in a Paradox form and now you need to make a few minor changes to it. To edit the object, you simply double-click the object in your form. What happens at this point depends on whether the *host program*—the program originally used to create that object—supports OLE 1.0 or OLE 2.0.

For applications that support only OLE 1.0, double-clicking on an embedded object starts the host program on your computer. Let's pretend that Paintbrush is the host program. Windows starts Paintbrush and soon shows the Paintbrush application window on your screen, with your drawing (object) as the active document. After making changes to the drawing, you save the drawing file and close Paintbrush before Windows shows you the revised version of the drawing in your Paradox form.

Paradox
Application
window

Embedded object

Paintbrush
application
window

Figure 14-2: Paintbrush, the program that created this object, appears in its own window because Paintbrush supports only OLE 1.0.

Host applications that support OLE 2.0, however, are a bit more intelligent. Let's now pretend that Word for Windows is the host program. In this example, double-clicking the object starts Word for Windows on your computer. But instead of seeing a separate Word for Windows application window, all you see are its menu bar and Toolbars. In fact, these Word for Windows screen elements replace the corresponding Paradox screen elements, and a Word for Windows document window appears behind the embedded object.

Word for
Windows
elements

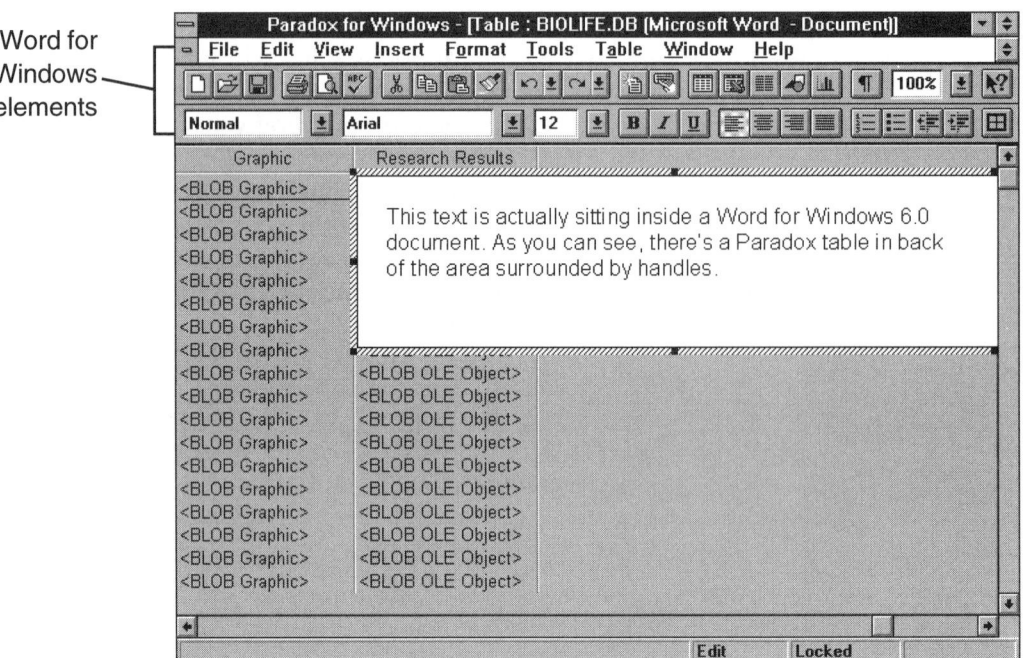

Figure 14-3: Look closely. Elements of the Word for Windows workspace appear when the embedded Word for Windows object is active in this Paradox table.

After making changes to the Word for Windows embedded document, simply click anywhere outside the object to recall the Paradox menu bar and Toolbar. As you can see, a document created in a host application that supports OLE 2.0 can be edited right in a Paradox table. Rather than bringing up the Word for Windows application window, the Word document is "live" right where it is.

Knowing When To Drag & Drop

In OLE 1.0, there are several ways to get data from the server program into the container program. Each technique involves the use of conventional copy-and-paste techniques that involve the use of conventional menus containing lots of conventional commands. Boring. If your goal is to achieve OLE nirvana, then you'll be happy to learn that OLE 2.0 makes it even easier to move data from program to program—you can simply drag and drop it.

Okay, so what's the big deal about dragging and dropping? you ask. Well, think about it. While you may be accustomed to dragging and dropping files in File Manager, or a range of cells in Excel, or a field in a Paradox table, when was the last time you dragged something from one program and dropped it into another program? Yeah, now you're getting it.

Suppose you wish to embed a Word for Windows document into a Paradox table. The best way to accomplish this feat is to arrange both application windows side by side on your screen. Once there, select the Word for Windows document and drag it into the Paradox application window. When you've positioned your mouse pointer near the area in the Paradox table where you wish to insert the embedded object, release your mouse button. Voilà! An embedded object in less than two seconds, and no menus and no commands up your sleeves.

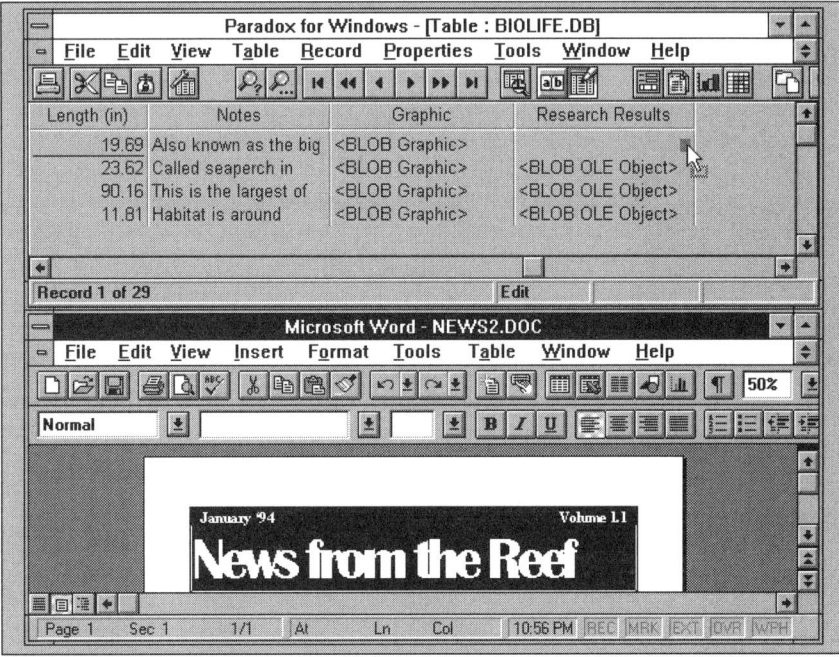

Figure 14-4: Dragging a Word for Windows document that appears selected in the lower window into the Paradox table in the upper window.

The mouse pointer shows the exact location where the Word for Windows document will be inserted.

Nesting Habits of the Spotted OLE

Catchy headings often precede complex explanations about esoteric computer topics. Not here, though. Actually this is the part where OLE 2.0 shows off a little bit. You see, with OLE 2.0 you can embed objects within objects within objects. This tiered arrangement of objects has come to be known as *nesting objects*. Why do that? you ponder.

Here's a simple example. Suppose you've embedded a Quattro Pro for Windows spreadsheet in a PowerPoint slide, and now you wish to use that very slide "as is" inside a Paradox form. Go ahead, do it. Now comes the cool part. Next imagine that you need to edit the Quattro Pro for Windows spreadsheet object that's embedded in the PowerPoint slide. Start by double-clicking the PowerPoint object in the Paradox form. Once the PowerPoint object is active, you can then double-click the embedded Quattro Pro for Windows object to edit the spreadsheet.

Try and think of it this way: you're a snake crawling along a tree branch that's holding a bird nest, and you're interested in a tasty meal. In order to get at the eggs, you first have to get into the nest. (Wow, was that nesting analogy a stretch, or what?)

OLE: The Next Generation

Although the future of OLE really isn't our concern today, it is fun to imagine where this technology is heading. It probably won't be too long before all your applications, Windows-based or otherwise, will be able to talk to one another with a minimum of effort on your part; you'll issue commands to your computer by voice, and the mouse will be relegated to an exhibit in a technology museum.

In the *near* future, we can realistically expect at least a few changes in OLE technology. How about a generic document structure that automatically accesses applications installed on your computer (Paradox, Word, PowerPoint, etc.) based on the information you key in at any one time? Or what about being able to quickly transport documents along a data channel without regard to the flavor of your network (Novell Netware, LAN Manager, BanyanVines, etc.)?

In any case, after a few experiments with OLE 2.0 in Paradox, you'll quickly come to appreciate the current state of OLE technology.

Paradox as a DDE Server

To use Paradox as a DDE server, copy a piece of data from a Paradox table, switch to the DDE client program and then choose the Edit, Paste Link command. The other program can be Quattro Pro for Windows, WordPerfect for Windows, Excel or any one of a number of other Windows programs you might have on your computer. The only condition is that the program must have the ability to act as a DDE client. It's as simple as that.

Pitfall Ahead

It's important to know that in order to successfully use Paradox as a DDE server, you must copy your data from a Table window. Although you can copy data from elsewhere in Paradox—say, while in a Quick Form window—when you switch to the DDE client, the Paste Link command on the Edit menu will be dimmed and unavailable to you.

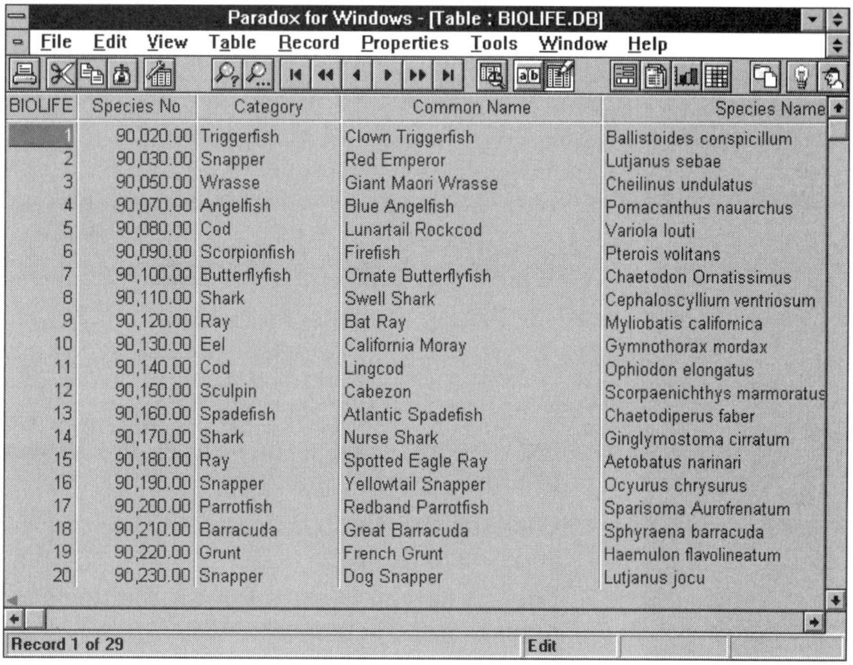

BIOLIFE	Species No	Category	Common Name	Species Name
1	90,020.00	Triggerfish	Clown Triggerfish	Ballistoides conspicillum
2	90,030.00	Snapper	Red Emperor	Lutjanus sebae
3	90,050.00	Wrasse	Giant Maori Wrasse	Cheilinus undulatus
4	90,070.00	Angelfish	Blue Angelfish	Pomacanthus nauarchus
5	90,080.00	Cod	Lunartail Rockcod	Variola louti
6	90,090.00	Scorpionfish	Firefish	Pterois volitans
7	90,100.00	Butterflyfish	Ornate Butterflyfish	Chaetodon Ornatissimus
8	90,110.00	Shark	Swell Shark	Cephaloscyllium ventriosum
9	90,120.00	Ray	Bat Ray	Myliobatis californica
10	90,130.00	Eel	California Moray	Gymnothorax mordax
11	90,140.00	Cod	Lingcod	Ophiodon elongatus
12	90,150.00	Sculpin	Cabezon	Scorpaenichthys marmoratus
13	90,160.00	Spadefish	Atlantic Spadefish	Chaetodiperus faber
14	90,170.00	Shark	Nurse Shark	Ginglymostoma cirratum
15	90,180.00	Ray	Spotted Eagle Ray	Aetobatus narinari
16	90,190.00	Snapper	Yellowtail Snapper	Ocyurus chrysurus
17	90,200.00	Parrotfish	Redband Parrotfish	Sparisoma Aurofrenatum
18	90,210.00	Barracuda	Great Barracuda	Sphyraena barracuda
19	90,220.00	Grunt	French Grunt	Haemulon flavolineatum
20	90,230.00	Snapper	Dog Snapper	Lutjanus jocu

Paradox for Windows - [Table : BIOLIFE.DB]
File Edit View Table Record Properties Tools Window Help

Record 1 of 29   Edit

Figure 14-5: Preparing Paradox to become a DDE server by displaying the Table window.

Here's an example you can follow along with. Using the BIOLIFE table that comes with Paradox, let's see how we can create a DDE link between Paradox and Quattro Pro for Windows. If you don't own Quattro Pro for Windows, use whatever spreadsheet program you own.

1. Launch both programs (DDE server and DDE client) on your computer.

2. Arrange the application windows side by side, or one on top of the other, to make it easy to see what's going on.

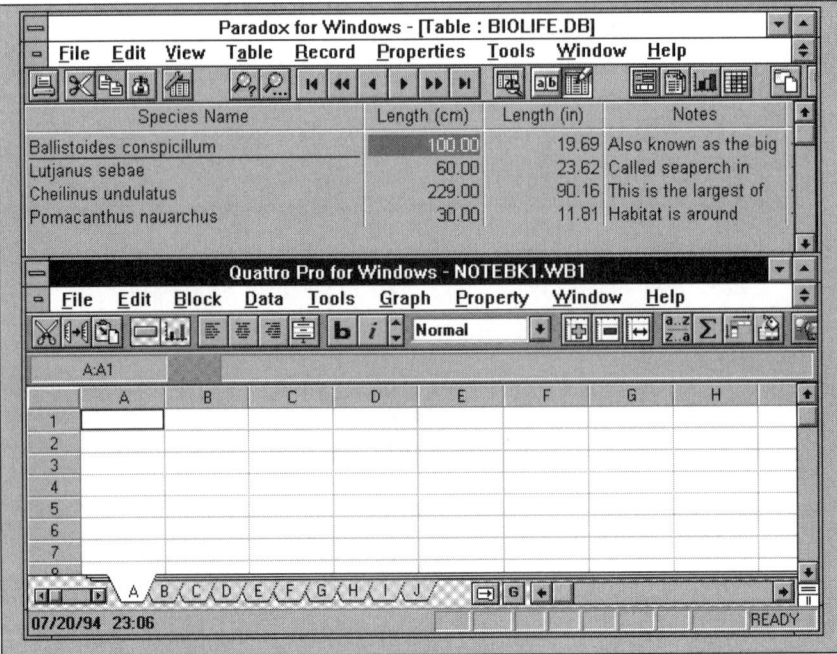

Figure 14-6: This arrangement of application windows makes it easy for you to navigate back and forth between the DDE server and the DDE client.

3. In Paradox, choose File, Open, Table and select the BIOLIFE.DB file from the Sample directory underneath your Paradox program directory.

4. Click the Length (cm) field in the table to activate it, then choose Edit, Copy.

5. Click inside the Quattro Pro for Windows application window to make it the active window.

6. Select cell A1, then choose Edit, Paste Link.

Soon the field name "Length (cm)" appears in cell A1 and beneath that appears the length value from the first row of the BIOLIFE table. Now here's the cool part. Click inside the Paradox window and move through the records in the BIOLIFE table. Every time you move to a new record, the DDE link in the Quattro Pro for Windows spreadsheet updates to show the length value in centimeters for the current record.

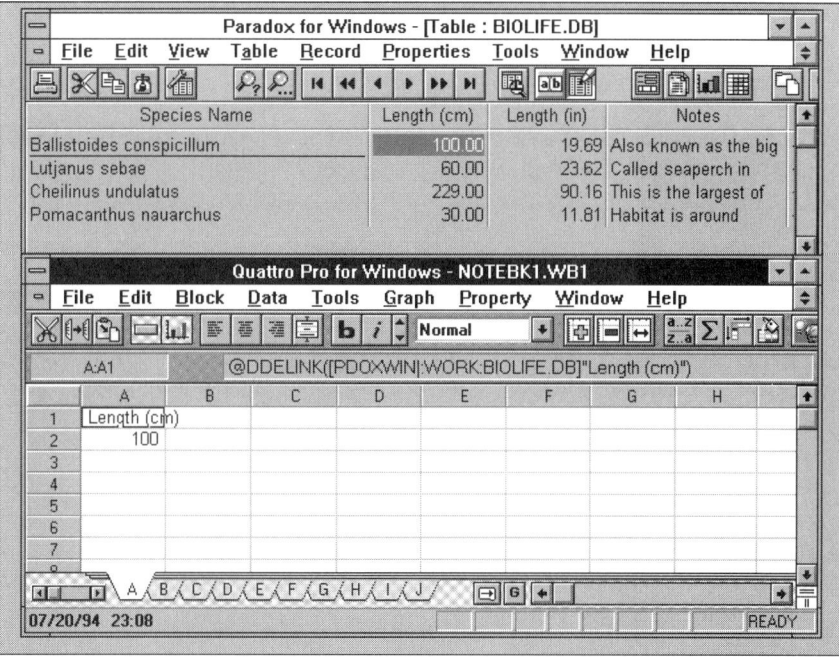

Figure 14-7: Here's the result of creating the DDE link with Paradox acting as server and Quattro Pro for Windows acting as client.

To see how this link works, move the cell selector back to A1 in the Quattro Pro for Windows spreadsheet. Now check out the entry shown in the input line:

@DDELINK([PDOXWIN|:WORK:BIOLIFE.DB]"Length (cm)")

This cryptic-looking entry is what's at the heart of the DDE link. It tells Quattro Pro exactly where to look for the link information; in this case, it points to a field named "Length (cm)" located in a file called BIOLIFE.DB that's stored in the \PDOXWIN\SAMPLE directory. In fact, when you paste a DDE link you aren't really pasting a value. You are pasting a piece of information that points the DDE client to the DDE server where the data can be found.

Inside Scoop

Because the alias for the SAMPLE directory on my computer (and probably yours, too) is WORK, the @DDELINK expression above shows WORK in the path name instead of SAMPLE.

This example is fairly simplistic because it only shows how to create a single DDE link. To really put this tool through its paces, choose Edit, Select All in Paradox to select the entire BIOLIFE table, then Edit, Copy; then switch to Quattro Pro for Windows and choose Edit, Paste Link. You've just linked an entire Paradox table to a Quattro Pro for Windows spreadsheet.

	A	B	C	D	E	F	G	H	I
1	#	Species N	Category	Common I	Species N	Length (cr	Length (in	Notes	Graphic
2	1	90020	Triggerfish	Clown Trig	Ballistoide	100	19.68504	NA	NA
3	2	90030	Snapper	Red Empe	Lutjanus s	60	23.62205	NA	NA
4	3	90050	Wrasse	Giant Mac	Cheilinus	229	90.15748	NA	NA
5	4	90070	Angelfish	Blue Ange	Pomacant	30	11.81102	NA	NA
6	5	90080	Cod	Lunartail F	Variola lou	80	31.49606	NA	NA
7	6	90090	Scorpionfi	Firefish	Pterois vo	38	14.96063	NA	NA
8	7	90100	Butterflyfis	Ornate Bu	Chaetodor	19	7.480315	NA	NA
9	8	90110	Shark	Swell Sha	Cephalosc	102	40.15748	NA	NA
10	9	90120	Ray	Bat Ray	Myliobatis	56	22.04724	NA	NA
11	10	90130	Eel	California	Gymnothc	150	59.05512	NA	NA
12	11	90140	Cod	Lingcod	Ophiodon	150	59.05512	NA	NA
13	12	90150	Sculpin	Cabezon	Scorpaeni	99	38.97638	NA	NA
14	13	90160	Spadefish	Atlantic S	Chaetodip	90	35.43307	NA	NA
15	14	90170	Shark	Nurse Sha	Ginglymos	400	157.4803	NA	NA
16	15	90180	Ray	Spotted E	Aetobatus	200	78.74016	NA	NA
17	16	90190	Snapper	Yellowtail	Ocyurus c	75	29.52756	NA	NA
18	17	90200	Parrotfish	Redband F	Sparisoma	28	11.02362	NA	NA
19	18	90210	Barracuda	Great Bari	Sphyraena	150	59.05512	NA	NA
20	19	90220	Grunt	French Gr	Haemulon	30	11.81102	NA	NA

Quattro Pro for Windows - NOTEBK1.WB1

File Edit Block Data Tools Graph Property Window Help

A:A1 @DDELINK([PDOXWIN]WORK:BIOLIFE.DB]"_TABLE")

07/20/94 23:10 READY

Figure 14-8: Here's what your Quattro Pro for Windows notebook might look like when linked to the entire BIOLIFE table in Paradox.

Inside Scoop

When you create a DDE link, Paradox enables its View, Notify On command. With this command in the "on" position, Paradox is able to update the DDE client (Quattro Pro for Windows, in this example) as soon as any data changes in the BIOLIFE table. If you wish, you can temporarily disable the View, Notify On command until you've finished making changes to the linked Paradox table. When you're ready, choose View, Notify On to reestablish the DDE link. The edited table data now appears in the DDE client.

Paradox as a DDE Client

To use Paradox as a DDE client, copy a piece of data from another program, switch to Paradox and open a target table, select an alphanumeric field where you wish to place the link, and then choose the Edit, Paste Link command. The result is another cryptic entry that might look something like this:

@DDE:QPW!|C:\QPW\SALARY.WB1!AA1!@

This message points Paradox to cell A1 on page A of a notebook named SALARY.WB1 that's saved in the \QPW directory on your C drive. Unfortunately, there's no way to cause this entry to resemble the cell value to which it's linked. In order to get to the DDE server (Quattro Pro for Windows, in this case), you press Shift+F2. After a moment, Paradox opens the DDE server program and the file that contains the value to which you're linked.

Again, the DDE server can be any one of the many Windows programs that support this capability. This DDE technique will come in handy when you have a list of data stored in a document created in another program, and you wish to perform queries on that linked data from within a Paradox table.

Paradox as an OLE Server

If you thought Paradox was powerful as a DDE server, wait until you see what it can do as an OLE server. Remember, a DDE link only creates a data bridge between Paradox and the container program. An OLE link allows you to use in-place editing so that you don't have to Alt+Tab to get back to Paradox whenever you need to make changes to an embedded table. In fact, what you can do is launch Paradox directly from inside the OLE container program by double-clicking the table object.

There are several ways to use Paradox as an OLE server. No one way is easier or more beneficial than any other. It all comes down to which applications are running on your computer and where you happen to be when you first decide to embed an OLE object. Suppose you're still in Paradox. Start by selecting the entire Paradox table you wish to embed as an OLE object, switch to the OLE container program, and then choose the Edit, Paste Link command. The other program can be Quattro Pro for Windows, WordPerfect for Windows, Excel or any other Windows program you might have on your computer. The only condition is that the program must have the ability to act as an OLE container. It's really that simple.

Inside Scoop

If you can't find the Edit, Paste Link command on your OLE container program's menu bar, look for the Edit, Paste Special or Edit, Paste command. Some programs use slightly derivative command names instead of the Edit, Paste Link command.

Here's a quick example you can follow along with. This example demonstrates another way to use Paradox as an OLE server—one where the OLE container program is the one showing on your screen. Let's return to the BIOLIFE table from an earlier example (this table comes with Paradox). Here's how we can create an OLE link between Paradox and Word for Windows. If you don't own Word for Windows, most other word processing programs will work fine.

1. Choose the Insert, Object command from the Word for Windows menu bar.
2. Since the Paradox table we wish to embed already exists, click the Create From File tab in the Insert Object dialog box.

Inside Scoop

The Create New option in the Insert Object dialog box allows you to create a new OLE server document directly inside the OLE container program. Unless you're working on a rush project, you're better off creating the document you intend to embed ahead of time (in the OLE server program) before you actually do the embedding. In-place editing is great for making a few changes here and there, but not necessarily for creating an entirely new document. It might not be worth the added strain on your computer's memory.

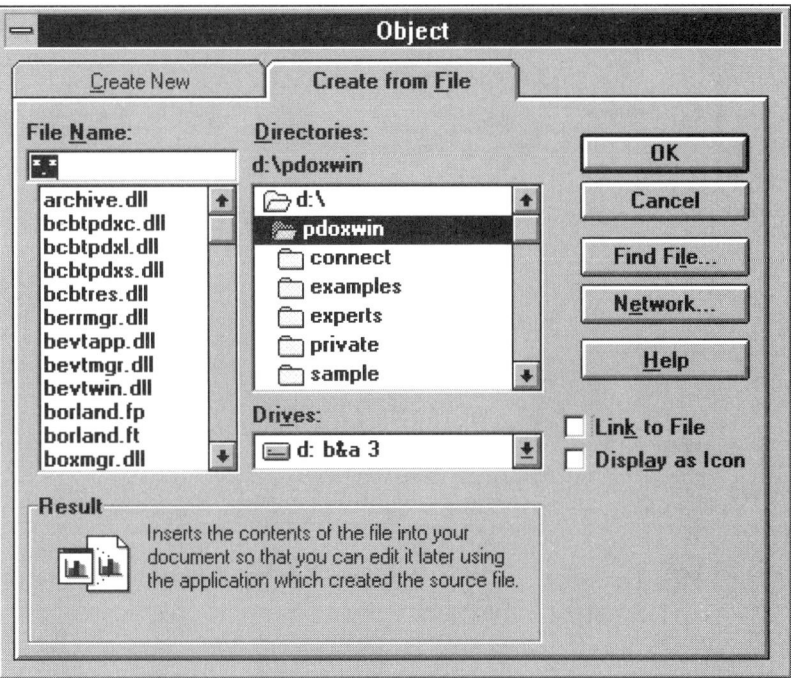

Figure 14-9: These Create From File options are available with the Insert Object dialog box in Word for Windows 6.0.

3. Click the Link To File check box. This tells both Word for Windows and Paradox that you intend to create an OLE link so that Paradox can update the embedded object in Word for Windows whenever it changes.

4. Scroll through the Directories list and locate the name of the directory where your Paradox table is stored. When the table name appears in the File Name list box, click it, then click OK.

After a moment or two you'll see a representation of your Paradox table inside the active Word for Windows document.

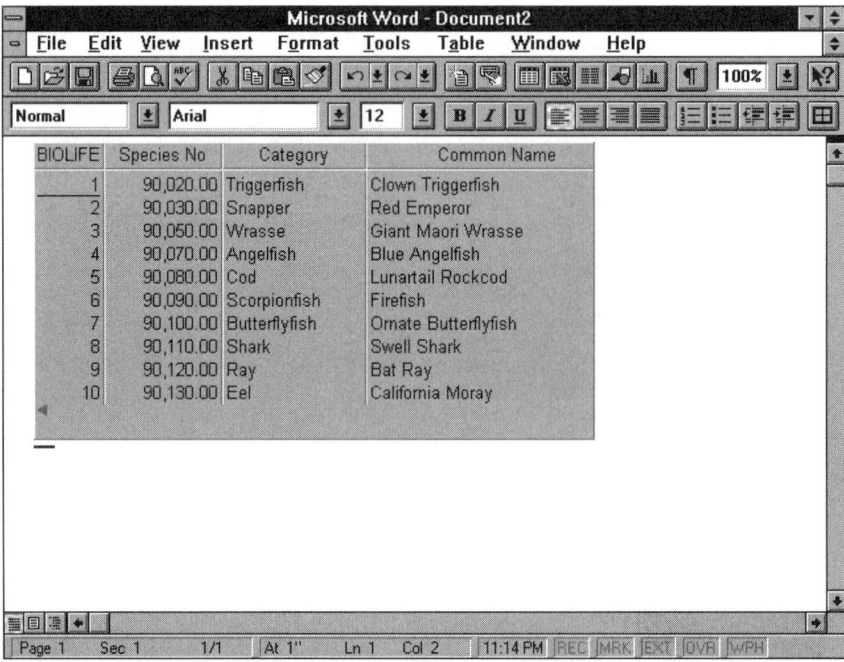

Figure 14-10: This Paradox table has been embedded as an OLE object inside the Word for Windows document.

Here's a list of the various things you can and can't do with the embedded Paradox table:

O Double-click the object to launch Paradox so that you can use the host program's menu bar and Toolbar to change data in the table. Remember, the OLE container must support OLE 2.0 for this feature to work.

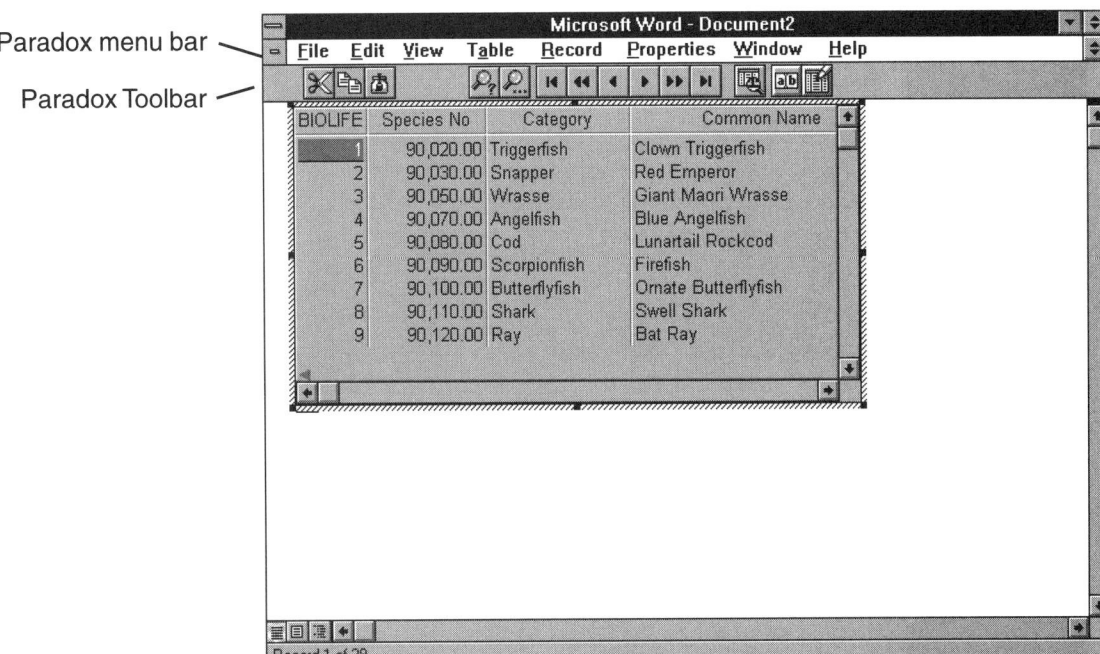
Paradox menu bar
Paradox Toolbar

Figure 14-11: The Paradox menu bar and Toolbar appear in Word for Windows once you double-click the embedded table object.

○ Right-click the object to display a shortcut menu for the OLE object. Depending upon which program you are using as the OLE container, you'll see a list of editing and formatting commands. In Word for Windows, the shortcut menu for our sample Paradox object offers the commands shown in the following figure.

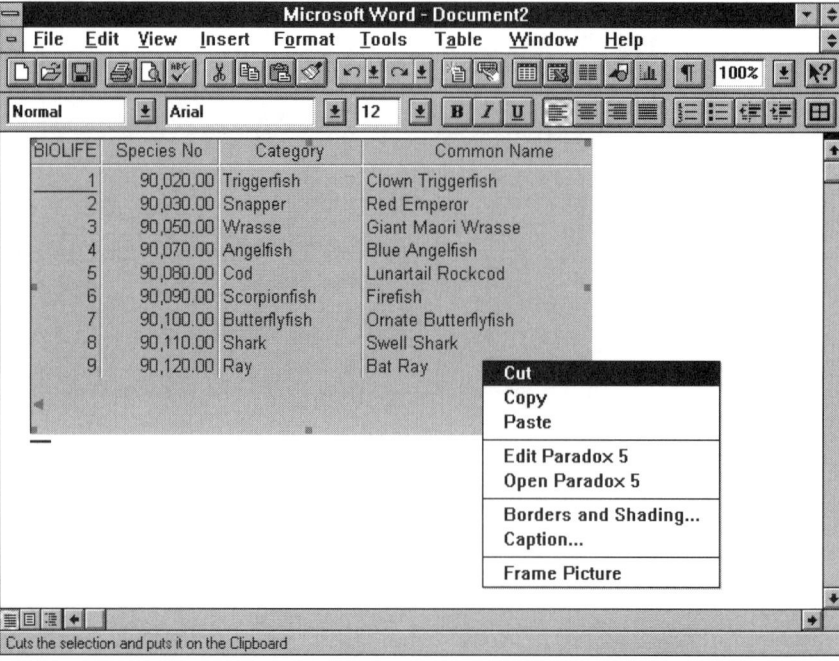

Figure 14-12: These commands appear on an OLE object's shortcut menu when Word for Windows is the OLE container and Paradox is the OLE server.

○ You can move and resize the object by dragging its border with a mouse; or you can delete the object simply by clicking it once and pressing the Delete key.

○ There also are several Paradox-specific things you can't do to an embedded table object. You cannot inspect the table's properties by right-clicking inside the table; you cannot enter Memo View; and you'll discover that certain menu commands (such as File, Print Preview, Edit, Copy To, and Edit, Paste From) are not available for use.

PARADOX AS AN OLE CONTAINER

When you wish to use Paradox as an OLE container, perhaps for the purpose of embedding a spreadsheet object or a bitmap graphic object, there are many different courses of action you can take depending upon your ultimate goal. You can create the embedded object directly inside a Paradox OLE field; you can use the Edit, Insert Object command to embed an existing object; and there's even a way to place a value in an OLE object in the Form Design or Report Design window.

The following few sections look at two different ways of handling Paradox in its role as an OLE container. In any example where you do not have the OLE server program discussed, substitute one of your own favorite made-for-Windows programs.

Embedding a New OLE Object in a Table

In order to embed an OLE object in a Paradox table or form, you first must name a field in your table as an OLE field. (Go back to Chapter 3, "Tables 101," if you don't remember how to do this.) In the following exercise, you'll retrieve the TRY_OLE.DB file and use it to test-drive this cool object-embedding technology. Here's a snapshot of this table—short and to the point, huh?

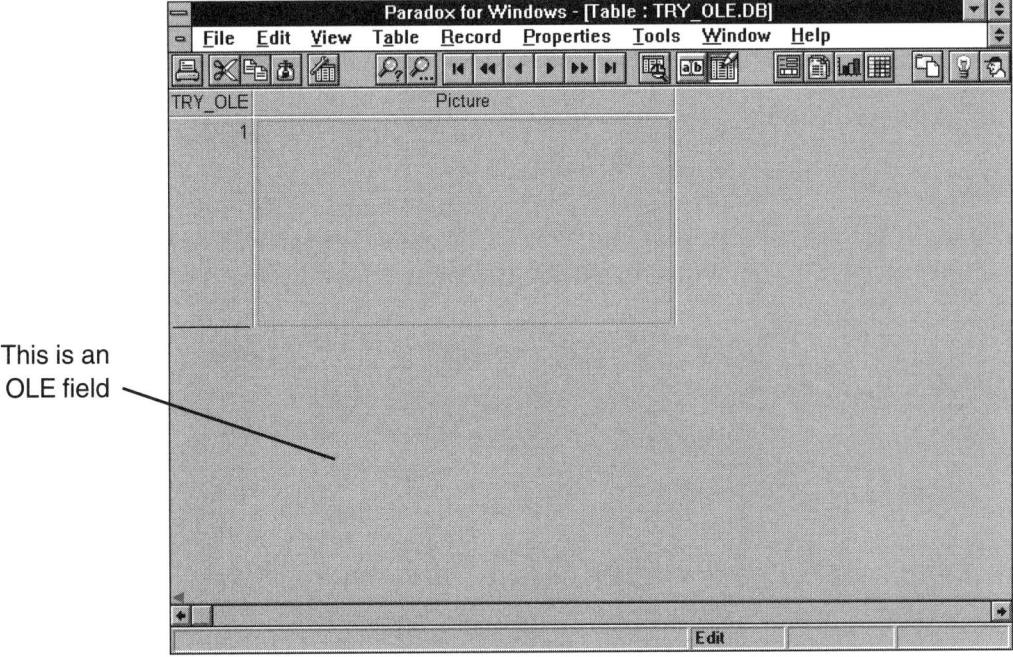

This is an OLE field

Figure 14-13: The Try_OLE table contains only a single field, Picture. I formatted this field as an OLE field and increased the row height and column width so you can quickly start your test drive of OLE.

The Graphic field in the BIOLIFE database, for example, is an OLE field that stores a color drawing of a fish in each record. Suppose you don't have a whole catalog of fish drawings handy, though. You could create each drawing in, say, Adobe Illustrator, and then return to Paradox to begin the embedding exercise. Or you could actually create each picture in Paradox, using Illustrator as the OLE server, right inside each OLE field.

Pitfall Ahead

I don't generally start out exercises with a pitfall anecdote, but in this case it's worth the negative karma. Before you can embed an OLE object in a table, remember that Paradox must be in Edit mode. I know, it's a rehash of basic material, but I can't tell you how many times I've jumped into a table raring to slap OLE objects all around the place only to discover a dimmed Edit, Insert Object command. Press F9 to enter Edit mode before you try your hand at embedding OLE objects.

Getting back to the positive karma of OLE object embedding, here are some steps for you to follow:

1. Press F9 to enter Edit mode.
2. Locate the OLE field into which you intend to embed the object, then click it once to activate it.
3. Choose the Edit, Insert Object command. Paradox displays the Insert Object dialog box (this one is nearly identical to the Word for Windows dialog shown in the previous exercise).

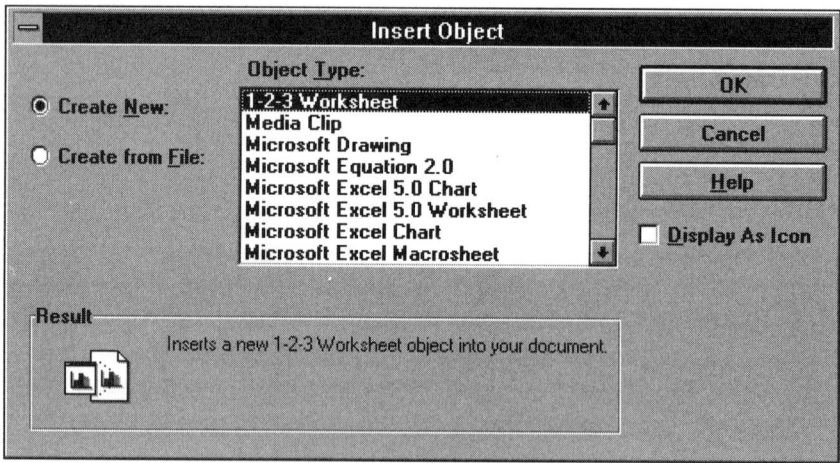

Figure 14-14: The Insert Object dialog box in Paradox.

4. Click the Create New radio button (it may already be selected) so that Paradox knows you want to create a new OLE object.
   You can display the OLE object as its host application's icon, rather than as a picture of a fish itself, by clicking the Display As Icon check box. Displaying an OLE object as an

icon does not affect how you edit the OLE object; instead of clicking on a picture of a fish you'd click on a picture of the Paintbrush icon. (Remember, this feature is available only if the OLE object's host application supports OLE 2.0.)

5. Now, locate the name of the OLE server program in the Object Type list, click it once, then click OK.

At this point, one of two things could happen:

One: if the OLE server supports OLE 2.0, then a new, blank document window for the OLE server will appear in the OLE field inside your table or form. Go ahead and create your document using the menu bar and Toolbar buttons that are available to you from the OLE server program.

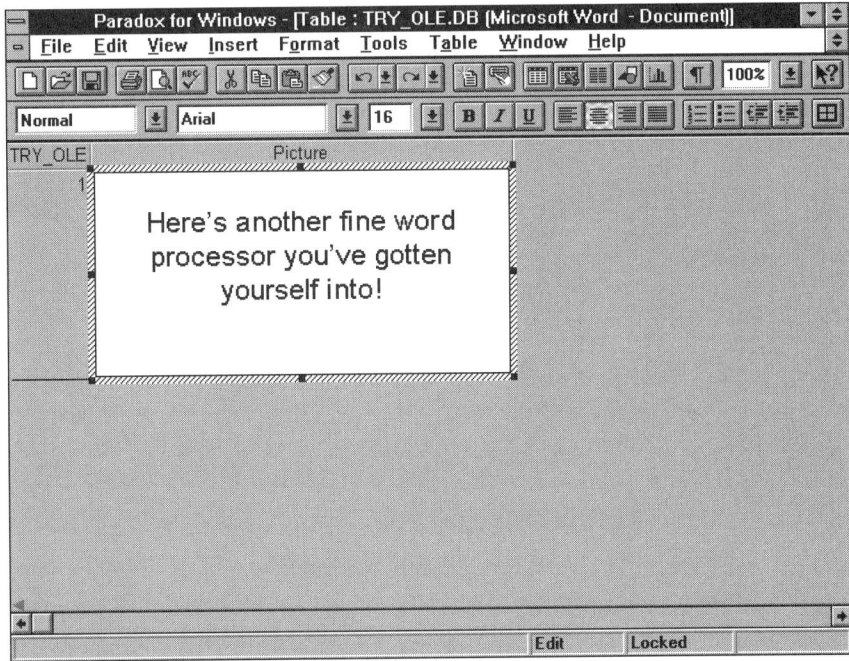

Figure 14-15: Word for Windows 6.0 uses OLE 2.0, so you can create your new document directly inside the blank area where you've embedded the OLE object.

Two: if the OLE server does not support OLE 2.0, then Windows launches the OLE server program and displays it inside its own application window right on top of your Paradox workspace. Go ahead and create your document inside the OLE server's application window.

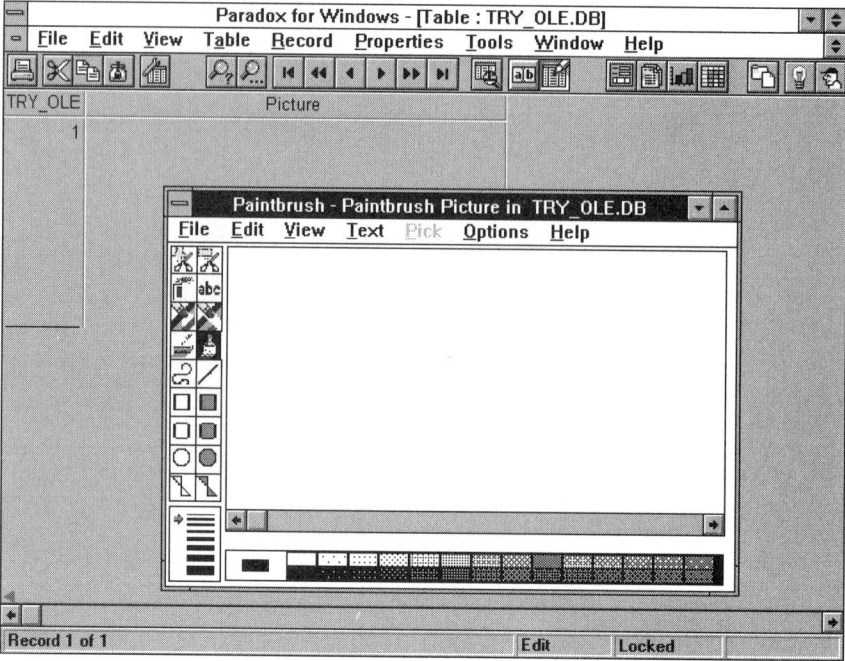

Figure 14-16: The Paintbrush applet that comes with Windows does not do OLE 2.0. So instead you see the entire Paintbrush application window.

When you are finished creating the new document in the embedded object, click anywhere outside of the object's frame to return to Paradox. Need to edit the OLE object again? Just double-click the object.

Inside Scoop

You also can use the standard Copy and Paste (or Paste Link) commands to embed OLE objects in Paradox. To start: from the OLE server, copy the item you wish to embed (it can be a document, a spreadsheet, a graphic, etc.). Now switch to your Paradox table and press F9 to enter Edit mode. Next, you must make a decision about whether or not to create a hot link between the two programs. To create a hot link, choose the Edit, Paste Link command. To simply embed the OLE object in the OLE field without maintaining a link, choose the Edit, Paste command. In order to determine what formatting and editing capabilities are available to you, simply double-click the OLE object.

Embedding an Existing OLE Object in a Table

You can embed or link an existing document in an OLE field by following these steps:

1. Press F9 to enter Edit mode.
2. Locate the OLE field into which you intend to embed the object, then click it once to activate it.
3. Choose the Edit, Insert Object command. Paradox displays the Insert Object dialog box.
4. Click the Create from File radio button so that Paradox knows you want to locate an existing file created by the OLE server program.
5. Click the Browse button, locate the name of the existing file in the Browse dialog box, and then click OK.
6. Click the Link check box to create a "hot link" between the OLE server and container programs. This way, any editing performed in one program automatically gets updated in the other program.
7. Click OK.

Again, one of two things can happen, depending on whether your OLE server supports the OLE 2.0 technology:

One: if the OLE server supports OLE 2.0, then a new, blank document window for the OLE server will appear in the OLE field inside your table or form. Go ahead and create your document using the menu bar and Toolbar buttons that are available to you from the OLE server program.

Two: if the OLE server does not support OLE 2.0, then Windows launches the OLE server program and displays it inside its own application window right on top of your Paradox workspace. Go ahead and create your document inside the OLE server's application window.

When you're finished creating the new document in the embedded object, click anywhere outside of the object's frame to return to Paradox. Need to edit the OLE object again? Just double-click the object.

Read on to learn some more tidbits about working with OLE 2.0-loving programs when you've joined them by a hot link.

MANAGING YOUR LINKED OLE DOCUMENTS

Information in a linked OLE object always stays current regardless of which program (OLE server or OLE container) you use to make changes. Put more simply, when you've linked a Quattro Pro for Windows notebook to an OLE field in a Paradox form, and you later modify the notebook in Quattro Pro for Windows, the changes you made will immediately appear in the linked OLE object on your Paradox form.

Windows programs update links in one of two ways: automatically or manually. The simplest way to deal with this issue is to allow the programs to do the updating automatically—that's the default method followed. But if for some reason you choose to update your linked OLE objects manually, that'll only happen when you tell Windows it must happen.

After you have completed adding a document into an OLE Object field as discussed in the previous section, you can specify whether you want it to be updated automatically or manually by choosing the Links menu item from the Edit menu. This displays the Links dialog box, where you can do any number of different things to a linked OLE document.

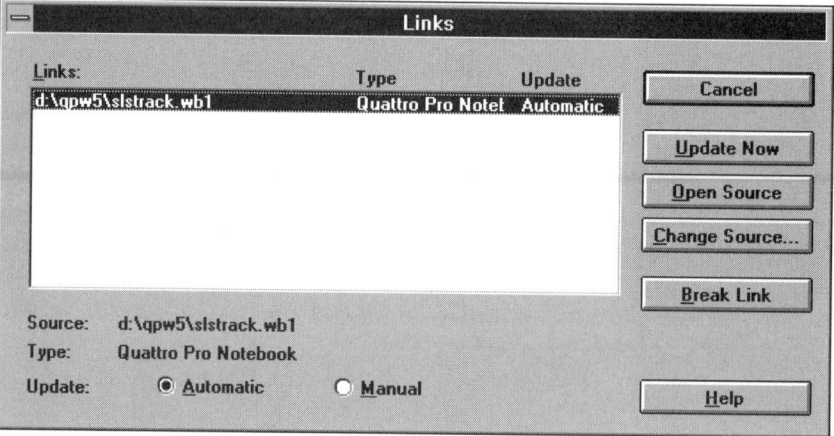

Figure 14-17: The settings in this Links dialog box show a link to the Quattro Pro for Windows notebook file, SLSTRACK.WB1, in the \QPW5 directory on drive D.

Here's a brief rundown of the other options in the Links dialog box:

Links list	Displays a list of all documents linked to the OLE container.
Update Now	Click this button every time you want to update the linked document's data.
Open Source	Opens the linked document in its host application (OLE server) for editing.
Close Source	Links the document to a different host application (OLE server).
Break Link	Completely disassociates the document from its OLE server.
Automatic	Updates linked data whenever it changes.
Manual	Updates linked data only when you click Update Now.

MOVING ON

This concludes your immersion into the language of DDE and OLE. Stick around and experiment for a while, if you have the time, using Windows programs that you own and have installed on your computer. You'll find that each program has its own little quirks when it comes to dealing with Dynamic Data Exchange and Object Linking and Embedding. Hey, we all have our own quirks, right?

Speaking of acronyms of the rich and famous, the turn of a page ushers you into the next level in your Paradox training. For the remainder of the book, you'll explore the strange and exotic world of ObjectPAL, a place where acronyms run rampant and where words like *syntax*, *methods* and *debug* become a part of your everyday vocabulary.

15 YOUR FIRST OBJECTPAL FORM

You already know that Paradox is powerful, and you've learned about its features: you know how to save queries, create fancy forms and print striking reports. But sometimes you may want even more. If something can't be accomplished using the features you've already mastered, it may be time to use ObjectPAL—to extend the natural abilities of Paradox for Windows.

By the end of this chapter you will have created a customized form using ObjectPAL—the programming language introduced with Paradox for Windows. The words "programming language" may conjure up images of professional programmers writing lines and lines of cryptic code. Fortunately, ObjectPAL isn't like that. One line of code is often all you need to perform a really useful task.

In order to use ObjectPAL effectively, you should be familiar with the interactive features. There have been times when I spent hours trying to do something using ObjectPAL without realizing that I could have used one of the Paradox features. Designing an application requires leveraging the natural abilities of Paradox with ObjectPAL programming—knowing when and how to use them together.

INTRODUCING OBJECTPAL

This chapter briefly discusses some of the important ObjectPAL concepts—objects, events and methods. It is not a complete discussion but it's enough to get you started. In later chapters, we'll refer back to these concepts and talk about them in more detail. Then the fun stuff—creating a form that uses ObjectPAL. We'll talk briefly about how the application was designed (planning and designing should never be overlooked), but mostly we'll see how ObjectPAL code works.

Chapters that follow present complex examples, ObjectPAL concepts and programming logic. Sample forms shown throughout the ObjectPAL chapters help you understand concepts by demonstrating the programming ideas. The focus is on useful forms with

ObjectPAL enhancements and on good programming practices. For now, let's start with the basics.

ObjectPAL gets its name from its object-based nature (more about objects very soon) and from the programming language used in Paradox for DOS—PAL (which is an acronym for Paradox Application Language). ObjectPAL is a very sophisticated programming language, so there's almost nobody who knows all there is to know about it. But it can also be a lot of fun if it's approached properly. Just a little bit of code is often all that's necessary to create really fancy applications.

Any time something can be done without programming, that's the best approach. For example, using ObjectPAL, you could tell Paradox to make the font color red when the value in a field is less than zero. But why bother? It is much easier to do that interactively using the field's Data Dependent property. The time to use ObjectPAL is when you want to change what Paradox would normally do.

For example, when you arrive on a field, all the text in the field is highlighted. If you wanted to modify this response so that when arriving on a field Paradox doesn't highlight it but instead displays an insertion point (as in Field View), ObjectPAL can be used to override the default Paradox response.

ObjectPAL can also get far more sophisticated than that: reports can be generated by clicking on a button, and custom dialog boxes can be displayed at any time. You could write ObjectPAL code that executes a query, performs calculations on the Answer table, compresses the table using PKZIP and sends it to company headquarters with your communications software (although this last example is beyond the scope of this book). You can even create applications that have nothing to do with databases—such as Reversi or Solitaire.

ObjectPAL & Forms

Because forms are used so frequently, ObjectPAL code is typically attached to forms and to various objects on forms. Perhaps you have created forms used mostly for displaying data. Or maybe your forms have been designed strictly for data entry.

Forms can be customized with graphic objects: they can display fields as radio buttons, drop-down edit lists and check boxes, and they can contain descriptive text and buttons. In short, forms can be designed for specific purposes.

You already know that you can place a button on a form and make the button perform a useful task, even though the button by itself is useless. It is common to attach ObjectPAL code to a button, but also any object on a form (including the form itself) can contain code.

Note: Forms, however, are not the only places to use ObjectPAL code. You can create *scripts* and *libraries* that contain ObjectPAL code stored in separate files. Both scripts and libraries are stand-alone files not associated with any form.

Let's say you frequently need to make all address fields in a table uppercase so they conform to postal regulations. You could create a script (similar to a *macro* in word processing or spreadsheet terminology) that does the work for you. Libraries contain lots of ObjectPAL code and are more complex than scripts. You'll learn more about scripts and libraries in Chapter 19, but I wanted to make the point here that ObjectPAL code isn't associated only with forms.

There are locations where you *cannot* place ObjectPAL code—reports, for example. Also, you cannot attach ObjectPAL code to a table or to queries. So except for the special cases of scripts and libraries, forms are typically where your ObjectPAL code will go. In fact, the first four chapters in this section of *The Visual Guide to Paradox for Windows* deal only with ObjectPAL code attached to forms and to objects on the forms.

ObjectPAL & Objects

Everything in Paradox is an *object:* a field, a line, a box, a button—anything. ObjectPAL interacts with these objects, frequently affecting their *default responses* (that is, the way in which Paradox responds to an action). For example, the default response of a button is to change its appearance when it's clicked on, so that it looks "pressed in." Any time you want to change (or add to) the default response of an object, ObjectPAL can do the job quickly and easily.

Objects Have Properties

This is true in the real world, and it's also true in programming. The chair you're sitting on may be wooden, metal or fabric-coated. Paradox for Windows doesn't have chairs, but its objects do have properties. A field may have specific font color, font style and text-alignment properties.

Different objects have different sets of properties, but all objects of the same type have the same properties. Right-clicking on any button (in the Form Design window) displays an identical pop-up menu. Right-clicking on fields displays a different pop-up menu, but the menu doesn't change from field to field. The properties may be set to different values (the font for one field could be 12-pt and another could be 10-pt), but the properties for fields are always the same.

You can see the form's properties (as you've no doubt done many times before) by right-clicking on an object in a Form Design window. If you want to see what properties are available for various objects, open OBJECT.FSL (on the disk that accompanies this book) in a Form Design window and right-click on each object. Every object type that can be placed on a form is on OBJECT.FSL.

If the properties of an object can be changed when designing the form, why would anyone use ObjectPAL? Let's say you have a form with lots of fields, and the person entering data might not be able to find the insertion point easily. To help make the field stand out, you decide you want to place a red frame around each field but only when that field is active (ready to accept input).

One solution you could consider in your original design would be to change the frame color to red and the frame style to a single line. But the problem is that when leaving the field, you want that frame to disappear and the frame for the next field to become red.

This is something you couldn't do when you originally designed the form because the field's frame property changes when the active field changes. The frame properties are initialized in a Form Design window, but the changes are implemented by ObjectPAL programming.

ObjectPAL & Events

An *event* is a "happening." Arriving on a field is an event. Opening a form is an event. Clicking on a button is an event. Events also *cause* something to happen—a response. In the example, where the field's frame turns red when it's active, the field's *arrive* event triggers the "turn frame red" response.

Just like properties, specific events are connected to specific types of objects. All Paradox objects respond to events. You don't tell an object to respond, you tell it *how* to respond to an event. And you tell it how only if you want a response that is different from the default response. That's a lot of customizing, but typically most events need no customization at all. Paradox just gives you that flexibility in case you need it.

Figure 15-1 shows the events available for a field object. You can get a general idea of what the events are by their names, but for now you don't need to know specifically what each one of them does.

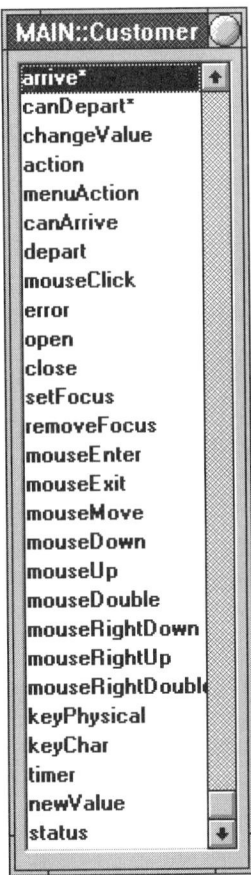

Figure 15-1: The Method Inspector shows the events for a field object.

Using OBJECT.FSL, you can also see what events each object responds to. In order to see these events, display the Methods Inspector by following these steps:

1. Open OBJECT.FSL in a Form Design window. (You could use any other form—it's just that OBJECT.FSL contains all the different types of objects you can place on a form.)

2. Right-click on any object and select Methods from the pop-up menu.

The Methods Inspector window displays the events for whatever object you right-clicked on. You may not see a long list like the one shown in Figure 15-1, because the list of events has two settings, which you'll learn about in a moment. For now it doesn't matter much what the setting is. What's important is that you see there are different types of events for different types of objects. However, if you want to, you can toggle between the two settings, like this:

1. Open a form in a Form Design window.
2. Click on the Properties menu and choose ObjectPAL. The ObjectPAL Preferences dialog box displays (see Figure 15-2).
3. The Level group box contains radio buttons for Beginner and Advanced. If the Beginner radio button is selected, the list of events is short; if the Advanced radio button is selected, a complete list of events is displayed by the Methods Inspector. Select whichever you want.
4. The Method Inspector group box contains a Keep Pinned check box, specifying whether to always display the Method Inspector when a Form Design window is active. (If Keep Pinned is not checked, you can still display it by right-clicking on an object and choosing Methods. But if you want to quickly see the events for several objects, check the Keep Pinned check box.)
5. When the settings in the ObjectPAL Preferences dialog box are the way you want them, click the OK button to close the dialog box.

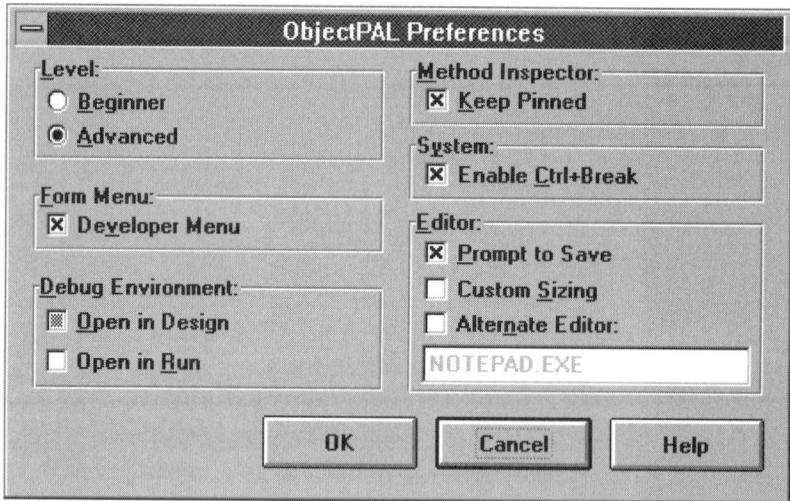

Figure 15-2: Various ObjectPAL settings can be changed.

Inside Scoop

Applications function the same regardless of whether you choose the Advanced or the Beginner setting in the ObjectPAL Preferences dialog box. The only difference is the size of the list in the Method Inspector.

ObjectPAL & Methods

So far, we have been talking about events listed in the Method Inspector. And indeed, the Method Inspector does list events that a particular object responds to. But events are internal to Paradox and cannot be controlled. No matter what customization you do, you cannot prevent events from happening, and when an event does occur, it always triggers a Paradox *built-in method*. The built-in method executes in response to an event, and that's when the customization is done. So the Method Inspector allows you to inspect an object's methods and attach ObjectPAL code as needed.

In Paradox lingo, the word *method* can mean several things. It can refer to the built-in methods (shown in the Method Inspector) that are triggered in response to an event. *Method* can also refer to many of the programming commands. Finally, you can create your own *custom methods*, but we won't get into that until Chapter 19.

All this will become clearer when you look at a form with ObjectPAL code attached to a built-in method. So let's open SALES.FSL, which is included on the accompanying disk (Figure 15-3). It looks like an ordinary form, but as you'll see in Table 15-1, some things are different from Paradox's normal default responses. Table 15-1 lists the changes that have been made.

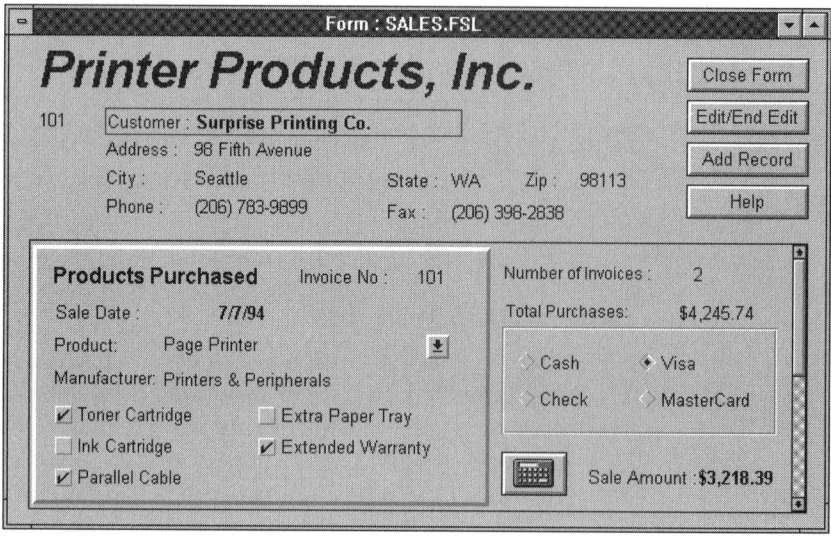

Figure 15-3: This form has ObjectPAL code in several locations. It will be used as an example throughout this chapter.

Default Responses Vs. ObjectPAL Modifications

Default Response	Response due to ObjectPAL code
1. When opening a form, Paradox is not in Field View.	When opening SALES.FSL, Paradox is palced in Fiield View.
2. Fiield View is only in effect for one field—when leaving a field, Paradox leaves field View.	SALES.FSL stays in Field View as you move from field to field.
3. When moving from field to field, the field's frame does not change.	SALES.FSL highlights the frame of the active field with a red border. When leaving the field, the border disappears.
4. Buttons normally don't do anything except change their shadow so that they look pressed in when clicked on.	Four buttons are added to the form, each of which performs a specific task in addition to the default response.

In the table, the built-in methods of some of the objects on the form are changed.

In order to understand how the form was designed and how it works, let's go through the design stages. We'll discuss some of the form's interactive features and how to use ObjectPAL to modify the built-in methods.

DESIGNING AN APPLICATION

Writing ObjectPAL code is only one step in the process of creating a useful application, so we'll touch on designing the interface but focus mainly on ObjectPAL. Four general steps are involved when designing an application:

1. Determine what data you need. A good data model is the foundation of a successful application.

2. Create forms and reports. Forms and reports help you visualize what the data will look like and the interaction with the user.

3. Write ObjectPAL code where necessary. Code is typically attached to the objects on the form, so the form needs to be created first.

4. Test the form and fine-tune it. Any time programming is involved, the chance for errors exists. You want to be sure the form looks and behaves the way you want it to.

Create the Form

Graphical computer environments such as Windows have ushered in an era where cosmetics, or "look and feel," have become important. You can spend a lot of time designing an appropriate interface, but the time is often well worth it. After all, an application should be easy to use.

When you first start designing applications, don't spend a lot of time placing objects precisely. Instead, get the general concept down; the fine-tuning can come later. As often happens, a substantial change in design or changing the display type of a field causes much of the fine-tuning to become obsolete. So you should save your tweaking for the end.

Choose Field Display Types

Paradox has several ways of displaying fields: labeled, unlabeled, radio buttons, check boxes, lists or drop-down lists (also known as combo boxes). With all these choices, you need to decide which are best. Here are some guidelines:

○ Labeled and unlabeled fields are used most frequently when creating forms. If a form is used only for viewing data, field labels are superfluous, so unlabeled fields will do. For example, you may not need the label "Address1" in front of an address. However, if the form is used for entering as well as viewing data, you are probably better off using labeled fields.

○ Don't confuse check boxes with radio buttons. Use check boxes for fields like "Retired" or "Self-Employed," where the answer can be either Yes or No. Check boxes may seem similar to radio buttons when there are several check boxes in a group, but the difference between them is that any, all or none of the check boxes can be checked, whereas only one radio button can be selected.

○ Drop-down lists display as many selections for a field as you want, and Windows adds a scroll bar, if necessary, to see all the choices. You'll see later that the list can display the contents of a Paradox table—and it takes only one line of ObjectPAL code. This is especially useful when a field's validity check specifies a Table Lookup.

○ Drop-down lists make choices clearer for the viewer than radio buttons do. With radio buttons, the only indication as to the selected option is a little black spot. If deciding between drop-down lists and radio buttons, use drop-down lists for ease of viewing and radio buttons for ease of data entry.

○ Table frame objects allow you to see more than one record at a time, and are especially useful for displaying the detail table in a one-to-many relationship. However, table frames can be used in conjunction with other field types when displaying a detail table. You can even place a drop-down list field in a table frame.

Other Interactive Features

Take another look at our sample form: the Tab Stop property is set to False for each of the following fields: Acct_no, Invoice Number, Sale Date, Manufacturer, Number of Invoices and Total Purchases. This was done by right-clicking on the field, choosing the Run Time option from the pop-up menu, and removing the check mark from the Tab Stop item, as shown in Figure 15-4. Under no circumstances should a user be allowed to enter data into Autoincrement or key fields. The Sale Date field automatically inserts today's date, so there is no need to move to that field either. Also, the Manufacturer field is automatically filled in with a lookup table when a product is selected.

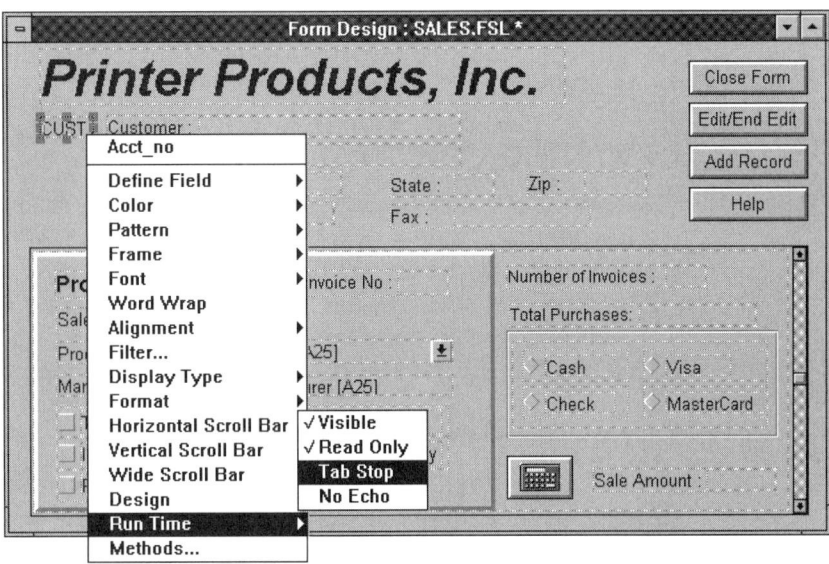

Figure 15-4: It's a good idea to remove the Tab Stop property any time a user would have the opportunity to change data that Paradox fills in automatically.

A lookup table (PROD.DB) is used by the Product and Manufacturer fields to ensure data integrity. When the Product is selected, the Manufacturer field is also filled in because the All Corresponding Fields option is selected. In this instance, all manufacturers in the lookup table were entered into the Define List dialog box that displays when the Drop Down Edit List field type is selected. ObjectPAL could be used to create a list from a Paradox table, but that's something you get to do in a later chapter. (If you're curious, though, feel free to look ahead—it's not complicated.)

Three special fields are placed on the form: Invoice Date, Number of Invoices and Total Purchases. The Invoice Date field automatically inserts today's date. This is done by the form rather than at the table level because there may be instances when you want a date that is not automatically today's date. However, as far as this form is concerned, it is assumed that a customer places an order the same day you enter the data.

The other two fields, Number of Invoices and Total Purchases, are calculated fields. Number of Invoices counts all linked detail records for the current customer; Total Purchases sums the Sale Amount field. Notice that for all three of these special fields, the label was edited so that it is clearer to the end user.

It was a conscious decision to have the user calculate the total sale because of the potential complexity. Prices change, sale prices need to be considered, different prices could apply for some clients, etc. However, to make the calculations relatively painless, a calculator button is added to the form.

WRITING OBJECTPAL CODE

If "writing code" sounds intimidating, it isn't really, because the first few methods will contain only one line of code. It's not even necessary to know the programming language for now. The concepts are far more beneficial in the long run because Paradox provides enough tools so that you don't need to memorize a lot of programming commands. So, let's start looking at the code attached to SALES.FSL.

Your First Line of ObjectPAL

This section outlines the steps necessary to write your first lines of ObjectPAL code—your first method. But before we do that, open SALES.FSL in View Data mode to see what happens. The default response for the field has two changes to it: the Customer field is surrounded by a red frame, and Paradox is in Field View. So far, those are the only changes. So let's see how Paradox does this. The first method to execute is the page's *arrive* method. Let's look at it by following these steps:

1. Place SALES.FSL in Design mode by clicking on the Design button.

2. Right-click anywhere on the page where there are no objects. A pop-up menu should display with #Page2 in its title (see Figure 15-5). If a different pop-up menu is displayed, try clicking somewhere else, where there aren't any other objects, until you are successful.

3. Click on the Methods option from the pop-up menu to display the Method Inspector.

4. In the Method Inspector, double-click on *arrive*. An Editor window displays, and it should look like Figure 15-6.

Figure 15-5: The page's pop-up menu lets you change its built-in methods.

```
SALES::#Page2::arrive
method arrive(var eventInfo MoveEvent)
    action(editEnterPersistFieldView)   ; always in Field View
endmethod
```
Edit | Line: 1 | Col: 1

Figure 15-6: The Editor window displays the code in the page's *arrive* method.

There are three lines of code in the page's *arrive* method, but the first line and the last line were supplied by Paradox. The only addition was line 2. For now, we are just going to ignore the first and third lines, because they are always there, and Paradox always supplies them. The important thing to know is that any customization you want should be between the *method* and *endmethod* lines.

The single line of code looks partially understandable. The easiest part is at the end—everything that follows the semicolon. In ObjectPAL, a semicolon tells Paradox to ignore the rest of the line. It is a comment for the reader of the code. Sometimes, especially if there are many lines, it can get confusing without comments about what the code is supposed to do.

Inside Scoop

If you get in the habit of regularly using comments, you will be doing better than most programmers. I have often thought, "I'll never forget what this code does," so I didn't comment it. A few weeks later, I'd be annoyed because I did indeed forget. (It took a while, but I learned.)

The ObjectPAL code is everything to the left of the semicolon. PersistFieldView causes Paradox to stay in Field View as you move from field to field. EnterPersistFieldView tells Paradox to enter (rather than exit) PersistField View. One of the common things for Paradox to do is to perform an *action*, and that is one of the Paradox programming commands. Don't worry about memorizing the command or about being able to recreate it. Just knowing that Paradox performs the action of entering (and staying in) Field View when the page opens is enough for now. While this method window is open, let's look at the editor that Paradox uses for writing ObjectPAL code.

Using the ObjectPAL Editor

You already know how to use Notepad, so you know how to type and edit code in Paradox. The ObjectPAL Editor is similar to Notepad—it's simple and easy to use. Dragging the mouse across text selects it, or you can hold down the Shift key while using the cursor-movement keys. Ctrl+X or Shift+Del cuts selected text, Ctrl+C or Ctrl+Ins copies selected text, and Ctrl+V or Shift+Ins pastes text. Or you can use the Edit menu. You can even paste text from another text file. The Search menu lets you search for text—again, similar to Notepad. There are many other options, but general typing and text editing should be familiar.

You have all sorts of tools available to help you write ObjectPAL code. You can look up commands, properties and syntax, and debugging tools are provided. For now, we'll just look at a couple of the most frequently used tools. As we go through future chapters, we'll look at more of them when we need to.

It always helps to have help at your disposal. In addition to a Help menu, Paradox also lets you look up help for whatever word the insertion point is next to. Just press F1 to browse through the ObjectPAL help screens for that word.

When writing code, syntax is vitally important. We're not going to get into syntax right now, but let's see how easy it is to check if everything is syntactically accurate (sort of like running a spelling check and a grammar check in a word processor). Right-click anywhere in the editor window. A pop-up menu like the one shown in Figure 15-7 displays. The options we care about for now are Check Syntax, Compile and Run.

Check Syntax
Compile
Next Warning
Add Watch
Toggle Breakpoint
Run
Types...
Properties...
Constants...
Keywords ▶
Methods

Figure 15-7: The pop-up menu for the ObjectPAL Editor.

456

Compiling is the process of converting programming code into a format that the computer can execute. In order to successfully compile ObjectPAL code, the syntax must be correct.

Choosing *Check Syntax* checks the ObjectPAL code in the current window; *Compile* compiles code in every method in the current form. If all is well, Paradox displays "No syntax errors" in the status bar. If there is an error, Paradox highlights the error and suggests what the problem might be. The suggestion is not always the answer, but sometimes it is. At any rate, it's better than nothing.

Pitfall Ahead

Don't assume that just because there are no syntax errors, your code will work as expected. Even if Paradox understands the code, it doesn't mean there are no logic errors. When running the form, something unexpected could still happen.

The *Run* menu option means, "Run the form." Paradox closes the Editor window and places the form in View Data mode. Choosing Run is the same as if you pressed F8 or closed the Editor window by double-clicking on the Control menu box and clicking on the View Data button on the Toolbar.

The page's *arrive* method did not do everything that is necessary to change the Paradox default behavior: there was no command telling the Customer field to turn its frame red. That's because the code to do that is attached to the field, rather than the page. Close the Editor window, and we'll take a look at what happens with the field to turn the frame red.

Arriving & Departing

When you move to a field, an *arrive* event occurs. You can freely type data if you're in Edit mode, or you can move to another field. Let's assume you're in Edit mode and that you typed a value into a field then pressed the Tab key. If the field has a lookup table or a picture and you type something illegal into it, an error message displays and the insertion point stays in the field until the error is corrected. Paradox tests whether it can leave the field before it actually does so—a *canDepart* event occurs, thereby triggering the *canDepart* method. (There are other events that happen when moving from field to field, but we'll get to them in Chapter 16.)

457

With this in mind, display the Method Inspector for the Customer field. It should look like Figure 15-8. If you have ObjectPAL Level set to Advanced, your list will be longer than the one shown, but either way, there will be an asterisk beside the *arrive* and *canDepart* methods. An asterisk beside a method means it has some code attached to it. So let's open both the *arrive* and *canDepart* methods.

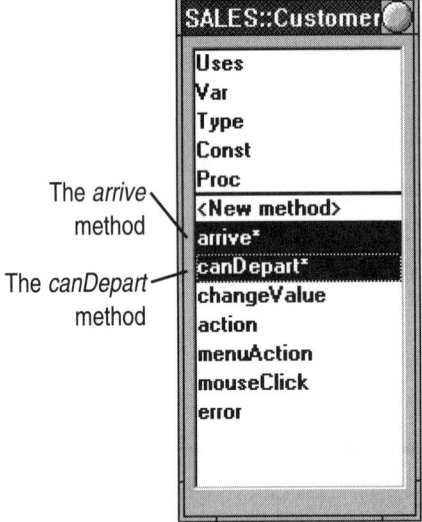

The *arrive* method

The *canDepart* method

Figure 15-8: The Method Inspector lets you open more than one Editor window.

1. Drag the mouse across the methods you want to open, or use Ctrl+click to select them.
2. Right-click on a highlighted method to display the pop-up menu.
3. Select Open from the pop-up menu to open an ObjectPAL Editor window for each method.

The two Editor windows are shown in Figure 15-9. Notice that the code for the *arrive* method is similar to the code in the *canDepart* method, and that neither of them mentions anything about turning the field's frame red. Why? When designing the form, the frame color was set to red and the frame-style option was no frame. (You can check this if you want to: display the color and frame-style palettes and click on the various fields.) Even with no frame, the color can be changed, so displaying and removing the frame turns on and off the red color for the frame.

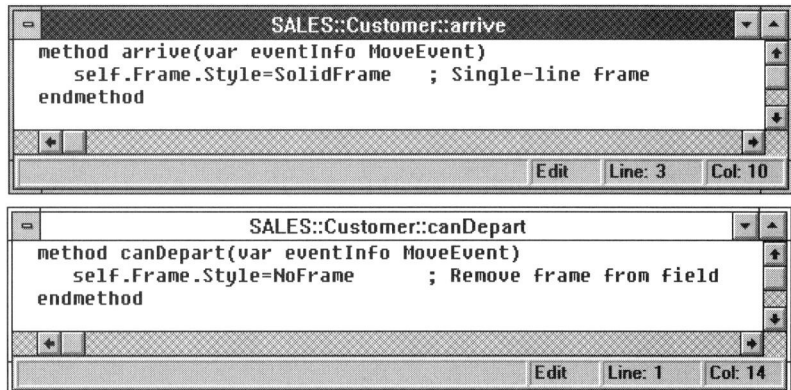

```
method arrive(var eventInfo MoveEvent)
   self.Frame.Style=SolidFrame    ; Single-line frame
endmethod
```

```
method canDepart(var eventInfo MoveEvent)
   self.Frame.Style=NoFrame       ; Remove frame from field
endmethod
```

Figure 15-9: The *arrive* and *canDepart* methods control the frame appearance for the active field.

The code looks a little more complex than the example in Figure 15-6, so here's a breakdown and definition of each component:

"self" refers to the current object—in this case, the Customer field. A dot separates the object from the property. "Fráme.Style" is one of the field's properties. "NoFrame" or "SolidFrame" is the value the frame-style property is to be changed to.

Again, learning more about the code that changes the frame style is coming in chapters that follow. At this point, you just need to get used to looking at ObjectPAL code.

Dot notation is something you see constantly in ObjectPAL. The dots are just separators, and the general syntax is *object.property=value*. You change properties interactively when you right-click on a field (the object), select Frame from the pop-up menu and then click on a frame style (the property value). Of course, you click on a picture of the frame, but ObjectPAL refers to these styles as NoFrame, SolidFrame, etc.

Inside Scoop:

When you copy objects that contain ObjectPAL code, the code is copied with the object. ObjectPAL is *modular*—you can create objects with programming code and copy them to other forms. Applications can, in part, be composed of these modules.

Each of the labeled fields has the same code attached to the *arrive* and *canDepart* methods, so it's easy to copy the code from field to field. (In later chapters, you'll discover better ways of applying the same code to multiple objects, but for now, copying text works well enough. You'll also see that *arrive* and *canDepart* methods are not typically used for fields, but they're used here because they're available in the Method Inspector when the ObjectPAL Level is set to Beginner.) When you're done with these two Editor windows, close them and we'll move on to the buttons, since there's no code attached anywhere else.

Making Functional Buttons

The built-in method used for the five buttons on this form is the *pushButton* method. Each button has one line of code attached to its *pushButton* method. Some of the buttons perform the same tasks as Paradox interactive features; others invoke features that are available only through ObjectPAL. We'll look at them one at a time.

The Edit Button

The Edit/End Edit button has three lines of code—just like the page's *arrive* method. The first and last lines are supplied by Paradox and the second line is the code that makes the button do something. The following command says, "Perform the following action: Toggle in or out of Edit mode."

```
method pushButton(var eventInfo Event)
    action(dataToggleEdit)                    ; Edit mode toggle
endmethod
```

The statement used by ObjectPAL that tells Paradox to do something is *action; dataToggleEdit* means that if in Edit mode, end Edit mode, but if not in Edit mode, enter Edit mode. You probably figured out that much without this explanation.

Clicking on the button, in this case, is no different from clicking on the Edit button on the Toolbar or pressing the F9 key. Actions that you perform interactively, such as pressing F9, also have an equivalent ObjectPAL command that uses an *action* statement. You'll see more examples of this when programming the other buttons on this form.

Buttons To Add New Records

Just like the Edit/End Edit button, the Insert Record button uses an action statement, but this time the action is *dataInsertRecord* as shown by the following code fragment. That makes sense. When the button is clicked on, it performs the action of inserting a new record in the Paradox table. Clicking on the button is no different from pressing the Ins key. The next line moves to the Customer field.

```
method pushButton(var eventInfo Event)
    action(dataInsertRecord) ; insert new record
    Customer.moveTo()        ; move to Customer field
endmethod
```

Try clicking on the Add Record button (in View Data mode) and see what happens. Oops ... nothing happens. Did the ObjectPAL method not work as expected? You cannot press Ins and expect a record to be inserted in a table unless Paradox is in Edit mode. The code attached to the Add Record button didn't test whether Paradox was in Edit mode. Paradox was not told to be in Edit mode, so it can't insert the record. Before you try to insert a record, click on the Edit/End Edit button, then on the Add Record button. Now it works!

In the next chapter you'll learn how to test to see if Paradox is in Edit mode, and if necessary, enter Edit mode before inserting a record.

Dialogs in a Flash

Communicating with Windows programs is done mostly through dialog boxes. So you need lots of dialog boxes and lots of options to choose from—probably more than you ever wanted to see. Paradox lets you create simple dialog boxes with only one line of code, so you too can add to the proliferation.

The dialog box in Figure 15-10 has four components: the title bar text, an icon, the message text and an OK button. This is the easiest type of dialog box to create because there is only one choice: press the OK button. (You could reboot your computer, but that's rather extreme if all you want to do is make the dialog box go away.) Dialog boxes like this are used to present information to the user. In later chapters, your dialog boxes will have more than one button, so a specific action can take place depending on which button is pressed.

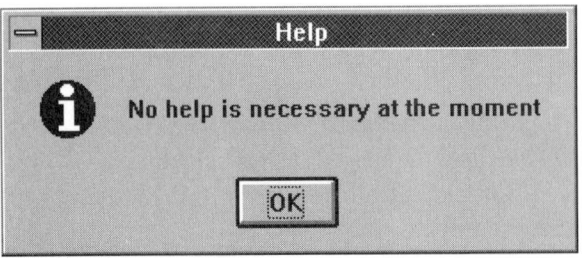

Figure 15-10: This type of dialog box is easy to create in Paradox; it's used simply to present information to the user.

The code to display the dialog box is shown below. This time, it's important to focus on the syntax. And that means we need to define a few terms. First, you need to know about *procedures* and *arguments*.

Procedures

Procedures are programming commands that tell Paradox to do something. They typically don't tell an object (such as a field or graphic) how to behave; instead they tell Paradox or the computer to perform a function. This will become clearer as you become more familiar with ObjectPAL.

Arguments

An argument is information you supply to Paradox—something that changes. A dialog box can have text in the title bar and in the message area, but there's no way the *msgInfo* procedure can know what text you want displayed. So *msgInfo* requires you specify the title and message text; otherwise an error will occur. The text strings you pass to the *msgInfo* procedure are known as arguments.

In the following, *msgInfo* displays a dialog box. It takes two arguments (or parameters).

```
method pushButton(var eventInfo Event)

    msgInfo("Help","No help is necessary at the moment")
endmethod
```

The two arguments *msgInfo* expects must both be text strings (rather than numbers). The first text string is the caption; the second text string is the message. Notice that both arguments have quotation marks around them and that a comma separates them. This syntax is used throughout Paradox (and programming languages in general). Text strings always have quotes around them. Arguments are always separated by commas. Without these syntax requirements, Paradox could easily get confused, so it's important to follow them. It's also important to perform syntax-checking when writing code.

The final note about syntax concerns parentheses. Arguments are always enclosed in parentheses, no matter how many arguments a procedure is expecting. Even if there are no arguments, parentheses are still used (with nothing inside them). For example, *beep( )* is a procedure that makes the speaker deliver its annoying sound to let you know you've gone astray. It requires no arguments, so nothing is included within the parentheses. But *msgInfo* requires two arguments, so both arguments are enclosed in parentheses.

In the *pushButton* method window, you can change the message. Figure 15-11 shows the syntax for the *msgInfo* procedure—you just need to add the text inside both sets of quotation marks. If you want to omit the title bar text or the message text, use open and close quotes, but don't include any text inside the quotes. If you changed the text for the msgInfo dialog box, check the syntax and run the form. When you press the Help button, a dialog box is displayed with the text you specified.

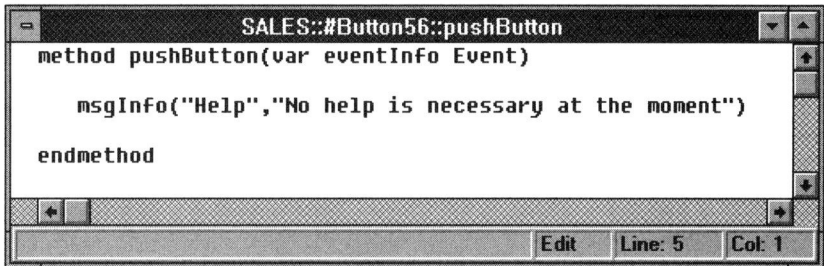

Figure 15-11: The syntax of a *msgInfo* procedure never changes—you just need to fill in the appropriate text between quotation marks.

Paradox automatically created the OK button and inserted the information icon in the dialog box. But what if you didn't want an information icon? There's another procedure called *msgStop*. The syntax is exactly the same whether you use *msgInfo* or *msgStop*; the only difference is the icon, as shown in Figure 15-12.

Figure 15-12: The *msgStop* procedure is identical to *msgInfo* except that a stop-sign icon is displayed instead of the information icon.

Dialog boxes with other icons can be displayed with similar statements; they're discussed in the next chapter, so you have something to look forward to.

The Close Button

Clicking on the Close Form button is supposed to close the form, and indeed it does. Paradox has a procedure that closes the form: its syntax is *close()* (see below). If you don't specify what to close, Paradox assumes you want to close the current form. Also notice that the *close* procedure takes no arguments, hence the empty parentheses.

```
method pushButton(var eventInfo Event)
    close()                          ; close the form
endmethod
```

Launching Other Programs

The final button, as you may have guessed from its picture, launches the Windows calculator. In fact, any Windows program can be launched by placing a button on a form and attaching one line of ObjectPAL code, like this:

```
method pushButton(var eventInfo Event)
    execute("calc")
endmethod
```

The executable file for the calculator is CALC.EXE. No path is necessary because Windows is in the path, but if you specify a program in a directory that isn't in the path, be sure to include the path name in addition to the program's executable filename.

Pitfall Ahead

People often delete accessory programs that ship with Windows. If the program you call with the ObjectPAL execute command is not found, an error will occur.

The ability to have a form with buttons that launch other Windows programs is quite useful. For example, if you wanted to take notes, you could have a Notepad button. Or a calendar. You could even launch your favorite word processor from a form, or get really carried away and use Paradox for Windows to launch all your favorite programs.

MOVING ON

That's all we'll do with SALES.FSL. In Chapter 16, we'll use another application that builds on what you learned here. However, we'll use programming logic to make decisions, and new concepts will be introduced. We'll also pay more attention to syntax and understanding the programming language. As we move along we'll continue to use the context of a form to introduce concepts as they come up.

16

LEARNING OBJECTPAL IN A HURRY

The one-line code samples in Chapter 15 showed only an inkling of ObjectPAL's potential power. To understand in greater depth what ObjectPAL can do for you, you need to delve into syntax, variables, methods, containers and objects. If this sounds like dry stuff, relax. By the end of the chapter, you'll have a functional database you can use to catalog movies and the actors and actresses who starred in them. This database will actually be useful—that is, if you like movies.

Within the context of the movies application, you will learn about variables—pigeonholes where you can store and retrieve information in the computer's memory. You will also learn about properties of objects and how to control them using ObjectPAL. In addition, several new programming commands will be introduced, and you will learn the necessary syntax to use them correctly.

CREATING A MOVIES APPLICATION

Time to have some fun. Let's create an application that can store all sorts of data about movies. A sneak preview is now showing in Figure 16-1. You'll be glad to know that the form is already created for you and is in the accompanying disk as MOVIES.FSL. The only thing that needs to be done is to learn about the code attached to the buttons. (If you really wanted to, you could ignore the rest of this chapter and use the application right away, but that would take the fun out of it.) Only the actual ObjectPAL code is discussed rather than the steps for writing it. But if you need a refresher in editing a method, refer to "Writing ObjectPAL Code" in Chapter 15.

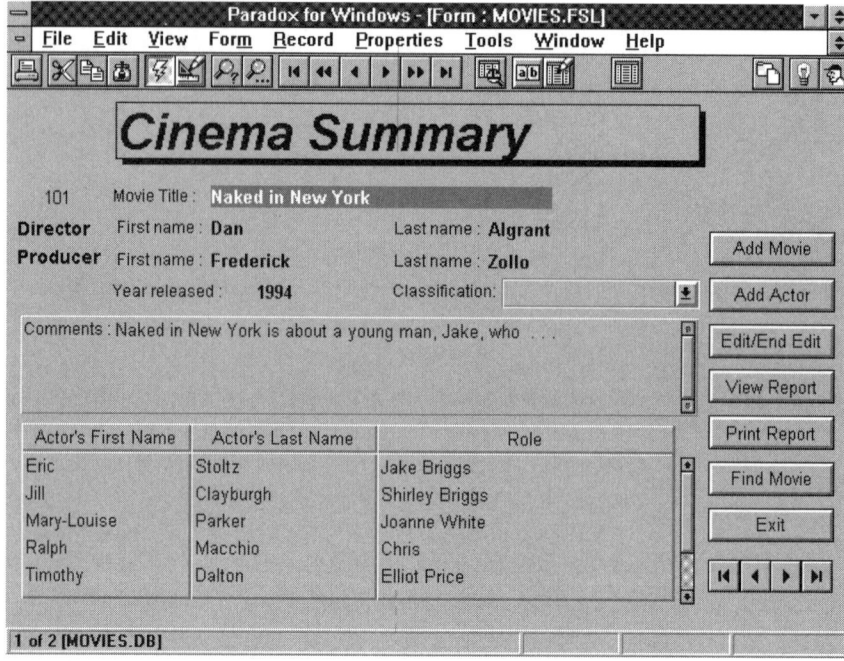

Figure 16-1: The form is ready for you to add code to buttons.

Copying Buttons

The Edit/End Edit button in this Cinema Summary application is no
different from the one in SALES.FSL in Chapter 15. The size of the
button may be different, but the ObjectPAL method is the same.
That's right, the *pushButton* method is *action(dataToggleEdit)*. But
you can create the button in either of two ways. You know how to
type code using the ObjectPAL Editor, so let's create the button
another way. Here's how:

1. Open the form SALES.FSL (from Chapter 15) in a Form Design
   window.
2. Click once on the Edit/End Edit button.
3. From the Edit menu, choose Copy or press Ctrl+Ins.
4. Move back to the form MOVIES.FSL by clicking in its window
   or selecting it from the Window menu.
5. Verify that the page is the selected item by clicking on it.
6. From the Edit menu, choose Paste, or press Shift+Ins.
7. Move the button to the desired location.

Pitfall Ahead

If you try to paste an object into Paradox and you get the message "Cannot paste from the Clipboard into the selected object," be sure to select the object you intend to paste into by clicking on it. If you still get the message, click on the page and choose Paste once again, then move the object to the desired location.

There are lots of advantages to copying objects from one form to another: the potential for errors is reduced, and you don't have to remember all of the syntax—you just need to know where you placed similar buttons. (Now you begin to see the value of object-based programming.)

Moving Among Records

A database isn't very useful if you can't move from record to record. The Paradox Toolbar buttons let you move to another record. However, there is one drawback to the buttons Paradox provides: if you are in a detail table (in this form, ACTORS.DB), the Next Record and Previous Record buttons move among the records in the detail table. But what if you want to move among the records in the master table (MOVIES.DB)? Here's how you do it: use one of the following lines in the *pushButton* method for each of the record movement buttons.

◄◄	action(dataBegin)	; Moves to first record
◄	action(dataPriorRecord)	; Moves to prior record
►	action(dataNextRecord)	; Moves to next record
►►	action(dataEnd)	; Moves to last record

These commands tell Paradox to move among the records of the *master* table, if it exists, rather than to move among the records of the *current* table. This is really useful in one-to-many relationships because typically when you want to move to the next record, you really want to move to the next record in the master table.

As we go through the various forms in this book, keep track of the buttons that may be useful for you. Create a new form and copy the useful buttons to it. Later, when you design other forms, simply copy buttons from your "button library" form into the form you're working on. No need to duplicate work.

Adding New Records

In Chapter 15, the Add Record button was a little awkward. It wouldn't work properly unless you were already in Edit mode. Being the sophisticated program that it is, one would think Paradox could determine whether it was in Edit mode, and if not, switch to Edit mode before trying to add a new record. It would also be handy to have the insertion point automatically positioned in the first field. Figure 16-2 shows the code for all of this.

```
                 MOVIES::#Button43::pushButton
method pushButton(var eventInfo Event)
var
   uio    UIObject
endvar

if not isEdit() then      ; If not in Edit mode
   edit()                 ;   go there
endif
uio.attach(movie_title)
uio.end()                 ; Move to last record in table
uio.moveto()              ; Move to the Movie Title field
uio.InsertAfterRecord()   ; Insert a new record as last rec

endmethod

                                          Edit   Line: 14   Col: 1
```

Figure 16-2: The Add Movie button places Paradox in Edit mode and moves to the first field in the movie table.

Variables

The *var ... endVar* block declares a variable, *uio,* of the type *UIObject.* A UIObject (User Interface Object) is any object placed on a Paradox form. The *uio* variable is the only variable used in this method. Although you don't *need* to declare variables, it's a good idea because Paradox can check different kinds of errors and your code executes faster.

To remind you about what a variable is: think back to when you last created a Paradox table. Field names described the data that would eventually be entered. And the value in a particular field could be anything, provided it conformed to the field type.

Given only a field name, there is no way to know what value it contains, but if a field is named logically, you know the type of data it contains. A phone number field either contains a phone number or the field is empty. In these respects, variables are similar to fields. A variable is given a name and it contains data or is empty; when looking only at its name, you don't necessarily know the value contained by the variable but you do know what type of data it is.

Fields can contain different data in each record; likewise, the contents of a variable can change. A variable is also like a field in that it contains only one item at any given instant. However, there's an important difference between a field and a variable: fields are typically stored in a table and written to disk, whereas variables are always stored in the computer's memory. There are other differences, too, as you'll soon discover.

Each field in a Paradox table has a data type. Variables are assigned data types also, but the data type for a variable is often different from the data type for a field. Variables can contain text (like alpha fields), numbers (like number fields), or they can be used to access UIObjects.

Once an association is made between a UIObject and a variable, the variable is used instead of the UIObject's name. The variable refers to the UIObject and is therefore a *handle.* "UIObject" is one of the many types of handles used by Paradox. Reports, tables, menus and forms are also commonly used variable types. We can see from this example that variables not only refer to text (strings, numbers, dates) but also to Paradox objects. Any Paradox object can be referenced with a variable.

Some common variable types are described in the following list. Other types of variables will be introduced as they become necessary. Understanding what type of data a variable can hold is important because if a variable is assigned a value that doesn't fit, an error results.

String	Any alphanumeric string up to 255 characters. Longer values can be assigned to strings, but it requires a trick or two.
Number	Floating-point values that are practically without bounds.
SmallInt	Integers ranging from –32,768 to 32,767.
LongInt	Integers ranging from –2,147,483,647 to 2,147,486,647.
Date	Dates ranging from January 1, 100, to December 31, 9999.

The rules for naming variables are similar to those for naming other Paradox objects. Even though you may not like rules, they must be followed. So here they are:

○ Names must be 32 characters or less.

○ The first character must be an uppercase or lowercase letter.

○ No spaces or tabs are allowed.

○ Names can contain letters, numbers, extended ANSI characters 161-255 and the characters $! _. Names cannot duplicate Paradox reserved words such as method names, property names or ObjectPAL language words.

In addition to these rules, common sense is helpful. Even though variable names can be 32 characters long, lengthy names become a little unwieldy. It's also easy to make typos. Avoid characters with accent marks; many of these are included in the extended ANSI character set, but they cannot be typed directly from the keyboard. (If for some reason you really want to, you can probably make changes to the international section of the Control Panel in order to more easily use accented letters.) Capitalization is used to make variable names more readable. It's difficult to read *getnextkeyfromuser,* so *getNextKeyFromUser* is preferable.

Variables typically exist only during the execution of the method. Once the method is done, Paradox forgets all about its variables. Although this may seem limiting, it is really very useful. If Paradox remembered variables forever, memory would be wasted on variables that are no longer needed. Furthermore, if two buttons referred to different forms by the same handle, Paradox wouldn't know which form to use. By purging unused variables from memory, the same variable name can be used over and over again without concern. (You'll learn more about this later, and you'll also learn about exceptions to this rule.)

A variable's *scope* refers to the objects that can access it. Variables are accessible only to the objects that declare them. Any number of variables can be declared in the *var ... endVar* block. Any time variables are declared, *var* indicates the beginning of the variable declaration block, and *endVar* indicates the end of the block.

Conditions

The word *if* is used frequently in conversational English; it's also used frequently in programming and means exactly the same thing. The general syntax of an *if* clause is this:

```
if <condition is true> then
    <do something>
else
    <do something else>
endif
```

The mandatory elements are the keyword *if* followed by a *condition* (something that evaluates to either true or false) followed by the keyword *then*. Any statements that follow are executed only if the condition is true. For true conditions, Paradox continues executing statements until it comes to the *else* keyword, if it exists. It is not necessary to use the keyword *else*, and if it is not used, no *else* conditions can be used either. The other mandatory component is the *endif*, which tells Paradox that the conditional statements are finished.

The following examples show how an *if ... endif* clause is useful.

```
if FirstName.value = "" then      ; If FirstName is blank
    msgInfo("Oops", "You must type a first name")
endif
```

In English, this reads, "If the value of the first name field is blank, then display a message alerting the user." Let's try another example.

```
if ClockSpeed >= 66 then
    message("You have a fast computer")
else                              ;executes this if ClockSpeed < 66
    msgInfo("Time Out", "You need a faster computer")
    BankAcct = BankAcct - 2500
endif                             ; end of if clause
```

In English, this reads, "If the variable ClockSpeed is greater than or equal to 66, then display a message in the status bar. Otherwise, display a msgInfo dialog box and subtract $2,500 from the variable BankAcct." Notice that two statements are executed in the *else* clause, but there could be as many statements as you want. There is no practical limit.

The *if ... endif* block in the *pushButton* method shown in Figure
16-2 tests whether Paradox is in Edit mode. The phrase *if not isEdit( )*
is a little confusing, so let's take a closer look at it. Remember that
whatever follows *if* needs to evaluate to either true or false. If Paradox
is in Edit mode, *isEdit( )* returns true; if Paradox is not in Edit mode,
isEdit( ) returns false. We want Paradox to be placed in Edit mode if
not there already, so *not in Edit mode* is what needs to be tested for.
If Paradox is not in Edit mode, *isEdit( )* would return false; therefore,
not isEdit( ) would return true. The line *Edit( )* executes only when
the *if* condition evaluates to true.

If this is confusing, look at the following example: these two code
fragments are functionally identical.

```
if not isEdit() then          if isEdit() then
      edit()                  else
endif                               edit()
                              endif
```

The next line in Figure 16-2, *uio.attach(movie_title)*, associates
the variable *uio* with the field *movie_title*. You're probably saying to
yourself, "Aha, so *uio* is a handle to the field." Paradox is told to move
to the last record in MOVIES.DB by *uio.end( )*, then the next line
moves to the field whose association has been made with the variable
uio. Finally *uio.InsertAfterRecord( )* inserts a new record as the last
record in the movies table.

The Add Actor button is similar to the Add Movies button, except,
of course, it would move to a different field. Also, there is no need to
move to the last record in the ACTORS table because the table is
sorted by actor name and Paradox has no idea what that will be.

At any rate, the easiest way to place code into the *pushButton* method of the Add Actor button is to copy it from the Add Movie button. Then you can change the *uio.attach(movie_title)* line, so that it says *uio.attach(Actor_Fname)*, delete *uio.end( )*, and change it to *uio.InsertRecord( )*. You can compare your code to Figure 16-3. Again, copying reduces the workload and the chance for error.

```
MOVIES::#Button47::pushButton*
method pushButton(var eventInfo Event)
var
    uio        UIObject
endvar
if not isEdit() then
    edit()
endif
uio.attach("Actor_Fname")
uio.moveto()              ; Move to Actor first name field
uio.InsertRecord()        ; Insert a new record

endmethod
```
```
                                    Edit    Line: 9    Col: 38
```

Figure 16-3: This code adds a new actor and is similar to adding a new movie.

The Report Buttons

The View Report and Print Report buttons are practically identical. Because they both refer to a Paradox object—a report—a report variable must be declared. But the custom method for the View Report button (see Figure 16-4) does not have any variables declared. It uses the variable *rpt* but does not declare it.

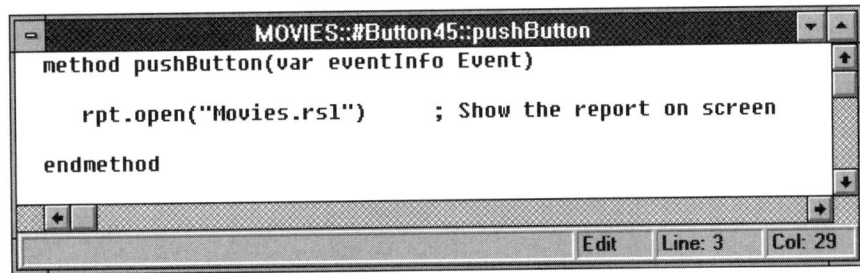
```
MOVIES::#Button45::pushButton
method pushButton(var eventInfo Event)

    rpt.open("Movies.rsl")    ; Show the report on screen

endmethod
```
```
                                    Edit    Line: 3    Col: 29
```

Figure 16-4: The View Report button's *pushButton* method uses the Report variable *rpt*, but it is not declared in this method.

Two buttons use the same variable, so the variable was declared on the page because the page contains both buttons. Figure 16-5 shows the Report variable declared on the page, and both the View Report and Print Report buttons have access to it. This is a useful practice when many objects refer to the same variable name. In this case, the report variable could just as easily have been declared in both buttons' *pushButton* method, but the concept of containership is important and worth working with.

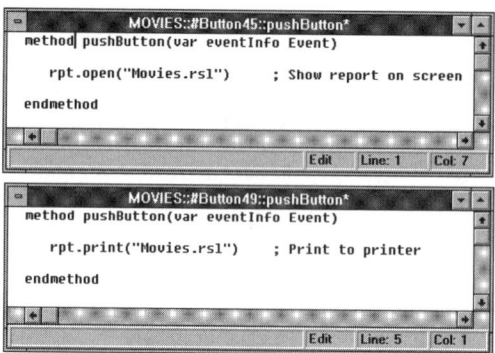

Figure 16-5: Both the View Report and Print Report buttons have access to the variable *rpt*, which is declared in the page's Var window.

Containers are an important concept in Paradox, and it's worth the time to review them. The object tree in Figure 16-6 shows that a field contains an edit region and a text label. What it doesn't show is that the page contains the field and the form contains the page. (For a refresher about the usefulness of object trees, refer back to the information on this subject in earlier chapters. The relationship in the object tree is typically the same as the visual relationship of objects. This containership feature makes it easy to move the field around on the form without having to move three independent objects.

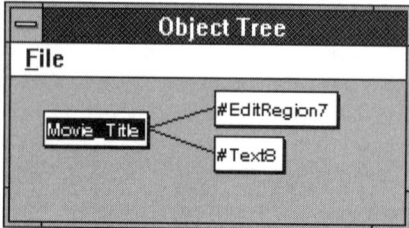

Figure 16-6: The field object actually is a container for two other objects: the text label and the edit region.

Containership serves other purposes, too. One of the bases of object-based programming is that an object doesn't rely on other objects and isn't affected by them. This self-sufficiency characteristic is known as *encapsulation*. Let's assume that you have a form with several buttons. Each button has custom *pushButton* methods that use variables, and because of encapsulation the buttons don't interact with each other. The same variable names can be used in each button's method without affecting the other buttons. You'll learn more about variables, containers and how the two interact later in this chapter.

Searching for Data

The *pushButton* method for the Find Movie button is the most complex so far. But don't worry! You have seen practically all the pieces before. You know you can click on Paradox's Locate and Locate Next buttons to move to a particular record. But before using them, you have to be sure you are in the field you want to search. The advantage of the Find Movie button is that it automatically searches through the Movie title field without your having to select the field. Figure 16-7 shows the code in all its glory.

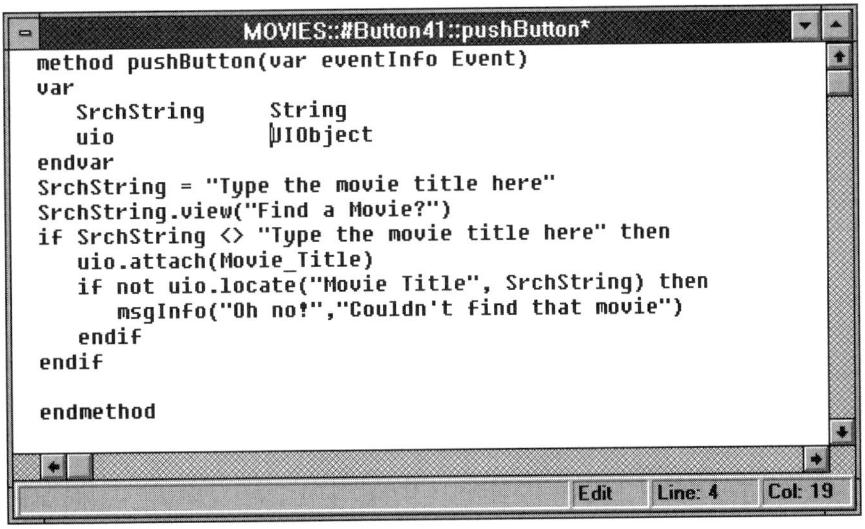

```
MOVIES::#Button41::pushButton*
method pushButton(var eventInfo Event)
var
    SrchString      String
    uio             UIObject
endvar
SrchString = "Type the movie title here"
SrchString.view("Find a Movie?")
if SrchString <> "Type the movie title here" then
    uio.attach(Movie_Title)
    if not uio.locate("Movie Title", SrchString) then
        msgInfo("Oh no!","Couldn't find that movie")
    endif
endif

endmethod
```
`Edit    Line: 4    Col: 19`

Figure 16-7: This method searches for the movie title that you type into a dialog box.

Two variables are declared in this method: *uio* and *SrchString*. Lines 6 and 7 display a dialog box ("Find a Movie?" is in the title bar) that lets you type in a variable. But notice that the dialog box (see Figure 16-8) has both an OK and a Cancel button. When the OK button is pressed, the value of the *SrchString* variable is changed to whatever you typed in the dialog box. When the Cancel button is pressed, the *SrchString* variable doesn't change, no matter what you typed in the dialog box. *SrchString* still equals its value before the dialog box was displayed—in this case "Type the movie title here."

Figure 16-8: The dialog box displayed by the *view* method doesn't change the value of the *SrchString* variable if the Cancel button is pressed.

Because there is no need to search for a movie if the Cancel button is pressed, line 8 tests to see whether the Cancel button was pressed by checking the value of the variable *SrchString*. If the value is the same as in line 6, either the Cancel button was pressed or the OK button was pressed but no text was entered. Either way, there's no need to search the database.

If a movie was typed, lines 9 through 12 are executed. Line 9 associates the variable *uio* with the field *Movie_Title* (just like the Add Movie button did). Line 10 performs the search, but the process may seem surprisingly complicated. Actually, *uio.locate("Movie Title", SrchString)* is all that's necessary to locate the value *SrchString* in the Movie title field.

But there's more to this line than just locating a record. Many Paradox commands return a value of true or false depending on whether the operation was performed successfully. Locate is no exception. If *SrchString* is located, Paradox moves to that record and returns a value of true. If *SrchString* was not located, a value of false is returned and line 11 displays a dialog box saying, "Couldn't find that movie."

Dialogs Revisited

One more button to go—the Exit button. Again, this is very similar to the Close button from Chapter 15. However, in Chapter 15, even if you accidentally click on the Close button, you're outta here! This could be devastating, or at least a nuisance. So, to refine the button a little, a dialog box was added, asking for confirmation. You see these dialogs all the time in Windows. Sometimes it is really advantageous; sometimes it's annoying. You be the judge, and add confirmation dialog boxes when you think it's necessary. Figure 16-9 shows the *pushButton* method for the Exit button.

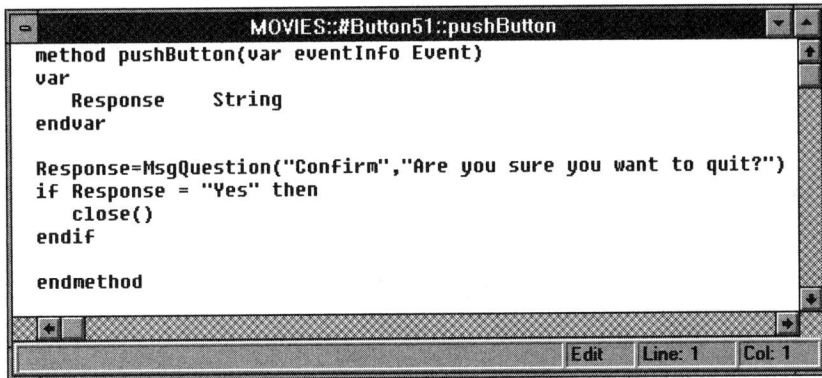

```
MOVIES::#Button51::pushButton
method pushButton(var eventInfo Event)
var
    Response     String
endvar

Response=MsgQuestion("Confirm","Are you sure you want to quit?")
if Response = "Yes" then
    close()
endif

endmethod
```

Figure 16-9: The Exit button displays a MsgQuestion dialog box asking for confirmation before exiting the application.

Not much code here, but to fully understand it, look at the MsgQuestion dialog box in Figure 16-10. It has two buttons: Yes and No. Line 5 in Figure 16-9 displays the dialog box. When one of the buttons is pressed, the variable *Response* is assigned to the text on the button that was pressed. *Response* must equal "Yes" or "No"—there are no other options. Also notice that the first text string for the MsgQuestion dialog box is the title bar text, then the message text. If the Yes button was pressed, line 6 closes the application. If the No button was pressed, the dialog box simply goes away.

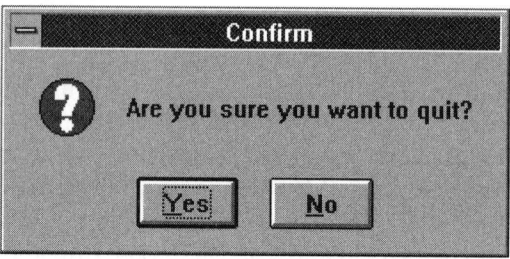

Figure 16-10: The MsgQuestion dialog box displays a message and returns a value of either Yes or No.

Other dialog boxes can be created just as easily as MsgQuestion—and they all use the same syntax. You can have msgYesNoCancel, which displays a dialog box with three buttons: Yes, No, and Cancel. Or msgRetryCancel displays a dialog box with two buttons: Retry and Cancel. You could also have msgAbortRetryIgnore. You get the idea—there are three buttons, and you know what they are.

That's it for the Movies application. If you want to embellish it, you're more than welcome to. In fact, in the next chapter, you'll learn more programming commands that will help you spruce up an application like this. But for now, let's look at some programming concepts that will make your work easier.

CONTAINERSHIP REVISITED

Let's take a look at a form that demonstrates containership principles. Refer to Figure 16-11: each button on CONT.FSL, which is included on the accompanying disk, uses the view method to assign a value to the variable *getText*. The descriptions to the right of the buttons indicate where the variable is declared. The purpose of this form is to show the importance of containership and its relation to declaring variables. Let's get on with the demonstration by following these steps:

1. Open the form CONT.FSL.
2. Click on the top button.
3. Type something into the dialog box and click on the OK button.
4. Click on the Display Variable button.

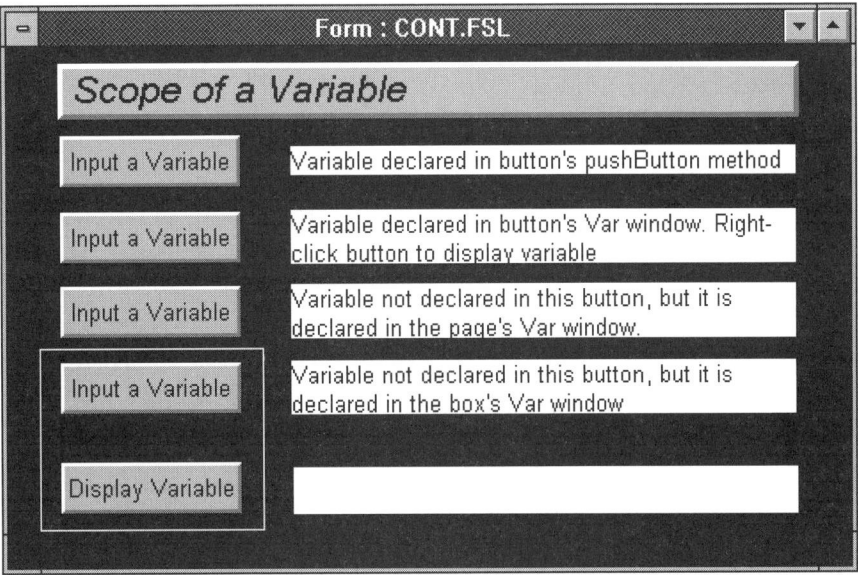

Figure 16-11: Each button on this form uses a variable named *getText*.

When you click on any Input a Variable button, you can assign a value to a *getText* variable; clicking on the Display Variable button displays a value.

The field displays a message that the variable was not assigned a value. You know that some variable was assigned a value because you typed something into the dialog box, so let's see what happened.

The top *pushButton* method shown in Figure 16-12 looks familiar. The variable *getText* is declared and assigned the value of whatever you typed in the dialog box. So far, this is identical to the Find Movie button on the Cinema Summary form *DisplayVar* is the field where the variable contents are stored. This method tries to display the variable *getText* in the field *DisplayVar*. If this is not possible (because the variable hasn't been assigned a value), the message "Variable not assigned" is displayed instead.

The main difference between this example and the Find Movie button is that this time the variable's contents are displayed by pressing a second button. Looking at the code, it seems reasonable to assume that because the same variable name is referenced, its value would be displayed in the field. So why were the variable contents not displayed in the field?

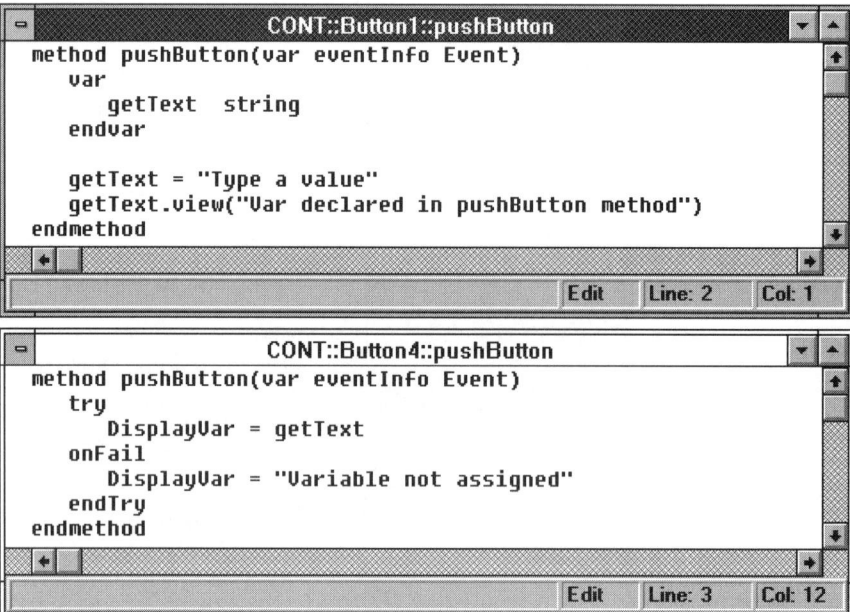

```
CONT::Button1::pushButton
method pushButton(var eventInfo Event)
    var
        getText   string
    endvar

    getText = "Type a value"
    getText.view("Var declared in pushButton method")
endmethod
```
Edit   Line: 2   Col: 1

```
CONT::Button4::pushButton
method pushButton(var eventInfo Event)
    try
        DisplayVar = getText
    onFail
        DisplayVar = "Variable not assigned"
    endTry
endmethod
```
Edit   Line: 3   Col: 12

Figure 16-12: The scope of the variable declared in the top window is limited to its method; therefore, the variable is not available to the Display Variable button (bottom window).

When declared in a method, the variable is only in existence as long as the method is executing. The Display Variable button does not have access to the variable declared in the Input a Variable *pushButton* method. Even though the name is the same, the variable is different. This is yet another example of encapsulation—the Input a Variable button is self-contained and does not affect the other buttons on the form.

Remember the View Report and Print Report buttons on the Cinema Summary form? Each button referenced the report variable *rpt*, but *rpt* was declared on the page rather than in the *pushButton* method. If the same variable is to be accessed by more than one object, you typically want it declared on the object which contains the objects that reference the variable. The Report buttons could just as easily have had the report variable declared in each *pushButton* method, but this example demonstrates a useful concept. However, if both Report buttons needed access to a variable *and its value*, declaring the variable on the page would have been essential.

Let's look at a different way of declaring variables. Notice in Figure 16-13 that the Method Inspector has an asterisk by two methods—*pushButton* and *mouseRightUp*—and also by Var (which stands for Variable) in the upper portion. The *mouseRightUp* method, as the name implies, is activated when the right mouse button is released with the mouse pointer located over the object. Variables can be declared in the Var window just as they are declared in a custom method. The difference is that variables declared in an object's Var window are accessible to all of the object's methods. If you look at the Var window as being attached to, or actually part of, an object and the methods contained by the object, this system fits in with the containership hierarchy.

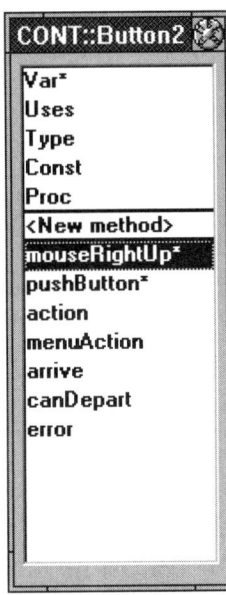

Figure 16-13: The Method Inspector shows that two built-in methods and the Var window have code attached to them.

Inside Scoop

Windows applications typically trigger events when the mouse button is released rather than when it is pressed. That's the reason Paradox has *mouseUp* and *mouseDown* events as well as *mouseRightUp* and *mouseRightDown*.

The two custom methods have access to the variable *getText* (see Figure 16-14). With this in mind, click on the second Input a Variable button and type something into the dialog box. Click on the Display Variable button and you see that once again the Display Variable button does not have access to the button's *getText* variable. Declaring a variable in the Var window did not give any other objects access to it. Encapsulation still makes the variable declared for the Input a Variable button invisible to the Display Variable button.

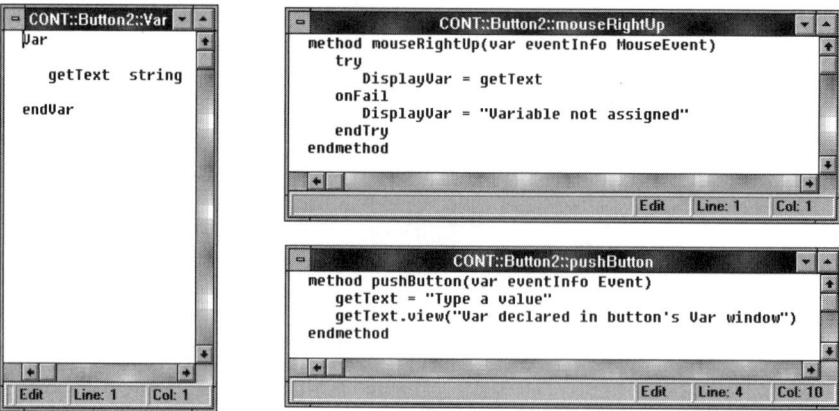

Figure 16-14: The variable *getText* is declared in the button's Var window so it is accessible to all the button's methods but inaccessible to other objects on the form.

Now, right-click on the second Input a Variable button. The variable is displayed in the field. This demonstrates that both the *pushButton* and *mouseRightUp* methods have access to variables declared in the button's Var window. By the way, every object has a Var window—rectangles, graphics, the form, everything. The relationship is the same. Any method attached to an object can access variables declared in that object's Var window.

Click on the Input a Variable button inside the yellow rectangle and type something into the dialog box. When you click on the Display Variable button, the value you typed is displayed in the field object. This is a first—two buttons having access to the same variable. Refer to Figure 16-15 and you see that the *getText* variable is declared in the rectangle's Var window. Both buttons are contained by the rectangle and therefore have access to the variable declared in that container—in this case a rectangle.

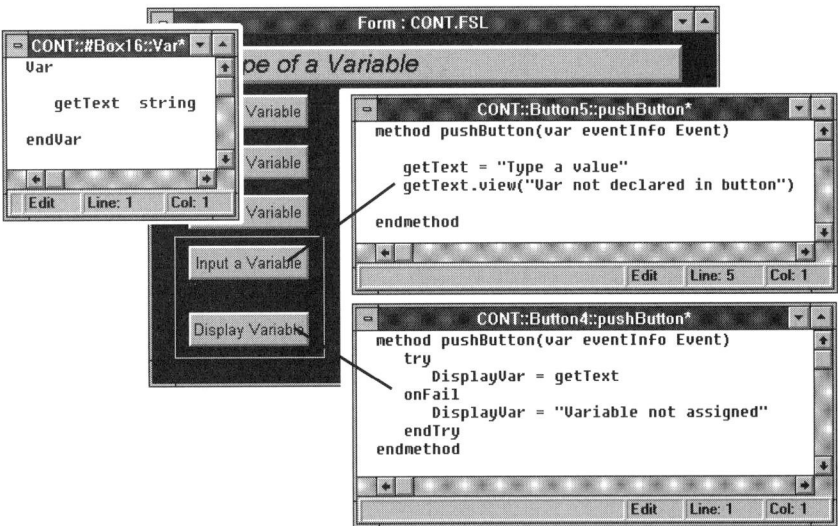

Figure 16-15: Neither button inside the Input a Variable rectangle declares the variable *getText*; it's declared in the rectangle's Var window instead.

There's still one button that has not been clicked on yet. It's getting lonely, so why not click on the third Input a Variable button and type something into the dialog box. When you click on the Display Variable button, the field doesn't change value. If that's a surprise, consider that the Display Variable button looks to its container for the *getText* variable. If found, it doesn't look any further. If not found, it looks at the container's container and so on. Paradox stops looking for the variable when it finds it or, alternatively, when there are no more containers. The page's *getText* variable is in fact set to the value you typed in the dialog box, but the Display Variable button doesn't see it—it only sees the *getText* variable in its container, the box.

Let's demonstrate that a value was actually assigned to the form's *getText* variable. To change the form so that the Display Variable button is not contained within the rectangle, follow these steps:

1. Open the form in a Design window by clicking on the Design button or by pressing F8.

2. Right-click on the rectangle to display its pop-up menu.

3. Click on the Design option from the pop-up menu (see Figure 16-16).

4. From the cascading menu, click on the Contain Objects option. The check mark is now removed.

5. Click the View Data button (or press F8).

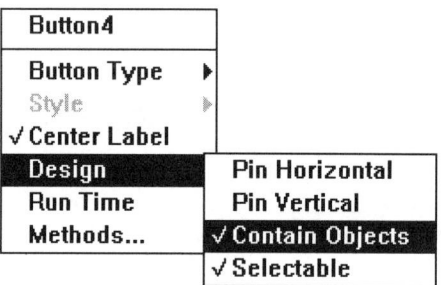

Figure 16-16: Contain Objects is a default property. However, it can be turned off by clicking on the Contain Objects menu choice, thereby removing the check mark.

Contain Objects is a property, just like color or font, and can be turned on or off at will. If the Contain Objects property is disabled, the rectangle no longer contains the Display Variable button. The fact that it is entirely inside the rectangle doesn't matter. Click on the fourth Input a Variable button and type something into the dialog box. This time when you click on the Display Variable button, the page's *getText* variable is displayed in the field object. The reason is the same as it was when you clicked on the Input a Variable button inside the rectangle. Both buttons were contained by an object where the variable was declared. In the first instance, the containing object was a rectangle. This time the containing object is the page. It doesn't matter what the containing object is; the relationship is what is important.

In summary, variables declared in a method are available only to that method. Variables declared in an object's Var window are accessible to all of that object's methods and to the methods of all the objects it contains.

PROPERTIES REVISITED

You have seen properties before. In fact, every time you right-click on an object, a pop-up menu of that object's properties is displayed. Figure 16-17 shows the pop-up menu for a circle. Any of these properties can be changed when the form is being designed, but they can also be changed while running the form using ObjectPAL. And with only one line of ObjectPAL at that.

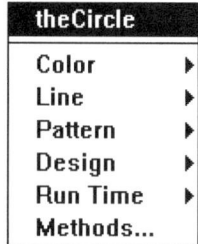

Figure 16-17: The pop-up menu for a circle lets you change its properties interactively, but the properties can also be changed using ObjectPAL.

PROP.FSL (included on disk and shown in Figure 16-18) changes many of an object's properties using ObjectPAL. Play with the form by clicking on the radio buttons to change the fill color, fill pattern and frame style. When you're through, let's see how this form works.

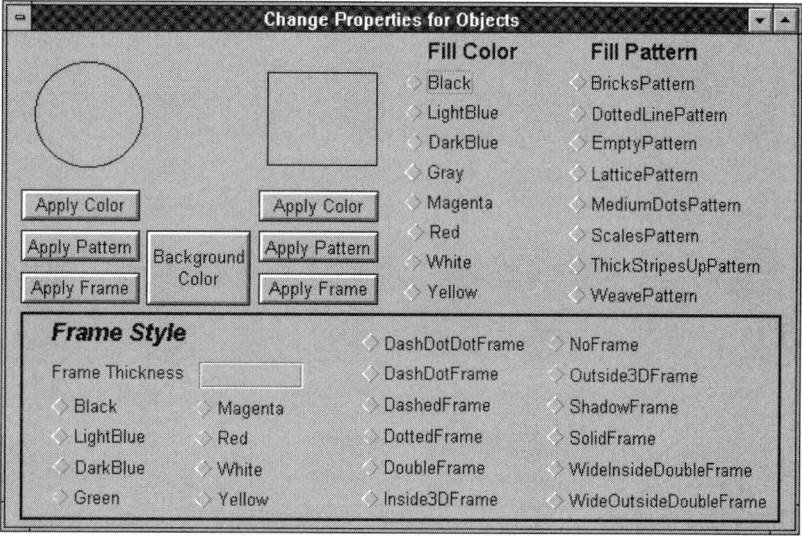

Figure 16-18: PROP.FSL lets you see what property changes look like.

The Apply Color button has one line of code, as shown in Figure 16-19. Periods separate the object from its property. What this says is, "Make the circle's color equal to the value of the selected radio button in ColorFld." (You'll learn more about the dot notation soon.)

```
method pushButton(var eventInfo Event)

    theCircle.color = ColorFld.value

endmethod
```

Figure 16-19: The color property of any object can be changed with a statement similar to the one shown here.

There are a lot of properties in this form, but there are many more available. For example, only a few of the frame colors are listed, but there are many more properties for the box and the ellipse that could have been changed. Paradox provides two different tools for determining what these properties are. When designing a form, right-clicking on any object displays its properties. However, when you are writing code, the ObjectPAL Editor doesn't understand right-clicking on an object on the form. Instead, right-click anywhere in the Editor window, and a pop-up menu is displayed. (You saw this menu in the previous chapter when checking syntax.) This time, click on the Properties menu option. The Display Objects And Properties dialog box (see Figure 16-20) is displayed.

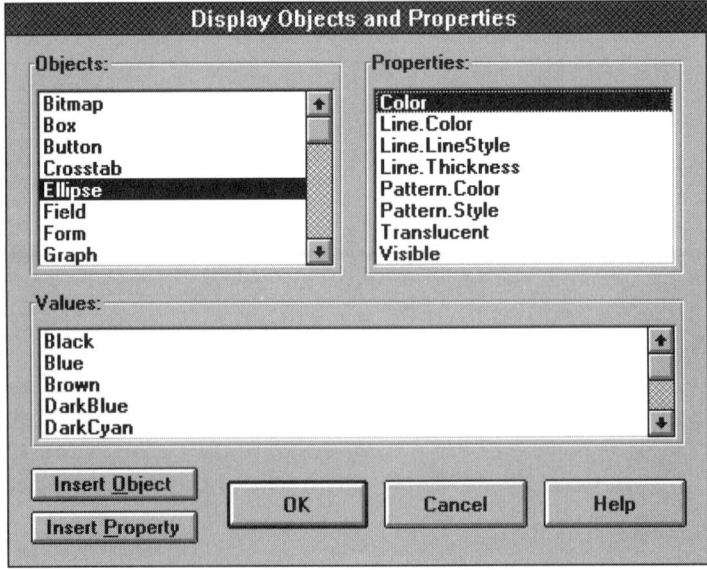

Figure 16-20: The properties of all Paradox objects can be determined when editing an ObjectPAL method. Different objects have different properties.

The Objects column lists all the Paradox object types. Double-click on an object type, and the properties for that object are displayed. Try double-clicking on various objects in the list to see what properties are available for that particular object. Notice that objects have different properties. Double-click on one of the properties; if values exist for the property, a list of them is displayed. This is a handy feature because there are so many objects with so many properties with so many values that no one could remember them all. Paradox lets you look them up easily. Also, notice that the dot notation used to specify the fill color of the Circle (Figure 16-19) corresponds to the syntax *object.property = field.value*. In fact, let's take a closer look at the syntax.

KEEP YOUR SYNTAX STRAIGHT

You have probably learned more about syntax than you think. You've created dialog boxes that display text strings (and remember the text strings were inside quotation marks). You've learned a little about dot notation, and you know how to assign variables. These are important concepts. This section goes into a little more depth, and introduces a few new concepts.

Dot Notation

The Display Objects and Properties dialog box is a wonderful tool to help you understand dot notation. The example in Figure 16-20 shows the Ellipse object, its Color property and the values for Color. The ObjectPAL syntax to make an ellipse's fill color black is this:

```
Ellipse.Color = Black
```

The statement is read: "Ellipse dot color equals black." Let's look at another example. Find the property for Frame.Style. Double-clicking on Frame.Style displays many values for frame style. To change the frame of an ellipse so that it's dotted, use the following statement:

```
Ellipse.Frame.Style = DottedFrame
```

Earlier in this chapter, fields were specified in ObjectPAL commands, and you want to know just by looking at the code whether a field or a variable was referred to. In an effort to program clearly, dot notation can be used to reference a field, even though it isn't really necessary. Let's assume the field named AcctNo is on a form, and you want to change its value. You could use the following syntax:

```
AcctNo = 101
```

However, with a statement like that there is no way of knowing whether AcctNo is a variable or a field. Because AcctNo is a field, it's best to make it clear. The following syntax is preferable:

```
AcctNo.value = 101
```

The two statements are functionally equivalent, but *value* is a property of a field and is not a property of a variable. In the Display Objects and Properties dialog box, find the Field object and you see that Value is one of its properties. Also look for the Variable object. It isn't listed because a variable is not a Paradox object and therefore cannot have a property. Dot notation for a variable is not permissible.

Another use for dot notation is to locate an object. The form in Figure 16-21 shows two objects with the name SmallEllipse (DOT.FSL on the disk). Assume you are referencing SmallEllipse from a button with the following syntax:

SmallEllipse.color = red

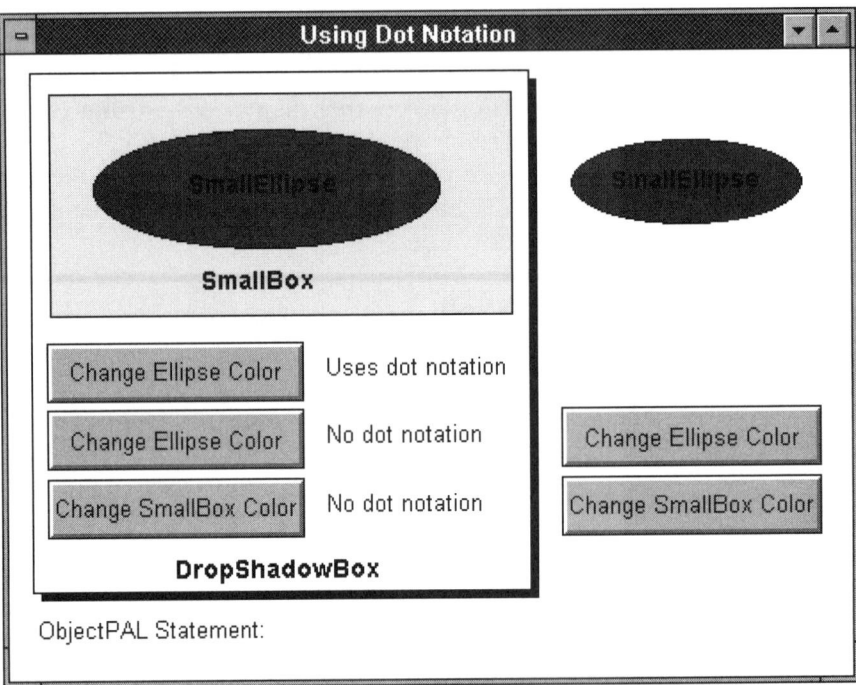

Figure 16-21: This form illustrates the usefulness of dot notation to reference an object when duplicate names exist.

Which SmallEllipse are you referring to when you ask Paradox to change the color to red? Both? The one closest to the button? An ellipse at random? Well, it's probably *not* one at random. When Paradox looks for an object, it follows the containership path. (If that explanation is as clear as split-pea soup, just wait a moment and you'll understand.) Using the form DOT.FSL, click on the right-hand Change Ellipse Color button. The ellipse above the button changes color. This is not particularly surprising. What do you think will happen when you click on the middle button on the left-hand side? Try it and see. The same ellipse changed color. Hmmm. Let's see what actually happened here.

When Paradox tries to find SmallEllipse, it first looks to see if the button contains SmallEllipse. It does not, so the button looks in its container. The object tree in Figure 16-22 shows that the right Change Ellipse Color button (#Button6) is contained by the page and the page contains the right SmallEllipse. The object is found.

When the other Change Ellipse Color button (#Button8) tries to find SmallEllipse, it too first looks to see if the button contains SmallEllipse. It does not, so the button looks in its container, BigBox. BigBox does not directly contain SmallEllipse, so Paradox looks at BigBox's container, #Page2. The page *does* directly contain an object called SmallEllipse, so Paradox changes its color. Either of these buttons finds the same SmallEllipse object.

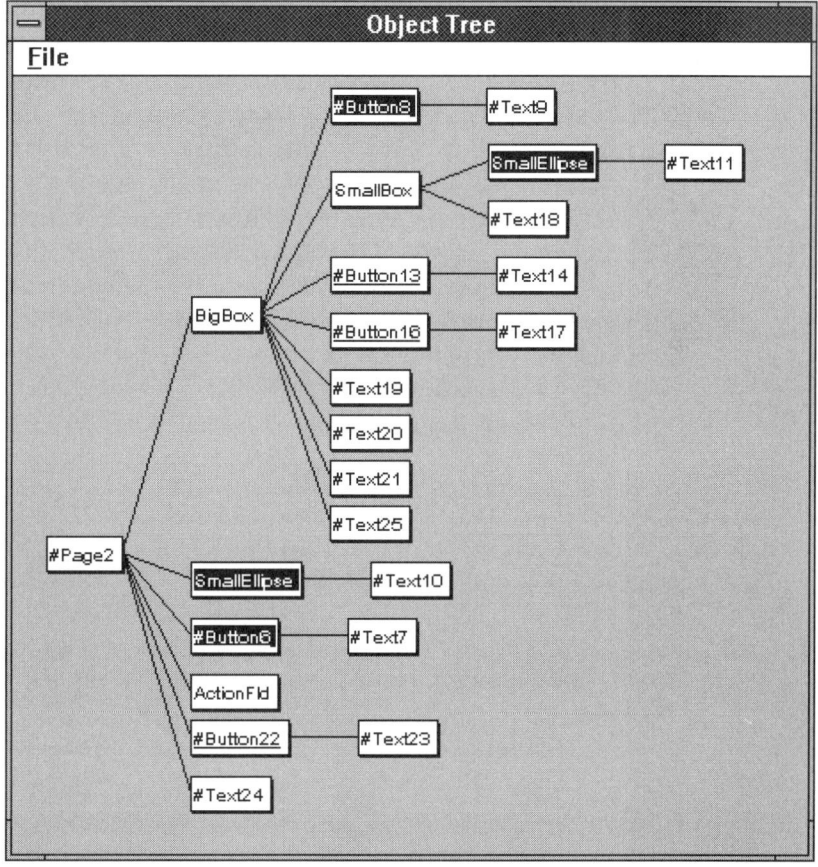

Figure 16-22: In the Object Tree both SmallEllipse objects and the buttons that change the color are highlighted.

If the desired result is to change the color of a specific object named SmallEllipse, dot notation is necessary. The Change Ellipse Color button that uses dot notation overrules the default behavior of Paradox and changes the color of the intended ellipse. The safest thing is to never use duplicate object names—for the same reason you wouldn't name both of your daughters Julie. At any rate, by taking advantage of containership and dot notation you can achieve exactly the results you want.

Other Syntax Requirements

Let's take a closer look at how variables and fields are assigned values. A mathematician would cringe at the following statement.

```
Counter = Counter + 1
```

In mathematics, the value on the left side of an equal sign is the same as the value on the right side. With computers, that is not necessarily the case. What the computer really does is evaluate the portion of the equation on the right of the equal sign, in this case *Counter + 1*. It then assigns that value to the variable *Counter* on the left side of the equal sign. The net result is that the variable *Counter* has increased in value by one. This idea is used constantly in the programming world. In fact, one of the most common things to do is to add 1 (one) to a variable (known as incrementing the variable).

In all the previous examples, when a text string was used, it was placed in quotes. When math was performed, no quotes were used. However, it is possible to perform addition with text strings. Consider the following example:

```
FirstName = "John"
LastName = "MacIntosh"
FullName = FirstName + " " + LastName
```

Both *FirstName* and *LastName* are text strings. When addition is performed with text strings, the text strings are added together to form one text string. In the example above, *FullName = "John MacIntosh"* (notice the space that was added between *FirstName* and *LastName*). Adding text strings is called *concatenation*.

The following example demonstrates a significant difference between text strings and numbers:

```
VarOne = "1"
VarTwo = "2"
VarResult = VarOne + VarTwo
```

What do you think the result is? If you said "12" you are correct. Even though you may recognize the contents of the variables to be numbers, they're really text strings because they are enclosed in quotation marks. Had there been no quotes, the answer would have been 3. By the way, notice that none of the variables have quotes around them—only the text strings are within quotes.

Inside Scoop

Throughout this chapter, examples of code have used white space to make the ObjectPAL code more readable. Normally, Paradox doesn't care about white space—you can use tabs to align text however you want. However, the code is easier to read when conditions in an *if ... endif* block are indented.

So far, addition and subtraction are the only operators that have been used. There are others. Division (represented by a forward slash) and multiplication (represented by an asterisk) can be performed on numbers and integers. Also, AND, OR and NOT are valid operators. For example:

```
if State = "NY" or State = "CA" then
    message("Lots of people in these states")
endif

if Var1 > "P" and Var1 < "S" then
    message("Var1 starts with Q or R")
endif

if not State = "HI" then
    message("No one living on islands included")
endif

if 2*3 = 12/2 then
    message("That's a true statement")
endif
```

This has been a lot of syntax, programming muckity muck. It is important stuff to know if you're going to continue with ObjectPAL programming, but for now enough is enough.

MOVING ON

Chapter 17 introduces a video rental application that shows you some wonderful ObjectPAL features. Because it is a more sophisticated application than anything introduced so far, planning the application will be discussed, but mostly the focus will be on ObjectPAL.

You'll learn how the *Event Model* determines the sequence in which events occur. You can make a button's label change. For example, instead of an Edit/End Edit button, its label could be either Edit or End Edit, depending on what it will do when you click on it. You'll also learn how to create a custom menu.

The video rental application is used throughout the rest of this book. Chapter 18 adds still more features. It's a great application for you to learn how to really make Paradox do what you want it to.

17  DESIGNING AN APPLICATION

In this chapter, you're going to create an application, from the ground up, for a hypothetical video rental business. The purpose of this app is to keep track of all video rentals and to print reports. It is not a simple application, so, once again, planning and designing will be stressed. When your design is complete, you'll create ObjectPAL methods that take advantage of Paradox's natural abilities. Specifically, here's what you're going to do:

○ Create a one-to-many-to-many relationship with a lookup table.
○ Design buttons whose labels change, depending on the current state of the application.
○ Automatically insert data in tables.
○ Create a custom menu.
○ Create a drop-down edit list that gets its data from a Paradox table.

PLANNING THE APPLICATION

We'll start the planning stage by focusing on how the application will be used and what data is necessary. Then, by looking at the reports, we'll see if we missed anything. We'll also consider the forms, but mostly their ObjectPAL methods. If you're thinking this will take forever, relax. Tables, forms and reports are already created. Figure 17-1 shows you the main form, but it's helpful to understand the thought processes that went into creating this application.

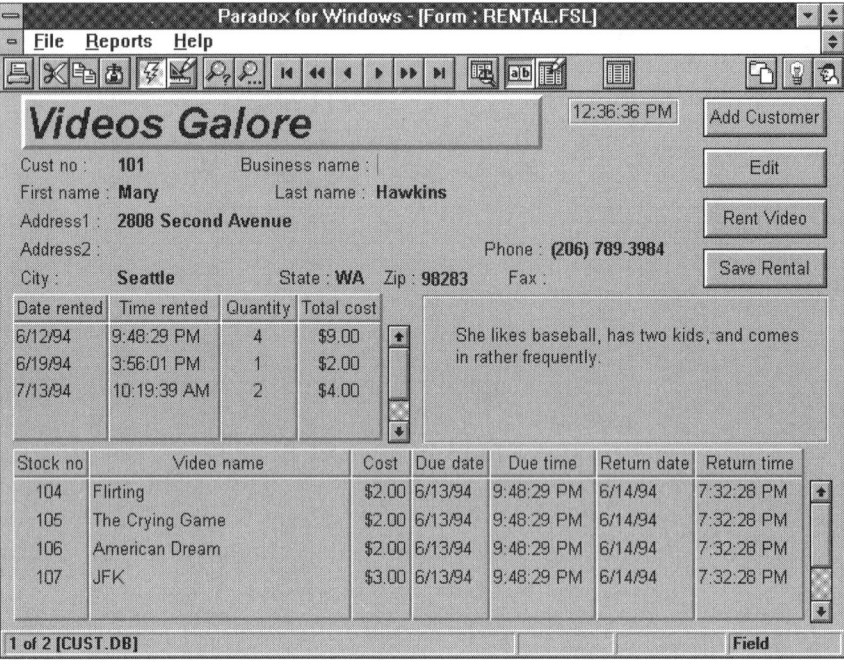

Figure 17-1: This is one of the forms used in the Video application—just to give you a taste of what you can create.

Choosing the Data

Who rents videos? Customers! So there's a Customer table (the master table) that stores the usual stuff. Name, address, phone and fax number, and comments.

The more difficult decision is how to keep track of the videos. Your store doesn't have a weekend surcharge or late fees. There are no special deals for renting lots of videos or renting them for an extended period. In other words, each video always rents for the same price, but there are different prices for certain videos.

Let's consider what happens when Bob and Mary come into the store to rent videos. They wander around, select videos from different sections of the store, and take them to the checkout counter. What information would be useful to collect from this transaction in order to quickly and easily retrieve and track the records of these videos?

The following is a list of possible fields:

    Date rented

    Time rented

    Video name

    Cost

    Number of days rented

    Due date

    Number of videos rented

    Total cost

This may be enough, but also consider the reports you want to produce. Remember that the reports can help determine the data you want to keep track of. Here are some possible reports:

○ Customer list—a simple list of all customers.

○ Daily income—so you and your accountant know how much you're taking in.

○ Most frequent rentals—so you know which titles are the most popular.

○ Overdue videos—so you can send a reminder to delinquent customers.

○ List of video titles—to publish a catalog of the videos you have available.

Let's look at these reports and see if the fields from the prior list are enough. The customer list needs only information from the Customer table. Daily income is a tally of sales for each day, so the Date rented and Cost fields should suffice. The most frequent rentals report can simply list all video names with a summary of the number of times they occur in the database, or it could summarize the income generated from renting each video. None of these reports add any new fields to the preceding list of fields.

Overdue videos is a more complicated report because Paradox needs to determine the tapes that haven't been returned by the due date. How can that be done? The fields above were chosen based only on tapes rented, not on tapes returned. Once Return date and Return time fields are added, a query could find all records with a blank Return date where the Due date is prior to today's date.

The final report, the list of videos, is actually a catalog. The video name is a necessity in the catalog, but none of the other fields seem appropriate. A video classification field would be helpful for grouping the videos, and a video description field would be helpful for customers. You probably also want to know how many copies of each video are available for rent. Again, this report adds fields that weren't in the preceding list.

The process of analyzing the reports has added five new fields to the original list: Return date, Return time, Video classification, Video description and Quantity. But the question remains: How are these fields going to be organized in tables? One possibility is to create two additional tables, Invoice and Videos. The table that follows lists the fields each table could contain. Now that reports have been analyzed, the following fields are included in this application; however, the structure of the tables still needs to be refined.

Invoice Table	Videos Table
Date rented	Video name
Time rented	Classification
Video name	Quantity
Cost	Video description
Due date	
Number of videos rented	
Total cost	
Return date	
Return time	

To see if this is good organization let's take a closer look, first at the Videos table (because it is simpler). Everything seems to be in order—there is enough data to publish a catalog, and there is no extraneous data. However, looking at the Invoice table, Video name appears there also. Uh oh, duplication of data. It might be preferable to link the Videos table to the Invoice table using a Stock number field. The cost differs from tape to tape, so it is also preferable to move the Cost field into the Videos table, especially since it will be linked to the Invoice table. Is there any other duplication?

Just looking at the fields, it seems OK, but consider that Bob and Mary rented three videos at one time. There you are, entering data at the checkout counter, typing Date rented, Time rented, Due date and Due time for each video. Duplicate information still exists, but it is hidden until the application is actually used. A better organization of fields is shown in this next table. This is the final organization of fields in the detail tables. Videos is a lookup table linked to Items.

Invoice Table	Items Table	Videos Table
Invoice number	Invoice number	Stock number
Customer number	Stock number	Video name
Date rented	Due date	Classification
Time rented	Due time	Video description
Number of videos rented	Return date	Quantity
Total cost	Return time	Cost

Notice that Customer number was added to the Invoice table. Can't forget that the Customer table is the master (or parent) table. It's just that we hardly talked about it because it was so much easier to figure out than these other tables. At any rate, the structure of the tables seems complete.

Designing Forms

The tables are designed, so now on to forms. Clearly a form is needed to fill in data at the checkout counter. But are there any other forms? Well, what else should this application do? Reports need to be printed, but that doesn't require forms. Reports are selected from a custom menu that you get to later in the chapter. What else may be necessary? Editing the Videos table requires an additional form because it is a lookup table on the form that is used at the checkout counter. Besides, updating the Videos table will be performed at a different time. It looks like two forms are enough—one for the check-out counter, one to edit the videos your store rents.

In order to design the forms, tables need to be created. Guess what? It's done! Figure 17-2 shows the structure of all four tables. But before we add ObjectPAL code to the two forms, let's look more closely at the data model.

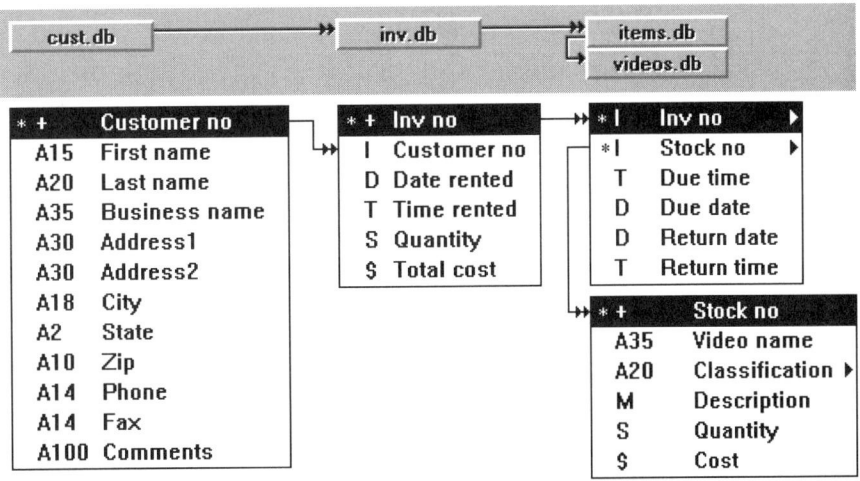

Figure 17-2: The tables used in this application are in a one-to-many-to-many relationship with VIDEOS.DB being a lookup table.

CUST.DB is linked to INV.DB in a one-to-many relationship, but unlike the other one-to-many relationships you have seen, both these tables have one key field. Normally that would create a one-to-one relationship (like ITEMS.DB to VIDEOS.DB), but the difference here is that CUST.DB is linked to the second field in INV.DB rather than its key field.

Paradox cannot link fields if they are not indexed, and because Customer no in INV.DB is not a key field, a secondary index was created. (Review Chapter 6 for more information on creating secondary indexes.) You have seen tables linked through their key fields, but Paradox lets you create a secondary index on any field, which lets you use that field to link tables.

INV.DB and ITEMS.DB are linked exactly like you would expect for a one-to-many relationship. The parent table has one key field and the child table has two key fields. VIDEOS.DB is a lookup table for the Stock no field in ITEMS.DB.

CREATING THE OBJECTPAL CODE

Code can be placed anywhere, but buttons are very common locations for code because they're useless without a little dab of ObjectPAL. This application is the first one we've looked at that has code tucked away in places other than buttons. The code for a custom menu is attached to the page, other code is attached to the form and still more code is attached to some of the fields' *arrive* and *depart* methods.

Adding a Customer

Providing a means of adding a customer is no different in this application than in any of the others, so the Add Customer button has code similar to other buttons you have already seen. Figure 17-3 shows the Add Customer button's *pushButton* method, which checks to see if Paradox is in Edit mode (line 2) and if not, turns on Edit mode (line 3). However, there is something new here—line 4 changes the Edit button's label to say "End Edit." This is handy because changing a button's label to reflect the action it will perform tells you exactly what the button will do. Line 6 inserts a new record in CUST.DB and line 7 moves to the business name field where you can start typing in new customer data.

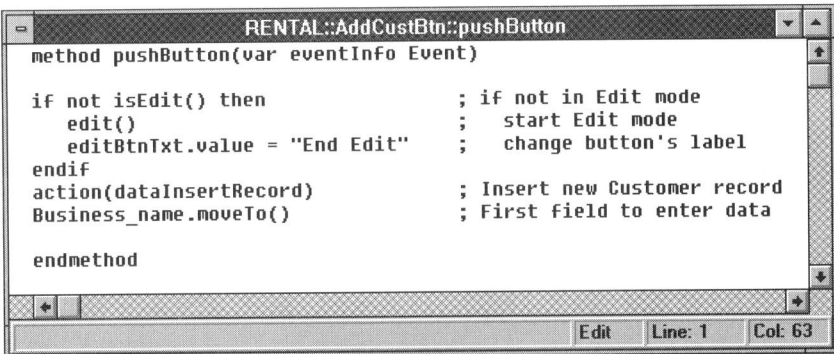

```
                     RENTAL::AddCustBtn::pushButton
method pushButton(var eventInfo Event)

if not isEdit() then               ; if not in Edit mode
   edit()                          ;    start Edit mode
   editBtnTxt.value = "End Edit"    ;    change button's label
endif
action(dataInsertRecord)           ; Insert new Customer record
Business_name.moveTo()             ; First field to enter data

endmethod
```

Figure 17-3: The Add Customer button's *pushButton* method is similar to what you have already seen, except that it changes the text label on the Edit button also.

Changing a Button's Label

Edit buttons in the other examples have used *action(dataToggleEdit)*. That works when the button is a toggle and if that is the only thing the button does. However, in this form, the button's label changes from "Edit" to "End Edit" depending on what the button will do when pressed. Figure 17-4 shows that when the form is in Edit mode, line 3 exits Edit mode and line 4 changes the button's label to say "Edit." However, when not in Edit mode (the *else* clause) line 6 changes to Edit mode and line 7 changes the button's label to say "End Edit."

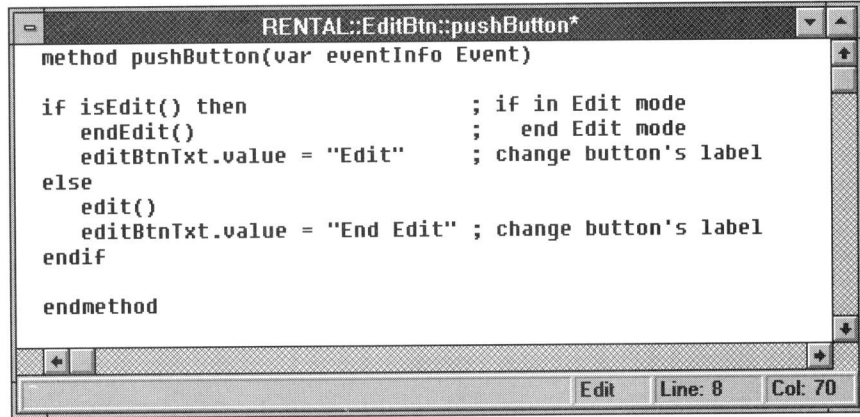

```
                     RENTAL::EditBtn::pushButton*
method pushButton(var eventInfo Event)

if isEdit() then                   ; if in Edit mode
   endEdit()                       ;    end Edit mode
   editBtnTxt.value = "Edit"        ; change button's label
else
   edit()
   editBtnTxt.value = "End Edit" ; change button's label
endif

endmethod
```

Figure 17-4: Pressing the Edit button enters Edit mode in addition to changing the button's label.

As you have already seen, other methods that change to or from Edit mode (such as the Add Customer button) must also change the Edit button's label. Figure 17-5 shows the Edit button's object tree (notice that the name of the button's label has been changed from the Paradox default). With the help of descriptive names, it's easy to reference the button's label with ObjectPAL.

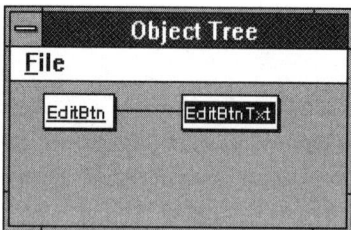

Figure 17-5: The Edit button's label has been renamed so it is easy to reference from ObjectPAL.

Inside Scoop

Typically there is no reason to change the default name of objects, unless they are referenced by your code. Looking at the page's object tree can often provide a clue as to which objects are manipulated with ObjectPAL.

What happens if you click on the Design button when the button's label says "End Edit"? The button still says "End Edit" even though you may have created the form with "Edit" as the button's label. When toggling back into View Data mode, the Edit button would start off saying "End Edit" just as it did in the Form Design window, even though it should really say "Edit." (When the form is first run, it is never in Edit mode.) When the form opens, the Edit button's label should be forced to say "Edit." This is done in the form's *open* method, but before looking at how the label's default values are set, we need to see what happens when a form opens.

Opening a Form

When Paradox opens a form, it also opens every object on the form. The *open* event for each object on the form is sent back to the form, causing the form to see lots of *open* events—one for the form and one for each object on the form. If this seems surprising, think back to Chapters 15 and 16 where the event model was briefly explained.

Chapter 15 showed that when a button is clicked, the form intercepts the mouse-click and then passes it to the button. This default behavior can be overruled, however, and default code in the form's *open* method (Figure 17-6) is one way of doing that.

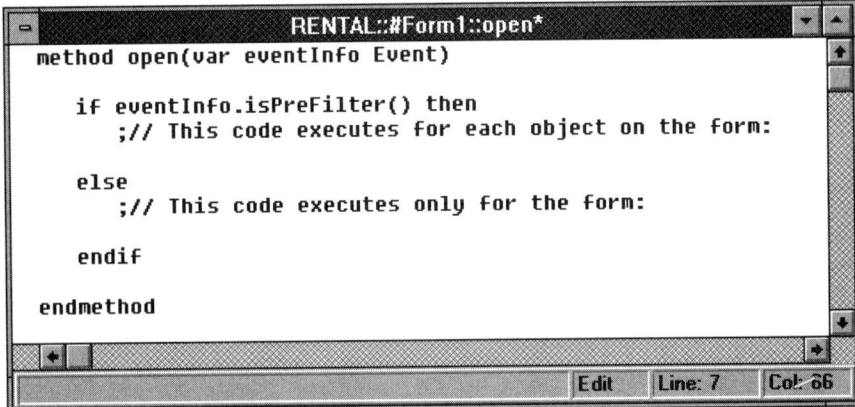

```
method open(var eventInfo Event)

    if eventInfo.isPreFilter() then
        ;// This code executes for each object on the form:

    else
        ;// This code executes only for the form:

    endif

endmethod
```

Figure 17-6: The default code in the form's *open* method segregates the form's *open* event from the *open* event of all other objects on the form.

Pitfall Ahead

Do not delete the default code. For example, if the *eventInfo.isPreFilter()* method is deleted from the form's *open* method, code placed in that method will execute when each object on the form opens.

isPreFilter( ) separates those events that are bubbled up from other objects on the form from the *open* event that occurs for the form itself. Open the form PREFLT.FSL (Figure 17-7), which demonstrates how *isPreFilter( )* works. The code shown in the text box is the code that Paradox places by default in the form's *open* method. (It also occurs in many other methods, but that doesn't matter now.) Click on each of the buttons to see how many *open* events occur depending on where code is placed. You can edit the form and add more objects to demonstrate that their *open* events are also included in the total displayed by the dialog box.

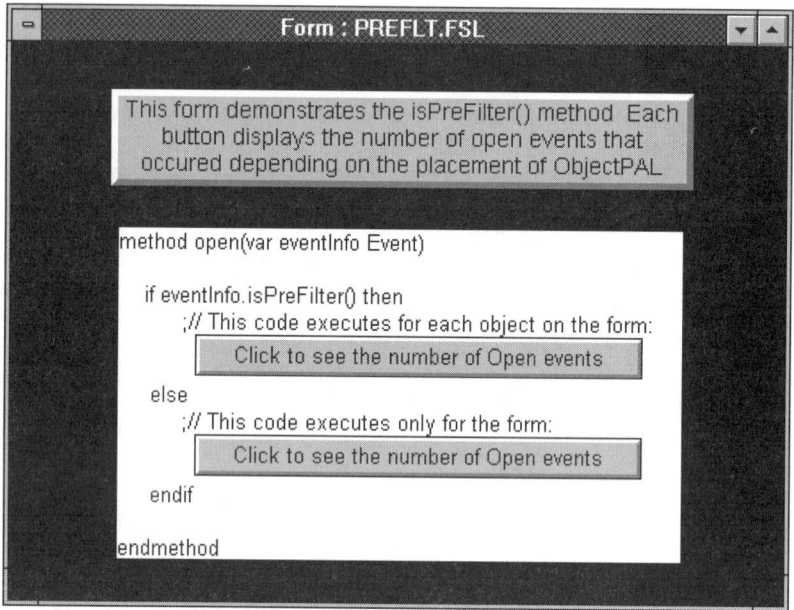

Figure 17-7: The form PREFLT.FSL demonstrates that placement of ObjectPAL code in the form's *open* method is critical.

The object tree for the page (see Figure 17-8) shows that there are seven objects on the form. The form itself is the eighth object, but when the top button is pressed, the form's *open* event is not included—only the seven objects on the form. However, when the bottom button is pressed, the form is the only object whose *open* event is processed.

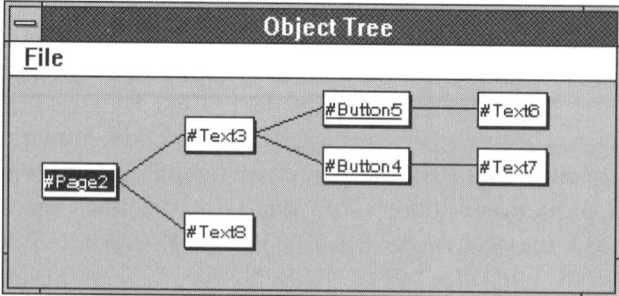

Figure 17-8: The object tree for the page on PREFLT.FSL shows seven objects—exactly the number displayed when clicking on the top button on the form.

Pitfall Ahead

If code is placed in the *if* clause of *eventInfo.isPreFilter( )*, it is executed for every object on the form. Sometimes this is useful, but if you intend the *open* method to execute only once, place code in the *else* clause. Otherwise, the same code could execute hundreds of times.

More events occur when opening a form than you would normally expect. Now that you know where to place code in the form's *open* method, let's get back to the labels on the Edit and Rent Video buttons. The labels need to be initialized each time the form opens, and Figure 17-9 shows how that happens—and that the code is executed only once.

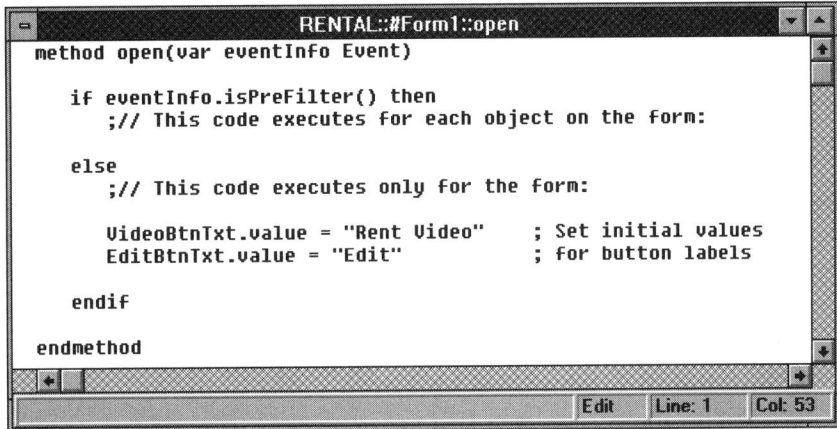

```
method open(var eventInfo Event)

    if eventInfo.isPreFilter() then
        ;// This code executes for each object on the form:

    else
        ;// This code executes only for the form:

        VideoBtnTxt.value = "Rent Video"    ; Set initial values
        EditBtnTxt.value = "Edit"           ; for button labels

    endif

endmethod
```

Figure 17-9: Button labels are initialized in the *else* clause of *eventInfo.isPreFilter.*

The Rent Video Button

The Rent Video button can perform two different functions. Click on it to start another video rental invoice (the button says "Rent Video"). Or, when you add another video to the current rental order (the button says "Add Video"), clicking on the button inserts a record into the ITEMS table frame. Notice that this button starts out like the others: it changes to Edit mode (if necessary) and changes the Edit button's label, as shown in lines 5 through 7 of Figure 17-10.

```
-                    Paradox for Windows - [RENTAL::RentVideoBtn::pushButton]           ▼ ▲
-   File   Edit   View   Search   Program   Properties   Tools   Window   Help           ▲
  ┌───────────────────────────────────────────────────────────────────────────────┐
  │ method pushButton(var eventInfo Event)                                          │▲
  │ var                                                                             │
  │    uioInv, uioItem    UIObject                                                  │
  │ endvar                                                                          │
  │ if not isEdit() then                        ; If not already in Edit mode       │
  │     edit()          editBtnTxt = "End Edit"  ;   go to Edit mode, change label  │
  │ endif                                                                           │
  │ if VideoBtnTxt.value = "Rent Video" then  ; First video customer is renting     │
  │     VideoBtnTxt.value = "Add Video"       ;   for this transaction--if more     │
  │     Date_rented.moveTo()                  ;   than 1 video, the 'Add Video'     │
  │     uioInv.attach(INV)                    ;   label is more intuitive.          │
  │     uioInv.end()                     ; Go to end of list of invoices            │
  │     uioInv.insertAfterRecord()       ;   and make a new last record             │
  │     INV.Date_rented.value = today()     ; Automatically insert date             │
  │     INV.Time_rented.value = now.value   ;   and time rented                     │
  │     INV.action(dataPostRecord)                                                  │
  │     stock_no.moveTo()               ; Field in ITEMS tableframe                 │
  │ else                                ; currently adding videos                   │
  │     uioItem.attach(ITEMS)           ; Tableframe of videos rented this time     │
  │     uioItem.Stock_no.moveTo()       ; Move to first field in tableframe         │
  │     uioItem.insertAfterRecord()     ; Insert a new record                       │
  │ endif                                                                           │
  │ endmethod                                                                       │
  │                                                                                 │▼
  ├───────────────────────────────────────────────────────────────────────────────┤
  │ ◄ ►                                                                         ◄ ► │
  └────────────────────────────────────────────────┬─────────┬──────────┬──────────┘
                                                    │  Edit   │ Line: 8  │ Col: 80  │
                                          ┌─────────────────────────────┐
                                          │    RentVideoBtn [Button]     │
                                          └─────────────────────────────┘
```

Figure 17-10: The Rent Video button's *pushButton* method.

Line 8 determines whether the button's label is "Rent Video," and if it is, that means this is the first video to be added to a new invoice. Line 9 changes the button's label to "Add Video," indicating that the next time the button is pressed, it adds another record to the ITEMS table frame instead. Paradox moves to the Date rented field in the INV table frame (Figure 17-11), and lines 12 and 13 insert a new record as the last record in the table frame.

The INV table frame contains all data that is pertinent to videos rented by a customer at a given time. Furthermore, this is information that Paradox should be able to calculate more accurately and more easily than the clerk at the checkout counter. So the decision is made: let Paradox do the work. Line 14 fills in today's date. Notice that the containership path, *INV.Date_rented* is followed by the property *value*. Specifying the container avoids ambiguity if another Date rented field is added to the form. Date rented is set to today's date with the *today()* procedure.

Date rented	Time rented	Quantity	Total cost
6/12/94	9:48:29 PM	4	$9.00
6/19/94	3:56:01 PM	1	$2.00
7/13/94	10:19:39 AM	2	$4.00

Figure 17-11: Because we're talking about this table frame, here's a picture.

One would think that if there is a procedure that fills in the current date, there would also be one that fills in the current time. But no such luck. It is possible to assign the current time to a field, so a field that looks like a digital clock is placed on the form. The value from the field can then be placed in the Time_rented field in the INV table frame, and line 15 does exactly that.

Once today's date and time are entered into the INV table frame, the record is posted to the table INV.DB (line 16) and the focus moves to the Stock_no field (line 17). Now that we're in the ITEMS table frame, let's look at some of the code attached to its fields.

Methods for the Table Frame

Table frames don't have *pushButton* methods, but they do have many other events you can attach code to. You can arrive on a field, depart from a field, change the field's value—the list is long. We'll look at both the event model when working with fields and the methods used in this application.

The *arrive & depart* Methods

These are new methods, and judging by their names, their actions seem rather obvious. For example, when Paradox departs from a field, it normally arrives on the next field. But what happens if something prevents Paradox from arriving on the next field—say, because a validity check said "oops"? Well, Paradox would not leave the field because the *canDepart* method prevents it from doing so. The table below shows the methods that are triggered when moving to and from fields. The following methods execute when moving from one object to another:

canArrive	The *canArrive* method executes when Paradox tests whether it is OK to arrive on the object.
arrive	The *arrive* method executes when the object first becomes active.
setFocus	The *setFocus* method executes after the *arrive* method, and indicates that the object has focus and can receive input from the mouse or the keyboard.
removeFocus	The *removeFocus* method executes when focus has left an object and it can no longer receive input from the mouse or the keyboard.
canDepart	The *canDepart* method executes when Paradox tests if it can leave the object.
depart	The *depart* method executes when the object is no longer active.

That's a lot of methods, and the order in which they're executed is not intuitively obvious. The form METHOD.FSL (Figure 17-12) demonstrates the order in which all these methods are executed. Arriving on a field is simple enough: *canArrive* is triggered first, followed by *arrive*, and finally *setFocus* allows you to type into the field.

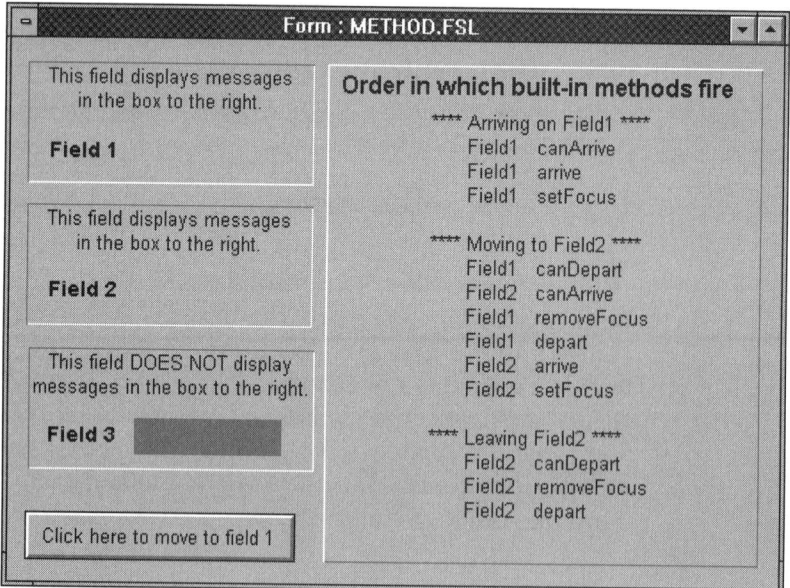

Figure 17-12: This form demonstrates what methods execute when moving from field to field.

However, when moving from one field to another, it gets a little more complicated. Here's what happens:

1. The *canDepart* method for field 1 (the field with focus) is executed. If it is OK to leave the field, then ...

2. The *canArrive* method for field 2 (the next field) is executed. If it's OK to arrive on field 2, then ...

3. The *removeFocus* method for field 1 is triggered.

4. The *depart* method for field 1 is triggered.

5. The *arrive* method for field 2 is triggered.

6. The *setFocus* method for field 2 is triggered.

In this scenario, notice that the *canArrive* method for field 2 executes before field 1 is left. It is easy to think of moving from one field to another as being really straightforward, but it's really a six-step procedure. And anywhere along the line, you can place code to override the default behavior of Paradox. Let's see how all this applies to the Video application.

Inside Scoop

The *setFocus* custom method (like all other methods) executes its code before performing the default behavior. To demonstrate this, look closely at the display in METHOD.FSL and you see that *setFocus* is printed in the box on the right *before* the field object becomes highlighted.

The Due date field has code attached to both the *arrive* and *depart* methods. The *arrive* method is simple. One day is the typical rental period for video tapes, so it displays a message in the status bar to press the Spacebar to insert tomorrow's date. If no date is typed into the Due date field, the *depart* method shown in Figure 17-13 fills in tomorrow's date.

```
RENTAL::Due_date::depart
method depart(var eventInfo MoveEvent)

    if self.value = "" then              ; If this field is blank
        self.value = Date_rented.value + 1  ;    insert tomorrow's date
    endif

endmethod

                                          Edit    Line: 4    Col: 71
```

Figure 17-13: The *depart* method fills in tomorrow's date as the due date for the video rentals.

509

This method uses a new identifier, *self*, which refers to the current object. Using *self* is often a good practice because if the name of an object changes, the code doesn't break. However, if the name of an object is explicitly used in a method and the object changes, the method would cause a syntax error because the reference would be to a nonexistent object.

After leaving the Due date field, Paradox arrives in the Due time field. This triggers the method shown in Figure 17-14, which inserts the time from the INV table frame into the Due time field. This makes sense because videos are rented for 24-hour time periods.

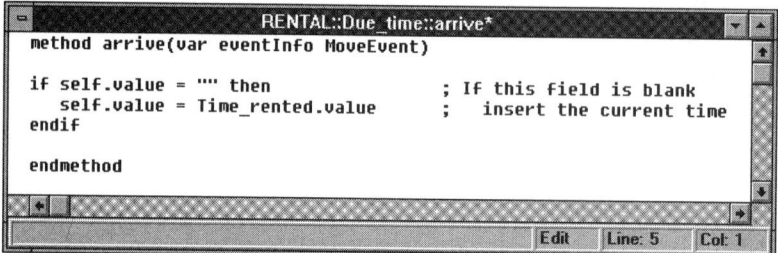

Figure 17-14: The *arrive* method inserts the time due automatically.

The Save Rental Button

Clicking on the Save Rental button is the final step in checking out videos to a customer. Like the other buttons, it ensures that Paradox is in Edit mode (see Figure 17-15). To close out this rental order, the number of videos rented is entered into the INV table frame (line 10). *nRecords()* is a method that counts the number of records in a table, but in this case, because it is counting records in a detail table, it counts only the records that are linked to the table's parent. In the Videos example, it counts those records that can be seen in the ITEMS table frame without changing records in the INV table frame. In Paradox terminology, it counts the records in the *restricted view*.

```
┌─────────────────────────────────────────────────────────────────┐
│ ▬          RENTAL::SaveRentalBtn::pushButton*              ▼ ▲    │
├─────────────────────────────────────────────────────────────────┤
│ method pushButton(var eventInfo Event)                         ▲ │
│ var                                                              │
│     uio        UIObject                                         │
│ endvar                                                          │
│                                                                 │
│ if not isEdit() then              ; If not in Edit mode         │
│    edit()                         ;   we gotta go there         │
│    editBtnTxt.value = "End Edit"  ;   and change the button's label │
│ endif                                                           │
│ uio.attach(ITEMS)                 ; Attach to the ITEMS tableframe │
│ Quantity.value = uio.nRecords()   ; Insert number of videos rented and │
│ Total_cost.value = InvAmount.value ;   total amount due in Quantity & │
│ endEdit()                         ;   Total_Cost field (INV tblframe) │
│ VideoBtnTxt.value = "Rent Video"  ; Reset the button's label    │
│ editBtnTxt.value = "Edit"                                       │
│                                                                 │
│ endmethod                                                     ▼ │
├─────────────────────────────────────────────────────────────────┤
│ ◄                                                             ► │
├─────────────────────────────────────────────┬──────┬────────┬──┤
│                                          Edit│Line: 2│ Col: 1 │  │
└─────────────────────────────────────────────────────────────────┘
```

Figure 17-15: Clicking on the Save Rental button totals the number of videos and sale amount and inserts the values in the INV table frame.

The dollar amount is inserted in the Total cost column in the INV table frame. InvAmount is a summary field just under the clock field that is hidden at run time. However, this hidden field can still be accessed using ObjectPAL. Its value is inserted in the table frame.

The final step is to leave Edit mode. At this point, all the data should be entered, with a little help from Paradox. Notice that all fields in the INV table frame were automatically filled in. The check-out clerk entered only the video's stock number and a date (if the videos were rented for more than one day). Pretty easy. But there are other things this application can do besides entering data. We'll look at them after creating a custom menu.

YOUR FIRST CUSTOM MENU

Custom drop-down menus created in Paradox look just like any other Windows menus. This is really cool because your applications look very professional. Admirers will call you asking for expert advice about Paradox. But let's get on with creating menus.

Every Windows application has a File menu, and every File menu has an Exit option. So you know you'll need a File menu—to exit the application.

Five reports are designed for this application, so a Report menu is a good idea also. Reports involve printing, so they could all be placed under the File menu. But what if you want to expand the report options? The File menu could become overburdened with reports.

A separate Report menu would do two things: provide a clearer indication of each menu's function, and allow for future expansion of the application.

The other common Windows menu is Help. It's beyond the scope of this chapter to provide context-sensitive help, but general information about filling out the form could be displayed. With these drop-down menus, the menu structure should look like Figure 17-16.

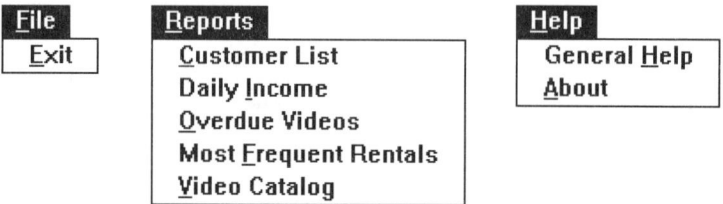

Figure 17-16: The menus for the Video Rental application look like this.

Programming the Menu

Now that the structure of the menu has been created, it's time to learn how to program it. First, the general ideas, and after that it's time to write code. The menu itself consists of two parts: the items in the menu bar (File, Report, and Help) and the choices for each menu. Paradox uses variables as handles to the menu items. The entire menu structure is referred to with the variable type *menu*. The list of items in each menu is referred to with the variable type *popUpMenu*. These are shown in Figure 17-17.

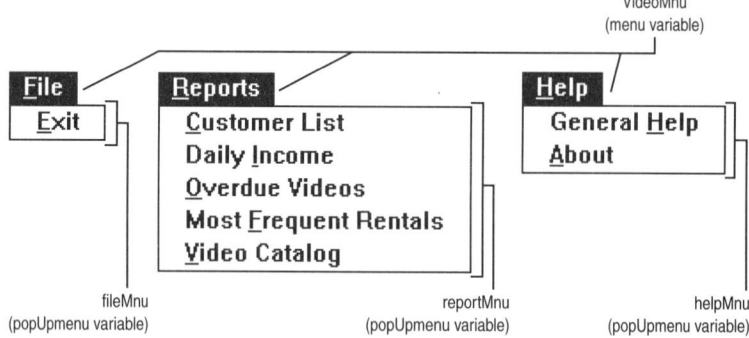

Figure 17-17: The entire menu is referred to with a *menu* variable. Each menu item plus its underlings are referred to with a *popUpMenu* variable.

Where is this menu defined? Normally, the menu is attached to one of two places—the *arrive* method of the form or the *arrive* method of the page. When the menu is attached to the form, the same menu is in effect for every page on the form. Obviously, this is a consideration only for forms that have more than one page, but it is important. You may run into circumstances where a multipage form needs a different menu for certain pages. In such an instance, the best place to attach the code for a menu would be on the page. That way, each page could have a different menu. In this application, it is uncertain whether other pages would be added at a later date, but because there is no foreseeable need for additional pages, the menu is attached to the page's *arrive* method. Typically, the menu is attached to the inner-most container, so it's best to use the page when possible–otherwise use the form.

When you click on a menu item in Paradox, the built-in method *menuAction* is triggered. In this case the menu is defined at the page, so the *menuAction* method for the page is triggered. (This is a simplification, but without getting into lots of detail, it is appropriate.) The *menuAction* event returns the text of a menu item that was selected, and an action is performed based on the selected menu item. So we have two places where ObjectPAL code for menus lives. Code in the *arrive* method of the page (or the form) displays the menu. Code in the *menuAction* method of the page (or the form) performs an action based on the selected menu item.

One really neat thing about menus, is that there is no programming involved with making the menus drop down or with making the items highlight as you scroll through the items in each menu. The default behavior of Paradox menus takes care of all that nit-picky stuff. All you need to do is tell Paradox what the menu should look like and what should happen when a menu item is selected.

Writing the Code

Now it's time to start writing code. First the code to define the menu, which is attached to the *arrive* method of the page. It looks like the screen shown in Figure 17-18:

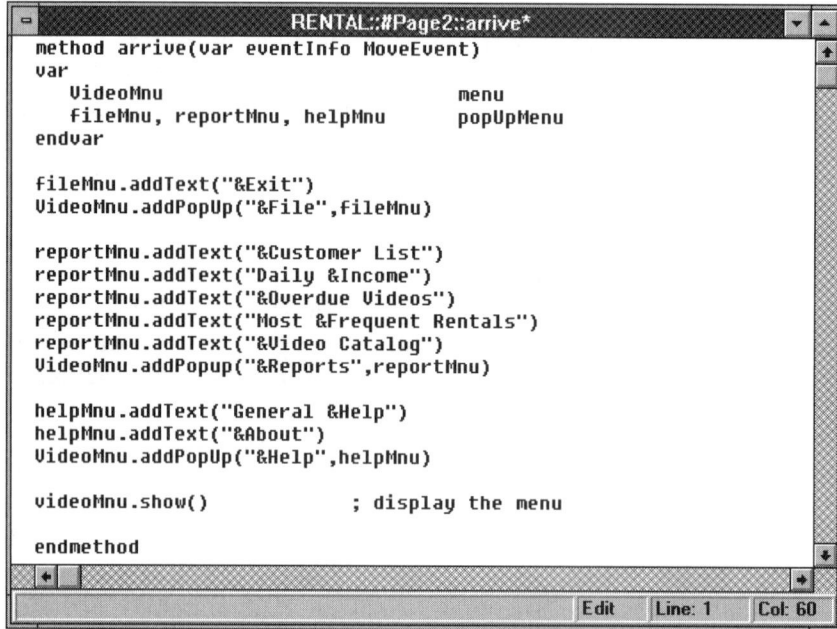

```
method arrive(var eventInfo MoveEvent)
var
    VideoMnu                        menu
    fileMnu, reportMnu, helpMnu     popUpMenu
endvar

fileMnu.addText("&Exit")
VideoMnu.addPopUp("&File",fileMnu)

reportMnu.addText("&Customer List")
reportMnu.addText("Daily &Income")
reportMnu.addText("&Overdue Videos")
reportMnu.addText("Most &Frequent Rentals")
reportMnu.addText("&Video Catalog")
VideoMnu.addPopup("&Reports",reportMnu)

helpMnu.addText("General &Help")
helpMnu.addText("&About")
VideoMnu.addPopUp("&Help",helpMnu)

videoMnu.show()                ; display the menu

endmethod
```

Figure 17-18: This code attached to the *arrive* method of the page creates and displays the menu.

Wow, that's a lot of code. But if you look closely, the lines are repetitive. So, what does this all do? The *var ... endVar* block declares the two variable types that were described in Figure 17-17 earlier. The *menu* variable is a handle to the entire menu (the menu bar); the *popUpMenu* variables are handles to each drop-down menu (they contain the items for each individual menu).

The bulk of the code adds text to the *popUpMenu* variable and when all menu items are added to the popUpMenu, that popUpMenu is added to the menu bar. The line *fileMnu.addText("&Exit")* adds the item Exit to the File drop-down menu (or pop-up menu, as the Paradox variable calls them). The ampersand tells Paradox to underline the following character and use it as a hot key. Line 7 associates the *fileMnu* variable with the word *File* in the menu bar. When the menu is displayed, the word *File* is displayed in the menu bar with Exit as the only option underneath it. Each menu has the same syntax—it's just that a different *popUpMenu* variable is used. Line 17 displays the menu.

Inside Scoop

If you want to add a horizontal separator line to a menu, use *addSeparator*. The syntax is *popUpMenuVar.addSeparator()*.

Run the form and see how this menu works. See, you have a fully functioning menu. The menus drop down, and you can scroll through the menu items and they become highlighted. The only problem is that none of the menu items do anything. More code is needed.

Now for the *menuAction* method. This is the real meat of the menu system. When a menu item is clicked on, *menuAction* needs to respond to the appropriate item. For example, if you click on the File menu and select Exit, *menuAction* needs to respond to the text string "Exit." (Actually, it needs to respond to the text string "&Exit" because that is the exact string specified in the *arrive* method.) Because there are gobs of menu items, using *if ... else ... endif* would be cumbersome. So you get to learn a new way of performing a similar function.

Enter the *switch ... endSwitch* command. This command is similar to *if ... endif*, but it's used when there are more than one or two choices. Why? Because that's what it was designed for. Any number of conditions can be tested, whereas if you use *if,* only one condition can be tested. Figure 17-19 shows the menu commands that actually tell Paradox to do something.

```
method menuAction(var eventInfo MenuEvent)
var
   mnuChoice    string
   f            form
   rpt          report
endvar
mnuChoice = eventInfo.menuChoice()
switch
   case mnuChoice = "&Exit" :                     close()
   case mnuChoice = "&Customer List" :            rpt.print("cust.rsl")
   case mnuChoice = "Daily &Income" :             rpt.print("income.rsl")
   case mnuChoice = "&Overdue Videos" :           rpt.print("overdu.rsl")
   case mnuChoice = "Most &Frequent Rentals" :    rpt.print("MFR.rsl")
   case mnuChoice = "&Video Catalog" :            rpt.print("Cat.rsl")
   case mnuChoice = "General &Help" :             f.open("Help.fsl")
   case mnuChoice = "&About" :                    f.open("About.fsl")
endswitch

endmethod
```

Figure 17-19: The *switch ... endSwitch* syntax is useful when more than one or two conditions exist.

Similar to *if ... endif*, the switch block begins with *switch* and ends with *endSwitch*. So far, only the words are different but the idea is the same in that the beginning and ending of the block need to be defined. The real meat of the *switch* block is the *case* statement. So let's take out our scalpels and dissect some of this syntax. Consider that the following two commands are identical:

```
case mnuChoice = "&Exit" : close()     if mnuChoice = "&Exit" then
                                           close()
                                       endif
```

The condition *mnuChoice = "&Exit"* is the same in both instances. So is the action *close( )*. The *case* keyword replaces the *if* keyword, and the colon replaces *then*. *Case* can have more than one command after the colon, just as there can be more than one statement between the keywords *if* and *endif*. So how does Paradox know when the list of commands ends? *endCase* causes a syntax error because it is not a Paradox keyword. The answer: the next occurrence of *case* or the end of the *switch ... endSwitch* block tells Paradox when to stop executing commands when a condition is true.

Understanding the syntax for a *switch ... endSwitch* block means you are ready to tell your custom menus to do something useful. After all, a menu that does nothing other than drop down is about as useless as a button that does nothing other than change its appearance when you click on it.

Printing the reports uses the same syntax you have seen before: *rpt* is a report variable that is a handle to the report, and *print* is a method that prints the named report. The Help menu opens two help forms—they display some text and have an OK button to close them. Again, this is something you have done before. The File menu has Exit as its only option, and this closes the form. In fact, there isn't really anything new in any of the things this menu can do—with the exception of the menu itself.

THE AVAILABLE VIDEOS FORM

The video rental store needs some way to update the list of videos available to rent. Figure 17-20 shows a form created exclusively for this purpose. It is a simple form compared to RENTAL.FSL. In fact, the only code attached to the form is on the Classification drop-down list. But it is really cool. The items that can be selected from the drop-down edit list are contained in a Paradox table. If the source table is changed, the choices in the drop-down list change also.

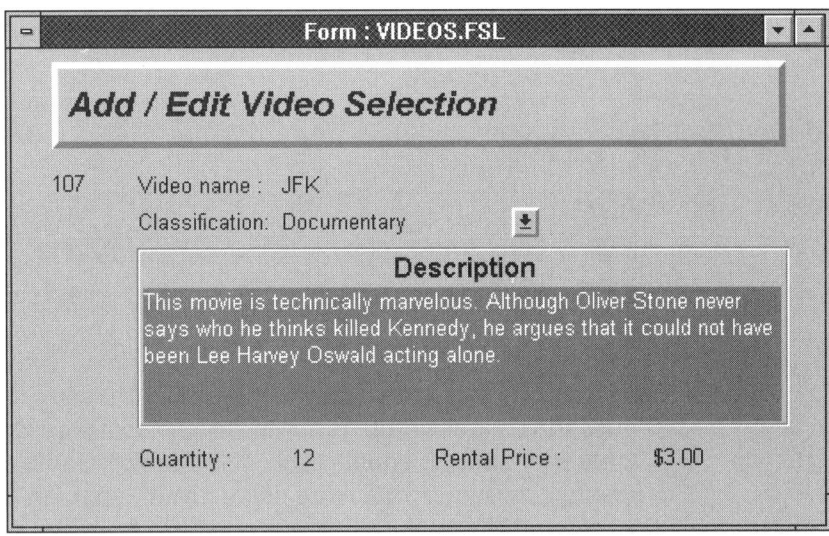

Figure 17-20: This form lets you make changes to VIDEOS.DB.

You have seen that fields are composed of more than one object unless their display type is Unlabeled. The drop-down edit list is no exception. As shown in Figure 17-21, it contains two objects: a field and a list. The field contains data selected from the drop-down list or data that was typed in from the keyboard. The list contains just that—a list.

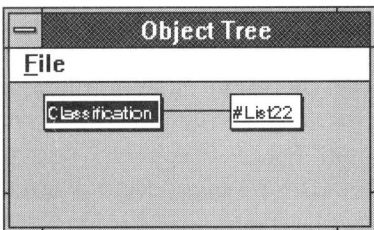

Figure 17-21: All drop-down edit lists are composed of two objects—a field and a list.

In Chapter 10, you saw how drop-down edit lists could be populated with values that you type in when designing the form. This example shows how the list can be populated from a Paradox table. It's really easy. One line of code does the trick—see Figure 17-22.

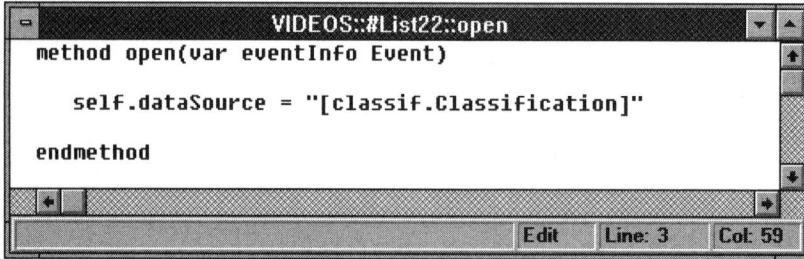

Figure 17-22: The drop-down edit list gets its data from the Classification field of CLASSIF.DB.

But why use a table instead of typing the data into the form? Good question. Using a table provides more flexibility and accuracy. If a table is created, it could be used as a lookup table for the field, which would prevent anyone from using a value that isn't in the list. The lookup table and the drop-down list are from the same source—if one changes, the other changes. Another reason is that you may want to add more video classifications in the future. If a table is used for the source data, it is easier to change. In fact, the next chapter shows you how to add a button to the form that will modify CLASSIF.DB, thereby changing the lookup table and drop-down edit list source data at once.

MOVING ON

You've learned a lot about events and methods. However, the Video application can be still be improved upon to make it even more useful.

The next chapter uses the same Video application, but adds a button to the Video form so that you can add a new video classification to the drop-down edit list. This is pretty neat because the button uses a *TCursor*, which writes to a table that is not attached to the form.

Several enhancements will be made to the Rental form as well. You will be able to search for customers by customer number, name, business name, ZIP Code and phone number. You will perform queries from ObjectPAL, and use the resulting Answer table for a report. But we'll start off learning about the *visible* property, which allows you to hide and display objects at will.

18 ADDING FANCY FEATURES

In Chapter 17, you created a useful application, and in this chapter it gets better and better. Four new features are added—one to the Video form and three to the Rental form. The videos form from Chapter 17 will soon have the ability to insert new video classifications in CLASSIF.DB. This feature uses the *visible* property of objects so they can be hidden and displayed at will. In addition to the *visible* property, error codes are used to prevent the user from moving off a field until it is OK to do so, and TCursors are used to manipulate a Paradox table without even displaying it.

In this chapter we add these three features to the Rental form:

Searching for customers: Searching for customers expands the use of the *visible* property and introduces methods similar to Locate.

Printing a receipt: When printing a receipt, Paradox prints a report for only the current customer. ObjectPAL queries come to the rescue.

Context-sensitive help: This is a really neat feature for the user, and surprisingly easy to implement. In this example, a table is created, listing every object on the form. When any object is right-clicked, a dialog box displays that object's H-help field from the table of all objects. We useTCursors once again.

THE VISIBLE PROPERTY

The *visible* property has two states—true and false. Objects are *visible*, or they are not. When designing a form, you can make any object invisible at run time by right-clicking on the object (in the Form Design window), selecting Run Time from the pop-up menu, and clicking on Visible, thus removing the check mark. You can also use ObjectPAL, which is what we do in this chapter.

Open VISIBL.FSL (Figure 18-1) to see a simple demonstration of the *visible* property. There are two objects on the form whose visible property changes: theEllipse and theBox. Initially, the form sets theEllipse to be invisible and theBox to be visible. This ensures that the appropriate object will be visible when the form is run. The button toggles the visible property of each object so that both objects are never seen at the same time. Whenever you use the visible property, code is attached to the form or the page's *open* (or *arrive*) method and to a button or whatever else controls the visible property.

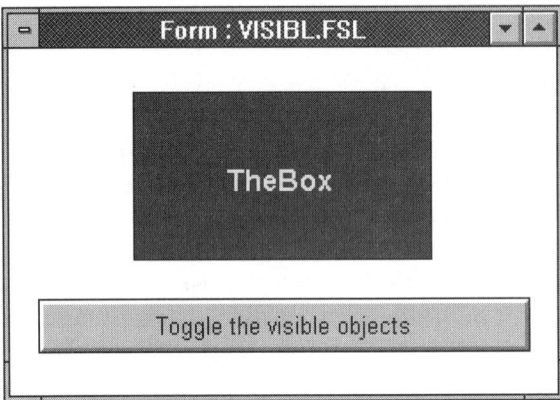

Figure 18-1: VISIBL.FSL in its initial state.

Let's look at the button's code (see Figure 18-2). The second line tests whether theBox is visible. If it is, the third line hides theBox and the fourth line makes theEllipse visible. If theBox is not visible, the reverse happens.

If many objects have their visible property changed, containership can tie all the objects together. In VISIBL.FSL, the visible property of each object changes simply because the visible property of its container is changed.

```
VISIBL.FSL::#Button5::pushButton*
method pushButton(var eventInfo Event)

    if theBox.visible = true then
        theBox.visible = false          ; make the box invisible
        theEllipse.visible = true       ; and the ellipse visible
    else
        theBox.visible = true           ; make the box visible &
        theEllipse.visible = false      ; the ellipse invisible
    endif

endmethod
```
Edit   Line: 7   Col: 67

Figure 18-2: This code changes the *visible* property of two objects on the form.

Figure 18-3 shows VISIBL.FSL in the Form Design window. Notice that there are lots of objects on top of one another. When objects will be piled on top of one another, it is a good idea to initially position them so they don't overlap. Be sure all ObjectPAL methods work properly before placing the objects in a position where they are obscured by other objects.

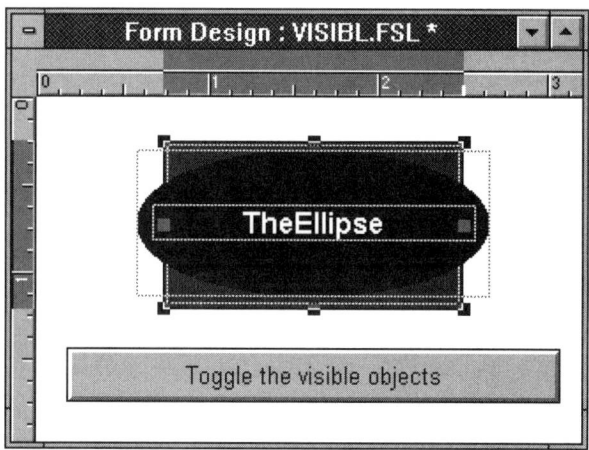

Figure 18-3: Objects placed on top of one another.

Inside Scoop

When you need to make changes to a form that has objects on top of one another, use the object tree to select objects. Using the object tree is often easier than selecting objects on the form. After an object is selected, you can easily change its properties, move the object, or use the Method Inspector to change its methods.

VISIBL.FSL is a simple example of the visible property. Using the *visible* property takes some getting used to, but it is really useful for several reasons: forms are less cluttered, only the appropriate objects are displayed at any given time, and users can be guided through multistep processes. Play with this sample form or create one of your own. Mastering the visible property will give your form's pizzazz.

EMBELLISHING THE VIDEO FORM

Looking at the completed VIDEO2.FSL form (Figure 18-4), the only addition from the last chapter appears to be an Add New Classification button. But there is a lot hiding on the form—quite literally—through extensive use of the visible property. This form also uses a new ObjectPAL concept—the TCursor, which is a pointer to a table that is not placed on the current form. It's really slick being able to manipulate tables behind the scenes, without the user even knowing that it's happening. This form will also show you more complex examples using techniques you have already learned.

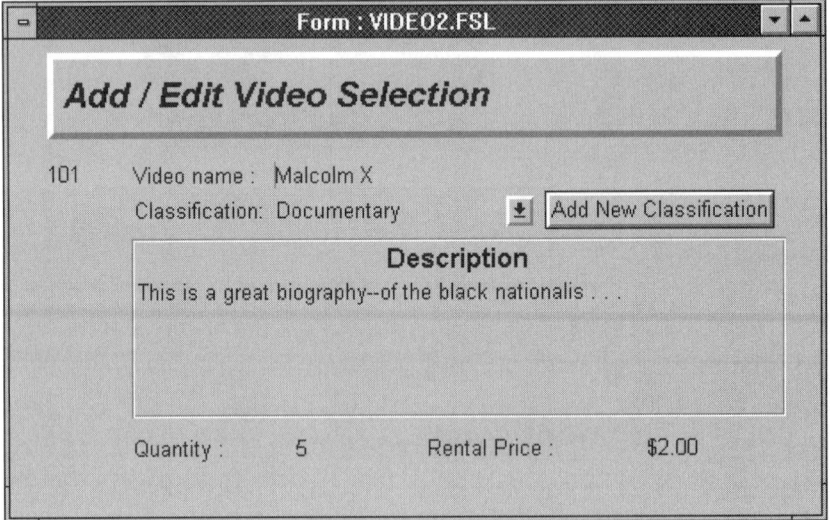

Figure 18-4: Many objects have been added to this form, but you can't see them because their *visible* property is set to false.

Using the Visible Property

Now that you are comfortable with the visible property, let's see how to use it along with some other really cool ObjectPAL stuff to improve the Video form. You can use the form from the last chapter if you want to add all your own code, or use VIDEO1.FSL, which has all the ObjectPAL code written (but objects still need to be moved to their final position). VIDEO2.FSL is a completed form with all objects in their correct positions; consequently, lots of objects are on top of each other and it's difficult to see what's there in the Form Design window.

For now, open VIDEO2.FSL in the Form window and add some video classifications to see how the form works. Notice that objects become visible, guiding you along the way. After you have used the form, you will have a better understanding of its ObjectPAL code. Then, in the Form Design window, open either the form from Chapter 17 or VIDEO1.FSL and use this form while working through this chapter.

The visible property of several objects can be changed simultaneously by drawing a box around all the objects. If you are starting with the form from Chapter 17, place a field object, a Save button and a Cancel button on the form and draw a box around them. Also place an Add New Classification button on the form and draw a box around it and the drop down edit list. Refer back to Figure 18-5 for the names of the objects.

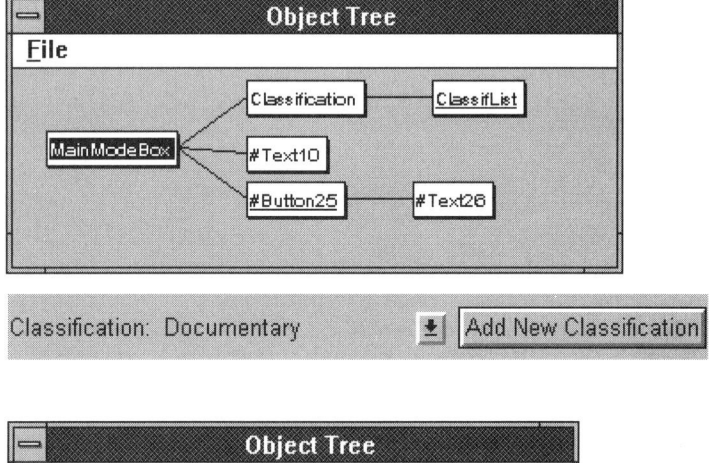

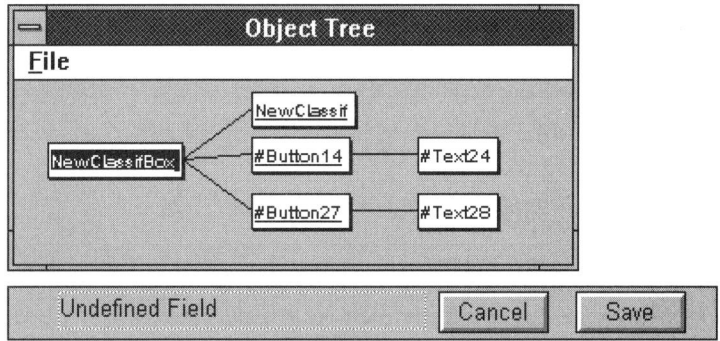

Figure 18-5: A frame is drawn around each object whose *visible* property changes.

Figure 18-5 shows the objects that are visible, depending on whether the Add New Classification button was pressed. Notice in the object trees that many objects have been renamed so they can be referenced easily from ObjectPAL. To make editing easier, objects are placed on the form so they are not overlapping other objects.

Inside Scoop

Paradox does not allow you to select or tab to objects that are not visible. Invisible objects can be controlled, but they must be controlled using ObjectPAL.

Now on to writing code for the VIDEO2.FSL form. The drop-down edit list and the Add New Classification button should be visible by default, so this status is enforced in the form's *open* method. Figure 18-6 shows the code that sets these defaults. It also shows that pressing the Add New Classification button reverses the state of the two boxes and moves to the NewClassif field object, enabling you to add a new classification.

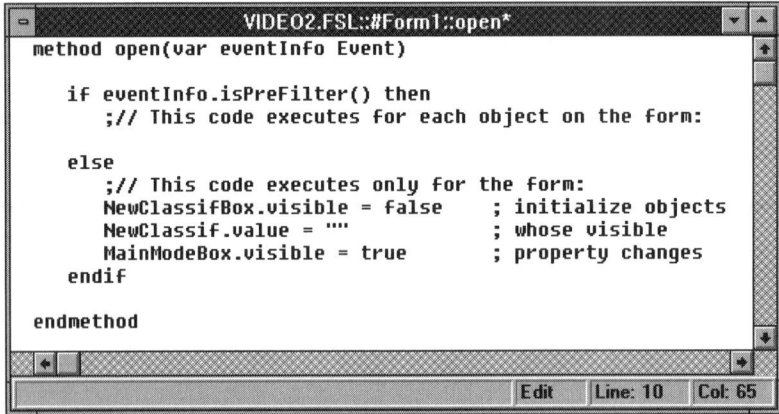

```
method open(var eventInfo Event)

    if eventInfo.isPreFilter() then
        ;// This code executes for each object on the form:

    else
        ;// This code executes only for the form:
        NewClassifBox.visible = false    ; initialize objects
        NewClassif.value = ""            ; whose visible
        MainModeBox.visible = true       ; property changes
    endif

endmethod
```

Figure 18-6: The form's *open* method sets the default *visible* properties. They are reversed by clicking the Add New Classification button.

Controlling User Action

The purpose of the Add New Classification button on the VIDEO2.FSL form is to enable the user to add a new category of videos by filling in data in the NewClassif field. When typing a new classification, the user shouldn't be allowed to do anything except type text in the NewClassif field, press the Cancel button or press the Save button. By modifying the *setFocus* and *canDepart* methods, you can prevent Paradox from leaving the NewClassif field.

The built-in method normally executes first, followed by the default behavior of the object. But in this example, the *setFocus* method for the NewClassif field (see Figure 18-7) first performs its default action. *doDefault* (in the second line) tells Paradox to perform the default behavior right now. Without *doDefault*, the message in the fifth line would be immediately erased by the default behavior of the field. Try commenting out *doDefault* and see what happens to the message. It flashes momentarily, then it's gone—replaced by the record count message from Paradox. The third line enters Field View so that a flashing insertion point is displayed, rather than highlighting the entire field.

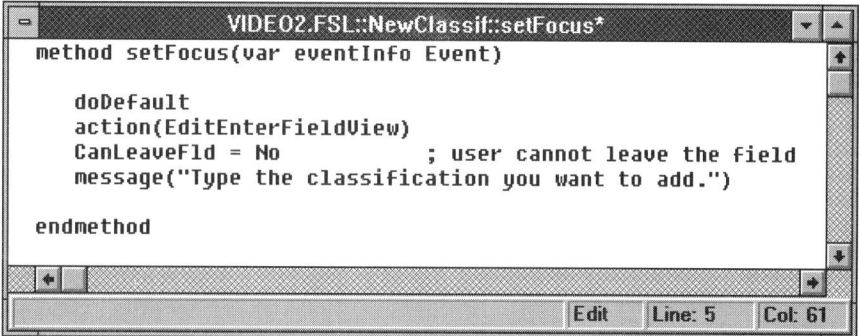

```
method setFocus(var eventInfo Event)

    doDefault
    action(EditEnterFieldView)
    CanLeaveFld = No               ; user cannot leave the field
    message("Type the classification you want to add.")

endmethod
```

Figure 18-7: The *setFocus* method of the NewClassif field, among other things, sets *CanLeaveFld* to No.

Inside Scoop

When moving to a field where data is entered, the user may expect to see an insertion point instead of the Paradox default behavior of selecting the entire field. To display the insertion point, enter Field View by adding *action(editEnterFieldView)* to the *setFocus* method.

But what we are really interested in is the fourth line in the *setFocus* method. *CanLeaveField* is a variable that was declared in the Var window of the box NewClassifBox, so all objects within the box have access to the variable. The field's *setFocus* method sets *CanLeaveField* to No, but alone this line does nothing. However, look at the *canDepart* method attached to this same field (Figure 18-8).

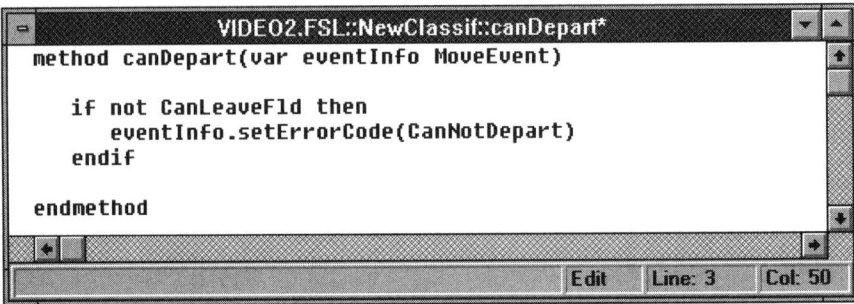

```
method canDepart(var eventInfo MoveEvent)

    if not CanLeaveFld then
        eventInfo.setErrorCode(CanNotDepart)
    endif

endmethod
```

Figure 18-8: The *canDepart* method of the NewClassif field tests the value of *CanLeaveFld* to see whether it can depart from the field.

eventInfo is something you've seen many times before. Just look at the first line of any method (something we have routinely ignored until now). Every event generates a packet of information about itself, and the default Paradox code uses *eventInfo* to store the packet. Line 1 of the *canDepart* method specifies that the type of event packet is a *moveEvent*. Various types of information are stored in the *moveEvent*, and they can be extracted or changed with a little help from ObjectPAL.

To find out what *eventInfo* stores, right-click in any editing window and select Types from the pop-up menu. The Types And Methods dialog box is displayed. Figure 18-9 shows the methods that are available for a *moveEvent*. All this information is included in the *moveEvent eventInfo* packet, and is accessible through ObjectPAL.

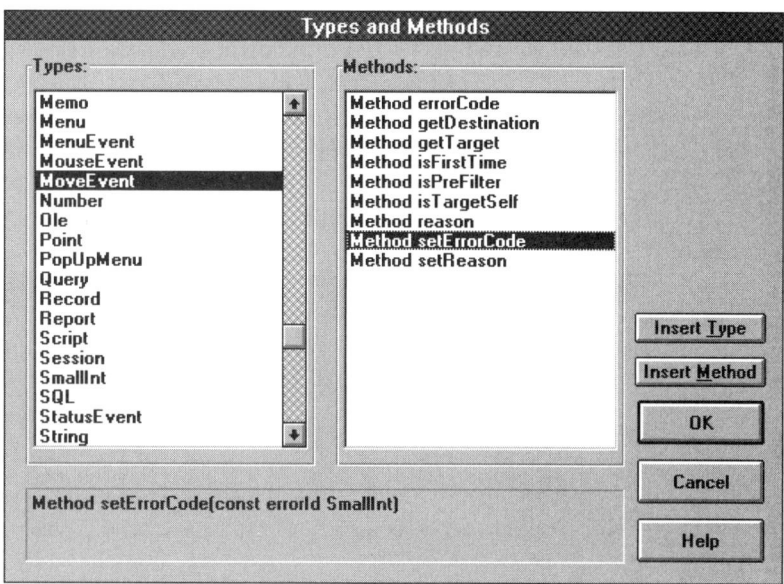

Figure 18-9: The Types And Methods dialog box displays methods that are available for all variable types and events.

The *canDepart* built-in method (shown in Figure 18-8) tests the value of *CanLeaveFld*. If *CanLeaveFld* has the value No, the *setErrorCode* method (that is included in the *eventInfo* packet) is set to *CanNotDepart*, preventing Paradox from leaving the field. This means that we must provide some way to set the value of *CanLeaveFld* to Yes, so that Paradox can leave the field. And we have done so. The Save and Cancel buttons on the VIDEO2.FSL form both have *pushButton* methods that among other things contain the code *CanLeaveFld = Yes*. This permits Paradox to perform one of its default behaviors—leave the field—but only after the user clicks either the Save button or the Cancel button..

Canceling an Action

In the VIDEO2.FSL form, when you press the Cancel button, a dialog box displays asking if you really want to cancel. In case you accidentally click the Cancel button, you won't lose any text you have typed. However, if you click the Cancel button without having first typed any text into the NewClassif field, there is no need for a confirmation dialog box because there is no data to lose. And no need for another one of those ubiquitous Windows dialog boxes. With this in mind, let's look at the code attached to the Cancel button in the VIDEO2.FSL form.

527

The fifth line in the *pushButton* method for the Cancel button (shown in Figure 18-10) determines whether the NewClassif field is blank. If the field is blank, NewClassifBox and MainModeBox are set to their default values—just as when you first opened this form. In addition, the *CanLeaveFld = Yes* line permits Paradox to leave the field. Without this line, you would have to press Ctrl+Break in order to leave the field, canceling the method in the process.

```
VIDEO2.FSL::#Button27::pushButton
method pushButton(var eventInfo Event)
var
   Response     String
endvar
if NewClassif.value = "" then          ; If nothing has been tyed
   NewClassifBox.visible = false       ;   hide box & its contents
   CanLeaveFld = Yes                   ; Enable leaving the field
   Video_name.moveTo()                 ; Move to the Video name field
   MainModeBox.visible = true          ; Make "classification" & its
   return                              ;   button visible then leave
endif
Response = msgQuestion("Confirm","Are you sure you want to quit adding to
if Response = "Yes" then
   NewClassifBox.visible = false       ; These are
   CanLeaveFld = Yes                   ;   the same
   Video_name.moveTo()                 ;   as above
   MainModeBox.visible = true          ;   except ...
   NewClassif.value = ""               ; Clear the value typed into field
   message = ""                        ; And clear the message
endif
endmethod
```
`Edit`   `Line: 12`   `Col: 94`

Figure 18-10: The Cancel button has lots of code, but most of it you have used before.

The tenth line (return) in the *pushButton* method is the last line to execute if the NewClassif field is blank. The *return* line simply means, "Stop executing this method and perform the default behavior of the object if that hasn't already been done." If return weren't there, the *pushButton* method would continue executing—which is not what we want.

However if the NewClassif field is not empty, the twelfth line displays a confirmation dialog box. If the user clicks the Yes button, the same steps occur that occur when the NewClassif field is empty. Notice that several lines of code are repeated. There is a way to eliminate this duplication (using procedures), but that will be covered in the next chapter.

Inside Scoop

Watch out for duplicate code. When code is in more than one location, debugging is more difficult and editing takes longer. But don't get paranoid about it. Eliminating redundancy is often not done until after the redundant code is written.

Using TCursors

The Save button in the example VIDEO2.FSL form writes the value of the NewClassif field to the Paradox table, CLASSIF.DB. This is a neat trick because the CLASSIF.DB table is not displayed on the form. The tool for accomplishing this trick is the *TCursor*, which is a pointer to a Paradox table. Using a TCursor, you can instruct Paradox to make practically any change to a table without ever displaying the table. The TCursor points to a table on disk rather than field or tableframe UIObjects. A TCursor is available only through ObjectPAL programming; TCursors are not available when using Paradox interactively. Let's look at the Save button's *pushButton* method to see how it uses a TCursor.

Before using a TCursor, a TCursor-type variable must be declared. In the *pushButton* method from the Save button, shown in Figure 8-11, *tc* is a handle to the TCursor. The seventh line (*tc.open("classif.db")*) opens the TCursor by associating it with a Paradox table, CLASSIF.DB. The eighth line places the TCursor in Edit mode, which is similar to placing a table in Edit mode by clicking on the Edit button, except that when using a TCursor, the table doesn't have to be in the form's data model. The ninth line (*tc.insertRecord()*) inserts a blank record in CLASSIF.DB, and the tenth line assigns the value in the NewClassif field on the form to the Classification field in the table CLASSIF.DB. Next, the record is posted, Edit mode ends, and the association between the TCursor and the Paradox table is discontinued.

```
━━━━━━━━━━━━━━━━━━━━━━━━━━━━━━━━━━━━━━━━━━━━━━━━━━━━
      Paradox for Windows - [VIDEO2.FSL::#Button14::pushButton]       ▼ ♦
 ▭  File  Edit  View  Search  Program  Properties  Tools  Window  Help    ♦
  method pushButton(var eventInfo Event)                               ▲
  var
      tc          TCursor
      msgClassif  String
  endvar

  if NewClassif.value <> "" then          ; If a new classification added
     tc.open("classif.db")                ; Open a TCursor to the table.
     tc.edit()        tc.insertRecord()   ; In edit mode, insert new record
     tc.Classification = NewClassif.value ; Classification fld in classif.db
     tc.postRecord()                      ;    is written to, record posted
     tc.endEdit()     tc.close()          ; Done editing, clean up
     msgClassif = NewClassif.value        ; Var containing new classificatio
     NewClassifBox.visible = false        ; Remove objects used for adding
     NewClassif.value = ""                ;    data & clear their values
     Video_name.moveTo()
     message(msgClassif + " was successfully added.")
     ClassifList.dataSource = "[classif.Classification]"
  else
     NewClassifBox.visible = false
     Video_name.moveTo()
  endif
  CanLeaveFld = Yes                       ; Allow leaving NewClassif field
  MainModeBox.visible = true              ; Original objects now visible
  endmethod                                                           ▼
  ◀                                                                   ▶
                                       Edit     Line: 13    Col: 74
                                      #Button14 [Button]
```

Figure 18-11: A TCursor is used to write to the table CLASSIF.DB behind the scenes.

Pitfall Ahead

It's important to close a TCursor when finished with it; otherwise an association will remain with that table. For example, if the line *tc.close()* were not included in the preceding example, you would be unable to restructure CLASSIF.DB because it could not be opened for exclusive use. This is especially important in a multiuser environment.

Try experimenting with TCursors. Here are some things you can do to see how TCursors work:

1. Open CLASSIF.DB in table view so that you can see it along with the form. Click the Add New Classification button and type something in the field, then click the Save button. Notice that the text you typed is placed in a new record in the table.

2. Click the Table View window. Click the Table menu and choose Restructure. Notice that you can restructure the table.

3. Edit the Save button's *pushButton* method and comment out the line, *tc.close()*. Click the Add New Classification button, type some text and click the Save button. Then try restructuring CLASSIF.DB. You get a message saying the table could not be opened for exclusive use. This demonstrates the importance of closing a TCursor when finished with it.

4. Edit the Save button's *pushButton* method and comment out the line, *tc.Classification = NewClassif.value*. Add a new classification and click the Save button. A blank record is inserted but nothing is entered into the field in the table. *tc.insertRecord()* inserted a blank record, but there is no longer a statement to fill that blank record with data.

Before you forget, be sure to remove any unwanted records from the table, and remove the semicolons from the lines in the Save button's *pushButton* method. It should be rather clear what a TCursor does. It is your friend. You'll find all sorts of uses for manipulating tables that are not associated with the active form.

Lines 14 through 18 in the Save button's *pushButton* method are similar to lines found in the Cancel button's *pushButton* method. The nineteenth line (*ClassifList.dataSource="[classif.Classification]"*) is new. It refreshes the list for the drop-down edit list's List object. Remember in Chapter 17 when the *open* event on the List object initialized the list? Well, the *open* event only occurs when the form opens, but we changed the underlying table and that needs to be reflected in the list. So line 19 does that. (The List object is referenced from ObjectPAL, so it has been given a name other than the default Paradox name.)

Using a TCursor to change a table is really a handy feature—in this case, both the field's lookup table and the drop-down edit list are updated simultaneously. Although new entries can be typed into the drop-down edit list, such a record could not be posted because CLASSIF.DB is a lookup table, and a validity check error would occur.

This VIDEO2.FSL form is now complete—let's move on to the rental form.

EMBELLISHING THE RENTAL FORM

By adding features to the rental form, we will review several concepts that we covered earlier in this chapter. In addition, we will explore several error-checking concepts. Keep an eye out for them. We will create a query interactively and paste the query into an ObjectPAL method. We'll also discuss a really cool way of implementing context-sensitive help. For now, let's add search capabilities to the main rental form.

Locating Records

There isn't much free space on the Rental form, so we need to create some space to place new fields and buttons for locating records. This can be done in a number of ways, including the following:

○ Rearrange, remove or reduce in size objects already on the form to create room for new objects;

○ Create a new form to contain the buttons and fields for finding a specific record;

○ Use the *visible* property.

Adding more objects to the form would make it really cluttered, and there are some tricks to using multiple forms. So we'll use the visible property to create a work area on top of the Comments field. A Find Customer button is all the user will normally see.

Two copies of the Video form are provided for use with this chapter. RENTL1.FSL has all the code written, but the objects are not all scrunched on top of each other. This way you can more easily get to the objects and their methods. RENTL2.FSL is the completed form. Both forms have all the code already written because there's a lot of it scattered all over. Use whichever form you want. This section shows you about locating records by pattern, shows another example of using *switch ... endSwitch*, and, of course, uses the visible property.

Working in a Confined Space

In our example rental form, RENTL1.FSL or RENTL2.FSL, clicking on the Find Customer button displays radio buttons showing which fields can be searched. After the user selects a radio button, the user clicks the OK button to display a field object in which to type the text string to be searched for. When searching a field other than the customer number, multiple matches could occur. How many people in the database might have "Smith" as their last name? Consequently, the form displays Find Previous and Find Next buttons. If the user clicks the Cancel button, the form removes all objects related to finding a record and redisplays the Comments field. Use RENTL2.FSL to see how it works. This is a really good demonstration of how space on a form can be maximized and superfluous objects can be eliminated—only those objects that are needed are displayed.

In the video form, discussed earlier in this chapter, we drew a box around several objects so we could change the visible property of these objects together. A different technique is used in the rental form. In the rental form, we first select objects that we want to treat as a group. Then click the Design menu and choose Group. Figure 18-12 shows the groups that are used for searching and the order in which they are displayed.

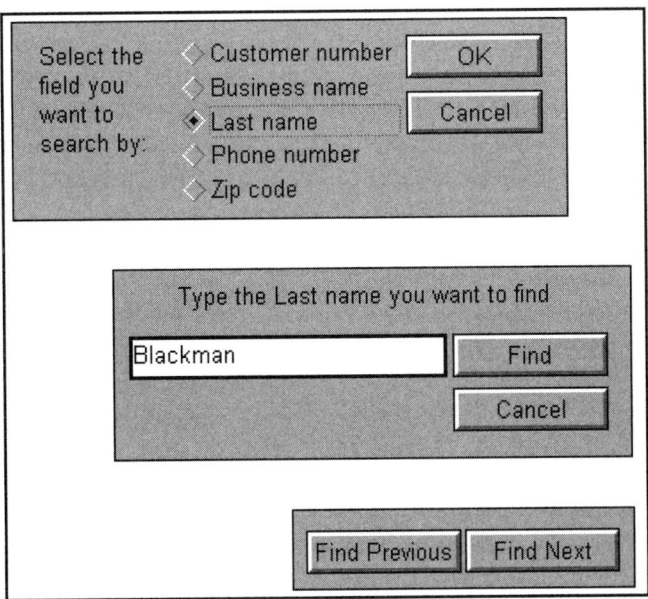

Figure 18-12: Selecting the field you want to search displays a text frame where you can type a search string. Find Previous and Find Next buttons are displayed when searching any field except Customer Number.

Clicking on the Find Customer button displays field selection radio buttons, an OK button and a Cancel button. Here's the code:

```
Comments.visible = false      ; Hide Comments field
SrchRb.value = ""             ; Clear value from Radio Btn
SelectSrchFld.visible = true  ; Radio button group
```

Notice from the code fragment above that the radio button field is cleared. The user is forced to make a selection because of the code attached to the OK button (Figure 18-13). After the user selects a radio button, clicking on the OK button hides the SelectSrchFld group, and displays a text box where the user can type a search string. However, if the user doesn't select a radio button, a dialog box informs the user that he must first select a radio button.

```
┌─────────────────────────────────────────────────────────────┐
│ □        RENTL1.FSL::#Button108::pushButton*          ▼ ▲    │
│ method pushButton(var eventInfo Event)                      ▲│
│ if SrchRB.value = "" then                                    │
│   msgInfo("Oops","You must select a radio button before proceeding")│
│ else                                                         │
│   SelectSrchFld.visible = false ; Hide radio button group    │
│   SrchByMsg = "Type the " + SrchRB + " you want to find"     │
│   FindBtnTxt.value = "Find"  ; Initialize text on Find button│
│   SrchString.value = ""       ; Clear the field              │
│   FindControl.visible = true ; Field, text, OK btn, Cancel btn│
│   SrchString.moveTo()         ; Field to type search string  │
│ endif                                                        │
│ endmethod                                                    ▼│
│ ◄                                                          ► │
│                                    │Edit   │Line: 3 │Col: 76│ │
└─────────────────────────────────────────────────────────────┘
```

Figure 18-13: *pushButton* method code attached to the OK button. If a radio button is selected, the form displays a text box in which the user can type a search string.

Notice that lines 7 and 8 initialize the text on the Find button and clear the SrchString field before they are displayed. This reduces screen redraws, making the application look cleaner. Note also that the *setFocus* and *canDepart* methods of the field object contain similar code to that of the NewClassif field on the Videos form so the focus cannot leave the field unless the Find or Cancel buttons are pressed.

Locating the Record

So far, we have discussed cosmetics and how to accept user input into the rental form. But we haven't yet dicussed how the form locates records. When you click the Find button, Paradox goes to work locating a record. The Find button needs a little explanation because it's capable of three different actions.

○ It can locate an account by customer number.

○ It can locate an account by a field other than customer number; if successful, it display Locate Next and Locate Previous buttons and changes the button's label to "Found It!"

○ While the button label is "Found It!" clicking on the button hide the fields and buttons associated with locating an account.

With all these possibilities, there's a lot of code; so let's proceed methodically and it'll all make sense.

The Find button can have either of two values: "Find" or "Found It!" The first line of code shown in Figure 18-14 tests whether the button's text is "Find," which would signify that this is the first time the button has been clicked on. (In the numbered list above, it could be either 1 or 2.) If the button's label is "Find," execution continues with the *switch ... endSwitch* block. When searching by customer number, Locate Next and Locate Previous aren't relevant, and the field type is AutoIncrement (which is equivalent to a *longInt* variable type). Searching through all other fields requires different code because Locate Next and Locate Previous *are* valid options, and the field type is string.

```
Paradox for Windows - [RENTL1.FSL::FindBtn::pushButton]
 File   Edit   View   Search   Program   Properties   Tools   Window   Help
If FindBtnTxt.value = "Find" then
   switch
      case SrchRB.value = "Customer number" :
         try FindNum = SrchString.value
         onFail  MsgInfo("Error","You must type a number.  Please try again")
                 return
         endTry
         if Customer_no.locate("Customer no",FindNum) then
            FindControl.visible = false   ; Hide field, text, 2 btns
            PrevNextBtn.visible = false    ; Hide 2 more buttons
            Comments.visible = true
            CanLeaveFld = Yes              ; So setErrorCode not set
            Business_name.moveTo()
         else
            MsgInfo("Find Account","No matches were found")
         endif
      case SrchRB.value = "Business name" :
         ignoreCaseInLocate()
         FindString = ".." + SrchString.value + ".."
         if Business_name.locatePattern("Business name",FindString) then
            FindBtnTxt.value = "Found It !"
            PrevNextBtn.visible = true
         else
            MsgInfo("Find Account","No matches were found")
         endif
```
```
                                                     Edit   Line: 1    Col: 1
                                           FindBtn [Button]
```

Figure 18-14: Some of the code associated with the Find button.

If searching for a customer number, the fourth line in Figure 18-4 (the ninth line in the Find button's *pushButton* method) tries to assign the variable *FindNum* to the value in the SrchString field. It may succeed, but only if the value typed in the SrchString field is an integer. If you display the Find button's *pushButton* method, you'll notice that *FindNum* was declared to be a *longInt*. If the value in SrchString isn't a legal value for a *longInt* variable, an error occurs. If Paradox is unable to successfully execute line 4, line 5 displays a warning dialog box. The sixth line, *return*, tells Paradox to stop executing this method. If the SrchString value is successfully stored in the variable *FindNum*, execution of the method continues.

The *locate* method in the eighth line in Figure 18-14 is used here as a condition for an *if* statement. *locate* returns a true or false value depending on whether Paradox was able to successfully locate the specified record. In fact, most Paradox methods return true or false values, enabling you to check for errors. In this example, if the customer number is found, Paradox hides all fields and buttons associated with finding an account and makes the Comments field visible. Focus then moves to the Business name field. If the customer number was not found, a *msgInfo* dialog box displays.

Inside Scoop

When run-time errors occur in ObjectPAL, the error dialog box often doesn't provide enough information to locate the error. To display more detailed error messages, before running the form, click the Properties menu and select Compile with Debug.

In this example, the code for finding a string in the Business name field is similar to the code for searching last name, phone number, and ZIP Code. Only the field name in the *locate* method changes.

Inside Scoop

Be sure to copy code whenever possible in order to reduce errors. It is often best to copy existing code even though it may seem to take longer because if you make a typo it can take a *long* time to find it.

The *locatePattern* method is used so that misspellings are less likely to cause an existing record to be unretrievable. Also, the user doesn't have to enter the entire field—just enough to whittle down the matching records to a handful. Then the user can move back and forth through all matching records until the correct one is located. Line 19 in Figure 18-14 adds the wildcard character ".." to the beginning and end of the search string, and line 20 tries to locate the record. When searching for the business name field, if the record is located, the Find button's label changes to "Found It!" and Find Previous and Find Next buttons are displayed. As was the case when finding records by customer number, a dialog box displays if no match is found.

Similar code is included in the *pushButton* method of both the Find Previous and Find Next buttons. A code fragment from the Find Previous button's *pushButton* method is shown below:

```
case SrchTxt = "Business name" :
    FindString = ".." + SrchString.value + ".."
    if not Business_name.locatePriorPattern("Business
name",FindString) then
        msgInfo("Find Account","No previous matches were found")
    endif
```

The Find Next button uses the *locateNextPattern* method instead of the *locatePriorPattern* method.. Also, the text in the msgInfo dialog box is changed to say "No more matches were found."

The example *pushButton* methods use many lines of code just to find a particular record. Much of it is repetitive, so we want to take a closer look to see what can be eliminated. As it turns out, the amount of code can be greatly reduced without altering functionality, but that will have to wait until Chapter 19.

Error-Checking Recap

The rental form we have been discussing demonstrates that you can work with many objects on a Paradox for Windows form in a confined space. This form also demonstrates a few important error-checking techniques. Error-checking is important in any computer application, so here's a quick recap:

○ When the user clicks the OK button, the button's *pushButton* method verifies that a search field radio button has been selected. If the user has not selected a search field, Paradox can't perform a search.

○ The *setFocus* and *canDepart* methods, attached to the SrchString field, work together using *eventInfo.setErrorCode(CanNotDepart)*, to prevent the user from leaving the field. Either the Find or the OK button must be pressed in order to leave the field.

○ The *try ... endTry* block of code in the Find button's *pushButton* method tests whether an integer value is typed in the SrchString field before searching through the customer number field. A dialog box displays an error if a noninteger value is typed.

All locate methods *(locate, locatePattern, locatePriorPattern,* and *locateNextPattern)* return a logical value indicating whether a record is successfully located. If Paradox is unable to locate a record, a msgInfo dialog box displays.

OBJECTPAL QUERIES

All the fancy new features in the rental form that we have been discussing don't help the video store's customer much. We have, therefore, implemented a feature that prints a receipt for the customer showing the videos rented. We've placed the code that prints receipts in the Save Rental button's *pushButton* method because we are presuming that only customers who rent videos want a receipt. A msgQuestion dialog box asks whether to print a receipt. If the user clicks the Yes button, a receipt is printed.

Printing a receipt involves printing the current record from CUST.DB, the current record from INV.DB and all linked records in ITEMS.DB. To extract the current records, we need to instruct Paradox to perform a query. In Chapter 8 you created queries with joined tables, and entered criteria into the query image. But now we want Paradox to perform queries using ObjectPAL.

Here are three ways to perform queries with ObjectPAL.

○ *Use a query file:* Any query that you create interactively and save to disk can be used in an ObjectPAL method. The *executeQBEFile* method requires only one argument—the name of the query file that is saved to disk. By default, an Answer table is created unless the optional parameter, Answer table name, is used.

○ *Use a query statement:* Queries can be placed in any method. The easiest way to create a query statement is to develop the query interactively and then paste it into a method (query files are ASCII files). You can use variables in a query statement by preceding the variable with a tilde (~). Using variables in a query statement provides more flexibility than just using a query file.

○ *Using a query string:* Like query files, query strings are placed in methods and can contain variables. However, query strings are more complex than query files. Query strings are created by concatenating strings to form a text string that, when evaluated, looks like a query statement. Query strings can be changed in more ways than just using tilde variables.

To create a receipt in the rental form, we decided to use a query statement because only the customer number and invoice number change from query to query. The query includes tilde variables in the customer number and invoice number fields. The rest of the query is the same. In general, use the simplest type of query that will perform all the functions you require.

Pitfall Ahead

When printing a report that is based on the Answer table, the report requires that the correct Answer table exists. If there is no Answer table (or the wrong one is found), opening the report will cause an error.

To create a query statement, the first step is to create a query interactively (the example query has been saved to disk as INV.QBE). The CUST.DB, INV.DB, ITEMS.DB and VIDEOS.DB tables are used in this query. It is a good idea to try the query and see if the resulting Answer table is what you expect. The query in Figure 18-15 shows that test values are entered in the invoice number fields. Another reason for typing a criterion into the query image is that it becomes a place-holder indicating where tilde variables will be placed.

When the query works properly, save it to a file. After you save the query file, you can edit a method and insert this query by choosing Paste From File from the Edit menu.

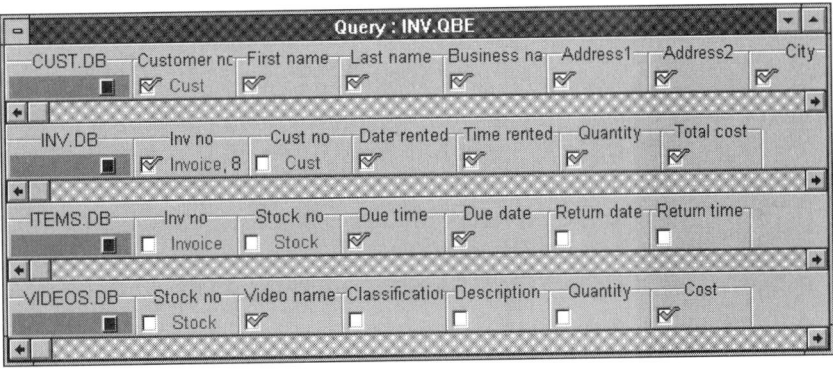

Figure 18-15: This query was created interactively and saved to disk, creating an ASCII file.

Now that you know how the query statement is created, let's look at the *pushButton* method for the Save Rental button (Figure 18-16) on the rental form. In lines 2 through 4 of the method, a variable of type Query is declared; this variable is a handle to the query. The second line shown in Figure 18-16 associates the variable *q* with the query. Notice that example elements are preceded with an under-score character, and that the blank lines are necessary. Remember, the blank lines in the query are necessary, and so are the lines after the *q = Query* line and before *EndQuery*.

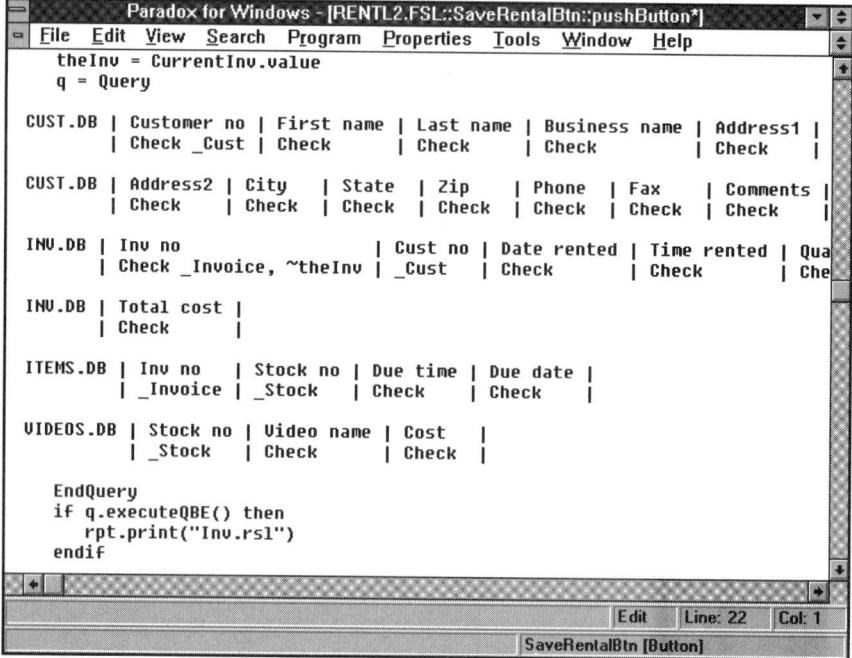

```
theInv = CurrentInv.value
q = Query

CUST.DB | Customer no | First name | Last name | Business name | Address1 |
        | Check _Cust | Check      | Check     | Check         | Check    |

CUST.DB | Address2 | City  | State | Zip   | Phone | Fax   | Comments |
        | Check    | Check | Check | Check | Check | Check | Check    |

INV.DB | Inv no                  | Cust no | Date rented | Time rented | Qua
       | Check _Invoice, ~theInv | _Cust   | Check       | Check       | Che

INV.DB | Total cost |
       | Check      |

ITEMS.DB | Inv no    | Stock no | Due time | Due date |
         | _Invoice  | _Stock   | Check    | Check    |

VIDEOS.DB | Stock no | Video name | Cost  |
          | _Stock   | Check      | Check |

    EndQuery
    if q.executeQBE() then
       rpt.print("Inv.rsl")
    endif
```

Figure 18-16: The code to execute a query was created interactively and pasted into this method.

The executeQBE line is the command that does all the work. It performs the query that is defined between *q = Query* and *EndQuery*. After the answer table is created, the *rpt.print("Inv.rs1")* command prints a report based on ANSWER.DB, using the INV.RS1 report on disk.

CONTEXT-SENSITIVE HELP

The help windows displayed by the Help menu in Chapter 17 were very simplistic. Furthermore, broad based-help is difficult to use because there is more information presented than the user may want. Context-sensitive help is a wonderful feature, and it's quite easy to implement. In the sample video store application, for example, right-click any object, in the Form window, to display a dialog box showing help for that object.

One way to provide context-sensitive help is to attach code to the *rightMouseUp* method. But then we'd have to edit the *rightMouseUp* method of every object on the form—and that's a lot of work.

The easiest way to provide context-sensitive help is to create a Paradox table with two fields—one for the name of each object on the form and another for the help text. Placing all the help text in one table makes it easier to maintain than if the help text were attached to every object. There are other benefits to this method, as you will soon see.

Enum ...

You might think its a lot of work to create a table with a record for every object. Fortunately, Paradox provides several methods that create tables with information about the current form. *enumUIObjectNames* creates a Paradox table with a record for each UIObject on the form. The first field is the object name; the second field is the object class— text, button, box, and so on. In our context-sensitive help scheme, the first field is what we really care about—the object name. To create a table with the name of every object on a form, follow these steps:

1. Open a form in the Form Design window.
2. Place a button on the form and change its label to "Enum."
3. Right-click the button and choose methods from the pop-up menu.
4. Double-click *pushButton* in the Method Inspector.
5. Look at the Project Viewer to verify that there isn't already a table called ENUMTBL.DB. If there is, in the next step, use a table name that doesn't exist.
6. Type the following text into the ObjectPAL Editor window:
   enumUIObjectNames("enumtbl.db")
7. Close the Editor window by double-clicking on its control menu or by pressing Ctrl+F4.
8. Run the form and click the Enum button.
9. Open the table ENUMTBL.DB to see a list of all objects on the form.

Pitfall Ahead

enumUIObjectNames writes to the specified table and, if the table already exists, overwrites it without asking for confirmation. The same is true of all the *enum* methods.

One potential problem with object-based programming is trying to keep track of code that is scattered about in many different objects. Also, there are often more objects to deal with than you can reasonably track. Because of this, the following *enum* methods help you keep track of the code and objects on each form. The following table lists all the *enum* methods:

Method	Fields in destination table	Function
enumSource	Object, MethodName, Source	Creates a table of source code for the methods for every object on a form.
enumSourceToFile	Destination is an ASCII file.	Creates an ASCII file listing the methods for each object on a form. This is similar to *enumSource* except that the destination is an ASCII file.
enumTableLinks	Name, Link, LinkType	Creates a table listing all tables linked to a form.
enumUIObjectNames	ObjectName, ObjectClass	Creates a table listing all UIObjects on a form.
enumUIObjectProperties	ObjectName, PropertyName, PropertyType, PropertyValue	Creates a table listing the properties of every UIObject on a form.

Before we can use the table created by the enumUIObjectNames command as a repository for help information, the table must be restructured. The ObjectClass field, which will contain the help information, needs to be larger. You could use a memo field or a formatted memo field to contain the help information. In the video store example help file, HELP.DB, an alphanumeric field with a length of 255 characters is used because the help text is displayed in a msgInfo dialog box.

HELP.DB contains several records that should contain the same help text. For example, HELP.DB contains a record for each button on the rental form as well as a record for each button's label. The help dialog box should display the same text whether a button or its label is clicked. The Help table is HELP.DB on disk; it has been edited so it contains help for every object.

Displaying a Help Dialog Box

Any time an event occurs to a UIObject, that event is first passed to the form. Typically, when code is placed in any of the form's methods, it is placed in the *else* clause of *eventInfo.isPreFilter,* causing the code to execute only for the form. (See "Opening a Form" in Chapter 17 for a review of events and the function of *eventInfo.isPreFilter*.) However, we want to be sure that right-clicks for every object on the form execute the same method; therefore, this time, code is placed in the *if* clause. Figure 18-17 shows the code that displays context-sensitive help.

```
Paradox for Windows - [RENTL2.FSL::#Form1::mouseRightUp*]
File   Edit   View   Search   Program   Properties   Tools   Window   Help
method mouseRightUp(var eventInfo MouseEvent)
var
   tc                     TCursor
   uio                    UIObject
   ObjectName, HelpMsg    string
endvar
disableDefault
if eventInfo.isPreFilter() then
   ;// This code executes for each object on the form:
   eventInfo.getTarget(uio)                  ; associate uio w/clicked object
   ObjectName = ".."+uio.name+".."           ; variable = "..uio.."
   message("Object name:   " + ObjectName)   ; Display message with object name
   if tc.open("Help.db") then                ; table containing all objects
      if tc.locatePattern("ObjectName",ObjectName) then
         HelpMsg = tc."ObjectClass"          ; Abbreviated help message
         msginfo("Help",HelpMsg)
      else
         msginfo("Help","No help available for that object")
      endif
   else
      msginfo("Error","Unable to open TCursor for Help.db")
   endif
else
   ;// This code executes only for the form:
endif
```
```
                                              Edit   Line: 15   Col: 67
                                              SaveRentalBtn [Button]
```

Figure 18-17: The form's *mouseRightUp* method displays help for any object that receives a right-click.

The *eventInfo* packet that is passed to the form's ***mouseRightUp*** method contains information as to the object where the event occurred–the target of the event. The target is always a UIObject, so a handle to the UIObject is used as the argument for *eventInfo.getTarget*. Line 10 then assigns the name of the target UIObject to a variable.

The table that was created using *enumUIObjectNames,* HELP.DB in our sample application, contains the complete containership path of each object. But the *getTarget* method returns the name of the object without any containership path. So there's no way to find the record in the Paradox table using *locate. locatePattern* allows you to find the object's name in the table. If line 11 locates a record in the

Paradox table that contains the variable, *HelpMsg* is assigned to the value contained in the ObjectClass field. The text in the variable is displayed in a msgInfo dialog box.

FINISHING UP

We're nearly finished with this application, but there are a few finishing touches to add. The rental form now enables the user to locate records, so the locate buttons on the Toolbar are no longer necessary. In fact, we could hide the entire Toolbar if we didn't still have a need for the Record Movement buttons. You could grab the Record Movement buttons from one of the forms in earlier chapters and paste them on RENTAL.FSL. Alternatively, you may have already designed a form that contains record movement objects that you can copy to the rental form.. For your convenience, I've included on the companion disk a form named COOL.FSL that contains record movement buttons as well as other useful objects.

The final thing to do is hide the Toolbar when the form opens. Consequently, the *open* method of the example rental form includes the *hideToolBar()* procedure. This procedure causes Paradox to hide the Toolbar until a command is issued to display the Toolbar again. A hidden Toolbar can be inconvenient to the user if the user needs to get into the Form Design window and make some changes to the form, or wants to open another form to do something else. So, we have added *showToolBar()* to the *close* method of the form. That way, the Toolbar is hidden only when the Rental form is open.

Inside Scoop

Any time the Toolbar is hidden, you can display it interactively by clicking the Properties menu and choosing Desktop. When the Desktop Properties dialog box displays, click the OK button. The Toolbar is displayed.

MOVING ON

That's all the new features for now. Chapter 19 will demonstrate more new programming concepts. For example, you'll learn how to add to the VIDEOS.FSL form the capability to add new records to the form's lookup table and drop-down list.

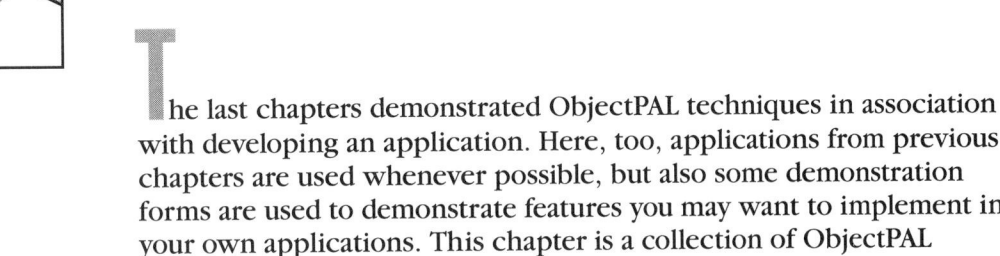

ADVANCED OBJECTPAL CONCEPTS

The last chapters demonstrated ObjectPAL techniques in association with developing an application. Here, too, applications from previous chapters are used whenever possible, but also some demonstration forms are used to demonstrate features you may want to implement in your own applications. This chapter is a collection of ObjectPAL concepts and techniques that either didn't fit in the prior chapters or were too complex at the time.

We'll focus on the following topics:

Procedures: Code that multiple ObjectPAL methods can call by name, reducing redundancy when many objects on a form perform the same action.

Libraries: A storage place for code fragments that can be called from more than one form. Libraries can also pass variables from one form to another.

Scripts: Scripts are like stand-alone custom methods. Scripts are not associated with a form but can be played at any time by simply selecting them from the Project Viewer or by calling them from a custom method.

Synchronization of records on two forms: You may run into circumstances in a multiform application where two forms display the same record.

USING PROCEDURES TO ELIMINATE REDUNDANT CODE

Paradox can use two types of procedures—those included in the ObjectPAL *run-time library* and custom procedures that you create on your own. You have already used procedures included in ObjectPAL's run-time library (RTL), probably without even knowing it. *msgInfo("Proc", "This is a procedure")* is a procedure. So is *close( )*. What do these two have in common? Neither procedure refers to a specific object. The close( ) procedure implies the current form, but the form is not specified because no dot notation is used. As a general rule, methods use dot notation; procedures do not.

Procedures in the Paradox run-time library are written by the folks at Borland, built into Paradox and can be called from any method. You can look up usage and syntax in Paradox's online help.

Each custom procedure is a block of ObjectPAL code that you write to perform a specific purpose. Custom procedures can be called by name just like the RTL procedures.

Procedures are great tools when the same code would otherwise appear in more than one method or in more than one place in the same method. One focus of good programming is to eliminate redundant code, and procedures help you achieve that goal. The trouble with duplicate code becomes apparent when you try to debug your code or add new features. If you want to add a new feature (say a message in the status bar), you may have to find every occurrence of the code that you want to modify and add the message to many different methods. However, if each of the methods calls the same procedure, the code needs to be modified only once—in the procedure itself. After you edit the message displayed by the procedure, any method calling the procedure displays the new message.

A procedure can be named anything you want as long as it conforms to the Paradox naming conventions described in Chapter 16. This means that something as simple as a descriptive name like *GetNextCustRecord( )* can be used, instead of several lines of code, to call a procedure.

Creating a Custom Procedure

Declaring a procedure is similar to declaring a variable. Variables can be declared in a method. So can procedures. Variables can also be declared in an object's Var window, whereas procedures can be declared in an object's Editor window.

Procedures follow the same scoping rules as variables:

○ Procedures declared in a method are accessible only to that method.

○ Procedures declared in an object's Editor window are accessible to all of that object's methods and to all methods of objects that the declaring object contains.

○ Procedures declared in the form's Editor window are accessible to every method of every object on the form.

Pitfall Ahead

Be careful where you declare procedures. Custom methods can be called from objects outside the containership of the object where the method is attached. Procedures cannot because they don't use dot notation.

The sample form SOUND.FSL (see Figure 19-1) has two field objects and two buttons. We used the following steps to build this form:

1. We placed one field object, named duration1, and one button on the form.

2. We added ObjectPAL code to the button's *pushButton* method which creates a series of sounds that play a C scale. The duration of each note is determined by the value that the user types into the duration1 field object.

3. After we tested the button and field to determine that they work properly, we made another copy of the button and the field objects on the form.

4. We named the second field duration2 and edited the second button's *pushButton* method so the notes played by this button have a duration determined by the value the user types in the duration2 field.

To test the form, switch to the Form window and type integers into the field objects (duration1 and duration2). Then click the buttons.

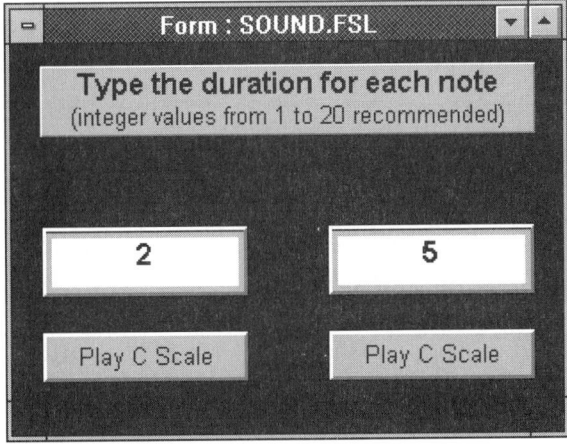

Figure 19-1: The SOUND.FSL form.

One slight problem exists with this form. Nearly identical versions of the code shown in Figure 19-2 exist in the pushButton methods of the form's two buttons. The reference to a field object is the only difference. If you want to change from a C scale to another scale, you have to edit both methods.

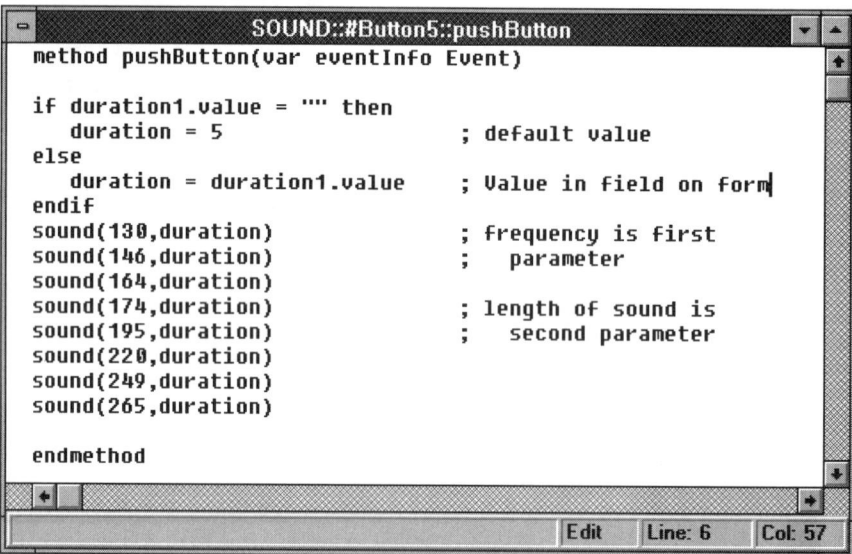

```
SOUND::#Button5::pushButton
method pushButton(var eventInfo Event)

if duration1.value = "" then
   duration = 5                    ; default value
else
   duration = duration1.value      ; Value in field on form
endif
sound(130,duration)                ; frequency is first
sound(146,duration)                ;    parameter
sound(164,duration)
sound(174,duration)                ; length of sound is
sound(195,duration)                ;    second parameter
sound(220,duration)
sound(249,duration)
sound(265,duration)

endmethod
```
Edit   Line: 6   Col: 57

Figure 19-2: The *pushButton* method is practically identical for both buttons.

Let's create a procedure that contains the *sound* procedures. (*Sound* is a procedure because it doesn't reference any Paradox objects.)

1. Open the form SOUND.FSL in the Form Design window.
2. Display the Method Inspector for the left button and double-click pushButton in the Method Inspector.
3. Select all the *sound* procedures, then click the Edit menu and choose Cut (or press Shift+Del).
4. Type *playTheScale(duration)* in place of all the *sound* lines.
5. Check the syntax by right-clicking in the Editor window and choosing Compile from the pop-up menu.

playTheScale should be highlighted, with the status bar displaying the message "Error: Unknown method name." This is expected because the procedure has not yet been declared. The syntax error doesn't matter right now. After the procedure is declared, there will be no syntax error. Now, let's continue:

6. Close the *pushButton* method window by double-clicking on the Control-menu box (or by pressing Ctrl+F4).

7. Display the page's Method Inspector, and double-click Proc in the Method Inspector. This opens an Editor window with the lines *proc* and *endproc* already filled in.

8. Click the Editor window's Edit menu and select Paste (or press Shift+Ins) to paste the *sound* procedures that you cut from the SOUND.FSL form's *pushButton* method.

9. Move to the first line in the Editor window after the word *proc*. Press the Spacebar, then type *playTheScale(duration longInt)*. There must be a space after the word *proc*. (This syntax will be explained in just a moment.)

10. Right-click in the Editor window and select Compile All from the pop-up menu. If you receive a syntax error, compare the code in your procedure to that in Figure 19-3. When there are no syntax errors, close the Editor window by double-clicking on the Control-menu box (or by pressing Ctrl+F4).

```
SOUND::#Page2::proc*
proc playTheScale(duration longInt)

sound(130,duration)          ; frequency is first
sound(146,duration)          ;   parameter
sound(164,duration)
sound(174,duration)          ; length of sound is
sound(195,duration)          ;   second parameter
sound(220,duration)
sound(249,duration)
sound(265,duration)

endproc
                                              Edit    Line: 1    Col: 1
```

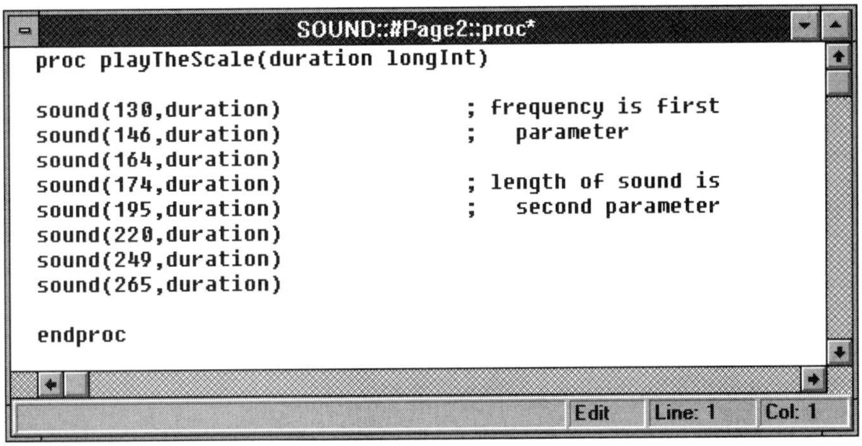

Figure 19-3: The completed procedure should look like this.

11. Use the form by typing an integer into the left field object and clicking on the left button.

12. When you are confident that the button plays the C scale with varying duration (depending on what value is typed into the field object), open the Editor for the *pushButton* method and copy the *playTheScale(duration)* line to the Clipboard.

13. Display the other button's Method Inspector, and double-click pushButton in the Method Inspector.

14. Select the eight *sound* lines, then click the Edit menu and choose Paste to replace the 8 *sound* lines with the call to your new custom procedure.

15. Check the syntax, and when there are no syntax errors, close the editor window and save the form with a different name. (You'll be using the original version of the form later in the chapter.)

How Procedures Work

Let's see how this procedure call works. The diagram in Figure 19-4 shows the sequence in which execution occurs. It is important to note that when you want the method to pass a value to the procedure, you must enclose the value in parentheses. Any number of values can be passed to a procedure, but they must all be listed inside the parentheses and separated by commas.

The *playTheScale(duration)* line is the line in the *pushButton* method that calls the procedure. Paradox looks through the containership hierarchy for the procedure, and finally finds it attached to the page. The method passes one value to the custom procedure, a longInt variable called *duration*. When the procedure is finished, control returns to the *pushButton* method that called the procedure.

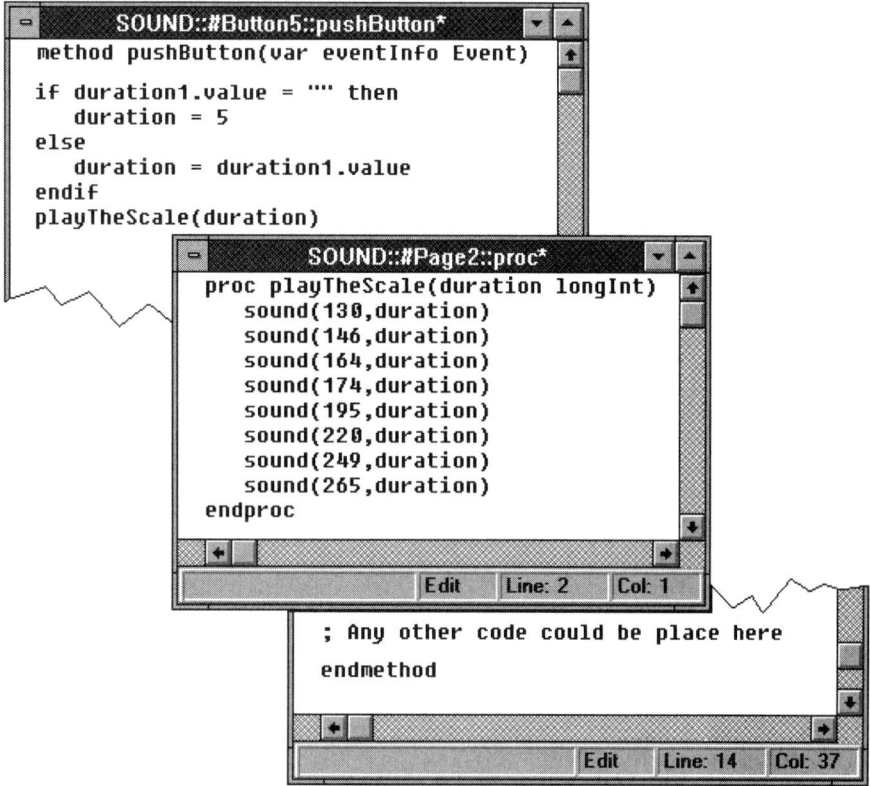

```
SOUND::#Button5::pushButton*
method pushButton(var eventInfo Event)

if duration1.value = "" then
    duration = 5
else
    duration = duration1.value
endif
playTheScale(duration)
```

```
SOUND::#Page2::proc*
proc playTheScale(duration longInt)
    sound(130,duration)
    sound(146,duration)
    sound(164,duration)
    sound(174,duration)
    sound(195,duration)
    sound(220,duration)
    sound(249,duration)
    sound(265,duration)
endproc
```
Edit   Line: 2   Col: 1

```
; Any other code could be place here

endmethod
```
Edit   Line: 14   Col: 37

Figure 19-4: When Paradox executes a custom procedure, it can be passed any number of variables.

When you declare a procedure in the Editor window, you can specify that the procedure will be passed a value from any method that calls the procedure. When you specify the value, you also specify the type of value. This is, in effect, the equivalent of declaring a variable. No var ... endvar block is used; the variable and its type are declared in the procedure declaration. It is imperative that the number of arguments (and types of the arguments) are the same in the calling method and the called procedure, otherwise a syntax error will occur. Furthermore, even if you declare a procedure that does not pass a value, you must still include parentheses after the procedure's name when you use the procedure in a method.

It seems like a lot of steps to create a procedure that is supposed to save time and simplify ObjectPAL. However, now you have reduced the amount of code in this form. Any time you want to change the scale, you need only edit the playTheScale procedure rather than both buttons. In addition, you can add another button that called the playTheScale procedure.

One More Procedure

Now let's look at RENTAL.FSL from the Video application. As the RENTAL.FSL currently stands (discussed in Chapter 18), it contains quite a bit of redundant code that you now know how to clean up. For example, when the user clicks the Find Customer button, radio buttons and associated fields become visible. When the customer is finally located (or when the Cancel button is pressed) all the "find customer" fields and buttons become hidden and the Comments field becomes visible once again. The code to do all this is repeated in three places: in both Cancel buttons and in the Find button. So let's make a procedure out of it.

Figure 19-5 shows three *pushButton* methods (the two Cancel buttons and the Find button from the Rental form) that contain nearly the same code. The code from the Cancel button on the right doesn't contain all the lines that the other two methods contain. We can reduce the repetitive code with a procedure. One option would be to place in the procedure only those lines that repeat. That would still leave two buttons, however, that contain some repetitive code. A better solution would be to place all the code from the Cancel button on the left in a procedure. That way, all code that pertains to removing the "find account" controls from the form is in one location—in a procedure. It doesn't matter that a couple of extra lines of code execute, because they don't change the state of the form at all.

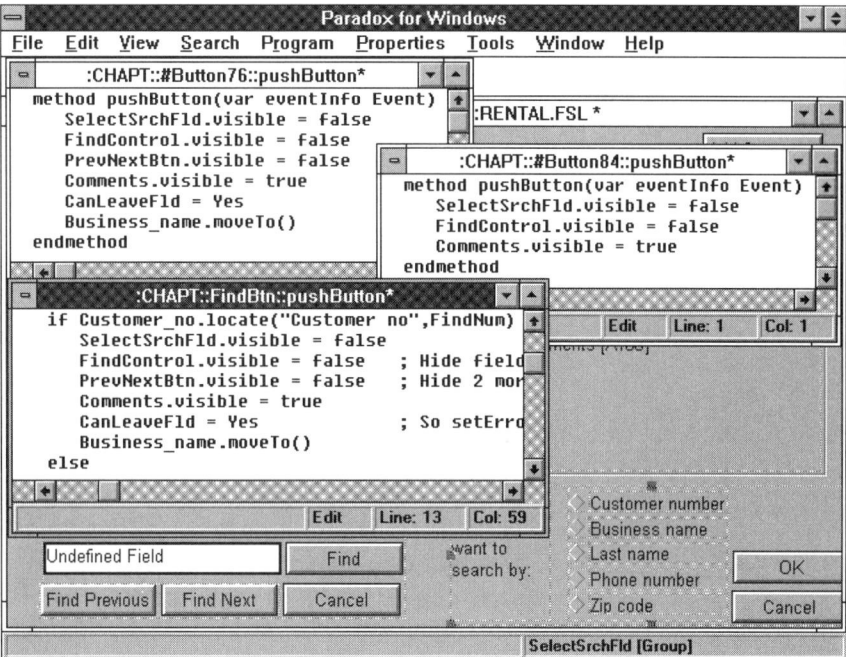

Figure 19-5: Code in three different locations can be replaced by one procedure.

Also notice that this is a procedure that doesn't take any parameters. It simply performs several actions. Let's add code that removes the "find account" objects from the screen.

1. Open RENTAL.FSL (from Chapter 18) in the Form Design window.

2. Open the *pushButton* method for the Find button and scroll to the bottom where the code to restore the form is located. Cut to the Clipboard the five lines beginning with *SelectSrchFld.visible = false*.

3. Type *clearFindObjects( )* where the five lines used to be, then close the Editor window.

4. Open the Method Inspector and click Proc to open the Editor window. To the right of the word *Proc*, press the Spacebar and type *clearFindObjects( )*. Starting on the second line, paste the five lines that you cut from the Find *pushButton* method. Copy the procedure name, clearFindObjects, to the Clipboard so it can be pasted into the other *pushButton* methods without retyping.

5. Delete the same lines of code in both Cancel buttons, and paste *clearFindObjects()* in their place.

6. Run the form to be sure everything works properly.

553

Eliminating Code Creatively

Sometimes it is not easy to see how to eliminate lines of code. Instead of simply looking for lines that are duplicated in two or more places, look for processes that are repetitive. It may be possible to restructure the code to eliminate a lot of programming. Consider, for example, the locate methods attached to three different buttons in the Video application. They can they be simplified, but some work is involved.

Open a copy of RENTAL.FSL and take a look at the code attached to the *pushButton* methods for the Find Previous and Find Next buttons. (The *if ... endif* clauses in both methods are similar. In each method a locate statement is used, and an error message is displayed if the record cannot be located. How can these similarities be used to create a procedure that all three buttons can call?

The field names are preceded by the *locate* method, but a UIObject could be used instead of the field names. Also, a variable could be used as the first parameter inside the parentheses. The primary difference between the two methods is that the Find Previous button uses *locatePriorPattern*, and the Find Next button uses *locateNextPattern*. Following is code from the Find Next button's *pushButton* method:

```
case SrchTxt = "Business name" :
    FindString = ".." + SrchString.value + ".."
    if not Business_name.locateNextPattern("Business
name",FindString) then
        MsgInfo("Find Account","No more matches were found")
    endif
```

There is also one other significant difference: The UIObject name doesn't contain spaces (Paradox replaces spaces with underscore characters) whereas the field name does contain a space. If variables are used, one would think that two different variables would be needed in the procedure to accommodate the two uses of the procedure. However, we can use an expression to calculate the field name from the UIObject name.

Let's look at a diagram of how all this can work together. Ideally, we want all three buttons to call the same procedure. The *pushButton* method of each button passes the procedure different information:

1. The *pushButton* method passes the type of *locate* (locate, locateNext, or locatePrior) and the field name to the procedure.

2. The procedure returns a value of true or false, depending on whether it successfully finds the record. If no record is found, the procedure returns the message "not found."

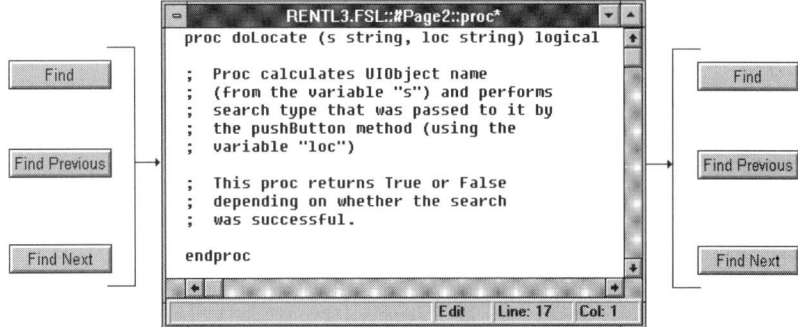

Figure 19-6: Diagram of how calls to the locate procedure are made.

Now let's look at the *pushButton* method's code, shown in Figure 19-7. Notice that the procedure is called from an *if* statement. In this example, the procedure returns a true or false value, depending on whether the locate operation was successful. The syntax is the same as using the *locate* method in an *if* statement. This time a custom procedure is returning a true/false value.

```
Paradox for Windows - [RENTL3.FSL::FindBtn::pushButton*]
File   Edit   View   Search   Program   Properties   Tools   Window   Help

If FindBtnTxt.value = "Find" then
    if SrchRB.value = "Customer number" then   ; FOR CUSTOMER NUMBER ONLY
        try FindNum = SrchString.value
        onFail   MsgInfo("Error","You must type a number.  Please try again.")
                 return
        endTry
        if Customer_no.locate("Customer no",FindNum) then
            FindControl.visible = false   ; Hide field, text, 2 btns
            PrevNextBtn.visible = false   ; Hide 2 more buttons
            Comments.visible = true
            CanLeaveFld = Yes             ; So setErrorCode not set
            Business_name.moveTo()
        else
            MsgInfo("Find Account","No matches were found")
        endif
    else                                  ; FOR ALL OTHER FIELDS (ALPHA)
        if doLocate(SrchRB.value,"locate") then   ; Call the Proc
            FindBtnTxt.value = "Found It !"       ; Change button label
            PrevNextBtn.visible = true            ; and show prev/next btns
        else
            MsgInfo("Find Account","No matches were found")
        endif
    endif

                                                    Edit   Line: 24   Col: 73
                            FindBtn [Button]
```

Figure 19-7: The *pushButton* method has been simplified by calling a custom procedure.

The *doLocate* procedure is shown in Figure 19-8. The procedure first Fdeclares variables that are in addition to the variables passed to the procedure from the *pushButton* method. The procedure then performs string calculations. Let's look at this procedure closely.

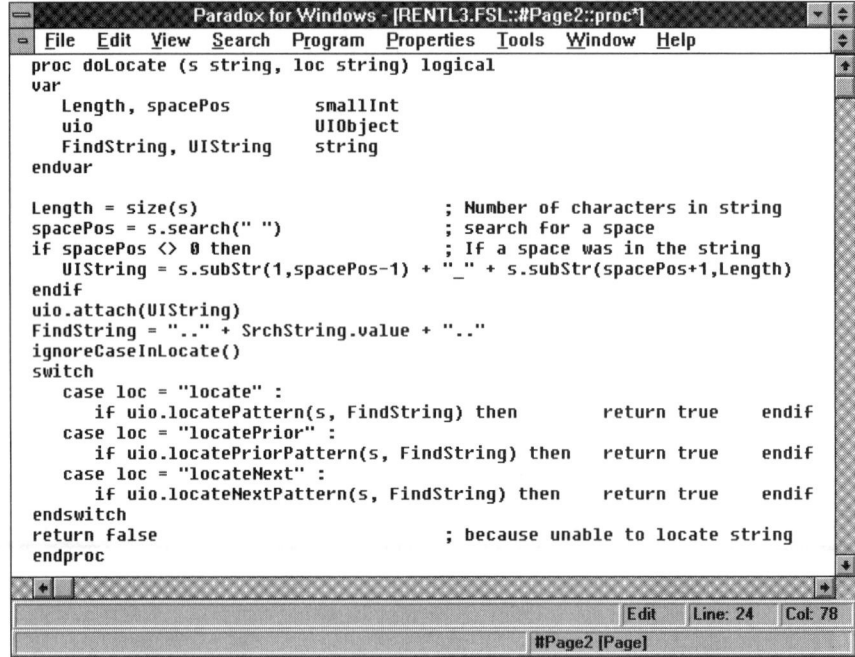

```
Paradox for Windows - [RENTL3.FSL::#Page2::proc*]
  File   Edit   View   Search   Program   Properties   Tools   Window   Help
proc doLocate (s string, loc string) logical
var
    Length, spacePos      smallInt
    uio                   UIObject
    FindString, UIString  string
endvar

Length = size(s)                      ; Number of characters in string
spacePos = s.search(" ")              ; search for a space
if spacePos <> 0 then                 ; If a space was in the string
    UIString = s.subStr(1,spacePos-1) + "_" + s.subStr(spacePos+1,Length)
endif
uio.attach(UIString)
FindString = ".." + SrchString.value + ".."
ignoreCaseInLocate()
switch
    case loc = "locate" :
        if uio.locatePattern(s, FindString) then      return true    endif
    case loc = "locatePrior" :
        if uio.locatePriorPattern(s, FindString) then  return true    endif
    case loc = "locateNext" :
        if uio.locateNextPattern(s, FindString) then  return true    endif
endswitch
return false                          ; because unable to locate string
endproc
```

	Edit	Line: 24	Col: 78
	#Page2 [Page]		

Figure 19-8: The *doLocate* procedure that is called by the three Find buttons.

The seventh line of the procedure assigns a variable *length* to the number of characters in the string. The purpose of this part of the procedure is to convert a field name to a UIObject name by replacing each space in the field name with an underscore. The *search* method in line 8 looks through the string *s* for the first occurrence of a space. If a space is found, the variable *spacePos* contains the position of the space in the string. For example, if the string is "First name," the variable *spacePos* contains the value 6. If the string *s* doesn't contain a space, the value of *spacePos* is 0.

So far, we have the length of the field name and the position of the space. That is enough information to perform the string calculation. The *subStr* method, used twice in the tenth line shown in Figure 19-8, returns a portion of a string between a starting character position (the first argument) and the ending character position (the second argument). In this case, *spacePos* contains the character position of the space, so *s.subStr(1,spacePos-1)* describes all characters in string *s* up to the space. The line then appends an underscore character to the string *s*, taking the place of the space, and appends the portion of the string that follows the space. As a result, the variable *UIString* contains the UIObject name.

The twelfth line shown in Figure 19-8 attaches the variable *uio* to the UIObject specified for this search, and the next line assigns *FindString* the value of the unbound field where the search string was typed. Next comes the switch ... endSwitch block. Instead of having *case* statements for each field, the *case* statements control the type of search to be performed. Notice the *return false* statements when the search string is not found. *return* causes the procedure to stop execution and the word *false* following it returns the logical value false. The procedure declaration specified that the return value was logical. Returning any other type of value (or not returning a value) would cause a syntax error.

Revamping the way the locate is performed has eliminated many lines of code and made the code easier to understand and maintain. All the locate code is in one place—in the procedure. The *pushButton* method of each button that finds a string has been streamlined. With a little creativity, applications can be made simpler. In fact, it is always possible to streamline an application that raises the question When is an application finished? And the answer is this: When you decide to stop working on it.

LIBRARIES: STORAGE PLACES FOR CODE

A *library*, like a procedure, is another location where ObjectPAL code lives. Also, as in the case of a procedure, you can call code in a library by name, pass it parameters, and return a value. But that is about as far as the similarities go. You can also think of a library as being similar to a form, in certain respects. A library stores custom methods, custom procedures and variables, as does a form. In fact, much of the code that is in a form could be placed in a library.

Creating a Library

Creating a library is much like creating a form. Either right-click the Library button in the Project Viewer or on the Toolbar and select New from the pop-up menu, or click the File menu, select New, and from the cascading menu select Library. An empty Library Design window, like that shown in Figure 19-9, opens. It looks just like a form, but the Toolbar is almost identical to the Toolbar that is displayed when ending a method. Also, right-clicking in the Library Design window automatically displays the Method Inspector if it is not already displayed.

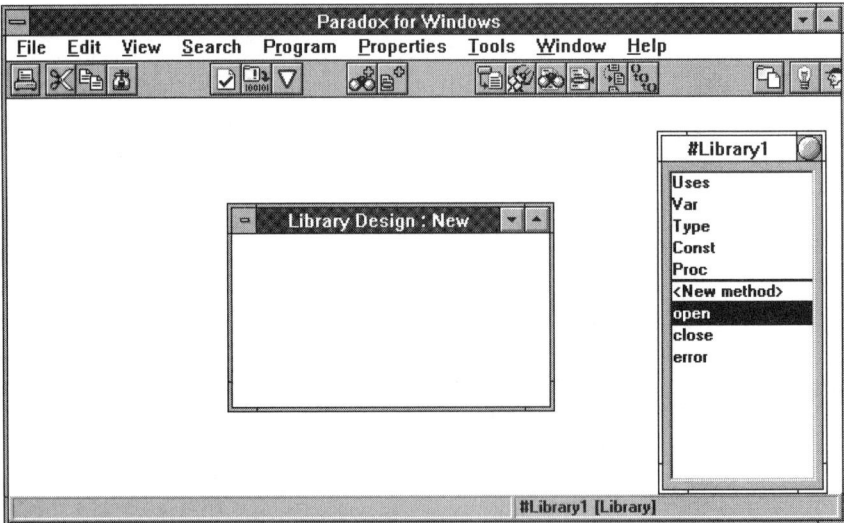

Figure 19-9: A new Library Design window resembles a form, but the Toolbar is more similar to the Editor's Toolbar.

Notice that when you're working in the Library Design window, the Method Inspector has only three built-in methods: *open*, *close* and *error*. The *open* and *close* methods work just like those in the Form Design window—in fact, everything in the Library Design window's Method Inspector works like it would in the Form window's Method Inspector, except that the error method, by default, returns to the calling object's error method. There are also differences in scope of variables and procedures between a Library window and the Form Design window, but we'll get into that later. Most frequently, <New method> is the option you choose from the Library Design window's Method Inspector.

You can place code on a form, so why would you want to use a library? Here are a few reasons:

○ Forms can contain a finite number of objects, so if forms start to get really big (several pages with lots of objects) it may be best to place some of the code in a library.

○ Libraries are stored in a separate file independent of a form, so if you have frequently used routines, they can be placed in a library and easily used with other applications.

○ Custom methods in a library can be accessed by more than one form.

○ Libraries can help with organization because similar types of routines can be stored in one location.

○ Libraries can be used to pass a parameter value from one form to another—something that cannot be done using forms alone. (You could write a value to disk in one form and read it with another form—but that's a different story.)

Calling a Library From a Form

Now we have a new library, but it doesn't have any code attached to it. Let's copy some ObjectPAL code from the SOUND.FSL form into the library and then edit a *pushButton* method for SOUND.FSL so that it calls the library. Here's how you place code in a library and call it from a form:

1. Open the SOUND.FSL form in the Form Design window.

2. Click the Form Design window and, if the Method Inspector is not displayed, right-click the window and choose Methods from the pop-up menu to display the Method Inspector.

3. Select both Var and Uses from the Method Inspector then press Enter to open both windows.

4. In the Editor window for the Uses item, edit the first line so that it says *Uses ObjectPAL*; then on a blank line type *playTheScale(duration longInt)* and check for syntax errors (by right-clicking the window and choosing Check Syntax from the pop-up menu). Close the Editor window when there are no syntax errors.

5. In the Editor window for the Var item, add a new line, *lib library* to declare a new variable *lib* of type *library*. Check for syntax errors. If there are none, close the Editor window.

6. Click the left Play C Scale button and open its *pushButton* method. Cut all eight *sound* lines to the Windows Clipboard. In their place, type *lib.playTheScale(duration)* and check for syntax errors. When there are no syntax errors, close the Editor window.

7. If you still have the Library Design window open, click in the Library Design window or select it from the Window menu. From the Method Inspector, double-click <New Method>. A dialog box like that shown in Figure 19-10 displays.

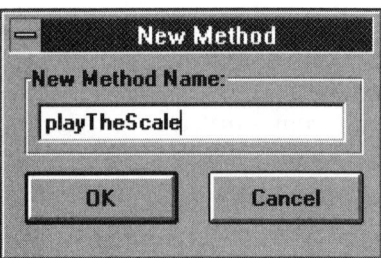

Figure 19-10: Type a name for the new custom method in the New Method dialog box.

8. Type *playTheScale* into the dialog box and click the OK button. A window opens where you can create the custom method.

9. Click the Edit menu and choose Paste (or press Shift+Ins) to paste the eight *sound* lines into the custom method.

10. Edit the first line of the custom method so it says *method playTheScale(duration longInt)* then check the syntax. When there are no syntax errors, close the Editor window.

11. To save the library, click in the Library Design window to select it, click the File menu and choose Save or Save As. Type *sound* in the Save File As text box and click the OK button. The library is automatically saved with the extension .LSL.

12. Click again in the form SOUND.FSL or select it from the Window menu.

13. Click the right Play C Scale button and open its *pushButton* method. Cut all eight *sound* lines to the Windows Clipboard. In their place, type *lib.playTheScale(duration)* and check for syntax errors. When there are no syntax errors, close the Editor window.

14. Edit the form's Open method. Type *lib.open("sound.lsl")* and check for syntax errors. When there are no syntax errors, close the Editor window.

15. Edit the form's Close method, type *lib.close()* and check for syntax errors. When there are no syntax errors, close the Editor window.

16. Save the form with a different name and run the form.

Again, that's a lot of steps, but you can no doubt see the similarities between libraries and procedures. The way you use a library is similar to the way you use a procedure, but you can use methods stored in a library from multiple forms. A procedure is stored in a form, while a library is stored as a separate file. The various windows used when calling the library SOUND.LSL from the form SOUND.FSL are shown in Figure 19-11.

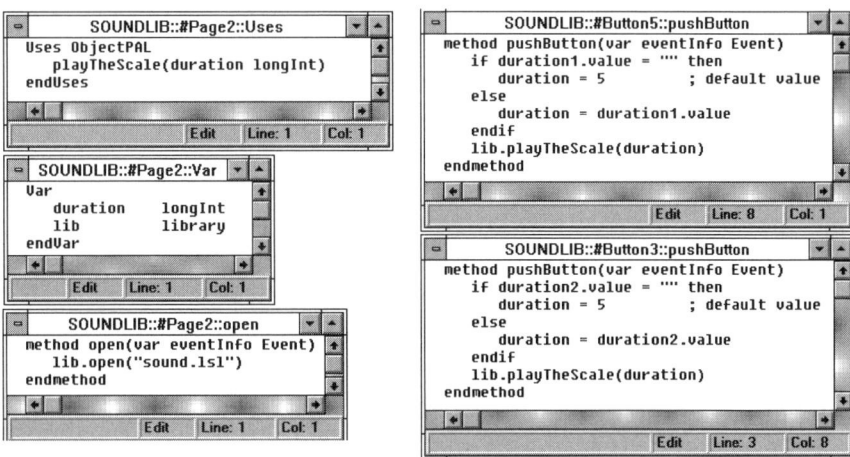

Figure 19-11: All the windows used to call a custom method in a library.

A library, like a form or a report, should be accessed using a variable—a handle to the library. Before a method can access the library, the method must open the library. Because the library can be called from more than one object, the handle variable is declared in the form's Var window. The library is opened in the form's *open* method so that the library doesn't have to be opened every time the method calls the library. By the time the user has a chance to interact with the form, the library is already open and ready for use.

Inside Scoop

Library names, variables and data types must be declared exactly the same in the Uses window as they are in the library itself. It is often a good idea to copy the declaration from one window and paste into the other to avoid typos.

Methods from a library cannot be called from a form until they have been declared. Place library method declarations in the Editor window for the Uses item in the form's Method Inspector (the *Uses window*). The Uses window tells Paradox where to look (which library [or DLL—but we won't get into that]) to find the declared method. When compiling the form, a syntax error will occur if a method or procedure refers to a library that is not declared in a Uses window. However, when compiling the form, Paradox does not check the contents of the disk to verify that the library actually exists or that the custom method has already been created in the library.

Inside Scoop

Custom methods in a library are accessible by any number of forms. However, each form must open the library and declare the library's methods in a Uses window.

Passing Variables Between Forms

Back in Chapter 16, I said that you needed a special tool to allow a variable to be seen by more than one form. That tool is a library. Two identical forms are included on disk—GLOBL1.FSL and GLOBL2.FSL. First, let's demonstrate that it is possible to pass contents of a variable from form to form. Open both GLOBL1.FSL and GLOBL2.FSL and position them so they are both visible on the screen. Type an integer value into the field object and click the button below it. Clicking the button passes the variable to a library. The value appears in the lower field object, indicating that the value can be read from the library. Now click the other form's Copy Variable From Library button and see what happens. The same integer is pasted into a field object. Figure 19-12 is a representation of what's happening—the variable is always being passed through the library.

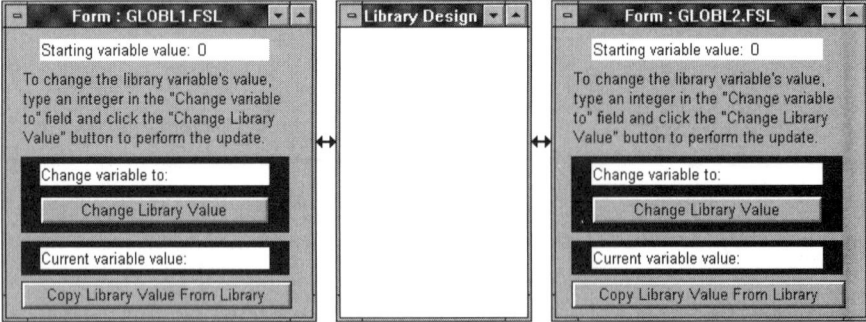

Figure 19-12: Libraries allow you to have variables with a greater scope than just the form.

Now, let's take a look at the code that passes a variable between forms. Unfortunately, it isn't as simple as declaring a variable in the library's Var window and using that variable name in each form, but that's sort of the idea. The first thing to do is declare a library variable, *lib*, in the form's Var window and declare the library's custom methods in the form's Uses window. Also, the form's *open* method (Figure 19-13) performs some initialization tasks.

```
method open(var eventInfo Event)

    action(editEnterPersistFieldView)
    lib.open("global.lsl")
    StartingValue.value = lib.copyNumber()

endmethod
```

Figure 19-13: The form's *open* method opens the library and it stays open while the form is open.

The second line places the form in Field View so that when the form opens, you see an insertion point. The third line opens the library and line 4 fills in the StartingValue field with the current contents of the library variable. So let's go look at the library and see what's there.

The library contains two custom methods in addition to a declaration in the Var window and an *open* method (see Figure 19-14). The *open* method simply initializes the variable *theNumber* that is declared in the Var window to be of type longInt. The work is done with the two custom methods, so let's take a closer look at them.

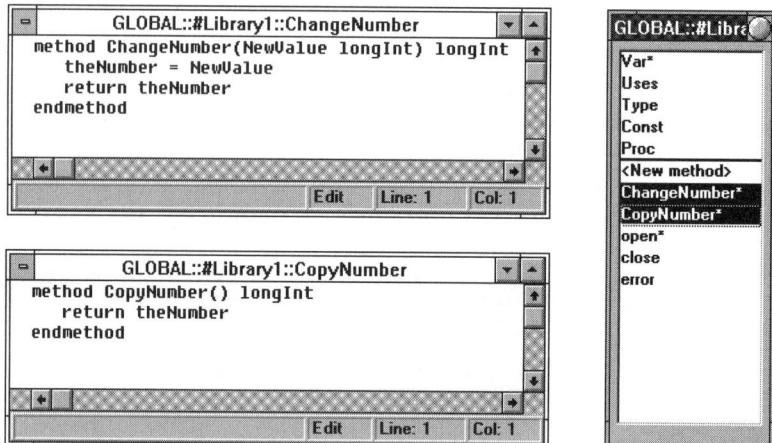

Figure 19-14: Two custom methods are responsible for changing a variable and making it accessible to more than one form.

When one of the form's methods calls the ChangeNumber method, the calling method passes one longInt parameter to the ChangeNumber method and is returned a longInt value. The second line assigns to *theNumber* (a variable declared in the library's Var window) the value passed to this library method in the *NewValue* parameter. At this point, *theNumber* (the library's variable) and newValue (the number passed to this method) are the same. Line 3 returns *theNumber* to the calling method. It could have just as easily returned newValue, but the purpose of this demonstration is to pass library variables to forms.

The CopyNumber method takes no arguments, and returns a longInt value–the library's global variable. Let's see what happens when a form calls the CopyNumber method. When the user clicks the Copy Value From Library button, the following code executes:

```
CurrentValue.value = lib.copyNumber()
```

This line simply displays the value returned by the library's copyNumber custom method in the CurrentValue field object. Any form that uses *lib.copyNumber()* returns the same value. But the benefit of variables is that they can change. You can cause the variable to change by clicking on the Change Library Value button, which executes the following code:

```
CurrentValue.value = lib.changeNumber(ChangeTo.value)
```

This line of code displays the value returned by the library's changeNumber method in the CurrentValue field. But it also changes the library's *theNumber* variable to the value in the ChangeTo field object. It is clear that using a library to provide global access to a variable is not as easy as declaring a variable in a form's Var window. If you need to share a lot of variables among forms, you may need to reconsider how the application is designed. Maybe a multipage form is preferable. Maybe there is some way to eliminate the need to use so many variables. Maybe you can write values to a table using a TCursor. Many options are at your disposal, and it is up to you to determine the best way of handling a particular situation.

POTPOURRI: SCRIPTS, LOOPS & STRINGS

Scripts are like macros—little automation routines that you can play from the Paradox menu or Project Viewer. The code in scripts is just like methods and procedures, so you already know a lot about writing scripts. When are scripts useful? Any time you want to automate a task that is not within the context of a form. For example, you may want to segregate a Name field into First Name and Last Name fields, without creating a form with a button just to do it. Or you may want to perform some kind of repetitive calculation. You probably won't use scripts a lot, but it's nice to know they're there when you need them.

In Chapter 18, the context-sensitive help located a pattern within the first field in order to find the current object. But there is a chance for error because the entire containership hierarchy is included in the field, and all that is necessary is the object's name. The table may contain *#Page2.Customer_no.#EditRegion4,* when all that is really needed is *#EditRegion4*. The table should be cleaned up because if you were looking for help on the page, this record might be found because it also contains the string *#Page2*.

Cleaning up the help table is not a function that is associated with a particular form; it is more closely related to the actual table, so using a script is a good choice. You certainly don't want to go through 100 or more records and edit them manually. The script ENUM.SSL is already created. It works with ENUM.DB from Chapter 18. Copy those two files to your current working directory and run the script by double-clicking the script's name in the Project Viewer. The script creates the table ENUMSC.SSL You can see the difference between the source table and the table created by the script by looking at Figure 19-15.

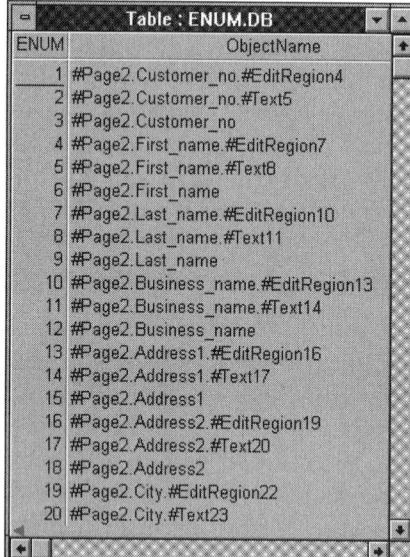
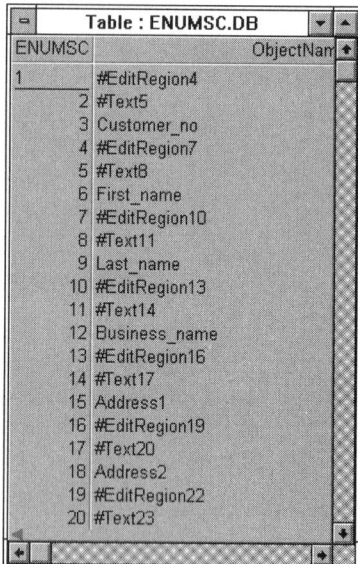

Figure 19-15: The script processes the table on the left, creating the table on the right.

Notice that the difference between the two tables is that everything to the left of the rightmost period is not included in the new table. Now that we see the results, let's see how it works. Figure 19-16 shows all the code in the script.

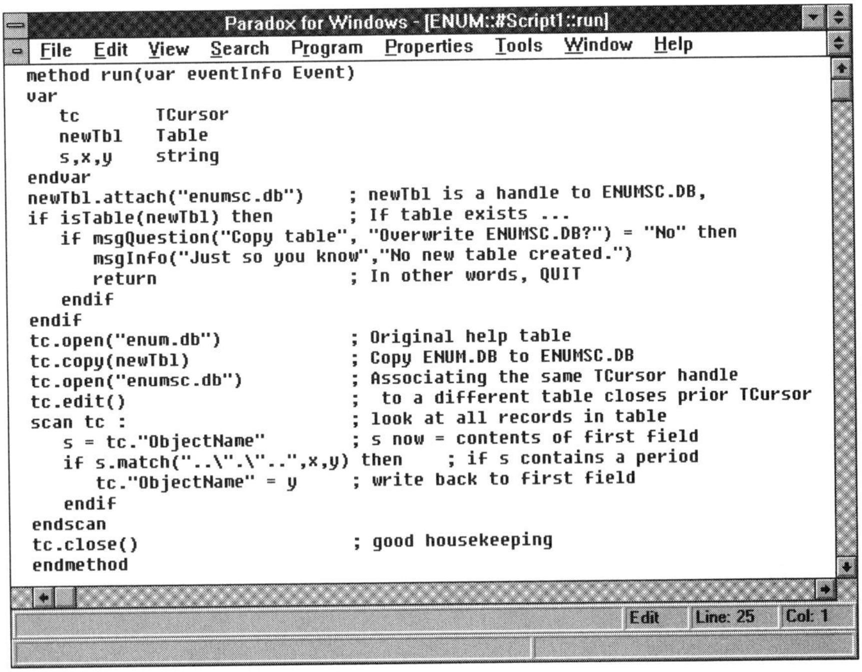

```
┌─────────────────────────────────────────────────────────────────┐
│  Paradox for Windows - [ENUM::#Script1::run]               ▼ ▲   │
│ ▬  File  Edit  View  Search  Program  Properties  Tools  Window  Help  ▲│
│ method run(var eventInfo Event)                                   ▲│
│ var                                                               ││
│     tc        TCursor                                             ││
│     newTbl    Table                                               ││
│     s,x,y     string                                              ││
│ endvar                                                            ││
│ newTbl.attach("enumsc.db")     ; newTbl is a handle to ENUMSC.DB, ││
│ if isTable(newTbl) then        ; If table exists ...              ││
│     if msgQuestion("Copy table", "Overwrite ENUMSC.DB?") = "No" then│
│         msgInfo("Just so you know","No new table created.")       ││
│         return               ; In other words, QUIT               ││
│     endif                                                         ││
│ endif                                                             ││
│ tc.open("enum.db")             ; Original help table              ││
│ tc.copy(newTbl)                ; Copy ENUM.DB to ENUMSC.DB        ││
│ tc.open("enumsc.db")           ; Associating the same TCursor handle│
│ tc.edit()                      ;  to a different table closes prior TCursor│
│ scan tc :                      ; look at all records in table     ││
│     s = tc."ObjectName"        ; s now = contents of first field  ││
│     if s.match("..\".\"..",x,y) then    ; if s contains a period  ││
│         tc."ObjectName" = y    ; write back to first field        ││
│     endif                                                         ││
│ endscan                                                           ││
│ tc.close()                     ; good housekeeping                ││
│ endmethod                                                         ▼│
│ ◄ ▭                                                            ► │
│                                      │Edit│  │Line: 25│  │Col: 1│ │
└─────────────────────────────────────────────────────────────────┘
```

Figure 19-16: Scripts look very much like methods.

The variable declaration block contains a new variable type—the *table* variable. Some methods that you can use for TCursors can also be used for table variables, but generally a table variable lets you work with the table as a whole, whereas a TCursor is a pointer to data in a table. Line 7 forms an association with the file ENUM.DB and line 8 tests whether that table actually exists.

Inside Scoop

Table variables are associated with a table by using *attach*. In English, the word *attach* implies that something already exists that you can attach to; but in ObjectPAL, attaching to a table only forms an association. It is possible to attach to a database file that doesn't exist.

The purpose of this script is to create a new Paradox table, but you want to be sure no other table is inadvertently overwritten. Lines 9 through 12 are the safety check. If a table exists that the script would overwrite, a dialog box asks for confirmation. If you click the No button, the script stops executing. Otherwise, the source table is copied and given the new name ENUMSC.DB.

Line 16 associates the same TCursor variable with the new table that was just copied, without closing the previous TCursor. The variable *tc* can only be associated with one table at a time, so if a second association is created, the first one is automatically closed.

A really powerful looping command is *scan*. When you use scan, Paradox executes every command between *scan* and *endscan* for each record in a Paradox table. *Scan* looks at every record, regardless of the number of records, the position of any table pointer, or the current record. In the script, TCursor is placed in Edit mode, with the *tc.edit( )* line before the scan loop starts. *tc.edit( )* only needs to be executed once—not once for every record.

Pitfall Ahead

Because *scan* executes commands for every record in a table, don't use commands like nextRecord in a scan loop. If you do, every other record will be skipped.

The twentieth line in the script (*if s.match(".. \ ".\ "... ",x,y)*) analyzes the string *s* to see if it contains a period. If it does, *match* extracts the portion of the string prior to the last period and assigns it to the variable *x*. It then extracts the portion of the string following the period and assigns it to the variable *y*. Searching for a period is complicated, so here's a simpler example:

```
s = "string to search"
msgInfo("Results", "s.match("..to.."))          ; displays True
msgInfo("Results", "s.match("..to"))            ; displays False
msgInfo("Results", "s.match("..hello.."))       ; displays False
msgInfo("Results", "s.match("@tring.."))        ; displays True
msgInfo("Results", "s.match("..to..",x,y))      ; displays True
        ; x = "string ", y = " search"
msgInfo("Results", "s.match("..s.."))           ; displays True
        ; x = "string to ", y = "search"
```

With letters and numbers as the search string, the match is a lot clearer. If the quoted string is found within the variable *s,* match returns a value of True. Two optional variables can be specified in the match statement, and if match returns True, the first variable equals the substring up to the last occurrence of the match. The second variable equals the substring following the matching characters. Using match to find a period is more awkward because *s.match(".....",x,y)* is not valid. To search for a period, surround the period with double quotes, and precede each quote with a backslash (\). Backslash means "Interpret the following character literally."

If a match is found, the TCursor writes the object name (stored in the variable *y*) to a table. The loop continues until all records are processed. If you want, you can uncomment the msgInfo line, which is there in case you want to see what the matching values are. Finally, the TCursor is closed and the script stops playing.

By the way, the example mentioned at the beginning of this section about breaking a Name field into First Name and Last Name fields is another good time to use the match method. Any time you want to manipulate values in Paradox tables, consider using scripts. And be sure to use the online help to find examples of other string and number manipulation methods.

Synchronizing Records on Two Forms

You may run into instances where you want two forms to display the same record. One instance might be if you display a dialog box with Find criteria. Or maybe two forms display data in different ways, and a multipage form is not practical. Consider the following example: You have a form that displays only a few fields, but occasionally you want to see the rest of the data. The two forms in Figure 19-17 illustrate this idea. The form with the table frame object can open a second form with more detailed information.

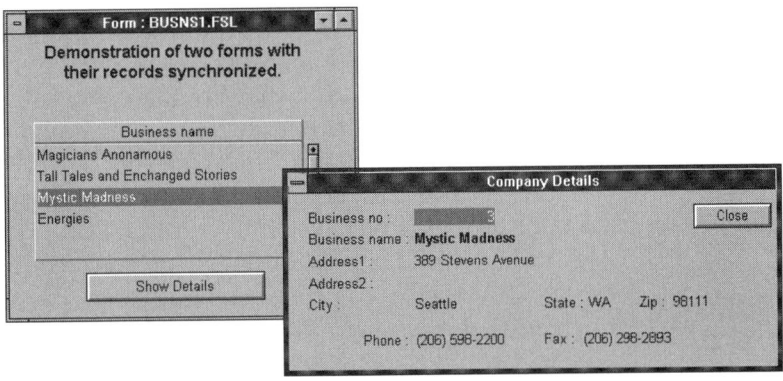

Figure 19-17: The Show Details button opens another form, with the records synchronized.

Open BUSNS1.FSL to see how this works. You can scroll through the records and select a particular record by clicking on it in the table frame. When you click the Show Details button, a form (actually, a dialog box) is opened, with more data for that business. Click the Close button on the dialog box and the dialog box closes. You can display more than one dialog box at a time by clicking on the Show Details button, with different records displaying. The only code in BUSNS1.FSL is on the Show Detail button's *pushButton* method. It looks like this:

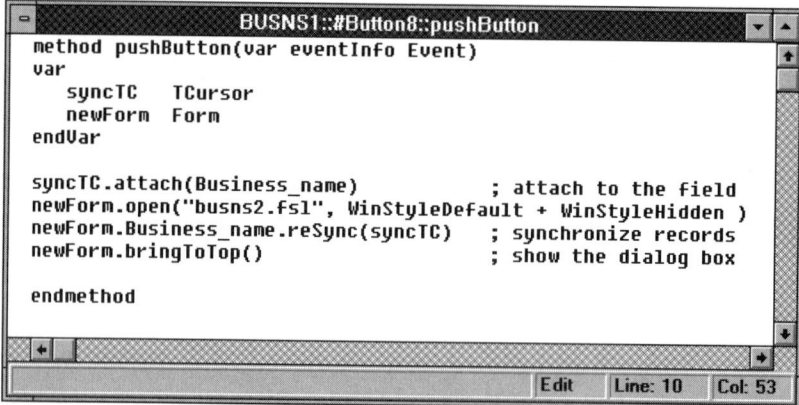

```
BUSNS1::#Button8::pushButton
method pushButton(var eventInfo Event)
var
    syncTC    TCursor
    newForm   Form
endVar

syncTC.attach(Business_name)             ; attach to the field
newForm.open("busns2.fsl", WinStyleDefault + WinStyleHidden )
newForm.Business_name.reSync(syncTC)    ; synchronize records
newForm.bringToTop()                     ; show the dialog box

endmethod
```
`Edit    Line: 10    Col: 53`

Figure 19-18: This is all the code necessary to display the current record in another form.

After declaring variables, the sixth line in the *pushButton* method attaches a TCursor to a UIObject. This is different from opening a TCursor. *Open* associates the TCursor with a Paradox table on your hard drive. *Attach* associates the TCursor with a UIObject on the form. Also notice that the UIObject is not enclosed in quotes.

The seventh line in the method opens a new form, but that new form is not displayed right away. Any time you use ObjectPAL to open a form, you can tell Paradox how that form should be opened and what the form attributes are. You won't need to use these parameters very often because Paradox lets you specify interactively form properties such as dialog box or window; thick border, sizing border, or dialog border; scroll bar; and title bar properties. (For a refresher on these attributes, refer to Chapters 9 and 10.) However, there are a few properties that are useful. WinStyleHidden is one of them. So are WinStyleMaximize and WinStyleMinimize. Use the same syntax shown in line 7 when using any of the ObjectPAL's window attributes, or in general form:

```
formVar.open("FormName.fsl",
WinStyleDefault+WinStyleAttribute1+WinStyleAttribute2)
```

Any number of attributes can be added in a similar manner. For a complete listing of all the window attributes, refer to online help. The eighth line in the *pushButton* method synchronizes the Business_name field on the dialog box with the Business_name field on the form by changing the record pointer of the UIObject (Business_name on the dialog box) to the record pointed to by the TCursor (syncTC).

After the record pointer points to the correct record, line 9 in the method causes the dialog box to display. The *bringToTop( )* method actually performs two functions: it moves the specified form to the top and also makes it visible. The line could just as easily have said *newForm.show( )*, but you want to be absolutely sure that the user didn't do something else that would have placed another form on top of the dialog box that is supposed to display.

MOVING ON

You have learned many neat things that can be done with ObjectPAL. These five chapters have not been exhaustively thorough, but they have shown you many of the important features and given you a springboard for creating custom applications. As you continue with ObjectPAL, look for new ideas and be sure to collect code fragments whenever you can.

The next two chapters walk you through two custom applications. The next one (on inventory applications) is designed to use very little ObjectPAL but use as many interactive features as possible. After that, the chapter on contact management uses lots of ObjectPAL, and will keep you busy for quite a while. You won't be writing any code for either of these applications–the next two chapters are more like a guided tour with explanations of what has already been done with ObjectPAL.

20

THE INVENTORY APPLICATION

The prior five ObjectPAL chapters presented applications that showed how ObjectPAL can be used to expand the power of Paradox. This chapter, and Chapter 21 walk you through two more applications. Although Chapter 21 uses lots of ObjectPAL code attached to many types of objects, this chapter's inventory application demonstrates that a little ObjectPAL goes a long way toward creating a professional application. Code is only attached to buttons and graphics and is intentionally kept to a minimum. Interactive features of Paradox are used whenever possible, illustrating the necessity that the developer thoroughly understand how to use Paradox interactively.

A useful application is not created just by placing fields on a form, but that is a good start. After the tables and forms are created, you usually have to add just a little bit. This inventory application demonstrates how you can almost create a complete application by creating forms interactively. In this Chapter you use filters, calculated fields, graphs, graphics and ObjectPAL code.

OVERVIEW

The inventory application lets you keep track of all your inventory—in this case, space ships. You can also keep track of your customers and what they purchase. Seven tables and four forms are used in this application. The Main Menu form, shown in Figure 20-1, enables you to select the task you want to perform.

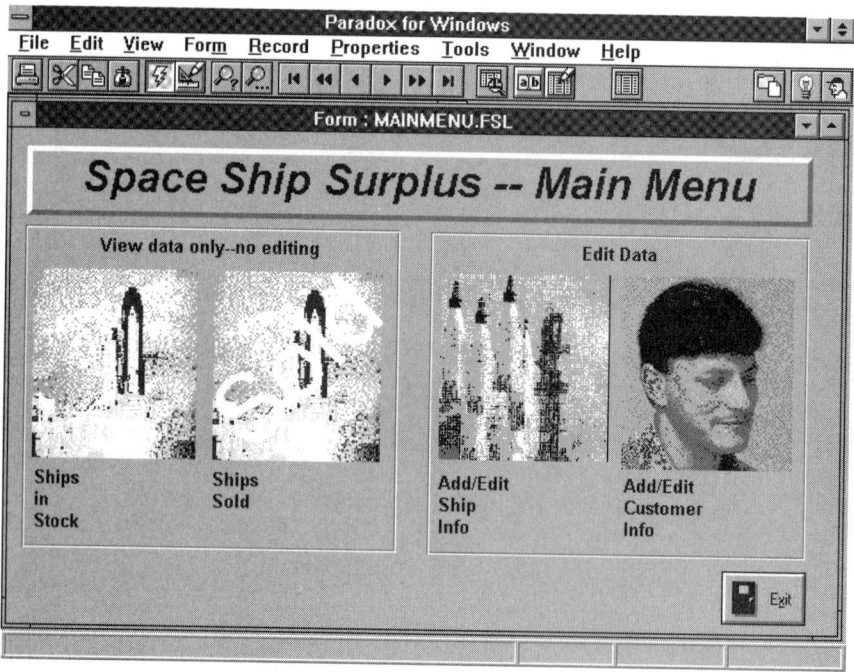

Figure 20-1: Clicking on one of the graphics on the Main Menu form starts that portion of the application.

Selecting one of the View options displays either the ships currently in stock or those that have already been sold. Both options open the same form (INVENTOR.FSL), but a different filter is used for each option. How does the filter separate space ships that have been sold from those that are still in stock? When a customer places an order, an order number is generated. In fact, the order number field is in two tables—Orders and Inventory. If the order number field in the inventory table is blank, the ship is still in inventory. However, if the field contains an order number, that space ship has already been sold. The filter selects either a blank Order Number field (ships in stock) or one that contains a value (ships sold).

The option to edit the ships in stock lets you add new space ships to your inventory, and edit existing data. It uses a form (EDITSTOK.FSL) designed for adding and editing records. Its data model is the same as INVENTOR.FSL.

The final option on the main menu allows the user to either add or edit customer data. The user employs this form, the CUSTVIEW.FSL form, to add new customers or purchases, or simply to look through customer data. This time the data model is different because you are looking through customer data. When using the form to add purchase items for each customer, you add space ships the customer wants to purchase by selecting the space ship from the Inventory form. INVENTOR.FSL is used a lot in this application—for viewing ships in stock, space ships that have been sold, and for adding a product to a customer's order.

Let's look now at the specifics of how the form works.

THE MAIN MENU FORM

The main menu doesn't look like a typical menu. There is no menu bar. The only button is the Exit button. Instead, the user clicks on pictures to perform an action. The pictures are simply bitmaps pasted into graphic objects.

ObjectPAL code on this form is attached to the *mouseClick* method of the graphic objects. The Add/Edit Ship Info and Add/Edit Customer Info graphics simply open another form. You already know how to do that. The two View graphics are a little more complex because, among other things, they set the filter for the form INVENTOR.FSL. The other interesting object on this form is the animated Exit button.

Filters With ObjectPAL

When you open INVENTOR.FSL, a large beveled text object contains a description for the form. For example, it may say "Ships in Stock" or "Ships Sold." The form has two buttons—OK and Cancel—but if the user is only viewing data, an OK button is all that is necessary, so the Cancel button is invisible (see Figure 20-2). These properties of INVENTOR.FSL are set when you click on one of the View Data graphics on the main menu. Figure 20-3 shows the *mouseClick* method for the View Ships In Stock graphic:

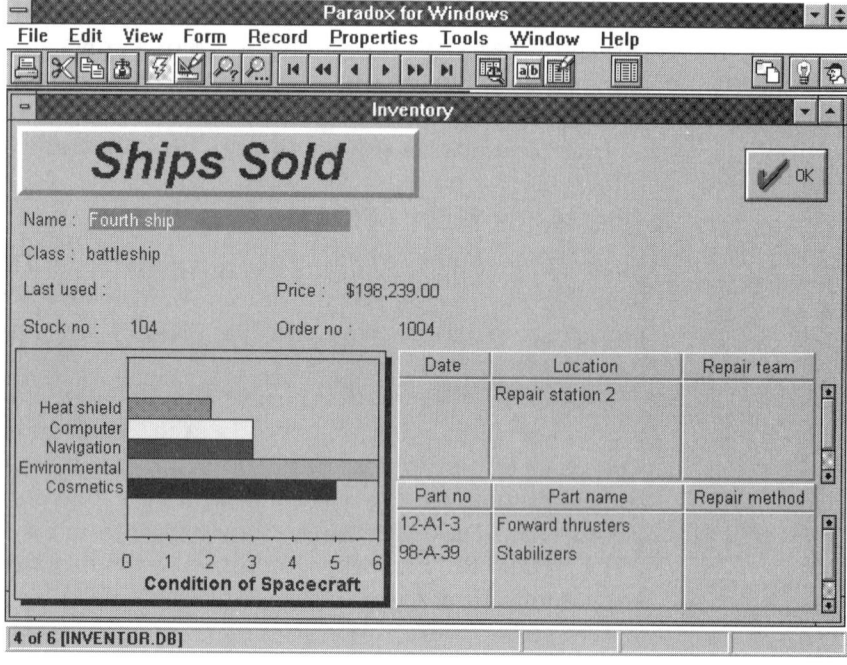

Figure 20-2: The Inventory form shows data from four tables.

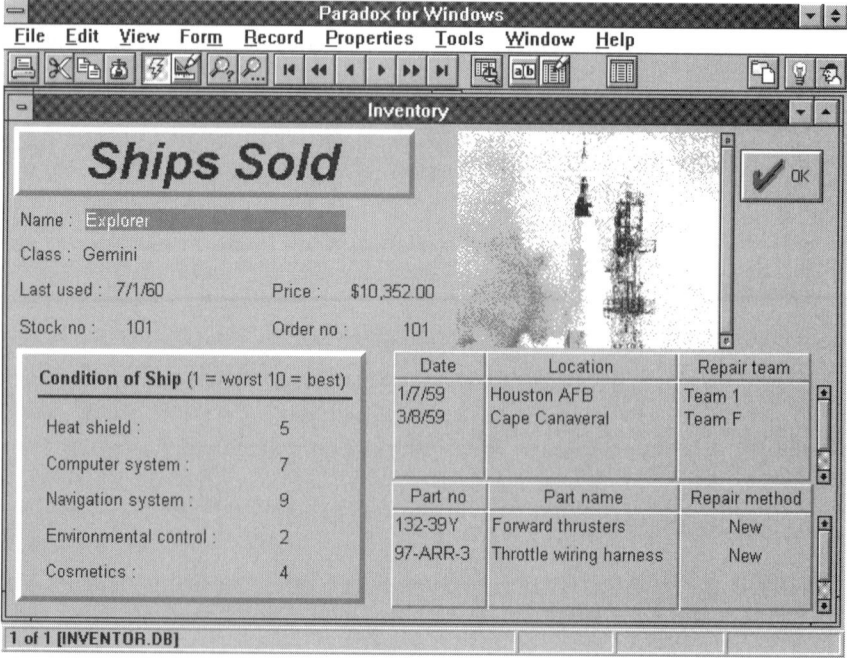

Figure 20-3: The filter for the Inventory form is set when you click on a graphic.

Here's how it works. The seventh line in the *mouseClick* method opens the Inventory form. The form is not visible because the parameter WinStyleHidden is used. The next line attaches the order number field so that it can be used as a filter; Line 9 sets a filter so that only records with blank order number fields are displayed. The *setRange* method in this example takes two arguments—minimum value and maximum value. The minimum value is blank and the maximum value is zero. The beveled text object is assigned a text string in line 10, then the Cancel button is hidden. Line 12 makes INVENTOR.FSL the top window, but it serves double duty—*bringToTop* also makes a form visible.

The code attached to the View Sold Ships is similar, except that lines 9 and 10 are changed to the following:

```
uio.setRange(1, 2147486647)
f.pg.InvTitle = "Ships Sold"
```

In this instance, *setRange* specifies different minimum and maximum values. Because sold ships have a value in the order number field, the minimum value is 1 (the lowest possible value for an Autoincrement field) and the maximum value is a very large integer. Using the maximum value for an Autoincrement field allows every record with a number in the order number field to be displayed. The form's title text object also specifies the appropriate text string.

Pitfall Ahead

When using *setRange*, be sure you don't specify a maximum value that is larger than the maximum value for the field type. If you do, the filter may not work and all records in the table are displayed.

Animated Buttons

Animated buttons add a finishing touch to your applications. You can freely copy animated buttons from form to form because the code that makes them work is all contained in the button. After you have designed the buttons, you don't need to change the animation code. You need to change the *pushButton* method only if you want to make the button do something different. The buttons appear animated because the picture looks different when the button is pressed.

An animated button is a normal button with two different bitmaps on it, only one of which is visible at any given time. When the button is pressed, the visible property of the two bitmaps is reversed—just like VISIBL.FSL in Chapter 17.

In order to understand animated buttons, you need to understand how a regular button works. Position the mouse pointer on top of a button and hold down the left mouse button. Keep holding down that left mouse button! The button looks depressed. Move the mouse off the button and the button looks released. If you release the left mouse button when the mouse pointer is not on the button, the button doesn't perform its normal function, but it doesn't look depressed any more either. The only time a button performs a function is when the left mouse button is pressed *and released* while the mouse pointer is over the button. Operating a button is not a simple mouse-click as it initially appears. Buttons are complex, and understanding a button really makes you appreciate what Paradox does for you automatically.

Several methods on this animated button have ObjectPAL code associated with them: *mouseUp*, *mouseDown*, *mouseEnter*, *mouseExit*, *open*, and *pushButton*. All the mouse methods determine which bitmap should be visible based on whether the button appears pressed or released, which is determined by whether the left mouse button is held down *and* the position of the mouse pointer.

Inside Scoop

Paradox does not provide a *mouseRightClick* method. If you want to perform an action when right-clicking, use the *mouseRightUp* method.

We won't go over all the code because the specific code is not that important. The animated buttons reinforce two concepts that are more important than the specific code. First, objects with code can be copied from form to form. An animated Exit button on one form will work exactly the same way on any other form. The only thing that you may need to change is the code that is attached to the *pushButton* method. All the other methods remain the same. Your applications can be created from pieces of other applications.

It is important that you understand all conceivable events that could occur. In this example, if the code that determines which bitmap is visible is only attached to the *pushButton* method, the bitmap would not revert to its normal state when holding the left mouse button, moving the mouse pointer off the button, then releasing the left mouse button. The *mouseExit* method is needed in that instance. This particular error is not critical, but it could be disconcerting. However, as you develop more applications, you could run into a situation that had not been anticipated, so watch out! Always test your code.

You have seen practically all the code attached to this form, so let's move on. Click on either of the View graphics to display the inventory form.

THE INVENTORY FORM

The Inventory table contains all spaceships that have ever passed through the hands of Space Ship Surplus, including ships that have already been sold. INVENTOR.FSL (Figure 20-2) displays the inventory table and tables that are linked to it. The data model isn't simple, but other than that, very little about the form is new to you. This form only has code attached to the buttons, but we'll look at the data model as well.

The OK Button

When called from the main menu, the OK button simply closes the form and returns to the main menu. However, there are many lines of ObjectPAL code attached to the OK button. This code is covered later when we look at how to use this form to add an item to a customer's invoice. (In the design mode you also see a Cancel button, but it is invisible in View Data mode because it does not apply when this form is opened from the main menu.)

The OK button performs two functions depending on which form opened it. The text string in the beveled text frame indicates the purpose of the form—to display data or to add an item to an invoice. The text string indicated which form opened INVENTOR.FSL, but that is discussed in a following section.

The Data Model

The INVENTOR.FSL form displays four tables, as shown in Figure 20-4. Each space ship is in INVENTOR.DB. Every time a ship is repaired, the repair date, crew and location are logged in REPAIRS.DB. Information about items that were replaced or refurbished is stored in REPITEMS.DB. The graph in the INVENTOR.FSL form represents the status of the major components.

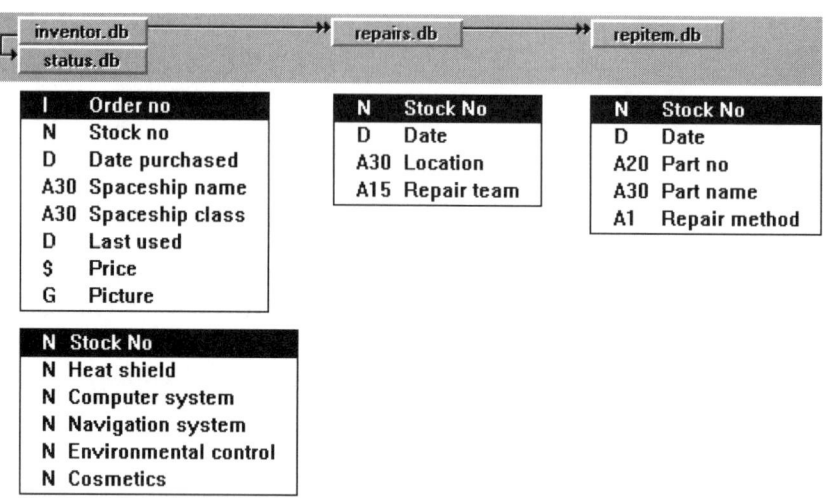

Figure 20-4: The data model shows the four tables displayed by the inventory form.

INVENTOR.DB has two key fields—Order No and Stock No. REPAIRS.DB has two key fields—Stock No and Date. REPITEM.DB has three key fields—Stock No, Date and Part No. STATUS.DB has only one key field because it is linked one-to-one to INVENTOR.DB.

You may be surprised that INVENTOR.DB has two key fields. Normally in a one-to-many relationship, the parent table only has one key field, and the child table is the one with two key fields. Here, the parent table has two key fields also. The Customer form, CUSTVIEW.FSL, also displays INVENTOR.DB, but in the data model for that form, INVENTOR.DB *is* a child table and as such needs two key fields. If this seems confusing for now, that's OK. We'll return to data models later when we look at how the Customer form works. The important thing is that you understand the relationship of these four tables.

INVENTOR.FSL is for viewing data, so no modifications can be written to disk. Each table in the data model has properties that are displayed by right-clicking on the button that represents the table. Right-clicking on the REPAIRS.DB button in the data model displays the pop-up menu shown in Figure 20-5. Selecting Read-Only prevents edits from being written to disk.

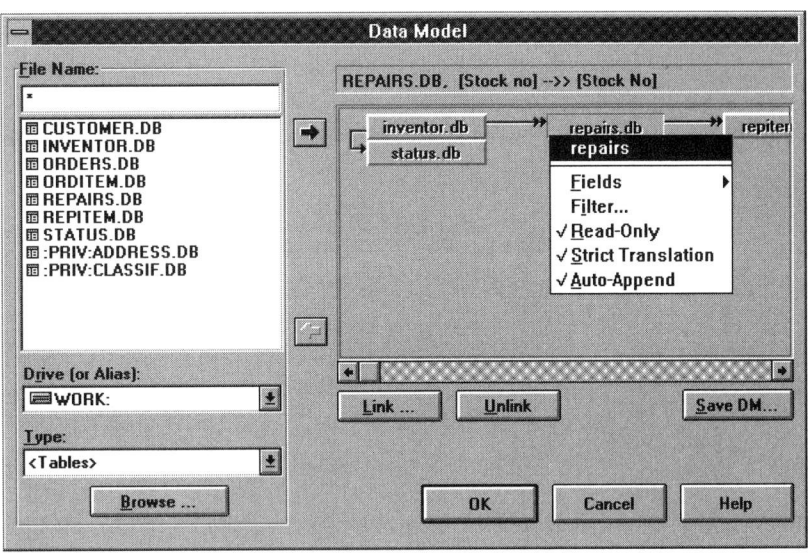

Figure 20-5: The Read-Only property prevents changes from being made to tables.

All tables have their Read-Only property set, including INVENTOR.DB. Entering the order number is necessary to indicate that a space ship is sold, but a TCursor is used. TCursors are not associated with objects on the form—instead, they write data to disk behind the scenes. The code to do this is discussed later in the Chapter.

Inside Scoop

The Read-Only property is automatically set for any tables that are linked one-to-one. Paradox assumes that a one-to-one relationship indicates a lookup table, and automatically sets the table to Read-Only. Tables linked one-to-many are not Read-Only by default. However, either of these defaults can be changed by inspecting the table in the data model.

For now, that's about all there is to this form. The data model has several tables. The OK button only closes the form when called from the main menu, and the Cancel button is hidden. A graph is used, but you saw that in Chapter 13. Let's close this form and return to the main menu. Then we'll see how to edit the data you just looked at.

THE EDIT INVENTORY FORM

The Edit Inventory form (EDITSTOK.FSL) is straightforward. As you can see from Figure 20-6, the form looks similar to INVENTOR.FSL, except that the graph is replaced by fields. This form is simple to create. It is a copy of INVENTOR.FSL, with a few modifications.

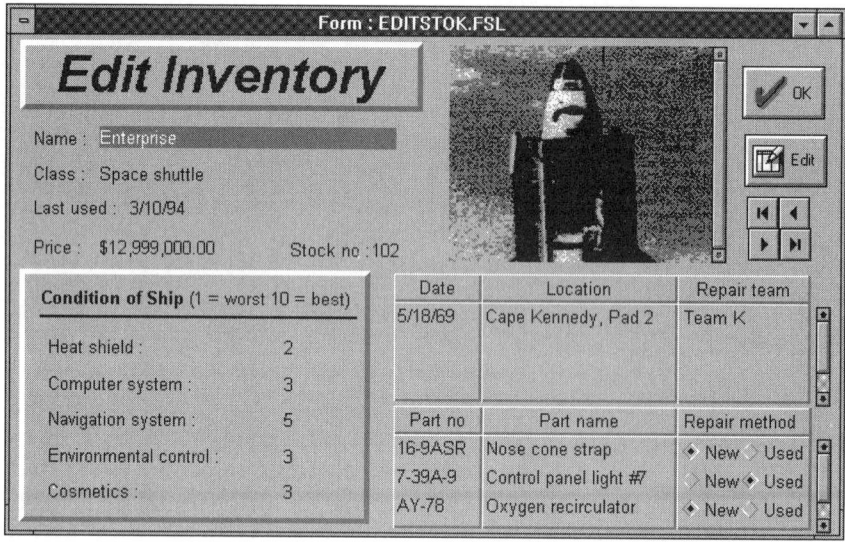

Figure 20-6: The Edit Inventory form is designed for editing data about space ships in stock.

The data model in the EDITSTOK.FSL form has the Read-Only attribute removed from all tables. (By default, STATUS.DB is Read-Only because it is a one-to-one link.) The only other difference between the EDITSTOK.FSL and INVENTOR.FSL is a formula that is used for the Order Number field. When the Order Number field contains a number, it means the spaceship has been sold. To make this clearer, the following formula is used:

```
iif([INVENTOR.Order no]>=1,"SOLD","")
```

This line reads, "If the order number is greater than or equal to 1 (one), which is the lowest possible number in an Autoincrement field, display the word SOLD, otherwise don't display anything." The field is placed on top of the picture of the spaceship because that is the item that was sold.

All this seems like it doesn't have much to do with ObjectPAL, but that's because we haven't looked at the Customer form yet. So let's do that now.

THE CUSTOMER FORM

The Customer form (CUSTVIEW.FSL) shows each Space Ship Surplus customer, every order they placed and all items in each order (see Figure 20-7). The user can add new customers, create new orders and add items to any new or existing order. Calculations are automatic, and the code attached to buttons maintains the relationships between key fields.

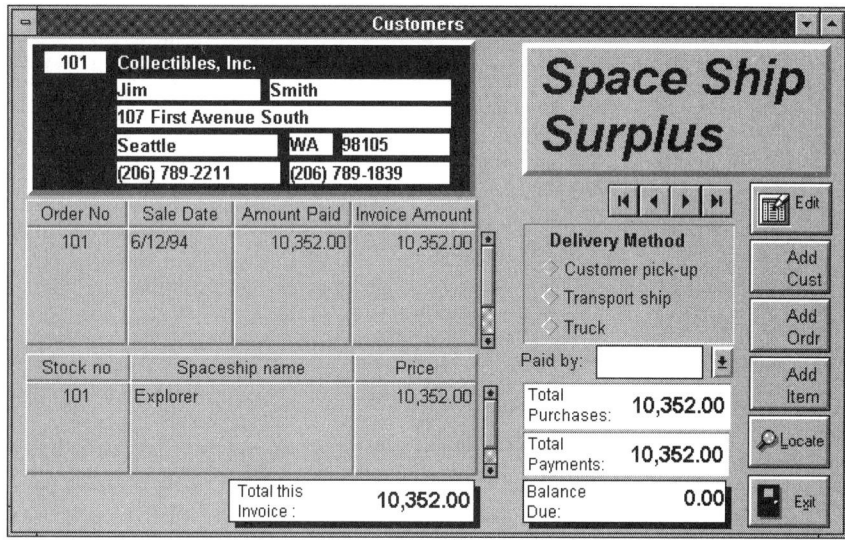

Figure 20-7: The Customer form is where the user views customers and adds orders.

One goal of this application is to keep code to a minimum, so not much error-checking is used. For example, you can delete an item from an order that a customer has already paid for. You can add an item to an order that is several years old. However, the assumption is made that you will use this application sensibly and not try to do such things.

Several components of this form are worth close examination. The data model is a one-to-many-to-many relationship. Calculated fields are placed on this form. Different field types are used, including drop-down lists, radio buttons, and fields in table frame objects. Buttons perform basic functions with a minimum of code. First things first. Let's look at the data model.

The Data Model

The data model for this form is perhaps the most important component. Figure 20-8 shows a one-to-many-to-many relationship. Each customer in CUSTVIEW.FSL may have placed any number of orders and each order can have many items. We need to look closely at what is happening here.

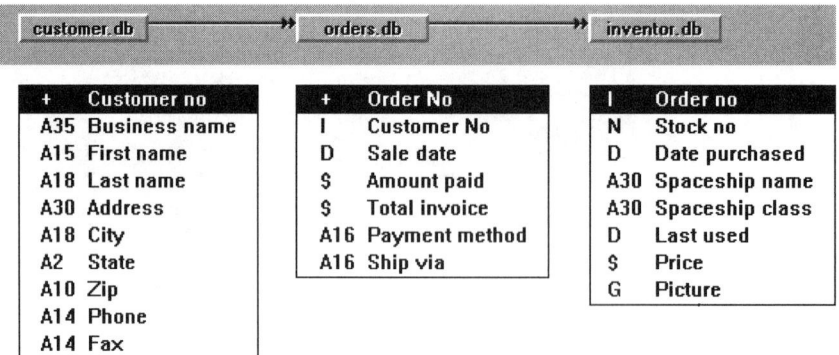

Figure 20-8: The data model for CUSTVIEW.FSL.

The field order is important. As you learned in Chapter 4, key fields must be the first fields in the table's structure. However, in a typical one-to-many relationship, the child table has two key fields. In this case the child table has only one key field. The Order Number field in ORDERS.DB must be unique or a key violation occurs. ORDERS.DB also needs a Customer Number field, because this is the field that links to CUSTOMER.DB.

Normally, when linking two tables, each of which has only one key field, you would expect a one-to-one relationship to be established. In this instance, a one-to-many relationship is established because the parent table is not linked to the key field in the child table. It is not necessary to link a key field to a key field, but each linked table must *contain* a key field. This is worth trying on your own.

Now let's focus on the many-to-many portion of this data model. INVENTOR.DB, the last table in this lineup, has two key fields: Order No and Stock No. This is exactly the relationship you learned earlier with one-to-many relationships. The parent table has one key field and the child table has two key fields.

It is also important to note that tables can have different relationships in different forms. Notice how INVENTOR.DB is the last table in the chain. However, in the Inventory form, it is the parent table.

(Remember that the parent table had two key fields, which seemed a little strange. Well, you now know the reason.)

Other Interactive Features

The customer number and order number shouldn't be edited manually or data integrity could be lost. In this form, the user is not permitted to move the cursor into those fields. How is it done? One of the properties of a field is Tab Stop—the ability to tab to a field, or move to it in any way. This property can be turned on and off. To do this, right-click the field in Design mode, select Run Time Properties, and deselect Tab Stop as shown in Figure 20-9. The Tab Stop property is also turned off for all fields in the inventory table frame because the only time these should be edited is when viewing the form that contains all the inventory information.

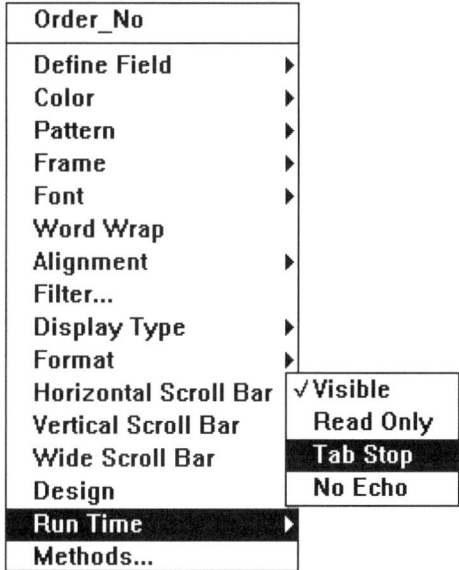

Figure 20-9: The tab stop property of a field can be turned on or off. Any time you don't want the contents of a field to be changed, turning tab stop off is a wise precaution.

Four calculated fields are placed on this form—the ones with white backgrounds. Calculated fields can calculate just about anything, including text strings and programming commands. Total this Invoice, Total Purchases, and Total Payments are simple summary fields (see Figure 20-10). Total this Invoice adds everything in the Price field of the INVENTOR tableframe object. Total Purchases and Total Payments add everything in the Amount Paid and Invoice Amount columns in the ORDERS table frame object. (Note that the table frame header has been edited so that the column headings are different from the actual field names.) The ObjectPAL code for the four calculated fields follows:

Field	ObjectPAL Code
[Total this Invoice]	Field name: Price, Calculation: Sum(INVENTOR.DB.Price)
[Total Purchases white box]	Field name: TotalPurchase, Calculation: Sum(ORDERS.DB.Total Invoice)
[Total Payments white box]	Field name: AmtPaid, Calculation: Sum(ORDERS.DB.Amount Paid)
[Balance Due drop-shadow box]	Field name: Balance, Formula: TotalPurchase - AmtPaid

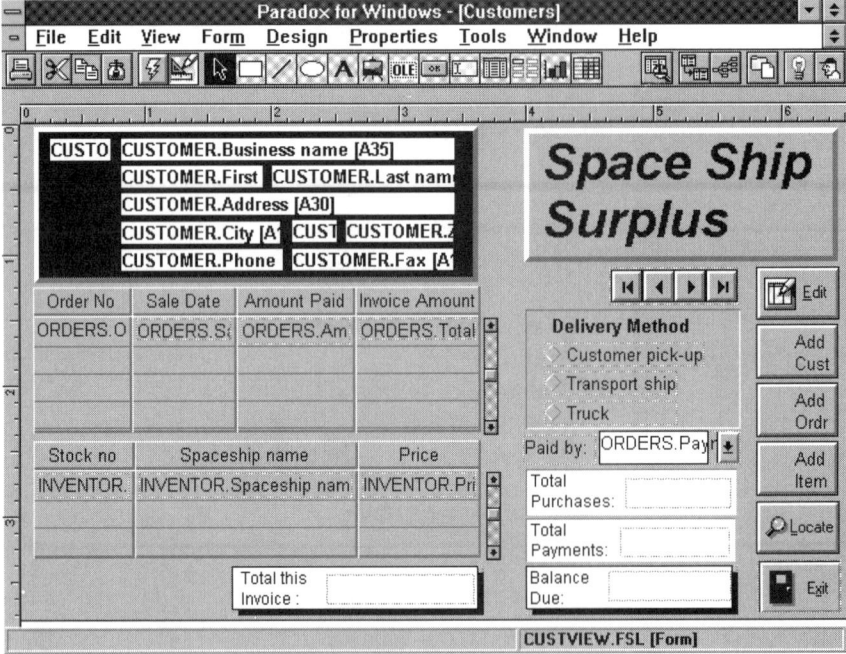

Figure 20-10: Summary fields and calculated fields are really useful—and don't even require ObjectPAL.

The Amount Due calculated field is a little different from the other three. It doesn't summarize data that is contained in Paradox tables—instead, its calculations are based on other calculations. In this case, a custom formula is used. The Total Purchases and Total Payments fields have been given a name other than the default Paradox name, and these named field objects are referenced by the formula for the Balance Due field.

Buttons That Add New Records

Buttons are really useless unless they have some code attached to them. So, the buttons on the Customer form contain some code. But no code exists anywhere else on this form. And only three buttons have code that is worth discussing in-depth. Those are the Add Cust, Add Order and Add Item buttons. Figure 20-11 shows ObjectPAL code attached to the other three buttons, which we won't dwell on.

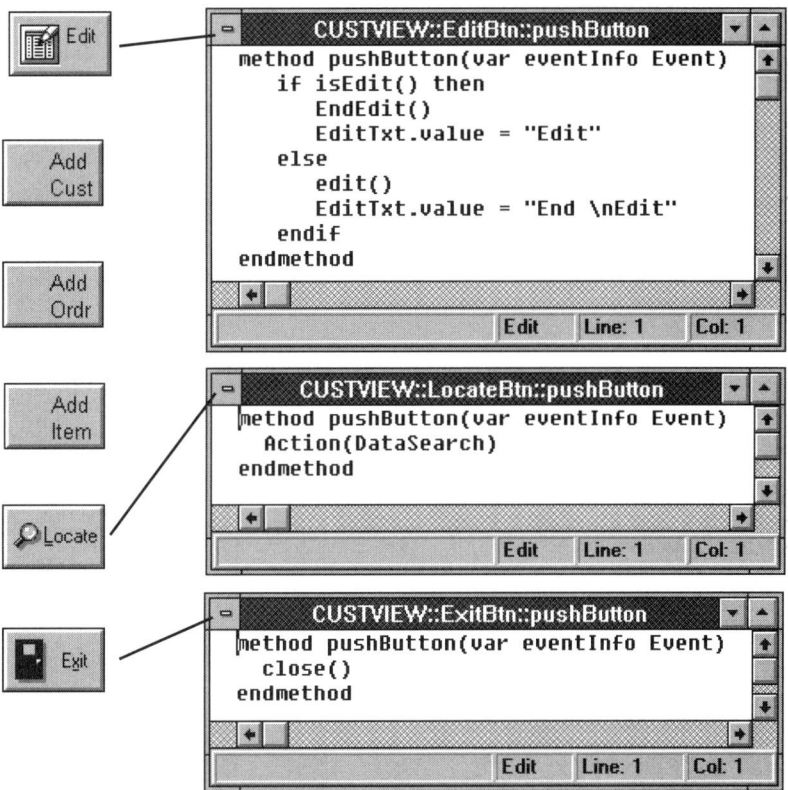

Figure 20-11: These three buttons contain code that is relatively straight-forward.

New Customer

The Customer table's key field is Customer No—an Autoincrement field type. That means that whenever a new record is posted, a new unique customer is automatically assigned. The only thing you really need to do with ObjectPAL is create the new record. The code to add a new customer is shown in Figure 20-12.

```
                  CUSTVIEW::#Button11::pushButton
method pushButton(var eventInfo Event)
var
    uio        UIobject
endvar

    uio.attach("Business_name")   ; Next field on the form
    uio.edit()                    ; Need to be in Edit mode to
    uio.insertRecord()            ;   insert a blank record
    uio.moveTo()                  ; Move to next field to enter data

endmethod

                                                    Edit   Line: 2   Col: 4
```

Figure 20-12: Adding a new customer is easy—just insert a new record.

Paradox must be in Edit mode to insert a new record, and once the new record is inserted, the insertion point is positioned in the business name field. You are now ready to type the data for a new customer. As soon as you leave Edit mode, the record is posted.

Order for a Customer

Adding an order for an existing customer is practically the same as adding a new customer. The order number is an Autoincrement field, so the order number is created automatically when the record is posted. A UIObject acts as a handle to the Sale Date field. However, there are a couple of differences that you can see by looking at Figure 20-13.

```
                  CUSTVIEW::#Button12::pushButton
method pushButton(var eventInfo Event)
var
    uio        UIObject
endvar

    uio.attach("Sale_date")
    uio.edit()                    ; Must be in Edit mode to
    uio.insertRecord()            ;   insert a new record.
    uio.value = today()           ; Assume order is placed today
    action(DataPostRecord)        ; Post record to assign order number
    uio.attach("Amount_Paid")     ; Next field where data
    uio.moveto()                  ;   will be entered manually

endmethod

                                                    Edit   Line: 1   Col: 1
```

Figure 20-13: Adding a new order is similar to adding a new customer.

The eighth line in the *pushButton* method inserts today's date in the Date field because it is assumed that the order is placed on the same day that you are entering a new record. Line 9 posts the record. Why is this record immediately posted to the Orders table? If you are going to add an item to this order, the order number needs to be inserted into the Inventory table to flag the space ship as sold. Because the Autoincrement field assigns a value when the record is posted, posting the record creates the order number that is placed in the order number field of the inventory table when you add items to this customer's order. Finally, the insertion point is moved to the Amount Paid field because that is the next field where you add data.

New Item to an Order

Adding a new item to an order is different from adding a new customer or a new order. In fact, clicking on the Add New Item button doesn't add any items to the order at all. Instead, it opens the Inventory form so you can select the space ship to add to the order. The code in Figure 20-14 is very similar to the code attached to the View Data graphics on the main menu.

```
method pushButton(var eventInfo Event)
var
    f       form
    uio     UIObject
endvar

if f.open("Inventor.fsl", WinStyleHidden) then
    if uio.attach(f.pg.Order_no) then      ; Filter only passes records
        uio.setRange("",0)                 ;    with blank Order_No field
        f.pg.InvTitle = "Ship to Sell"     ; Beveled text frame text
        f.pg.CancelBtn.visible = true      ; Cancel button showing
        f.bringToTop()                     ; Show the form as topmost form
    endif
else
    msgInfo("Program Error","Unable to open Inventory form")
endif

endmethod
```

Figure 20-14: Clicking on the Add Item button opens the inventory form so you can select the ship to sell.

When the Inventory form displays, there is both a Cancel button and an OK button. Clicking on the Cancel button simply closes the form. However, clicking on the OK button is more complex because it calculates the total invoice cost and inserts the order number in the Order Number field in INVENTOR.DB. The ObjectPAL code attached to the OK button is shown in Figure 20-15.

589

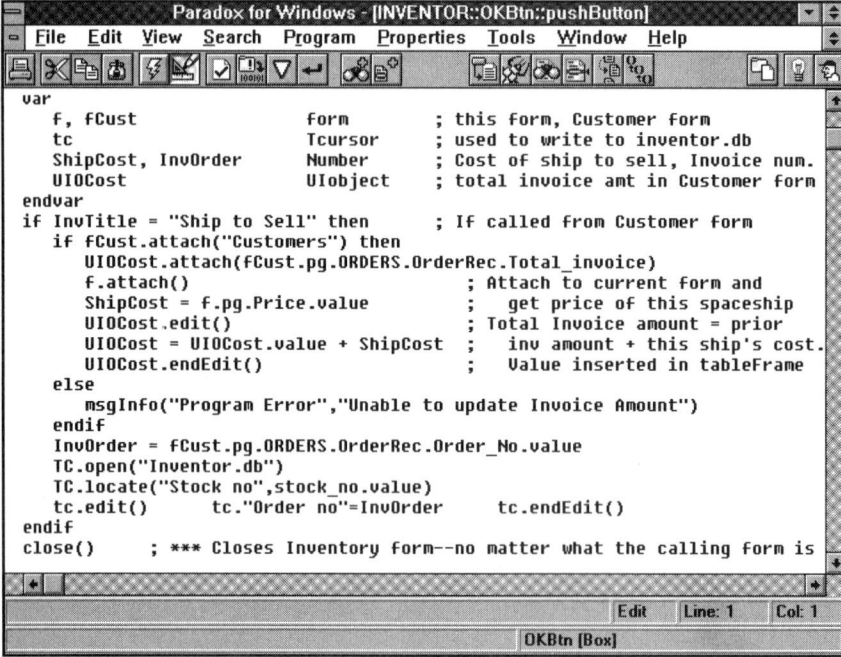

```
var
    f, fCust                    form        ; this form, Customer form
    tc                          Tcursor     ; used to write to inventor.db
    ShipCost, InvOrder          Number      ; Cost of ship to sell, Invoice num.
    UIOCost                     UIobject    ; total invoice amt in Customer form
endvar
if InvTitle = "Ship to Sell" then          ; If called from Customer form
    if fCust.attach("Customers") then
        UIOCost.attach(fCust.pg.ORDERS.OrderRec.Total_invoice)
        f.attach()                          ; Attach to current form and
        ShipCost = f.pg.Price.value         ;   get price of this spaceship
        UIOCost.edit()                      ; Total Invoice amount = prior
        UIOCost = UIOCost.value + ShipCost  ;   inv amount + this ship's cost.
        UIOCost.endEdit()                   ;   Value inserted in tableFrame
    else
        msgInfo("Program Error","Unable to update Invoice Amount")
    endif
    InvOrder = fCust.pg.ORDERS.OrderRec.Order_No.value
    TC.open("Inventor.db")
    TC.locate("Stock no",stock_no.value)
    tc.edit()       tc."Order no"=InvOrder        tc.endEdit()
endif
close()        ; *** Closes Inventory form--no matter what the calling form is
```

Figure 20-15: This code on the Inventory form's OK button adds the selected ship to the customer's order.

Remember that this button serves double duty. When INVENTOR.FSL is opened from the main menu, the OK button closes the form—nothing more. However, when it is opened by clicking the Add Item button on CUSTVIEW.FSL, clicking the OK button adds the selected item to the customer's order. The seventh line in the method makes that decision based on the contents in the beveled text frame. If this form is not called from the Customer form, only the last line executes, and the form is closed. However, if you are adding an item to a customer's order, line 8 attaches to the Customer form, and line 9 is a handle to its Total Invoice field (the one in the table frame object). The tenth and eleventh lines work together to assign the variable ShipCost to the price of the space ship. Line 13 inserts the new total invoice amount into the table frame object on the Customer form.

Now, the order number needs to be updated in the Inventory table. Because the Read-Only property is set in the data model for every table on the form, a UIObject cannot be used. It is impossible to write changes using a UIObject when its table is Read-Only, so a TCursor is used. Line 18 assigns the variable InvOrder to the order number in the table frame object in the Customer form. A TCursor is opened to INVENTOR.DB and the record currently displayed in INVENTOR.FSL is located. When the TCursor is synchronized with the displayed record, line 21 places the TCursor in Edit mode, writes the value in InvOrder to the order number field, and ends Edit mode.

When line 23 returns you to the Customer form, you see that a new record has been added to the table frame that shows the items purchased with each order. In addition, the calculated fields are updated, and all that is left is to type in the amount paid, select how you are paid, and select the delivery method.

MOVING ON

In this chapter, you have seen that an application can be very useful without resorting to lots of ObjectPAL. In fact, planning the data model was as important as the ObjectPAL code. Filters were changed for the Inventory form using ObjectPAL so that the form could be used for three purposes. You have seen some animated buttons and can now copy them to your own applications, along with the buttons to insert records in tables. Finally, the sample application used a form that displays all inventory items, allowing you to page through the items and when the desired item is displayed insert it into LINEITEM.DB and recalculate the total amount for the invoice.

In the next chapter, you learn about another application—a contact manager. There's a lot of ObjectPAL in it, but don't worry. Pertinent code fragments are discussed in detail. The rest will be left for you adventurous people to learn about on your own.

21

THE CONTACT MANAGEMENT APPLICATION

Imagine that you run a business. You know from past experience that you need to be in constant contact with your customers and prospective customers or prospects. That isn't easy. Your customers are scattered all over. You want to use Paradox to keep track of the contacts you make, what transpires and the products you sell. You also need to send letters and print reports. Finally, you want the database to be foolproof and uncluttered. You only want to see what is necessary—no extraneous clutter.

If you haven't used the contact management application included on the companion disk, do so now by running MAIN.FSL. After you use the application, (or at least look through the various forms, you will be more familiar with the topics in this chapter.

The contact management application consists of many components. Tables, forms and reports are the most obvious. Queries are also used extensively throughout the application as well as a custom menu. There is a lot of ObjectPAL code attached to forms, buttons and other objects. That's a lot to keep track of. So that you are not overwhelmed, we'll divide the application into segments, then proceed methodically from form to form.

THE MAIN MENU

When you run the application, the first form you open is MAIN.FSL shown in Figure 21-1), which is the main menu for the application. This form is rather straightforward and not based on a Paradox table. (The Blank option was selected when creating the form.) Let's look at what happens when the form opens and when you click one of the big buttons.

Figure 21-1: The main menu has two big buttons—each of which opens a different form.

The Form's Methods

When you open MAIN.FSL, the Paradox menu and Toolbar are hidden. The menu and Toolbar have no functions that are applicable to this form. Hiding the menu and Toolbar is beneficial because: users of the application cannot use Paradox features that are not pertinent or that may be confusing. Also, the available screen space is larger and the display is less cluttered with these features out of the way.

The *open* method of MAIN.FSL, shown in Figure 21-2, associates a null string with a menu variable (the sixth line) and displays the empty menu (the seventh line). This line is necessary. If you just had *m.show( )*, without *m.addText*, an undefined variable error would result. Because an empty menu is displayed, no menu is visible.

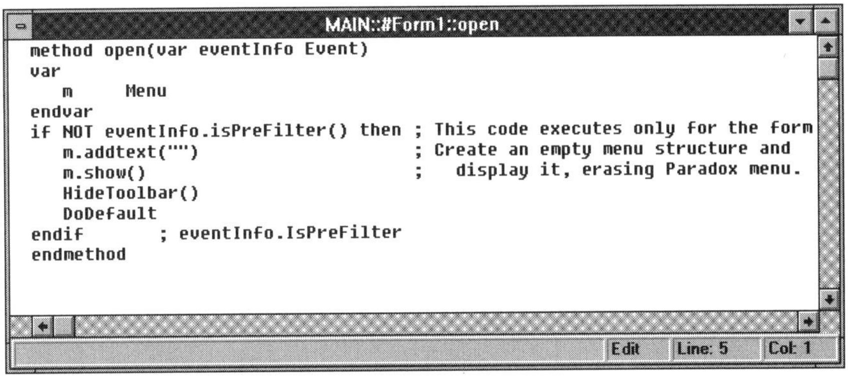

```
┌─────────────────────── MAIN::#Form1::open ──────────────────▼─┬─┐
│ method open(var eventInfo Event)                                 │ │
│ var                                                              │
│     m       Menu                                                 │
│ endvar                                                           │
│ if NOT eventInfo.isPreFilter() then ; This code executes only for the form
│     m.addtext("")                    ; Create an empty menu structure and
│     m.show()                         ;   display it, erasing Paradox menu.
│     HideToolbar()                                                │
│     DoDefault                                                    │
│ endif          ; eventInfo.IsPreFilter                           │
│ endmethod                                                        │
│                                                                  │
│                                                                ▼ │
├─┬──────────────────────────────────────────────────────────┬──┤
│◄│                                                            │►│
│  │                                        │ Edit │ Line: 5 │ Col: 1 │
└─────────────────────────────────────────────────────────────┘
```

Figure 21-2: The *open* method of MAIN.FSL clears the default Paradox menu and hides the Toolbar.

Inside Scoop: ·

You may occasionally see procedures named hideSpeedbar() and showSpeedbar(). They are relics from earlier versions of Paradox when the Toolbar was called SpeedBar. Procedures that reference the SpeedBar still work, for compatibility reasons.

· ·

The MAIN.FSL form's *menuAction* method disables the Close option in the form's control menu. Not only does this code fragment (shown below) prevent choosing Close, it also disables double-clicking the control menu and Ctrl+F4. You can't even press Alt+F4 to leave Paradox because that would close the form also. In other words, the Close event, not just a particular *way* of closing the form, is disabled.

```
If EventInfo.ID() = MenuControlClose then
    DisableDefault
Endif
```

The Close event is disabled for consistency with the other forms and also to force you to use the animated Exit button. The Exit button's *pushButton* method displays a msgQuestion dialog box confirming that you want to exit the application (another reason that Close is disabled). If you choose Yes, the Toolbar is displayed (using *showToolbar*) and the form is closed.

Form Displays

When the user clicks either of the big buttons on the main menu, another form, exactly the same size and in the same location as MAIN.FSL, is displayed. That's sort of neat—clutter on the screen is reduced because forms don't overlap. Let's see how this is done. Figure 21-3 shows the *pushButton* method for the Reports and Letters button.

```
                    MAIN::ReportBtn::pushButton*
method pushButton(var eventInfo Event)
var
   f, fMain       form
   x, y, w, h     longInt
endvar

fMain.attach()                            ; Attach to the current form
fMain.getPosition(x, y, w, h)             ;   and get its size and location
f.open("REPORTS.FSL",WinStyleDefault, x,y,w,h)  ; Open next form and
fMain.hide()                              ;     hide current form

endmethod

                                              Edit   Line: 12   Col: 7
```

Figure 21-3: This code opens another form with the same size and location as MAIN.FSL.

The *pushButton* method shown in Figure 21-3 declares two types of variables: form and longInt. After attaching to MAIN.FSL (the sixth line), *getPosition* assigns values to the variables x, y, w and h. As you can see from Figure 21-4, the variables x and y specify the upper left corner of the form; w and h specify the width and height. After the size and location of MAIN.FSL is determined, these values are used when opening REPORTS.FSL. Finally, the *pushButton* method hides MAIN.FSL (the ninth line) so that even if the user moves REPORTS.FSL, MAIN.FSL cannot be seen. When the user close REPORTS.FSL, the method makes MAIN.FSL visible using the *show* procedure.

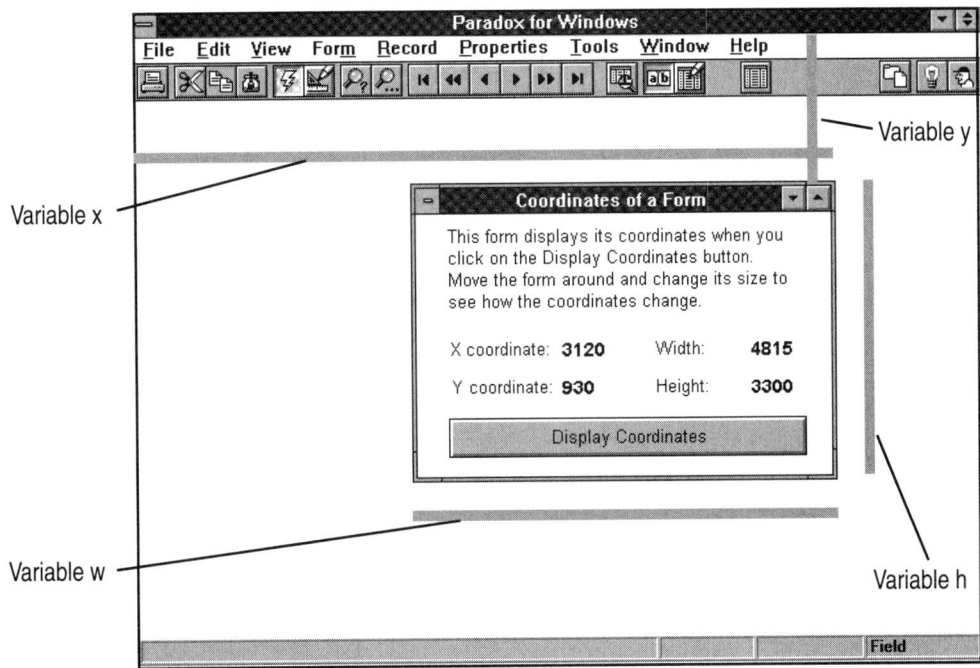

Figure 21-4: A form's size and position are determined using four variables—x, y, w and h.

You probably still have questions about positioning forms. What unit of measurement is used? Where is the coordinate 0,0 (known as the origin) located? A reasonable assumption is that pixels (dots on the screen) are the measurement and that the origin is the upper left pixel. The problem with pixels is that you may be using VGA resolution (640 pixels across and 480 pixels top to bottom), Super VGA resolution (for example, 800 pixels by 600 pixels), or something else. If pixels are the unit of measure, locations of objects would change based on the screen resolution. Forms would change proportions when displayed at different resolutions. This is a problem.

Paradox uses a measurement called a *twip*. I know, you think I'm joking because it's such a weird word. But it's true. A twip is 1/1440 of an inch or 1/20 of a point (as in 12-point text). This is a very small measurement (the form in Figure 21-4 is almost 5,000 twips wide), which explains why longInt is used as the variable type for x, y, w and h. A twip is also device-independent. The screen resolution doesn't matter. A twip is a twip is a twip.

The coordinate system also needs a little explaining. If you are referring to the position of a form, the origin is the upper left corner of the Paradox desktop, which starts just below the Toolbar. Dialog boxes (special kinds of forms) and the Paradox application use the upper left corner of the screen as the origin. Ever notice how, even if you are running an application in a window that is positioned toward one side of the screen, that dialog boxes for that application appear in the center of the screen? Dialog boxes use a coordinate system based on the screen rather than the application window.

Figure 21-5 shows screen coordinates. Notice the Y coordinate is the same value for both the dialog box and the form. In the Figure, Paradox is maximized, so the Y coordinate of the dialog box is measured down from the top of the title bar (the same as the top of the screen). This seems like nit-picky stuff, but if you want to position forms and dialog boxes in a specific location, it is important information.

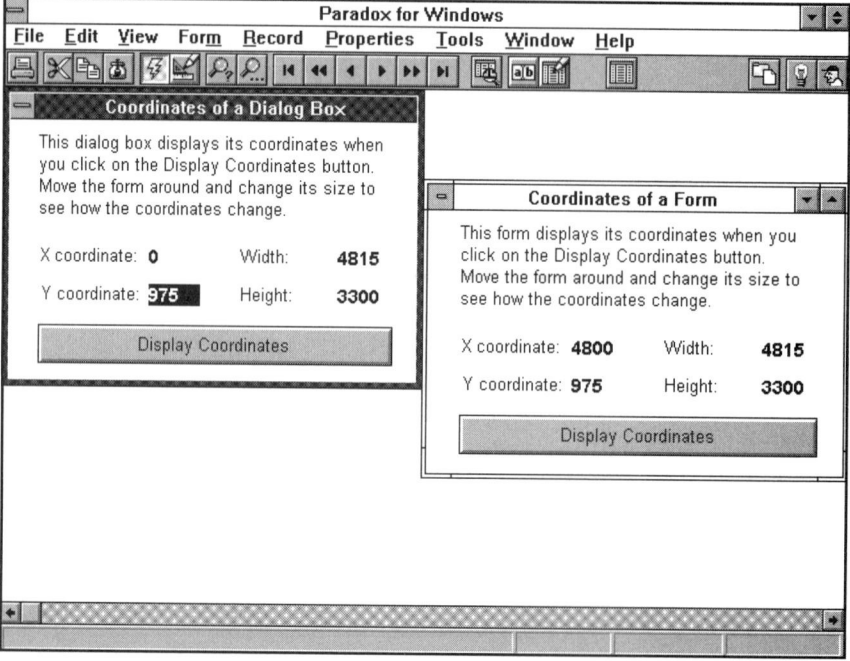

Figure 21-5: The coordinates for a form are relative to the Paradox desktop, whereas the coordinates for the application and for dialog boxes are relative to the screen.

So far, we have discussed ObjectPAL code and concepts for MAIN.FSL, so let's continue exploring the contact management application. From this opening main menu form, click the Display Customer Info button, and you'll see the information you want to track and the programming that makes it possible.

CUSTOMER INFORMATION FORM

The customer information form (CUSTVIEW.FSL) displays customer data, all customer contacts, and follow-up tasks. The user can edit and delete data in this form. Interesting features of the form include the formulas used to display data, the data model, custom menus and more. CUSTVIEW.FSL has several ways of looking at data. Figure 21-6 shows all data in the customer table, along with the most recent contact information. There are also other views, if you haven't seen them already.

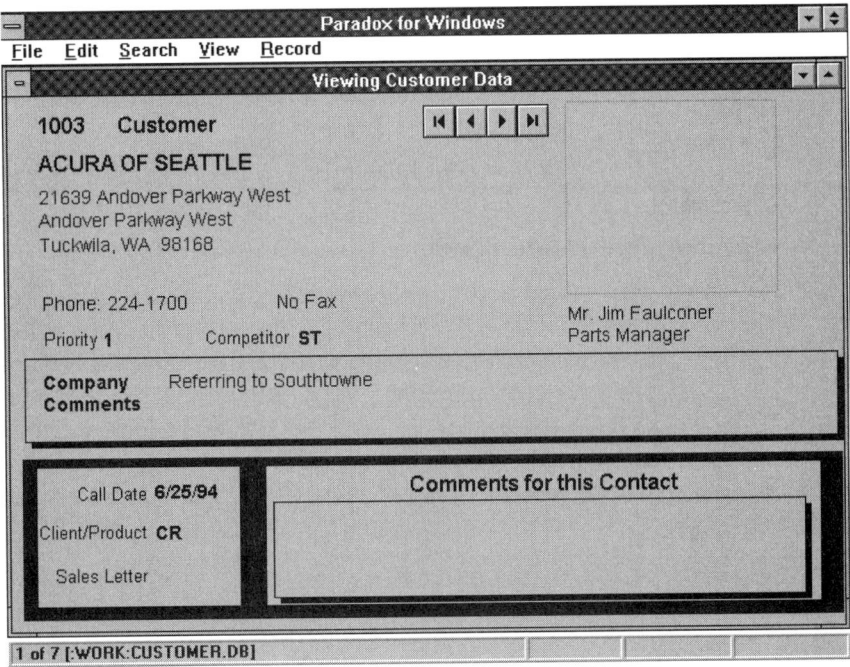

Figure 21-6: The CUSTVIEW.FSL form uses field labels only when necessary, and formulas display fields such as the decision-maker's name, phone and fax number.

Formulas to Display Data

It is easier to find information when there is not a lot of unnecessary text on the screen. Who needs clutter? Notice that the form shown in Figure 21-6 uses labels for field names only when necessary for clarification: no Mr/Ms, First Name or Last Name field labels are used. The following formula displays the name in the cleanest possible way:

    [:WORK:CUSTOMER.Mr_Ms]+" " +[:WORK:CUSTOMER.First name]+"
    "+[:WORK:CUSTOMER.Last name]

On first glance, the phone number appears to be preceded by a label. However, a formula is used to print the word "Phone" in front of the phone number. The phone number and the word "Phone" display only if the phone field contains data.

The form displays "No Fax" when the fax field contains no data. The fax field uses the same type of formula. Here's the formula:

```
iif([:WORK:CUSTOMER.Fax]="","No Fax","Fax:
"+[:WORK:CUSTOMER.Fax])
```

Also look at the formula for the customer/prospect field. The database contains either a C or a P, but the form displays "Customer" or "Prospect." You're right—it uses the formula shown below. Try opening CUSTVIEW.FSL in design mode and looking at these formulas. Although formulas are a little more work, when you're done, your application looks really clean.

```
iif([:WORK:CUSTOMER.Prospect Cust]="P","Prospect","Customer")
```

Multipage Forms

Forms can be one page or many pages and are typically organized by function. CUSTVIEW.FSL displays data in different ways; it consists of several pages—each page with a different view of the data. You can view all customer data, view four or eight sales calls at a time, or view follow-ups. Figure 21-7 shows these choices. Regardless of the way the data is displayed, this form serves one purpose—to display data. That's why all of these views were included on one form. Use the View menu to select other pages on this form.

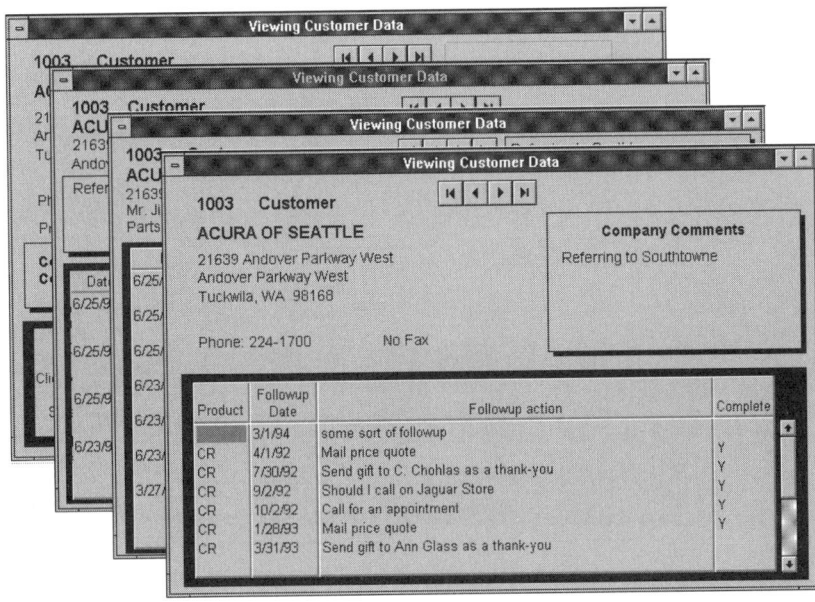

Figure 21-7: CUSTVIEW.FSL has several pages—each with a different view of the data.

CUSTVIEW.FSL not only lets you view data—you can edit contact and follow-up information also. Consequently, adding contact information is on yet another page on the same form. To access the page for adding contact information, select the Edit menu and choose Add New Contact/Follow-Up.

Data Model

As you certainly must have noticed, one page of the CUSTVIEW.FSL form displays four sales calls at a time. Another page of the form displays eight sales calls at a time. In order to be able to add the fields from CALLS.DB to the form twice, we added CALLS.DB to the data model twice. The data model for CUSTVIEW.FSL is shown in Figure 21-8. (If you have questions about data models, refer to Chapter 4.) Notice the one-to-many relationship between Customer and the two instances of CALLS.DB. The third one-to-many link is with FOLLOWUP.DB.

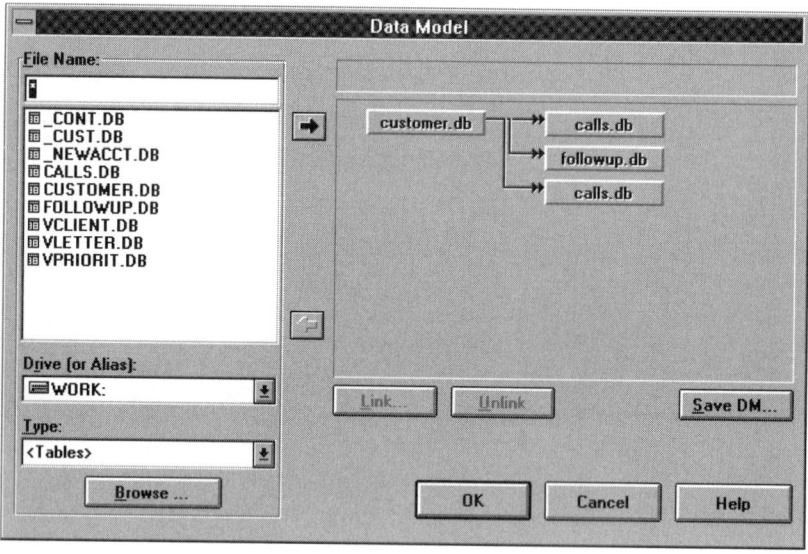

Figure 21-8: The data model shows three one-to-many relationships. The table CALLS.DB has been added to the data model twice.

Inside Scoop:

The same table can be added to the Data Model as many times as you want. A table can even be linked to itself. Let's say you have a customer table with a referral field that contains a customer number in the customer table. Instead of displaying the customer number, you display the customer name. But then you want to see who referred *that* customer so you link the customer table to itself a third time. And so on.

Menu Bar

You learned how to create a simple custom menu in Chapter 17. However, those menus had no fancy options like check marks, grayed items or disabled selections. You could not use the same menu option in two different menus. For example, it was not permissible to place an Open option on both the File and Form menus. The menu in our sample contact management application is not limited in this way. Even though expanding the menu is a little more work, the extra work is well worth it.

To create a custom menu, follow these steps:

1. Define variables and constants. When referring to menu items, refer to the constants rather than the actual menu text. Use two menu variables to the menu items: PopUpMenu for each drop down menu (such as the File menu) and Menu for the menu as a whole.

2. Create the menu using the variables and constants defined in step 1. Define menus by adding text items, such as Main Menu, Report Menu and Print, to the PopUpMenu variable. Associate the PopUpMenu variable with a Menu variable.

3. Show the custom menu. Use the Menu variable in a one-line command to display the menu.

These three steps can be performed in any order, but typically constants and variables are assigned first. The only other step is to write code that performs an action when the menu item is selected.

These three main steps are followed in order to create a full-featured menu. Constants (or ID numbers) are assigned to all menu items. Like the name implies, they don't change even if the menu text changes. Later, when using the menu, the menu options are accessed by the constants rather than the text string that is displayed in the menu. The Const window in Figure 21-9 shows menu items assigned to integers. Notice that constants are declared in the Const window for the form because the menu is the same for every page on the form. If you want different menus for each page, you should use the page's Const window instead.

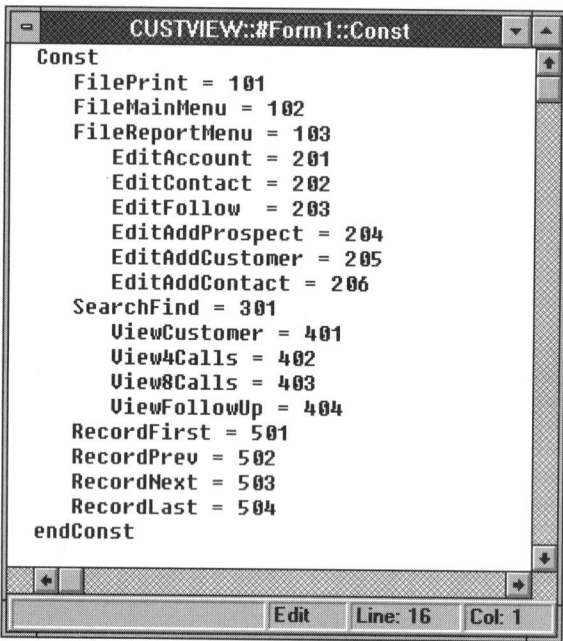

Figure 21-9: The form's Const window defines constants—one for each menu item.

The Var window for the form (Figure 21-10) has two variable types defined, so they are available to every object on the form. The menu variable is a handle to the entire menu. Several PopUpMenu variables (FileMenu, EditMenu, SearchMenu, and so on) are handles to each menu item.

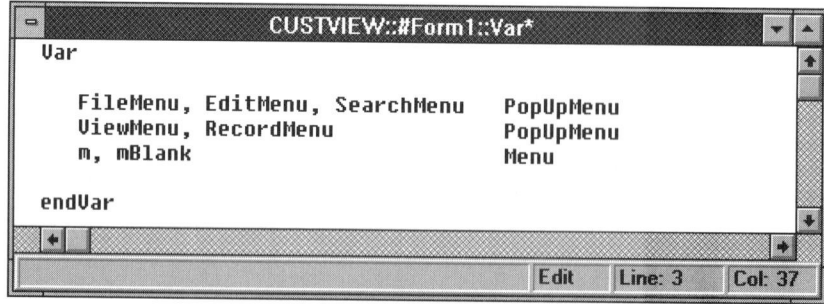

Figure 21-10: The form's Var window declares all menu variables used on this form. The PopUpMenu variable is a handle to the items in each menu. The Menu variable is a handle to the collection of PopUpMenu variables.

Now that constants and variables are defined, it's time to build the menus using *addText*, which adds items to a pull-down menu.

addText takes three arguments: the menu text, display attribute and ID number (constants). Figure 21-11 shows how the menu is built in this contact management application. Enclose the menu text in quotation marks. An ampersand tells Paradox to underline the letter that follows and use it as a hot key. Pretty powerful stuff—you just type an ampersand and Paradox handles menu keystrokes, allowing you to use these menus just as you'd use menus in any other Windows application. The second argument is the display attribute. In this application, MenuEnabled is used for every menu option, but you could have used MenuGrayed, MenuChecked, MenuDisabled, or any number of other attributes. This application does not use any of the special menu attributes, but you can add them if you want to. Refer to online help for more details. The third argument is UserMenu plus one of the constants declared in the form's Const window.

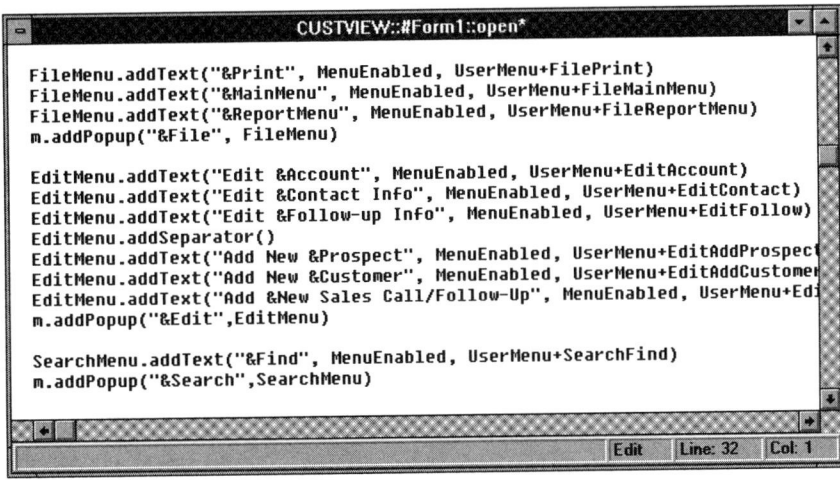

```
CUSTVIEW::#Form1::open*

FileMenu.addText("&Print", MenuEnabled, UserMenu+FilePrint)
FileMenu.addText("&MainMenu", MenuEnabled, UserMenu+FileMainMenu)
FileMenu.addText("&ReportMenu", MenuEnabled, UserMenu+FileReportMenu)
m.addPopup("&File", FileMenu)

EditMenu.addText("Edit &Account", MenuEnabled, UserMenu+EditAccount)
EditMenu.addText("Edit &Contact Info", MenuEnabled, UserMenu+EditContact)
EditMenu.addText("Edit &Follow-up Info", MenuEnabled, UserMenu+EditFollow)
EditMenu.addSeparator()
EditMenu.addText("Add New &Prospect", MenuEnabled, UserMenu+EditAddProspect
EditMenu.addText("Add New &Customer", MenuEnabled, UserMenu+EditAddCustomer
EditMenu.addText("Add &New Sales Call/Follow-Up", MenuEnabled, UserMenu+Edi
m.addPopup("&Edit",EditMenu)

SearchMenu.addText("&Find", MenuEnabled, UserMenu+SearchFind)
m.addPopup("&Search",SearchMenu)
```

Edit   Line: 32   Col: 1

Figure 21-11: The *open* method is where the menu is built.

Each menu item is assigned an ID number (the third argument). What is UserMenu? Paradox menu IDs must be within a specific range, and this range may change with future versions of Paradox. So Paradox has a built-in constant called UserMenu that makes sure the menu's ID is within the accepted range. You have to help out, too by not defining menu constants that are larger than 2047—otherwise, the menu ID will be above the accepted range.

After all the items for a specific menu are created, *addPopup* adds them to the pull down menu. Its arguments are the menu name (in quotes) followed by the PopUpMenu variable. I know, there is a lot of code, but once you understand *addText* and constants, you understand almost all you need to know about building menus.

The final task in creating a menu is to display it. Figure 21-12 shows you how to display a menu. In Chapter 17 you learned that *isPreFilter* determines whether the code executes for each object on the form or only for the form itself. The menu code shouldn't execute for each object on the form, because clicking a button or moving to another field would redisplay the menu.

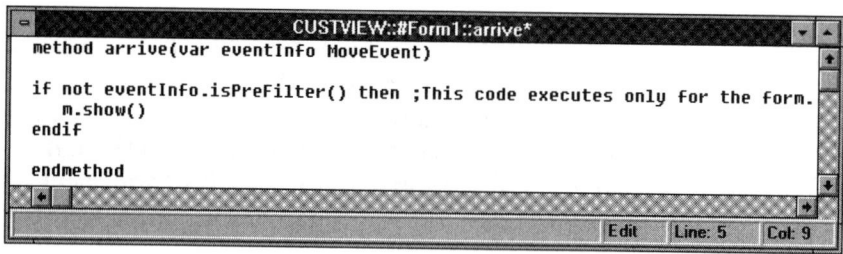

```
CUSTVIEW::#Form1::arrive*
method arrive(var eventInfo MoveEvent)

if not eventInfo.isPreFilter() then ;This code executes only for the form.
   m.show()
endif

endmethod
```
Edit   Line: 5   Col: 9

Figure 21-12: The easiest part of creating a menu is displaying it. Typically the menu is displayed on the *arrive* method.

Inside Scoop

In the previous chapters you have seen text placed in the *else* clause of *eventInfo.isPreFilter*. However, the syntax in Figure 21-12 is far more concise than the following:

```
if eventInfo.isPreFilter() then
     ;// This code executes for each object on the form:
else
     ;// This code executes only for the form:
endif
```

Notice that *m.show()* is attached to the *arrive* method of the form. *open* only occurs once, but if the form does not have the focus (for example, because another form or dialog box is displayed), *arrive* occurs when you come back. This is important because another form may have changed the menu, and the custom menu always needs to be displayed when using this form.

We now have a custom menu to which you can add all the bells and whistles you desire; but the form does nothing. We need to tell Paradox what to do when a menu item is selected.

When you select a menu item, Paradox places the value assigned in the *addText* statement (UserMenu + the constant defined in the form's Const window) in an *eventInfo* packet. When Paradox triggers the *menuAction* method, that value is passed to the *menuAction* method via the *eventInfo* packet. The switch block in the *menuAction* method, a portion of which is shown in Figure 21-13, tells Paradox what to do when a menu item is selected.

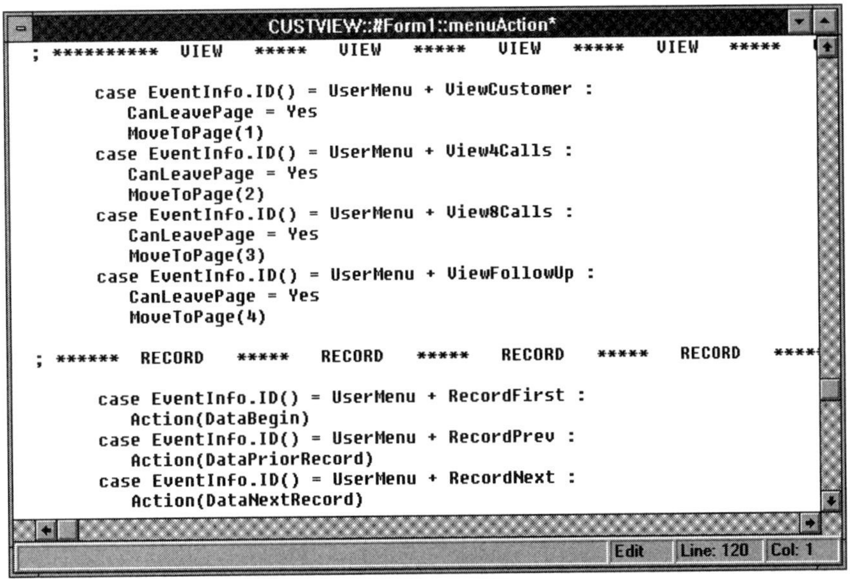

```
                         CUSTVIEW::#Form1::menuAction*
; ********** VIEW ***** VIEW ***** VIEW ***** VIEW *****

        case EventInfo.ID() = UserMenu + ViewCustomer :
            CanLeavePage = Yes
            MoveToPage(1)
        case EventInfo.ID() = UserMenu + View4Calls :
            CanLeavePage = Yes
            MoveToPage(2)
        case EventInfo.ID() = UserMenu + View8Calls :
            CanLeavePage = Yes
            MoveToPage(3)
        case EventInfo.ID() = UserMenu + ViewFollowUp :
            CanLeavePage = Yes
            MoveToPage(4)

; ****** RECORD ***** RECORD ***** RECORD ***** RECORD ****

        case EventInfo.ID() = UserMenu + RecordFirst :
            Action(DataBegin)
        case EventInfo.ID() = UserMenu + RecordPrev :
            Action(DataPriorRecord)
        case EventInfo.ID() = UserMenu + RecordNext :
            Action(DataNextRecord)

                                            Edit    Line: 120    Col: 1
```

Figure 21-13: Selecting a menu item triggers this code in the form's *menuAction* method. The switch block makes the menu perform an action.

All this work has its rewards. In Chapter 17, the text in menus was typed in two locations. If you want to change a menu item, you have to change the text in two places. In this example, the menu text is in only one place—the *open* method of the form. The code is less likely to break during future revisions, and that is a really nice benefit!

There is more to this form, but it is for you to discover on your own. As a hint, look at the *menuAction* method attached to the form to see what happens each time you select a menu option. You will notice that another form is called if you want to edit customer data. Also look at how new contact information and follow-ups are added.

The next form to discuss in depth is the Find Customer form. The only way to go there is by clicking the Search menu and choosing Find. Do that now. Or take a break and do it when you come back.

THE FIND CUSTOMER FORM

When you are looking through customer data, you need to be able to quickly search for a specific customer. The Search menu is available only on the Customer Information form. (Even though adding contact information and follow-ups is on a page of this form, you can't search for a customer from that page.) When you click the Search menu and choose Find, a dialog box displays at the lower portion of the screen (see Figure 21-14).

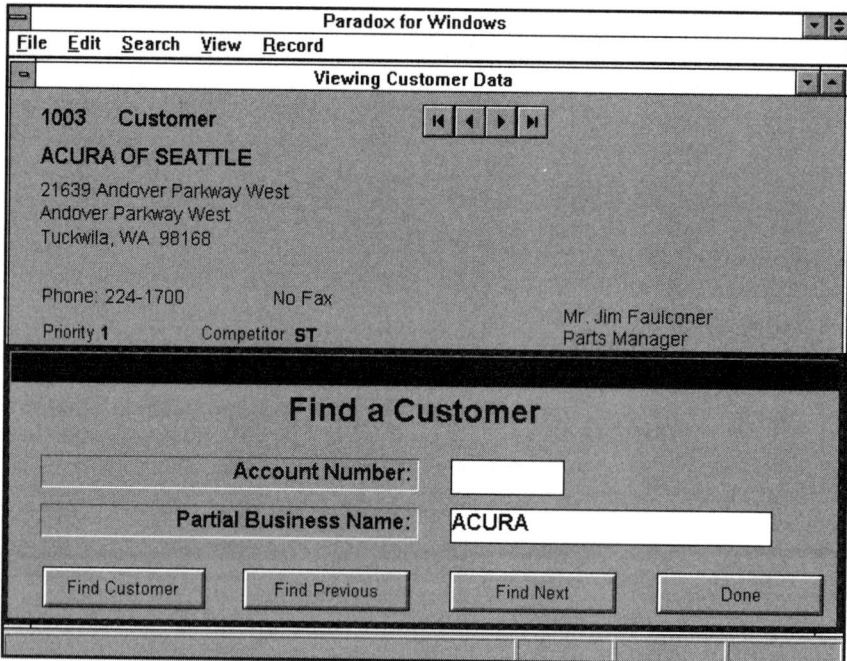

Figure 21-14: The Find Customer dialog box only displays the Find Previous and Find Next buttons only when searching by business name.

When designing an application, you want to be sure that future changes won't break existing code. The height of FINDCUST.FSL might change in the future, to accommodate more search fields, for example. You want the Find Customer dialog box to display properly, without regard to its size. The bottom of the dialog box should always be at the bottom of the screen.

The Find Customer form is opened from the *menuAction* method on CUSTVIEW.FSL, so let's see how that works. FINDCUST.FSL opens it in a specific position, using the variables x, y, w and h, (just like opening CUSTVIEW.FSL). Figure 21-15 shows the code fragment that opens the form.

```
┌─────────────────────────────────────────────────────────────────────┐
│ ═          CUSTVIEW::#Form1::menuAction                          ▼ ▲ │
│ ; ******* SEARCH  *****  SEARCH  *****  SEARCH  *****  SEARCH  ***│   │
│                                                                       │
│         case EventInfo.ID() = UserMenu + SearchFind :                 │
│            f.attach()                                                 │
│            if f.getTitle() = ViewData then                            │
│               CanLeavePage = Yes                                      │
│               ap.GetPosition(x, y, w, h)      ; origin relative to screen │
│               f.GetPosition(x1, y1, w, h)     ; origin relative to form │
│               f.open("FINDCUST",WinStyleDefault+WinStyleHidden)       │
│               f.GetPosition(x2, y2, w1, FindH)                        │
│               f.setPosition(x+x1+60, y+y1+h+585-FindH, w-20, FindH)   │
│               f.show()                         ; display FindCust dlg box │
│               f.wait()                         ; wait until dlg box closes │
│            else                                                       │
│               msgInfo("Wait","You must first click the Save Data button") │
│            endif                                                      │
│                                                                   ▼   │
│ ←                                                                 →   │
│                                          Edit │ Line: 104 │ Col: 62   │
└─────────────────────────────────────────────────────────────────────┘
```

Figure 21-15: The Find Customer form is precisely positioned, and even if its size changes this code doesn't have to be changed.

Let's look at how FINDCUST.FSL is positioned—first along the X axis (horizontally). This is not as easy as it might seem at first. FINDCUST.FSL is a dialog box, so its origin is relative to the screen. However, it needs to be positioned relative to the Viewing Customer Data form, whose origin is relative to the application. This can be done by getting the position of the application *and* the form (the sixth and seventh lines). The X-coordinate used to position FINDCUST.FSL is the X-coordinate of the application plus the X-coordinate of the form plus a few twips to account for the form's border.

The Y-coordinate is a little trickier because you first need to find the position of the bottom of the form (which should be the same as the bottom of the dialog box when it displays). Then measure up the height of the Find Customer dialog box to determine what the Y-coordinate of the dialog box should be. The bottom of the form is calculated by adding the Y-coordinate of the application plus the Y-coordinate of the form plus the height of the form plus the height of the menu bar and the title bar (585 twips). Subtracting the height of the dialog box (FindH) determines its Y-coordinate. Once the X and Y coordinates are calculated, the position of the Find Customer dialog box can be determined no matter how its height may change.

The other important aspect of the code fragment is in the twelfth line. *Wait* tells Paradox to stop executing the method until control is returned from the form that was just called. Because FINDCUST.FSL is a dialog box, this line has the effect of making the computer beep any time you click outside the dialog box. Without line 12, you could still use the menu and move from record to record in the customer form. Try commenting out line 12 and notice the difference.

The Find buttons are similar to those in the Video Rental application. They include error-checking (a value must be typed into one of the criteria fields). When searching for a business name, if locatePattern finds a match, Find Next and Find Previous buttons display. Clicking the Cancel Find button closes the dialog box.

The next form to explore is the Report form. The easiest way to get there is by clicking the File menu and choosing "Report Menu." Alternatively, you could return to the Opening form and click the Reports and Letters button.

THE REPORT FORM

The report selection form, REPORTS.FSL, lets you create many different reports. REPORTS.FSL is a multipage form. The first page contains buttons so that you can select the report you want. After you have selected a report, a different page of the form is displayed and asks for more information. In effect, you are entering query criteria. Queries are performed before producing any of the reports generated by this application. In just a moment we'll look closely at how this works.

A lot of code is attached to this form. In fact, too much to cover in this chapter. For those of you who feel like exploring, open the form and see what's there. If you really like to go exploring, open the library TRACKER.LSL. For the rest of us mere mortals, we will cover some key code fragments, progressing from the report selection page to filling in report criteria, and finally viewing the report on screen.

Code Global to the Form

Did you notice that whenever the mouse pointer is positioned over a button, a message describing the button's function is displayed in the status bar? When the mouse pointer is moved off the button, the message is erased. Each button has code attached to the *mouseEnter* method that displays a message. The *mouseEnter* method is where you attach code that executes whenever the mouse pointer enters an object. Each button could also have code attached to the *mouseExit* method that clears the message when the pointer is moved off the button. But that's a lot of work because the same code would have to be attached to every button. Who needs to do the same thing several times? Paradox to the rescue!

If you examine the methods for buttons, you see that code is attached to *mouseEnter*, but *mouseExit* is empty. Remember how events bubble up to the form level and are then dispatched to the target object? (Refer to Chapter 16.) We can use that to our benefit in this case. We really want to tell Paradox, "If the mouse pointer is moved off any button on the form, remove the message from the status bar and delete any text in the report description box. Do this for every button but not for any other objects." Figure 21-16 shows the code attached to the *mouseExit* method of the form; and notice that it executes for each object on the form.

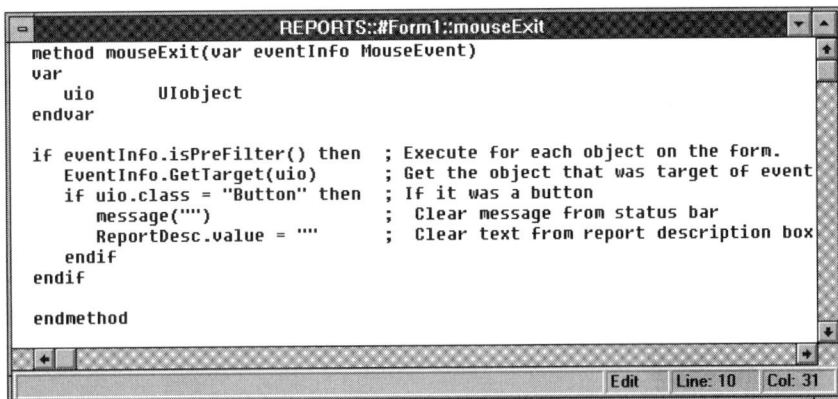

```
method mouseExit(var eventInfo MouseEvent)
var
    uio        UIobject
endvar

if eventInfo.isPreFilter() then    ; Execute for each object on the form.
    EventInfo.GetTarget(uio)       ; Get the object that was target of event
    if uio.class = "Button" then   ; If it was a button
        message("")                ;    Clear message from status bar
        ReportDesc.value = ""      ;    Clear text from report description box
    endif
endif

endmethod
```

REPORTS::#Form1::mouseExit   Edit   Line: 10   Col: 31

Figure 21-16: To clear the status bar message and report description text for each button on the form, code is attached to the *mouseExit* method of the form. Even though the code executes when the mouse leaves a button, no code is attached to the *mouseExit* method of the button.

How does this code work? When an event occurs (in this case, a *mouseExit* event), a packet of information about the event is created and passed to built-in methods. The *getTarget* method returns the handle of the UIObject where the most recent event occurred. If the type of UIObject is a button, a blank message is displayed and a blank text string is displayed in the report description box. This erases any previously existing text.

This example of code attached to the form actually modifies the behavior of other objects on the form. Any time it is possible to write code once and make it visible to all objects that need to access it, you've done yourself a favor. There are fewer mistakes, application development is faster, and the final application is easier to maintain. You'll see other examples of this as we continue exploring this form.

Report Criteria

Let's see what happens when you create a Sales Call report. From the Report Menu, click the Sales Call Report button to display the page shown in Figure 21-17. The form looks pretty simple, but there is a lot going on behind the scenes. A sales call report is created by filling in the blanks on page 2 of REPORTS.FSL. Valid dates must be typed in the Starting Date and Ending Date fields. Any time the drop-down list for the Product Code field is selected, a list displays all products that have been sold between the dates specified. Let's discuss the error-checking for each of these fields.

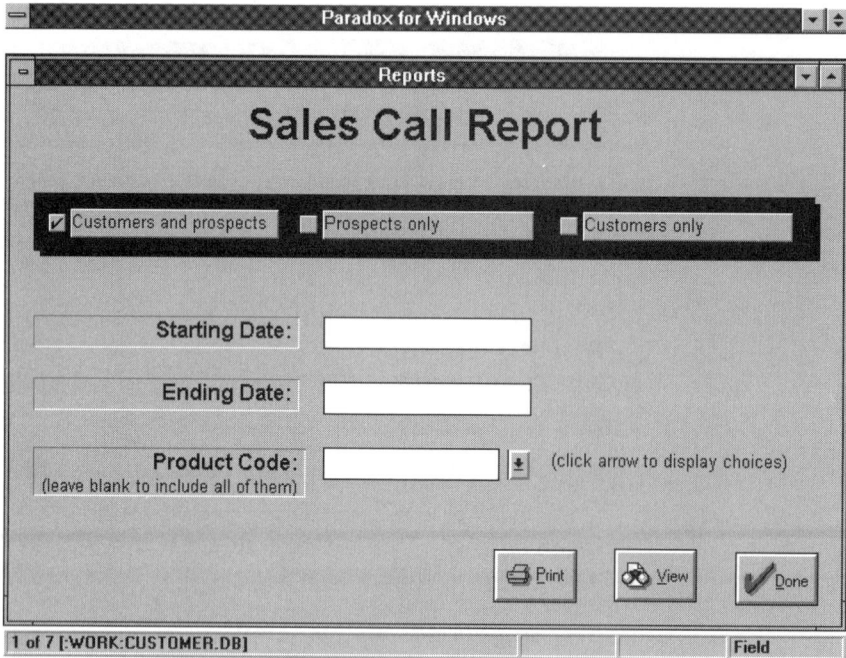

Figure 21-17: The Sales Call report page verifies each field before proceeding to the next field.

The form is filled out from top to bottom. First, the prospect/customer check box. The default is always Customers and Prospects. The variable PorC is set in the page's *arrive* method. The check boxes don't need any error-checking. Customers and Prospects is already checked. Whatever happens, one check box always remains checked. The only possible error is that the user might select the wrong option accidentally. It's hard to test for that.

The Start Date and End Date fields must contain a date. What if someone types something other than a date? Or they type 2/30/95, which is in date format but is not a valid date. This should not be allowed. To test for valid dates, you tell Paradox, "Try to convert the value in this field to a date. If that's not possible, display an error message and don't leave the field." Figure 21-18 shows the code for this error checking.

```
╔══════════════════ REPORTS::SCStartDate::canDepart ══════════════╗
  method canDepart(var eventInfo MoveEvent)

  TRY
     self.Date()          ; Try to convert the value in this field to a date
  OnFail                                      ; If not possible,
     MsgInfo("Oops","Please type a valid date")   ;   Error dialog
     EventInfo.SetErrorCode(CanNotDepart)         ;   Don't leave field
  endtry

  endmethod
╚══════════════════════════════════════════════════════════════════╝
                                          Edit    Line: 3    Col: 1
```

Figure 21-18: If an invalid date is entered, the Start Date field's *canDepart* method displays a dialog box and prevents the user from leaving the field.

The sixth line tells Paradox, "Do not leave the field." Since Paradox tests whether it can depart from an object before actually departing, the error code prevents Paradox from leaving the field. The same code is also attached to the *canDepart* method of the End Date field.

By now, prospects or customers have been selected, and no invalid dates have been entered into the Start Date and End Date fields. It's time to select a product code for this report. Drop-down lists are used throughout REPORTS.FSL. They display only valid choices. In this example, you can type a value into the Product Code field or select from the drop down list.

What is the best way to create the drop-down list? You could use a lookup table just like the Video application in Chapter 17. That way the list would display all values in the lookup table. This seems like a good solution. After all, a lookup table is linked to CALLS.DB. But what if not all values in the lookup table are in the CALLS.DB table? An inaccurate selection list is displayed. The user could pick a value that would not be in CALLS.DB, and a query using that criterion would not return any records. Furthermore, the list does not change based on the dates or the prospect/customer radio buttons. This application uses a query similar to the one in Figure 21-19.

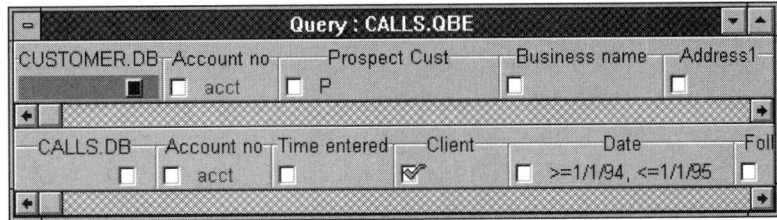

Figure 21-19: The list object's query is created interactively, saved and pasted into its *setFocus* method.

Let's look at the code attached to the *setFocus* method of the list object (see Figure 21-20). The seventh line calls a procedure that tests whether the dates are valid (for example, both fields are filled in, the start date is prior to the end date, and so on). If the dates pass the test, the variables StartDate and EndDate are assigned values. Next comes a query statement like what you saw in Chapter 18. Three tilde variables are used in the query: ~PorC, ~StartDate, and ~EndDate. PorC determines whether Customers and Prospects (PorC is blank), Prospects only (PorC="P"), or Customers only (PorC="C") is selected. ~StartDate and ~EndDate contain the dates that were entered into the form. When the query is performed, it will contain one field, Client, which is the field that contains the product code. Line 16 displays the drop down list.

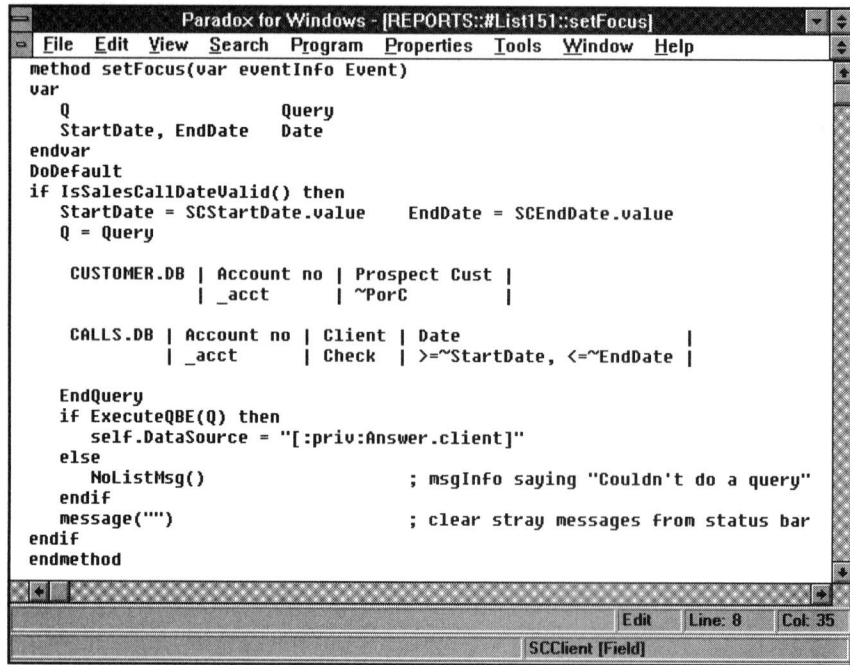

```
Paradox for Windows - [REPORTS::#List151::setFocus]
 File  Edit  View  Search  Program  Properties  Tools  Window  Help
method setFocus(var eventInfo Event)
var
    Q                       Query
    StartDate, EndDate      Date
endvar
DoDefault
if IsSalesCallDateValid() then
    StartDate = SCStartDate.value      EndDate = SCEndDate.value
    Q = Query

    CUSTOMER.DB | Account no | Prospect Cust |
                | _acct      | ~PorC         |

    CALLS.DB | Account no | Client | Date                      |
             | _acct      | Check  | >=~StartDate, <=~EndDate  |

    EndQuery
    if ExecuteQBE(Q) then
       self.DataSource = "[:priv:Answer.client]"
    else
       NoListMsg()                     ; msgInfo saying "Couldn't do a query"
    endif
    message("")                        ; clear stray messages from status bar
endif
endmethod
```
Edit   Line: 8   Col: 35

SCClient [Field]

Figure 21-20: ObjectPAL code attached to the list object of the Product Code field.

The View and Print buttons also call the IsSalesCallDateValid procedure, which is created in the Proc window of the page so the list and both buttons can find it. Figure 21-21 shows the procedure. You see that this procedure checks for many date errors. It also demonstrates a benefit of procedures—elimination of redundant code. If everything passes the test, it's time to generate the report.

```
┌─────────────────────────── REPORTS::Pg2::proc* ───────────────────┐
│ proc IsSalesCallDateValid() logical                                │
│ var                                                                │
│    msgChoice    String                                             │
│ endvar                                                             │
│ if SCStartDate.isBlank() then                                      │
│    msginfo("Insufficient Info","You must type a starting date")    │
│    SCStartDate.moveTo()                                            │
│    return false                                                    │
│ endif                                                              │
│ if SCStartDate.year() < EarliestDate then                          │
│    MsgInfo("Oops","Starting date is too far in the past")          │
│    SCStartDate.moveTo()                                            │
│    return false                                                    │
│ endif                                                              │
│ if SCStartDate.value > Today() then                                │
│    MsgInfo("Oops","Starting date cannot be in the future.")        │
│    SCStartDate.MoveTo()                                            │
│    return false                                                    │
│ endif                                                              │
│ if SCEndDate.isBlank() then                                        │
│    MsgChoice = MsgQuestion("Insufficient Info","NO ENDING DATE. Use today'│
│    If MsgChoice = "Yes" then                                       │
│       SCEndDate.value = Today()                                    │
│       SCClient.MoveTo()                                            │
│       return false                                                 │
│    else      ; "No" button on dlgBox pressed                       │
│       SCEndDate.MoveTo()                                           │
│       return false                                                 │
│    endif                                                           │
│ endif                                                              │
│ if Date(SCStartDate.value) > Date(SCEndDate.value) then            │
│    MsgInfo("Oops","The starting date cannot be more recent than the ending│
│    SCStartDate.moveTo()                                            │
│    return false                                                    │
│ endif                                                              │
│ if SCEndDate.value > Today() then                                  │
│    MsgInfo("Oops","Ending date cannot be in the future.")          │
│    SCEndDate.MoveTo()                                              │
│    return false                                                    │
│ endif                                                              │
│ if SCEndDate.year() < EarliestDate then                            │
│    MsgInfo("Oops","Ending date is too far in the past")            │
│    SCEndDate.moveTo()                                              │
│    return false                                                    │
│ endif                                                              │
└──────────────────────────────────────── Edit │ Line: 42 │ Col: 1 ─┘
```

Figure 21-21: The list object, as well as the View and Print buttons call this custom procedure attached to the page.

This has been a lot of work just to enter criteria into a form. It's amazing that something that seems so simple can actually be very complex. A lot of the work so far was simply error-checking: checking for valid dates, ensuring that a correct drop-down list is displayed, and verifying that the form is completely filled out before creating the report. But there is one more error-checking routine—verifying that capital letters are entered into fields.

Keystrokes

When typing text into fields on REPORTS.FSL, the text is always capitalized. Type text into any field and see what happens. Text strings entered in fields are used in queries, so the case should match that of the Paradox tables (which is uppercase). Although each field could have a picture statement, you must be sure every field has the same picture. It's a judgment call, but like the *mouseExit* example, global code is attached to the form.

Before delving into the actual code, it is important to understand that each printable character is represented by a number. If you subtract 32 from the value for a lowercase letter, you get the value for the uppercase letter. With this in mind, let's look at the code.

We want to modify the result of keystrokes (if the keystroke is a lowercase letter) so code is attached to the form's *keyChar* method. Figure 21-22 shows that, once again, we make use of *eventInfo*. This time, the method *char* is used. *char()* returns a string that represents the key that was pressed. The code, in English, says "If a lowercase letter was typed, replace it with an uppercase letter," and line 6 does the work.

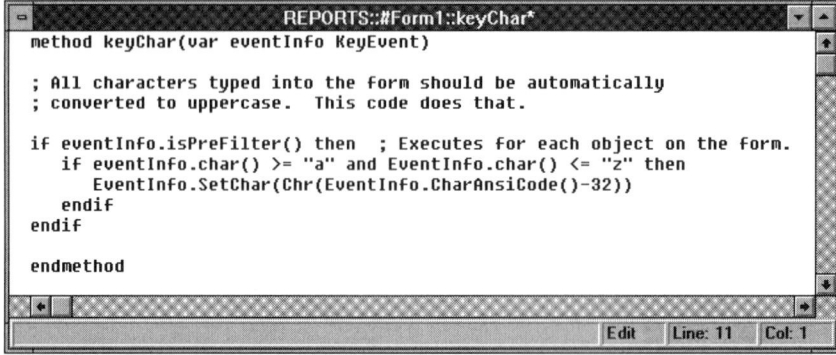

```
method keyChar(var eventInfo KeyEvent)

  ; All characters typed into the form should be automatically
  ; converted to uppercase.  This code does that.

  if eventInfo.isPreFilter() then   ; Executes for each object on the form.
    if eventInfo.char() >= "a" and EventInfo.char() <= "z" then
      EventInfo.SetChar(Chr(EventInfo.CharAnsiCode()-32))
    endif
  endif

endmethod
```

Figure 21-22: The *keyChar* method attached to the form converts lowercase letters to uppercase for every field on the form.

Let's take this one step at a time. When analyzing code that has nested parentheses, it is easiest to start with whatever is in the inner-most parentheses—in this case *EventInfo.CharAnsiCode()-32*. Figure 21-23 shows how to figure o

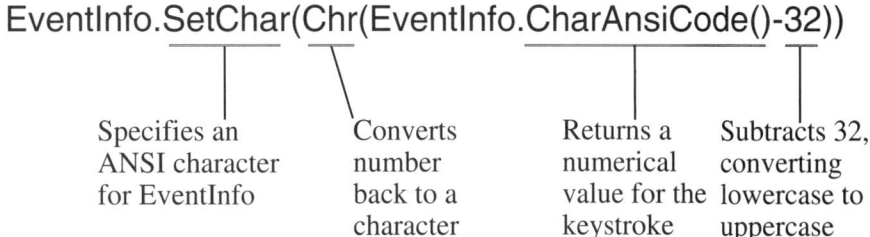

EventInfo.SetChar(Chr(EventInfo.CharAnsiCode()-32))

| Specifies an ANSI character for EventInfo | Converts number back to a character | Returns a numerical value for the keystroke | Subtracts 32, converting lowercase to uppercase |

Figure 21-23: This chart describes what's going on within the nested code segments.

By now, the form is filled out, you have seen copious error-checking, and it is time to view a report on the screen.

Sales Call Report

The fields you just filled in are the criteria for a Sales Call report. But they are also the criteria for the Sales Call Summary report. In fact, page 2 of REPORTS.FSL is used for the Sales Call report and the Sales Call Summary report. (The *pushButton* method on page one sets the text string in the title object so it indicates the proper report.) This means that when the View button is pressed, the appropriate report (and consequently, its associated query) must be selected based on the text string in the title. That's exactly what happens in the *pushButton* method of the Print and View buttons. Different custom methods are called depending on the text string in the heading– "Sales Call Summary Report" or "Sales Call Report."

Let's take a closer look and see how this works. Figure 21-24 shows the code associated with the View button's *pushButton* method. Line 3 tests the text string in the text frame to determine which report to view. A different custom method in a library is called for each report. The custom method performs a query and returns true or false depending on whether the query executed successfully. Then the RptShow procedure displays the report onscreen.

```
━━━━━━━━━━━━━━━━━━━━━━━━ REPORTS::btnView::pushButton ━━━━━▼▲
  method pushButton(var eventInfo Event)                            ▲

  if IsSalesCallDateValid() then
     if SalesCallRptTxt = "Sales Call Summary" then
        if lib.QSalesCallSum(SCStartDate.value, SCEndDate.value, SCClient.va
           RptShow("Summary.rsl")
           f.show()
        endif

     else                    ; Sales Call Report
        if lib.QSalesCall(SCStartDate.value, SCEndDate.value, SCClient.value
           RptShow("Calls.rsl")
        endif

     endif
  endif

  endmethod
                                                                    ▼
◄►                                                                  ►
                                            │Edit  │Line: 16│Col: 6│
```

Figure 21-24: The code attached to the *pushButton* method of the View button creates and displays a report based on the text string in the page's title text object.

If you haven't created a Sales Call report, do so now. Fill in the blanks and click the View button. When reports are displayed on the screen, a button bar is positioned above the report (see Figure 21-25). When you close the report, the button bar disappears. You have already seen a similar feature in this application. MAIN.FSL is hidden when another form displays, then when that form closes, MAIN.FSL is displayed again. In this case, the button bar (BUTTONS.FSL) is shown and then hidden again. MAIN.FSL's *open* method also determines the location of a form it opens. When displaying BUTTONS.FSL, it too is precisely positioned. Although the same ideas are used with the button bar, there are a couple of new twists.

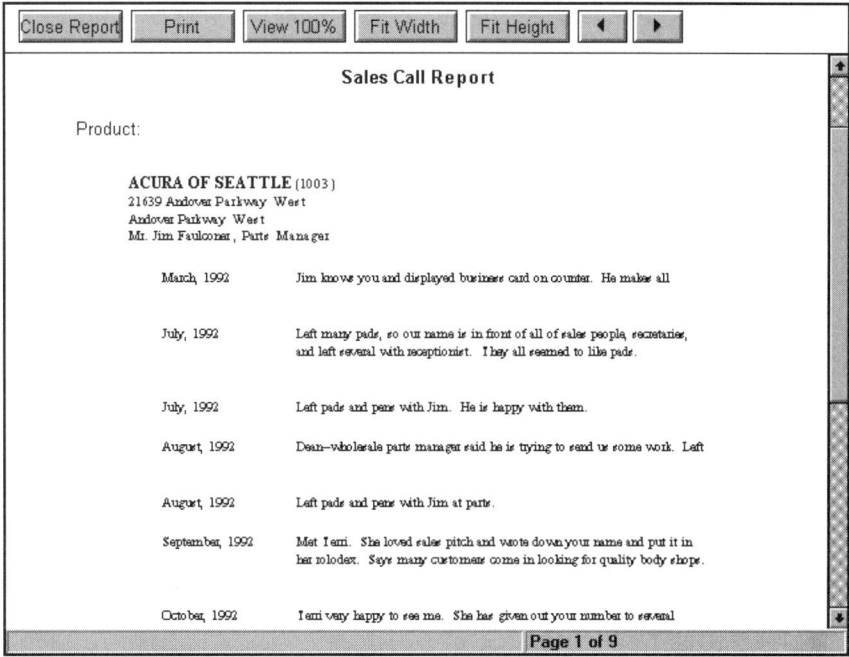

Figure 21-25: When viewing a report onscreen, the report window is maximized and a button bar form displays.

When REPORTS.FSL is loaded, BUTTONS.FSL is loaded also. You don't see this happen, but it does. The assumption is that several reports may be viewed and that BUTTONS.FSL should be loaded only once. The following code fragment attached to the *open* method of REPORTS.FSL opens BUTTONS.FSL. However, no screen redraws occur because the window style is WinStyleHidden. The form is loaded into memory, but you don't see it.

```
var
    fBut    Form
endvar
if NOT eventInfo.isPreFilter() then      ; This code executes only for
                                              the form.

        fBut.open("Buttons", WinStyleHidden) ; ButtonBar form for
                                                    viewing
        fBut.hide()
endif
```

When clicking any of the View buttons, the button bar is displayed in the appropriate position. Because the same code is executed from every View button—and there are several—the code is placed in a

619

procedure that is accessible to all objects on the form. (Chapter 19 discusses procedures in more depth.) This modular approach makes it easy to modify the code because you only need to look in one location, rather than code attached to several buttons. Figure 21-26 shows the library code that displays the button bar. The button bar is first positioned, then displayed.

```
┌─────────────────── REPORTS.FSL::#Form1::proc ──────────────── ▼ ▲
│ proc RptShow(RptFile string)                                        ↑
│ var
│     app            Application
│     x, y, w, h     LongInt
│     m              menu
│     ButForm        form
│     Rpt            Report
│ endvar
│ HideSpeedBar()     m.AddText("")   m.show()
│ app.getPosition(x,y,w,h)
│ if Rpt.open(RptFile, WinStyleMaximize + WinStyleVScroll) then
│     Rpt.SetTitle("Selected Report")
│ endif
│ if ButForm.attach("Viewing Report") then
│     ButForm.setPosition(x+65,y+65,w-135,560)
│     ButForm.show()
│     ButForm.wait()
│     ButForm.hide()
│     rpt.close()
│     if f.attach() then
│         f.SCStartDate.moveTo()
│         MenuAction(MenuControlRestore)
│     else
│         msginfo("Program Error","Unable to attach to report form")
│     endif
│ else
│     msginfo("Program Error","Unable to attach to button bar")
│ endif
│ endproc                                                             ↓
│ ←                                                              →
│                                          Edit    Line: 56   Col: 4
```

Figure 21-26: The custom procedure, RptShow, determines the coordinates of the application, positions the button bar, and suspends operation until the button bar returns control back to this method.

The eighth line in the procedure hides the Toolbar and creates a blank menu—just in case either of them are visible. Line 10 opens the report maximized and with a vertical scroll bar, and line 11 sets the title bar text. The ninth line gets the location of the application so the button bar dialog box can be positioned over the blank menu bar and the Paradox title bar. Yes, it is possible to position a form that is hidden (invisible). Again, the reason is to reduce the screen redrawing.

The *wait* method tells Paradox to keep BUTTONS.FSL active until the Close button is pressed. The Close button's *formReturn* method returns control back to REPORTS.FSL, as shown below. The Find Customer form automatically returned control back to the calling form when it closed, but because BUTTONS.FSL stays open, *formReturn* must be used.

```
method pushButton(var eventInfo Event)
    FormReturn()                  ; Return control back to RptShow
endmethod
```

You have seen a lot of ObjectPAL attached to this form. You have seen how the Sales Call report works, but there are six other reports on this form. You can explore them on your own if you wish.

ODDS & ENDS

REPORTS.FSL is a multipage form. The only appropriate time to leave the page is when the Print, View or Exit buttons are pressed. Under no other circumstances do we want to move from the page (for example, by pressing Shift+F4). This is not really difficult, but pieces of code are placed in various locations.

The first thing to do is declare a Logical variable. That variable, in effect, states "Yes, it is OK to leave this page" or "No, you can't leave this page." *canLeavePage* is declared in the form's Var window so that each object on the form can access it.

The *setFocus* method for each page sets *canLeavePage* to No. As soon as a page receives focus, you cannot leave. Well, that's not quite true. If you click the Print, View or Exit buttons, the *pushButton* method sets *canLeavePage* to Yes, allowing you to leave. But, if you look at the code for the *pushButton* method, you don't see any reference to *canLeavePage*. Hmmm. Where is it? The isFormComplete procedure attached to each page sets *canLeavePage* to true. Two buttons call this procedure, so setting *canLeavePage* in the procedure eliminates a line of code. The Exit button doesn't call this procedure, so *canLeavePage* is set to True in the Exit button's *pushButton* method.

MOVING ON

We have covered a lot of ground, and still haven't exhausted this form. You learned how to position forms in exact locations and what the differences are between forms and dialog boxes. Forms are opened with different attributes from other forms. This application contains a custom menu that can be further refined to include check marks, grayed items or any other attribute that you have seen in any other Windows programs. Query criteria is entered just by filling in the blanks on a form—the ultimate in ease for those who use the applications you create. And, you have a contact management application that you can customize for your own needs.

There is more lurking in the depths of ObjectPAL code just waiting for you to open the form and explore. However, that's something for you to do on your own. We are now finished with ObjectPAL. If you want to explore it further, the two applications included with this book give you some good tools. ObjectPAL is great for expanding the power of Paradox. Have fun with it. There is always more to learn.

WHEN & HOW TO HIRE A CONSULTANT

You've learned a lot in this book about Paradox features, and you're well on your way to developing custom applications. Some applications take only a day to implement; others take much longer. By now, you're probably comfortable with smaller projects, but what about a complex automated application? The more sophisticated the application, the more critical the planning becomes. This chapter focuses on the importance of the people—either in-house staff or outside professionals—who can help you with your project.

PLAN, DON'T PANIC

It's easy to feel pressured to produce an application more quickly than you consider humanly possible. For this reason, it's important to look first at what is required of a database project rather than what is desirable. In other words, first solve the user's problems; refinements can come later. If you're in the hot seat to complete an application project *right now*, start by asking some questions.

Answering these questions will help reduce the pressure on you because the answers can mean less work for you to do. Explore all the possibilities to offload work and simplify the project in order to get it completed rapidly. People unfamiliar with application development often don't understand how long it can take. Be sure to set realistic expectations.

What's Required?

Planning and prototyping are important steps in designing an application because database projects are notoriously open-ended. You need to anticipate as much as possible everything you want the system to do. In addition, you have other things to keep in mind. Do you need to get an application up and running as quickly as possible? Do you need to learn more about Paradox using a custom application as a learning tool? How much time do you have? What is your budget? These questions must be answered before deciding whether you need to hire outside help.

First, establish and document minimum requirements. It may well be that the requested project is overly ambitious and that you can streamline it enough to deliver the project within the requested time frame. You don't want to begin work with only part of the "picture," only to find yourself subject to ever-expanding application requirements.

If you proceed carefully in this way, serious design flaws can be caught before programming starts. Change orders will be kept to a minimum (it's next to impossible to eliminate them altogether, but reducing them will help a lot). All too often, a change can ricochet throughout an application, wreaking havoc that results in added expense and delays in implementation.

Can You Use Existing Elements?

How about copying existing forms, reports and code? Any time you can borrow work that's already been done, you save time—not only in creating the application but in debugging and testing it as well. The two applications included with this book give you some code fragments you can copy into your custom applications.

You may be able to locate similar applications elsewhere in your company that you can use or modify. And chances are that an outside consultant will have many applications to copy from. Another option is to purchase an application from a third-party vendor and customize it for your particular needs.

Any database project consists of many smaller projects. The checklist at the end of this appendix lists some of the components a database application, but they vary with each application. Use tl table throughout the chapter to determine what components already exist, what needs to be created and who can perform specific tasks.

And again, a reminder about the importance of planning: if adequate planning has already been completed, much of this prototyping can be used in your application.

Who Can Help You?

In-house corporate developers can be helpful for rapid application development. However, they are often under extreme pressure and don't have the luxury of offering several days or weeks of their time to develop an application. Frequently, anywhere from a few hours to a couple of days is all you could expect. In-house developers do give you certain advantages that an outside consultant could not. They're likely to be more experienced with the application requirements and the skill level of potential users. They're also more familiar with the framework in which the application will be used. An outside consultant would need to learn that basic information.

How Much Consultant Do You Need?

There are several possible approaches when hiring a consultant. You could hire someone full time or only on a consulting basis. Hiring a full-time employee is a viable option only for a large long-term project. You have to calculate the cost of a full-time salary, benefits and taxes against the cost of a contractor. And regular permanent employees may resent such arrangements. Hiring for less than two years is often a losing proposition—for the potential employee and your company. If you don't expect to keep someone employed for at least two years, use a consultant.

For very large projects, it might be best to hire a project manager and give that person overall responsibility for designing, integrating, implementing, testing and modifying the system. That person should then have the authority to hire people on either an as-needed or a permanent basis.

You could also hire a consultant to work along with you, performing those tasks that you don't feel comfortable with. For example, you could create the forms, reports, table and queries, and place buttons on the forms but have the consultant write the ObjectPAL code.

Or you could plan to do most of the work yourself but have the consultant provide advice when needed. Referring once again to the table, you can determine who does which parts of the project.

PREPLANNING SAVES TIME & MONEY

Saving time and money returns us once again to planning the application. When hiring a consultant, he or she needs to fully understand your business and the purpose of the custom application, know the application specs, and be able to produce credentials showing past experience in working with similar projects.

One of the main advantages of hiring someone experienced in a similar project is that you'll be assured that he or she realizes the scope of the project without running into change orders and cost overruns.

In all likelihood, the consultant won't be able to give a fixed fee and will probably prefer working on a time and materials basis.

FINDING THE RIGHT PROFESSIONAL

Where do you start looking for a consultant? Referrals from friends, associates in trade and professional groups and other business professionals are good sources. A consultant hired by referral would feel a responsibility not only to you; failure to meet your expectations would reflect poorly on the referring person as well. The consultant knows this and would have even more incentive to do a good job.

Another good source is your local Paradox user group. Check with the Chamber of Commerce. The Independent Computer Consultants Association has chapters in many cities, and many offer referral service. Also, there may be brokers or agencies in your area who specialize in computer consulting. Once you have several people in mind for a project, you need to start interviewing prospective candidates.

What To Look For

Probably the first thing to look for in a prospective candidate is a positive and congenial attitude. It's very important to choose someone you'll get along with. You need to feel comfortable and confident that when the project is underway, the consultant will address your concerns and allocate time to deal effectively with the issues.

Ideal Qualifications:

○ Expertise in developing software.

○ Successful previous experience with projects of a similar nature and scope, preferably a similar application.

○ Experience with the tools to be used.

○ Understanding of the concepts—the big picture—and how the pieces of the application must work together within your company.

○ Willingness to learn from you, your staff and your business.

It would be helpful to get several references and visit all potential clients, if possible.

In dealing with technical topics, it's often difficult to determine who really knows what they are talking about and whether they can communicate that information to others. Have your best techies go to lunch with applicants you're interested in. Some informal chit-chat and techie talk can reveal valuable insights about the candidates' qualifications. Typically, your techies' feedback and evaluations will be correct.

If you're really pressed for time, you can arrange for an applicant to talk with one of your technical people while you're "on the phone" or "in a meeting." Make it an informal interview without any decision-makers present. You may be surprised at how much you can learn about the candidate in this kind of setting.

Consider having a series of short interviews, one right after the other. Have your most senior technical person talk with the consultant and get a sense of how compatible he or she is, as well as how technically competent.

You could also have one of your most flexible users spend some time with the candidate to get a sense of whether they would "fit" in a work situation. The more people involved, the better the result. It is important that the consultant makes a good team player, as well as being technically competent.

THE CONTRACT

The purpose of a contract is to ensure mutual understanding between you and a consultant. However, there is no typical job. Consequently, contracts vary. You want to be sure the consultant gets paid appropriately, that you get the application you want and that you retain the rights to the work you've paid to have done.

When consultants bid on a job, they bid a fixed fee, time and materials or some combination of the two arrangements. Many times, consultants work strictly on a time and materials basis. This arrangement doesn't specify the exact amount a project will cost, but you will very likely be given a price range.

For a fixed-fee arrangement to be successful, here are some rules to follow. Most important, you need to write very detailed specs derived from adequate preplanning. If the consultant writes the specs, expect him or her to complete the project for the specified price. However, if you or a third party writes the specs, the consultant may want to allow for unforeseen circumstances such as charging for change orders (to avoid feature creep).

The fixed-fee method is a good pricing mechanism; it is value pricing in its purest form. You don't know how many hours the consultant spends on the project, and in fact it doesn't matter. This works well for companies that have arbitrary limits on how much they can pay for a consultant's time.

Another approach is to separate a project in stages—such as application requirements, conceptual design, development, documentation and training. Once one stage is complete, the following stage is negotiated. This is a practical approach because changes in one stage will cascade throughout the other stages. Don't use this method to try to cut costs by switching consultants for each particular phase (in order to get the lowest prices). This ploy will backfire. Choose your consultant, and if you're satisfied with the work don't change consultants in the middle of a project.

As you can see, there are several ways that a consultant can charge for a project, and the particulars should be clearly stated in the contract. You must be realistic and work with the consultant. Inadequate compensation is a sure way to end up with an unacceptable or inferior product.

It's also important for you and the consultant to mutually understand the application specs for the project—the specifics of the work and the completion dates for each phase of the work. Be sure that as the project progresses, you monitor what has been completed. Write a clause in the contract creating a feedback mechanism to ensure that the consultant doesn't stray fom your desired goals.

Include in the contract your rights to the source code, or at least your right to modify it. The consultant may charge extra for signing over all rights to the source code, but you want the capability to make changes to the application if it becomes necessary. Be careful, though. Modifying the application could void the warranty. The important thing is that you don't want to be in the position of having to re-create work you've already paid for.

MANAGING A CONTRACTED DEVELOPER

A person you hire to develop the software for a project must be self-reliant. Sometimes this can be a problem. Many people have difficulty organizing and completing a project if they're given only a general concept rather than strict guidelines. Even though they are technically great at programming, they have trouble creating solutions to problems.

This type of person may need things laid out to some extent. Lack of organization or technical incompetence can leave you with a poor product. To prevent this kind of situation, set intermittent goals so that you are informed on the progress and can keep the product under your control at all times.

Determining What "Done" Means

If the application has been adequately prototyped, the contract is specific and the end product is well defined, both you and the developer will know when each stage is complete and when the entire project is done (see the checklist that follows).

If adequate communication is lacking during the project, it becomes difficult to determine what *done* means because requirements may have changed. You could have one understanding and the developer could have another. Communication with the consultant will help to assure a successful project.

Good luck!

Application Requirements
○ What is the purpose of the application?
○ What should the interface look like?
○ What is the user's knowledge of Paradox?
○ Is the application multiuser or single-user?
○ What error checking is needed?

Conceptual Database Design
○ What data goes in which table?
○ What lookup tables, val checks, RI, etc. are necessary?
○ What forms are needed?
○ What reports are necessary?
○ What queries are necessary?
○ Will custom menus be used?
○ Will custom libraries be used?

Application Development
○ Creating tables, validity checks, RI.
○ Designing the forms' interface.
○ Writing ObjectPAL methods for the form.
○ Creating reports.
○ Creating queries.
○ Writing custom menus.
○ Writing ObjectPAL libraries.

Testing the Application
○ Creating test data.
○ Verifying test results.
○ Testing in a multiuser environment.

Documentation
○ Documenting application components.
○ Documenting ObjectPAL code.
○ Documentation for the end user.
○ Creating online help.

Implementation & Final Testing

○ Installing the application.

○ Running a new application side by side with a previous application.

○ Training end-users.

○ Final tweaking of the application.

INDEX

Colophon

The Visual Guide to Paradox® for Windows was produced using PageMaker 5.0 on a Macintosh Quadra 700 computer with 20mb of RAM and a Pentium PC-compatible with 32mb of RAM. The video system used by the PC is a Cornerstone Dual-Page 120 grayscale monitor driven by an Image-Excel controller. The body copy is set in Garamond and headlines are Kabel and Bernhard Fashion, all from the Digital Typeface Corporation collection.

Pages were proofed on a Hewlett Packard LaserJet 4M. Final output was produced on film using a Linotronic 330.

INTERNET.
HERE.
NOW.

Internet Membership Kit™

$200 Value!
- Free access offer — one month plus 5 hours free from CERFnet!
- Easy E-mail software
- Graphical Search
- File transfer and compression software
- Two bestselling guide books
- Internet Visitors Center

Access and tools! Your on-ramp to the information superhighway!

1-800-209-3342

Uncover the secrets buried deep within your software! Slash through the jungle of your user manuals and unveil hidden productivity treasures you never knew were right under your nose! Whether you're a novice or a veteran, you can learn a lot from Ventana's

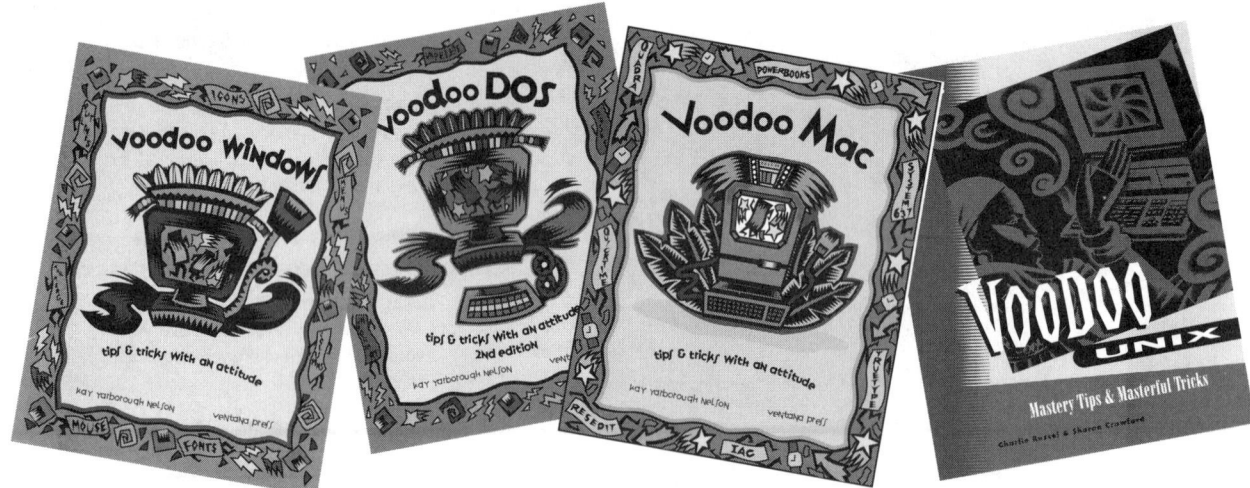

Voodoo Windows

$19.95
282 pages, illustrated
ISBN: 1-56604-005-1
A unique resource, *Voodoo Windows* bypasses the technical information found in many Windows books to bring you an abundance of never-before-published tips, tricks and shortcuts for maximum Windows productivity. A one-of-a-kind reference for beginners and experienced users alike.

Voodoo Mac

$21.95
307 pages, illustrated
ISBN: 1-56604-028-0
Whether you're a power user looking for new shortcuts or a beginner trying to make sense of it all, *Voodoo Mac* has something for everyone! Computer veteran Kay Nelson has compiled hundreds of invaluable tips, tricks, hints and shortcuts that simplify your Macintosh tasks and save time, including disk and drive magic, font and printing tips, alias alchemy and more!

Voodoo DOS

$21.95
325 pages, illustrated
ISBN: 1-56604-046-9
Increase your productivity with the "magic" of *Voodoo DOS*. Packed with tips, tricks and shortcuts for all versions of DOS through 6.0, this book offers a variety of time-saving techniques designed for all users. An excellent reference for users who want to juice up their computing power without wading through obtuse technical information.

Voodoo UNIX

$27.95
310 pages, illustrated
ISBN" 1-56604-067-1
Unleash the 32-bit power of UNIX with tips, tricks and shortcuts from *Voodoo UNIX*. Written for intermediate UNIX users, *Voodoo UNIX* shows readers how to streamline their work and increase productivity with invaluable, time-saving tips for getting the most from their system resources.

To order any Ventana Press title, fill out this order form and mail it to us, with payment, for quick shipment.

	Quantity		Price		Total
Internet Membership Kit, Macintosh Version	_____	x	$69.95	=	$ _____
Internet Membership Kit, Windows Version	_____	x	$69.95	=	$ _____
The Visual Guide to Visual Basic for Applications	_____	x	$27.95	=	$ _____
The Visual Guide to Visual Basic for Windows, 2nd Edition	_____	x	$29.95	=	$ _____
The Visual Guide to Microsoft Access	_____	x	$29.95	=	$ _____
The Visual Guide to Visual C++	_____	x	$29.95	=	$ _____
Voodoo Windows	_____	x	$19.95	=	$ _____
Voodoo DOS, 2nd Edition	_____	x	$21.95	=	$ _____
Voodoo Mac	_____	x	$21.95	=	$ _____
Voodoo UNIX	_____	x	$27.95	=	$ _____
The Windows Internet Tour Guide	_____	x	$24.95	=	$ _____
The Mac Internet Tour Guide	_____	x	$27.95	=	$ _____
The PC Internet Tour Guide	_____	x	$24.95	=	$ _____
			Subtotal	=	$ _____

SHIPPING:

For all regular orders, please *add* $4.50/first book, $1.35/each additional.	=	$ _____
For Internet Membership Kit orders, *add* $6.50/first kit, $2.00/each additional.	=	$ _____
For "two-day air" on books *add* $8.25/first book, $2.25/each additional.	=	$ _____
For "two-day air" on the IMK *add* $10.50/first kit, $4.00/each additional.	=	$ _____
For orders to Canada, *add* $6.50/book.	=	$ _____
For orders sent C.O.D., *add* $4.50 to your shipping rate.	=	$ _____
North Carolina residents must *add* 6% sales tax.	=	$ _____
TOTAL	=	$ _____

Name_____ Company_____

Address (No PO Box)_____

City_____ State_____ Zip _____

Daytime Telephone _____

___ Check/money order enclosed (no cash) ___VISA ___MC   Exp. Date _____

Card # _____

Signature _____

Mail or fax to: Ventana Press, PO Box 2468, Chapel Hill, NC 27515 ☎ 919/942-0220 Fax 919/942-1140

CAN'T WAIT? CALL TOLL-FREE ☎ 800/743-5369 (U.S. only)

巨揚

（近台北火車站）
Tel:(02)331 ·
Fax:(02)361-3007
台北市懷寧街
3 6 號 2 樓
550